Spiritual Dimensions of Bediuzzaman Said Nursi's *Risale-i Nur*

Spiritual Dimensions of Bediuzzaman Said Nursi's *Risale-i Nur*

Edited and with an Introduction by
Ibrahim M. Abu-Rabi'

STATE UNIVERSITY OF NEW YORK PRESS

Published by
State University of New York Press, Albany

Printed in the United States of America

For information, contact State University of New York Press, Albany, NY
www.sunypress.edu

Production by Kelli W. LeRoux
Marketing by Anne M. Valentine

Library of Congress Cataloging in Publication Data

Spiritual dimensions of Bediuzzaman Said Nursi's *Risale-i Nur* / edited and with an introduction by Ibrahim M. Abu-Rabi'.
p. cm.
Includes bibliographical references and index.
ISBN 978-0-7914-7473-0 (hardcover : alk. paper)
ISBN 978-0-7914-7474-7 (pbk. : alk. paper) 1. Nursi, Said, 1873–1960. Risale-i Nur. 2. Nurculuk—Doctrines. I. Abu-Rabi', Ibrahim M. II. Nursi, Said, 1873–1960. Risale-i nur. English. Selections.

BP252.S65 2008
297.8'3—dc22

2007042270

10 9 8 7 6 5 4 3 2 1

CONTENTS

Editor's Introduction

History, Politics, and Charisma in Risale-i Nur

Ibrahim M. Abu-Rabi‘

The objective of the chapters included herein is to present the reader with a picture of the spiritual dimensions of a major religious movement in the contemporary Muslim world by focusing on the spiritual ideas of its leader, Bediuzzaman Said Nursi. The Nur community is one of the most significant religious and social movements in contemporary Turkey, with millions of adherents and a strong institutional and educational system running across the country.

Modernity poses a curious set of problems to the modern and contemporary Muslim world. It is nearly impossible to summarize modernity in a few statements; however, it suffices to say that a great number of intellectual forces, institutions, and ideas have emerged within modernity since its historical beginnings in the fifteenth century. Throughout its long history in modern European societies and during European colonialism in various regions in the world, modernity has given birth to such modern phenomena as secularism, nationalism, capitalism, socialism, imperialism, colonization, and modern criticism.

There were several Ottoman responses to the nineteenth-century question of European modernity and the threat it posed to the integrity of the Ottoman state: first was the response of the modernizing elite in the Ottoman Empire, which opted to modernize the infrastructure of the Empire while preserving the status of Islam in that society. The second response was aimed at preserving the Ottoman Empire without giving any central role to Islam in either society or politics. The third response was nationalist in orientation and was mainly represented by Turkish nationalists who did not much care about empire or religion.

The fourth was more mass-oriented than the previous positions, and focused on religious community, text, and Shari'ah.

It is within these four major configurations that one must locate Ottoman debate about religion, civil society, constitution, modernization, and progress. Also, it is within this tumult that a critical appreciation of the Islamic tradition among a small but influential number of Ottoman Muslim intelligentsia emerged. This critical examination of tradition took place on at least on two fronts: (1) the Sufi front, especially the Naqshebandia tariqah and the efforts of Mawlana Khalid al-Naqshebandi to revive Sufism in the nineteenth-century Ottoman empire, and (2) on the front of dialectical theology, or *ilm kalam* or *yeni Osmanli kelam* pioneered by a number of Ottoman intellectuals in the nineteenth century.

This critical examination of Muslim tradition was necessary because the empire itself was going through some major changes, and the Muslim intelligentsia felt that it was their duty to revive the Muslim notion of *ummah* and connect it to nation and state. One may argue that *ummah*, nation, and state are the three terms that most aptly summarize Ottoman political philosophy in the nineteenth century. Nursi himself dealt with these three concepts in various ways throughout his religious and intellectual life. However, after the defeat of the Ottoman army in World War One, Nursi turned his attention to Islamic spirituality and the spiritual mission of Islamic communities in a new era marked by radical secularism and Westernization.

Nursi scholars are fond of dividing the philosopher's life into the "Old Said" and the "Young Said" periods. In his "old" phase, Nursi was totally immersed in traditional Islamic sciences and was actively pursuing a single mission: saving the Ottoman Empire from further decay and loss. In his "young" phase, Nursi focused less on saving the Empire and more on saving Islamic spirituality and ethics in a secular age. In his first phase, Nursi fought on many different fronts. He understood that there were deep gaps between 'center' and 'periphery' in the Ottoman Empire. As someone who belonged to the periphery, he sought to remedy the situation by advocating far-reaching educational, constitutional, and social reforms.

Nursi did all this with a view toward solidifying the bond between *ummah*, nation, and empire in the Ottoman state. That is, he did what he did in the name of Islamic solidarity. He tried to revive the Ibn Khaldunian notion of solidarity in a new age, and he did this on the basis of his understanding of Islamic identity. He thought that it was possible to accept the tremendous institutional and social changes that began within the Ottoman Empire at the beginning of the nineteenth century while reviving the great bond between *ummah* and empire. Nursi argued that religion (i.e., Islam) must be organically linked to empire to preserve its identity in the modern era. He basically did not see any contradiction between Islamic bondage and the major changes that had been taking place in the empire since the early days of Tanzimāt.

However, Nursi went through a radical transformation after World War One. Generally speaking, Nursi was disappointed with the failure of the empire to preserve Islam and began to look into new ways to promote Islam and its spirituality in a radically new phase of modern Turkey. Right after World War One, Nursi became well aware of the fact that it was a matter of time before the empire would be dismantled; that there were powerful forces, both internal and external, that were no longer interested in preserving the political integrity of the Ottoman Empire. He was aware of all of this because he was captured for two years during World War One while fighting for the Ottoman army.

While at some point Nursi was ready to let go of the empire, he was not ready to give up on Islam and the Muslim *ummah*. These two concepts began to acquire strong spiritual meaning for him. He still thought of the Muslim world in a universal sense and was anxious to preserve the great bond between the Turkish nation and Islam. He still thought of the Turkish nation not in nationalist terms, but in ummatic terms. And clearly, this went against the grain of the leading political authorities in the post-Ottoman phase of Turkey. The most dominant political current, epitomized by Kemal Ataturk and his comrades, defended the notion of severing ties between the Turkish nation and the Muslim world and attempted to relegate religion to a secondary status in the lives of the Turkish people.

Said Nursi and his comrades, on the other hand, were the only group to intellectually defend the traditional bond between the Turkish nation and the Muslim *ummah*. As we know, Nursi refused to subscribe to the European notion of nation when he denied assistance to the Shaykh Said rebellion, a Kurdish rebellion against the state in the mid-1920s.

As mentioned, empire, nation, and *ummah* played significant roles in Nursi's intellectual life, especially before World War One. With the progress of years, a new constellation of forces came to the fore in Nursi's life and that of his community in a secularized Turkey. This new constellation of forces can be called text-individual-community.

The text is, of course, Nursi's magnum opus, *Risale-i Nur*, which begins to take shape from the 1920s on. And the *Risale-i Nur* must be seen as Nursi's deep reflection on the Quran in light of the modern and rapidly changing conditions in Turkey. However, there is a central dimension of the text that many scholars have overlooked. The text was not a simple exegesis of the Quran; it was a product of Nursi's crisis, imprisonment, exile, and alienation. I believe his experiences give *Risale-i Nur* a unique edge. The text is similar in this sense to the works of Antonio Gramsci in Italy and Dietrich Bonhoeffer in Germany under Nazi authorities. It is a text forged from tremendous pain and suffering in the extreme. This is the main reason why the text is so charismatic.

Despite his spiritual, psychological, and emotional struggles, Nursi had an objective goal, which was to preserve the integrity of Islam in the high age of radical secularism. He immersed himself in the infinite treasures of the Islamic sacred to express his new position and achieve his goal. In so doing, he was also expressing the feelings of numerous people who were not affected by the new secular formula of nation, Turkification, and Westernization.

It is in this context that we must read the chapters in this book. The world is indeed fortunate that leading scholars of Nursi's work and spirituality shed light on a spiritual tradition in modern and contemporary Turkey that has steadfastly survived the secular project of Kemalism.

In conclusion, I sincerely thank Dr. Faris Kaya of the Istanbul Science and Culture Foundation for conceiving of the idea for this book and supporting its progress from the beginning.

ONE

A Survey of the Main Spiritual Themes of the *Risale-i Nur*

Şükran Vahide

Written at a time that the drive for Westernization and secularization was gaining momentum in Turkey, the primary purpose of the *Risale-i Nur* is the revitalization of the faith of the ordinary believers, along with moral renewal. Employing a method derived largely from the Quran, Bediuzzaman Said Nursi (1877–1960) aimed to expound and prove the fundamental truths and tenets of the Islamic religion and instill a Quranic worldview based on the affirmation of divine unity (*tawhid*), at the same time disproving the basic assumptions of such materialist philosophies as positivism and naturalism, with which the government of the time intended to replace Islam. Supporting all his assertions with proofs and reasoned arguments, Nursi set out to demonstrate the logical coherence and validity of the Quranic view of existence and the falsity of the scientistic view underlying Western modernity. The greater part of the *Risale-i Nur* deals with these questions, and is designed to offer a "direct" way, relevant to contemporary needs, of gaining conscious, affirmative belief in, and knowledge of, God by means of reflective thought on "the book of the universe" and the divine names manifested on its pages. From this it may be seen that for the most part the contents of the *Risale-i Nur* may be subsumed under the rubric of spirituality.

Thus, in this chapter, by spirituality is meant that dimension of Islam that encompasses the endeavor to gain and increase in faith in God, and in knowledge and awareness of Him, sometimes called its inner dimension, rather than its dimension related to legal matters, its scholarly disciplines, or the formal practices of the religion, which by the same token are said to be its outer dimensions.

Nursi, however, only uses the term "spiritual" (*rūhānī*) in this sense, in reference to Sufism and to the saints (*evliya*) and people of sainthood (*ehl-i velāyet*), by which he almost invariably means followers of the Sufi paths. For instance,

> Underlying the terms Sufism, path, sainthood, and spiritual journeying is an agreeable, luminous, joyful, and spiritual sacred truth (. . . *rūhānī bir hakikat-i kudsiyye*).[1] The aim and goal of the Sufi path is—knowledge of God and the unfolding of the truths of belief—through a spiritual journeying (*bir seyr ü sülūk rūhānī*) with the feet of the heart. . . . and all the saints of his community make their spiritual journeyings under the shadow of the Ascension, with the spirit and heart (*rūhānī ve kalbī bir tarzda*).[2]

Nursi does not use the term spiritual in reference to the *Risale-i Nur* and its way, and is at pains to illustrate the differences between it and the Sufi way, as shall be shown. A term that may be considered an equivalent is "mānevī," which he uses in its sense of pertaining to meaning, as opposed to material, physical, or related to form (*maddī*). The term, which is fundamental to Nursi's general method or approach and is an important concept if not actually a theme, is mentioned in several contexts below.

Moreover, Nursi argues against the view that Sufism is the inner dimension of Islam, and the Shari'ahh, as the body of formal injunctions and ordinances, its outward dimension:

> The ways of the Sufi orders (*tarikat*) and of reality (*hakikat*) are like means, servants, and steps for reaching the truths of the Shari'ah, till at the highest level they are transformed into the meaning of reality and essence of the Sufi way, which are at the heart of the Shari'ah. . . . it is not right to think of the Shari'ah as an outer shell, and reality as its inner part and result and aim, as some Sufis do.[3]

It may be added in connection with connotations of the word spiritual, which infer opposition or conflict between matter and spirit, that since Islam admits no dichotomy or opposition between corporeality and spirit, or between the visible, manifest world (*ālem-i şehadet*) and the nonmaterial worlds hidden from human perception (*avālim-i gayb*), all forming an indivisible whole and being various faces and gradations of the same reality, and making every aspect of "the world" and existence in a sense sacred, neither faith or belief (*imān*), nor knowledge of God, nor the purification of the self, can be disembodied or isolated from the so-called outer dimensions of Islam, or indeed from the physical world. This, too, should be borne in mind when using the terms spirituality and spiritual. To reiterate, the terms are used in this chapter in a broad sense to refer to the endeavor to attain to and increase in faith in God, and in knowledge of Him and awareness of His presence.

With the *Risale-i Nur*, Said Nursi was attempting to construct a way of comprehending and practicing Islam at a time when, with the abolition of the Ottoman medrese system and the interdiction on the Sufi orders, an effective stop had been put to religious education, and, moreover, there were sustained assaults on religious belief and Islam on both the ideological and practical levels. He therefore made it first a general way that addresses all classes and types of people, and second, in his writings in order to achieve his main purpose of the revitalization of faith, he sought to bring together or, more accurately perhaps, perform the essential functions of various traditional religious sciences such as *kalām*, *'aqā'id*, *uṣūl-al dīn*, and *tafsīr*. He sought, too, to incorporate modern scientific knowledge, and with his overall method, which was derived from the Quran, satisfy inner spiritual needs. Thus, while constructing a system of thought that would answer the needs of the day, Nursi drew on existing institutions and traditions and in many cases took existing terms and concepts and adapted them to suit his way. Some of these will be mentioned in the course of this chapter. The introductory section of the survey will examine three basic themes of the *Risale-i Nur*: belief/faith; the way of the *Risale-i Nur* and reality; and the Quran. This will be followed by four main sections that, within the framework of the four fundamental principles of the *Risale-i Nur*'s "way," will attempt to investigate its main spiritual themes.

Belief/Faith

Belief or faith (*imān*) is the central theme of the *Risale-i Nur*, and the renewal and strengthening of belief its purpose and primary function. Nursi states this explicitly in many places in the work. For example: "The *Risale-i Nur*'s function is to strengthen and save belief. We are charged with serving [the cause of] belief."[4] And, "With the assaults of science and philosophy, and the contagion[s] of materialism and naturalism spreading through humanity, [its function] is first and foremost to save belief in such a way as to silence philosophy and materialistic ideas."[5] So, too, he attributes the present weak state of Islam first to the damage it has suffered over a thousand-year period from the infiltration of alien ideas, and second to the intellectual assaults of the present and to those furthering the ends of such currents. The purpose of the *Risale-i Nur* is to repair that vast damage by "striving to cure with the medicines of the Quran and belief . . . the collective heart and generally-held ideas . . . and general conscience."[6] In other words, it is to revitalize the faith of the mass of believers by offering certain proofs of the fundamentals of belief by means of a method derived from the Quran, relevantly to the present situation, in a way that addresses both the intellect, the heart, and the conscience.

As a Quranic commentary the chief aim of which is the renewal of faith, the *Risale-i Nur* interprets and elucidates the Quran's call to men to believe in the world's Maker, its central message. Indeed, according to verse 51:56, "I created not jinn and mankind except that they might worship [Me]," faith is the central issue of creation. In expounding this verse, Nursi points out that to recognize, believe in, and worship the Creator of all things is "man's primordial duty" and is a requirement of his inborn nature.[7]

Thus, a theme running through Nursi's proofs of "the pillars of belief," around which most of the discussions in the *Risale-i Nur* revolve, is the necessity of faith; that is, he not only marshals all the elements of his method—logical proofs, reasoned arguments based on observation of the natural world, allegorical comparisons, and so on—to persuade his readers of the necessary truth of the Creator's existence and unity and other truths of belief; he also shows that the universe itself and its beings including man—and indeed the findings of science—necessitate them.[8] However, this necessity becomes clear only when beings are observed in the manner of the Quran. This crucial element of Nursi's method, called the "indicative viewpoint or meaning of things (*māna-yı harfī*)," is discussed in greater detail below. In addition, Nursi sets out to demonstrate the invalidity and impossibility of the ideas and concepts underlying unbelief.[9]

Another theme related to the pillars of belief is the interrelation and indivisibility of those pillars. For Nursi, "Belief is a single truth, which, composed of its six pillars, cannot be divided up. It is a universal that cannot be separated into parts. . . . In which case, an invalid idea that cannot shake all the pillars together with all their proofs, cannot in reality negate any one of the pillars, or even a single of their truths, and cannot deny them."[10] This interrelation is pointed out and demonstrated in most of the discussions of the *Risale-i Nur*.

A matter to which great importance is attached in the *Risale-i Nur* is that since the true nature of man and the cosmos is fully disclosed by the divine revelation of the Quran and is to be seen by the eye of belief, it is only in faith in this sense that human beings can find true happiness and fulfillment. In other words, if man himself and the world in which he finds himself are not "illumined" by belief and the meaning and purpose it imparts to them, he remains in the "darkness" of purposeless transience. The means Nursi most often employs to persuade his readers of this are comparisons between belief and unbelief or "philosophy,"[11] which analyze both states and illustrate their results from various angles.

The emphasis in the *Risale-i Nur* is on the strengthening and renewal of faith, and on inculcating Quranic morals and teaching the basics of "universal worship," yet it contains little discussion about "works (*amel*)" in the legal and formal sense. One can say that it deals with questions of faith to the exclusion of works. It allots minimal space to discussion of classic questions of debate such as the nature and relation of faith and works, though in reply to a question Nursi restates the orthodox position on the mutual relation of faith (*imān*) and Islam.[12] He does not enter into the debate on the possible increase and decrease of faith,[13] but he does offer illuminating discussion on "the degrees" of faith and certainty. It is probably fair to say that since Nursi was addressing all levels and classes of people at a time when the fundamentals of religion were under threat, he deemed it necessary to limit the discussions of the *Risale-i Nur* to questions directly related to its primary purpose.

For this same reason, since the *Risale-i Nur* is a popular, didactive work and was written at a time when people had no access to religious education, Nursi brought together and encapsulated the gist of various traditional religious sciences[14] so that it might perform their essential functions. His intention was to combine these with both modern scientific knowledge and the knowledge of the Quran, and to utilize all of them in proving his main theses.[15] However, because his propositions were mostly related to the truths of belief and were derived from the Quran, he termed the knowledge of the *Risale-i Nur* "the sciences of belief (*ulūm-u imāniye*)," which he informs us, is "the type of knowledge that the Quran teaches."[16] Besides its curative properties for spiritual wounds,[17] the particular characteristic of this knowledge is its being "the sustenance and light for numerous human inner faculties, in addition to the intellect."[18]

Nursi thus acknowledges the role of knowledge in belief and accords it an important place in his scheme. Indeed, as is well known, the cognitive elements of faith have always been emphasized in Islam.[19] Making one of his frequent comparisons, he emphasizes that faith is "knowledge, pertains to existence, and is an affirmation and a judgement,"[20] while for unbelief he uses such terms as "an evil, a destruction, and an absence of affirmation,"[21] and "denial, ignorance, and negation."[22]

The knowledge of the *Risale-i Nur* is the corollary of the powerful faith or belief that Nursi was aiming to gain for people, which he calls *imān-ı tahkikī*; that is, certain, affirmative belief or belief by investigation. As a conscious assent and verification, it is the opposite of belief by imitation (*taklidī iman*), which Nursi felt could be easily negated by the skepticism of the scientific age. The strength of such belief lies in its suffusing man's heart, spirit, and other inner faculties as well as satisfying his intellect, which all then become immune to the whisperings of Satan.[23]

Aided by "the sciences of belief," certain, affirmative belief has innumerable degrees and levels; it may grow from being merely seed-like to resemble a mighty date-palm. It is related to thousands of the divine names and to the truths of the universe related to the pillars of faith. Ultimately it may unfold to a degree in which the whole universe will be read as though it were a Quran.[24] Further light will be thrown on this in the section on reflective thought.

THE *RISALE-I NUR*'S WAY

Said Nursi characterizes the *Risale-i Nur* as being a "way" or "method," which, proceeding on the four principles of impotence, poverty, compassion, and reflection, is a direct way to reality (*hakikat*). According to Nursi, "all true paths are taken from the Quran, [but] some are shorter, safer, and more general than others."[25] He places this way within "the legacy of prophethood," rather than in the Sufi tradition, and frequently when explaining it compares and contrasts it with the latter. "It is reality (*hakikat*) rather than *tarikat*. It is Shari'ah." Thus, *hakikat* and various derivatives of the same root referring to aspects of the *Risale-i Nur*'s way form another major theme that should be examined here. The meaning he attaches to *hakikat* will I hope become clear in the course of this chapter. Nursi's use of this threefold categorization of Shari'ah, Tarikat, and Hakikat,[26] which is generally associated with Sufism, yet adapting it to fit his own system, suggests his intention to update and renew the existing traditions, rather than to innovate completely.

In the years following the demise of the Ottoman Empire, it was Nursi's immersion in certain works of Shaikh Ahmad Sirhindi, Shaikh 'Abd al-Qadir Gilani, and presumably others, and his constant reading of the collection of prayers and litanies of leading Sufi figures, *Majmu'āt al-Aḥzāb*,[27] that led him to take the path of reality and resolved his spiritual crisis, allowing the New Said to emerge. The works he wrote thereafter expounded this way of gaining knowledge of God, which is derived from the pure *tawhid* of the Quran and its verses mentioning the divine names. He amplified and elaborated it when he started to write the *Risale-i Nur*, making it a general way based on reflective thought on the natural world that aimed to prove the fundamentals of belief.

According to Nursi, the way he propounds in the *Risale-i Nur* consists of "knowledge of [or the science of] reality (*ilm-i hakikat*)," and receives "the effulgence of the legacy of prophethood (*verāset-i nübuvvet*), [known as] the greater sainthood."[28] Nursi quotes Sirhindi as specifying three grades of sainthood (*velāyet*): "The greater sainthood (*velāyet-i kübrā*) is to open up by way of the legacy of prophethood a direct way to reality without entering the intermediate realm of Sufism."[29]

This very short though elevated path "looks to the unfolding of divine immediacy (*akrebiyet*)."[30] For there are two ways of passing from the apparent to reality: one is to traverse the degrees through spiritual journeying, as in Sufism. The second is to pass directly to reality without entering the intermediate realm of Sufism. According to Nursi, this way is particular to the Companions of the Prophet and those who succeeded them.[31] It was Nursi's wish that the *Risale-i Nur* possessed the qualities necessary to effect this.[32]

In establishing his way of reality derived from "the highway of the Quran," Nursi was, besides eloquently defending "the rights of beings" against materialist philosophy's accusations of meaningless and purposelessness, pointing out some of the inconsistencies of Ibn 'Arabi's ideas concerning the Unity of Existence, which, according to Nursi, "in order to truly affirm divine unity and fully enter God's presence . . . relegates the universe to the level of imagination and casts it into non-existence."[33]

Nursi argues that the realities (*hakikat*) of beings are rays of the divine name of Truth (*Hakk*) and the manifestation of His names and attributes. The reality of each and every thing, including man, is based on a name and relies on its reality. Things are not merely insignificant forms without reality.[34] The universal rule of this highway of the Companions and their successors is "the reality of things is constant (*thabita*)." Almighty God has a manifestation through all His names in actuality. Such names as Merciful and Provider are real and actual, and require actual mirrors—beings needy for sustenance and beneficence. Through His creativity, all things have accidental existence. Relatively to His necessary existence it is extremely weak and unstable, but it is not imagination.[35]

In addition, Nursi describes this way by contrasting it with the purely rational methods of the Islamic philosophers (*hükema*) and the ulama. These he likens to bringing water from the far reaches of the world by means of pipes and conduits, which may get broken or blocked. Through an instance of the miraculousness of the Quran's meaning (*Kur'an'ın bir i'caz-ı mānevisiyle*), the way it teaches causes the water of life to flow forth wherever it strikes, like Moses' staff; "it opens a window yielding knowledge of God in everything."[36]

THE QURAN

The third major theme of the *Risale-i Nur* to be examined in this introductory section is the Quran. Since his youth, it had been Nursi's goal in life to demonstrate to the world the Quran's miraculous nature and inimitability, and that it was the source of true knowledge and of the guiding principles for human life. His aim was to update Quranic exegesis and other Islamic sciences in order to explicate it in the light of contemporary advances in knowledge. *Isharat al-I'jaz*[37] (1913–1914) was one fruit of his endeavors. It was in the course of his transformation into the New Said that on the indication of Sirhindi he took "that most lofty guide and holy master" as his sole guide and dedicated himself to the study of it and to finding a way of expounding and proving its truths to the people of the present. He absorbed its meanings to such an extent that when writing the *Risale-i Nur* he claimed that it "had no source but the Quran";[38] that it had "issued from the Quran";[39] and that its verses had been his "absolute master directly."[40]

In response to queries about the *Risale-i Nur*, arising from its original form and styles, Nursi characterized it as being "a true and powerful commentary [on the Quran]";[41] a type of commentary that "expounds, proves, and elucidates with powerful arguments, the Quran's truths related to belief";[42] and "a commentary on the Quran's meanings (*mānevī tefsir*) that silences obstinate philosophers in unprecedented manner."[43]

As has been noted, Nursi made wide use of the term "mānevī" in a variety of contexts and with varying meanings such as nonmaterial or pertaining to meaning. It gives a clue as to what he was trying to achieve with the *Risale-i Nur*. He uses it also in connection with the *Risale* and the Quran's miraculousness, apparently ascribing the *Risale-i Nur*'s efficacy to the miraculousness of the Quran's meanings. For instance, he says: "As a miracle of the Qu'ran's meanings (*Kur'an'ın bir mānevī mucizesi olarak*), the *Risale-i Nur* saves the fundamentals of belief";[44] the *Risale-i Nur* is "one ray of the miraculousness of the Quran of Miraculous Exposition's meanings (*i'caz-ı manevisinin bir şuāı*)";[45] and the *Risale-i Nur*'s solving numerous riddles of creation and mysteries of religion was "directly the work of the miraculousness of the All-Wise Quran's meanings."[46]

The inimitability of the meanings the Quran expresses is only one aspect of its miraculousness. Nursi expounds numerous aspects of it. He claimed to have pointed out almost forty aspects in the first works of the New Said, written in Arabic and later put together in *al-Mathnawī al-'Arabī al-Nūrī*, and in *Ishārāt al-I'jāz*, which deals chiefly with literary aspects of the Quran's miraculousness;

its word-order, eloquence, and use of various literary devices. The Twenty-Fifth Word is the part of the *Risale-i Nur* that is proved and elaborated in greatest detail. Other aspects that he mentions are its youth and its addressing all classes and levels of men in every age;[47] its solving the riddles of the universe;[48] numerous aspects of its eloquence, and also its conciseness;[49] and its use of allegorical comparisons.[50]

The attribute of the Quran that is most emphasized in the *Risale-i Nur*, however, so that it has almost become identified with the *Risale*, is the Quran's being what Nursi calls "the pre-eternal translator of the book of the universe"; in other words, the Quran's interpreting and making meaningful the processes of the natural world with its verses describing the divine acts and the names from which they proceed. This question will be dealt with in greater detail in the section on reflective thought.

A further theme of the *Risale-i Nur* that may be subsumed under that of the Quran is its comparisons between the wisdom of the Quran and philosophy and science. These comparisons, which should be distinguished from the allegorical comparisons of a more abstract nature, are an effective device designed to illustrate the true wisdom of the Quran in several respects and the unwisdom of philosophy and the differences between them. Nursi makes wide use of them to illustrate the wisdom and purposes (*hikmet*) of things, which are a manifestation of the divine name of All-Wise, and a theme underlying many of his discussions. His emphasis on the purpose and use of teleological proofs was probably a response to the denial of ultimate causes by materialist thinkers like Büchner, who were influential in early twentieth-century Turkey, and their refutation of the order of the universe.[51] Seen through the filter of such thinkers' works, scientific discoveries had caused everything to be questioned.

Impotence and Poverty

Impotence and poverty are two of the four main principles of the *Risale-i Nur*'s way. Signifying man's powerlessness and incapability before his Maker, and his want and neediness, they are two basic concepts in Nursi's system of thought. He describes impotence as being a path that, like ecstatic love, leads to winning God's love by way of worship, but is safer. Poverty leads to the divine name of All-Merciful.[52]

According to Nursi, infinite impotence, weakness, poverty, and need are instrinsic to human nature,[53] for "The essence of humanity has been kneaded" with them. One of man's innate duties is to recognize this and proclaim it before the Most Merciful One by seeking his needs. To do so is, in Nursi's words, "to fly to the high station of worship of God and servitude to Him (*ubūdiyet*) on the wings of impotence and poverty."[54]

This is the path of prophethood, inspired by divine revelation, which is the origin of sheer worship. It teaches "that the aim of humanity and duty of human beings is . . . knowing their impotence to seek refuge in divine power, by seeing their weakness to rely on divine strength, by realizing their poverty to trust in divine mercy."[55]

Just as the darkness of the night is a perfect mirror for displaying electric light, so man's vast impotence and poverty have the reverse function of allowing man to act as an extensive mirror to "the innumerable manifestations of the All-Powerful and Compassionate One Whose power is infinite, the All-Generous and Rich One whose wealth is boundless."[56]

References to man's mirror-like essence are found throughout the *Risale-i Nur*. For example, "Through its impotence, weakness, poverty, and need, my life acts as a mirror to the power, strength, wealth, and mercy of the Creator of life."[57] Not only human beings, all creatures act as mirrors to the Maker's power and riches through their impotence and poverty.[58]

Further, it is because of man's innate weakness and impotence that beings have been subjugated to him by divine mercy, not because of human power and dominance.[59] Thus, Nursi argues that human progress and civilization have been achieved not through man's conquering them or through combat but because he has been assisted by divine compassion and mercy due to his impotence; they have been given them due to his need.[60]

Another point Nursi frequently draws attention to is man's need to have recourse to the power and mercy of the All-Powerful and Compassionate One due to his innumerable enemies and needs on the one hand, and his impotence and poverty on the other.[61]

It is because of this that, after belief, man's primary innate duty is supplication. And supplication, Nursi informs us, "is the basis of worship of God and servitude to Him."[62] That is, the reason Almighty God made man infinitely weak and impotent was so that "he would perpetually seek refuge at the divine court and beseech and supplicate."[63]

Man and His Faculties

Before examining the major themes of worship, servitude, and supplication, it will be useful to look at Nursi's treatment of man and his abilities and faculties.

With the *Risale-i Nur*'s way as one of universal worship (*ubūdiyet-i külliye*), Nursi assigns much space to analysis and descriptions of the human being, his comprehensive nature and many faculties, and his duties and functions. For, in Nursi's view, it is because of his duties and rank that man has importance. In respect of his face that looks to the ego and the life of this world, and to the soul (*nefs*) and physicality, he is insignificant.[64] If he is perfected through belief and Islam, and in regard to humanity and servitude to God, he may rise to universality within his particularity and to a position whereby he discerningly reads the book of the universe and oversees its creatures and benefits from them. In this way, according to Nursi, he rises to "the highest of the high and becomes the Most Excellent Pattern of the universe (*ahsen-i takvim*–Quran, 95:4)." Here, to illuminate this question, we will take a brief look at Nursi's interpretation of, first, the 'I' or ego; second, the evil-commanding soul (*nefs-i emmāre*); and third, man's comprehensive nature.

*The 'I' (*ene*)*

According to Nursi, man's 'I' or ego is one component of the Trust mentioned in Quran 33:72, and is the key both to the divine names and what he calls "the locked talisman of creation." Thus, when the 'I' is understood correctly, so may the mysteries of the universe be solved, and the divine names be understood. Crucial to the understanding of this fundamental question is the concept of the indicative meaning of things (*māna-yı harfī*), and the nominal meaning, which is related to viewpoint and was Nursi's major finding during his intense inner search as the New Said was emerging following World War One. It is one of the pivotal concepts of the *Risale-i Nur* and is discussed further in the section on reflective thought. As far as the 'I' is concerned, what it means is that the 'I' should be seen as possessing only apparent or imaginary power and other attributes, and as being mirror-like, indicating the true power, knowledge, and ownership of its Maker. That is, the 'I' "is a sort of scale or measure that makes known the absolute, all-encompassing attributes of the Necessary Being." When perceived in this way, the 'I' abandons its imaginary ownership and, ascribing both itself and other beings to their True Owner, sees the universe as it is in reality and "the duties it is performing." It purifies the soul, carries out the Trust, and achieves true worship. If, however, it fails to do this, as it ascribes power and ownership to itself, so it does to causes in the outside world. Thus, it betrays the Trust and, not seeing the universe as it is in reality, attributes partners to God on a grand scale.[65]

The Evil-Commanding Soul

Being the way of the Companions of the Prophet, the *Risale-i Nur*'s method is to purify and cleanse the evil-commanding soul, rather than to kill or annihilate it as with the Sufis and saints. For by virtue of the many faculties within the soul, the Companions performed a greater variety of worship, thanks, and praise, while the saints' worship acquires a simplicity and plainness.[66] According to Nursi, although the human soul is dense like earth, on condition it is purified, it may rise above all the other subtle faculties because of its comprehensiveness.[67]

Thus, Nursi's analyses and discussions of the sicknesses and tricks of the unregenerate soul and his suggestions for its cure and purification form another major theme of the *Risale-i Nur*. The Addendum describing the path of impotence, poverty, compassion, and reflection, which consists of four steps, is Nursi's most systematic exposition of his method of purifying the soul.[68] Other references and remedies are found scattered through the volumes of the *Risale-i Nur*. In the Addendum he gives brief explanations of the four steps, each of which is inspired by a verse from the Quran, and then explains how it is shorter, safer, and more universal than various Sufi paths, for by means of it a person may find a way leading to God in everything.

Nursi points out the positive functions of the soul, one of the most important of which is its being a means of perpetual striving and therefore of moral and spiritual progress,[69] and he suggests that a person should train his soul with compassion while seeing its shortcomings,[70] but he still does not fail to draw attention to its evils and pitfalls.

A final matter that may be cited as a related theme is Nursi's condemnation of "philosophy," and modern civilization, which springs from it, for their gratifying and inflating the appetitive soul.[71] He equates philosophy with the soul,[72] and the soul with nature, as put forward by the naturalists, in the world.[73]

Man's Comprehensive Nature

Nursi dwells at length on the comprehensive abilities and faculties given to man, which make him the center and conscious fruit of the universe,[74] and "the chief pivot of the works of [divine] dominicality"[75]—that is, the center of the Sustainer's administration and regulation of all beings. "Most of the wisdom, aims, purposes, and benefits in the universe look to man." The reason for their focus on him in this way is his comprehensive nature, by virtue of which he can understand and experience all the divine names manifested in the universe.[76]

Reworking the theme of man's virtual worthlessness regarding his transitory physical being and his supreme importance in regard to the duties and rank he assumes through belief and Islam, Nursi in many places lists the rising levels of divine bounties and expanding spheres from corporeal life up through humanity, which extends as far as the mind can reach, then Islam and belief, which encompass the spheres of contingency and of the divine names and attributes, to knowledge and love of God. At each he describes the human senses and faculties with which man may weigh the divine gifts and understand the divine names manifested in it. In this way, he is raised up from petty particularity "to an exalted luminous universality."[77]

Since man possesses the faculties and abilities to receive all those bounties and to reflect the divine names manifested in the cosmos, he is like a point of focus displaying together all the names in the mirror of his essence, thus proclaiming God's oneness (*ehadiyet*).[78]

There are thus two main aims in the creation of man's senses and faculties: the first is thanks and worship, and the second is to make known to him the divine names so that he should believe in them.[79] He has many other duties and functions;[80] his heart, spirit, intellect, imagination, and other subtle faculties each has duties of worship peculiar to it.[81]

> The perfect man is he who, driving all those subtle senses towards reality on the different ways of worship particular to them, marches heroically like the Companions in a broad arena and rich fashion towards the goal, with the heart as commander and the subtle faculties as soldiers.[82]

WORSHIP, SERVITUDE, AND SUPPLICATION

We have seen how man is created with a comprehensive disposition, as a comprehensive mirror, thus being prepared for universal worship. That is, Nursi counts as worship (*ubūdiyet*) all the acts a person performs with his limbs, members, senses, and faculties, physical, mental, and spiritual, when he perceives both the latter and the objects in the outside world as mirror-like creatures reflecting the divine names, and he performs his actions consciously offering thanks, praise, and worship. Now we will examine a number of other themes related to worship and supplication.

As has been mentioned, in expounding the Quran, Nursi points out that all the branches of knowledge and sciences, being based on the divine names, are in essence truth and reality. Thus, part of man's universal worship is the practicing and advancing of knowledge and science.[83] For this reason, he describes as "valuable worship" the work of "craftsmen and artists and inspired inventors who purely for the benefit of God's servants, serve the general interest and public well-being and betterment of social life."[84]

Furthermore, in a short treatise on supplication, in which he explains its three main sorts, Nursi says: "The greater part of human progress and most discoveries are the result of a sort of supplication. . . . They were asked for with a sincere tongue of latent ability and so were given."[85]

A key theme running through Nursi's expositions of worship is the exalted worship of the Prophet Muhammad (PBUH), who is shown to be the model in many matters. According to Nursi, the comprehensive worship performed by the Prophet was at the very highest degree and earned for him the title of God's Beloved.[86] Moreover, just as his messengership was the reason for the creation of this world, so his worship was the cause of the foundation of the next.[87] Nursi also frequently cites the Prophet's prayers and supplications, the essence and basis of worship, as being the reason for the creation of eternal felicity.[88] He even extends this prayer to include all beings, saying: "[The Prophet] is beseeching for a need so universal that . . . all beings join in his prayer . . . he supplicates with such want . . . that he leads the whole cosmos to join in his prayer."[89]

Nursi looked on the reading of the *Risale-i Nur* itself, and the practice of the reflective thought it teaches, as worship,[90] and this "sacred" aspect of the work is enhanced by the fact that each part of it is concluded by a verse, or verses, from the Quran and sometimes a short prayer. Parts of it are actually in the form of supplications or invocations, such as the Twenty-Ninth Flash, in Arabic, and the Third Ray, in Turkish. These latter are summarized versions of the reflective journeys through the cosmos described in various parts of the *Risale-i Nur*, and reiterate some of the arguments and ideas they put forward. Furthermore, Nursi considered the recitation of such supplications as *al-Jawshan al-Kabīr*,[91] and particularly the litanies (*tesbihat*) recited following the five daily prayers, to be an essential part of the *Risale-i Nur*'s "way."[92]

Cosmic Worship and Glorification of God

The reading of the tongues of beings and the glorifications of God they utter through displaying manifestations of the divine names is the purpose of the reflective thought on the universe that is discussed below. Here is included a brief outline of what this worship of beings consists of.

First, according to Nursi, it was only through the light brought by Muhammad (PBUH) that the universe was raised to life and "transformed into a place where God's names are recited in joy and ecstasy." Previously to the sending of the Quran, it had been a dark place of mourning, filled with dumb, dead, insensate creatures.[93]

Second, from Nursi's descriptions it seems that the beings of the universe perform worship and glorifications in myriad ways. For instance, "the perfect worship and obedience of the angels and spirit beings" on the one hand, and the conformity and submissive obedience to the divine laws and general order of all beings animate and inanimate on the other, are forms of worship that indicate the existence of an object of worship.[94]

In expounding Quran 22:18, which "states explicitly that everything from . . . planets to particles prostrates, worship, praises, and glorifies God," Nursi divides beings into four categories and explains their duties of worship, which, he tells us, "vary according to their capacities and the divine names that they manifest." The four categories of beings employed in the palace of the universe are the angels, the animals, plants and inanimate creatures, and human beings.[95]

One of the most frequently mentioned of the angels' functions is their representing in the angelic tongue in the World of the Inner Dimensions of Things (*melekūkiyet*), and presenting to the divine court, the glorifications of the external beings of the universe. Another is their being bearers of the divine command. In interpreting certain allegorical hadiths, Nursi explains their duties of representation in terms of universals as well as particulars, thus showing that "although external beings are outwardly inanimate and unconscious, they all perform extremely vital, living, and conscious duties and glorification."[96]

Nursi explains causality in terms of supplication, with the refutation of nature and causality being one of the main purposes of the *Risale-i Nur*. He says that the gathering together of causes is a supplication for the creation of the effect. For a tree, for example, "which is a miracle of divine power," cannot be attributed to the lifeless substances surrounding it. This is a form of supplication through the tongue of latent ability. Supplication through the tongue of innate need, made by all living creatures, is another sort. In fact, Nursi says: "All that rises to the divine court is supplication. Those things that are causes seek the effects from God."[97]

Compassion

Compassion (*şefkat*) is the third principle of the *Risale-i Nur*'s way. "Compassion is a path like ecstatic love is a path, but it is swifter and broader, and leads to the name of All-Compassionate (*Raḥīm*)."[98] It is a means together with the other principles of impotence, poverty, and reflective thought of attaining to the names of Most Merciful and All-Compassionate.

In Nursi's view, compassion is far superior to passionate love, for three reasons: first, "it is gentle and pure, whereas many sorts of love and passion are beneath one's dignity." Second, compassion is wide and embracing, whereas passionate love either restricts its gaze to its beloved and sacrifices everything for it, or so elevates it that it denigrates everything else. And third, compassion is sincere and pure and wants nothing in return, whereas passionate love wants remuneration. It is presumably for these reasons that he considers it a swifter and broader path.

While some aspects of compassion in the *Risale-i Nur* look to communal and social life and are beyond the scope of the present chapter, here it may be noted that overwhelming emphasis is placed in the work on the Creator's compassionate munificence and merciful benevolence, and on the wisdom, art, beauty, and sublimity of His works, rather than divine wrath, vengeance, and punishment. Indeed, Nursi said of the *Risale-i Nur* that it "is a manifestation of the names of All-Compassionate and All-Wise," and that "numerous flashes and mysteries of the truth of [divine] compassionateness have been expounded and proved in many parts of [it]."[99]

Reflective Thought

Reflective thought or reflection is the fourth principle or component of the *Risale-i Nur*'s way and, according to Nursi's definition, "is a path like passionate love is a path, but it is richer, more brilliant, and broader, and leads to the name of All-Wise."[100] In another place, he says that "it proceeds on the principles of wisdom (*hikmet*) and order (*intizam*),"[101] that is, the order of the universe.

One of "man's fundamental duties" is to "gaze on the miracles of dominical power in things, [and] to ponder over them as objects from which lessons may be drawn."[102] For the Maker fashioned the universe in such a way, "adorning it with endless varieties of embellished wonders," that conscious creatures would "reflect on it and take lessons."[103] Nursi reminds his readers that the Quran frequently refers its verses to the faculty of reason so that people will reflect on them.[104] He was hopeful, too, after having written *Ayetü'l-Kübrā*, that he had succeeded in capturing the meaning of the hadith: "A hour's reflection is better that a year's [supererogatory] worship."[105]

A large part of the *Risale-i Nur* consists of arguments, proofs, and allegories describing aspects of the natural world from numerous angles, and is therefore related to this question. Here, an attempt will be made to pinpoint some main elements and themes.

Doubtless in response to Western science and post-Enlightenment thought, which had stripped the world of all sacredness and meaning, Nursi's prime intention was to depict and restate its meanings and purport in the light of the Quran, so as to demonstrate how the universe may be a means of gaining belief in the Maker and knowledge of Him. Indeed, he supplies proofs based on "reading" the meanings stated by beings, of all the main pillars and matters of belief.

Thus, a theme to mention here is the concept of the indicative meaning of things (*māna-yı harfī*) and the nominal meaning (*māna-yı ismī*), which is related to viewpoint and was noted earlier in connection with the 'I'. Nursi deduced it from the Quran and explained it as follows:

> All things other than God, that is, the universe, should be looked at as signifying something other than themselves (*māna-yı harfī*) and on His account. It is an error to looke at them as signifying only themselves (*māna-yı ismī*) and on account of causes. . . . Thus, when considering bounties, the Bestower of the bounties should spring to mind . . . when looking at causes, one should think of the True Causer of Causes.[106]

When regarded in this way, the 'I' becomes "shadow-like and a mirror reflecting one other than itself," as mentioned, while nature in the outside world becomes "divine art and a code of natural divine laws."[107]

The metaphor of a book to describe the universe and its function of conveying meaning follows on logically from this. In fact, Nursi uses many metaphors to depict its various functions, such as an exhibition, a guesthouse, a palace, a factory, a clock, a country, and a tree, but a book is the one he employs most extensively. He also makes wide use metaphorically of the parts, features, and instruments of books and writing to make his points. For example,

> Just the same is the mighty book of the universe; we see with our eyes a pen at work that writes on the face of the earth, which is a single of its pages, and on the spring, which is a single folio, the . . . plant and animal species, which are like . . . different books, all together . . . with complete order, and sometimes writes an ode in a word like a tree, and the complete index of a book in a point-like seed.[108]

Thus, beings become "words of power"[109] and "embodied words."[110] They also "speak" their testimony to their Maker's existence, unity, and other attributes through what Nursi calls "the tongue of disposition," that is, through the meanings expressed by the manner of their creation and the functions they perform. The universe in this sense is a "speaking book." The *Risale-i Nur* interprets their words and testimony, and shows how to read them. However, this is in its capacity as a Quranic commentary, for, as Nursi emphasizes, the Quran and the universe have a mutually interpretative relationship. That is, just as the Quran is "the interpreter of the verses of the book of the universe,"[111] and explains its meanings,[112] and expounds its order and art;[113] so "the cosmos [is] so meaningful and well-ordered, [it is] an embodied book of the Glorious One, an incarnate dominical Quran."[114] Expressing the same meanings in different form, one, the Quran, proceeds from the attribute of Speech, while the other, the Quran of the universe, proceeds from Power.

In this way, the universe itself is shown to offer innumerable proofs and evidences of the divine existence and unity and other truths of belief, and to be a powerful means of gaining knowledge of God. For example, according to Nursi, the most striking thing about the cosmos is its "universal and perfect order . . . everything exists within a precise order and delicate balance and measure." Many of his arguments show this to be an incontrovertible proof of divine unity.[115] And the persistence of the precise order in things despite the constant motion and change, at the same time as following innumerable aims, purposes, and benefits, indicates such attributes as universal wisdom, and justice, comprehensive knowledge, and absolute power.[116]

The wisdom and purposes apparent in beings form another major theme; many different questions are elucidated in this regard. They are also very often shown to necessitate matters of belief. For example, the wisdom in things in many respects necessitates the existence of the hereafter;[117] it necessitates a teacher, that is, a divine messenger, to make known the purposes in them;[118] and the wisdom and purposes of things necessitate the attribute of will, and disprove the efficacy of causes.[119]

The works of divine mercy and providence, to which much space is given, are also shown to necessitate and prove the pillars of belief, particularly the resurrection of the dead and life of the hereafter.[120] Indeed, the manifestations of very many of the names are described with this aim in view.

Thanks

A final section should be allotted to thanks, which in some places is given as one of the basic principles of the *Risale-i Nur* together with some or all of the four discussed earlier, and is another of its major themes. In a short treatise devoted to thanks,[121] Nursi quotes verses from the Quran and says that it is the thing the Merciful Creator wants most from His servants. He recalls the severe threats the Quran directs at ingratitude, showing it to be denial of the divine bounties and favors.

As with other moral qualities and precepts, Nursi deals with thanks in a cosmic context. He persuasively argues that thanks is "the most important result of creation" and "the most important fruit of the tree of creation and the most elevated product of the factory of the universe." For the vastly rich treasury of sustenance, which is at the center of human and animal life—with all the beings of the universe looking to life—subsists through thanks and produces thanks.

Man, who is most needy for all the varieties of sustenance and is a comprehensive mirror to all the divine names and has been given the faculties to weigh up all their subtleties, may be raised up to the highest of the high through thanks. Thanks is the most essential of the four principles of the way of worship and winning God's love.

NOTES

1. Bediuzzaman Said Nursi, *Letters 1928–1932* (Istanbul, 2001), 518.
2. Ibid., 362.
3. Ibid., 528. This coincides with Shaikh Ahmad Sirhindi's view that "the Shari'ah defines what religious life truly is, and what are its constituents and what they really mean. Shari'ah is not just a code of rules and regulations that govern external action. It also explains what faith, *tawhid*, love, trust, gratitude, patience, worship, *dhikr*, *jihad*, *taqwa*, and *ihsan* are, and shows how to realise these realities." Muhammad Abdul Haqq Ansari, *Sufism and Sharī'ah. A Study of Shaykh Ahmad Sirhindi's Effort to Reform Sufism* (Leicester, 1986), 75; also 71. William C. Chittick, however, discusses Islam in terms of three dimensions, with Sufism in the broadest sense being "Islam's third and innermost dimension." See Chittick, *Faith and Practice of Islam. Three Thirteenth Century Sufi Texts* (Kuala Lumpur, 1994), 168.
4. Nursi, *The Rays Collection* (Istanbul, 2002), 416.
5. Bediuzzaman Said Nursi, *Emirdağ Lahikası* (Istanbul, 1992), i, 266.
6. Nursi, *Rays*, 200.
7. Ibid., 125.
8. For further discussion of this, see the section on reflective thought.
9. For Nursi's refutation of nature and causality, see Treatise on Nature, in *The Flashes Collection* (Istanbul, 2000), 232–54.
10. Nursi, *Rays*, 256.
11. Nursi's use of the term "philosophy" is pejorative since he employs it mostly to signify naturalism, positivism, or other currents of materialistic Western thought that have been hostile to revealed religion, or to signify a materialistic interpretation of science. It represents the dominance of human reason and the rejection of divine revelation.

12. See Nursi, *Letters*, 53; *Barla Lahikası* (Istanbul, 1994), 349.
13. See *TDVİA*, xxii, 213–14.
14. See Nursi, *Emirdağ Lahikası*, i, 91.
15. This undertaking of Nursi is perhaps a contemporary example of previous endeavors to integrate different disciplines in the Islamic scholarly and spiritual traditions in order to demonstrate and teach religious truths. See, for example, *The Conclusive Argument from God: Shah Wali Allah of Delhi's Hujjat Allah al-Baligha*. Tr. Marcia K. Hermansen (Islamabad 2003), xv–xvi.
16. Nursi, *Words*, 402.
17. Nursi, *Letters*, 422.
18. Nursi, *Emirdağ Lahikası*, i, 65.
19. See, for example, Chittick, *Faith and Practice of Islam*, 6.
20. Nursi, *Rays*, 127.
21. Nursi, *Words*, 329.
22. Nursi, *Rays*, 127.
23. Bediuzzaman Said Nursi, *Kastamonu Lahikası* (Istanbul, 1994), 18; Nursi, *The Key to Belief* (Istanbul, 1998), 111–12.
24. Nursi, *Key to Belief*, 104–15; Nursi, *Emirdağ Lahikası*, i, 103–4.
25. Nursi, *Words*, 491.
26. For explanations of these, see Najm al-Din al-Razi, *The Path of God's Bondsmen from Origin to Return*, tr. Hamid Algar (North Haledon, 1982), 28 fn 16; Annemarie Schimmel, *Mystical Dimensions of Islam* (Chapel Hill, 1975), 16, 98–99, 334–35.
27. Gümüşhaneli Shaikh Ahmed Ziya'üddin (ed.), *Majmu'at al-Ahzab*, three vols. (Istanbul, 1311).
28. Nursi, *Flashes*, 22.
29. Nursi, *Letters*, 40.
30. Ibid., 71–72.
31. For elucidation of this "obscure mystery," see ibid., 72. For similar statements by Sirhindi, see Ansari, *Sufism and Shari'ah*, 218–19, quoted from *Maktubat*, vol. I, no. 313.
32. Ibid., 420.
33. Ibid., 392.
34. Nursi, *Words*, 188–89, 655, 660.
35. See Nursi, *Letters*, 107–9.
36. Bediuzzaman Said Nursi, *Mesnevi-yi Nūriye* [Turk. Tr. Abdülmecid Nursi] (Istanbul: Envar Neşriyat, 1994), 8–9; *Letters*, 389.
37. For English translation: *Signs of Miraculousness. The Inimitability of the Quran's Conciseness*. Tr. Şükran Vahide (Istanbul, 2004).
38. Bediuzzaman Said Nursi, *Sikke-i Tasdik-i Gaybī* (Istanbul, 1994), 94.
39. Nursi, *Letters*, 434.
40. Ibid., 441.
41. Nursi, *Rays*, 399, 512.
42.Nursi, *Rays*, 512; also *Emirdağ Lahikası*, ii, 75.
43. Nursi, *Rays*, 513.
44. Nursi, *Kastamonu Lahikası*, 11.
45. Ibid., 60.
46. Nursi, *Letters*, 438–39.

47. Nursi, *Words*, 419–24, 461; *Rays*, 159, 263.
48. Nursi, *Words*, 153; *Rays*, 259.
49. For example, Nursi, *Words*, 255ff., 206; *Letters*, 374–76.
50. Nursi, *Letters*, 443–44; *Words*, 209.
51. Süleyman Hayri Bolay, *Türkiye'de Ruhçu ve Maddeci Görüşün Mücadelesi* (Ankara, 1995), 152 ff.
52. Nursi, *Words*, 491.
53. See ibid., 564.
54. Ibid., 324, 326, 334.
55. Ibid., 562, 563.
56. Ibid., 330.
57. Nursi, *Rays*, 81.
58. Nursi, *Letters*, 286.
59. Nursi, *Rays*, 65.
60. Nursi, *Words*, 337; also, 245.
61. See, Nursi, *Words*, 16, 172, 324, 719; *Rays*, 651.
62. Nursi, *Words*, 324.
63. Nursi, *Flashes*, 274.
64. Nursi, *Words*, 330, 337–38.
65. Ibid., 559–60.
66. See ibid., 508.
67. Ibid., 514.
68. Ibid., 491–94.
69. Nursi, *Letters*, 387–88.
70. Nursi, *Words*, 678.
71. See ibid., 420, 566.
72. Nursi, *Words*, 70; *Flashes*, 306.
73. Nursi, *Words*, 239–40.
74. Nursi, *Flashes*, 456.
75. Nursi, *Rays*, 78.
76. Nursi, *Flashes*, 456.
77. Nursi, *Rays*, 6–8. Also, *Flashes*, 456–57; *Words*, 369–70.
78. Nursi, *Letters*, 279.
79. Nursi, *Words*, 139.
80. See, for example, *Flashes*, 457–59.
81. See Nursi, *Words*, 331.
82. Ibid., 511.
83. Ibid., 272.
84. Ibid., 274.
85. Nursi, *Letters*, 354.
86. Nursi, *Letters*, 533; *Words*, 603, 72.
87. Nursi, *Words*, 83–84.
88. For example, ibid., 247.
89. Ibid., 247–48.
90. See, for example, ibid., 168; *Rays*, 262, 432.
91. *al-Jaushan al-Kabir* is a long supplication that is ascribed to the Prophet Muhammad (PBUH) and consists of verses from the Quran and the divine names. Nursi

himself read it constantly and said it was a source of inspiration for the *Risale-i Nur*. See *Rays*, 596; *Emirdağ Lahikası*, i, 72, 210.

92. Nursi, *Words*, 491.
93. Ibid., 244–45.
94. Ibid., 690–91.
95. See *Words*, 361–67.
96. Ibid., 530–32.
97. Nursi, *Letters*, 353–54.
98. Nursi, *Words*, 491.
99. Nursi, *Rays*, 197.
100. Nursi, *Words*, 491.
101. Nursi, *Sikke-i Tasdik-i Gaybī*, 117.
102. Nursi, *Words*, 334.
103. Ibid., 604.
104. See ibid., 428, 430, 433, 434.
105. al-'Ajluni, *Kashf al-Khafa'*, i, 143; al-Haythami, *Majma 'al-Zawā'id*, i, 78; al-Ghazali, *Ihya' 'Ulum al-Din*, iv, 409.
106. Nursi, *Mesnevi-yī Nūriye*, 51.
107. Nursi, *Mesnevi-yī Nūriye* [Turk. Tr. Abdülkadir Badıllı] (Istanbul, n.d.), 262.
108. Nursi, *Rays*, 228. See also *Rays*, 577; *Flashes*, 176; *Words*, 302, etc.
109. Nursi, *Words*, 230, 320, 572, etc.
110. Nursi, *Rays*, 169.
111. Nursi, *Words*, 136.
112. Ibid., 251.
113. Ibid., 151.
114. Nursi, *Rays*, 163.
115. For example, Nursi, *Words*, 716; *Flashes*, 406.
116. Nursi, *Letters*, 273–74; *Signs of Miraculousness*, 164–65; *Mesnevi-yī Nūriye*, 252–53.
117. See, for example, Nursi, *Flashes*, 432.
118. See, for example, ibid., 410.
119. Ibid., 408–9.
110. See, Nursi, *Words*, 75–76, 540–41; *Rays*, 208, 231, 248, etc.
111. Nursi, *Letters*, 428–32.

TWO

The Six-Sided Vision of Said Nursi

Toward a Spiritual Architecture of the Risale-i Nur

Colin Turner

If the definitive history of twentieth-century Islamic movements is ever written, one wonders whether its author would be both perspicacious and brave enough to argue a point that, while held in private by many Muslim thinkers and writers, is rarely if ever mooted openly, namely, that the Islamic resurgence that is said to have occurred over the past forty or fifty years should be seen primarily in terms of a *resurgent identity* that has little to do with any surge of interest in, or affiliation to, the faith beneath Islam per se. One presumes that Muslims have not suddenly become better believers or more proficient in their outward expressions of submission, although clearly this may have happened in various individual cases. What does appear to have occurred in the Muslim world, however, is a sustained attempt on the part of certain groups to reassert their collective identity in the face of external threats. Some have accentuated their inextricable ties—be they religious, cultural, or a mix of the two—to Islam, while others have taken advantage of the centrality of Islam to the sociopolitical and cultural dynamics of the Muslim world in order to advance their own political and ideological agendas.

As Muhammad Shabistari points out, seen in this way, the numerous movements of the past 150 years, characterized almost without exception as Islamic movements, have had little if anything to do with the resurgence of religious faith as such. Most of these, Shabistari argues, have actually been political movements, with leaders whose underlying goal has been to solve a specific problem: the problem of the perceived backwardness of the Muslim peoples and their subservience, politically and culturally, to the West.[1]

While none of the groups that operate within the definitional matrix of Islamic movements can claim to be identifiable primarily as a faith movement, various individuals have appeared sporadically with the avowed aim of fostering renewal of belief—often to the extent of dedicating their whole life's work to that aim—and around some of these individuals, movements of considerable size and import have accreted. Bediuzzaman Said Nursi is one such individual.[2]

Almost half a century after his death, Nursi continues to defy any attempts to locate him precisely within the generally accepted milieu of Muslim scholars. While his magnum opus, the *Risale-i Nur*, is for all intents and purposes a commentary on the Quran, it is not a work of exegesis in the technical sense of the word, although he was clearly an accomplished exegete. And while Nursi was well versed in the principles of *kalām* and the methods of the *mutakallimūn*, and devotes the lion's share of the *Risale* to what he claims are rational proofs for the unity (*tawḥīd*) of God, it is not a work of traditional theology either.

In fact, on one level, the *Risale* is as resistant to compartmentalization as the Quran itself, which it claims to mirror and to elucidate. And if, as Nursi often asserts, the aim of the Quran is to guide man to belief, then the teachings of the *Risale* should be seen as consonant with that aim.

> The three supreme matters in the worlds of humanity and Islam are belief, the Shari'ahh, and life. Since the truths of belief are the greatest of these, the Risale-i Nur's select and loyal students avoid politics with abhorrence so that they should not be made the tool to other currents and subject to other forces, and those diamond-like Quranic truths not reduced to fragments of glass in the view of those who sell or exploit religion for the world, and so that they can carry out to the letter the duty of saving belief, the greatest duty.[3]

Part of Nursi's appeal lay in his uncompromising belief that it is belief (*īmān*) that must be renewed and protected, and that all other endeavors must be approached with the primacy of belief in mind: the fact that, unlike many of the popular Muslim thinkers of his own epoch, he repudiated the dubious art of politics—and, more important, the dubious art of politicking that is buttressed by religion—earned him respect and conferred on him a sense of authenticity that would perhaps be found wanting in so many other Muslim thinkers. Another part of his appeal lay in his shrewd interpretation of the forces ranged against him. For Nursi, unlike many of the Muslim scholars, leaders, and ideologues who came later, realized that if there is a conflict between Islam—or belief—and modernity, it is not a conflict fought over issues of government or technology, over science or democracy. As Nursi's own evaluation of the problems facing the Muslim world shows, the conflict is ultimately over transcendence, with the post-Enlightenment experiment claiming a centrality in the universe's affairs for man that Islam, with its emphasis on the dependence of man on God, cannot countenance. Man is faced with a choice: belief in the sovereignty of God or belief in the sovereignty of man, with all that such a choice entails. For Nursi, the way to salvation consists solely in choosing the Other over the self, and it is in the dynamics of this choice that the key to an understanding of Nursi's take on spirituality may be found.

DEFINING THE SPIRITUAL

The extent to which any discussion on spirituality can succeed—whether in the context of Islam in general or Said Nursi's *Risale* in particular—depends on the degree to which the definitional opacity surrounding the term can be cleared. There are as many approaches to, and manifestations of, Islam as there are Muslims, and the same applies, mutatis mutandis, to the notion of Islamic spirituality.

Definitions of spirituality abound: like the term "mysticism," overuse has rendered it almost inutile, particularly in Western secular milieus, where it is employed to denote anything and everything—from the contemplative traditions within Christianity to the vague feelings of religiosity claimed by those who do not adhere to any institutionalized faith yet continue somehow to feel at one with a 'higher force'. However, while we need to steer clear of the more essentialist a priori conceptions of the term "spirituality"—particularly those that, in the context of Islam at least, connote some kind of false division between the material and the spiritual, or, more misleadingly still, between the worldly and the religious—discussion cannot take place in a vacuum. Arguably the most convenient and germane place to locate the basic premises on which a workable definition of the spiritual in Islam can be found is the Quran itself. If the word spiritual means "connected to or concerning the spirit," then the Islamic revelation makes it abundantly clear that the human spirit is an uncreated entity, breathed into man by God himself. Man's spirit is thus that uncreated "breath of the Compassionate" (*nafas al-raḥmān*) within him that connects him to the divine, and that transforms an otherwise transient material being into the 'vicegerent' (*khalīfa*) of God on earth, capable of rising above all other beings to take his rightful place in eternity, the highest of the high. In the Quranic—and, by extension, the Nursian—schema, spirituality involves man's quest to uncover the reflection of the divine within himself.

The creation of human beings took place, it is held, not merely that they should affirm the existence of a Creator and bow down to His laws through various rites and rituals: for Nursi, God is not merely a principle that is to be accepted, or a giver of laws who is to be obeyed. While the God of the Quran is infinite, absolute, theoretically unfathomable, and ultimately unreachable in the very real sense of those terms, He can be understood through His creation and, more important, His reality can be gradually 'uncovered' by man, who is able to approach God and become ever more aware of what He is simply by virtue of the fact that he is created *in imago Dei*, with the capability of communion with the very Source of his own being. In the cosmology adumbrated by the Quran, and confirmed by the *Risale-i Nur*, man is the reflection whose purpose in life is to perceive and understand the Reflected, and by so doing solve the existential riddle of his own being.

Quranic—and, by extension, Nursian—spirituality is therefore not about becoming more God-like. In fact it would appear to be quite the reverse. It is about realizing that those attributes in man that appear to make him like a God belong in reality to another. The spiritual journey of man toward God, then, is not about becoming more like Him; rather, it is about purifying oneself of all possible claims to Godlikeness and making room for Him to reveal Himself through the medium of the spiritualized soul. It means not acting like Him, but acting in His name; it involves not being like Him, but manifesting or revealing Him.

> Man has been created to open and unveil (the treasuries of Divine Names and Attributes), be a luminous sign (guiding to God), receive and reflect (Divine manifestations),be a light-giving moon reflecting the Eternal Power, and be a mirror for the manifestations of the Eternal Beauty.[4]

For manifestation to be realized, one has to clear out the clutter of the self—the imaginary ownership that man exercises over his own attributes—so that His image may be reflected in the mirror of man's being. It is this handing back or surrender to God of man's imaginary ownership over his own self that forms the bedrock of Nursi's approach to the spiritual, to which we now turn.

The Spiritual Architecture of the *Risale-i Nur*

With the individual treatises that compose the work described variously as rays, gleams, and flashes, the *Risale* models itself as a sort of hermeneutical prism, catching what its author considers to be the effulgence of divine light from the Quran and refracting it as colors visible to, and understandable by, the eye of the human heart. Inspired by the sense of drama that underpins the landscaping of his work, and by his description of the Quran as a six-sided entity,[5] I suggest that we approach the *Risale* as one would a building. In fact, the *Risale* is not one building, but a whole complex of edifices, constructed at various points along the author's career. In the West it remains largely unknown, although there have been attempts in recent years to excavate, rather as one would some fabulous desert palace, lost for years beneath the sands and uncovered gradually, brick by brick. As such, the complex is largely intact. True, the earlier structures—those that date to Nursi's formative period, when the self-styled Old Said was by his own admission preoccupied with the natural sciences and speculative philosophy—are showing signs of wear and tear. The more recent additions to the complex, however, are as impressive now as they must have been when first erected. Nevertheless, many of the buildings that make up the complex remain unexplored, and even those that have been open to the public for years contain rooms, passages, and tunnels that remain locked to this day.

While the extended allegory of the *Risale* as a complex of buildings may appear to be little more than a decorative literary conceit, it is not without its utility. It is in keeping with Nursi's own extensive and often flamboyant use of allegory and metaphor, and reminds us that he was first and foremost a communicator, with a communicator's sense of what best facilitates understanding of the message being communicated. It also conveys something of the unity of composition and design that underpins the *Risale*, with each of its component structures adding strength and sense of purpose to the other, while contributing to a whole that is most definitely more than just the sum of its parts.

More important, the allegory allows this author to talk in terms of the spiritual architecture of the *Risale*, and to offer an overview of those crucial aspects of the Nursian weltanschauung that inform the work and bestow on its unique character. Like the foundations, pillars, and buttresses that support St. Paul's Cathedral, say, or Sultanahmet, certain features in the *Risale* stand out as key to the whole complex. I have identified six of them. On one level, six is a purely arbitrary figure; on another level, however, it is in keeping with Nursi's own assertion of the six-sided nature of the Quran, of which the *Risale* is held up as a mirror. And while these six concepts are not the only 'pillars' holding up the edifice of the *Risale*, they are, I believe, the most conducive to our understanding of what this methodologically fascinating piece of extended Quranic exegesis is all about. They are also woefully understudied, and it is to be hoped that this tour through the buildings of the *Risale-i Nur* will prompt further research in these areas.

The First Pillar: Nursi and "the Most Beautiful Names"

The first pillar represents Nursi's uncompromisingly theocentric portrayal of the cosmos as a divinely penned book, composed of words or verses that, once deconstructed, are revealed as nothing less than embodiments or individuations of the beautiful names (*asmā al-ḥusnā*) of God himself. Nursi's view of creation is thus a wholly sacramental one, in which the transcendent sacred—the Divine—imbues all things.

That God possesses innumerable beautiful names, and not just the ninety-nine mentioned in the *hadith* or counted on the rosary, is nothing new in the theology of Islam. Emphasis on the centrality of the divine attributes of perfection is clearly Quranic in origin, where passages that enumerate the divine bounties, or that describe the workings of God in the world, end invariably in the mention of one or more of the divine names. Acknowledgment of the utter indebtedness of the cosmos to the manifestation of those names appeared relatively early on in Muslim liturgy, finding particular resonance in the invocations of Muhammad and the prophetic household. In the *Invocation of Kumayl*, for example, taught by 'Ali b. Abi Talib to one of his disciples, we read that "the beautiful names of God are the pillars which hold up all things," while countless supplications attributed to the Imams of the Alid line are constructed around the names and attributes of God.[6] Later, of course, meditation on the names of God became a staple of Sufi literature, with whole cosmologies being founded on the premise of manifestation and the created world as mirror for the reflection of the divine.[7] Nursi's view of the cosmos as a multiplicity of loci for the ceaseless and ever-changing manifestation of the divine names is to an extent informed by the teachings of a number of major gnostic thinkers, including Ibn al-'Arabi and Imam Ahmad Sirhindi, although the literary and didactic means he employs to articulate it are undoubtedly his own.

In the Nursian scheme, the visible realm (*'ālam al-shahāda*) is akin to a full-length mirror in which the hidden treasure that is God manifests himself in order to contemplate His own perfection.[8] While on the level of divine essence, this act of contemplation is self-reflexive, on the level of divine acts, contemplation is mediated through creation, at the pinnacle of which stands man. For Nursi, all created beings manifest God's names to some degree: the whole of the cosmos becomes a hierophany, with each created being hymning the praises of God through its innate disposition. However, unlike Eliade's perception of the hierophanic, which posits each of the constituent beings in the cosmos as *potentially* indicative of the sacred, Nursi's vision is one in which all things *actually* and *actively* reflect the Other, yet without compromising their own distinct otherness.[9] Acutely aware that the perception of the world as God's personal mirror may tempt some to dismiss the created realm as a phantasm and declare, along with some of the more extremist advocates of "unity of being" (*waḥdat al-wujūd*), that "all is God," Nursi is at pains to draw clear lines of distinction between his own schema and that of the pantheists.[10] Nursi's own delicate balancing act, in which he juggles the declaration of God's incomparability (*tanzīh*) with that of His similarity (*tashbīh*), serves to ensure on the one hand that in His immanence, God is not confused with His creation, and on the other hand that, in His transcendence, He is not seen as absent or unconcerned with the day-to-day workings of the cosmos.[11]

Nursi also devotes huge swathes of the *Risale* to eloquent expositions of the book of Creation—*kitāb-i kāinat*—in which all of God's 'words'—expressions of His attributes—are written for all to read. Man's understanding of God is thus posited as experiential, for everyone is tasked with the interpretation of the same cosmic text, in which the attributes of perfection are made manifest for all to ponder. Yet while all read, only some come to the desired conclusion. For Nursi, it is only by pondering the countless divine names made manifest in the created realm, with their seemingly numberless permutations and gradations that man, using his own receptivity to the attributes of perfection, is able to reach the truth of belief and fulfill his true destiny, which is to act as a conscious mirror for the reflection of his Creator:

> Now the true meaning of your life is this: its acting as a mirror to the manifestation of Divine oneness and the manifestation of the Eternally Besought One. That is to say, through a comprehensiveness as though being the point of focus for all the Divine Names manifested in the world, it is its being a mirror to the Single and Eternally Besought One.[12]

For Nursi, the key to belief consists, inter alia, of deciphering the signs that exist "in the self and on the horizons" in order to unlock the talisman of creation and reveal the true worth of man, which is his position as vicegerent of God. By knowing what he is, and, more important, what he is not, he can, to paraphrase the words of the *hadith*, come to know his Lord.[13] From the Nursian perspective, the attainment of belief, and the strengthening of belief once it is attained, is contingent on man's ability to read the cosmic text "in the name of God" or *bismillah*—a phrase that he must assimilate into his consciousness if he is to sustain the vicegerency entrusted to him:

> Yes, this phrase is a treasury so blessed that your infinite impotence and poverty bind you to an infinite power and mercy; it makes your impo-

> tence and poverty a most acceptable intercessor at the Court of One All-Powerful and Compassionate. The person who acts saying, 'In the Name of God', resembles someone who enrols in the army. He acts in the name of the government; he has fear of no-one; he speaks, performs every matter, and withstands everything in the name of the law and the name of the government.[14]

Nursi's portrayal of the cosmos as a vast book replete with signs (*āyāt*) for man to decipher complements the Quran's own portrayal of itself as a book replete with verses (*āyāt*) that describe and point to its author. The intertextuality of the revealed Book that is the Quran and the created book that is the cosmos was clearly not lost on the author of the *Risale*, who on numerous occasions alludes to their complementary relationship.[15]

It is tempting, in the light of this near-conflation of the two divine texts, to read into what was allegedly the first verse revealed to Muhammad—*iqrā*, or "read!"—a second layer of meaning. For if we take a Nursian approach, surely it does not strain exegetic credulity too much to suppose that what Muhammad was being asked to read was not only the words of God revealed through the medium of Gabriel, but also the words of God as made manifest in the created realm. And in this command to read there was also the command to interpret. His inability to comply with the divine command has often been cited as proof of his illiteracy, the almost sacred unlettered state that has served to bolster his claim to prophethood. But Muhammad's inability to comply with the command *iqrā!* goes much deeper than his inability to read in the usual sense of the word. It is, I believe, possible to understand the inability that Muhammad pleaded on Mt Hira was the inability to read in the interpretive sense of the word: what he lacked was a suitable epistemological framework with which to make sense of his own being and the cosmos around him. "How should I read?"—Muhammad's supposed answer—becomes "How should I interpret?," to which the response of the Divine is in "In the Name of God"—interpret the cosmos as a manifestation of One Who created you; interpret it as a vast book, replete with Signs that point to Me. For Nursi, the words "*bismillah al-rahman al-rahim*" are much more than just a formulaic phrase of initiation that in Muslim tradition is prescribed before the performance of certain actions: it indicates an epistemological framework for Quranic theology that was possibly in place from the very outset of the Prophetic mission, and which informs most of the popular theology in the *Risale*.[16]

For Nursi, then, man is truly fulfilled only with the attainment of belief, and belief is contingent on the correct interpretation of the cosmic narrative: to read anything but the words of God inscribed on the pages of the universe, or to see anything but the signs of God in the mirror of created beings, is to betray one's role as vicegerent and to fall short of what it means to be the conscious mirror in which the hidden treasure that is God can be made manifest.

THE SECOND PILLAR: NURSI AND THE TALISMAN OF THE HUMAN 'I'

The second pillar upholding the Nursian structure is his elucidation of the seemingly impenetrable mystery of *anā*—the ethereal amalgam of qualities and characteristics in man that constitute his I-ness or sense of self. Nursi's exposition of *anā* in his seminal *Ene Risalesi* complements his theology of divine names with what amounts to a spiritual psychology of man—an exposé of the human soul that is designed on one level to clarify for Muslim believers the true nature of the relationship between man and the Creator, and on another as a trenchant critique of the anthropocentric premises that, he claims, underpin both classical philosophy and the whole project of modernity. As such, it is arguably the key pillar of Nursian thought.

In deconstructing this *anā*, this "*alif* from the book of the character of mankind"[17] which owns nothing yet claims everything, Nursi shows what happens when man tries to wear the "clothes of God," unaware that they neither suit nor fit him. For every soul, he asserts, possesses the wherewithal to appreciate, receive, and reflect the names of God. Yet if the connection between man and God is severed, man appropriates the attributes of perfection for himself, believing erroneously that he is the owner of all that he has, and all that he is. Rather than give back or surrender these attributes by reflecting them in God's Name, he keeps them for himself and attempts to augment and perfect them, not by manifesting God but by acting as though he himself were worthy of worship. Indeed, in order to be able to consider his attributes his own, he must constantly bow down before others and acknowledge them as masters of their own fate, even if this means abasing himself before them.

THE DIVINE TRUST

The ability of each human individual to talk about himself or herself as 'I', Nursi contends, was given to man as part of the divine trust: "We did indeed offer the Trust to the Heavens and the Earth and the Mountains; but they refused to undertake it, being afraid thereof: but man undertook it—he was indeed unjust and foolish" (33:72). A trust is something that is given to an individual, and over which he has power of disposal: he is expected to use it in the manner prescribed by the giver of the trust, although he also has the power to go against the giver's wishes and dispose of the trust in any way that he likes. In the context of the Creator–creature relationship, what is this trust that man agreed to take on himself, after cosmic phenomena such as the heavens and the mountains had refused it? Nursi is not alone in defining the trust as man's God-given ability to act as divine vicegerent; in accepting the trust, man takes it on himself to act as God's representative on earth.

To understand exactly what the Nursian conception of representing God entails, we have to look to those verses in the Quran that refer to the creation of mankind. Several passages discuss the drama of man's first appearance on the cosmic stage, but none is quite so succinct as the account given in verses 30 to 40 of the second *sura*, al-Baqara.

> Behold, thy Lord said to the angels: "I will create a vicegerent on earth."
> They said: "Wilt Thou place therein one who will make mischief therein and shed blood?—whilst we do celebrate Thy praises and glorify Thy holy (name)?" He said: "I know what ye know not."
> And He taught Adam the names of all things; then He placed them before the angels, and said: "Tell me the names of these if ye are right."They said: "Glory to Thee, of knowledge We have none, save what Thou hast taught us: In truth it is Thou Who art perfect in knowledge and wisdom." He said: "O Adam! Tell them their names." When he had told them, God said: "Did I not tell you that I know the secrets of heaven and earth, and I know what ye reveal and what ye conceal?"
> And behold, We said to the angels: "Bow down to Adam." (2:30–34)

The key that unlocks the meaning of this passage lies in the names that God taught to Adam, who as the first man represents the totality of humankind. For Nursi, like other gnostic thinkers in the Muslim tradition, the names taught by God to man are none other than the beautiful names of God Himself. In imparting knowledge of His names, not only does God teach man to recognize all of the divine attributes of perfection, but He also gives him the ability to display those attributes consciously and, in so doing, act as God's 'representative' on earth. In other words, man is able to recognize divine attributes of perfection such as power, wisdom, mercy, beauty and the like simply by virtue of the fact that he is, in one sense, created in God's image.

It is on account of man's potential to act as God's representative that the angels were asked to acknowledge man's creational status by bowing down to him. In the cosmology of the Quran, angels are endowed with limited knowledge of God's names, and while they worship God with perfect sincerity and awareness, they do so because they lack the free will to disobey. Man, on the other hand, is endowed not only with knowledge of all of God's names, but also with free will: if man uses his knowledge of the names wisely and bows down to God of his own volition, he rises above the angels and fulfills his destiny as the jewel in the crown of creation. However, if he abuses his knowledge of the names and fails to fulfill his part of the trust, he sinks to a position described by the Quran as the "lowest of the low."

The trust, then, offers whoever accepts it the ability to know God and to experience Him through His beautiful names and attributes of perfection. But whoever accepts a trust must also undertake the responsibility to dispose of what he is given in accordance with the wishes of the giver: should he discharge his responsibility successfully, he will reap the reward; should he fail, he must face the consequences. In the context of the trust offered by God, the responsibility is a momentous one, for what it actually means in practice is assuming the attributes of God and acting not only in His name, but in complete accordance with His will. It is only when man grasps the significance of the trust and what it means in practice to accept such an undertaking that he can see why cosmic phenomena such as the heavens and the mountains—both symbols of might and grandeur—refused the challenge.

THE FUNCTION OF THE HUMAN 'I'

The 'I', then, is considered by Nursi to be part of the trust given to man by God. The 'I', he goes on to say, is not only the means through which we are able to understand of the 'names' of God, but it is also the "key to the locked talisman of creation." When we understand the meaning of 'I', Nursi assures us, the locked doors of creation will open and the riddle of cosmic existence will be solved. The ability of the 'I'—the self—to know God stems from the fact that it contains within it what Nursi calls "indications and samples" that reflect the attributes and functions of God. In this sense, the 'I' is like a unit of measurement that exists solely for the sake of revealing the existence and measure of something else. Like any other unit of measurement, the 'I' does not have a concrete material existence:

> It is not necessary for a unit of measurement to have actual existence. Rather, like hypothetical lines in geometry, a unit of measurement may be formed by hypothesis and supposition. It is not necessary for its actual existence to be established by concrete knowledge and proofs.[18]

Whether the 'I' is part of the soul or the spirit, or whether it is a function of the conscience or the psyche, Nursi never elucidates. What is clear, however, is that the 'I' is an abstract entity whose sole function is to act as a kind of yardstick against which God's names can be measured. Such a yardstick is necessary because, it would seem, in dealing with God we are dealing with a being who is absolute and all-encompassing. The very fact that something is absolute and all-encompassing, without shape or form, means that under normal circumstances it cannot be perceived. If the whole of the cosmos were colored red, we would be unable to perceive it, simply because there would be nothing against which red might be compared and thus distinguished: if everything were red, we would not be able to perceive it as such. Nursi uses the example of endless light to elucidate his argument: "For example, an endless light without darkness may not be known or perceived. But if a line of real or imaginary darkness is drawn, it (i.e. the light) then becomes known."[19] Light is discernible only because it exists in degrees. In other words, without the existence of darkness, light would remain imperceptible. Darkness is needed in order to reveal or render perceptible the existence of light. In that sense, it is, like the human 'I', a yardstick. And, like the human 'I', darkness has no concrete material existence. Darkness is simply an absence of light: in and of itself it does not exist.

The yardstick of the human 'I' is needed, then, because the attributes and names of God, such as knowledge, power, mercy, compassion, and wisdom, are all-encompassing, limitless, and without like. In order to discern them, man must impose on them an imaginary limit, like the line of darkness that is used to make known the light. This imaginary limit is placed on the divine attributes of perfection by the human 'I'.

How the 'I' does this, Nursi contends, is perfectly simple: it imagines that it is the owner of its own self. In other words, it claims ownership over all of the attributes of perfection that it experiences as part of its own existence. The human self looks at the power, beauty, wisdom, compassion, and knowledge within its own being and claims to be the owner of them all. This ownership appears to be very real, but, as Nursi contends, it is illusory, its function being simply to reveal or indicate the true Owner of the attribute:

> For example, with its imagined dominicality over what it owns, the 'I' may understand the dominicality of its Creator over contingent creation. And with its apparent ownership, it may understand the true ownership of its Creator, saying, "Just as I am the owner of this house, so too is the Creator the owner of this creation."[20]

Similarly, through his own knowledge, man may understand the knowledge of God; through his own art, man may understand the art of the Creator, and so on.

Man looks at his own creative powers and extrapolates from them, concluding that whoever or whatever is responsible for the creation of the universe must possess similar powers, but on a truly cosmic scale. At this embryonic stage of man's spiritual journey, he 'shares' the attributes between himself and God, reasoning that since he has power, God too must have power, but on a scale befitting God; the same applies to all of the divine attributes of perfection.

According to Nursi, the 'I', then, is nothing but a mirror-like unit of measurement, or a tool through which man is able to discover the Creator: it has no meaning in itself, and exists only to reveal the existence and meaning of the absolute. However, the 'I' is a double-edged sword, as Nursi points out, for while it is designed to lead man to God, if misunderstood, it may lead man in the other direction.

If man uses his 'I' to journey toward God, at some stage—either through his own reasoning or through the grace of revelation—he will realize that only One who is absolute in every sense of the word can be the creator and nurturer of the cosmos. In other words, those attributes of perfection that the 'I' was once content to 'share' conceptually between itself and God now have to be surrendered in their entirety to God alone, whose possession of such attributes must, of necessity, be absolute.

But where does this leave human attributes? Nursi argues that man's power is imaginary: the ownership he appears to exercise over his attributes is an illusion, there only to reveal the very real and absolute attributes of man's Maker. Realization of this truth is, according to Nursi, the kernel of real worship and true submission:

> That is to say, the 'I' . . . realises that it serves one other than itself. Its essence has only an indicative meaning. That is, it understands that it carries the meaning of another. Its existence is dependent; that is, it believes that its existence is due only to the existence of another, and that the continuance of its existence is due solely to the creativity of that other. Its ownership is illusory; that is, it knows that with the permission of its owner it has an apparent and temporary ownership.[21]

THE SUBMISSION OF 'I'

The issue of ownership is key here, for it is the metaphorical surrender of man's temporary and illusory ownership over his own attributes that underpins the notion of *islām* or submission. For it is only by giving up one's claims to ownership of one's attributes that one can begin to comprehend the idea of purification of the self, which lies at the heart of Quranic—and, by extension, Nursian spirituality.

True surrender is only possible if the 'I' is realized for what it is, namely, a nebulous, insubstantial mechanism that exists solely to indicate its Creator. Once it has truly accepted this, the 'I' will abandon its imaginary ownership and admit that all attributes belong to God alone. It will realize that whatever it appears to own is there in the form of a loan, to be given back to its rightful Owner. To give back the attributes means to use them in a manner dictated by the One who gave them in the first place. To submit one's (imaginary) knowledge, for example, means to nurture it for God's sake and to use it in accordance with His will alone. It also means to attribute it to Him at all times and under all circumstances, and not to appropriate it for oneself or to imagine that one has any real power of disposal over it. Submission involves the conscious attribution of all of the attributes of perfection to God, thus turning the self quite consciously into a mirror through which God's attributes can be reflected for others to see. The surrendered *anā* forms the basis of what Nursi calls the line of prophethood—the current of thought that bases itself on a reading of the cosmic narrative that is mediated through acceptance of Divine sovereignty.[22]

THE UNREGENERATE 'I'

The alternative, as Nursi points out, is for the 'I' within man to hold onto its illusory ownership and deny that there is a Creator with greater claim to sovereignty. This happens when the 'I' fails or refuses to recognize its true function and sees itself solely in the light of its nominal and apparent meaning. If the 'I' believes that it owns itself, it cannot act consciously and sincerely as the vicegerent of God, and thus fails the trust.

For Nursi, it is not difficult to understand why an 'I' would choose the path of self-assertion rather than self-submission. If man is created in God's image, with small samples or reflections of the divine attributes deposited in his innermost being in order to allow him to recognize God, is it not surprising that he should want to claim these attributes as his own? When one is so used to power, wisdom, beauty and the like, to be told that they belong elsewhere and must be surrendered is to invite incredulity, often followed by rebellion and denial. The longer that the 'I' claims ownership, the more difficult it will become to submit. Eventually, the 'I' swells, puffed up by its imaginary sovereignty, until it transforms the person into a creature that is propelled purely by considerations of self. Rather than using the 'I' as a yardstick to indicate God, it begins to measure all other things against itself, and becomes the center of its own universe. It is the unregenerate *anā* that fuels what Nursi calls the line of philosophy, which is the outcome of man's attempt to read the cosmic narrative through the prism of his own self, without reference to God. As such, it is completely antithetical to the line of prophethood mentioned earlier.

Furthermore, in order to retain the ownership it believes it exercises over its attributes, it begins to divide the absolute sovereignty of God between itself and other beings. Instead of attributing power to God, for example, it attributes it to nature, to causes, and to other beings. As Nursi puts it:

> It is just like a man who steals a brass coin from the public treasury: he can only justify his actions by agreeing to take a silver coin for each of hisfriends that is present. So the man who says, "I own myself," must believe and say, "Everything owns itself."[23]

Therein lies the way of *shirk*, or the ascription to God of partners—the cardinal and unforgivable sin that the heavens and the mountains were terrified of committing should they accept the trust and fail. Nursi's exposition of *anā*, outlining as it does his take on the Quranic spiritual psychology of man, is key to the spiritual character of the *Risale*, yet remains virtually unexplored by Western writers.

THE THIRD PILLAR: THE SELF-REFERENTIAL AND THE OTHER-INDICATIVE

The third pillar is Nursi's elucidation of the twin concepts of *ma'nā-ye ismī* and *ma'nā-ye harfī*, which represent the two diametrically opposed hermeneutical positions open to man as reader of the cosmic narrative. For Nursi, the polarity is stark and simple: either one interprets the individual verses in the cosmic narrative as Other-indicative (*ma'nā-ye harfī*), namely as signs pointing to the Creator; or one deracinates them from their Divine origin and imposes on them a self-referential meaning (*ma'nā-ye ismī*), claiming that they indicate none other than their own existences. To grasp the dynamics of Nursi's treatment of *ismī* and *harfī* 'meanings' allows us insights into his approach to the sacred/profane dichotomy, and provides us, inter alia, with a fresh understanding of the Quranic term *hayāt al-dunyā*—a notion that is on one level the complete antithesis of Quranic spirituality as adumbrated by Bediuzzaman.[24]

Arguably the most salient example of the *ismī/harfī* polarity used by Nursi appears toward the end of the First Principle of the Twelfth Word, where he juxtaposes the Quranic view of the cosmos with the view espoused by natural philosophy or science:

> Yes, the All-Wise Quran . . . regards beings, each of which is a meaningful letter, as bearing the meaning of another, that is, it looks at them on account of their Maker. It says, "How beautifully they have been made! How exquisitely they point to their Maker's beauty!," thus showing the universe's true beauty. But the philosophy they call natural philosophy or science has plunged into the decorations of the letters of beings and into their relationships, and has become bewildered; it has confused the way of reality. While the letters of this mighty book should be looked at as *bearing the meaning of another*, that is, on account of God, they have not done this; they have looked at beings as *signifying themselves*.[25]

For Nursi, interpretation of the constituents of the cosmos as self-referential is a corollary of the skewed epistemological framework imposed on creation by the unregenerate *anā*, and underpins the endeavors characterized by the line of philosophy. In contradistinction, an interpretation of the cosmos that is mediated by revelation will see all things as being Other-indicative, or as signs (*āyāt*) that indicate their divine origin. For Nursi, the truth of this Quranic claim is self-evident, and the only truth that man can choose, if he is honest to himself, and if he wishes for salvation. For, according to Nursi, "Belief makes man into man; indeed, it makes man into a king. Since this is so, man's basic duty is belief and supplication. Unbelief makes man into an extremely impotent beast."[26]

If, as Nursi claims, man's quest should be to see all things as Other-indicative, the result is a vision in which all things in the created realm are invested with sacrality, pointing as they do the transcendent Sacred, or God; the Nursian "theology of the Beautiful Names," in which all created beings are manifestations of the divine attributes serves to complement this. However, one does not find in Nursi the kind of treatment of the dialectic of the sacred that we find, for example, in Eliade.[27] For Nursi, the profane is in the eye of the beholder, and lacks any real existence. To see things through the telescope of *ma'nā-ye ismī* is to see them as *mulk* alone: it is to impose on them meanings that are inherently false and based on an illusion. Existentially, the profane is simply another way of conceptualizing what for Nursi is *sharr*, or evil; and evil, in Nursi's theodicy, is nothing more than the lack of good, with no external existence to talk of.[28]

Nursi's explanation of *ma'nā-ye ismī* also helps to throw light on the much contested term "*hayāt al-dunyā*." Miscomprehension of the term—and its mistranslation into English as "the worldly life"—may have given rise to the notion that Nursi's attitude to material existence is a world-denying one. What Nursi rejects, however, is not the world per se, but the *ismī* attitude that bestows on created beings what amounts to virtually a life of their own—hence the word *hayāt*—and an existence that is celebrated without any reference to the divine. For Nursi, the world has three faces: "One is the mirror to Almighty God's Names, another looks to the hereafter and is its arable field, and the third looks to transience and non-existence."[29] This third face represents the world of those who worship of the world, Nursi asserts, and who invest it with self-referential meanings alone, thus turning it into "the source of all wrongs and the spring of calamities."[30]

However, Nursi's notion of the self-referential and the Other-indicative has equal resonance for *homo religiosus* when applied to the behavioral domain, particularly in the context of practice or righteous deeds. For in the Nursian vision, what is true of the material constituents of the cosmos is also true of human behaviors, and particularly true of acts of worship. In fact, while Nursi does seem to preserve the notion of formal acts of worship, he asserts that all actions—so long as they do not contravene the sacred law—are worthy of being termed worship so long as the intention that fuels them is pure and Other-oriented: "Intention is a mysterious elixir changing ordinary acts and customs into acts of worship."[31]

An action—any action—is thus considered sacred if it is connected directly to God and carried out in His name, and becomes profane only when that connection is broken or ignored. Nursi, like his coeval Eliade, thus avoids the dichotomy of the religious versus the secular by positing a world in which all things and behaviors are able to partake of sacrality so long as they are approached from the perspective of the Other-indicative rather than the self-referential. As a result, sacredness and profanity become states of mind rather than states of existence.

THE FOURTH PILLAR: NURSI AND CAUSALITY

The issue of causality, or, more precisely, the necessity and efficacy of the causal nexus, is a long and vigorously contested problematic in the history of Muslim theological and philosophical debate. When fire touches paper, and paper ignites, is the fire the cause of the ignition, or is the effect—namely, the flames that consume the paper—produced directly by God?[32] The Asharite *mutakallimun* were arguably the first to deny the existence of a necessary connection between cause and effect independently of God, who, as *musabbib al-asbāb*, they alleged, creates the effect directly. Centuries later, Ghazali championed the Asharite cause in his anti-Peripatetic tract, *Tahāfut al-Falāsifa*. There, predating David Hume by several centuries, but for considerably different reasons, Ghazali theorized that the causal nexus to which we are all inured is only apparent: a human construct born out of the habit we have of linking events that occur together, such as the striking of the match, the touching of the match to paper, the ignition of the paper, and its subsequent destruction by fire. To claim that the fire is in reality the cause of the paper's being reduced to ashes constitutes, in Ghazali's view, a slur on divine omnipotence and sovereignty. If causes actually possess the potency and duration needed to bring an effect into being, the role of God becomes virtually redundant: at best God then becomes a Prime Mover in the truly Peripatetic sense of the term, with a nominal sovereignty akin to that of modern-day constitutional monarchs, who are king of all they survey in name alone.[33]

Nursi's repudiation of causality is informed by both the atomistic theology of the Asharites and the syncretism of Ghazali, whose disavowal of Peripatetic philosophy was articulated to a certain extent in their own language and on their terms. His motivation, too, was something that he shared with his ideological predecessor. Unlike the Asharites, whose sole objective seems to have been their desire to save divine sovereignty from the onslaught of the philosophers, Ghazali was fuelled in all of his endeavors—including his debunking of the Peripatetics—by an avowed intention to revivify belief among the Muslim masses. Eight centuries later, Nursi was moved to echo Ghazali's teachings on causality for almost identical reasons. However, the goalposts had now changed, and the old bête noire of Peripatetic philosophy had been joined by what Nursi claimed was one of its ideological offspring, scientific materialism. Founded on the premise of causal efficacy, scientific materialism was considered by Nursi to be the major threat to Muslim faith at the outset of the twentieth century. His rejection of the claims of scientific materialism runs through much of the *Risale* like a leitmotif, but finds its most trenchant expression in his treatise on nature and the causal nexus, *Tabiat Risalesi*.

Nursi's treatise on nature rests on his refutation of a series of propositions that are, he says, "commonly used and imply unbelief." These include: the belief that causes create; the assertion that things form themselves; and the assumption that beings exist because 'nature' has created them. Furthermore, he adds, such propositions are forwarded by believers, who fail to understand the implications of their own words.[34]

By invoking, inter alia, the cosmological argument, the anthropic principle, and the argument from design, and by employing the kind of dialectic championed by Ghazali in his refutation of the philosophers some seven centuries earlier, Nursi takes each proposition in turn and attempts to demonstrate what he considers to be the bankruptcy of these three central planks of naturalist-atheist belief in causality—his ultimate goal being to show that once reason has rejected these three, it has no option but to accept the fourth way: the way of divine unity.

According to this fourth way, the created realm is a realm in which God's works are constant and continuous. Nursi says that God has two ways of creating: the first is through origination and invention, or *'ibdā*: "That is, He brings a being into existence out of nothing, out of non-existence, and creates everything necessary for it, also out of nothing, and places those necessities in its hand."[35]

The second way is through what Nursi terms "composition" or *inshā*:

> That is, he forms certain beings out of the elements of the universe in order to demonstrate subtle instances of wisdom, like displaying the perfections of His wisdom and the manifestations of many of His Names. Through the law of Providing, He sends particles and matter, which are dependent on His command, to these beings and employs the particles in them.[36]

The creational modality known as *ibdā* may be understood in the sense of instantaneous or ex nihilo creation, while *inshā* may be termed "developmental" insofar as it connotes growth and change *over time*. One is able to locate the Quranic antecedents for the Nursian schema of *ibdā* and *inshā* in verses such as 36:82, where the formula of kun fa yakun stands for *ibdā*, and where verses such as 23:78—and, indeed, any verse that includes derivates of the verb *khalaqa*—stand for *inshā*.[37]

There is, however, a certain ambiguity in the Nursian take on these two kinds of creation. If, as he seems to imply, the modality of creation described as *ibdā* corresponds to the ex nihilo creation suggested in several Quranic verses, his assertion that "certain beings" are formed "out of the elements of the universe" would appear to be at odds with this. While, it may be argued, the Quran is equally ambiguous on this score, there is nothing in its verses to suggest—as Nursi seems to do—that the two kinds of creation may be irreconcilable.

One possible solution would be to posit two modalities of creation working in tandem. On one level—the level of *inshā*—each being is seen to be formed from other beings and developed over time: the nourishment and concomitant growth and evolution of the embryo in the womb *over time* is a salient example. On a more fundamental level, however, beings are created—and re-created—from instant to instant ex nihilo. On the level of *inshā*, the creation of a being is analogous to the unfolding of a feature film: it is developmental, with one scene giving rise to the next in an unbroken causal sequence. On the level of *ibdā*, however, each being is made up of a succession of instants that are causally unrelated, much like the individual frames of a film. Our perception of creation as the formation of beings from other beings persists partly because of our inherent inability, as creatures immersed in the space-time continuum, to discern the direct hand of God, which, the Quran asserts, creates all beings simply by commanding them to "Be!" In short, we see the moving film, and not the individual frames.

On the level of *mulk* or *shahāda* (the visible realm), therefore we see God's creative act in terms of a causal sequence; on the level of *malakūt*, or *ghayb* (the hidden realm) God creates each effect directly, ex nihilo, and re-creates continuously: with nothing persisting for more than an instant.

The logical corollary of any disavowal of a truly efficient causal nexus can only be a form of occasionalism—be it Asharite, Ghazalian, or Malebranchian—in which God creates and re-creates the world continuously from instant to instant. Unfortunately for us, while Nursi gives us many tantalizing glimpses of what may indeed amount to a kind of inchoate Nursian occasionalism, no such theory is ever articulated explicitly in the *Risale*. Whether one is excavated in the future depends on the skill and tenacity of those who take it upon themselves to delve more than surface-deep into Nursi's writings.

In short, Nursi's disavowal of causal efficacy brings creaturely focus back on God, who is seen not as one who created the world in six days and then rested on the seventh, but one whose creation and re-creation of the world is continuous and continual: were He for one second to withdraw from His creation, all would topple into oblivion. The enigma of the continuous effulgence of divine light—however it is presented philosophically or theologically—serves to prevent man from attributing ownership to causes and, by extension, to himself. Indeed, as the Nursian strictures on *anā* have shown earlier, the human predilection to attribute efficacy to causes stems from man's innate desire to claim ownership over everything he is and everything he does. The rejection of any necessary causal relationship between beings, implied by the notion of continuous creation, is also a rejection of the notion of human ownership of personal acts and attributes. Thus, continuous creation strips man of all claims to godhood and returns the true ownership of all attributes of perfection to their rightful Owner.

The Fifth Pillar: Nursi on Belief (*Īmān*) and Submission (*Islām*)

The fifth pillar is Nursi's emphasis on the essential difference between belief (*īmān*) and submission (*islām*), and on their interdependence as a means for human salvation.

Implicit in the general Nursian discourse on Islamic orthopraxy is the notion that external submission to the will of God is predicable only on the possession of true, sustained, and constantly reaffirmed belief, and that the externalia of

Islam—the practice of prayer, fasting, and the like—are devoid of meaning without it. Belief in turn must be based on investigation and introspection, on deliberation and contemplation: without knowledge, belief cannot obtain, and without belief, submission is of little value.

In contrast to certain classical scholars who argued that belief is static, Nursi is one with the Hanafite theologians in his assertion that belief is subject to increase or decrease. Again, as with much of his general discourse, Nursi's writings on the subject are didactic and quasi-sermonical rather than academically theological: he writes not to prove some arcane point of *kalām*, but to guide and instruct:

> Since man himself and the world in which he lives are being continuously renewed, he needs constantly to renew his belief. For in reality each individual human being consists of many individuals. He may be considered as a different individual to the number of years of his life, or rather to the number of the days or even the hours of his life. For, since a single individual is subject to time, he is like a model and each passing day clothes him in the form of another individual.[38]

Belief in turn should, in the Nursian schema, lead to submission—*īmān* precedes *islām*—but not every believer in God will necessarily express submission to God's will in the form of adherence to the practical dictates of the *Shari'ah*. Nursi describes such an individual as *gayr-ı müslim bir mümin*, or someone who affirms intellectually the fundamentals of belief, such as divine unity, prophethood and the existence of the Last Day, but who falls short of implementing the pillars of Islam.[39] By the same token, not everyone who claims to adhere to Islam is necessarily a believer. In verses such as those that outline the opportunism of the Banu Asad, the Quran uncovers the possibility of external submission without inner conviction, which means that while one is encouraged to assume that deeds of righteousness—the indicator par excellence of external submission—are the concomitants of belief, they are not necessarily so. In reality, deeds of righteousness are in and of themselves no guaranteed indication of belief, as the response to the Banu Asad shows.[40] Nursi's *dinsiz bir Müslüman* or unbelieving Muslim presumably fits this bill.[41]

Similarly, there are two modalities of submission—the formal and the internal, or uppercase-I Islam and lowercase-i *islām*, with the concomitant possibility, first, that some Muslims are not actually *muslim* in the Quranic sense of the word; and, second, that non-Muslims may also be considered *muslim*. While this more nuanced approach to the belief-submission issue is as far as I can discern absent from the *Risale*, Nursi was clearly aware of the difference.[42]

Nursi is also clear on the need for both components—belief and submission—to be present as criteria for salvation: "Just as Islam without belief cannot be the means of salvation, neither can belief without Islam be the means of salvation."[43] That belief should exist without external submission is anathema to Nursi, for "Islam is taking the part of the truth and is submission and obedience to it."[44] Similarly, Nursi fulminates against those who follow blindly, advocating at all times "belief through investigation" (*tahkikī iman*) rather than "belief through emulation" (*taklidī iman*).[45] Both states—belief without submission and submission without belief—are seen by Nursi as inherently self-defeating, leading ultimately to the ossification and gradual disappearance of belief.

While Nursi's teachings on belief and submission are significant on a purely religious level, they also offer important insights into the sociocultural development of Muslim society as a whole, particularly in the context of the development of Muslim scholarship. For as I have attempted to show elsewhere, the *īmān-islām* issue not only renders explicable the bifurcation of the so-called religious sciences into the rational (*'aqlī*) and the scriptural (*naqlī*), but it also helps to explain why the *faqīh* or jurist was able to attain such a high profile in the Muslim world of learning, and why the pursuit of jurisprudence came to be more prized than any other academic endeavor.[46]

Furthermore, it provides a theoretical framework in which the phenomenon of nomocentrism—the expression par excellence of Muslim religious externalism—can be analyzed and understood. Ghazali was the first scholar of note to bemoan the semantic shifts that had contrived to divest words such as *fiqh* of their spiritual significance and turn them into designations for *farḍ al-kifāya* sciences that pander to the ego of the practitioner on the one hand and to the religious externalism of the masses on the other; Mulla Sadra was another.[47] Nursi's elucidation of the *īmān/islām* dichotomy is a contemporary variation of this age-old theme.

Nursi and the "Closed Doors of Creation"

The sixth pillar comes in the form of a simple sentence that appears in *Ene Risalesi*, embodying an assertion that informs the whole Nursian endeavor, and in which can be found the subtext for the author's interpretation of the divine book that is the cosmos, as well as the exegesis of the Quran by which that interpretation is paralleled. The assertion is made in an almost throwaway manner and, given the weight of the conceptual material on *ene* in which it is embedded, is quite easily overlooked. The key to understanding the world, Nursi says, is in the hand of man, and is attached to the enigmatic *anā*, which is a yardstick enabling him to grasp the measure of all things, including the names and attributes of God. This is a key that man must use, Nursi asserts, for "while being apparently open, the doors of the universe are in fact closed" (*Kāinat kapıları zāhiren açık görünürken, hakikaten kapalıdır*).[48]

For Nursi, the myth of the open doors of creation is one of the biggest obstacles to human felicity, simply because it appears to demystify the world through the provision of spurious answers to the fundamental questions that man poses of himself and his surroundings while attempting to come to terms with the basic existential dilemma of his own being. Underpinning the open doors paradigm is the assertion that the lion's share of man's most searching existential questions (Where am I from? Where am I now? What must I do? Where am I going?) have been answered in one way or other, and that those questions that remain unsolved will, one day, yield to human knowledge and achieve closure. Key to this future achievement are arguably what for Bediuzzaman must seem to have been two of the Enlightenment's most obdurately assertive and recalcitrant offspring: materialist—and, particularly, Freudian—psychoanalysis, which places man as the center of his own universe, in obvious contradistinction to the Nursian view of *anā* hitherto outlined; and scientism, which bestows absolute epistemological primacy on science, advocating the application of scientific theory and methods in all fields of inquiry about the world, including areas—such as morality, art, ethics, and religion—which, its detractors claim, are outside its remit.[49]

At the heart of scientism, of course, lies the acceptance on purely a priori grounds of the necessity of the causal nexus and the ubiquitous yet ethereal laws of nature, an ideological position that appears to repudiate all attempts to define the universe in any but the most mundane and material of terms. For the scientistically minded scientist, the efficacy of causes and the primacy of natural processes are taken as givens, and all subsequent discourse is mediated by those unquestioned assumptions. Attempts to bring God into the equation in any serious discussion with advocates of the scientistic approach are hampered from the outset by the uncontested premises upon which materialist science is founded. This, as the following passage shows, and as Nursi would presumably agree, would appear not only to close the door to future discussion, but to double-bolt it as well:

> The first thing we must do in order to discuss the matter at all, of course, is to contrast the hypothesis of a creator with others supposedly competing with it. In thinking about this, we at once encounter two problems. First, *the events we usually call instances of 'creation' are themselves natural processes*, and this makes it a little difficult to get

> the intended contrast off the ground. Mary baking pies is a creative process, of a minor but nice sort; we don't think any magic is involved there. The pie grows *by purely natural processes*.[50]

Implicit in this positivist paradigm, of course, is the notion that the material world is the only world that we can really comprehend *in and of itself*, and that man merely wastes his time thinking that anything mysterious, esoteric, or otherworldly is at play in the universe. The concept of disenchantment—the *Entzauberung* discussed by Weber[51]—can be traced back to the Romantic movement, where it was considered to be an unwanted and unnecessary effect of scientific progress. For Nursi, it is not scientific progress per se that is to blame for the tendency to see the doors of the universe as open, but rather the hubris that attends a scientistic approach to such progress. He himself advocates a form of "re-enchantment through revelation" that involves seeing past superficialities and acknowledging the Ground from which all things spring:

> Know, O friend. Most of the knowledge of people about the earth and what they see as evident are based on a superficial familiarity, which is a veil spread on compound ignorance. They do not have any real foundations. For this reason, the Quran draws the attention of man to the usual and the ordinary. With its piercing expressions it draws aside the veil of superficial familiarity, shows man how things seen as usual and ordinary under the veil of familiarity are in fact extraordinary.[52]

For Nursi, the open doors paradigm is both a cause and a consequence of the apparent triumph of the *ismī* approach to the cosmic narrative over the *ḥarfī*, and can be combated only in the light of revelation and belief. For in Nursi's view, it is only by reading the cosmic narrative according to the epistemological precepts outlined by the line of prophethood that man, desensitized by the claims of the line of prophethood, may regain his birthright and attain salvation through belief.

However, the myth of the open doors of creation is germane not only to Nursi's repudiation of causality and avowal of continuous creation, as discussed earlier. In the domain of disciplines such as jurisprudence, theology, and exegesis, to claim that the teachings of any individual represent the last word on a particular subject is to lay the same kind of obstacles before the inquiring minds of men as the champions of scientism. Nursi's stance becomes clear in the occasional jeremiad leveled at certain iconic figures from the history of Muslim philosophy, whose elevated status in the collective memory of the Muslim *umma* tends, for Nursi at least, to conceal the fact that they are not all that they seem.

Speaking of the predilection of certain renowned Muslim philosophers for the line of philosophy and their implicit affirmation of the primacy of reason over revelation, Nursi berates them in no uncertain terms:

> It is because of these rotten foundations and disastrous results of philosophy that geniuses from among the Muslim philosophers like Ibn-i Sina and Farabi were charmed by its apparent glitter and were deceived into taking this way, and thus attained only the rank of an ordinary believer. *Ḥujjat al-Islām* al-Ghazzali did not accord them that rank, even.[53]

While Nursi's apparent disdain for philosophers such as Ibn Sina, Farabi, and their Peripatetic peers is evidence not of any personal malice toward these individuals, but rather of his visceral approach to the question of authenticity, it can also be seen as a confirmation of his belief that no scholar or thinker can ever be said to have a monopoly on the truth. More important, his refusal to take on board the teachings of the "great and the good" merely on account of their reputation in the eyes of the Muslim masses reveals an intellectual iconoclasm as refreshing as it is rare. Nursi wrote that if anyone were to challenge him as to why he thought he was able to challenge such famous philosophers in this way, he would say:

> While having a pre-eternal teacher like the Quran, in matters concerning truth and the knowledge of God, I do not have to attach as much value as that of a fly's wing to those eagles, who are the students of misguided philosophy and deluded intellect. However inferior I am to them, their teacher is a thousand times more inferior than mine. With the help of my teacher, whatever caused them to become submerged did not so much as dampen my toes. An insignificant private who acts in accordance with the laws and commands of a great king is able to achieve more than a great field marshal of an insignificant king.[54]

For Nursi, the truth is where it lies, regardless of whose hands it lies in. And to locate the truth only in the hands of those whose iconic status overshadows their actual claim to authenticity is to consider those doors of creation to be closed, and all matters dealt with and understood. This is why the issue of orthodoxy in Islam is such a vexed and contentious affair: as soon as one fixes in intellectual aspic the contents and confines of orthodoxy, one proclaims that the ink has dried on the issue, and all other bets are off. By following the example of Ghazali and exposing the erstwhile stars in the Muslim philosophical firmament as less than their champions claim them to be, Nursi remains true to his own strictures on the closed doors of creation, leaving room for the human intellect to explore the possibilities and discern its own truth on its own terms.

Conclusion

These are, to my mind at least, the defining features of Nursi's worldview, and the central pillars that support his teachings. That they are key to Nursi's perception of the spiritual is understood from the centrality of one or more of these concepts to each and every treatise that goes to make up the complex of epistles known as the *Risale*. They are concepts that, when understood as a unity, offer a framework in which the Creator/created relationship can best be understood. And it is the decipherment and deconstruction of man's position vis-à-vis the Ground of his being that provides the opportunity for *communion*, which is the objective of all spiritual endeavor. Without the Nursian conception of the human 'I', for example, his exposition of the *asmā al-ḥusnā* is little more than eloquent but ultimately meaningless gnostic theology, while without the repudiation of efficient causality, Nursi's teachings on the wiles and deceits of the human 'I' lose most if not all of their potency. Consonant with his rejection of the efficacy of causes is his affirmation of the Other-indicative over the self-referential, thus completing his sacramental view of creation. Each pillar lends credence to the other, and to Nursi's overarching spiritual edifice as a whole.

Each of the six pillars discussed represents a concept, notion, or principle that Nursi clearly deems essential for man in his quest for meaning, authenticity, and salvation, and central to his attempt to solve man's most pressing existential dilemmas. They may not be concepts originated by Nursi himself, although it is tempting to consider them his by virtue of the innovative, eloquent, and highly idiosyncratic way that he expresses them.[55] Furthermore, they are concepts that, despite their importance, have not received the kind of scholarly attention they warrant. While important work has now begun on the *Risale*, with commendable exploratory studies such as *Islam at the Crossroads* preparing the ground for future endeavors, it is still almost completely virgin territory.[56] Whether the concepts that constitute the six pillars under scrutiny here are of crucial importance for every individual is a matter of personal belief and private conscience. On a purely academic level, however, they are concepts that researchers in the field of contemporary Muslim thought cannot afford to overlook. From the tenor of his writing, there can be little doubt that they are concepts that Nursi himself considered seminal—not only in the sense of their centrality to his own weltanschauung, but also as conceptual foundations for an authentic interpretation of the Islamic revelation and, consequently, a hermeneutic of the cosmic narrative that, as Nursi suggests, man has no option but to try to decipher. As such, unless these concepts are subjected to rigorous critical appraisal by philosophers, sociologists, and psychologists of religion, as well as theologians and scholars of Islamic gnosis, the surface of the *Risale* will remain barely scratched, and, in the West at least, Nursi's magnum opus will continue to be seen as little more than a fascinating yet poorly understood curio.

NOTES

1. Muhammad Mujtahid Shabistari, *Dīn wa Āzādī* (Tehran, 1999), 122.
2. For biographical information on Nursi, and for an analysis of the development of Nurculuk, the faith movement composed of his followers, see: Şükran Vahide, *Bediüzzaman Said Nursi* (Istanbul, 2000). This excellent biography remains the sole English language source for information on Nursi's life, times, and works.
3, Quoted in Vahide, op.cit., 261.
4. Said Nursi, *Epitomes of Light* [*Mathnawī al-Nūriyya*] (Izmir, 1999), 300.
5. Bediüzzaman Said Nursi, *The Rays* (Istanbul, 1998), 159.
6. For the *Supplication of Kumayl*, see Abbas Qummi, ed., *Kulliyāt-i Mafātīh al-Jinān* (Tehran, n.d.), 127–39. The *Mafātīh*, the most popular book of liturgy among the Shi'ites, is a veritable treasure-trove of invocations, supplications, and meditations based on or around the beautiful names, including the famous *Jawshan al-Kabīr*. The *Jawshan*, an invocation that involves the recitation of a thousand divine names and attributes, and which is usually traced back to Muhammad through Ali's great-grandson, Zayn al-'Abidin, is a clear source of inspiration and support for much of Nursi's theology of Names. He cites it frequently and its impact on him is evident in the tenor of his writing. For Nursi's take on the importance of the *Jawshan*, see Bediuzzaman Said Nursi, *Risale-i Nur Külliyatı*, two vols. (Istanbul, 2004), vol. two, 1745–1746.
7. Ibn al-Arabi's *Fuṣūṣ al-Hikam* is a prime example, among many others.
8. For Nursi's treatment of the *ḥadīth qudsī* "I was a hidden treasure . . . ," see Bediüzzaman Said Nursi, *Risale-i Nur Külliyatı*, vol. two, 1161.
9. For Eliade's exposition of the hierophanic nature of creation, see Douglas Allen, *Myth and Religion in Mircea Eliade* (London, 2002), 74–83.
10. Nursi's views on *wahdat al-wujūb* are well documented and appear at various points throughout the *Risale*. See, for example, his Second Important Example in the Eighteenth Letter of *Mektubat*, published as B. Said Nursi, *Letters 1928–1932* (Istanbul, 1994), 106–109.
11. On the balance between *tanzīh* and *tashbīh* insofar as it pertains to Ibn al-Arabi's conception of *wahdat al-wujūd*, see William C. Chittick, "Ibn Arabi" in S. Hossein Nasr and Oliver Leaman (eds.), *History of Islamic Philosophy* (London, 2001), 501–503. Nursi's disavowal of *wahdat al-wujūd* and espousal of the Sirhindian notion of *wahdat al-shuhūd* would profit from further research. To my mind it is by no means clear that Nursi rejected in toto the thesis of unity of being put forward by Ibn al-Arabi, although it is clear that he did repudiate the more extreme variations of the theory, such as that proposed by pantheists such as Ibn Sab'īn.

12. Bediuzzaman Said Nursi, *The Words* (tr. Ş. Vahide) (Istanbul, 2002), 141.
13. "Whosoever knows his own self, knows his Lord" [*Man 'arafa nafsahu qad 'arafa rabbahu*] is a staple of Naqshbandi thought, which is claimed to have been influential on Nursi in his formative years. It should be noted, however, that the authenticity of this tradition is contested by many mainstream Sunni scholars.
14. Nursi, *The Words*, 16.
15. Nursi often uses the term "cosmic book" (*kāinat kitabı*) to describe the created realm, but on several occasions goes so far as to describe the universe almost as a kind of *über*-Koran, as in the phrase "the mighty Quran inscribed by Divine power and called the universe" in Nursi, *The Words*, 484.
16. For one of his many elucidations of the *bismillah*, see Nursi, *The Words*, 15–17.
17. Nursi, *The Words*, 559.
18. Bediuzzaman Said Nursi, *Man and the Universe* (Sozler Neshriyat, Istanbul, 1987), 22.
19. Ibid.
20. Ibid., 23
21. Ibid., 29.
22. For Nursi's exposition of the line of prophethood and its antithesis, the line of philosophy
23. Ibid., 26
24. There are sixty-four occurrences of this term in the Koran. See, for example, 7:51 or 46:20.
25. Bediuzzaman Said Nursi, *The Words*, 145. The italics are mine.
26. Ibid., 323.
27. For an overview of Eliade's teachings on the sacred and the profane, see Allen, op. cit., 65–99.
28. Nursi, *The Rays*, 39–40.
29. Nursi, *The Words*, 355.
30. Ibid., 356.
31. Nursi, *Epitomes of Light*, 132.
32. The complexity of the issue is such that any attempt to summarize it in space as limited as this is bound to lead to oversimplification. Interested readers who wish to gain more insight into the classical debates on causality may refer to Majid Fakhry's seminal *Islamic Occasionalism* (London, 1958).
33. Causality according to the Ghazalian perspective is a relatively well-covered area of research, although articles are of vastly differing quality. One of the more accessible is Stephen Riker, "Al-Ghazali on Necessary Causality." In *The Monist*, vol. 79, no. 3, 315–24.
34. Bediuzzaman Said Nursi, *The Flashes Collection* (Istanbul, 2000), 233.
35. Bediuzzaman Said Nursi, *The Staff of Moses* (Istanbul, 2002), 232.
36. Ibid.
37. 36:82—Verily, when He intends a thing, His Command is, "be," and it is! 23:78—It is He Who has created for you (the faculties of) hearing, sight, feeling and understanding: little thanks it is ye give!
38. Bediuzzaman Said Nursi, *Letters 1928–1932* (Istanbul, 1994), 391.
39. Nursi, *Risale-i Nur Külliyatı*, vol. one, 360.

40. 49:14—The desert Arabs say, "We believe." Say, "Ye have no faith; but ye (only)say, 'We have submitted our wills to God,' For not yet has Faith entered your hearts. But if ye obey God and His Apostle, He will not belittle aught of your deeds: for God is Oft-Forgiving, Most Merciful."
41. Nursi, *Risale-i Nur Külliyatı*, vol. one, 360.
42. Ibid., vol. 2, pp. 1553–54. For an analytical survey of the various theological and jurisprudential positions on this issue in classical Islam, see Colin Turner, *Islam without Allah? The Rise of Religious Externalism in Safavid Iran* (London, 2000), 1–20.
43. Nursi, *Letters 1928–1932*, 53.
44. Ibid.
45. Nursi, *Risale-i Nur Külliyatı*, 1511–12 and 1721.
46. See: Turner, op.cit., 23–35.
47. On Ghazali and his approach to this issue, see Turner, op.cit., 25–31. Mulla Sadra's strictures on nomocentrism and the problem of religious externalism appear in his treatise *Sih Asl* [Three Principles], a translation of, and commentary on, which is currently in preparation.
48. Nursi, *Risale-i Nur Külliyatı*, vol. one, 241.
49. A workable definition of scientism is given by Michael Shermer as "a scientific worldview that encompasses natural explanations for all phenomena, eschews supernatural and paranormal speculations, and embraces empiricism and reason as the twin pillars of a philosophy of life appropriate for an Age of Science." See Michael Shermer, "The Shamans of Scientism." In *Scientific American*, 2002, 35.
50. Jan Narveson, "God by Design" in Neil A. Manson (ed.), *God and Design: The Teleological Argument and Modern Science* (London, 2003), 90. [Italics added]
51. "*Entzauberung* refers mainly to the 'contents' aspects of culture and describes the demystification of the conception of the world connected with growing secularism, with the rise of science, and with growing routinization of education and culture": S. N. Eisenstadt, "Introduction," in Max Weber, *On Charisma and Institution Building* (Chicago and London, 1968), li.
52. Nursi, *Epitomes of Light*, 323.
53. Nursi, *The Words*, 565.
54. Ibid., 568.
55. An in-depth study of the intellectual and spiritual influences on Nursi awaits the time and effort of future researchers of the *Risale*.
56. Ibrahim M. Abu-Rabi', ed., *Islam at the Crossroads: On the Life and Thought of Bediuzzaman Said Nursi* (Albany, 2003).

THREE

Grounded Spirituality

The Challenge of Bediuzzaman Said Nursi

Ian Markham

For many in America today, spirituality is the way forward. For secular Americans and many in the liberal mainline churches, spirituality offers an alternative to conservative religion. Indeed, spirituality is often contrasted to religion. Spirituality is linked with an experience of the transcendent that brings meaning to a life, while religion is seen as an institution that often supports patriarchy and oppression. In this chapter, I contrast this "religionless" spirituality of secular America with the account of spirituality advocated by Bediuzzaman Said Nursi. For Nursi, the category of spirituality is very important; however, he is equally adamant that the spirituality must be grounded in the revelation of God found in the Quran. I will show that Nursi's account of spirituality provides an important challenge to the religionless spirituality of secular America—a challenge that needs to be taken seriously.

Religionless Spirituality of Secular America

For modern America, spirituality is very much in fashion. Whereas religion seems complicated and tied to morally ambiguous institutions, spirituality is the simple connection with God. Increasingly one hears individuals describe themselves as "spiritual but not religious." For these individuals, the point is that God or the divine or the transcendent still matters; however, the institution of the Church or the official beliefs of a certain religion are deeply problematic.

This spirituality that is separate from religion has become very popular among the specialists in certain professions. Healthcare professionals talk about treating the whole person holistically, of which the spiritual is a much neglected and important aspect.[1] Educationalists talk about the centrality of the spiritual in the creative or knowing process.[2] Often the meaning of the term "spirituality" for healthcare professionals and educationalists is very imprecise. However, there seem to be two main features. First, the term "spiritual" is opposed to the reductionist scientific accounts of personhood. In part, it is a reaction against the propensity of the sciences to reduce the complexity of humanity to some biological or genetic account. Or as Larry and Lauri Fahlberg (two advocates of spirituality in healthcare) put it: "Evidence of an overriding emphasis on the sensate realm—the turf of the five senses—manifests itself in philosophy as materialism, in science as scientism, in social and behavioral science as behaviorism, and in the popular world as the material triumvirate. . . . Although health professionals have the desire to go beyond the sensate realm, they are often frustrated in their efforts, given the pervasive philosophical materialism in both professional and scholarly influences. However, these influences often seem to leave us humanistically destitute and spiritually deprived."[3] The project for the Fahlbergs is to construct an account of spirituality that is not overtly religious: so spirituality becomes, "that which is involved in contacting the divine within the Self or self—'Self' referring to realms of consciousness well beyond the ego."[4]

Second, the term "spiritual" is intended to stress the human quest for meaning and the ways in which life is given value. Another healthcare professional, Pamela Reed, defines spirituality as "the human propensity to find meaning in life through self-transcendence; it is evident in perspectives and behaviors that express a sense of relatedness to a transcendent dimension or to something greater than the self, and may or many not include formal religious participation."[5] L. Ross, working in the same field, takes a similar line: "the spiritual dimension is described and is interpreted as the need for: meaning, purpose and fulfillment in life: hope/will to live: belief and faith."[6]

So why is this religionless account of spirituality so popular? There are several reasons. First, it appeals to the secular side of America and Europe. For some, the fact that many religious institutions have been (and continue to be) cruel to women and minorities is the problem. For others, the package of beliefs that a person is required to affirm is increasingly difficult in a scientific age. Some find the Trinity or Virgin Birth improbable given our contemporary historical and biological understanding of the world. Yet these people still enjoy a sense of the transcendent. So talk of spirituality separate from religion seems very liberating and helpful. And in the United States where it is constitutionally required that church and state are separate, a religionless spirituality is a neat way of talking about the transcendent without violating the Constitution. Second, it is believed that a religionless spirituality solves the problem of pluralism. We live in a religiously diverse world. And often the differences between religions are a source of continuing conflict. If, the argument goes, we could just see that underpinning our different religious experience is the same Spirit, then perhaps we could move beyond the differences and recognize the ultimate unity. The assumption implicit in this argument is that religions cause problems in ways that the idea of "spirituality" might be able to solve. And the third reason is that many suspect that it was the spiritual sense that predates the emergence of organized religion. Our ancestors had a sense of the divine that religion then organized, codified, and used. In other words, religion is parasitic on the spiritual. The time has come, so the argument goes, for us to recover our authentic spiritual roots unencumbered by the religious overlay.

One can and should recognize that there is force in these arguments. The strongest is the dark side to religion; it is so often intolerant, cruel, and reactionary. Given what we believe about God, it is not surprising that some believe that for "God's sake" they should flee religious institutions. However, we must be more careful with the other arguments. Although it is true that religion builds on spiritual experience, the spiritual experience becomes religious very quickly. For example, the Hebrew Bible is a record of the Jewish experience of God, which was then written down and given the status of scripture. However, although the experience is prior to the interpretation, the moment the experience is communicated it must be interpreted. Even in an oral culture, words will be found to describe the experience so that others can understand and, in a vicarious way, participate in the experience. This means that the spiritual rapidly becomes religious. If I name the experience "God," then this implies theism, which a Buddhist might find problematic. The act of just naming the experience is a religious act. Once concepts are found to describe the experience, then beliefs rapidly follow. The spiritual becomes religious the moment it is communicated.

The argument from pluralism also needs to be handled with some care. A religionless spirituality is deeply unattractive to the orthodox of most faiths. As we will see in a moment, Nursi would disagree strongly with it. However, let us concede there is a legitimate issue here. There have been three major responses to pluralism in the spirituality debate.[7]

The first is the religionless account of spirituality, which seeks to invite everyone to name the experience as they wish, while recognizing that it is the same experience for everyone. So someone might say "life-force," another "Buddha nature," and yet another might say "Allah"; but all should agree that it is same underpinning experience. There are several problems with this. On the epistemological level, how do we know that it is the same experience? Some experiences of the divine involve a sense of fear, others a sense of love: so how can we be sure it is the same underpinning experience? In addition, a Buddhist and a Muslim do not agree that the label for the experience is describing the same ultimate reality. The Bodhisattva is not a Creator God. And, for Buddhism, theistic belief is often seen as an inappropriate form of attachment.

The second is the common denominator model. This involves finding an account of spirituality that most religious traditions could share. Naturally it will be very minimal, but at least it avoids disagreement. The problem here is that the religious are very diverse in their description of the spiritual. In Judaism, the stress is on recognizing in the mundane the holy. So the food laws turn the practice of eating a meal into a sacred holy moment. Meanwhile, in Protestant Christianity, the stress is on an experience of Jesus that elevates the spirit and enables one to transcend the world and the flesh. The account of the spiritual in these two cases is different. It is not obvious how one can reconcile the two.

The third model involves standing in a certain tradition and advocating a particular account of spirituality from that perspective. Now advocates of a religionless spirituality find this model deeply imperialist and insulting. It is imperialist because it is assuming that a particular religion is true; it is insulting because it is not taking other faith traditions seriously. One purpose of comparing the religionless account of spirituality with the account found in the writings of Nursi is to see whether these criticisms are justified. Nursi's approach to pluralism is to take position three; however, as we will discover, this is neither imperialist nor insulting to those of us in other traditions.

Spirituality in the *Risale-i Nur*

Turning now to Nursi, we find a supreme example of—what I am calling—a grounded spirituality. It is a spirituality grounded in a particular tradition. Nursi has a vibrant spirituality. Readers of his magnum opus the *Risale-i Nur* are repeatedly exhorted to experience the intimacy of God. So in the fourteenth note of the Seventeenth Flash, Nursi explains that our immortality is not for ourselves "but for the manifestation of the Enduring One of Glory."[8] And while we are here on earth, we should not be worshipping the causes (e.g., ourselves), instead "man's true object of worship, place of recourse, and savior can only be the One Who rules the earth and the heavens, and holds the reins of this world and the next."[9] In addition to these general exhortations to experience God, there are particular moments in Nursi's life when he is clearly a mystic.[10] In the *Sixth*

Letter, for example, he writes about an experience that came to him while alone in the mountains; he talks about the five forms of exile. He writes:

> The first: due to old age, I was alone and a stranger away from the great majority of my friends, relations, and those close to me; I felt a sad exile at their having left me and departed for the Intermediate Realm. Then another sphere of exile was opened within this one: I felt a sad sense of separation and exile at most of the beings to which I was attached, like last spring, having left me and departed. And a further sphere of exile opened up within this, which was that I had fallen apart from my native land and relations, and was alone. I felt a sense of separation and exile arising from this too. Then through that, the lonesomeness of the night and the mountains made me feel another pitiable exile. And then I saw my spirit in an overwhelming exile, which had been prepared to journey to eternity both from this exile and from the transitory guest house of the world.[11]

In this passage, Nursi is highly sensitive to the transitory nature of life. Taken out of context, it might seem almost Buddhist (or perhaps worthy of Existentialist philosophy) in his awareness of the power of attachment (to others, to country, and to life). However, it is important to look more closely. The first exile is the sense of loss due to old age (many who were close to Nursi are no longer alive); the second is the inevitable separation (as people come and go); the third is the sense of dislocation that Nursi felt in his country (exacerbated due to his antagonism to the secular nationalism of the government); the fourth is the contrast between the insignificant human life and nature (especially mountains and the night); and the last exile is the conflict between the spirit ready for eternity and life that must still be lived here.

Now although this is a good comprehensive description of the human predicament, it is important to note how it confronts this pervasive sense of "anxiety." He writes:

> Suddenly the light of belief, the effulgence of the Quran, and the grace of the Most Merciful came to my aid. They transformed those five dark exiles into five luminous and familiar spheres. My tongue said: *God is enough for us, and He is the best disposer of affairs.*[12]

The point is that his intense experience of dislocation is transformed by his recollection of a verse from the Quran (in this case surah 3, verse 173). This illustrates a central theme of Nursi. The experience of God needs to be rooted.

Unlike the religionless spirituality of secular America, spirituality, for Nursi, must be grounded in the truths found in the Quran.

To illustrate this, we now examine the main features of Nursi's account of spirituality. We have already noted the awkwardness of defining the word "spirituality." In his sustained discussion of Sufism, Nursi links spirituality with the quest for sainthood using the Sufi path. He explains that there are two ways. The first is the Inner Way:

> The Inner Way starts from the self, and drawing the eyes away from the outer world, it looks at the heart. It pierces egotism, opens up a way from the heart, and finds reality. Then it enters to outer world. The outer world now looks luminous. It completes the journey quickly. The reality it sees in the inner world, it sees on a large scale in the outer world. Most of the paths which practice silent recollection take this way. The most important basis of this is to break the ego, give up the desires of the flesh, and kill the evil-commanding soul.[13]

The picture here is that the act of introspection makes one realize the divine origin of all reality, which then transforms the lens through which one looks at the outer world. The Second Way, Nursi explains thus:

> The Second Way starts from the outer world; it gazes on the reflections of the Divine Names and attributes in their places of manifestation in that greater sphere, then it enters the inner world. It observes those lights on a small scale in the sphere of the heart and opens up the closest way in them. It sees that the heart is the mirror of the Eternally Besoughted One, and becomes united with the goal it was seeking.[14]

In this way, it is as we move from ourselves "up" to God, we are then equipped to recognize in the heart a mirror of the Divine light, which is then united to God.

Spirituality, then, for Nursi involves a fundamental recognition of a link between the Creator and the heart of a person, which then transforms the way in which the person sees the world. Unlike those strands of Islam, which are suspicious of Sufi spirituality, Nursi believes that this account of spirituality is authentically Islamic. Although he has a nuanced view of Sufism, he never deviates from affirming this basic insight.

It is in his criticisms of Sufism that his grounded spirituality emerges. It is tempting, explains Nursi, to juxtapose the Sufi spiritual against the observation of the law. He talks of those who are so tempted as people "carried away by the brilliant pleasures of the Sufi path and the way of reality, and since they cannot attain to the pleasures of the truths of the Shari'ah . . . they suppose them to be dull formalities and are indifferent towards them."[15] However, this is a temptation that must be resisted. So Nursi writes, "The ways of the Sufi path and of reality are like means, servants, and steps for reaching the truths of the Shari'ah, till at the highest level they are transformed into the meaning of reality and essence of the Sufi way, which are at the heart of the Shari'ah."[16] Therefore the daily prayers are still obligatory, even if the Sufi mystic has experienced the divine. Indeed, explains Nursi, the mystical experience should help the observation of the obligatory prayers. Nursi writes:

> The rules of behavior of the Sufi path and the invocations of Sufism should be a solace and means to true pleasure within those obligatory acts, not themselves be the source. That is, his *tekke* [a Sufi prayer lodge] should be the means to the please and correct performance of the five daily prayers in the mosque; one who hurriedly performs the prayers in the mosque as a formality and thinks he will find his true pleasure and perfection in the *tekke*, is drawing away from reality.[17]

For Nursi, the thrill of the mystical experience must remain grounded. It cannot and should not displace the ritual obligation. The experience must be firmly located within the Islamic tradition.

This grounded spirituality is a key characteristic of Nursi's account of spirituality. There are four further elements:

1. God has made spirituality possible by creating us complex beings open to the divine.
2. Spirituality makes atheism much harder.
3. Spirituality helps Reason to see the truth.
4. Spirituality is an all-embracing disposition that challenges every area of your life.
5. Spirituality must be grounded in the Quran.

Each of these will now be discussed in turn.

On the first, Nursi writes:

> Since man is a comprehensive index of the universe, his heart resembles a map of thousands of worlds. For just as innumerable human

> sciences and fields of knowledge show that man's brain in his head is a sort of center of the universe, like a telephone and telegraph exchange for innumerable lines, so too the millions of luminous books written by the incalculable saints show that man's heart in his essential being is the place of manifestation of innumerable truths of the universe, and is their means, and seed.
>
> Thus since the human heart and brain are at this center, and comprise the members of a mighty tree in the form of a seed in which have been encapsulated the parts and components of an eternal, majestic machine pertaining to the hereafter, certainly the heart's Creator willed that the heart should be worked and brought out from the potential to the actual, and developed, and put into action, for that is what He did. Since He willed it, the heart will certainly work like the mind. And the most effective means of working the heart is to be turned towards the truths of belief on the Sufi path through the remembrance of God in the degrees of sainthood.[18]

For Nursi, it is science that is demonstrating the complexity of the mind; and it is the mystics who are demonstrating the complexity of the heart. And in the same way that the Creator requires humanity to use the mind for the purposes of understanding; so the Creator requires that we use the heart so that we might experience God. This means that all people (given that everyone has a heart) have the capacity to experience to God and should be aspiring to enjoy that experience.

Now this is important. This tradition-located account of spirituality that Nursi is advocating is not imperialist or insulting to those of us who are not Muslim. For Nursi recognizes that every person has the capacity to sense and experience the divine. This includes non-Muslims who identify with a different faith tradition. Although his account is located and, as we will see later, Nursi believes that an accurate description of the experience is found the Quran, it does recognize a universal sense of the transcendent, which has been hard-wired into all of us.

On the second, we find a familiar Nursi theme. He was deeply disturbed by the European propensity toward atheism, which he described as corrupt due to the "darkness of the philosophy of Naturalism."[19] Safeguarding the faithful from the temptation of atheism is a key theme of the *Risale-i Nur*. Although he is confident that a rational person should see the overwhelming arguments for the truth of theism and, in particular, the divine origin of the Quran, he also sees the value of an experience of God. One advantage of the Sufi way, Nursi explains, is that atheism becomes impossible. So he writes:

> A sincere ordinary follower of the Sufi path preserves himself better than a superficial, externalist person with a modern, scientific background. Through the illumination of the Sufi path and the love of the saints, he saves his belief. If he commits grievous sins, he becomes a sinner, but not an unbeliever; he is not easily drawn into atheism. No power at all can refute in his view the chain of shaykhs he accepts, with a strong love and firm belief, to be spiritual poles. And because no power can refute it, his confidence in them cannot be destroyed. And so long as his confidence is not shaken, he cannot accept atheism.[20]

Nursi believes it is important that faith touches both the mind and the heart. One should have good arguments for faith, but one should also have a sense of God made possible through a careful discernment and listening to the Divine.

It is the relationship between reason and experience that makes up the third element of Nursi's account of spirituality. Much of the *Risale-i Nur* comprises proofs for the resurrection,[21] the existence and unity of God,[22] the prophethood of Muhammad,[23] and the miraculousness of the Quran.[24] However, despite this robust defense of the intelligibility, coherence, and explanatory power of Islam, he does concede that reason has its limitations. Given that our subject matter is God, Nursi does concede that the human mind is working at the outer limit. It is all so much easier to talk about science or engineering. In a very striking passage, Nursi suggests "witnesses and proofs of knowledge of God are of three sorts."[25] The first is water: "it is visible and palpable, but cannot be held with the fingers. For this sort, one has to detach oneself from illusions and submerge oneself in it as a whole."[26] The second is air: "it may be perceived, but it is neither visible, nor may be held. You should turn yourself towards it with your face, your mouth, your spirit, and hold yourself before that breeze of mercy."[27] And the third sort is light: "it is visible, but it neither palpable nor may it be held. So you should hold yourself before it with the heart's eye and spirit's vision: you should direct your gaze towards it and wait. . . . For light cannot be held in the hand nor hunted with the fingers; it can be hunted only with the light of insight and intuition."[28]

Nursi wants believers who use their whole body—both their minds and their hearts. We should struggle and formulate good arguments for the positions we hold; but we should also trust and open ourselves to the divine. God ultimately provides the decisive evidence about God by surrounding us with the cosmic, divine love.

The fourth element is the all-embracing aspect of Nursi's spirituality. Spirituality is often criticized as individual and indulgent. It is sometimes set against justice. For Nursi, this is an impossible opposition. Spirituality embraces the obligations to create a just world. This comprehensive sense of spirituality is captured when Nursi shares a text on which he meditates daily. He writes:

> I have hung it above my head for the wisdom it teaches. I look at it every morning and evening and receive instruction:
>
> **If you want a friend, God is sufficient.** Yes, if He is the friend, everything is a friend.
>
> **If you want companions, the Quran is sufficient.** Indeed, for in the imagination one meets with the prophets and angels in it, observes the events in which they were involved, and becomes familiar with them.
>
> **If you want possessions, contentment is sufficient.** Yes, one who is content is frugal; and one who is frugal, finds the blessing of plenty.
>
> **If you want an enemy, the soul is sufficient.** Yes, one who fancies himself is visited with calamities and meets with difficulties. Whereas one who is not fond of himself, finds happiness, and receives mercy.
>
> **If you want advice, death is sufficient.** Yes, one who thinks of death is saved from love of this world, and works in earnest for the hereafter.[29]

This is an all-embracing outlook, which links the spiritual with the obligations to live simply. Moving from one's friendship with God, Nursi weaves together the centrality of the Quran, the need for a lifestyle of simplicity, the dangers of self-love, and the need to have one's perspective on the life to come. Spirituality for Nursi is not simply an intense experience, but a life-changing disposition.

It is the last element that is vital for Nursi's account of grounded spirituality. When Nursi sets out his definition of the Sufi path, it is firmly located in key Islamic beliefs about the Prophet Muhammad and the Quran. Nursi writes:

> The aim and goal of the Sufi path is—knowledge of God and the unfolding of the truths of belief—through a spiritual journeying with the feet of the heart under the shadow of the Ascension of Muhammad (PBUH), to manifest the truths of belief and the Quran through illumination and certain states, and to a degree by "witnessing;" it is an elevated human mystery and human perfection which is called "the Sufi path" or "Sufism."[30]

As we have already noted, he chides Sufis when they start assuming that their experience of God is more important than ritual obligations. This is because he wants to firmly locate the experience of God in the context of the disclosure of the nature of God in the Quran.

One reason why this is so important for Nursi is that the correct interpretation of an experience depends on revelation. In the *Eighteenth Letter*, Nursi muses on the question: Why did some great mystical saints describe the universe in ways that we now know are wrong? Nursi answers: "They are the people of truth and reality. They are also saints and those who witness the realities. They saw correctly what they saw, but since they were not correct in declarations they made while in the state of illumination and witnessing, which is without comprehension, and in their interpretations of their visions, which were like dreams, they were partially incorrect."[31] He then concludes this section by making it clear that the only safeguard against inaccurate interpretations of religious experience is the firm foundation of an infallible and reliable revelation. So he writes:

> The uncomprehending illuminations of some of the saints relying only on "witnessing" do not attain to the statements about the truths of belief of the purified or exact scholars, who are the people of the legacy of prophethood and who rely on the Quran and Revelation, not on "witnessing". . . . The balance of all illumination, mental states, visions and witnessing are the Book and the *Sunna*.[32]

Although the insights of the mystic are important (and Nursi always stresses the value of the mystical discoveries), they might be mistaken. Ultimately, true knowledge of God depends on God's disclosures to us: God must tell us what God is like. Our mystical experience of the Divine might be mistaken; ultimate certainty depends on trusting God's revelation.

THE CHALLENGE: SPIRITUALITY NEEDS REVELATION

It is at this point that the secular religionless spirituality is being challenged. For Said Nursi, any knowledge learned through religious experience must be corroborated by the Quran (i.e., by revelation from God). In this respect there is an echo of the famous argument offered by the Swiss theologian Karl Barth (1886–1968). For Barth, modernity had a choice: it must either trust a revelation or resign itself to agnosticism. In the end, argued Barth, if we want to know what God is like (however partially, given that God is unlimited), then we must trust that God has revealed himself (or herself—because of course God is beyond gender) to humanity. The alternative is a human attempt to "guess" or "speculate" what God is like, which we cannot be sure is true. This alternative, argued Barth, is tantamount to agnosticism.[33] Said Nursi would concur with Barth's argument at this point. Knowledge of God depends on the revelation; our mystical experience requires interpretation, which can be difficult, and therefore cannot count as knowledge.

For Nursi, there are two controls on legitimate interpretation of a spiritual experience. The first is the Quran; the second is the community. One should test the discovery or insight by that which is revealed in the Quran. And given the danger of private or unconventional interpretations, it is important to test the spiritual disclosure with others who are wiser and perhaps more mature in the community; this is of course the whole point of the *Risale-i Nur*—it is to provide a reliable interpretation of the Quran for other Muslims. On these points (namely, the importance of an authoritative revelation and the judgment of a community), Nursi would be in agreement with the Christian mystic Mother Julian of Norwich (1342–1413). She agonizes about the appropriate interpretation of her visions of the dying Christ. At every stage, she tests out her interpretations against the Bible and in the context of the Church. So although she believes that her spiritual experience discloses the truth about the all-embracing love of God, she struggles with the doctrine of hell out of respect to the biblical text and the teaching of the Church.[34] Both Said Nursi and Mother Julian are in agreement: our experience of God must be located.

It is my view that they are both right. Testing out your experience in the context of a community that accepts an authoritative text is important. An extreme illustration of the challenge may help at this point. In 1975, the Englishman Peter Sutcliffe received a religious experience from God that instructed him to kill prostitutes. Over the next five years, he killed thirteen women. Now the question is: did Peter Sutcliffe receive an authentic experience from God? Nursi has a clear answer: this is not an authentic experience from God because the exhortation contradicts what we know God requires from the Quran. Given God is the author of the Quran, we know that Peter Sutcliffe must be mistaken. Now Peter Sutcliffe is both tragic and extreme. But, for Nursi, the point holds in general. We need to locate our spirituality.

At this point, it may be objected that these authoritative "revelations" have problematic passages—passages that might justify inappropriate ethical behavior. It is for this reason it is important that it is both the text and the community, which are essential for an appropriate interpretation of a religious experience. The *Risale-i Nur* is a remarkable exercise in Quranic exegesis. The whole point of the text is that Nursi is providing well-thought out interpretations of the Quran, including all its difficult passages. The entire project assumes that the text needs some interpretation because the revelation of God found in the Quran is not always easy and obvious. (And of course any text about God is bound to complicated; this is because God and God's relations with the world are the most complicated topics there can possibly be.) So then the control on an experience is not simply the text, but also the community.

Our experiences of God need to be judged by the authorities provided by a tradition. If we want confidence that the experience of God is authentic, then the experience must be compatible with what we know about God from revelation.

CONCLUSION

This is a grounded spirituality. Nursi clearly had a strong sense of God; he endlessly exhorted others to seek a comparable experience. He saw many advantages in these experiences. However, the context of ritual prayers, the Quran, and the supreme significance of the prophet Muhammad remained important. The experience was prohibited from displacing the revelation. Indeed, the experience, argued Nursi, needed always to be checked by the revelation. Furthermore it is not simply a "private interpretation" of the Quran that is sufficient, but one should seek to be informed by those who have training and the skill to interpret the Quran accurately. This is the reason why the *Risale-i Nur* exists at all: it is an exercise in Quranic exegesis to help Muslims interpret the Quran accurately. Therefore one finds in Nursi the dual check on personal spirituality—the check of revelation and the check of community.

Many other mystics in other religious traditions would agree with Nursi on this point. In Christianity, it is not simply Mother Julian of Norwich, but also St. John of the Cross (1542–1591) and St. Teresa of Avila (1515–1582). In all these writers there is a real concern about experiences treated as authoritative, which are not first checked out with the revelation and the community.

Nursi provides an important challenge to much of the talk about spirituality in America and Europe today. He would disagree with those who want to disentangle spirituality from religion. Instead Nursi would argue that it is only by standing within a tradition that we can know exactly which experiences to trust. The need for our experiences of God to be located and grounded is the challenge of Nursi. It is a challenge, I suggest, we all need to face. Spirituality needs a home. It needs a community in which the interpretation of the experiences can be explored; it needs a revelation by which we can ensure that our experiences really are from God.

Notes

1. For an extended discussion of the term spirituality in contemporary healthcare discussions see my "Spirituality and the World Faiths" in Mark Cobb and Vanessa Robshaw, ed., *The Spiritual Challenge of Health Care* (London, 1998), 73–87.
2. For a good recent illustration, see Elizabeth J. Tisdell, *Exploring Spirituality and Culture in Adult and Higher Education* (San Francisco, 2003).
3. Larry and Lauri Fahlberg, "Exploring Spirituality and Consciousness with an Expanded Science: Beyond the Ego with Empiricism, Phenomenology, and Contemplation," in *American Journal of Health Promotion*, March/April 1991, vol. five, no. 4, 273–74.
4. Ibid., 274.
5. Pamela Reed, "Spirituality and Mental Health in Older Adults: Extant Knowledge for Nursing," in *Fam Community Health,* 1991; vol. fourteen, no. 2, 15.
6. L. Ross, "The Spiritual Dimension: Its Importance to Patients' Health, Well-being and Quality of Life and Its Implications for Nursing Practice," in *International Journal of Nursing Studies*, vol. 32, no. 5, 457. Quote from the abstract.
7. For a discussion of these three options see my "Response to Clive and Jane Erricker" in Adrian Thatcher (ed.), *Spirituality and the Curriculum*,
8. Said Nursi, The Seventeenth Flash—Fourteenth Note in *The Flashes Collection* (Istanbul, 1995), 185.
9. Ibid., 184.
10. The term "mystic" is a difficult one. I am using it to describe a person who had certain intense experiences that conveyed insights into the ultimate nature of reality.
11. Said Nursi, The Sixth Letter in *Letters*, 2nd edition (Istanbul: Sözler Neşriyat A.Ş 1997), 42–43. I am very grateful to Dr. Ibrahim M. Abu-Rabi' in directing to me to this passage.
12. Ibid., 43.
13. Said Nursi, The Twenty-Ninth Letter—Ninth Section in *Letters* (Istanbul,1997), 522.
14. Ibid., 522.
15. Ibid., 530.
16. Ibid., 528.
17. Ibid., 529.
18. Ibid., 518–19.
19. Said Nursi, The Seventeenth Flash—Fifth Note in *The Flashes Collection*, 160.
20. Said Nursi, The Twenty-Ninth Letter—Ninth Section in *Letters*, 2nd edition, 520–21.
21. Said Nursi, The Tenth Word in *The Words* (Istanbul,1992), 59–131.
22. Ibid., The Twenty-Second Word, 287–318.
23. Ibid., The Nineteenth Word, 243–52.
24. Ibid., The Twenty-Fifth Word, 375–474.
25. Said Nursi, The Seventeenth Flash—Tenth Note in *The Flashes Collection*, 175.
26. Ibid., 175.
27. Ibid., 175.
28. Ibid., 176.
29. Said Nursi, Twenty-Third Letter in *The Letters*, 334.
30. Said Nursi, The Twenty-Ninth Letter—Ninth Section in *Letters*, 2nd edition, 518.
31. Said Nursi, The Eighteenth Letter in *Letters*, 2nd edition, 104.

32. Ibid., 106.
33. It is important to note that there are significant differences between Barth and Nursi. Karl Barth insisted that a commitment to revelation must exclude natural theology (i.e., any attempt to reflect on the nature of the universe and deduce the nature of the creator), while Said Nursi believed in natural theology and talked about the "book of the universe." Furthermore, for Barth, the revelation is located in the life, death, and resurrection of Jesus—the Word of God; for Nursi the revelation is located in the Quran.
34. See Julian of Norwich, *Revelations of Divine Love.* Mother Julian is responsible for the famous analogy of everything that is with a hazelnut sustained simply by the love of God. She writes: "Also in this He shewed me a little thing, the quantity of an hazel-nut, in the palm of my hand; and it was as round as a ball. I looked thereupon with eye of my understanding, and thought: *What may this be?* And it was answered generally thus: *It is all that is made.* I marvelled how it might last, for methought it might suddenly have fallen to naught for little[ness]. And I was answered in my understanding: *It lasteth, and ever shall [last] for that God loveth it.* And so All-thing hath the Being by the love of God. In this Little Thing I saw three properties. The first is that God made it, the second is that God loveth it, the third, that God keepeth it. But what is to me verily the Maker, the Keeper, and the Lover,—I cannot tell; for till I am Substantially oned to Him, I may never have full rest nor very bliss: that is to say, till I be so fastened to Him, that there is right nought that is made betwixt my God and me." (Text taken from http://www.ccel.org/ccel/julian/revelations.pdf.)

FOUR

At the Heart of the Matter

Faith and Belief in the Poetic Imagery of Bediuzzaman Said Nursi

Jane I. Smith

No concept in the Quran is more basic to the understanding of God's revelation through Prophet Muhammad than faith. As the core of the truly good or moral life, faith is generally understood to encompass both affirmation and response. According to the Quranic perspective, nothing of virtue is conceivable that does not arise directly from faith in the being and revelations of God. Such faith as it is articulated in the Quran in its most basic sense means acknowledgment of the reality of the oneness of God and of the fact that humans will be held accountable for their lives and deeds on the day of resurrection. These two integrally related concepts frame the message of the Quran and thus the religion of Islam itself.[1]

True to both the letter and the intention of the Quran, Nursi has made faith (generally rendered in the English translation of his works as "belief")[2] central to his life, his theology, and his writings. Indeed he is often referred to as "the renewer of belief,"[3] and, in his later persona as the New Said, has dedicated his efforts to explicating the relationship of faith to the individual and his or her role in society.[4] In this brief chapter, I propose to consider the ways in which Nursi has applied the Quranic portrayal of *imān* to his own understanding of what it means to live out of a position of deep faith. As is true of his writings in general, Nursi locates his discussions of faith/belief in the contemporary world in which he lived, and in which those who read his writings have lived, enriching his explanations with a wealth of imagery and metaphorical language that bring his ideas to life and make his message relevant.

Nursi's later writing specifically and by his own acknowledgment constitutes a full and rich commentary on the Quran. It is part of a long heritage of such commentary, called *tafsīr*, written in Nursi's case with both the intellect and with the heart. His creative imagery brings the reader into direct touch with Nursi's own beliefs, sensibilities, and understanding of the importance of living immediately in the world of today. His writing is straightforward, yet rich in interpretive symbolism. In the extended *Risale-i Nur* collection, Nursi draws extensively on the use of allegorical comparisons, employed for the express purpose of helping the reader understand more directly and personally the truths of the Quran. These images are powerfully rendered in Nursi's many references to the dramatic contrasts between faith and the absence of faith, and the consequences of each for human life.

While constantly employing a range of metaphors, Nursi intends his exegesis of the Quran to be homiletic and didactic rather than to offer specific descriptions of what is or is to come. He is both an interpreter and a teacher, and throughout his writings he employs examples from everyday life as well as references to the farthest reaches of the universe to help portray his understanding of the deep and absolute distinction between having faith and being without faith. The distinction is clear in Nursi's mind, though he certainly is well aware of the complexities and subtleties of faith, to which he gives extended attention in his writings, sometimes including personal reflections about his own personal struggles to be a man of faith and belief. He understands through experience that faith is a matter not of one-time attainment, but of degree, of achievement, and of continual realization.

Nursi's metaphors, analogies, and parables come into play consistently in his discussions of the importance of faith or belief, which is arguably the underlying and most crucial message he has to relay. One favorite example is the comparison between the selfish man and the godly man. The first he describes as able only to see the negative—the land around him seeming to be a house of mourning, full of enemies, corpses, torment, and despair. The godly man, devout with fine morals, sees the same land as full of rejoicing drumbeat and chanting that God is most great. The first man, of course, is an unbeliever, one without faith, who is depraved and heedless. The second is a believer who recognizes and affirms God. Their respective visions represent the Zakkum tree found in the depths of hell, and the Tuba tree located in the exalted realms of paradise.[5] Belief is like a valuable antique work of art of God, he says elsewhere, while unbelief is like brilliant diamonds that have become dull glass. Belief turns man into a king, while unbelief makes him an impotent beast.[6]

Updating his metaphors to reflect his twentieth-century location, Nursi frequently urges his readers to understand his meaning by looking through the telescope of belief. When he himself looked with the eyes of belief, he relates, he found his minuscule being was really the mirror of an infinite existence, even myriad existences, in fact, everlasting, immaterial existences. The absence of belief, on the contrary, leaves one totally lost in nonexistence.[7] Extending the eyewear analogy, he later says that while philosophy is a pair of dark glasses through which everything appears ugly and frightful, "belief in God is a transparent, clear, luminous pair of spectacles which shows everything to be beautiful and familiar." He continues to elaborate how the various aspects of reality (past, future, heavens, earth, etc.) are all revealed in their richness and fullness through these spectacles of faith.[8] Changing from the oral to the aural, he insists elsewhere that the absolute certainty brought about by faith or belief provides one with a way to communicate with elevated spirits through the telephone of the heart.[9]

How, then, do Nursi's rich and often allegorical descriptions of the reality of faith correspond to the more concise and immediate directives of the Holy Quran as it distinguishes between the dramatic alternatives of faith and its rejection?

Faith as Safety

The Arabic noun used in the Quran for what we render in English as faith or belief is *imān*. It is from the verb *amāna*, which in its several forms means to be faithful, to be reliable, to be safe and secure from fear. The fourth form of the verb carries the meaning of rendering secure and of putting trust in someone/something, the latter understood as having faith. The one who is faithful, therefore, is he or she who understands and accepts the content of God's basic revelation and who thereby has entered a state of security and trust in God. "The faithful are the ones whose hearts, when God is mentioned, are filled with awe," says Quran 8:2. "And when His revelations are recited to them, their faith is strengthened and they put their trust in their Lord." Because the Quran speaks to the faithful through commandments, admonitions, or words of counsel, the message most commonly begins with the address "O you who are faithful [yā ayyuha alladhīn āmanu]." And so Said Nursi sprinkles his commentary with the admonition "O people of belief!," urging them to use faith as the most effective weapon to ward off the attacks of the awesome and ever-tempting destructive forces of Satan.[10]

While Nursi does not always use the term "safety" itself in his discussions of faith and belief, it can certainly be argued that no concept is more basic to his understanding of what it means to be in right relationship to God. One is rendered safe from many things, including that yawning maw of the hell of unbelief, from a severing of connection from one's maker, one's fellow beings, and one's universe, and from the dangers posed by the temptations of Westernism, secularism and modernism all facing Turkish Islam in the tumultuous times in which both the Old and the New Said were writing. He refers often to the model of the Prophet, who in his own extraordinary faith had strength, certainty, and conviction that rendered both him and the believing Companions the safety of faith.[11] Belief in the truths of the Quran itself, Nursi argues, provides protection and safety from external extinction in the hells of both this world and the hereafter.[12] "Thus, all the truths of belief and Islam," he says, "basing their matters on the grandeur and sublimity which are their requirements, deliver themselves from the awesome absurdities, the fearsome superstitions, and the tenebrous ignorance of unbelief that confronts them, and take up their place in sound hearts and straight intellects, through utmost submission and assent."[13]

Faith as Thankfulness

Many verses in the text of the Quran attest that one of the primary ways in which faith is to be understood and expressed is by recognition that the world is the manifest gift of God, and that its constituent elements are the signs (*āyāt*) by which God makes evident his beneficent favors to humankind. The person who has faith is the one who sees these signs and understands with his intelligence or intellect their nature as a gift from God. Those who are lacking in faith are the ones who fail to recognize and be grateful for these signs. Faith in God in its Quranic understanding, then, contains as an important ingredient the element of thankfulness to God for the bounties He has bestowed on humanity and praise of God in response. Appreciation is expressed not only in the heart and by individual praise and prostration, but by active participation in helping support the faithful of the community.

"All praise be to God!" affirms Nursi on numerous occasions, for the bounty of belief that He has made available to the world.[14] Discussing belief as the key to eternal happiness, he affirms the importance of instruction in belief for purposes of its strengthening, and says that those who are so learned will perform their duties "not with ingratitude" or assuming that the Divine bounties that have been bestowed on them, and the virtues arising from belief, are to be counted as nothing.[15] Under what he calls the "seventh hope" of the twenty-sixth flash, in a section written specifically to bolster the spirits of the elderly who may see nothing but death and destruction in their future, Nursi describes some of his own experiences. Alone on the Pine Mountain of Barla, he relates, his situation of old age and exile lay heavily on him as he wept for his dead associates and for his own grievous and sorrowful exile from his country. Suddenly God came to his assistance with a consolation that, in extreme gratitude, Nursi says would have been sufficient if it had been only one thousandth of its magnitude. Looking from past to future—and here he seems to be speaking of himself personally, of his native country, and of all of humanity—he finds hope in desolation and thanks God for providing the remedy of faithfulness to the pain of his affliction. "To my very utmost, with all the particles of my being, I offer praise and thanks to my Creator for the light and bounty of belief, for it shows me that this world and the Hereafter are overflowing with bounties and mercy, and allows me and all true believers to benefit from those two vast tables with the hands of all their senses, which develop and unfold through the light of belief and Islam."[16]

FAITH AS FEAR OF GOD

It is important to underscore the importance of fear as a Quranic component of faith. The word generally rendered as piety, godliness, or devoutness is *taqwa*, which comes from the verb meaning "to fear," especially God. "O you who have faith," says Quran 59:18, "fear God." Fear, however, is not a state in which a person of faith is terrorized or left in a pitiable condition with no consolation. It is rather an attitude of trembling before the power and majesty of God and the reality of the events to come at the end of time, including those signaling the coming of the resurrection, judgment, and final consignment. Fear as an element of faith in the Quran has the implication of a kind of unshakable reliance on the fundamental goodness, justice, and mercy of God. "In God let those who are faithful put their trust" (Quran 14:11).

As Nursi discusses fear, it is most often to warn of the wiles of Satan and to put the fear of the consequences of a lack of faith into the hearts and minds of his readers. With the certainty of belief, one cannot be harmed, he affirms, but the unfortunate person who is exposed to the Satanic whisperings may fear that he has lost his certainty in the truths of belief. Nursi tries to provide assurance that such fears do not mean that one has lost contact with God or with the basis of his or her faith, but that the fearful person must hold high the truths of belief and the incontestable matters of the Quran, in effect waving them in the face of the crafty Satan. "And so, O people of belief! Fully confident and with belief enter under the protection of the Quran, which will save you from eternal extinction and the Hells of this world and the Hereafter."[17] The God that Nursi suggests seems to be one before whom one would come not with fear and trembling, but certainly with awe, which perhaps best expresses the Quranic intent, and with rejoicing and thankfulness that the fear of a life of unbelief can be overcome.

Faith as Protecting Friends

The faithful are described in the Quran as those who are "protecting friends one of another," as specified in 9:71. This verse continues by putting on male and female believers the responsibility for carrying out what was to become one of the signal responsibilities for Muslims as these were developed in the schools of law and theology, namely, to enjoin and to do what is right and forbid and abstain from what is wrong. Thus doing good and avoiding evil, in the general Quranic understanding, is essential to an understanding and expression of faith. And the next verse clearly spells out the reward for this discernment, namely, the promise of God that faithful men and women will abide in the blessed dwellings of the gardens of paradise.

With the exception of certain theological interpretations, Muslims have generally avoided the trap of having to determine which is weightier in the mind of God: faith or works. The very recognition of God is often expressed by the term *tawḥīd*, meaning both God's oneness and human acknowledgment of it through the act of faith. It presupposes that there is no other being similar to God, that God is utterly unique, and that humans must not only testify to that uniqueness but must reflect their acknowledgment of it through their own lives and actions. As God alone is lord and creator of the universe, so the Muslim acknowledges that oneness by living a life of integratedness, of integrity, of ethical and moral responsibility. Nursi expresses the relationship between human and divine in the concept of *tawḥīd* when he says that "belief illuminates man and allows him to rise to the highest of the high."[18] Belief demonstrates the relationship between the Creator of all things and all the works of art in man, reflecting from the dominical to humans whose virtue serves as a mirror of that art.

The Quranic equation of believers with protecting friends finds deep resonance in Nursi's commentary. He expresses throughout the *Risale-i Nur* the connectedness among people of faith, and the corresponding pain caused to everyone when unbelief or lack of faith prevails. "While all beings are dominical officials charged with elevated duties, through unbelief, the people of misguidance cast them down, and showing them to be lifeless, transitory, meaningless creatures, they in a way violate the rights of all of them."[19] If belief involves protection, misguidance hurts everyone and, as Nursi goes on to say, "the universe becomes angry at the people of rebellion and misguidance, as do all beings and creatures." Faith for Nursi is not a solitary activity, but has inevitable consequences not only for those whom one knows, but for the universe itself. "Cry out at that," he says in a later section, "for all the beings in the world are connected with your heart, spirit and soul."[20] Searching for a cure for the illness of unbelief is not only for the healing of one's own soul and for assurance of one's eternal felicity, but has a direct relationship on the state of the entire universe.

FAITH AND ITS ANTITHESIS

The Quran is replete with the kind of absolute dichotomy represented both by the choices of right and wrong, and by the ultimate consequences of those choices in the consignment to the Garden or the Fire. Faith becomes the ultimate criterion by which one is aligned either with the positive or the negative. Thus, in many verses, one sees the sharp contrast drawn between the person of faith (*mu'min*) and the one who lacks faith (*kāfir*), who actively disbelieves, who thereby rejects the message and the promise of God. Lack of faith is sometimes said to be the response of those whose intellectual reasoning does not enable them to believe, to adopt a position of faith. Those who are without faith are also described in the Quran as the ungrateful. As we saw earlier, gratitude and the corresponding attitudes of praise are fundamental to faith. "He gives you all that you ask for," says Quran 14:34. "If you count the favors of God you will not be able to number them. Man is truly a wrong-doer, an ingrate (*kāfir*)." As the person of faith allows the promises of God to assume reality, however difficult that may be for reason to accept, and to engender in him or her a grateful response, so the *kāfir* both rejects what reason cannot allow and is actively unaccepting of and ungrateful for the bounty of God's gifts to humankind. "Then remember Me," says God, "and I will remember you. Give thanks to Me, and do not reject [Me]" (2:152). In this striking negative parallelism found throughout the Quran between the concepts of faith and rejection/ingratitude, one can find the definition of the qualities of the one in the negation of the qualities of the other.

Nursi's writings are suffused with these dramatic alternatives of faith and rejection; it might be argued that no theme is more prominent in the *Risale-i Nur*. In one analogy he describes two brothers, one with a believing spirit and righteous heart, and the other with an unbelieving spirit and a depraved heart. The first follows the road to the Quran and faith in God, the other to rebellion and denial. What to the one are the calamities of this world, are for the second gentle divine warnings and favors. "Whoever makes this fleeting life his purpose and aim is in fact in Hell even if apparently in Paradise. And whoever is turned in all seriousness toward eternal life receives the happiness of both worlds."[21] Nursi applies a great wealth of imagery to describe the dramatic difference between faith and rejection: health versus illness; illumination versus darkness; kingship versus an impotent beast; freedom versus severe punishment; and so on.[22] "Just as belief saves man from eternal extinction at the time of death, so it saves everyone's private world from the darkness of annihilation and nothingness."[23]

Faith (*Imān*) and Islam

Islam is the only religion whose very name suggests a bidimensional focus of faith. On the vertical axis it refers to the individual and personal human response to God's oneness, often described as the "faith" dimension, and on the horizontal axis it means the collectivity of all those persons who together acknowledge and respond to God to form a community of religious faith. Muslims acknowledge that the religious response of all of those persons throughout the ages who have affirmed the oneness of God in faith can be understood as personal *islām*. It was only with the official beginning of the community at the time of the *hijra* to Medina, however, that there came to be a specific recognition that Muslims together form a group, an *umma*, although the term "Islam" itself was not much used in that sense until considerably later. Nonetheless, it was over the question of who is a legitimate member of the *umma* that some of the most serious controversies arose. Implicit in that discussion was the issue of whether there is a distinction between *islām* and *imān*.

In the Quran there is no clear distinction between these two terms except perhaps in 49:14, where the desert Arabs are enjoined to say "We submit" (*aslamna*) rather than "We have faith" (*amāna*), as faith had not yet entered their hearts. Among the early traditions of the community, however, the distinction between *islām* and *imān* began to be made more sharply, often based on a tradition of the Prophet in which *islām* was given lowest priority, then *imān*, and finally *iḥsān* [goodness] as the highest level of personal response to God. Only a few Quran commentators, notably Fakhr al-Din al-Razi, have argued for the essential identity of faith and submission (while different in generality, he says, they are one in existence). Most agree with the giant of classical Quran exegetes, Abu Ja'far Muhammad al-Tabari, that on one level *islām* signifies the verbal submission by which one enters the community of Muslims, and on the other it is coordinate with *imān*, which involves the total surrender of the heart, mind, and body.

As is true in the Quran, Nursi generally seems to understand that the person who acts out of faith or belief is by definition a Muslim, and that Islam is that religion by affiliation with which one understands not only the scripture but the life of Prophet Muhammad as normative. Occasionally, however, like the Quranic reference to the desert Arabs, he presses the discussion to the point of understanding some distinction between the terms "*imān*" and "*islām.*" In the Letters, for example, he acknowledges that the relationship has been the topic of discussion among many Islamic scholars, one group arguing for their identity and another for their distinction. "I myself have understood the following difference," he says. "Islam is a preference, while belief is a conviction. To put it another way, Islam is taking the part of the truth and is submission and obedience to it, and belief is acceptance of and assent to the truth." Posing the question whether belief without Islam can be the means of salvation, he responds that in effect neither can be true without the other. The *Risale-i Nur* itself, he argues, has demonstrated "the fruits and results of the religion of Islam and Quranic truths in such a way that even if someone without religion does not understand them, it is not possible for him not to be sympathetic towards them . . . if a non-Muslim even understands them, he is certain to assent to them. Although he would be a non-Muslim, he would believe."[24] He concludes that the fruits of both belief and Islam are as sweet and delectable as the fruits of the Tuba tree of Paradise.

FAITH AND THE CONNECTEDNESS OF THE UNIVERSE

As has been suggested several times in this chapter, for Nursi, faith is not simply a single act of volition but an affirmation and a realization of the relationship of all the elements of time and the universe. He ties together the Quranic testimony to God's lordship over all the worlds, and His creation of the elements of nature for the wholesome enjoyment of all believers, with a strong affirmation of the connectedness of human beings with all that exists around us as well as before and after us. Nursi's relationship with Sufism is the topic of another chapter, but it is certainly fair to say, as Dale Eickelman acknowledges, that he saw Sufism as a valid avenue to religious truth, though inferior to the revelation of the Quran.[25] It is also clear that he relied on some of the wisdom of Sufism to expand the focus of the believer beyond the requirements of conduct to a view of the physical universe as displaying the sublime presence of God.[26] But Nursi's intuitions are his own, and as Taha 'Abdel Rahman has observed, "He enjoyed a unique capacity for astonishment, which enabled him to ponder the wonderful secrets of his particular life and that of nature around him."[27]

Some weeks before I wrote this chapter, I happened to watch a public television presentation on the work being done at a planetarium in the high mountains of Peru. To my utter astonishment, as one who knows little about most branches of the natural sciences, I was shown pictures of the light of stars and other celestial fragments reflected from so many millions of years ago that the numbers were far beyond my counting. "In effect we are seeing," said the commentator, "the light of the first stars of creation from the beginning of time." Time and space seemed to dissolve for me, and in some real consternation I turned off the television and tried to contemplate what such stunning images actually have to say about us tiny, finite, and fragile humans. As luck, or perhaps God's mercy, would have it, shortly afterward I took up Said Nursi's *Risale-i Nur* to prepare for a conference. I opened the Fourth Letter to read these often quoted words from the Andalusian poet ("I have no ability to write poetry," Nursi disclaims) and mystic-theologian:

> Then listen to the stars, listen to their harmonious address!
> See what wisdom has emblazed on the decree of its light.
> Altogether they start to speak with the tongue of truth,
> They address the majesty of the All-Powerful, All-Glorious One's sovereignty;
> We are each of us light-scattering proofs of the existence of our Maker,
> We are witnesses both to His Unity and His Power,
> We are subtle miracles gilding the face of the skies for the angels to gaze upon.
> We are the innumerable attentive eyes of the heavens which watch the earth, which study Paradise.[28]

This, says Said Nursi, is what can be seen with the eyes of faith. Through the insight of belief, and as belief allows us to be connected to the Maker of the heavens and earth, Nursi understood himself and all of the faithful to be the work of art of "a craftsman who adorns the skies with stars and the earth with flowers and exquisite creatures, and demonstrates a hundred miracles in every one of his artifacts."[29] It is clear that, for Nursi, it is faith that opens our eyes to the reality of the universe, its Maker, and our full participation in it.

Notes

1. Much of the material on the Quranic understanding of faith and belief is taken from my article for Jane Dammen McAuliffe's *Encyclopedia of the Quran* entitled "Faith," volume two (Leiden, 2002).

2. The four collections in the *Risale-i Nur* (translated by Şükran Vahide) referred to here are I. *The Words. On the Nature and Purposes of Man, Life and All Things* (Istanbul, 1992), rev. 1998 [hereafter *Words*]; 2. *Letters 1928–1932* (Istanbul, 1994), rev. 1997 [hereafter *Letters*]; 3. *The Flashes Collection* (Istanbul, 1995) [hereafter *Flashes*]; 4. *The Rays Collection* (Istanbul, 1998) [hereafter *Rays*].
3. Fred A. Reed, "In the Footsteps of Said Nursi," in Ibrahim M. Abu-Rabi', ed., *Islam at the Crossroads. On the Life and Thought of Bediuzzaman Said Nursi*, 42.
4. See Dale Eickelman, "Quranic Commentary, Public Space, and Religious Intellectuals in the Writings of Said Nursi." *The Muslim World* LXXXIX/3–4 (July–October 1999):260.
5. *Words*, 27–28.
6. *Words*, 320–22.
7. *Rays*, 78–79; cf. *Flashes*, 324.
8. *Rays*, 648–49.
9. *Flashes*, 379.
10. See, for example, *Flashes*, 107.
11. *Letters*, 265.
12. *Flashes*, 115.
13. *Rays*, 129.
14. See, for example, *Rays*, 650 ff.
15. *Flashes*, 229.
16. *Flashes*, 320.
17. *Flashes*, 113–15.
18. *Words*, 320. See Farid al-Ansari, "Man and the Relationship of Belief in the View of Said Nursi," *The Quranic View of Man, According to the Risale-i Nur*, Fifth International Symposium on Bediuzzaman Said Nursi, p. 139.
19. *Flashes*, 119.
20. *Flashes*, 271.
21. *Words*, 50.
22. The *Words* Collection is particularly rich in such imagery.
23. *Rays*, 274.
24. *Letters*, 53.
25. Eickelman, 261.
26. Reed, 42.
27. Taha 'Abdel Rahman, "The Separation of Human Philosophy from the Wisdom of the Quran in Said Nursi's Work," in *Islam at the Crossroads*, 201.
28. *Letters*, 38.
29. *Rays*, 80. As Imtiyaz Yusuf has said, "Said Nursi addressed the subject of the relation between Islam as a religion and science at an elemental level. In other words, he engaged in 'philosophical hermeneutics' of the Quran for the purpose of delineating the relationship between nature, human beings and the Creator." Yusuf, "Bediuzzaman Said Nursi's Discourse on Belief in Allah: A Study of Texts from Risale-i Nur Collection," *The Muslim World* LXXXIX/3–4 (July–October 1999), 343.

FIVE

Faith Development and Spiritual Maturation in the Works of Said Nursi

Marcia Hermansen

The idea that an individual's capacity for faith and trajectory of spiritual development unfold over the course of a lifetime is found in many of the traditional religions. In the twentieth century, those interested in theology and spiritual direction drew on Western psychology and models of cognitive development to describe the maturation of faith and spirituality according to a developmental or stage model. The hypothesis that the capacity for faith emerges in tandem with increasingly sophisticated powers of analysis coupled with concomitant notions of Self and Other arose in the twentieth-century West based on the insights of the Swiss researcher Jean Piaget (d. 1980), regarding cognitive development in childhood. Prominent theories in this vein have included Lawrence Kohlberg's stages of moral development and James Fowler's model of stages of faith.[1]

In the case of Islamic tradition, the notion of changing situations and responsibilities over the life cycle is present, for example in Shari'ah rulings concerning a person's accountability being based on their age and ability to reason. More detailed ideas of development may be found in the concepts of suitable approaches to training and educating (*tarbiyyah*) children and adolescents. In general, the specific topic of spiritual development over the life cycle has not received extensive attention in classical works, although in philosophical ethics, *adab* manuals, and Sufi literature one may find some material. In addition, we may note the quasi-evolutionary perspectives of Sufis such as Mawlana

Jalal al-Din al-Rumi[2] as well of the writings of Imam al-Haddad[3] that take the concept of spiritual development beyond the confines of the human condition by extending it further than the individual's life cycle on earth.

In this chapter, I will consider the writings of Nursi, whose magnum opus, the *Risale-i Nur* is the basis of some of the most important and active movements for social, moral, and spiritual reform in Turkish Islam. The maintenance of faith in the face of the onslaught of modernity and Westernization is an important and pervasive element in his writings and teaching activities. During Nursi's lifetime and in the successive development of movements inspired by his teachings, the importance of education has been stressed as providing the basis for this faith and for developing ethical, sound, and dedicated individuals.

At times the use of the English word "spirituality" for aspects of the Islamic tradition has been challenged since an exact parallel sense of "*rūḥiyyah*" or "*rūḥaniyyah*" is not found in classical Muslim writings. The word "*rūḥ*" is related, as it is in other Semitic languages, to the word for breath, and is sometimes, but not always, equivalent to "spirit." There are indications in many classical Muslim writers that there are various aspects of levels of this spirit,[4] and that it is the animating force of the body as well as the source of humanity's connection with God. Quranic verses that describe Allah as breathing his spirit into Adam (15:29, 32:9, 38:72) form the basis for these understandings.

The word "*nafs*" is used in the Quran and in classical Islamic texts in ways that correspond either to the concepts of "soul" or "ego" in English. Based on certain Quranic references, the Muslim mystics developed a model of progressive psychospiritual development through levels of soul beginning with the soul commanding to evil, then the blaming soul, and on to the soul pleasing to God and the contented soul.[5] There are some traces of this Sufi psychology in the works of Nursi—for example, his frequent mentioning of the "soul commanding to evil."[6]

The idea of the "spiritual" or "spirituality" as being something distinct from religion itself has become current in the contemporary West.[7] According to this understanding, spirituality is often separated from organized religion and represents a more personal and individual encounter with the sacred. The use of the term "spiritual" or in Turkish, "*manevi*," in Nursi's works should not be understood as having this connotation. He rather opposes the spiritual to the material or worldly, but certainly feels that spirituality emerges from a religious foundation and within the bonds of units such as the family.

Speaking of the "spirituality" of a figure such as Nursi leads to a discussion of the mode of his personal practice as well as the currents in the Islamic tradition to which he responded. For example, the relationship of Nursi's teachings to

Islamic Sufism both personally and in his own practice has been a matter of attention and interest to many who have studied his career.[8]

Nursi's relationship to the ideas and even the idealized images of saintly figures such as Abd al-Qadir Jilani, Rumi (1273), and Shaikh Ahmad Sirhindi (1625) has often pointed out.[9] The milieu in which Nursi developed was permeated with Naqshbandi Mujaddidi Sufi teachings continuing the transmission of Shaikh Khalid (1776–1827),[10] and Nursi certainly studied with learned teachers in this tradition. In his own practice, however, he seems to have eschewed the system of *piri-muridi*, that is, the discipleship and charismatic authority of traditional tariqa Sufism, declaring it unsuitable for the changed conditions of modernity.[11] In contrast, Nursi sometimes offered a positive evaluation of the methods for Sufi training "*tarikat*," for example, stating that it "is under the name of *tasavvuf*, a mystery offered to humans and a step in the maturity of mankind."[12]

NURSI, THE INDIVIDUAL, AND SOCIETY

In classical Islamic mystical philosophy, the individual was thought of as a little universe or microcosm, and thus the adage "know thyself" or, as a Sufi hadith puts it, "the one who knows himself knows his Lord" was the basis of gnosis (*'irfān* or *ma'rifah*).[13] Nursi has an interesting articulation of this principle, in that each individual carries an inner world within the larger world. "Moreover everyone has his own vast world in this world. Simply, there are worlds one within the other [corresponding} to the number of human beings. But the pillar of everyone's private world is his own life."[14]

Sherif Mardin analyzes the notion of society according to Nursi's view as constituting a network of personal relationships rather than as an entity in itself. According to Mardin, Nursi in the *Risale-i Nur*

> portrays society as made up of constituents such as "fathers and mothers," "our ruler" or "rulers." It mentions the Master and his Pupils, master craftsmen and hard working artisans. The linkages between these figures are pictures of consisting of "filial piety," "keeping one's engagements." The sacredness of an oath, establishing "bonds of friendship" "fitting into the neighborhood," and "trying to establish a respectable status as a member of a (partly) religious community."[15]

An important element in Mardin's analysis of Nursi is the focus on personal development rather than on direct social or political action.

> Seen as a system of social relations, the personalistic element explains some aspects of the religious strategy of Said Nursi, i. e. his special emphasis on changing man's inner world as the touchstone of a revitalized Islam. Here again, two forces worked concurrently: the mobilized self was one of the requirements that had been brought about by the modernization of the social structure, but the best way to implement the mobilization was to anchor it in persons by making faith something that was cultivated by truly autonomous individuals. The importance of this internalization followed logically from the personalistic system, for where there are no holistic concepts of society to work with—other than "Islam"—then the end one pursues is not to change society as a whole but the individual and his "heart." It is this set of opportunities for the mobilization of the heart that Said Nursi seems to have had in mind when he shifted from politics to the conversion of individuals.[16]

Here Mardin is describing the shift in Nursi's focus from political activism to individual transformation as a key element. This distinction is often characterized in terms of Nursi's own characterization of his transformation from the Old Said to the New Said[17] that corresponded to his changing response in the wake of the replacement of Ottoman rule by the republican period.

The inner "conversion" of individuals as characterized by Mardin is a powerful element of Nursi's spirituality, both in his own personal experience and the impact of his philosophy and teachings on others. This conversion, however, is not that of a sudden "snapping," a spontaneous or involuntary shift,[18] but rather is a growing awareness and commitment transformation, based on information, education, and the impact of a model or ideal teacher. This latter sort of conversion is often correlated with what the contemporary theorist James Fowler would consider to be spiritual or faith maturation.[19]

The more autonomous modern self referred to by Mardin is one that yearns for a spirituality able to address personal needs rather than merely emphasize traditional conformity to group codes and rituals. This in turn relates Nursi's spirituality to Fowler's model of levels of faith in the sense that for Fowler religious maturation is achieved through an individual's obtaining some distance from their initial context.

Broadly summarized, Fowler's stages of faith are as follows.

Stage 1 of intuitive-projective faith is the fantasy-filled, imitative phase in which the child can be powerfully and permanently influenced by examples, moods, actions, and stories of the visible faith of closely related adults.

Stage 2 or mythic-literal faith is the stage in which the person begins to take on for him or herself the stories, beliefs, and observances that symbolize belonging to his or her community. Beliefs are appropriated with their literal interpretations, as are moral rules and attitudes

In Stage 3, synthetic-conventional faith, a person's experience of the world now extends beyond the family. Faith must synthesize values and information; it must provide a basis for identity and outlook.

Stage 4 of individuative-reflective faith is particularly critical for the late adolescent or adult who must begin to take seriously the burden of responsibility for his or her own commitments, lifestyle, beliefs, and attitudes.

Stage 5 or conjunctive faith involves the integration into self and outlook of much that was earlier suppressed or unrecognized. There must be an opening to the voices of one's "deeper self." Unusual before midlife, Stage 5 is that of a person who has experienced defeat and knows the reality of irrevocable commitments and acts. What the previous stage struggled to clarify, in terms of the boundaries of self and outlook, this stage now makes porous and permeable.

Stage 6 is exceedingly rare. The persons best described by it have generated faith compositions in which their sense of an ultimate environment is inclusive of all being. They have become the actualizers of the spirit of an inclusive and fulfilled human community.[20]

Considering the societal implications of Nursi's spirituality in the light of Fowler's model makes us aware of the fact that Fowler assumes faith throughout, and in general privileges individual spiritual development over traditional conformity to norms and rules. Nursi, on the other hand, is concerned with the threat of modernity, secularism, materialism, and alienation, and so on, to the faith of the young person. Therefore it seems that Nursi affirms traditional belief as a response to these challenges.

This may be observed in the following example. At one point, Nursi portrays a division of society that is based both on age and life situation. Having sorted society into five or six groupings, he asserts that the rejection of faith (irreligion) only appeals to the youth segment. He states that the other sectors of society, including the elderly, the weak and poor, children, and the pious are neglected and vulnerable to the arrogance and roughness of those (young people) who turn from belief, and who, by implication, loosen traditional bonds and values.[21] From this we may extrapolate one of the reasons for Nursi's emphasis on education in the earlier stages of life as a cure for both individual and social ills. The specific treatises addressed to youth, the elderly, and the sick that Nursi composed seek to reinforce hope and belief among these groups.

At the same time, we may note a convergence of the higher levels of faith and moral reasoning according to the respective models of Fowler and Kohlberg with Nursi's idea that an individual must transcend self-interest for the betterment of society. This commitment to betterment of the external society for Nursi represents a component of maturity,[22] and at the same time is said to be the implementation of the prophetic legacy in the Islamic tradition.[23] Individual moral and spiritual improvement is, according to Nursi, the foundation and prerequisite for service to others.

Nursi's Psychology

Nursi's psychology is largely drawn from classical views in Islamic thought derived from Ibn Sina (d. 1037) who synthesized Aristotelian and Quranic elements. These concepts were further spiritualized by the Sufis in the light of Quranic terms. For example, Nursi speaks of natural and spiritual faculties in a way reminiscent of the distinction made between the animalistic and angelic components of the person in the writings of al-Ghazzali and others.[24]

> Furthermore, man's nature and spiritual faculties show that he is created for worship. For in respect of the power and actions necessary for the life of this world, he cannot compete with the most inferior sparrow. While in respect of knowledge and need, and worship and supplication, which are necessary for spiritual life and the life of the hereafter, he is like the monarch and commander of the animals.[25]

As further evidence of Nursi's spiritual psychology in his preface to the *Mathnawi al-Nuriyya* he mentions "additional spiritual senses."

> The inner and outer human senses are not confined to the well-known five senses; such as hearing, taste, seeing, and so forth. In addition to these man has many others that are like opened windows looking out onto the world of the unseen. This means that he has many unknown senses.[26]

Said Nursi refrained, however, from a lengthy discussion of these senses according to either Naqshbandi Sufi or Islamic philosophical models and seemed to consider them too esoteric to be helpful to the majority of people.[27] At the same time, Nursi's idea of perfection attained through spiritual journeying[28] is reminiscent of the Sufi concept of *sulūk* or traveling the spiritual path. Sufis themselves state that *sulūk* is not for everyone. For most people obedience to the divine law would suffice to restrain their animalistic instincts and produce paradise-worthy actions.[29] This is echoed in Nursi's view of the relationship between faith and Sufism: "No one can enter Paradise without faith, whereas there are innumerable people who would go there without Sufism. In that case, Islam is like bread, a basic sustenance, without which man cannot live, while Sufism is like a fruit with which man can dispense."[30]

Therefore, Nursi promoted the path of the Quran over that of Sufism, which, along with kalam (Islamic theology), had been "sullied by human thought which rendered them tedious and problematic, and not without delusions and doubts."[31]

In another place he points out the differences between the *Risale-i Nur* and the Sufi orders: "Serving the Risale-i Nur saves belief, while the Sufi orders and sheikhdom win the degrees of sainthood [for people]. It is more important and more meritorious to save one man's belief than to raise ten believers to the rank of sainthood."[32]

It is also noteworthy that Nursi pays particular attention to the experience of spiritual wounding or inner wounding as being transformative in a person's life and in the development of faith.[33] Nursi's own "spiritual storm" is mentioned in *Flashes*, in connection with the effect of following the specific practices of the prophetic Sunnah.

> At a time this poor Said was trying to emerge from the Old Said, his intellect and heart were floundering among truths in a terrible spiritual storm resulting from lack of a guide and the pride of his evil-commanding soul. They were being tossed around, rising and falling, sometimes from the Pleiades to the ground, sometimes from the ground to the Pleiades.
>
> At that time I observed that like *qibla*-directing compasses showing the course to be followed in ships, each of the matters of the Practices, and even small points of conduct, were like electric switches among innumerable hazardous, dark ways. And when, at the time on that spiritual journeying I saw myself under awesome pressure overwhelmed by truly burdensome loads, I followed the matters of the Practices touching on that situation, I experienced a lightness as though all my burdens were being lifted from me. Through submitting to them, I was saved from doubts and scruples, that is, from anxieties like: "Is such a course of action right, is it beneficial, I wonder?" Whenever I drew back my hand, I looked and saw that the pressure was intense. There were numerous ways, but it could not be known where they led. The load was heavy, and I was utterly powerless. My view was short, and the way, dark. Whenever I adhered to the Practices of the Prophet (PBUH), the way was lit up and seen to be safe. I experienced a state of mind as though the load was being lightened and the pressure lifted.

> And so at those times I confirmed through my own observations what Imam-i Rabbani had said.[34]

In addition, life's trials such as illnesses are understood by Nursi to be a form of spiritual training.[35]

In his study, Mardin portrays Nursi's "new phase" in life as one based on faith and spiritual experience as opposed to mere rationality. "The new Said was taking leave from the intellectualization of religion to grasp the bedrock of the *mysterium termendum*. For him, faith now overtook religion as reasonable."[36] In some ways, this description evokes al-Ghazzali's autobiographical account in *Deliverance from Error* in which lived religious experience (*dhauq/zevk*) becomes the touchstone of faith rather than the credulousness of the masses or the rational proofs of the theologians.[37]

Ibrahim Abu-Rabi' gives us an even broader interpretation of Nursi's transformation through suffering, as representing the crisis of the religious person in the era of modernity.

> One can read the *Risale* as the product of suffering, exile, imprisonment, and alienation, a process reflective of the deep historical and social changes engulfing the Muslim world since the nineteenth century. Crisis predicates every major idea of the *Risale*. Nursi's thought was born of historical fluctuations and nourished by a deep-seated desire to achieve the Sacred in a secular age.[38]

Nursi's View of Faith over the Life Cycle

In considering how we might extract the contours of a developmental spirituality from the works of Nursi, I have decided to focus on his discussions relating to the specific life stages that he addresses most often, childhood, youth, and old age. Both infancy and old age are characterized by Nursi as the periods of life that most evince the divine mercy, for in fact powerlessness and dependence are evidence of closeness to God and His merciful qualities.[39]

As noted by Mardin: "We can understand now how, in Said Nursi's writings, 'children' and the 'aged' both functions of the concept of *insan* (human) are two basic analytical categories used by him to conceptualize social relations."[40]

In his treatise on the benefits of belief in the hereafter, Nursi divides the human life cycle into the major stages of childhood, youth, maturity, and old age and estimates proportions of the total population at each stage. Children and the elderly are each said to represent one-quarter of humanity, while youth constitute one-third, and the remaining one-sixth consists of the sick and the oppressed.[41]

Childhood is a time that is both blessed and vulnerable according to Nursi.[42] Children are strongly impacted by the attitudes of their parents. Like the elderly, children are "innocents."[43] The attitude of parents toward children, therefore, should be tender and protective. This is a natural response to beauty and similarity of kind, according to his analysis. This quality of atmosphere surrounding childhood will, in turn, produce healthy and functional adults rather than distorted and traumatized spirits.

> Children, which form a quarter of mankind, can live a human existence only through belief in the hereafter, and sustain their human capacity. They otherwise live only childish, empty existences, blunting their grievous pains with trifling playthings. For the effect of the constant deaths around them of children like themselves on their sensitive minds, and weak hearts which in the future will nurture far-reaching desires, and their vulnerable spirits, makes their minds and lives into instruments of torture. But then, through instruction in belief in the hereafter, in place of their anxieties, and the playthings behind which they hid so as not to see those deaths, they feel a joy and expansion.[44]

The sense of responsibility for the young and their impressionability translates into Nursi's focus on childhood and education.

Youth for Nursi is a time of impressionability when the passions run high. "turbulent emotions [should be] checked by the fear of Hell."[45] Youth are said to heed emotion rather than reason.[46] However, the stage of youth is fleeting and will depart, and this is something that the young should bear in mind.[47] In this context, Nursi counsels seriousness, restraint, and consciousness of death for the young while instilling hope in the elderly.[48]

To impress the reader with this transience of youth, Nursi at one point describes a vision he saw in Emirdag. In this he invokes the image of being in a cinema that would show conditions fifty or sixty years hence. In such a case, we would realize how this present time must be spent meaningfully.

> Yes, what I saw was reality, not imagination. Just as the summer and autumn are followed by winter, so the summer of youth and autumn of old age are followed by the winter of the grave and Intermediate Realm. If there was a cinema which showed the events of fifty years in the future, the same as those of fifty years ago are shown in the

present, and the people of misguidance and vice were to be shown their circumstances of fifty or sixty years hence, they would weep in horror and disgust at their unlawful pleasures and those things at which they now laugh.[49]

Another aspect of this stage of life is that youth and adults are those most likely to receive "slaps" or "blows." This concept in Nursi's psychology seems to refer to a supernatural or synchronistic[50] response to moral lapses on the part of a person that result in his or her suffering some sort of calamitous reprove from forces of destiny.[51] This concept is not so familiar in high tradition Islamic thought, but seems derived from the folk or popular conceptions that Mardin noted are important in Nursi's thought.[52]

In one section of the *Rays* collection Nursi cites specific instances of such slaps being received by those in his circle.

> [The unruly youths themselves confirm that nine slaps they received related to the five matters in the *Risale-i Nur*'s Guide For Youth and Fruits of Belief are a subtle instance of the *Risale-i Nur*'s wonder-working.]
>
> ***The First*** is Feyzi, who sometimes assists me. At the start I told him: You have attended a reading of The Fruits, so don't get into trouble. He did get into trouble, and received a slap: he could not use his hand for a week.
>
> Yes, it's true
> ***Feyzi***
>
> ***The Second*** is Ali Riza, who assists me and writes out The Fruits. One day I was going to teach him about what he had written. Out of laziness, he made an excuse about cooking the food and did not come. He suddenly received a slap: although his saucepan was in good shape, the bottom suddenly fell out together with the food.
>
> Yes, it's true
> ***Ali Riza***[53]

The slaps seem to be of varying levels of intensity, and there are "compassionate" and "restraining" types.

> **The Third Sort is this:** Whenever those who work sincerely in this service become lax, they receive a compassionate slap. So coming to their senses, they again start working. Incidents of this sort number more than a hundred. Of only twenty incidents, thirteen or fourteen received "compassionate slaps," while six or seven received "restraining slaps."[54]

The concept of the slaps suggests deeper and important elements of Nursi's metaphysics, his grasp of how the universe works. In fact, elements of the "slaps" that we might term "supernatural" or cosmic were alluded to during one phase of Nursi's court defense.[55]

In terms of Nursi's construction of youth, binary categories are employed of "wasted youth" versus youth that is guided and channeled into productive learning and service.

In fact, the young should:

> Dwell on the Hadith, the meaning of which is: "*The best of the youths among you are those who imitate those of mature years, while the worst of your elderly are those who imitate the young.*"[56] That is to say, "The best of your youths are those who resemble the elderly in self-restraint and abstaining from vice, while the worst of your elderly are those who resemble the young in plunging themselves into dissipation and heedlessness.[57]

Old age is portrayed by Nursi as a time of blessing, due to the innocence and vulnerability of the elderly. "The weakness of old age attracts divine mercy."[58] The very presence of the elderly is also said to repel disasters,[59] while the prayers of the elderly are most likely to be answered.

> And so, O elderly men and women! Know that the weakness and powerless of old age are means for attracting Divine grace and mercy. The manifestation of mercy on the face of the earth demonstrates this truth in the clearest fashion, just as I have observed it in myself on numerous occasions. . . .
>
> I have had experiences which have given me the absolutely certain conviction that just as the sustenance of infants is sent to them in wondrous fashion by Divine mercy on account of their impotence, being made to flow forth from the springs of breasts, so too the sustenance of believing elderly, who acquire innocence, is sent in the form of plenty.

> This truth is also proved by the Hadith which says: "*If it was not for your elderly folk with their bent backs, calamities would have descended on you in floods*."[60] It states both that a household's source of plenty is its elderly inhabitants, and that it is the elderly that preserve the household from the visitation of calamities.[61]
>
> My elderly brothers and sisters! There is a Hadith which says: "*Divine mercy is ashamed to leave unanswered the prayers offered to the Divine Court by elderly believers of sixty or seventy years*."[62] Since Divine mercy holds you in such respect, you too be respectful towards this respect by performing your worship![63]

Old age is something to be thankful for and a major theme of Nursi's advice to the elderly is that they should develop hope. Among hopeful aspects is the promise of the afterlife where there will be "immortal" or "eternal youth."

> It is only in belief in the hereafter that the elderly, who form another quarter of mankind, can find consolation, in the face of the close extinction of their lives and their entering the soil, and their fine and loveable worlds coming to an end. Those kindly, venerable fathers and devoted, tender mothers would otherwise feel such a disturbance of the spirit and tumult of the heart that the world would become a despairing prison for them and life, a ghastly torture. But then belief in the hereafter says to them: "Don't worry! You have an immortal youth; a shining, endless life awaits you. You will be joyfully reunited with the children and relatives you have lost. All your good deeds have been preserved and you will receive your reward."[64]

Many of Nursi's writings were composed when he considered himself to be one of the elderly and hence a "brother" to them. This could be dated from his forties in all likelihood as he speaks of old age commencing with the first signs of graying in his hair.[65] Speaking of the sense of the autumn or winter arriving in his own life seems to have a particular poignancy for Nursi.

> SECOND HOPE
>
> One day at the time I entered upon old age, in the autumn at the time of the afternoon prayer, I was gazing on the world from a high mountain. Suddenly I was overwhelmed by a plaintive, sorrowful and in one respect dark state of mind. I saw that I had become old. The day too had grown old, and so had the year; and so too had the world become old. With the time of departure from the world and separation from

> those I loved drawing close within these other instances of old age, my own old age shook me severely. Suddenly Divine mercy unfolded in such a way that it transformed that plaintive sadness and separation into a powerful hope and shining light of solace. Yes, you who are elderly like myself! The All-Compassionate Creator presents himself to us in a hundred places in the All-Wise Quran as "The Most Merciful of the Merciful," and always sends His mercy to the assistance of living creatures on the face of the earth who seek it, and every year fills the spring with innumerable bounties and gifts from the Unseen, sending them to us who are needy for sustenance, and manifests His mercy to a greater degree relative to our weakness and impotence. For us in our old age, therefore, His mercy is our greatest hope and most powerful light. This mercy may be found by forming a relation with the Most Merciful One through belief, and through performing the five daily prayers, by being obedient to Him.[66]

In this instance, a sense of mercy is imparted by the hope of a returning spring that restores his spirits. A more melancholy note is sounded in his meditation composed on climbing the Ankara citadel:

> I climbed to the top of Ankara citadel, which was far more aged, dilapidated, and worn out than me. It seemed to me to be formed of petrified historical events. The old age of the season of the year together with my old age, the citadel's old age, mankind's old age, the old age of the glorious Ottoman Empire, and the death of the Caliphate's rule, and the world's old age all caused me to look in the most grieved, piteous and melancholy state in that lofty citadel at the valleys of the past and the mountains of the future. . . . As I sought consolation looking to the right, that is, to the past, my father and forefathers and the human race appeared in the form of a vast grave and filled me with gloom rather than consoling me. . . . I looked at the present day. It appeared . . . as a coffin bearing my half-dead, suffering and desperately struggling corpse.[67]

All, however, is not negative. We find in Nursi's own words a hope for continuity when he speaks of many "young Saids" emerging among his students to replace the Old Said.[68]

The special blessings of weakness, poverty, and compassion associated with the life stages of childhood and old age are reflected in the following analysis of Nursi's path.

> As far as Nursi's own path is concerned, it is by all means based on the Quran, and is relatively shorter and safer than the others. His path consists of four progressive stages, beginning with that of inability (*acz*), then traversing through two intermediate stages of poverty (*fakr*) and compassion (*sefkat*), and culminating at last with that of contemplation (*tefekkür*).[69] Each stage is also regarded by Nursi as an independent path leading to one particular aspect of God, for instance, inability leading to His all-encompassing Love, poverty to His overall-Mercy, compassion to His Compassion, and contemplation to His all-comprehensive Wisdom.[70]

While weakness, poverty, and compassion are natural stages experienced regularly by humans due to their life circumstances, the stage of *tefekkür* seems to be one that must be specifically cultivated and that is induced by both the revealed book and the book of nature. Elsewhere Nursi characterized his four stages as a "reality" (*haqiqat*) rather than a Sufi path (*tariqat*). Instead of traditional Sufi methods of either the loud or silent recitation of divine names or pious litanies (*dhikr*) that induce states of ecstatic love, Nursi defines his four steps in terms of psychospiritual attitudes.[71] The main focus of these attitudes is on the person's understanding of his autonomy and relationship to God. All sorts of egotism such as self-justification, forgetting God, arrogance, and sense of permanence must be overcome. It seems that acts of worship, morality, and service to others are key here. The final stage, however, seems mystical, "if he gives up egotism and sees that he is a mirror of the manifestations of the True Giver of Existence, he gains all beings and an infinite existence. For he who finds the Necessary Being, the manifestation of Whose names all beings manifest, finds everything."[72]

Nursi on the Role of Hope and Belief

Some of the repeated themes in Nursi's work when speaking of the life stages of childhood and old age are the necessity of hope and the vulnerability and powerlessness that attract to a person a disproportionate element of divine mercy. At the abstract level, both hope and mercy are spiritual qualities, hope on the part of the human being and mercy ultimately derived from the divine Bestower.

In general, hope in classical Islamic thought was not perceived as being an entirely positive attitude. The classical discussion, from the hadith through Sufi works, usually paired hope (*rajā'*) with the counter balance of fear (*khauf*), sometimes depicted in the image of two wings that allow a bird to soar higher. According to al-Ghazzali:

> Hope and fear are two wings by means of which those who are brought near (to God) fly to every praiseworthy station. (As in the early saying—hope and fear are like the two wings of a bird, when they are equal the bird is in balance an the flight is perfect.) Fear and hope are two mounts on which every steep ascent of the path of the next world is traversed.[73]

An important dimension of hope is suggested by Quran 71:13:

> "Why do you not hope (*tarjauna*) for dignity (*wiqar*) from God
> when He created you in diverse stages,
> Don't you see how Allah has created the seven heavens in harmony."[74]

The meaning of this Quranic verse is that the contemplation of nature inspires hope. This is resonant with Nursi's repeated evocation of natural phenomena—plants, butterflies, and spring itself as representing and inspiring hope.

Along with the more rational or argument-from-design element in Nursi's presentation we find a more emotive quality in his assertions that beauty and affinity are sources of hope and inspiration. This is reminiscent of sayings such as that of the Sufi, al-Qushayri, "Hope is seeing the divine splendor with the eye of beauty."[75]

According to al-Ghazzali's analysis, hope is a "*maqām*"—a permanent spiritual station and an acquired attitude. Al-Ghazzali says that the station of hope comes to dominate a person through:

1. Reflection (*I'tibār*) on God's blessings, for example, the beauty and complexity of the created world
2. Recitation of those Quranic verses and traditions that encourage hopefulness.[76]

Both of these strategies of the self-cultivation of hope are exhorted to by Said Nursi in his discussion of belief, and in his advice to the elderly and children. According to Nursi, hope is closely linked with belief.

> And so, the light of belief was sufficient for me and all my sorrows arising from old age and the pains of separation; it gave me an inextinguishable hope, an unassailable faith, an unquenchable light, unending solace. Belief then is certainly more than enough for you in the face of the darkness, heedlessness, sorrows, and griefs of old age. In reality, the old age which is utterly black and lacking in light and solace, and the

> most grievous and terrible separation, is the old age and separation of the people of misguidance and the dissipated. Experiencing the belief which affords such hope, light, and solace, and its effects, is possible through adopting a consciously worshipful attitude, worthy of old age and appropriate to Islam. It is not possible by trying to imitate the young, plunging one's head into heedlessness, and forgetting old age.[77]

Imtiyaz Yusuf, in his analysis of Nursi's writings on belief, comes to the following summation: "Placing trust in God leads to personal integration, contentment, confidence, peace, and security."[78]

Conclusions

Western scholars of personality theories have suggested a number of models into which most theories fall. Some of these models are based on the attribution of traits to an individual, others are more philosophical or metaphysical. These latter models portray the human condition within scenarios either of competing forces in irresoluble conflict (e.g., Freud) or as part of a system in which one great force ultimately guides individual development in the cultivation of an ideal (Jung, most religious theories).[79] The classical Muslim thinkers such as al-Ghazali, and especially those following Shaykh Ahmed Sirhindi (Imam-e rabbani), combine these two types of models (conflict and one great force) by positing conflict at lower levels of human development that ultimately may be resolved. Thus, the arena of conflict is the material or earthy realm, where the animalistic, corporeal side, or what is termed "the soul commanding to evil" clashes with the angelic or spiritual forces. Through moral and spiritual development, the one great teleological force toward perfection is able to prevail as these conflicts are resolved. Nursi is clearly within this latter tradition.

Perhaps it may be appropriate here to briefly consider Nursi's view of spiritual development in comparison with Kohlberg's view of moral reasoning. For Kohlberg, the first level of moral thinking is that generally found in children. At this level, people behave according to socially acceptable norms because they are told to do so by some authority figure (e.g., parent or teacher). Obedience in this case is compelled by the threat or application of punishment.

The second level of moral thinking is that generally developed through socilization, hence the name "conventional." A first stage of this level is characterized by an attitude that seeks to do what will gain the approval of others while the second stage is one oriented to abiding by the law and responding to the obligations of duty.

Kohlberg felt that the next or third level of moral thinking is one that was not reached by the majority of adults. Its first stage is an understanding of social cooperation and an interest in the welfare of others. The final stage is based on respect for both universal principles and the demands of individual conscience.

Kohlberg believed that individuals could only progress through these stages one stage, in sequence, at a time. Thus, they could only come to a comprehension of a moral rationale one stage above their own. According to Kohlberg, it was important in order to develop moral understanding to present students with ethical dilemmas for discussion that would help them to see the reasonableness of a "higher stage" of morality and thereby encourage their growth in that direction.

In fact, Kohlberg saw this as one of the ways in which moral development could be promoted. In addition, Kohlberg believed that most moral development occurs through social interaction based on the insights that individuals develop as a result of overcoming cognitive conflicts confronted at their current stage.[80]

The similarity of this model to Nursi's concepts is seen both in the idea of overcoming conflict and in the importance of moral education. Unlike Fowler and Kohlberg, however, Nursi upholds traditional religious tenets as the best way of resolving spiritual and moral conflict while he believed in absolute revealed truth. Interestingly, the Islamic moral practice of *muḥāsaba*, the regular reviewing and assessment of one's activities and attitudes that Nursi's followers practice among themselves, was an element of classical Sufism and is similar, although more personal, than Kohlberg's educational model of forcing students to struggle with moral conundrums.

Another way of considering Nursi's spirituality and techniques for moral development is in the light of David Carr's analysis of three conceptions of spirituality that inform contemporary discussions of spiritual education in the West. These are:

1. Traditional spirituality, that of religious models.
2. Postmodern and pluralism notions of awe and wonder at a range of experiences that transcend what is traditionally defined as religious.
3. Constructivist, more formal or systematic psychologies of experience and development.[81]

I would characterize Nursi's approach to spiritual education as melding elements of all three. The basis of his system is traditional Islam, while his focus on youth, development, and education contain implicitly "systematic psychologies" whose application in a broader public educational system were new to Muslim society. Nursi's openness to science and nature as ultimately confirming and strengthening religious belief may be associated with the second element in

Carr's descriptive model. Of course the "argument from nature" as a source of awe and a proof of the existence of a Creator is nothing new in religious education. In fact, Carr's second point is only novel in its attempt to decouple the "spiritual" from a faith position.

In summary, an analysis of Nursi's spirituality indicates the compatibility of his model of spiritual development with its Islamic and cultural context as well as with contemporary attempts to address moral and spiritual dimensions of human maturation.

Notes

1. Lawrence Kohlberg, *The Psychology of Moral Development: The Nature and Validity of Moral Stages* (San Francisco, 1984). James W. Fowler, *Stages of Faith: The Psychology of Human Development and the Quest for Meaning* (San Francisco, 1981).
2. See, for example, Franklin D. Lewis, *Rumi: Past and Present, East and West* (Oxford, 2000), 416–17.
3. Imam al-Haddad, *The Lives of Man* (Louisville, 1991). Al-Haddad, a Yemeni scholar, died in the early 1700s.
4. Marcia K. Hermansen, "Shah Wali Allah's model of the Subtle Spiritual Centers (Lata'if): A Sufi Model of Personhood and Self-Transformation," *Journal of Near Eastern Studies* 47 (1, January 1988): 1–25.
5. Annemarie Schimmel, *Mystical Dimensions of Islam* (Chapel Hill, 1975), 112. The blaming soul (Q 75:2), the soul inciting to evil (Q 12:53), the contented soul (Q 89:27), and the pleasing soul (89:28). For an interpretation in terms of contemporary psychology see Robert Frager, *Heart, Self, and Soul: The Sufi Psychology of Growth, Balance, and Harmony* (Wheaton, 1999), 47–93.
6. Said Nursi, *Rays*, 500. *Letters* 21, 309. A recent translation of the *Mathnawi al-Nuriyya* by Ali Unal prefers the usage "carnal soul" in English where Nursi apparently used the "soul commanding to evil" *Epitomes of Light* (Izmir, 1999), passim, index ix.
7. Wade Clark Roof, *A Generation of Seekers: The Spiritual Journeys of the Baby Boom Generation* (San Francisco, 1993).
8. Hamid Algar, "Said Nursi and the *Risale-i Nur*" in *Islamic Perspectives Studies in Honour of Sayyid Abu'l-A'la Mawdudi*, Khurshid Ahmad and Zafar Ishaq Ansari (eds.) (Leicester, 1979), 313–33. Bilal Kuspinar, "Nursi's Evaluation of Sufism," Third International Symposium on Beduizzman Said Nursi, vol. 2, http://www.saidnursi.com/symposium/s10c.html
9. Şerif Mardin, *Religion and Social Change in Modern Turkey: The Case of Bediuzzaman Said Nursi* (Albany, 1989), 54–56, 66, 72, 94.
10. Mardin, 57–60, 158.
11. *Letters*, 41, 85, Mardin, 181–82.
12. Mardin, 187 citing *Mektubat*, 415.

13. This macro/microcosmic interpretation is easily derived from Quran (41:43). "We shall show them Our signs sings upon the horizons and in themselves."
14. Said Nursi, *A Guide for Youth* (Istanbul, 1991), 60.
15. Mardin, 163 ff.
16. Ibid., 165.
17. M. Hakan Yavuz, "Print-Based Islamic Discourse and Modernity: The Nur Movement" in *Third International Symposium on Bediuzzaman Said Nursi* (Istanbul, 1997), 324–50. Sukran Wahide, *The Author of the Risale-I Nur: Bediuzzaman Said Nursi* (Istanbul, 2000), 164 ff.
18. For a discussion of theories of conversion see Larry Poston, *Islamic Da'wa in the West* (New York, 1992), 145–57.
19. Ibid., 151.
20. Adapted from Joann Wolski Conn (ed.), *Women's Spirituality: Resources for Christian Development* (Mahwah, 1986), 226–32.
21. *Letters*, 492–95. *Flashes*, 486.
22. Which with respect to the Prophet Muhammad's biography he sets at the age of forty, and we can assume this as a general benchmark. *Letters*, 333.
23. Especially following the ideas of Shaykh Ahmad Sirhindi on the role of the Prophet and subsistence (*baqā'*) versus annihilation (*fana'*).
24. Discussed explicitly in Bilal Kuşpinar, "The Concept of Man: Mevlana Jala al-Din and Said Nursi" in Ibrahim M. Abu-Rabi', ed., *Islam at the Crossroads: On the Life and Thought of Bediuzzaman Said Nursi* (Albany, 2003), 157–59.
25. *Words* #5, 35.
26. Said Nursi, "Preface to the *al-Mathnawi al-'Arabi al-Nuri"* trans. Redha Ameur in *Islam at the Crossroads*, ed. Ibrahim M. Abu Rabi', 335–50, 347.
27. *Flashes*, 155, *Words*, 491.
28. *Letters* #15, 72; #9, 535.
29. Marcia Hermansen, "Shah Wali Allah's Concept." Note that Shah Wali Allah (d. 1762) was a Naqshbandi in the tradition of Sirhindi.
30. Cited in Bilal Kuspinar, "Nursi's Evaluation" based on *Letters*, 41.
31. *Letters*, 344.
32. Ilhan Yildiz, "The Search in the Transitional Period (1924–1950) for a Religious Educational Model," Fifth International Symposium on Bediuzzaman Said Nursi.
33. *Flashes* #2, 22 and #26, 288.
34. *Flashes*, 2–3, 81–82. Imam-i Rabbani, Ahmad Faruqi (May God be pleased with him) said: "While traversing the degrees in my spiritual journeying, I saw the most brilliant, splendid, subtle, and sound among the levels of the saints to be those who took following the Practices of the Prophet (PBUH) as the basis of their way. Even the ordinary saints of that level appeared to be more splendid than the highest saints of the other levels."
35. *Flashes* #25, 284.
36. Mardin, 146.
37. Nursi uses a formulation quite similar to this in the Mathnawi al-Nuriyya; see Ameur's translation, in I. Abu-Rabi', *Islam at the Crossroads*, 348, 350—where *dhauq* is translated as "spiritual taste."
38. I. Abu-Rabi', *Islam at the Crossroads*, x.

39. *Flashes*, 301.
40. Mardin, 166.
41. Said Nursi, *Rays*, 245–46, also see *Words*, 110.
42. The vulnerable spirits of children are mentioned in *Rays*, 244.
43. *Rays*, 372.
44. *Rays*, 245.
45. *Rays*, 204.
46. *Rays*, 475.
47. *Rays*, 225.
48. *Rays*, 247. *Letters*, 334.
49. *Rays*, 219.
50. A perfect Arabic/Turkish equivalent is provided in the translator's note. " 'Coincidences' (*tevāfukat*): the unintentional correspondence of words or letters in lines or patterns on one or several pages, or the 'coinciding' of apparently unrelated events. [Tr.]" *Rays*, 407.
51. *Rays*, 357.
52. Mardin, 166.
53. *Rays*, 357.
54. *Flashes* #10, 70.
55. *Rays* #14, 407.
56. Hadith cited from 'Ali Mawardi, al-Ghazzali's *Ihya 'Ulum al-Din*, and other sources in *Flashes*, 321.
57. *Flashes*, 320–21.
58. *Flashes*, 301.
59. Ibid.
60. Hadith cited from al-'Ajluni, *Kashf al-Khafa'* ii, 163, and other sources. In *Flashes*, 301.
61. *Flashes*, 301.
62. Hadith cited from al-'Ajluni, *Kashf al-Khafa'*, I, 244 in *Flashes*, 321.
63. *Flashes*, 320–21.
64. *Rays*, 245–46.
65. *Flashes*, 296.
66. *Flashes*, 287.
67. *Rays*, 437.
68. *Rays*, 335.
69. On *tefekkür* see Umit Şimşek, "The Style of Reflective Thought in the Risale-I Nur" in *The Reconstruction of Islamic Thought in the Twentieth Century and Bediuzzaman Said Nursi* (Istanbul, 1997), 27–39.
70. Bilal Kuspinar, "Nursi's Evaluation of Sufism" http://www.saidnursi.com/symposium/s10c.html, *Letters* Addendum, 536.
71. *Words*, 491–93.
72. Ibid., 493.
73. Al-Ghazzali, *Ihya 'Ulum al-Din*, Book 33. Translated by William McKane in *al-Ghazzali's Book of Fear and Hope* (Leiden, 1962), 1.
74. Franz Rosenthal, *Sweeter than Hope: Complaint and Hope in Medieval Islam* (Leiden, 1997), 79.

75. Al-Qushayri, *Risala*, translated by Barbara von Schlegell as *Principle of Sufism* (Berkeley, 1990), 66.
76. Al-Ghazzali, *The Book of Hope and Fear*, *Ihya 'Ulum al-Din*, tr. William McKane (Leiden, 1962), 11.
77. *Flashes*, 320.
78. Imtiyaz Yusuf, "Bediuzzaman Said Nursi's Discourse on Belief in Allah: A Study of Texts from *Risale-i Nur* Collection" *Muslim World* 89 (3–4, July–October, 1999): 336–49, 345, citing *Words*, 45.
79. Salvatore Maddi, *Personality Theories: A Comparative Analysis* (Long Grove, 1996).
80. Summary based on W. C. Crain, *Theories of Development: Concepts and Applications* (Englewood Cliffs, 1985), 118–36.
81. David Carr, "Three Concepts of Spirituality" in *Spirituality, Philosophy and Education*, eds. David Carr and John Haldane (London, 2003), 217.

SIX

THE SPIRIT OF WORSHIP AND THE RESULT OF SINCERE BELIEF

Nursi's Mathnāwī al-'Arabī al-Nūrī *as a Handbook for the Contemplative Life*

Lucinda Mosher

For Nursi, now in his early forties, 1920–1921 C.E. would be an interval of purposeful withdrawal from the intense public activism that had characterized the previous two decades of his life. While, from 1925 onward, exile and imprisonment would be his lot all too frequently and for periods all too long, the 1920–1921 sojourn was by his own choice. It would be for him a spiritual retreat, a period of profound theological reflection and personal transformation. Now calling himself the New Said, and writing in Arabic, he spent these months working out his ideas in a number of *rasā'il* (epistles; sing., *risālah*), which were then published in 1922 and 1923.[1]

From the outset, Nursi had it in mind that these individual items would be brought together as a book: in these separate epistles, he explains, "I have recorded a handful of spiritual intuitions, and [have] brought forth various chips of glass that are awaiting to be put together in [a beautiful collage]"; eventually, he asserts, people will emerge whose duty it is to "compose them in a well-edited and illustrious fashion."[2] In 1955, the collected *rasā'il*—(roughly a dozen of them) now edited and collated—would indeed be published as the single-volume compendium *al-Mathnāwī al-'Arabī al-Nūrī* (or *Mathnawi al-Nuriye*).[3] The result is a relatively concise starting-point for studying Nursi's appreciation of the Quran as holy mystery and daily guide, or his understanding of such themes as theological anthropology and ecology. However, because its contents are not solely didactic, Nursi's *Mathnawi al-Nuriye* is as well a devotional manual—a relatively compact handbook for the student embarking on the contemplative life.

Viewed as such, Nursi's *Mathnāwī* stands alongside other classical devotional manuals by well-regarded spiritual masters of various faiths—for example, the various compendia of al-Jilānī's treatises and supplications, or al-Ghazālī's *Mishkat al-Anwār* (Niche of Lights), or Ibn al-Sabbagh's collation of the prayers and epistles of al-Shādhilī,[4] or (from my own Anglican Christian tradition) Lancelot Andrewes's *Preces Privatœ*, or Jeremy Taylor's pair of guidebooks: *Holy Living* and *Holy Dying*. This chapter will introduce the reader to the *Mathnawi al-Nuriye* itself, and to the resources it provides for the life of supererogatory supplication and remembrance—most especially for theological reflection on God's beautiful names.

The Structure of the *Mathnawi*

Technically, *mathnāwī* names a literary genre characterized by rhymed couplets, the most famous example of which is Jalaluddin Rūmī's *Mathnāwī Ma'nāwī*—a six-volume devotional poem of some 25,000 verses. Nursi did compose a verse-*mathnāwī*: his *Lemeāt* (Flashes), composed in Turkish during Ramadan in 1921 C.E., now available as something of an appendix to the Sözler edition of his *Words*.[5] It is indeed a poem, but not formally so. Nursi describes it as "natural verse, like a hymn, [which] was pleasing to my spirit."[6] Nursi's *Mathnawi al-Nuriye,* the opus of concern in this chapter, is not a poem, however—despite its name. Nevertheless, its name is a conscious reference to Rūmī's *Mathnāwī* as a creative project of theological reflection and Quranic exegesis.[7] Nursi's calling his work an "Arabic *mathnāwī*" is also a nod toward Rūmī, whose own *mathnāwī* is in Farsi.

Various editions and translations of Nursi's *Mathnawi al-Nuriye* are now extant, but the numerical order of the essays does not reflect the order in which they were written, nor are the editions consistent in how the material is subdivided and numbered. We are clearer, therefore, if we refer to its individual entries by name. Treatise titles as given in the Sözler Yayınevi Arabic edition (1999), the primary source for this chapter, are:

1. *Lama'āt min Shamsi 'l-Tawhīd* (Sparks from the Realm [lit., Sun] of Tawhīd).
2. *Rashaħāt min Bahri Ma'rifati 'l-Nabi'* (Splashes from the Prophet's Sea of Knowledge).

3. *Lā Siyyamā* (In Particular).[8]
4. *Qatrah min Bahri'l-Tawħīd* (A Drop from the Sea of Tawhīd).
5. *Ħabābun min 'Ummāni'l- Quran al-Hakīm* (Grain from the *Depth* of the Wise Quran).[9]
6. *Ħabbah min Nawatāt Thamarah min Thamarat Jinān al-Quran* (A Seed from pits of the fruit from the Gardens of the Quran).[10]
7. *Zahratun min riyađ al- Quran al-Hakīm* (A Flower from the Meadows of the Wise Quran).
8. *Dharratun min Shu'ā' Hidāyat'l- Quran* (An Atom from the Rays of the Guidance of the Quran).
9. *Shammatun min Nasimi Hidāyat'l- Quran* (A Whiff from the Breeze of the Guidance of the Quran).
10. *Al-Qit'atu'l-Thalithatu min Shammah* (A Third Fragment from "A Whiff").[11]
11. *Shu'latun min Anwāri Shamsi'l-Qur'an* (A Torch from the Lights of the Sun of the Quran).
12. *Nuqtah min Nuri Ma'rifati'llahi* (A Point from the Light of the God's Knowledge).
13. *Nūrun min Anwāri Nujumi'l-Quran* (Light from the Lights of the Stars of the Quran).

It is also worth noting at this point that one treatise in *Mathnawi al-Nuriye* is entitled *Lama'āt*—the same name given to Nursi's "other *mathnāwī*" (the versified composition), and to a particular volume of his *Risale-i Nur*. When talking about Nursi's works, we need to be clear about which *Lama'āt* we mean.

Style-wise, the prose of Nursi's *Mathnawi al-Nuriye* is characterized by dense paragraphs, a great many of which begin with the vocative "Know." Analogies abound. Figurative language is plentiful. Outlining devices are commonplace—as they are in the *Risale-i Nur* as a whole—both to aid the reader and to facilitate oral discussion, making it easier to pinpoint a particular argument or example in a lengthy epistle. For example, each of the fourteen sections of the *Lama'āt* is numbered; the discussion in the *Rashaħāt* works its way through fourteen "Droplets." The first of the four "chapters" of *Qatrah* features a fifty-five-part cosmological argument, with each step of the argument numbered explicitly;[12] this is followed by two short essays: one on the human condition, with subheadings demarcating discussion of each of four "diseases," the other on insights gleaned from the spiritual journey, again with subheadings demarcating discussion of each of four "truths." Such outlining devices both aid the reader and facilitate oral discussion, making it easier to pinpoint a particular argument or example in a lengthy epistle.

The internal structure of the *Mathnawi* treatises themselves, however, is not formulaic. Some treatises are concise and through-composed; others are multi-part, with formal introductions, divisions, subdivisions, formal conclusions, appendices, and the like—and can quite logically stand alone as small books in themselves.[13] In two cases—*Rashahāt* and *Lā Siyyamā*, Nursi opens simply by leaping right into his discussion. In all other cases, however, he prefaces his thoughts with praise of God or testimony or supplication. In the case of *Lama'āt,* he does this by means of Quran verses drawn from several *sūrahs.*[14] In other cases, this preface is in effect a lengthy litany: the six-part psalm that opens *Zahratun*, the series of eight vocatives with which *Shu'lah* commences, and the testimony at the beginning of *Nūrun* (the final treatise), which is in essence a *credo.* Except for *Lama'āt* and *Qatrah,* all treatises close with one or several supplications—some of these quite lengthy. It is to the place of supplication in the *Mathnawi al-Nuriye* that we now turn.

Illumination and Supplication

Anyone familiar with Nursi's biography knows how vigorously he eschewed the label of Sufi.[15] On one level, this simply was prudent: in 1925, the Turkish government banned Sufism; to claim to be a Sufi in this climate was dangerous.[16] Nursi, however, voiced a different reason for caution: the Sufi way might be "most luminous and radiant," but it was not for everyone. "Only the highest of the elite could take that way," he said, and the way he was advocating was open to all.[17] So, while he would mount an elegant apology for Sufism in his *Twenty-ninth Letter*, over the years he defended himself repeatedly—in court and in his treatises—against numerous charges of having violated the anti-Sufism edict.[18]

Nevertheless, Nursi was a mystic—if we concur with well-accepted scholarly understandings of the term.[19] In her seminal study, *Mysticism: The Nature and Development of Spiritual Consciousness*, Evelyn Underhill notes how often mysticism is defined by means of "metaphors of pilgrimage to a goal—of a road followed, distance overpassed, fatigue endured [as] the traveling self in undertaking the journey is fulfilling a destiny, a law of the transcendental life, obeying an imperative need."[20] Mystics, whatever their religion, exhibit deep commitment to a life of contemplation, she says, characterized by "oscillations between 'states of pleasure' and 'states of pain'," as they strive to spiral ever closer to the Ultimate.[21]

Nursi's *Mathnawi al-Nuriye*—its story and content—helps us locate Nursi as a mystic according to Underhill's explication of the term. While, as Underhill stresses, paradigms for analyzing the stages through which mystics pass are several, and no two of the great mystics of yore fit into any of these paradigms in quite the same way, commonalities do exist. It is typical for the life of the mystic to include the experience of awakening markedly to the fullness of divine beauty, and sustained experiences that are profoundly purgative and illuminative.[22] Classical outlines of the mystical life account for this as three *stages*. In our examination of Nursi's biography, his early literary legacy, and the life he commends to his students, we will find that *Purgation* and *Illumination*—Stages One and Two in the oldest paradigms—are useful descriptors. *Unitive* (the term for the third stage in most ancient systems) is problematic because, despite any effort to define it with care, it runs the risk of being misunderstood as deification or annihilation (*fanā'*)—neither of which obtains here. For Nursi, Stage Three is better understood (to borrow language from Underhill) as "joyous apprehension of the Absolute: that which many ascetic writers call 'the practice of the Presence of God'."[23]

Certainly the period of withdrawal, reflection, and transition that produced the *Mathnawi al-Nuriye* can be understood as a purgative period for Nursi—his Stage One as a mystic. Years as a soldier and a prisoner of war, compounded by the emotional upheaval occasioned by the demise of the Ottoman Empire, took their toll. Contemplation of death and the material world's transitory nature initiated for him an experience he likened to travel through a subterranean tunnel and across a suffocating desert. He immersed himself in devotional materials from many great spiritual masters, and found valuable aid in some.

From al-Jilānī's *Futūh al-Ghayb* (Revelations of the Unseen), Nursi learned that if he would heal the hearts of others, he first would need to find a physician to heal his own ailing heart. From the *Maktubat* (Letters) of Shaykh Ahmad Sirhindī (also known as Imam-ī Rabbānī), he learned that if he would find his way out of his spiritual confusion, he would need to limit himself to one *qiblah* (one focal point or guide). On the basis of this advice, Nursi emerged from what he called the "tunnel" and the "desert," turned decisively from the "Way of Naturalism" and the "Way of the Philosophers" (i.e., reason alone), and declared the Quran to be his "most elevated guide and most holy master"—his only *qiblah*; he would travel exclusively on the "Way of the Quran."[24] As Nursi worked out these insights in his Arabic treatises of 1920–1921, the very exercise of writing would prove instrumental in his winning the battle against what he called the "idols" of "ego within humanity" and "nature in the outer world."[25] With the publication of the Arabic treatises, Nursi was pulling out of the Way of Purgation, and entering the Way of Illumination (in his terms, "the luminous highway of the people of the Qur'ān").[26]

The Way of the Quran includes many mandates regarding supplication, instructing the faithful to call upon God, or otherwise pointing to the practice of private, supererogatory devotion. This given, the New Said would maintain for himself and commend to his students an ardent discipline of supererogatory prayer. In the *Mathnawi,* he asserts: "Verily, *du'ā'* is a sample of the secrets of *tawhīd* and *'ibādah* (worship). Whoever supplicates silently should believe firmly that the One-Called-Upon does indeed hear, and has the power to supply what one requests and is in need of. Whoever does this needs to know that the One-Called-Upon is knowledgeable of everything and capable of doing everything." That is, Nursi says, if we would make supplication, we must be convinced of God's omniscience and omnipotence.[27]

For Nursi, supplication is crucial to the illumined life. This will become a major theme of the *Risale-i Nur* as a whole. For example, in his *Twenty-fourth Letter*, he asserts that "supplication is a mighty mystery or worship; indeed, it is like the spirit of worship";[28] later in the essay, he continues in this vein:

> Supplication is the spirit of worship and the result of sincere belief. For one who makes supplication shows through it that there is someone who rules the whole universe; One Who knows the most insignificant things about me, can bring about my most distant aims. Who sees every circumstance of mine, and hears my voice. In which case, He hears all the voices of all beings, so that He hears my voice too. He does all these things, and so I await my smallest matters from Him too. I ask Him for them.[29]

In *Mathnawi al-Nuriye*, Nursi explores this theme in the treatise *Habābun*. In order to assert God's generosity to the supplicant, Nursi cites a verse from the Quran *Who is it that answers the distressed when they call upon Him? Who removes their suffering?* (27:62). By way of an answer, Nursi offers: "The One who hears and responds to the concerns of the heart and the innermost self is as well the One who governs the movements of the sun and the moon."[30] In the treatise *Shu'lah*, Nursi makes the point that all of God's creatures make supplication to their Creator—either with the tongue of speech, the tongue of necessity, or the tongue of readiness (by which he means the natural process of developing and growing, of transformation and progression). In fact, he says, everything has a means by which it calls upon and thanks God.[31]

From Nursi's perspective, human beings may and should supplicate in the tongues of consciousness and neediness. He alludes to this in his addendum to the treatise *Habābun*, when he asserts that God "has created you surrounded by concentric circles of needs." God, he continues, has equipped us with means by which we can satisfy the smallest circle of needs through reliance on our own will and power. However, other needs constitute a circle so large that its diameter stretches eternally from past to future, and its radius from the center of the earth to the Throne of God. To deal with these needs, Nursi explains, "God has provided [us] with *du'ā'*." Pointing to the Quran's rhetorical question, *What are you to my Lord without your supplication?* [25:77], Nursi reminds us that "a toddler would call to his parents for help in getting what his hands cannot reach, so the servant [i.e., any believer] may call upon his Lord for what one lacks the capacity to get on his own."[32]

Having commended "the luminous highway of the people of the Qur'ān," Nursi asserts that the community of believers gathered in worship and supplication yields a result far greater than the sum of its parts, and illustrates this in the treatise *Shu'lah* by way of analogy. Each believer is like a single stone in solid masonry, he asserts. Just as the individual stones create a solid structure when mortared together, so each individual believer will benefit from his or her brothers and sisters, and millions more. Collective work will benefit everyone in millions of ways. If this gathering becomes organized and systematized, "everyone will become part of the collective that asks for mercy, and makes requests, and issues praises, and gives endorsements."[33]

The Prophet Muhammad as role model for all Islamic spiritual disciplines is, of course, a recurring and well-developed theme throughout *Mathnawi-al-Nuriye*.[34] But we also find Nursi noting that, over the centuries, the light of the Prophet's guidance has informed and been transmitted by great spiritual masters in every century since. He names more than a dozen examples.[35]

We can extract from the *Mathnawi al-Nuriye* some twenty supplications of varying lengths: some appropriated from the Quran; others, from the *Hadīth*; and still others from the *du'ā'* legacies of some of the masters Nursi lists. A *hizb* attributed to al-Jilānī is said be one of Nursi's favorite supplications, one he would recite daily.[36] Nursi uses it to close *Shammatun*, prefacing it with a supplication of his own in which he indicates that he feels more confident beseeching God by means of al-Jilānī's much stronger voice; furthermore, he knows God is indeed "familiar" with this supplication because God has heard al-Jilānī pray it already.[37] This given, we can presume that Nursi expects readers of *Mathnawi al-Nuriye* to experience this same lack of confidence, this same need for resources with which to approach God, and expects them to use the devotional material he includes in these treatises in their own devotional exercises. Just as he has stressed that there is benefit in making supplication in league with others, so also there is benefit to linking our requests to supplications God has heard repeatedly from the lips of those in the past on whose shoulders we now stand, metaphorically.

The *Mathnawi* also contains supplications in Nursi's voice. For example, he concludes the main section of *Habābun* by addressing his reader: "Know! Verily, helplessness gives rise to entreating [*nadā'*] and need causes praying [*du'ā'*]."[38] He then addresses God:

> *Yā Rabbī, wa Yā Khaliqī, wa Yā Malikī* [O Lord, O Creator, O Owner]! My plea with my summons is out of my necessity. My resources for my supplication stem from my poverty. You are my means when my resources are disrupted. My treasure is my weakness. You are my capital, [source of] my hopes and my pains. My intercessors are Your Beloved [i.e., the Prophet Muhammad] and Your Mercy. Pardon me, forgive my sins, and have mercy on me, *Yā Allah, Yā Rahmān, Yā Rahīm.*[39]

As he nears the end of the treatise *Zahrah*, Nursi explains why he commits his supplications to writing. He ought to keep them secret, he admits, but, he says, "I write the entreaties of my heart to my Lord . . . in a hope that the Almighty's Mercy will accept the speech of my book, once death has silenced my tongue."[40] He concludes the treatise with a four-part *du'ā'* in which he speaks as though he is a very elderly man: "O my Merciful Lord, O my Generous God! My life and youth have been wasted in calamity of my own accord"—although later in the prayer he reveals that he is only in his forties.[41] Three times he tells God that he is already wearing his burial shroud—and is either already in his grave or ready to climb in. If it be that God take pity on him, forgive him, and admit him to Paradise, says Nursi, it will happen because this is what has come to be expected of the Most Compassionate of the Compassionate. After all, Nursi concludes, what other door is there on which to knock?[42] On the one hand, this is demonstrative of the mystic's Way of Purgation. On the other hand, by embedding such a supplication in a treatise destined for publication and distribution, the still comparatively young Nursi is modeling for his growing circle of students the boldness with which they are to call upon God as they travel the Illuminative Way.

When it comes to the discipline of supplication informed by rigorous study, Nursi exhibits a knack for speaking with what one scholar calls the authority of one who has assimilated the things about which one is speaking—something one does by way of two unifications: the unification of one's own faculties, thinking, feeling and willing, into a single movement of assent and adoration; and the unification of oneself with the subject that one is considering.[43]

Joyous Apprehension: *Mathnawi al-Nuriye* and God's Beautiful Names

According to Evelyn Underhill's thinking, the third stage or dimension of the contemplative life may be described as the Way of Joyous Apprehension of the Absolute. For Nursi, part and parcel of this Joyous Apprehension of the Absolute was sheer delight in the Quran itself—its mystery, its beauty, its efficacy. Even before his sojourn of 1920–1921, he had already published important volumes of Quranic exegesis and commentary: *Proceedings* and *Signs of Miraculousness*, both written in Arabic, date from 1911 and 1913 C.E., respectively.[44] Traveling "the luminous highway of the Qur'ān" with Nursi leads us quite directly, not just to *du'ā'*-study, but also to consideration of such terms as *dhikr* and litany; thus to contemplation of God's beautiful names—a major occupation for him, and a major theme of *Mathnawi al-Nuriye*.

That the Quran includes repetition and reiteration is one of the themes of the treatise *Rashahāt*.[45] The Quran does this, Nursi explains, because it is—among other things—"a *dhikr*-book, and a *du'ā'*-book, and a *da'wah*-book." (That is, it is a book of invocation, supplication, and invitation.) The more one reads it, the better, says Nursi; in fact, he asserts, it is a *must* to read it over and over, since invocation, supplication, and invitation all are enhanced and intensified by repetition: "*Dhikr* is to be repeated, and *du'ā'* is to be reiterated, and *da'wah* confirmed. In repetition of *dhikr* there is illumination [*tanwīr*]; and in reiteration of *du'ā'* there is repose [*taqrīr*]; and in the confirmation of *da'wah* there is assurance [*ta'kīd*]."[46] By extension, repetition of the devotional material incorporated into *Mathnawi al-Nuriye* is commendable—a point Nursi will make more explicitly in the *Risale-i Nur*.

Dhikr, as this audience well knows, is the technical term for remembering and contemplating God's attributes. In the concluding section of the treatise *Qatrah*, Nursi alludes to the custom of congregational *dhikr* while seated in a circle. It is easy enough, he says, to envision the whole surface of the earth as a mosque, and oneself praying within it; to envision the totality of the believers, and see oneself in that grand community. Go a step farther, he urges, and "envision within it all the prophets and saints repeating *There is no god but God.* And from the harmony of these voices the devotee becomes inspired to see time as a *halqah dhikri* [47] [a circle of rememberers] under the guidance of the Imam of All Prophets. On the right hand of the past, 'the prophets' are seated; on the left hand of the future, 'the saints' are sitting down, remembering God with an audible voice received by those who are all ears—that is, by one whose one's hearing is strong: he is a witness. Verily, the one who has keen hearing and insight hears the *dhikr*, takes in everything around, and sees oneself in a *halqati dhikri* itself."[48]

For Nursi, one purgative aspect of his spiritual sojourn of 1920–1921 was what he called the smashing of the idols of ego and nature. Just as *du'ā'* helps to accomplish this, he says, so does *dhikr*. In *Habābun*, he explains that *dhikr* pierces the ego, arrests its growth, and stems its rebelliousness against the Compeller-of-the-Heavens-and-the-Earth. One can perform *dhikr* silently or aloud, and Nursi commends both methods. Either way, *dhikr* yields both conscious and unconscious benefits, and is in fact "the sum total" of Islam's liturgical practices.[49]

Discussion of *dhikr* leads, typically, to a discussion of the Islamic notion that God's names are "beautiful," and that they are ninety-nine in number. The most common list of these ninety-nine beautiful names comes to us in a *hadīth* transmitted by Abū Hurayrah;[50] and when we encounter a list of God's names, that list is apt to follow the order set down by him.[51]

Perhaps the definitive exposition of the traditional list of God's attributes is the great al-Ghazali's *al-Maqsad al-asnā*.[52] Because he is wedded to the notion that God's names number ninety-nine, al-Ghazali is concerned with reconciling pairs of synonyms and variant traditions such that, in the end, the list of God's names has only ninety-nine entries.[53] Nursi would have been familiar with al-Ghazali's thinking on all of this. However, when it comes to denoting God's attributes, Nursi is never particularly concerned about "ninety-nine" as an operative term. And where, in explicating God's beautiful names, al-Ghazali proceeds systematically through the list defined by Abū Hurayrah's *hadīth*, submitting it to painstaking exegesis, when Nursi discusses God's names, he has a different list in mind.

The key to all of Nursi's reflections on God's beautiful names—insight into his method—lies in *Qatrah* (which, as we have noted, is the earliest of the entries in *Mathnawi al-Nuriye*). There Nursi stipulates that "all things other than God, that is, the universe, should be looked at as signifying something other than themselves (*māna-yi harfī*) and on His account. It is an error to look at them as signifying only themselves (*māna-yi ismī*) and on account of causes . . . when looking at causes, one should think of the True Causer of Causes."[54] Nursi asserts that the reason why so many verses of the Quran conclude with one or several of God's beautiful names is that in this way the Quran calls attention to the origin of whatever divine work it has just laid before the reader. "Thus it spreads out before humanity the textiles of [God's] design, then envelops this in the Names. And [again], thus it categorizes [God's] acts, then sums them up through the Names."[55]

Nursi's favorite vehicle for contemplation of God's names is the *Jawshān al-Kabīr*,[56] a 100-stanza supplication. Like Abū Hurayrah's list of God's beautiful names, the *Jawshān* is likewise a *hadīth*: reportly, it is a supplication of the Prophet himself,[57] the chain of transmission (albeit somewhat weakly established) proceeding through Zayn al-'Ābidīn and his father Husayn to Alī.[58] The *Jawshān* is important to our present discussion because it encourages us to conceive of the notion of divine beautiful names in much broader terms than does Abū Hurayrah's *hadīth*.

It is important to our understanding of *Mathnawi al-Nuriye* to be aware that, while he may have known of the *Jawshān al-Kabīr* beforehand, it was during his profoundly transitional sojourn of 1920–1921 that Nursi cultivated his deep and abiding fondness for it.[59] From then on, he recited it regularly; from then on, it served as a source of inspiration for writing projects. Nursi himself says that, in a sense, the *Risale-i Nur* was born of the *Jawshān,* and that it was the source of the *Risale*'s brilliance.[60]

Given that *Jawshān al-Kabīr* means "the great armor," it is not a leap to liken it to the Celtic *lorica* (breastplate prayer)—the sort of prayer to be chanted while getting dressed in the morning, or while arming oneself for a physical or spiritual battle. The *Jawshān* is precisely armor of this latter sort. Armor for daily spiritual battle seems to be the purpose to which Nursi put it.[61]

There are those who are known to take the notion of *Jawshān* as armor more literally than metaphorically, wearing a tiny copy of this long prayer as a pendant. In the *Risale-i Nur*, Nursi will caution against treating the *Jawshān* as a talisman. The reason for reciting such a supplication, he stresses, is for God's good pleasure, and for the "fruits and benefits" of the hereafter. If this-worldly fruits and benefits happen to accrue to the person who maintains this spiritual discipline, that is fine, "so long as they are not the ultimate reason and not intentionally sought." In fact, a yield of this-worldly fruits may even "encourage the weak and make them choose worship." However, if this-worldly fruits and benefits are the reason for reciting a supplication—or even just part of the reason—then doing so is invalidated as worship. It becomes mere recitation.[62]

Nursi refers to the *Jawshān al-Kabīr* as a *wird*—a near synonym of *hizb*.[63] The English term *litany* translates both.[64] Regardless of the label, Islamic prayers of this kind are characteristically through-composed. For example, al-Shādhilī's litanies typically meander for pages and pages, alternating between sections of didactic and vocative material. Nursi employs this technique in *Mathnawi al-Nuriye*, as in his appendix to treatise *Habbah*, which includes a litany on the theme, "There is no force and strength save God."[65] The treatise *Qatrah* is something of a *du'ā'* manual in itself; much of it can indeed be prayed: its second, third, and fourth chapters are, to all intents and purposes, litanies.[66] When we survey the entirety of the Nursi corpus, we get a clear sense of the importance of the role played by litanies in his own devotional discipline, and in the life of contemplation he advocates.[67]

When scholar Titus Burckhardt discusses *wird* as a literary genre, he asserts that it is characterized by "its monotonous rhyme and complex metre."[68] Burckhardt's description is particularly appropriate to the *Jawshān*. Different from the litanies of al-Shādhilī, for example, the *Jawshān*'s form is strictly stanzaic. Its 100 stanzas are punctuated by two different refrain patterns. The refrain concluding every stanza is shifting and supplicatory; the other, which inaugurates each quartet of stanzas, is constant and assertive.

What is most obvious about the formal elements of the *Jawshān* is that each of its 100 stanzas consists of ten invocations, and within a stanza those ten invocations are parallel in format. The first stanza of every quartet comprises ten "single names" rather than phrases. Successive stanzas are constructs—sometimes just a noun and its modifier, other times a longer phrase. In addition to such unifiers as length, word order, and phrase complexity of the honorifics (all of which work together to produce a unity of rhythm for that stanza), stanzas may also be unified by word endings (creating rhyme). Sound patterns take pride of place over the traditional order of the beautiful names in the list recorded by Abū Hurayrah. According to Ahmet Eren Kademoğlu's assessment, the disregard of the traditional order, plus the use of various grammatical constructs instead of single names only, interweaves descriptions of the divine and plays one off another with such variety that the *Jawshān* provides the devout supplicant with a total of 160 (rather than a mere ninety-nine) divine names by which to invoke God.[69] In the *Risale-i Nur,* Nursi makes an even bolder claim: from his perspective, the *Jawshān* speaks of God's 1001 names "both explicitly and allusively"; and they in turn provide "a thousand and one proofs of *tawhīd*."[70]

Islamic theology, it is scarcely necessary to reiterate, gives pride of place to *tawhīd*—the fact of God's absolute Oneness (and everything that fact implies). Add this to Nursi's love of the *Jawshān* as a tool of contemplation, and it will be unsurprising to learn how much attention he pays in *Mathnawi al-Nuriye* to the relationship between the notion *tawhīd* and the plethora of names of God—always stressing that recognition of, delight in, and contemplation of the latter is in no way a violation of the notion of God's absolute unicity. What may be surprising—and what may indeed delight—are the analogies with which he makes this point, as when he says:

> The whole tends to be unified by virtue of the making of the part—which is a sample of the whole. This is similar to the relationship of a

> tree to its fruit. A whole will become a whole of its genre, as well as a part of the genre *per se*. For example, sunlight spreads out in the sky. Each particle of light can contain all of the parts of that light in the likeness of the sun. So every little parcel of twinkling light is a partial sun, connected with each other to make light—and God is the Highest Example. This is how the Names of the Light of the Eternal Lights reflect themselves; and this is how the Names can be apprehended in two ways: each and all as part and whole.[71]

Returning, however, to the *Jawshān*'s formal elements: when it is chanted aloud, God is praised by patterns that expand and contract, interlock and interweave, creating aurally the geometry and arabesque so characteristic of Islamic art visually. This is a text's "sound vision"—a term I borrow from Michael Sells, who employs it in his discussion of the aural dimension of the Quran.[72] Many parts of *Mathnawi al-Nuriye* exhibit a sound vision similar to the *Jawshān*. Nursi has a propensity to play with assonance, to pair terms for their mutual resonance, to pull out obscure terms (or even to coin them) for their rhythmic value. We might characterize the effect this achieves as "the mystification of language"—a term used occasionally by anthropologists and others in reference to the phenomenon of preaching in which rhythm, alliteration, and other auditory effects trump surface clarity of meaning.[73]

"Mystification of language" can leave one's reader mystified, and in two *Mathnawi* treatises Nursi responds to criticism that his rhetoric is obscure. In the preface to *Habbah*, he states: "Know that it has been reported to me that people are saying 'we cannot comprehend much of his writings, and so they [get printed in vain]'"; and, in *Nūrun min Anwāri,* he says: "It is often said: 'Your *kalām* can not be clearly understood!' Agreed, but what to do?! This is the way insights come into the heart!" One solution Nursi offers is this: let the reader "send his imagination to me; that way I could add him on as a guest to my own eyes and he would, at last, see things the way I see."[74]

The *Jawshān*'s own "sound vision" informs the *Mathnawi al-Nuriy*'s own felicity of aural effect. Consider the pairing of name-sounds in this example from *Nūrun: "Allah Akbar: Huwa'l-'Adl al-Hākim. Huwa'l-Hukmu al-Fard. Huwa'l-Ādl al-Hakīm.*"[75] And again, "*Allahu Akbar: Huwa'l-Qādir al-Muqīm. Huwa'l-Barī' al-'Alīm. Huwa'l-Latīf al-Karīm. Huwa'l-Wadūd al Rahīm Huwa'l-Jamīl al-'Adīm Huwa'l-Naqqāsh al-'Ālim.*"[76]

In the treatise *Qatrah*, on the other hand, the sound vision is not so dominant, yet echoes of the *Jawshān* can be heard therein nevertheless, as a description of God by means of long, complex sentences tapers into a list of "single names" reminiscent of the first of each quartet of Jawshan stanzas: "They affirm that surely He is God: al-Waajib, al-Wujuud, al-Qadeem, as-Sarmadī, al-Badī, al-Waahid, al-Ahad, al-Fard, as-Samad, al-'Azāz, al-Jabbār, al-Mutakabbir, al-Qahhār."[77]

Mathnawi al-Nuriye not only echoes the *Jawshān*, it includes commentary on it—particularly in the essay *al-Qit'at'l-Thalthah min Shammah*, also called "Whiff (3)." Here Nursi likens the *Jawshān*'s many stanzas to as many jewel-cases containing "gems of *tawhīd*": each gem being a descriptor of God. He explains that, "just as a Sultan has diverse titles for his dominion in the bureaus of his government and classes of his protectorate and ranks of his sultanate and the duties of his principality—as if he were an available presence and overseer of what is taking place in every domain," so it is with God's names. Each name is dominant in its department; the others then are subordinate. God exercises His governance in each domain by manifesting the Beautiful Name peculiar to that level—as if it were particular to that level alone. On some other level this Name will be subdominant to whichever name is peculiar to *that* level. The names correspond to and reflect one another, Nursi stresses; and the *Jawshān al-Kabīr* is a supplication that hammers this reality home.[78]

It is not unusual for pious persons enhance their practice of *dhikr* by using a *tasbīh*—a rosary. Nursi makes note of this in *Mathnawi al-Nuriye*, but asks: Why bother with rosaries? At best they only have ninety-nine beads, and as the *Jawshān* demonstrates and he himself has asserted, God has far more names than that! In the treatise *Zahratun*, he argues:

> Instead of an ordinary *tasbīh*, the Quran puts in the hand of its students beads in an amount equal to the atoms of all the creatures of the earth who supplicate to God. Instead of a ninety-nine-bead *tasbīh*, God gives them 'the chain of the entirety of the atoms of [all] beings', and they recite their litanies using that marvelous *tasbīh.* And they mention their God a number of times equal to the number of the creatures in the universe—and even more! So, look at such saintly students of *Tanzīl* (Revelation) as al-Jilānī, or al-Rufā'ī, or al-Shādhilī—how they took in their hands chains of atoms and drops and breaths of the creatures as an alternative to an ordinary *tasbīh,* remembering God by means of them.[79]

Nursi discusses the use of comparatives and superlatives when speaking of God's attributes, and assures his students that the practice in no way impinges on divine ultimacy and unity. This lesson vis-à-vis God's beautiful names brings him eventually to expound on the greatest name of God—which is unknown. He picks up this theme in the treatise *Habbah*, using an analogy of light passing through a prism to make his point:

> The Beautiful Names—each one of them—each contain the whole in general. Just like white light contains the 'seven colors' [i.e., the whole of the color spectrum], so each name contains the whole list. Therefore, each one is itself a reference to, and a result, of all of them. [God's Beautiful Names] reflect each other like mirrors. So, they can be invoked in a manner similar to the way measurement can lead to sequential results. And, just as a verdict emerges from solid evidence, so the Greatest Name contains the whole of the list [the whole of the general included information]. Some can reach the light of the Greatest Name through the other Beautiful Names. In this reaching, the Greatest Name would be relative to the level of the seeker reaching it. And God knows best![80]

Truly, Joyous Apprehension of the Divine—profound engagement with the many ways to describe God—is a blissful pursuit for Bediuzzaman Said Nursi. We have but scratched the surface of the ways in which he works out this theme of the importance and interlocking nature of God's beautiful names.

CONCLUSION

Nursi's *Mathnawi al-Nuriye* provides the rationale and the resources for the student of what he calls the "luminous highway of the Qur'ān." Its story and its content allow us insight into Nursi's contemplative life as having involved periods of Purgation, Illumination, and Joyous Apprehension of the Divine—stages very much in harmony with classical, scholarly paradigms of the mystic way. As rationale and resource, *Mathnawi al-Nuriye* is (among other things) a *dhikr*-book, and a *du'ā'*-book, and a *da'wah*-book (to echo Nursi's own characterization of the Quran itself). That is, *Mathnawi al-Nuriye* is (among other things) a handbook of invocation, supplication, and invitation—one that demonstrates the spirit of worship and the result of sincere belief.

Thematically, this set of Arabic essays was the seed (*nawāh*)—that is, the starting-point or nucleus—of the *Risale-i Nur*, as Nursi himself explains; he saw it as "a seedling (*ghirs*)" which would bear much fruit as time passed.[81] As the "seedbed of the *Risale-i Nur*," it is a transitional work, and a curious one. On the one hand, it is the first opus of the New Said (as Şükran Vahide considers it).[82] On the other hand, it is an opus of the elderly Said (in that its first appearance in collated form came just five or so years before his death). The *Risale-i Nur* does not (actually, cannot) cite *Mathnawi al-Nuriye* by name, but does mention the names of many of its constituent treatises;[83] oddly, (unless one is mindful of the distance between composition and collation) *Mathnawi al-Nuriye* cites the *Risale-i Nur* a number of times. Regardless, the set of treatises collated as *Mathnawi al-Nuriye* are indeed a prelude to the outpouring of Quran commentary and theological reflection now known as the *Risale-i Nur*. Even before one digs into the discussions, the correlation is apparent in key words employed in titles and outlining devices.

What is needed now is a scholarly critical edition of *Mathnawi al-Nuriye*. Such an edition would situate the individual treatises, providing a chronology of their composition, and likewise would situate the project of compilation some thirty years later. Its scholarly apparatus would include cross-referencing of discussions begun in the Arabic essays that are amplified in the *Risale-i Nur*. If such an edition could be a translation as well, it would be scrupulously consistent in rendering the dozens of names (and combinations of names) by which Nursi refers to God, making easier for the reader of the translated edition the task of discerning how many are at play, and which are used most frequently. Such a translation would do its best to honor *Mathnawi al-Nuriye*'s sound vision and rhetorical intricacy as well. My own meager attempt at a close reading of *Mathnawi al-Nuriye* has convinced me that such a scholarly edition in English would itself be "a seedling (*ghirs*)" that could bear much fruit as time continues to pass.

We have in Nursi's *Mathnawi al-Nuriye* a digest—an epitome—of the *Risale-i Nur*.[84] As a form of commentary, the *Risale-i Nur* introduces, expounds the mystery of, and comments on various portions of the Quran. Obviously, *Mathnawi al-Nuriye* does this, too. But the *Risale-i Nur* is as well a project of theological reflection and spiritual direction; as such, it is a window into the spiritual disciplines of a great exemplar, thus a project of spiritual direction for his disciples. *Mathnawī al-'Arabī al-Nūrī* is a window into that window.

Notes

1. Şerif Mardin, *Religion and Social Change in Modern Turkey: The Case of Bediūzzaman Said Nursi* (Albany, 1989), 177.
2. Said Nursi, Preface to *Habbah min Nawatāt Thamarah min Thamarat Jinān al-Qur'ān*. See Redha Ameur, translator, "Preface to the *Al-Mathnawī al-'Arabī al-Nūrī*." In *Islam at the Crossroads: On the Life and Thought of Bediuzzaman Said Nursi*, edited with an introduction by Ibrahim M. Abu-Rabi' (Albany, 2003), 336–37.
3. Şükran Vahide, "A Chronology of Said Nursi's Life" in *Islam at the Crossroads*, op. cit., xix. (Hereafter: Vahide, *Chronology*.) Some Turkish references to this work spell

the title *Mesnevī-i Nūriye*. All citations of *Mathnawi al-Nuriye* will refer to the Arabic-language edition: Badī'uzzamān Sa'īd al-Nursī, *Al-Mathnawī al-'Arabī al-Nūrī* (Istanbul, 1999)—hereafter, *Mathnawi al-Nuriye*. Unless otherwise noted, all paraphrasing and translation of *Mathnawi al-Nuriye* are my own, and most was prepared in consultation and collaboration with Hashim Al-Tawil, Ph.D., of the faculty of Henry Ford Community College, Dearborn, Michigan. Where these paraphrases and translations are felicitous, Dr. Al-Tawil has my deepest thanks. Where there are errors, they are mine alone.

4. *Durrat al-Asrār wa Tuḥfat al-Abrār* (The Pearl of Mysteries and the Treasure of Righteousness).
5. The full English title given for this composition in the Sözler English edition of *The Words* is "Gleams from between Crescents of Ramadan and the Festival: Flowers from the Seeds of Reality," with the subtitle "A short 'Mathnawi' and a collection on the subject of belief for the Risale-i Nur students." Bediuzzaman Said Nursi, *The Words: On the Nature and Purposes of Man, Life, and All Things*, translated from the Turkish *Sözler* by Şükran Vahide (Istanbul: Sözler Neşriyat, 1992). Throughout, any quotations from the *Risale-i Nur* will be Şükran Vahide's translation (Sözler Neşriyat), and hereafter will be cited simply as *Words*, *Letters*, *Flashes*, and *Rays*.
6. See *Words*, op. cit., 725 and 726.
7. Interestingly, scholars are as likely to draw parallels between Rūmī's *Mathnawi* and the *Risale-i Nur* as a whole, as between the Rūmī and Nursi *mathnawis*. A case in point is Bilal Kuşpinar, who asserts: "One could even justifiably declare that the Mesnevi is the former's interpretation of the Quran in verse, while the *Risale* is the latter's in prose"; and, in so doing, one would be "concurring with the opinions of various writers on Rumi and Nursi." See Bilal Kuşpinar, "The Concept of Man: Mevlānā Jalāl al-Dīn and Said Nursi," in *Islam at the Crossroads*, op. cit., 151.
8. That is, "particular arguments for the Resurrection."
9. Nursi seems to have coined two words here. *Habābun* is an atypical plural; and, because the meaning of the noun *'Ummān* is ambiguous, its translation (*depth*) has been italicized.
10. Again, we have in *nawatāt* an atypical plural; the standard plural of *nawah* is *nawayāt*.
11. "A First Fragment" and "A Second Fragment" comprise appendices to the previous treatise. The Kaynak English translation (1999) does not treat "A Third Fragment" as a separate treatise, but rather as yet another appendix to "A Whiff." The Sözler edition refers to this material by the shorthand "Whiff (3)."
12. *Mathnawial-Nuriye*, op. cit., 108.
13. An example is *Qatrah* (No. 4), which has four chapters, a conclusion, and an addendum; another is *Habbah* (No. 6), which has two addenda.
14. *Al-Zumar* (39) 62–63, *Yā Sīn* (36) 83, *al-Hijr* (15) 21, *Hūd* (11) 56.
15. See, for example, Nursi's remarks in his Sixteenth Letter. He is adamant: for years he has eschewed politics and he is not a Sufi shaykh. "I have told everyone who has come to me: Belief is necessary, Islam is necessary; this is not the age of Sufism." *Letters*, op. cit., 84–85.
16. Vahide, *Author of the Risale-i Nur*, op. cit., 202, 239.
17. Ibid., 168.
18. Ibid., 239–40. See also *Letters*, 518–35.

19. To assert this is to stand with scholars of Islamic thought and practice who distinguish between Islamic mysticism and Sufism. Professor Dr. Homayoun Hemmati of Tehran University, for example, defines Islamic mysticism as "an intellectual heritage, cultural system, outlook, a set of beliefs, values and ontology," whereas Sufis are mystics who establish (or are initiated into) an order and maintain "special organizational behavior and customs." Homayoun Hemmati, "Hafez and Nursi on Mysticism," unpublished paper presented in Istanbul, August 2005.
20. Evelyn Underhill, *Mysticism: The Nature and Development of Spiritual Consciousness* (Oxford, 1999), 132.
21. Ibid., 168. In a 1963 essay, Joseph Ratzinger (now Pope Benedict XVI) juxtaposes the "way of mysticism" with the "way of monotheism," thus polarizing monotheism and mysticism. See his *Truth and Tolerance: Christian Belief and World Religions* (San Francisco: Ignatius Press, 2004), 36–38. On the other hand, as I use the term *mysticism* in the present chapter, any such notion of its being something somehow necessarily different from monotheism is rejected. Homayoun Hemmati's attitude on this matter is similar to mine: he describes the mysticism of Nursi as "quite faith-centered and faith-based. We can call it a *monotheistic* practical mysticism." Hemmati, op cit., emphasis mine.
22. Ibid., 169–70.
23. Ibid., 240.
24. Nursi, *Letters*, op. cit., 418–19; Vahide, *Intellectual Biography*, 10–11. By "naturalism," Nursi means preoccupation with the study of nature, particularly preoccupation with any notion that nature is the cause of its own existence (cf. *Mathnawi al-Nuriye*, 184). It is important to realize that this awakening was informed by earlier profound Quran study. See the discussion of the Way of Joyous Apprehension.
25. Vahide, *Intellectual Biography*, op. cit., 11; See also *Mathnawi al-Nuriye*, 220.
26. *Words*, 569. See also Vahide, *Intellectual Biography*, op. cit., 11.
27. *Mathnawi al-Nuriye*, 178.
28. *Letters*, 353.
29. *Letters*, 357.
30. *Mathnawi al-Nuriye*, 212.
31. *Mathnawi al-Nuriye*, 403.
32. *Mathnawi al-Nuriye*, 210.
33. *Mathnawi al-Nuriye*, Arabic 406.
34. See, for example, *Mathnawi al-Nuriye*, 62–63.
35. *Mathnawi al-Nuriye*, 315. His list includes Abu Hanīfah (700–768 C.E.), al-Shāfi'ī (767–820 C.E.), al-Jilānī (1077–1166 C.E.), al-Ghazālī (1058–1111 C.E.), Ibn al-'Arabī (1165–1240 C.E.), al-Shādhilī (1196–1258 C.E.), Shah al-Naqshband (1316–1389 C.E.), and Rūmī (1207–1273 C.E.), among others.
36. During a conversation in Saylorsburg, Pennsylvania, during the summer of 2000, translator Ali Ünal indictaed that the source of this supplication is *Al-Majmu'a al-Ahzab: A Collection of Supplications* (Istanbul, date uncertain, but definitely before the republic)—a three-volume anthology of supplications and litanies compiled by Gümüshane'li Ahmed Ziyauddin (d. 1893). See also note 70.
37. *Mathnawi al-Nuriye*, 331–32.
38. *Mathnawi al-Nuriye*, 195.
39. *Mathnawi al-Nuriye*, 195.

40. *Mathnawi al-Nuriye*, 281.
41. *Mathnawi al-Nuriye*, 281.
42. *Mathnawi al-Nuriye*, 282.
43. A. M. Allchin, adapted slightly. Allchin is making this remark of the Anglican spiritual master, Lancelot Andrewes, but I have long thought that it transfers to Said Nursi without loss of integrity. See A. M. Allchin, "Anglican Spirituality," in *The Study of Anglicanism*, revised edition, eds. Stephen Sykes, John Booty, and Jonathan Knight (London, 1988), 354.
44. Vahide, *Chronology*, op. cit., xviii. *Muhākemat* and *İşārātū'l-İ'caz* are the common Turkish iterations of these titles.
45. Nursi takes up this question as well in his essay "A Flower of Emirdağ"—an open letter to disciples of the *Risale-i Nur*, written during Ramadan in the Denizli Prison. It is published as the Eleventh Ray, and appears as well in the *Words* collection (after the Twenty-Fifth Word).
46. *Mathnawi al-Nuriye*, 70.
47. A technical term for the kind of collective liturgical exercise performed by a gathering of Sufis. Nursi puts it in quotes.
48. *Mathnawi al-Nuriye*, 162.
49. *Mathnawi al-Nuriye*, 179.
50. Al-Bukhārī, 4:419.
51. *Allāh, ar-Rahmān, ar-Rahīm, al-Malik, al-Quddūs, as-Salām, al-Mu'min . . . an-Nūr, al-Hādī, al-Badī', al-Bāqī, al-Wārith, ar-Rashīd, as-Sabūr;* etc. See the classic commentary on the divine names: Abū Hamid Al-Ghazālī, *The Ninety-Nine Beautiful Names of God*, trs. David B. Burrell and Nazih Daher (Cambridge, 1995). For a list with limited commentary, see Shems Friedlander, *Ninety-Nine Names of Allah: The Beautiful Names* (San Francisco, 1993).
52. The Most Radiant Import, consisting in an Explanation of the Beautiful Names of God.
53. Al-Ghazālī, op. cit., 24–26, 51.
54. Vahide emphasizes this point. See her *Intellectual Biography*, 11.
55. *Mathnawi al-Nuriye*, 339.
56. *Cevşenü'l-Kebīr* in Turkish transliteration.
57. See Nursi, *Rays*, op. cit., 596.
58. Zayn al-'Ābidīn is the honorific for Ali ibn al-Husayn—a great-grandson of the Prophet and a survivor of the Battle of Karbala. His grandfather Ali is revered by Sunni Muslims as the Fourth Rightly Guided Caliph, and by Shi'ah as the First Imam. His own supplications (cherished by Sunni and Shi'ah alike) are published as *Al-Sahīfat al-Kāmilat al-Sajjadiyya*. For a thorough scholarly analysis of the *Jawshān al-Kabīr*, see Ahmet Eren Kademoğlu, *The Textual and the Spiritual Structure of the Jawshān al-Kabīr: A Study on Jawshān al-Kabīr and Its Translation* (Licence diss., Rome, 2000). See also William C. Chittick, Introduction to Alī ibn Al-Husayn, *The Psalms of Islam: Al-Sahīfat al-Kāmilat al-Sajjadiyya*, tr. William C. Chittick (London, 1988), xix.
59. Vahide notes that the *Jawshān* was readily available to Nursi by virtue of its inclusion in (and his access to) *Majmu'at al-Ahzāb*. See note 42; see also Vahide, *Intellectual Biography*, 30, 11. In the introduction to her translation of the *Jawshān*, Vahide notes Nursi's role in popularizing it in the twentieth century. See Şükran Vahide, *A*

Supplication of the Prophet Muhammad (Peace and blessings be upon him): Al-Jawshan al-Kabīr (Istanbul, 2003), 3. This supplication is also available as a small devotional manual in Arabic alone, and in Arabic with Turkish translation, and on the Internet in English, Arabic, and Turkish. (There may be other editions.)

60. Nursi, *Rays*, op. cit., 596.
61. It is reported that it was his routine to arise at 3:30 each morning to pray the *Jawshān*—an exercise that requires at least an hour.
62. *Flashes*, 180.
63. See, for instance, *Flashes*, 180. As with *hizb*, the usual English translation for this term is "litany."
64. While some might argue that that there is a distinction between the *hizb* and the *wird*, they are often used interchangeably. See Constance E. Padwick, *Muslim Devotions: A Study of Prayer-Manuals in Common Use* (Oxford, 1996; originally published, 1961), 20–25, 98, 170.
65. *Mathnawi al-Nuriye*, 248–49.
66. The second chapter comprises twelve exclamations of praise, each beginning *Subhan Allah*; the third chapter features nine, each beginning *Al-Hamdu li-llah*; and the fourth chapter, fourteen beginning *Allahu Akbar*. See *Mathnawi al-Nuriye*, 132–39.
67. In the *Rays*, for example, Nursi quotes part of al-Ghazali's *Hizb al-Masūn*. He mentions the *Hizb al-Nūri*, a forty-five page Arabic supplication, which, according to Vahide, manifested for Nursi the validity of the *hadith* that says, "An hour's reflective thought may be better than a year's [supererogatory] worship." Nursi called it "a luminous proof of the *Risale-i Nur*, a supreme invocation springing from it, and a small sample of it." (See *Rays*, 329; 501, n. 78.) He also discusses a *Hizb al-Qur'ān*, which seems to have been a collection of Quranic verses he and his students compiled, the result being to make something of a *du'ā'* manual. Putting together *du'ā'*-booklets like this, Nursi explains, "is an Islamic custom that has been practiced since the time of the Prophet." Şükran Vahide observes that many of the verses in that collection "form the basis of, and are expounded in, the *Risale-i Nur*." (See Nursi's own comments and translator's note in *Rays*, 322.)
68. Titus Burckhardt, *Mirror of the Intellect: Essays on Traditional Science and Sacred Art*, tr. and ed. William Stoddart (Albany, 1987), 246
69. Kademoğlu, op. cit.
70. *Rays*, 51, 593, 596; also *Words*, 344.
71. *Mathnawi al-Nuriye*, 209.
72. Sells also discusses this notion as "aural intertextuality." He bases his ideas on the work of Roman Jakobson and Linda R. Waugh, *The Sound Shape of Language* (Bloomington, 1979). See Michael Sells, *Approaching the Qur'ān: The Early Revelations* (Ashland, 1999; and his "A Literary Approach to the Hymnic Sūras of the Quran: Spirit, Gender, and Aural Intertextuality," *Literary Structures of Religious Meaning in the Qur'ān*, ed. 'Issa Boullata (Richmond, 2000), 3–25.
73. Professor Claude F. Jacobs, Ph.D., Chair of the Anthropology Department and Director of the Center for the Study of Religion and Society at the University of Michigan–Dearborn, offered this explanation in a conversation with Dr. Hashim Al-Tawil and the author in Dearborn, June 27, 2005.

74. Mathnawi al-Nuriye, 218, 480, translated by Redha Ameur. See Redha Ameur, translator, "Preface to the *Al-Mathnawī al-'Arabī al-Nūrī*" in *Islam at the Crossroads*, op. cit., 336, 337.
75. He is the Wise Justice. He is the Lone Judge. He is the Fair Knowledgeable One.
76. He is the Powerful, the Enduring. He is the Creator, the Omniscient. He is the Kind, the Noble. He is the Loving, Merciful One. He is the Exalted Beautiful One. He is the Artist of the Universe. See *Mathnawi al-Nuriye*, 473.
77. The Necessarily Existing, the Sempiternal, the Perpetual, the Incomparable, the One, the Unique, the Single One, the Refuge, the Mighty, the Compeller, the Proud, the Subduer. See *Mathnawi al-Nuriye*, 134.
78. *Mathnawi al-Nuriye*, 342–43.
79. *Mathnawi al-Nuriye*, 271.
80. *Mathnawi al-Nuriye*, 236.
81. See "Author's Introduction" in *Mathnawi al-Nuriye*, 31. As such, the methodology in both cases is encyclopedic theological reflection more so than systematic analysis in course. The degree to which the Nursi corpus succeeds as Quran commentary is best left to others.
82. Vahide, *Author of the Risale-i Nur*, 168.
83. Specifically, Nursi opens his Seventeenth Flash (dating from 1933, and penned in Turkish) by explaining that, in 1921, he had written in Arabic about Divine Unity "in such treatises as *Zühre, Şu'le, Habbe, Şemme, Zerre*, and *Katre*." The Seventeenth Flash comprises "Fifteen Notes taken from *Zühre*"—a portion of one treatise that would be included eventually in *Mathnawi al-Nuriye*. Thus we have mention of half the eventual contents of *Mathnawi al-Nuriye*, but not the anthology per se. Then, under the rubric "The Thirty-Third Flash," is the note that this entry comprises the six Arabic essays mentioned in the Seventeenth Flash, and their appendices; and, that a Turkish translation of this material has been "included in *Mesnevi-yi Nūriye*, part of the Risale-i Nur Collection, and published." *Flashes*, 157, 461. The translation from the Arabic, in the 1950s, was the work of Abdülmecid Nursi (Said's younger brother). See Şükran Vahide, *Islam in Modern Turkey: An Intellectual Biography of Bediuzzaman Said Nursi*, edited and with an Introduction by Ibrahim M. Abu-Rabi' (Albany, 2005), 166, 323. According to Vahide, "When completed [in the mid-1930s], *The Flashes* numbered thirty treatises." Ibid., 212. This given, the Thirty-Third Flash (with its reference to *Mathnawi al-Nuriye*) may be seen as a later appendix to *The Flashes Collection*.
84. It is this sense of the relationship between the compilation of Nursi's Arabic essays of 1920–1921 and the compilation of all of his output thereafter that informs Ali Ünal's choice of *Epitomes of Light* as the title for his English translation of the Mathnawi al-Nuriye (Kaynak, 1999).

SEVEN

The Chief Characteristics of Spirituality in Said Nursi's Religious Thought

Bilal Kuşpınar

> You should know, O honorable, that I had been in constant struggle for thirty years against the two *idols*: one is in man, the Ego (*ana*), the other is in the cosmos, the [physical] Nature (*Ṭabī'at*). By looking at the former idol rather in its *literal* significative meaning (*harfiyyan*), I have conceived it as a shadowy mirror. But, those who had seen it in its *nominal* apparent form (*ismiyyan*) have transgressed and become like Nimrods and Pharaohs. As for the second idol [i.e., the Nature], I have seen it as a work of art, divinely designed, and as a piece of embroidery, mercifully patterned. However, those who looked at it simply with a heedless eye saw it as a Nature [in itself and by itself] and thus perceived it [wrongly], like the materialists, as a deity. A perception as such leads eventually to the denial of God and the ungratefulness to His favors. Praise be to God and thank is due to Him, my struggle has come to a successful end, with the extinction of these two idols, by virtue of the effusions emanated from the Noble Qur'an.

In this chapter, I will sketch out the most essential components and distinctive features of Nursi's conception of spirituality, along with the foremost foundations that he has envisioned as necessary for the construction of his spiritual system. We plan to undertake this formidable task at first with a short inquiry into the meaning of spirituality within the writings of Said Nursi and then proceed to identify and analyze the elements and faculties that are pivotal for the author's general understanding of spirituality. In the end we intend to determine as accurately as possible the major spiritual parameters within which Nursi has operated throughout his intellectual journey and developed at both theoretical and practical levels his religious thought, as well as his weltanschauung. Such a study, I hope, will modestly serve for the readers of Nursi to both better contextualize his spirituality in his own writings and better situate it in the centuries-long spiritual tradition of Islam.

The Importance of the Heart and the Mind

One of the immediate questions we are expected to answer in such a study involves the definition of spirituality. As implied in its very name, spirituality has to do mainly with the act, state, and condition of the spirit and in particular the human spirit, called in Arabic '*al-ruh al-insani*', which is defined in the classical technical dictionaries of Islam as a subtle force that enlivens and activates human body, and whose nature is hardly comprehensible to the human mind. But Nursi's spirituality does not simply deal with the act and state of the human spirit, which in fact constitutes only a small portion of it. His conception of spirituality goes far broader than the realm of the spirit and includes virtually all the inner faculties of man with concentration, though, on the heart itself. For him, as for many religious thinkers, man is first and foremost a spiritual being possessed of a heart (*kalb*), an intellect or a mind (*akıl*), a spirit (*ruh*), an inner heart (*sırr*), and a soul (*nefs*), all of which operate in human body under the aegis of the heart.[1]

The heart, on the other hand, is not merely the pine-shaped flesh located generally in the left-hand side of the human body, which is undoubtedly a vital organ indispensable for the operation of the entire human system and is, like all other limbs and organs of the body, liable to death, too. What concerns Nursi and other spiritual masters most, however, is the symbolic heart, which stands for the immaterial divine subtle entity and is connected with the above-cited physical heart in the way accidents are connected with corporeal bodies and attributes are connected with their bearers. As such, it constitutes the very *spiritual* reality of every human being.[2] It is this second meaning of the heart that is mostly intended in the Quran and the Ahadith.[3]

Many of the Muslim spiritualists prior to Nursi had taken up this symbolic heart very seriously and developed profound mystical theories entirely on the basis of it, some of which are today available either in the form of separate books and treatises or as part of compiled works or manuals on Sufism.[4] A small portion of this literature has already become the subject matter of various academic writings, though a considerable part of it still remains to be studied. Apparently, Nursi, as a faithful but critical representative of the Islamic tradition, appears to have been well informed of and well trained in most of this literature. He has even subjected some of them to his own critical examination as is noticeable in several places of his *Risale*. He has furthermore developed his own conception of the heart, which may be characterized as an elaborate synthesis of the previous conceptions, concentrating more on the spiritual function of it, rather than its nature.

In other words, Nursi, who always takes the Quran as his sole guide, engages himself chiefly with understanding the function and the role of the heart as presented in the Scripture. His extensive study of the verses and the ahadith, dealing with the heart, leads him to forming his fundamental conviction, that is, in order for the human being to progress spiritually he must possess at first a sound heart (*kalb-i selim*)—a noteworthy Quranic element—and then a straightforward [thinking] mind (*akl-i mustaqim*)—another important element derived from the Quran.[5] These two are required, for Nursi, not only for the attainment of spiritual perfection but for the honest interpretation and the appropriate comprehension of the wisdom of God. One who is equipped with the two, he vigorously stresses, would be able to both understand the divine truths and realities and consent wholeheartedly to all the decrees of God.[6]

Nursi at the same time concurs with the generally held opinion that the mind or the intellect functions as a faculty of reasoning and theoretical thinking (*tafakkur*) while the heart works as a mirror for contemplation (*mushahada*) and spiritual witnessing (*kashf*). But he goes further and states that they both are necessary for a balanced, holistic, and in-depth comprehension of reality, as well as a deep and sober internalization of the divine truths. As a matter of fact, such a harmonious combination of the two seems to have been demonstrated in the very life of Nursi himself, who even testifies it on several occasions. All the truths the Old Said had once conceived, as he declares, through his intellect and acquired by virtue of certain syllogistic arguments, appear to be corresponding with all that the New Said has later contemplated and witnessed in his heart by the light of his conscience.[7] So, the two Saids, one representing chiefly for the period of his intellection and the other for that of his contemplation, have become eventually reconciled in the personality of Nursi, who has then made it clear that, although the intellect and the heart have their own respective domain of function, they ought to work together as complementary to each other. After all, the heart deciphers and appreciates the secrets of both the microcosm, namely, the human being, and the macrocosm, that is, the world, and thus lets man perceive them as well as all that exists in them as likeable things, while the intellect conceives them as mere objects and thus makes them intelligible to itself. Moreover, the heart is for remembering God and beholding His Beauty, as the intellect is for reasoning about God and observing and interpreting His signs. By the same token, supplications to God are made in the heart, while religious creeds and dogmas are formulated by the intellect. Again, longing for and yearning constitute part of the activities of the heart, whereas meditating and deliberating make up part of the activities of the intellect.

Such a well-balanced unification of the heart and the mind and their jointly and harmoniously executed application are also manifest in the *Risale-i Nur*, which has in effect resulted from Nursi's *intellectual* erudition and *spiritual* witnessing and as such it can conveniently be characterized as a book of *spiritual philosophy* or, to look at it from the other angle, a book of *philosophical spirituality*. For the *Risale*, as the author himself distinguishes it, does not resemble other scholarly works that are written only on the basis of reasoning and discursive thinking. Nor is it comparable to other saintly works that stem merely from the heart's intuition and unveiling. The distinctiveness of the *Risale* lies in that it has emanated from the harmonious fusion of both the heart and the intellect along with the cooperation of the spirit and other subtle entities of the human being. Accordingly, the message it contains is so high and so sublime that it almost transcends the boundary of the human realm, where the truths pertaining to faith can be better understood and appreciated.[8] And at that stage, he says, these truths even become visible to the eyes of the atheist philosophers.[9]

As has been noted, Nursi never tires of mentioning the importance of equilibrium between the mind and the heart and the necessity of their alliance in embarking on a spiritual training. His insistence on this particular point is made not simply for a theoretical reason or a hypothetical purpose but definitely because of the practical experience that he had gone through during his spiritual quest. In numerous places of his *Risale*, especially in his *Mesnevi-i Nuriye*, he expressly states how important it is to travel on the spiritual path with the legs of both the mind and the heart and not just with one of them. He says, "While my mind proceeds through this [spiritual] journey, it becomes a friend of my heart. The heart passes its own intuitive experience onto the mind which in turn, as expected, turns such experience into presentable and defendable proofs."[10] In other words, according to Nursi, it is necessary that the mind's discursive thinking (*nazar-i 'akli*) be infused in a balanced manner with the heart's instant intuition (*hads-i kalbi*)[11] in journeying on a spiritual path to God. For even if the mind stops thinking for a while and occupies itself with something else, the heart, along with the conscience (*wijdan*), continues to remember and contemplate God to Whom it also turns longingly. Besides, intuition occurs to the heart instantly as a result of its recollection of God.[12] It is also through this recollection that the veil of the heedlessness will be removed and thereby the divine truths and secrets that lie behind the luminous words of the Scriptures will be disclosed to the eye of the heart. And the intellect for its part will interpret them in an intelligible fashion.[13]

If, however, one prefers to rely exclusively on one's heart and attempts to travel on the spiritual path with it only, then, Nursi asserts, one may fail to attain to the spiritual perfection for an obvious reason: man does not consist of a heart only; on the contrary, as we have mentioned earlier, he possesses, apart from the heart, numerous senses and subtle faculties, such as the mind, the spirit, the soul, each of which is charged with certain duties. If man directs all these senses and faculties to God according to their respective functions and in different forms of obedience and worship pertaining to them, he can conveniently advance on the spiritual path toward perfection. Nursi further illustrates his thesis with an analogy and says that the heart is comparable to a soldier and all other faculties, including the mind, to the soldiers working in collaboration with the former but under its control. So, the heart, Nursi argues, cannot neglect its soldiers and proceed on its own just to save itself; otherwise this would cause harm to itself and the rest.[14]

THE SPIRITUAL JOURNEY IN THE HEART

Nursi, as we have thus far observed, vehemently warns of the danger of traveling on the spiritual journey only through heart, which, he believes, leads ultimately to relinquishing all but God, as is well articulated in the celebrated Naqshbandi quadruple principle: *abandoning the world, abandoning the hereafter, abandoning existence, and abandoning (the very act of) abandoning.* If we analyze each of these precepts closely and separately, we could realize that *first* we should renounce this world for the fear that it may captivate our soul with its transient pleasures. *Second*, we should give up on the hereafter; lest it may take us away from God and make us live only for the sake of the heavenly pleasures. *Third*, we should renounce our very being in order not to fall into self-pride and vainglory. *Fourth and last*, we should renounce the very act of renunciation so that we may keep ourselves free from all concerns. In this case, the full practice of all of these four steps would push us into what certain Sufis call "annihilation" (*fana'*) or passing away from our individual conscious being. Therefore, as Nursi indicates, these four relinquishments, even if they might be accepted as the practices of self-mortification, are not sufficient to serve as a comprehensive means to attain true knowledge of God and the spiritual perfection, since they all take place within the heart only.[15]

On the other hand, abandoning this world means, according to Nursi's interpretation, abandoning the lustful pleasures of this world that, if not curbed, not only hinder the spiritual progress of the faithful but eventually ruin his entire life, too. And the heart, which is supposed to be the mirror of God's glance, as if it were a minuscule *ka'ba* of the believer, should not be filled with and swayed by the love of the worldly pleasures. As noticed, Nursi regards this world as a means to facilitate man's understanding of himself and his Creator and, as such, he stresses, it cannot be a cause of loss but a land of profit, provided that man fulfills his responsibility there in accordance with his ability and capacity. This being the case, then the above-cited Naqshbandi principle can be better comprehended if it is interpreted from Nursi's perspective. He says that if one looks at this world in terms of its significance for the world to come and in terms of its function as a theatre for the manifestation of God's names and acts, then one would adopt a positive attitude toward the world and make good use of it, rather than entirely disparage and abandon it as some of the Sufis had done it. One's knowledge and worship of God depends on how deep one looks at this world from the *purposeful* and *reflective* vantage points.[16] Such a perception will be treated later under the title of the *ma'nay-i harfi*.

We have so far explained the importance of the two key faculties, the heart and the mind, in Nursi's spiritual sytem. As we have shown, it is mainly with the leg of the former, that is, the heart, that the spiritual journey commences; it, nevertheless, proceeds together with that of the mind or the intellect and advances further for the human perfection in the harmonious cooperation of the two. In the meantime, it must be stated that, as has been noticed, we have made no distinction between the mind and the intellect in this study. Rather, we have used them both interchangeably for the English rendition of the Arabic word *'aql*, which Nursi conceives either as an independent internal faculty or as one of the pivotal faculties of the heart. All in all, the role of the symbolic heart, which works as a subtle entity in the human being, like the mind, is indisputably formidable in the weltanschauung of Nursi, who, having been inspired by the Quran and the Hadith, proclaims that it is the seed of the seed of the cosmos. In other words, the heart is the seed of man who is both the fruit of the tree of the world and the raison d'être of its creation. As such, the heart, indicates Nursi, has not only limitless ties and connections with the world and its various aspects but virtually endless aspirations, as well. So much so that nothing other than the Absolutely Rich, Self-Sufficient God can satisfy it, as is nicely articulated in the sacred hadith that is widely circulated among the Muslim mystics: "Neither my earth nor my heavens contain Me; but the heart of the believer does contain Me."[17] In terms of its potential capacity, it is like a map or index of the whole world, latently comprising and encapsulating all the parts of the universe in the form of a seed, and serving at the same time as a mirror of manifestation of innumerable realities of that world.[18] Hence, the heart can only consent an everlasting existence and permanent life that can be obtained only after it is awakened by belief and fostered and cultivated with sincere worship, whose essence is the remembrance of God, which Nursi conceives, like Abu Talib al-Makki, as its nourishment.

In this case, the heart, which is as tiny as a seed in size, as precious as a jewel in value and as spacious as a globe in capacity, needs to be kindled with the light of faith, cultivated with the devotional acts and services to God and polished with the recollection of Him, if it is to be, truly speaking, a locus-mirror of God's beautiful names. A heart that does not go through such a process of spiritual training remains what Nursi calls "a dry and raw seed" and becomes even a burden for its bearer, while leaving at the same time all of its auxiliary members and faculties dull and idle and letting them eventually die off. If, on the other hand, it is well trained and well cultivated, then all of its faculties will be able to perform their respective functions. Nursi gives among others the example of the faculty of imagination, which, he says, works under the command of the heart and enables the heart to travel all around the world in joy, provided that the latter, that is, the heart, is fostered and flourished by the love (*muhabba*), contemplation (*tafakkur*), and remembrance (*zikr*) of God.[19] Besides, the man possessed of such a heart attains to the stage of intimacy with God where he, being fully at peace and tranquil in himself, witnesses the signs and realities of God within himself (*anfusi*) and outside (*afaki*).[20] And he who ascends up to such an elevated stage remains fully sober and conscious of his own existence and sees everything in unity as pointing toward God. The people who travel on this kind of spiritual path are generally known as the people of the unity of witnessing (*waḥdat al-shuhūd*), such as Ahmad Sirhindi, whom Nursi highly praises and prefers over those of the unity of being (*waḥdat al-wujūd*), such as Muhyi al-Din ibn al-'Arabi, on the ground that, though their journey takes place entirely within the realm of the heart, the spiritual attainment of the former comes about at the end of witnessing the signs of God and hence results *positively* in sobriety (*sahw*) and distinction (*farq*) between themselves and God, whereas that of the latter comes about at the end of an overwhelming contemplation of God's Essence and hence results *negatively* in total obscurity (*sukr*) and obliteration (*mahw*) of their individual beings in God. The purest and safest path between the two, therefore, is that of the unity of witnessing, since the exponents of this path, as Nursi argues, instead of meditating on the nature of God, ponder deeply on His diverse creation and thereby come to the realization of an underlying divine unity in them. After all, there is no way for man to penetrate into God's Essence, which is utterly unfathomable and inscrutable. Because of this, the Prophet Muhammad has also cautioned about it when he said: "Reflect on the signs of God but not on His Essence at all, because you have no ability to do so."[21]

Having thus approved of the sober form of spirituality, Nursi goes on further to construct his own spiritual system on the basis of his thirty-year long study and personal experience. For this purpose, he initially lays down what he calls four expressions (*kalimat*) and four maxims (*jumal*), which I consider, respectively, as the four major epistemological foundations and the four chief ethical principles of his view of spirituality. In the remainder of our present survey, therefore, we will examine, rather in a review fashion, all of these foundations and principles, the roots of which are of course traceable to certain precepts of the Quran and the Sunna. In the meantime, it must be pointed out that it was through these illuminative precepts that Nursi, as he himself confesses, was able to overcome all the hardships and adversities he had encountered during the tumultuous period of his life and that he was able to gain victory against the temptations of the Satan and the lustful desires of his carnal soul.

The Three Epistemological Foundations

The whole edifice of Nursi's spirituality appears to be built on three solid foundations, if we look at it strictly from an epistemological perspective. Although, as we have just mentioned, Nursi terms them, probably for the sake of simplicity and clarity, four words or expressions, we label them the three major epistemological foundations of his spirituality. The first one is twofold: (1) *al-ma'nā'l-harfi*, the significance of letter and *al-ma'nā'l-ismi*, the significance of name. The other two are (2) intention (*al-niyyah*), and (3) reflection (*al-nazar*). These are further supported, as will be later explained, by the four chief ethical maxims or principles as follows: (1) *Genuine ownership*: I am not the owner of myself; (2) *Reality of death*: Death is truth; (3) *Oneness of God*: My Lord is One; and (4) *Denunciation of Ego*: Ego or I is a black dot.[22] When we examine them more closely, we may find that the former, that is, the epistemological grounds, seem to be corresponding to Nursi's horizontal mystical journey (*seyr-i afaki*) and the other four principles appear to accord with his vertical mystical journey (*seyr-i enfusi*).[23] Now let us explore and analyze each of these foundations and principles at first in their own context and then in conjunction with Nursi's whole system of spirituality.

The essentiality of al-ma'nā'l-harfi *(literal-significative meaning) vis-à-vis* al-ma'nā'l-ismi *(nominal-apparent meaning)*

It must be remarked at the outset that these two expressions, which occupy considerable space in Nursi's works and also constitute significant part of his intellectual and spiritual thought, cannot be easily translated into English with accuracy. Literally, we can render the first one as "the meaning of letter," namely "the meaning implied in the letter" and the second one as "the meaning of name," that is, "the meaning conveyed by the name." Technically speaking, however, the first expression denotes a sort of meaning that is associated with the reality of a being or the cause of its existence, while the second one imparts simply the meaning of a being that is derived directly from its name. Hence, without losing sight of their original connotations we wish to identify them with somewhat arbitrary but fairly descriptive appellations, such as spiritual meaning or real meaning for the *ma'nay-i harfi* and phenomenal meaning or nominal meaning for the *ma'nay-i ismi.*

By these two expressions, Nursi at first draws a general distinction between the corporeality of a thing and its spirituality and then tips the scale toward the latter. If one looks at everything besides God, he suggests, in terms of the meanings that are implied in their very letters, one would be able to see them as pointers, indicating their Creator and Maker. But to perceive them simply as beings in themselves and without seeing in the background their ultimate cause is obviously a defect, if not a sheer failing altogether, on the part of the perceiver. For every being, ontologically speaking, has at least two sides, one looking to the Ultimate and Absolute Reality *(al-Haqq)*, the Creator and the other to the creation (*al-khalq*). The side that looks to the creation must be perceived as pointing toward the Creator. When, for instance, one looks at provision, one has to see its Provider, and when one looks at a work of art, one has to see its Maker. Likewise, all the secondary causes should be conceived as mirrors reflecting their ultimate Cause. The letters of this grand cosmos, Nursi maintains, should be perceived as imparting the meaning of their origin.

Nursi goes on to elaborate on the importance of perceiving beings in their real and essential status, and not simply qua beings, but rather as the reflectors of their Creator. This time he takes up the world itself and says that it can be perceived from three different aspects. One aspect looks to the hereafter and hence it is seen as the land of cultivation and preparation for the latter. The other aspect looks to the divine names and thus it is perceived as the theatre for the manifestations of those names. Finally, it has the third aspect that looks to itself. The first two aspects are not only spiritual but significant, too, since they reveal the existential and real meaning of the world, along with the reason and the cause of its creation. But the last aspect is rather corporeal and less important, merely because it conveys nothing else than the phenomenal and nominal meaning of the world. So, if it is looked at from this last aspect only, it is seen as, for instance, an open market available to man's desires, fancies, and entertainments, as well as a spacious arena for his performance. Every human being, therefore, ought to look at the world, emphasizes Nursi, from its existential and real aspects together with the light of his faith, so that he can see it as a garden of paradise. To such a man the world per se, that is, in its nominal state, carries almost no value.[24]

As has so far been discussed, all beings, in Nursi's view, should be observed and examined first and foremost in their *real* and *spiritual* dimensions and not merely in their *nominal* and *corporeal* state. Such an observation would lead to the Oneness of the Creator. For, as Nursi quotes, everything has an obvious sign indicating that He is One. He further says that the Scriptures are replete with numerous examples illustrating this point. Suffice it to say that the staff of Moses, though it appeared to his rivals as a mere object in its corporeality, became like the water of life in its spirituality. How is it possible for man then to see things in their spirituality? Is there a way or are there means whereby man can attain such insightful perception? These questions bring us to the other two foundational expressions of Nursi's spiritual thought.

*Reflection (*Nazar*) and Intention (*Niyyah*)*

Reflection and intention are stipulated by Nursi as important criteria for a healthy and accurate perception of the world. For they both may alter, as he argues, the natures of things; they may turn what is bad into what is good, just as the elixir may turn the earth into gold. Similarly, intention may change a mundane motion to an act of worship. Reflection, in like manner, may convert knowledge pertaining to the created beings into knowledge about God. Looking at things and objects in the material world with just the physical eye and perceiving them merely within their immediate causes and intermediaries is in fact tantamount to overlooking their Creator. But looking at them with an eye of the heart, namely, the spiritual eye, and conceiving them as originating from God leads to the attainment of knowledge of God.

Nursi again confesses that the question of intention took him forty years to study and comprehend in its all ramifications. The importance of intention has often been emphasized in many sayings of the Prophet Muhammad, too. The first hadith of the *Sahih al-Bukhāri*, the most reliable of all of the Hadith collections, focuses on intention: "Actions are to be judged according to the intention. One's actions will be recompensed according one's intention." Being well cognizant of this Prophetic wisdom, Nursi even goes one step further and cites another hadith, saying that "a believer's intention is better than his actions."[25]

In response to a hypothetical question, "how can man respond to countless and universal bounties of God with his limited and particular gratitude?" Nursi furnishes an answer, which underlines forcefully the importance of intention:

> Man can respond to these endless bounties with a universal intention and limitless conviction. Imagine, for example, a man comes to the presence of a king with a gift worth five cents, and he sees many other gifts worth millions given by famous people and all displayed there. He feels in his heart that his gift is nothing as compared to others. He then suddenly says: "My master! I offer all of these valuable gifts to you in my name. For you deserve them. If I had the means and power, I would have offered you gifts equal to them in value." Thus, the king, who in fact has need of nothing and yet receives the gifts from his subjects as a sign of their loyalty and respect, accepts that poor man's great and universal intention and wish, as well as his beautiful gesture and faithfulness as the greatest gift. . . . So, intention and belief are most comprehensive universal thanks. The seeds and grains of plants are their very intentions. A melon, for instance, utters a thousand intentions in its heart in the form of the nuclei of its seeds: "O my Creator! I want to announce [and expose] the embroideries of Your Most Beautiful Names in many places on the earth." Since God Almighty knows how future things will come about, He accepts their intention as actual worship.[26]

Thus, Nursi, as has been noted, places intention at the center of his spirituality and even compares it to a kind of elixir that transforms habitual manners, ordinary movements, and even mundane acts into the deeds of worship. Moreover, it is like a vital spirit, which revives the deadly states and dormant actions and renders them lively divine rituals. Intention has a special particularity that changes the evil to the good. It is a spirit and the spirit of that spirit is nothing but sincerity. No salvation can be attained except through sincerity. Many good deeds can be performed in a short period of time with good intention and sincerity. So, man in his short lifespan can attain to the pleasures of Paradise by virtue of his sincerity. It is only through his intention that man can turn into an ever-thankful servant of God. In such a state of gratefulness, he always perceives the worldly provisions and pleasures as gifts bestowed on him by the All-Providing.

All of these favors, as he says with full conviction and sincere intention, are extended to his service from the hands of the Infinitely Good and All-Merciful. Consequently, he moves from the perception of these favors to the contemplation of their Provider. His contemplation of the Provider becomes much more delightful to him than his perception of the favors. This is the station of gratefulness to which a servant could attain with his elixir-like intention. What is important for Nursi is to transcend beyond the physical appearance of things by looking at them with a spiritual penetrative insight and thus perceive them in their spirituality, rather than in their mere corporeality. If a person confines his perception only to the worldly provisions themselves, he takes them for granted and consumes them without any gratitude. When the food is exhausted, his taste fades off. If, however, his perception of the food goes beyond and deeper than that of the simple nourishment, his spiritual taste remains with him forever, even if the physical taste disappears with his consumption of the food. For he ponders on the Provider of the food, rather than the food itself and at the same time anticipates to receive more from Him. As he further elucidates,

> When this-worldly provisions and the other-worldly pleasures are looked upon with the luminosity of faith, they are seen as constantly turning in a circular movement while being followed by their likes, one substituting the other. As such, the quiddity of these provisions does not go to perdition.[27]

Throughout his *Risale*, Nursi stresses, besides intention and sincerity, the importance of the penetrative eye in observing all beings in the world, living and non-living alike, a penetrative eye that is needed for deep reflection and sincere intention. A person, who is equipped with such an insight, he says, perceives and conceives everything in their primordial nature (*fitra*) and in their relation to God. If we look at closely a cat, continues Nursi, we can see how it worships its Lord with its innate disposition. You see the cat approaching its master friendly and entreating him for food. But as soon as it obtains its food, it adopts an unusual attitude, distancing itself from its master, as if it did not know him at all, and even displays no sign of appreciation to him. Notwithstanding its seemingly indifferent attitude, it still feels grateful in its innate state to its Real Provider of the food and continues to worship Him in that original state forever. Its meowing sounds to the penetrative listener, "O Most Caring! O Most Caring! O Most Caring!" as the Quran articulates it: "There is no living being on the earth whose sustenance is not provided by God." (11:6)

As a result of his emphasis on intention and reflection, Nursi's conception of the world, unlike that of some Sufis, seems quite affirmative and optimistic.

He regards it at first as an obvious proof and an open theatre for all Divine perfections. He further delineates his tripartite division of the world in terms of its function and meaning in another place with more concrete examples. Among the three faces of the world, he says, the first one that looks to God, displays the imprints of His Names, and reflects as mirror of their meanings, and as such it is perceived as utterly beautiful and hence worthy of love. The second face looking to the hereafter serves as the seedbed and arable soil for Paradise, and as such it is also seen as beautiful and deserving of love, too. But the third face looking to man's base appetites becomes not only a veil of neglect but also a plaything for satisfying this-worldly desires, and as such it appears as ugly, transient, mortal, deceptive and full of pain. It is this third face of the world, proclaims Nursi, that has been loathed by the saintly people and that has also been spoken of critically in the hadith of the Prophet. Otherwise, the world as a whole, on account of its first two faces, has often been held in high esteem by the people of truth, including the Companions of the Prophet.[28]

Nursi treats both this world and the present life with due care and attention and regards them as contributing positively to man's spiritual progress. That is why the aforementioned famous Naqshibandi quadruple renunciation (*terk*) of the world, the hereafter, existence (*hesti*), the very act of renunciation (*terk-i terk*) is substituted by Nursi with his alternative quadruple proclaimation as absolute poverty (*fakr-i mutlaq*), absolute inability (*acz-i mutlaq*), absolute gratitude (*şükr-ü mutlaq*), and absolute longing (*şevk-i mutlaq*). Since we have examined at length these four primary mystical concepts of Nursi in another chapter, we will skip them here. It must be noted, nevertheless, that according to Nursi, one would have to preserve one's life as the most precious capital and comprehensive treasury yielding eternal life and perfection. One should consider this world, as stated earlier, in its real and spiritual dimension and thus take it willingly and lovingly, he stresses emphatically, as the tillage for the hereafter and as a mirror of the divine names, as well as a temporary guesthouse. More important, it is an open book full of letters, each of which is constantly pointing to a meaning beyond themselves, a meaning that draws man closer to God. But all of these can be discerned only by the inner heart and not by the mere mental faculties or the soul.[29]

Having delineated up to now the three foundations of Nursi's spirituality, we move on to discuss the four ethical principles that in fact reinforce and crystallize those foundations with some details. These principles at the same time represent Nursi's personal spiritual convictions. Each of them, as we have mentioned several times, essentially springs forth from the Quran to which Nursi has always remained faithful. Without the guidance of the Quran, it is unthinkable that Nursi should construct any idea, let alone write his voluminous works.

The Four Ethical Principles

Nursi discusses all of the following ethical principles either separately or collectively at various places in his *Risale*, but especially in his *Mesnevi-i Nuriye*, we find him more elaborate and intensely concentrated on them. For our part here we will offer a summary of these principles as presented to us in both Arabic and Turkish versions of the *Mesnevi*. Let us return now to the relevant passages of this work and see how Nursi formulates these principles.

1. *Principle of real ownership*: I am not the owner of myself: My real owner is the Owner of all dominions, who is the Most Generous and Majesty. I may, however, envisage for a while that I am owner, in order that I can comprehend by way of comparison the attributes of my real Owner and that I can discern the finitude of my imagined ownership against the unlimited ownership of my Lord, as if the real daylight outshines the light of the imaginary lamp.[30]
2. *Principle of the reality of death*: Death is a reality. Neither this corporeal body nor this ephemeral life is capable of sustaining themselves forever. Besides, this world was not constructed on these two pillars, that is, the body and life. They are composed of flesh, blood, and bones. Shortly, they will all be decomposed and dispersed. How can then man build up his long aspirations on the basis of this short life?[31]
3. *Principle of God's unity*: My Lord is One. The happiness of everyone in this world comes about as a result of his or her submission to One Lord. Were it not so, man would be in need of many lords due to his complex nature driving him to seize all things around him. He is also imbued with emotions, sentiments, and pains that he may feel or he may not feel. Being in such a state, he is amenable to all sorts of difficulties. He comes out of this adverse situation only if he submits himself to One Lord.[32]
4. *Principle of I-ness*: I-ness is described with "egoism" and usually conceived as a black point [in human being]. It means that one ascribes to oneself a sort of 'being' and 'value.' In reality, however, it is a central apparatus or a yardstick of self-awareness through which man knows his real Owner and in which he witnesses the acts of that real Owner and realizes that He is closer to him than his own self.[33]

Nursi furthermore expounds all four principles in conjunction with the spiritual path he has devised for himself on the basis of the Quran. An in-depth analysis of each of these principles reveals to us at the same time his persistency and consistency in unifying the heart and the mind and maintaining the equilibrium between the two, as well as combining between the theory and the practice in his own spirituality.

Nursi's *practical* spirituality traverses, along the lines of the above-listed *theoretical* foundations and *ethical* convictions, through a path that consists of four progressively advancing stages leading ultimately to God. They are, (1) inability or powerlessness (*acz*), (2) poverty or indigence (*fakr*), (3) compassion (*şefkat*), and (4) contemplation (*tefekkur*). Each of these stages, which Nursi bases on a particular verse of the Quran, serves as a short way to reach one of the names of God and thus attain to a direct awareness of God's presence. The first stage, inability, inspired from the verse "*you should not justify yourselves*" (53:32), when it is practiced through worship, leads to "winning God's love." Poverty, the second stage, which is derived from the verse "*be not like those who forget God, and He therefore makes them forget themselves*" (59:19), leads to God's name, All-Merciful (*al-Rahmān*). The third stage, compassion, sprung forth from the verse "*whatever good happens to you is from God, but whatever evil befalls you is from yourself*" (4:79), leads to the All-Compassionate (*al-Rahīm*). As for the last stage, contemplation, it draws on the verse "*everything will perish save His Face* (countenance*)*" (28:88) and leads to the divine name, All-Wise (*al-Hakīm*).[34] Each of these practical stages imparts individually a profound spiritual message and a candid moral exhortation. As a whole, however, they serve as explicit reminders for man that he must always remain vigilant against the harmful and vicious demands of his carnal soul and that he must continue to improve his spiritual well-being toward perfection.

The first stage of Nursi's spiritual journey, as seen above, begins with a heartfelt confession, as if he is saying, "Despite my apparent physical strength, I am utterly powerless in reality." A confession as such, when conjoined with the ethical principle of 'real ownership' and supported with the epistemological foundation of 'existential meaning,' leads man to self-examination whereby he stops praising himself and begins to see his own faults, instead of those of others. In the second stage of utter indigence, man is warned of the possible harmful consequences of forgetting himself and his *real* condition, which is caused by the deception of his evil-commanding soul. Nursi emphasizes the importance of this stage by referring to the moral principle of 'the reality of death.' Man, proceeds Nursi, due to his forgetfulness,[35] thinks of death usually in relation to others and somehow becomes oblivious to the fact that it is inevitable for every man, including him, too. It means that since he has no power at all to change this inevitable fate, it would be better for him to concentrate on the improvement of his spiritual well-being, rather than fancying endless permanent plans on such a short ephemeral life. In other words, this kind of forgetfulness is a serious weakness of every human being, and it can be treated with its twofold antidote: the realization of one's utter need of God and the reality of death.

Man's another weakness is disclosed in Nursi's analysis of the third spiritual stage, which is the corollary of the preceding stage—that is, he attributes goodness to himself, due to the evasive nature of his evil-commanding soul and thus becomes self-conceited. By reflection on the verse cited above, "*whatever good occurs to you is from God and whatever bad befalls you is from your own self*" (4:79), he immediately sees his faults and defects and thus realizes that all goodness, including all his good qualities, are granted to him from the All-Glorious Creator. Consequently, instead of being conceited and boastful, he in utter humility offers his thanks and praises to his Lord. In accordance with the meaning of the verse "*Truly he succeeds who purifies it [i.e. his soul]*" (91:9), man begins to understand that his purification lies in imperfection, his power in inability, and his wealth in poverty. It must be noted that the spiritual admonition of the fourth stage is elucidated by Nursi along the lines of his conception of 'existential meaning.' That is, man's profound reflection on the verse "*everything will perish except His Face*" will not only make him abandon his egotism (*enāniyet*) but elevate him from his phenomenal temporal state to his existential permanent state as being a mirror of the manifestation of the true Donor of Existence and procuring at the same time an infinite existence thereof. In the very end of this four-stationed journey, one is saved from utter heedlessness, as he enters the Divine presence permanently, where he finds and sees a way leading to God in everything.[36]

Practical Key Elements and Devotional Practices

At the center of Nursi's spiritual system lie several key elements and devotional acts, such as faith (*iman*), worship (*ibade*), sincerity (*ikhlas*), love (*muhabbet*), remembrance (*zikr*), and contemplation (*tefekkür*). Among them we will deal with only four, faith and worship, leaving the last two aside, which we have already discussed in connection with Nursi's spiritual journey. First, Nursi generally identifies faith with a kind of light and maintains that without it no spirituality can ever be thought of. It is through the light of his belief that man rises up to the highest of the high and thus becomes worthy of Paradise. It is again with his belief that he connects himself with the All-Glorious Creator, and hence belief, indicates Nursi, is man's true affiliation with God, with which he gains value and importance in the eyes of God and with which the imprints of the divine art and the inscriptions of the divine names become manifest in him. As for disbelief, it is the quite opposite of belief—namely, it is cutting off the affiliation with God, resulting consequently in the concealment of the inscriptions of the divine names and divine art. The value of a person who has no faith is measured in respect to the matter of his corporeal being. Since the matter itself is only transitory, fleeting, and temporal, its worth is nearly nothing. Nursi offers an illustrative analogy here between the value of the materials used in a piece of art and the art itself. Take, for instance, an old coin whose material value as iron is one dollar or less, yet its antique value is probably worth a million. Thus, man is an antique work of the divine art. When the light of faith enters in man, all the significant inscriptions that are hidden in him become readable and meaningful with that light. A believer, therefore, reads all the signs with awareness of and affiliation with His Creator, as if he is uttering, "I am a fine art wrought and fashioned by the All-Glorious Maker and hence I am worthy of His Mercy and Generosity." If this is the case, then the value of man rests on his spirituality and first and foremost on his faith, which is defined as his heart-bound affiliation with his Creator. For it is faith, Nursi underscores, that makes man a true human and even a sultan.[37]

The second key element that constitutes the backbone of Nursi's spirituality is worship, which we have previously touched on together with sincerity. Worship is of two kinds: one is positive, the other is negative. The positive one is quite well known. As for negative type of worship, it takes place at a time when one is afflicted with sicknesses and misfortunes, in which case one feels weak and helpless and thus turns to one's Compassionate Lord and seeks His protection from it by meditating on Him and offering a sincere prayer to Him with no pretension at all. His steadfast endurance in the face of all these unfortunate hardships accrues him so many benefits, one of which is that his short life becomes a long one in the sense that his one-minute endurance procures for him the reward of a day-long worship.[38]

Next comes sincerity, which Nursi regards as another important element and indispensable means for the spiritual journey. He emphatically declares that one who is not sincere and has not achieved sincerity cannot travel the vertical and horizontal journeys. On the other hand, the most effective power that initiates and advances this journey, Nursi points out, is love, which seeks no pretext for its beloved and always desires to become the part of its beloved. Without love, it is even almost impossible to start the journey, let alone proceed through. Again, it is love, stresses Nursi, that will dispel all kinds of doubts and objections from the mind of the traveler when he turns toward his Beloved. Thanks to love that stems from the illuminative knowledge of God (*marifetullah*), which serves for the traveler as the most needed leaven and elixir, all sorts of hardships that might hinder the journey would easily be eliminated.[39]

Love, furthermore, helps to bind the devotee's heart exclusively to its real Beloved (i.e., God) and elevate him or her to the state of self-effacement, which is, in fact, as Nursi rightly puts it, the essence of worship. If it is, on the other hand, directed toward things other than God, then it would become a veil, to say the least, if not an obstacle altogether, for the spiritual perfection. In order to redirect love toward its real Owner, Nursi consistently and persistently suggests that we look at all the objects insightfully and meaningfully, in terms of their existential meanings, and with the eye of the heart and thus observe them as reflective mirrors of God and His names.[40] Only then can we discern that all these objects cannot deserve to be loved in themselves, but they can serve at best as the means for the love of the real Beloved. As noted, in Nursi's religious weltanschauung, the temporary love of mundane objects, if they are considered in their very roots, namely, in relation to their Creator, rather than in their mere appearances, leads to the permanent love of God, which again contributes quite significantly to the spiritual well-being of man.

Concluding Remarks

Nursi, as we have shown, has developed his own spiritual system on the basis of the three epistemological foundations and the four ethical maxims, a system that considers man in his entirety and cares to maintain the balance between the heart and the mind, the intuition and the reasoning, gnosis (*ma'rife*) and knowledge (*'ilm*), and the heart's recollection (*zikr-i kalbi*) and the mind's contemplation (*tefekkür-ü akli*). With its well-articulated theoretical structure and self-experienced practical guide, it aims to perfect the spiritual condition of man. To this end, it at first stipulates that man posses a sound heart (*kalb-i selim*) and a straightforward thinking mind (*akl-i mustaqim*) and that he adopt a positive attitude toward all beings and the world itself and ponder on them with deep reflection (*nazar*) and perceive them in their *real* meaning as related to God (*ma'nay-i harfi*) and behave toward them with good intention. All of these in fact constitute the theoretical and horizontal aspect (*afaki*) of Nursi's spiritual system. In its practical and vertical side (*enfusi*), his system offers an ascending four-staged spiritual journey, beginning with that of utter impotence, moving upward with the stages of indigence and compassion, and culminating in that of contemplation. Once man has traversed through these four stages and thus completed his spiritual journey, he not only delivers and cleanses himself from hypocrisy, ostentation, dishonesty, and all types of base traits, but also purifies his soul from all sorts of lustful desires and saves his body from the dangers of his evil-commanding soul and the perils of his ego. Then all of his faculties, which are mainly centered in the heart, become activated and start rendering their respective functions in accordance with their originally created form, namely, according to the *fitra* (primordial disposition). Furthermore, he henceforth begins to appreciate the significance of the subtle truths contained in religious obligations and hence fulfills them lovingly and longingly and without any feeling of compulsion. Again, he, having gained a sense of divine presence in his heart, utilizes the capital of his life all the time for noble causes and good deeds, turning every minute of his time, in Nursi's own expression, into seeds that will sprout and grow for the eternal felicity and even transforming his habitual actions into worship and his so-called mundane affairs into worthy sublime acts. At this state, he not only seeks the pleasure of God in his every word and act but finds, as Nursi depicts, special delight, as well in the gnosis of God (*marifetullah*) and the love of God (*muhabbetullah*). Finally, the end result of this spiritual journey rises man up to such a sublime and lofty state, where he becomes, in Nursi's own articulate words,

> a true believer and a perfect Muslim, far removed from superficiality and formality (*suri*), who has grasped the real meaning of faith (*hakikat-i iman*) and the real meaning of Islam (*hakikat-i Islam*); a straightforward servant of the Glorious Creator and His real representative in the universe, His direct addressee, His friend, His beloved and His mirror . . . thereby proving that man, having been created on the best mould, can surpass the angels in superiority provided that he attains to such a highest spiritual progress and hence deserves to earn felicity here as well as in the hereafter.[41]

NOTES

Source of epilogue: Bediuzzaman Said Nursi, *Al-Mathnawi al-'Arabi al-Nuri*, ed. by Ihsan Qasim al-Salihi (Istanbul, 1994), 221; Cf. Turkish Translation by Abdülmecid Nursi (Istanbul, 2000), 103.

1. Nursi, *Barla Lahikası* 2/1481. Unless otherwise indicated, all references for Nursi are to his *Risale-i Nur Külliyatı*, published in two volumes, by Nesil Basım Yayın in Istanbul, 1996. For the sake of convenience, we cite first the main text, followed by the volume and page numbers. We occasionally state more specifically the number of the chapter righter after the main text.
2. Some of the Sufis seem to be somewhat inconsistent in their understanding and conception of the heart. For whenever they speak of the heart, they sometimes mean by it "the soul," sometimes "the spirit," and sometimes "the intellect." However, in reality, they employ all of these epithets and others only metaphorically and not necessarily as the real name of the heart. They call it at times, for instance, the soul

because they compare it with the body and view it as interior to the body, and thus they refer to it as the heart of the body or as the meeting place of all the attitudes and activities. In some of the theological and mystical lexicons we find this commonly accepted definition of the heart: "It is an immaterial luminous substance, mediating between the spirit and the soul." It is a spiritual substance through which manhood becomes fully realized, as it collects and combines between the corporeal realities and the temperamental faculties and the spiritual realities and the soul-related properties. As such, it might as well correspond to the philosophers' concept of 'the rational soul.' For a detailed coverage of the subject, see al-Tahanawi, *Kashshaf Istilahat al-Funun*, 3/496–497.

3. "On that Day neither wealth nor children will avail, but only the one who brings to God a sound heart." (al-Shu'ara 26: 88–89); "They have hearts with which they understand not, eyes with which they see not, and ears with which they hear not" (al-A'raf 7:179); "There is a piece of flesh in the body; if it is good and sound, the whole body is good and sound. But if it is spoiled [or corrupted], the whole body would be spoiled; that is the heart" (*Sahih al-Bukhari* 2/44).
4. Among the early Muslims who dealt with the issue of the heart, the most prominent ones were: H{asan al-Basri (d. 110/728) who was probably the first in the Muslim world to speak about 'the knowledge of the hearts' (*'ilm al-qulūb*) in a technical sense and focused on the purification of the heart via repentance (*tawba*), which, he believed, was necessary for the sound preservation of the heart from its possible fluctuation. Then comes next Harith b. Asad al-Muhasibi (d. 243/857) who occupied himself predominantly with the self-reckoning (*nafs al-muhasaba*) on workint at the same time the heart, which he considered the locus of reason (*'aql*) and of illuminative knowledge (*ma'rifa*) and which he separated from the soul (*nafs*) in the sense that it desires this worldly appetites while the heart longs for the divine.. Another important Sufi was Hakim al-Tirmidhi (d. 300/910), who developed a more systematic theory of the heart within concentric circles, which he called "the stations of the heart" (*maqamāt al-qulūb*). He devoted to this subject, among other small treatises, a sizeable work entitled *Bayan al-Farq Bayn al-Sadr wa'l-Qalb wa'l-Fu'ad wa'l-Lubb* (*The Explanation of the Difference between the Chest, the Heart, the Inmost Heart and the Inmost Intellect*). In this work, al-Tirmidhi provided a map, so to speak, of the heart as well as a mystical journey traversing through the concentric layers of the heart converging ultimately in the centrality of the Divine. For a recent study on this subject, see Natalie A. Pavlis, "An Early Sufi Concept of Qalb: Hakim al-Tirmidhi's Map of the Heart," MA thesis, submitted to McGill University, Montreal 2001. To the list we can still add more personalities such as Abu Talib al-Makki (d. 996), who composed his famous work, *Qut al-Qulub* (*the Food for the Hearts*), Abu Hamid al-Ghazali (d. 1111) who assigned a large portion of his magnum opus *Ihya 'Ulum al-Din* to the subject of the heart, and so on.
5. "Only he who brings to God a sound heart will prosper," al-Shu'ara 26:89. "Behold! He (Abraham) approached his Lord with a sound heart," al-Saffat 37:84. See also Qaf 50:37; al-A'raf 7:179; al-Ra'd 13:28; al-Hajj 22:46; Muhammad 47:24;
6. Nursi, *Barla Lahikası*, 2/1516.
7. Nursi, *Barla Lahikası*, 2/1517.
8. *Kastamonu Lahikası*, 2/1574.
9. Ibid.

10. *Mesnevi-i Nuriye*, *Şule*, 2/1366.
11. It is worth mentioning that Nursi considers '*hads*' (intuition) as one of the functions of the heart instead of the mind or the rational soul, a significant point of divergence between him and the Muslim philosophers such as al-Farabi and Ibn Sina.
12. Ibid.
13. *Mesnevi-i Nuriye*, *Şule*, 2/1365
14. Sözler, 1/220.
15. Ibid.
16. Sözler 1/219; cf. *Words* 510. In accordance with such a perspective, the well-known hadith, "the love of this world is the principal cause of all error" has been interpreted by Nursi in a quite different but profoundly meaningful fashion. When conceived from purposeful standpoint, the world is seen in its useful face as an arable land to be cultivated for the harvest of the hereafter; when considered from the reflective standpoint, it is viewed in its permanent face as a mirror to be gazed at yearningly for the disclosure of the divine names. All the existents in the world then would become necessary for the spiritual progress of man. Apart from these two perceptions of it, there is the third face of this world, which is transitory and looks to man's bestial instincts and lustful desires. If taken only from this last point of view, the world would become, as the hadith indicates, head of all error. (Sözler 1/220; *Words* 511)
17. *La yasa'uni 'ardi wa la sama' wa lakin yasa'uni qalbu'l-mu'min*. *Mesnev-i Nuriye*, 2/1390–1391.
18. *Mektubat*, 29, 1/561.
19. See, for more, *Mesnevi-i Nuriye*, *Habbe*, 2/1325.
20. *Mektubat* 29, 1/562.
21. *Mesnevi-i Nuriye, Nokta*, 2/1373.
22. *Al-Mathnawi al-'Arabi al-Nuri*, pp. 105–106; Turkish 2/1297.
23. The spiritual journey of the heart takes place in two directions: vertical or inner (*enfusi*) and horizontal or outer (*afaki*). In the vertical one, the journey starts within the self by taking one's eye away from the outer world and turning it entirely to the heart. In doing so, it pierces egoism, opens up a path from the heart that leads to reality. Then it turns his glance to the horizons, that is, the external world, which now looks to him luminous. Thus, he completes the vertical journey. The most fundamental basis of this journey is to crush the ego, abandon lustful desires of the flesh, and mortify the carnal soul. As for the horizontal journey, it starts from the external world by observing thereon the reflections of God's Names and Attributes. Then it turns its glance into the inner world and beholds those luminous reflections in the sphere of the heart on a relatively smaller scale and finds the shortest path leading to them. In the end, the heart sees itself as the mirror of God and thus arrives at the goal it was seeking for. (*Mektubat* 29, 1/563.)
24. *Al-Mathnawi al-'Arabi al-Nuri*, p. 168; Turkish 2/1309.
25. Sözler 1/24, p. 158; cf. *Words* 24, p. 371.
26. Sözler 1/24, p. 158; cf. *Words* 24, pp. 370–71.
27. *Al-Mathnawi al-'Arabi al-Nuri*, pp. 159–60; Turkish, p. 2/1305.
28. Sözler 32, 2/ 285; cf. *Words* 32, pp. 653–54.
29. *Words* 32, p. 670.
30. *Al-Mathnawi al-'Arabi al-Nuri*, 106; Turkish, p. 2/1297.
31. Ibid.

32. Ibid.
33. Ibid.
34. Sözler 26, 1/210; *Words*, 490.
35. Nursi speaks about various forms of forgetfulness and, like his predecessors, holds that the Arabic word *insan* (man) derives from the word *nisyan* (forgetfulness). This being the case, man is afflicted with the weakness of forgetfulness. The worst of all forgetfulness, he believes, is forgetting one's soul. Forgetting the soul only at the time of reward right after the services and works would be a sign of perfection. Therefore, the people of perfection completely forget about their souls at the time of the distribution of the rewards and benefits, but they always keep them in check and under control during work, contemplation, and spiritual journey (*Mesnevi-i Nuriye, Şule*, 2/1365).
36. Sözler 26, 1/ 210–11; *Words*, pp. 491–92.
37. See, for the further importance of faith, *Sözler* 23, 1/132–35.
38. *Lem'alar* 2, 1/ 581; *Flashes*, pp. 23–24.
39. Ibid., 1/ 565.
40. Ibid., 1/ 565.
41. Ibid., 1/ 568–69.

EIGHT

Dreams and Dream Interpretation in Said Nursi's *Risale-i Nur*

Islamic, Judaic, and Universal Resonances

Yehezkel Landau

This chapter is conceived as part of a longer study in comparative spirituality exploring the phenomenon of dreams, dream imagery and symbolism, and the art of dream interpretation in the three major monotheistic faiths. Christianity is not addressed here,[1] and the section on Jewish tradition is abbreviated. The conclusion, also, only adumbrates how our dreams can help us reduce estrangement among adherents of the different Abrahamic traditions. For the purposes of this reflection, I focus on Nursi's own teachings and their wider Islamic context, along with some Jewish parallels and resonances.[2]

In her intellectual biography of Nursi, Vahide presents the following account:

> In September 1919, Nursi had a "true dream" or sort of vision, which he subsequently recorded and included in Sunuhat [a section of his magnum opus, the *Risale-i Nur*]. He tells us there that he was at the time greatly distressed at the course of events [the Ottoman Empire, synonymous with the Muslim caliphate, had been defeated in World War I] and was "searching for a light in the dense darkness." In his dream, Nursi was summoned by "a great assembly" made up of representatives of the leading figures of Islam from each century and called upon to give an account of the present state of Islam.

> Contrarily to what might be expected, Nursi's reply pointed out positive aspects of the defeat, including the strengthening of Islamic brotherhood and the Ottomans being saved from being carried away to a greater extent by "the tyrannical current" of capitalism. Then, in order to show why Islam rejects modern Western civilization, which was epitomized by the ugly and exploitative capitalism and aggressive imperialism of the time, he made a comparison of the principles on which Western civilization and Islamic civilization are based and their results. This extremely interesting and original exposition was greeted with approval by the assembly in the dream, and one of the deputies declared: "Yes, be hopeful! The loudest and strongest voice in the coming upheavals and changes will be that of Islam!"[3]

From Nursi's inclusion of this dream in his public writings, we can infer that he took the dream seriously and that it reinforced his confidence in the triumph of Islam over its cultural adversaries, the ideologies of materialism and atheistic communism. The timing of this dream is significant, as it coincided with Nursi's transition from his period of political activism under Ottoman rule (what he termed the Old Said) to his more mature years of spiritual inwardness and withdrawal from politics (the New Said). This latter period, lasting until the mid-twentieth century, was lived mostly under the harsh conditions of imprisonment and isolation, as Nursi suffered for his religious convictions at the hands of the secularist regime in postwar Turkey.

Nursi devoted his career to integrating the classical Islamic disciplines with the insights of modern science. Given this holistic approach, embracing both faith and reason, tradition and modernity, one might be surprised to encounter such a passage, with its confessional sharing of a private dream. But an examination of other parts of the *Risale-i Nur* demonstrates that this account in *Sunuhat* conforms with Nursi's understanding of the role that dreams play in the spiritual life.

As a Jewish reader of Nursi's writings, I find this particular topic fascinating and of great practical importance. The subject of dreams and dream interpretation has interested me for many years. In recent decades, it is the psychologists, far more than theologians, who have engaged this subject—much to the detriment of theology, I would argue. My own graduate studies at Harvard Divinity School in the 1970s focused on the interdisciplinary field of psychology and theology, along with Jewish-Christian relations. Among the courses I took were two on "Myth and Dreams" and "God and Psyche," both taught by Professor Leighton McCutchen.[4] One of the assignments for those courses was to keep a dream journal, recording nighttime dreams upon waking in the morning. This is a discipline that I began in 1974 and continue until today. Over the years, these nocturnal symbolic messages have nourished and deepened my own spirituality considerably. And it is this personal experience that has, in turn, stimulated my scholarship in the area of dream symbolism and interpretation. In my research, I have tried to integrate insights from both theology and psychology. Since I am also active, as teacher and scholar, in promoting mutual understanding among Jews, Christians, and Muslims, the interreligious dimension of this research has also held profound meaning for me. I believe that a comparative study of Jewish, Christian, and Muslim teachings on dreams and dream interpretation would yield fruitful insights on both the scholarly and practical levels.

This chapter, which is a first attempt at such comparative analysis, has four parts. In the first section, I examine Nursi's views on dreams and dream interpretation; in the second, I place Nursi's teachings within the wider context of Islamic tradition on the subject; third, I present some parallels and resonances from Jewish tradition; and in the last section I offer some thoughts on how Jews and Muslims, heirs of a common monotheistic heritage, can find ways to share and to actualize their dreams of a peaceful future. Christians should participate in this conversation as well, and I hope that this stimulus will encourage them to contribute their insights to a three-way exchange.

NURSI'S VIEWS ON DREAMS AND DREAM INTERPRETATION

The Twenty-Eighth Letter

Nursi's personal account in *Sunuhat* is not the only reference to dreams and their religious significance in the *Risale-i Nur*. A more general discussion of the subject is presented in the First Matter/Part of *The Twenty-Eighth Letter*. This discourse was written in response to a dream shared with Nursi by one of his male students, who requested help in understanding the dream symbolism. The letter opens with the traditional Muslim affirmation of faith, "In the name of God, the Merciful, the Compassionate," and then Nursi cites a portion of a Quranic verse (12:43): "If it be that you can interpret dreams." This citation is from *Sura Yusuf*, the only chapter of the Quran to explicitly refer to dream interpretation, and is part of Pharaoh's charge to his counselors to help him understand his own dream (of the seven fat and seven lean cows, plus the seven green and seven withered ears of corn). Nursi then begins his response to the student's request:

> You want me to interpret now the dream you had three years ago, three days after meeting me, whose meaning has long since become apparent. That beautiful, happy, and auspicious dream has been consigned to the past, so am I not right to say the following in the face of it, since it has demonstrated its meaning?
>
> *I am neither the night nor a lover of the night; I am a servant of the Sun; it is of the Sun that I speak.*
>
> *Those illusions which are the snare of the saints, Are the moon-faced reflections of the garden of God.*
>
> Yes, my brother, we have become accustomed to discussing with you teachings concerning pure reality. Since to discuss in investigative fashion dreams, the doors of which are open to fancy and illusion, is not completely in keeping with the way of investigative scholarship, in connection with that minor incident of sleep, we shall explain Six Points of Reality about sleep, the small brother of death, according to scholarly principles and from the angle indicated by verses of the Qur'an. In the Seventh we shall make a brief interpretation of your dream.[5]

From this introduction we learn that Nursi was very cautious when broaching this subject, since even "saints" were deceived and ensnared by dreams. In the accentuated couplet, dreams are associated with the nocturnal moon, which only reflects the sun's light, but does not give its own light directly. Nursi's apprehension of true or pure reality (revealed in the Quran) is linked with the light of the sun, of which he is its "servant." I will try to summarize or paraphrase Nursi's seven points (with appropriate citations), offering commentary, in brackets, where warranted.

THE FIRST. The dream of Yusuf/Joseph is significant, and the Quran as a whole demonstrates "in veiled fashion," through verses like "And We made your sleep for rest" (78:9), that sleep and dreams contain important truths.

THE SECOND. The "path of reality" is not in accordance with dreams or omens that undermine true belief. The "All-Wise Qur'an" disabuses nonbelievers of their superstitious falsehoods, and they fall into despair and confusion. "Dreams, too, while good, since they sometimes appear to be opposed to reality, are thought to be evil, causing a person to fall into despair, destroying his morale, and causing him to think badly of things." [Here lies the problem or danger: dreams are inherently good or positive, but people's ignorance of their true meaning can lead them astray.] Since people generally do not know the proper way of interpreting dreams, including those whose forms are "terrifying, injurious, or unclean" but which may actually be "very good," they may "become unnecessarily anxious, despairing and unhappy." It is because of this negative effect on morale, and the potential estrangement from truth, that Nursi reiterates, "*I am neither the night nor a lover of the night*" (italics in the original).[6]

THE THIRD. Nursi cites "an authentic Hadith" that states that "true dreams during sleep" contain "one-fortieth part prophethood" [prophecy, *nubuvvet* in Turkish, *nubuwwah* in Arabic]. "This means that true dreams are both truth and they are connected with the function of prophethood. Being extremely important, long, profound, and connected with prophethood, I am postponing this Third Point to another time, and not opening this door for now."[7] [This is a crucial point for our consideration. I am not aware of another place in Nursi's writings where he further develops this theme, though it would be very helpful if such a source were to be found. As we will see in the second section, the prophetic element or fragment in dreams is a subject richly developed in Hadith literature, though there the fraction usually cited is one-forty-sixth or, in at least one source, one-forty-ninth. In the third section we will cite a Talmudic teaching that professes yet another fraction of prophetic truth within dreams. This statement by Nursi in the *Twenty-eighth Letter* is the only textual source I have found that cites the number one-fortieth.]

THE FOURTH. In line with earlier Islamic teachings, Nursi identifies three kinds of dreams. "Two of these, in the words of the Qur'an [Pharaoh's counselors in 12:44], are *a confused medley of dreams*" and are not worth interpreting. Whatever meaning they may have is unimportant, deriving either from an ailment or from "some stimulating event which occurred to the person that day" or at an earlier time. But the third category of dreams are "true dreams." In sleep, the senses that connect us to the "Manifest World" (*alem-i shehadet*) are inactive, and "the dominical subtle faculty in man's essential nature finds a direct relation with the World of the Unseen (*alem-i ghayb*) and opens up a window onto it. Through the window, it looks on events whose occurrence is being prepared; it encounters the manifestations of the Preserved Tablet" [the divine template from which revelation, including the Quran, derives] and receives some kind of message of "Divine Determining" [Providential intent]; "it sees some true occurrences. Sometimes the imagination governs in those occurrences, dressing them in the garments of form. There are numerous types and levels of this sort of dream. Sometimes they turn out exactly as dreamed; sometimes they turn out slightly concealed, as though under a fine veil; and sometimes they turn out heavily veiled." Citing various Hadith compilations,

Nursi notes that the dreams that the prophet Muhammad himself (PBUH) had "at the outset of the [Quranic] Revelations turned out as true and clear as the breaking of morning."[8]

THE FIFTH. Although everyone, even animals, according to Nursi, has premonitions, true dreams are "a higher development." He asserts that at one time he "discovered scientifically" two senses in addition to the known ones, including premonition [clairvoyance]. These sixth and seventh senses are not "natural instinct," he says, but rather "Divine Determining impels man and animals through a sort of innate inspiration." He mentions cats, which, even when blinded, find plants that help heal their eyes; and predatory birds like eagles that locate animal carcasses that are "a day's distance away"; and newly born bees that return to their hives after flying long distances. Among human beings, Nursi writes that "it happens frequently to everyone" that, when speaking of another person, suddenly that person will come through the door unexpectedly. This is an unconscious, involuntary faculty of premonition. Some "intuitive" people's abilities in this regard can appear "like wonder-working." And then he adds: "At one time in myself, even, sensitivity of this kind was acute. I wanted to incorporate the condition into a principle, but I could not adapt it and was unable to. However, in the righteous, and particularly in the people of sainthood, premonition develops to a high degree, showing its effects wondrously." [Here Nursi indicates that he himself took an interest in extrasensory perception or parapsychological phenomena, since he was prone to such experiences, but he gave up the attempt at formulating some generalizing principle to explain such phenomena. In this discourse, he connects ESP in the waking state with the uncanny ability to apprehend elements of the supernatural in some dreams.]

Nursi emphasizes that even "ordinary people" can experience a kind of "sainthood" in this regard, in that "they dream of things pertaining to the Unseen and the future in true dreams." People "with good morals" tend to harbor good thoughts and dream of good things; whereas those "with bad morals" harbor bad thoughts and dream of bad things.

"Furthermore," he writes, "for everyone, true dreams are a window in the Manifest World looking into the World of the Unseen. For restricted and transitory human beings, they are also an arena of infinite proportions manifesting a sort of eternity, and a place for gazing upon the past and the future as though they were the present." For people facing hardship in life, this kind of experience, given by God, makes sleep a spiritual relief as well as physical rest, and for this reason "the All-Wise Qur'an teaches the reality of sleep, giving it importance."[9]

THE SIXTH AND MOST IMPORTANT. Here Nursi becomes very personal, using powerfully confessional language that I will reproduce in full:

> Experiencing them numerous times, true dreams became for me like decisive proofs at the degree of 'absolute certainty' that Divine Determining encompasses all things. Yes, especially the last few years, these dreams have reached such a degree that has become certain for me that the most insignificant events and unimportant dealings and even the most commonplace conversations I will have the following day are written and recorded before they occur, and that by dreaming of them the night before, I have read them not with my tongue but with my eyes. Not once, not a hundred times, but perhaps a thousand times, the things I have said in my dreams or the people I have dreamt of at night, although I had not thought of them at all, turned out exactly or with little interpretation the following day. It means that the most insignificant things are both recorded and written before they happen. That is to say, there is no chance or coincidence, events do not occur haphazardly, they are not without order.[10]

[Nursi's spiritual or psychic gifts were, without doubt, highly developed—his followers called him "Bediuzzaman," Wonder of the Age—and his prolonged isolation probably accentuated his innate talents. A religious believer would probably maintain that he was graced by God with such acute extrasensory faculties in order to fulfill his divinely ordained mission in this world. It is beyond the scope of this chapter to elaborate on the basic question, or mystery, which Nursi's confession raises: how, if human beings have free will, can actions be foreseen or known in advance? Rabbi Akiva, a second-century Jewish luminary living in the Holy Land, expressed the irresolvable paradox in this pithy statement: *Hakol tzafui ve'hareshut netunah*, "Everything is foreseen (by God), and (at the same time) free will is granted (to human beings)." Nursi seems to be affirming here that, under certain conditions, human beings can be favored with a Godly kind of knowledge that transcends time and space, an apprehension through "true dreams" that blurs the distinctions between past, present, and future and attains a vantage point on reality that is ordinarily associated only with the Eternal One, Creator of space, time, and all there was, is, and will be. In fact, the most holy name for God in Judaism, *Yod-Heh-Vav-Heh*, transliterated YHVH, is traditionally understood to convey the essential infinity and eternity of God, the One Who Was, Is, and Will Be.]

THE SEVENTH. To conclude the First Part of *The Twenty-Eighth Letter*, Nursi returns to the subject that prompted it: the dream reported by his student. He writes, "Your beautiful, blessed, and auspicious dream was very good for the Qur'an [Nursi's primary loyalty] and for us." Nursi indicates that subsequent events have served to interpret the basic elements of the dream, so there is little for him to add. But then he proceeds to offer a rather detailed interpretation, translating the symbols of the dream into personalities and events in the life of the student, one of the disciples who was helping to disseminate the Words of Nursi's *Risale-i Nur*. I will cite only the last part of his interpretation.

> The congregation [in the mosque seen in the dream], like wireless receivers, were the indication and fact of wanting to make the whole world hear [the Words'] teachings, which God willing, will turn out at a later date. If the individuals now are like small seeds, with Divine assistance, in the future they will each be like tall trees. And each will be like a telegraph office. As for the turbaned youth, he is someone who will work together with [the disciple] Hulusi, or even surpass him; he is destined to become one of the students and those who disseminate the Words. I can think of some of them, but I cannot say definitely. The youth is someone who will come into prominence through the force of sainthood. You can interpret the remaining points instead of me.

Nursi then closes the first part of his letter by acknowledging how "agreeable and acceptable" it is to converse with "friends like you," and it is for that reason that he has "spoken at length about this brief matter, and perhaps I have been prodigal. But since I began with the intention of indicating a way of expounding the Qur'an's verses about sleep, God willing, that prodigality will be forgiven, or even not be prodigality."[11]

EXCERPTS FROM OTHER PARTS OF THE *RISALE-I NUR*. Although Nursi evidently did not fulfill his declared intention (in the third of his seven points) to open the door to further discussion of dreams and prophecy, other parts of his *Risale-i Nur* collection offer some indication of how he viewed our capacities for grasping transcendent knowledge, that is, knowledge from a divine source outside our personalities and beyond apprehension by our five senses. A few excerpts from the first volume, *The Words*, offer some complementary perspectives to what was previously discussed.

In the Second Ray, Fifth Flash, Fifth Glow of the *Twenty-Fifth Word*,[12] Nursi affirms that philosophy and science will never succeed in rending, as the Holy Quran has, the "veils of the habitual and the commonplace," for the Quran "sees reality, is familiar with the Unseen, bestows guidance, and shows the truth." And in the First Ray, Second Flash, of the same *Twenty-Fifth Word*, Nursi writes: "Since the Qur'an is a pre-eternal address, and sitting above and beyond the centuries, which, layer upon layer, are all different, addresses and instructs all of mankind lined up within them, for sure, it will include and intend numerous meanings, according to those varying understandings, and will make allusions to what it intends. . . . The Qur'an has placed allusions to each of those meanings according to its degree. They are either literal or figurative."[13] We can see from these statements that Nursi's loyalty to the truth of the Quran is based on his belief in its transcendent, unqualified, "pre-eternal" nature, beyond the limitations of history and geography and beyond the qualified subjectivities of human beings. At the same time, his unwavering loyalty to the Quran as the divine blueprint for Creation allows for a diversity of interpretation and an acknowledgement that different saints and scholars over time understood the Quran's message in different ways.

In the Third Branch, Eleventh Principle, of *The Twenty-Fourth Word*, Nursi discusses the obscure nature of both Quranic verses and hadith teachings. He uses the analogy of dreams to illustrate that such sacred sources of revealed truth require, like dreams, careful interpretation. He writes:

> Indeed, just as someone who is awake interprets the dream of another who is sleeping, so too, sometimes one who is sleeping hears the words spoken by those near him who are awake, but he gives them a meaning and interprets them in a way that applies to his own world of sleep. And so, O man stupefied in the sleep of heedlessness and philosophy! Do not deny in your dream what One saw, who manifested the meaning of, His eye [or sight] never wavered nor did it swerve (Qur'an 53:17, referring to the Prophet), and My eye sleeps, but my heart sleeps not, and who was truly awake and aware, interpret it. Yes, if a mosquito bites someone who is asleep, he sometimes dreams, which has a reality in sleep, that he has received terrible wounds in war. If he was to be questioned, he would say: "Truly I have been wounded. Guns and rifles were fired at me." Those sitting by him laugh at his anguish in sleep. Thus, the sleep-stained view of heedlessness and thought of philosophy certainly cannot be the criterion for the truths of Prophethood.[14]

In this passage, Nursi is disparaging the truth-value of nocturnal dreams, in order to construct an analogy that elevates the All-Wise Quran above the speculations and assertions of "sleep-stained" philosophers. He is clearly not referring to the "true dreams" that contain some portion of prophetic inspiration. Earlier in this Word, at the end of the Third Branch, Eighth Principle, Nursi makes the simple, yet fundamental, assertion: "*None knows the Unseen save God*" (italics in the text[15]). It is a central and basic principle of faith for Nursi that human beings cannot fully fathom the mind and will of God, and that the truest repository for what *can* be grasped by human faculties is the All-Wise Quran. He therefore argues, again and again, that Islam, as the historical carrier of that Quranic wisdom, has a superior grasp of genuine truth than any human pursuit of knowledge, whether philosophy, science, or, for that matter, extrasensory means such as dreams, visions, or premonitions.

Nursi understands that even the greatest saints (mystics) and scholars, while authentic believers and practitioners of Orthodox Islam, differed in their subjective apprehension of the truth. He considers this a "mystery," which he poses as follows:

> Why do the saints differ in their visions and illuminations although they are unanimous on the principles of belief? Why are their illuminations, which are at the degree of witnessing, sometime[s] opposed to reality and contrary to truth? And why in their ideas which they consider to be the truth, establishing them through decisive proofs, do thinkers and scholars see and show reality in a way that contradicts one another? Why does one truth take on numerous colours?[16]

Nursi's answer is long and detailed, too extensive to present here.[17] He develops a poetic metaphor using the archetypes of flower, droplet, and atom to illustrate how different aspects of creation, including humans, are recipients of varying manifestations of divine truth. He also uses the contrasting archetypes of sun and moon to argue that some manifestations are direct and reliable (like the sun's light, which is "pure, universal, and without shadow"), while others are indirect (like the moon's reflected light) and are more obscure, cloaked in shadow, and hence less reliable. This sun–moon typology conforms with his references to these heavenly bodies in the *The Twenty-Eighth Letter*, where he declares that he is the "servant of the Sun" and not a "lover of the night."

His reflection on why even great mystics and scholars differ in their understandings of truth includes these observations:

> for sure man is the place of manifestation of all the [divine] Names, but since his power is slight, his will partial, his abilities various, and desires different, he searches for reality among thousands of veils and barriers. And so, in uncovering reality and witnessing the truth, barriers intervene. Some people cannot by-pass the barriers. Their abilities are

> all different. The abilities of some cannot support the unfolding of some of the truths of belief. . . . Also, the manifestations of the Names takes on different forms in respect of universality, particularity, shadow, or originality. . . . For the reality of the Resurrection and Last Judgement is the manifestation of the Greatest Name and of the supreme degree of certain other Names. Whose-ever (*sic*) gaze cannot rise there is compelled to believe it by way of imitation. While whose-ever mind can enter there, sees the Resurrection and Last Judgment as easily as day and night, and spring and winter, and accepts it with ease of mind.[18]

Tying these teachings to his reflections on dreams, true ones or a "confused medley," we can say that Nursi understood that people, even spiritual giants, exhibit a wide spectrum of capacities to grasp the higher truths of the unseen realm. As a result, their dreams will correspondingly exhibit varying degrees of truth or falsehood, beyond the normal variation caused by residues of daily activity or psychological mechanisms at work in the unconscious (what Freudians would call wish fulfillment or the processing of repressed desires). Even ordinary people can dream dreams that contain a fraction of prophetic revelation (for Nursi, one-fortieth), but what is "one-fortieth part prophecy" for one person is likely to be very different for another person on a higher level of receptivity and discernment. How much is divine intentionality in directing dream-prophecy to one dreamer versus another, and how much is determined by the spiritual level attained by the dreamer remains an open question. It is likely to be interrelated in some way that is virtually impossible to determine empirically.

One additional passage from the *Risale-i Nur*, this time from *The Eighteenth Letter*, sheds further light on Nursi's overall cosmology and how it might relate to his statements on dreams ten letters later. Nursi is again wrestling with the challenge of how mystics can describe realms ("seven levels of the globe of the earth and the white earth beyond the 'Kaf mountain") that have no corresponding reference points on the plane of reality that we all inhabit. Nursi asks: "Are these true? But these places do not exist on the earth. Furthermore, these things that they say are not accepted by geography and science. And if they are not true, how can they be saints? How can people who say things contrary to reality and the truth in this way be 'people of reality'?"[19]

His answer begins:

> They are the people of truth and reality. They are also saints and those who witness the realities. They saw correctly what they saw, but since they were not correct in declarations they made while in the state of illumination and witnessing, which is without comprehension, and in

> their interpretations of their visions, which were like dreams, they were partially incorrect. People of illumination and witnessing of that sort cannot interpret their own visions while in such a state, just as a person cannot interpret his own dream while dreaming it. Those who can interpret them are the exact scholars of the legacy of prophethood, called 'the purified ones.' For sure, when they rise to the rank of the 'purified ones,' the people of witnessing of that group understand their errors through the guidance of the Qur'an and the Sunnah, and they correct them; and they did correct them.[20]

Further on, Nursi explains that these "people of illumination" are not describing physical places or realms that cartographers can map. "For instance, they said that one of the earth's levels is that of the *jinns* and demons, and that it has a breadth of thousands of years." (Notice the confusion of the spatial and temporal dimensions.) He continues:

> But if we supposed the globe to be like a pine-seed in the World of Meaning, the World of Similitudes, the Intermediate Realm, and the World of Spirits, the similitude of the tree that would be formed from it would be like a huge pine-tree in relation to the seed. Thus, in their spiritual journeyings, some of the people of witnessing have seen some of the earth's levels in the World of Similitudes to be extremely extensive; they have seen them to stretch over a distance of thousands of years. What they saw was right, but because superficially the World of Similitudes resembles the physical world, they saw the two worlds blended together, and interpreted them thus. When they returned to the realm of sobriety, since they lacked balance, and since they wrote exactly what they witnessed, it has been considered to be contrary to reality.[21]

This single passage is material enough for an entire chapter, focusing on Nursi's cosmology. Since that is not the primacy focus of this reflection, I will highlight only two aspects of this teaching.

First, Nursi is offering a typology of (at least) four "worlds" or dimensions, of reality: (1) the world of our conceptual categories and interpretations (Nursi uses the term *alem-i mana,* world of meaning, to designate this first dimension); (2) a world of corresponding or parallel "similitudes" (*alem-i misal*, a world of symbols and associations perhaps like Plato's world of Forms); (3) an intermediate realm or world, *alem-i berzah*, where souls reside between death and the Day of Judgment; and (4) a world of spirits, *alem-i ervah*, that may be related to what

Nursi calls *alem-i ahiret*, a realm or world beyond the Day of Judgment. This four-level cosmology, which we see parallels Jewish mystical teachings, makes more variegated and tantalizing the two-dimensional polarity of Manifest and Unseen Worlds that Nursi posits in other contexts.

The second aspect to consider, and the last point for this first section, is the connection between this four-dimensional cosmology and the phenomenon of dreaming, especially the experience of "true dreams" that convey some portion of prophetic truth. A statement that makes this linkage is another from the *Sunuhat* section of the *Risale-i Nur*, which appears in the Turkish original but not in the English edition.[22] Nursi states: "**The world of dreams** (*alemi-i ruya*) **is the shadow** (*zill* in Arabic, *golge* in Turkish) **of the World of Similitudes** (*alem-i misal*)," while "**the World of Similitudes is the shadow of the Intermediate World** (*alem-i berzah*)"[23] (emphasis mine).

Here Nursi qualifies the prophetic truth and value of dreams in two ways: he uses his cosmological typology to set up a hierarchical gradation of veracity and credibility, plus he uses the term "shadow" to indicate that the prophetic element in dreams involves some inherent distortion; that is, the messages in dreams are moon-like reflections of the sun-like truths at best, and refractions or even subjective fabrications of pseudo-truth (if we can coin an oxymoron), at worst.

Piecing together the various strands of the discussion so far, we can summarize Nursi's teachings on dreams as follows: his own 1919 dream, along with the letter to his student, indicate that he took the spiritual dimension of dreams seriously enough to write about it. He based these reflections on traditional teachings in the Quran and hadith collections. Nursi regarded many, if not most, dreams as spiritually meaningless, or even deceitful in the worst cases, while some dreams he deemed portals onto supernatural or unseen realms of reality, but in an indirect, shadowed, moon-like way. To construe them correctly requires expertise and discernment in interpretation, and people—even saints and scholars—vary in their possession of such spiritual capacities. Whatever tiny element of prophecy our own dreams convey, they are only partial and obscure pieces of the sun-like wisdom that is revealed fully in the All-Wise Quran. Hence, Nursi prefers to be a "servant of the Sun," not a "lover of the night," and to rely on the Quran's wisdom as the ultimate arbiter of truth. Dreams can be the "snare of the saints," leading even faithful mystics and scholars astray, so Nursi cautions spiritual seekers against putting too much stock in the alluring images of our nocturnal imaginations.

It could be that Nursi's warnings made his followers equally cautious when approaching their own dreams as potential sources of spiritual insight and guidance. From my limited knowledge of the Nur community, I have the impression that the subject of dreams and their interpretation is not a major concern. At the same time, my conversations with Nursi disciples in Istanbul yielded some fascinating information that is worth sharing here. It might be considered part of the "oral tradition" within Nursi circles, rather than teachings committed to paper.

Şemsettin Turkan, who works with various educational NGOs in Ankara, cited for me a Turkish saying: "If forty saints see the same dream for forty nights, one should take it seriously but not follow it blindly." The circumspection reflected in this statement parallels Nursi's own skepticism and caution regarding dreams. Turkan then proceeded to tell me that three Nur community members—two of whom he knew and one of whom he had not met—saw Said Nursi in their own dreams. One of them also heard Nursi speaking in the dream. All three instances occurred some time after Nursi's death, and none of these three had ever met him personally. The person whom Turkan had not met reported that he recognized Nursi from a photograph, and that in his dream Nursi was waving regards to him. The dream, according to Turkan, led the man to start reading Nursi's writings, and later he joined the Nur community.

Ihsan Kasim issued a four-volume collection of Nursi's students' recollections, focused mainly on the life of their spiritual master. He told me that they include occasional reminiscences of Nursi appearing to the disciples in dreams, before and after his death.

The most meaningful encounter I had with a Nur community member on the subject of dreams was my conversation, in August 2005, with one of Nursi's closest disciples, Mehmet Nuri Güleç, known as "Firinci" (the "baker") by everyone in the community. With Semsettin Turkan translating, he told me that on February 22, 1952, Nursi himself came to Istanbul for some legal proceeding, and that is when Firinci met him for the first time. "I was young," he recounted to me. Nursi "showed patience and love to us. He hugged both of us [Firinci and another student] and we spent about two and a half hours together." Nursi spoke of his own life and the impact of his *Risale-i Nur* collection. He gave Firinci some flour and sugar and asked him to bake some sweet cakes. The following summer, Firinci went to his native town of Inegol in the district of Bursa. There he discovered that his family members were arguing with neighbors. An elderly relative wanted to fight on behalf of the family using a pistol, and he asked Firinci to help him practice firing the gun in a remote mountainous area. That night, Firinci had a dream in which Nursi came to the door of his home in Inegol, took hold of Firinci's arm with one hand, and slapped him in the face with his other hand. "The slap felt so sweet," Firinci recalled. To him, the message of the dream was clear: no violence was to be used to settle the dispute between the two families. The next day Firinci shared this dream with his relative and affirmed his decision to abandon "the violent way." Then he went to the other family and told them, too, about his dream. This helped the two families resolve their quarrel and become friends.

These personal accounts indicate that at least some of Nursi's disciples also took their dreams seriously, especially when their spiritual teacher appeared in them. Now let us turn to the wider cultural matrix, rooted in Islamic tradition, for these nocturnal messages and their interpretation.

BROADER ISLAMIC RESONANCES: THE CONTEXT FOR NURSI'S VIEWS ON DREAMS

Since the *Risale-i Nur* is intended to be a commentary on the Quran, it is only natural that Nursi cites Quranic verses to buttress his views on the nature and purpose of dreams. In The First Matter or Part of *The Twenty-eighth Letter*, examined earlier, he also cites Hadith sources twice: he cites various Hadith collections to support his statement about the "one-fortieth part" prophecy or prophethood in "true dreams," and he mentions the dreams "as true and clear as the breaking of morning" that "God's Most Noble Messenger" was having at the same time that he received the initial revelations of the Quran.[24]

For Nursi, the Prophet Muhammad (PBUH) was "the cause of pride of mankind and truly the perfect man"[25] and, because of his extraordinary qualities and unique status, he was graced by God to receive the Quranic revelations. No one else, even in prophetic or "true" dreams, can claim to have similar access to divine truth. Yet Islamic tradition presents a fascinating paradox: it was Muhammad (PBUH) himself who taught that, after his earthly life and the fulfillment of his role as God's Messenger, dreams would be the primary medium for receiving communication from the divine, although they would not attain the unique status of Quranic revelation (*wahy*).

John C. Lamoreaux has written an exemplary study, probably the most comprehensive to date in English, of the Islamic tradition on dreams and how it developed over the centuries. His book, *The Early Muslim Tradition of Dream Interpretation*, examines a wide range of Muslim dream manuals compiled by such writers as Ibn Qutaybah, Sijistani, Qayrawani, and Kharkushi. These guidebooks drew mainly on Hadith teachings about the Prophet, his wives, and his Companions. They also offered standardized interpretations of various symbols that appear in dreams. Ibn Qutaybah (b. 213 A.H./828 C.E. in Kufah, d. 276/871 in Baghdad) explains why he wrote his manual:

> Among the types of knowledge and the varieties of wisdom with which humans occupy themselves, there is none more obscure, none more

> refined, exalted, and noble, none more difficult . . . than the dream, for it is one of the parts of revelation (*wahy*) and one of the modes of prophecy (*nubuwah*).[26]

Lamoreaux offers some common elements of the various dream manuals he has found and studied closely:

> All Muslim dream manuals are in accord that there is no person who is not able to receive divinely sent dreams. It matters not whether one is a North African shoemaker, an Afghani holy warrior, or a menstruating woman. Various circumstances, however, can cause a person to be particularly receptive to divine influence, or contrariwise, particularly unreceptive. . . . There are, too, certain people by nature more receptive to dreams. The most systematic treatment of this subject is found in the work of Sijistani [b. 326/937, d. 399/1008], who ranked dreamers as follows:
>
> 1. A Muslim's dreams are more truthful than a non-Muslim's.
> 2. Among Muslims, the dreams of prayer leaders, judges, jurists, and religious scholars are most truthful.
> 3. The dreams of freedman are more truthful than those of slaves.
> 4. The dreams of a man are more truthful than those of a woman.
> 5. Among women, those who are veiled have truer dreams than those who are not.
> 6. The rich have more truthful dreams than the poor.
> 7. The elderly have more truthful dreams than the young.[27]

This parochial, sexist, ageist, and elitist hierarchy is clearly colored by the era in which Sijistani lived. If he were alive today and compiling a dream manual, what kind of ranking might he present? Lamoreaux offers some general observations about this genre of Islamic literature, read widely throughout the Muslim world for centuries:

> All Muslim dream manuals . . . concur that the knowledge gained in dreams is a form of prophecy (*nubuwah*) and revelation (*wahy*), two highly charged terms also used to describe the nature of the Koran. . . . Such sweeping claims are occasionally qualified, usually by specifying that dreams provide only a fraction of prophecy—one forty-sixth or some variant on that figure. Invariably an appeal is made to prophetic [Hadith] tradition on this point: "The dream of the Muslim is one of the forty-six parts of prophecy (*nubuwah*)"—the standard against which

> they are measured being the Koran. There are, also, certain kinds of dreams particularly laden with prophetic significance. Usually these are identified as dreams in which Muhammad appears. The standard proof text for this is likewise a prophetic tradition: "Whosoever has seen me in a dream has seen me in truth, for Satan is not able to imitate me in a dream." Sometimes dreams of the Koran and other exalted objects are included among these invariably true dreams. Ibn Qutaybah, for instance, suggests that Satan can appear to the dreamer neither as God or the Koran, nor as the sun, moon, heavens, earth, or clouds.[28]

What is the connection, if any, between the written revelation (the Quran and the *Sunnah* or the records of the Prophet's life) and the messages conveyed in dreams? Here is Lamoreaux's answer:

> Not only are dreams understood to be forms of prophecy and revelation, they are also usually considered to be nothing less than the chronological successors of Koranic revelation. [Such was the conviction of those who authored dream manuals, and this belief was evidently shared by countless readers over the centuries.] Prophetic traditions to this effect abound and are widely cited in the dream manuals. Perhaps the most famous takes as its setting the penultimate day of Muhammad's life. The prophet, now quite ill, is carried into the mosque on the shoulders of two companions. He tries to lead the prayer, but is too weak. He delegates his duties to Abu Bakr, and as he leaves, proclaims: "[When I am gone] there shall remain nought of the glad tidings of prophecy, except for true dreams. These the Muslim will see or they will be seen for him." Dreams are, in short, the primary mode through which God will communicate with His community following Muhammad's death and the cessation of Koranic revelation. They are, in short, the successors of Koranic revelation. Ibn Sina alone seems not to have shared this view, in large part as a result of his neoplatonic understanding of the function and character of prophecy.[29]

As Lamoreaux notes, the interconnectedness between the dream world and the "real" world that we experience while awake is simply assumed, without any substantiation beyond the classical texts, by the Muslim dream interpreters. The ambiguity of the Arabic term *ruya* is one factor that lends itself to such blurring of boundaries, for the word may mean "dream" or "vision" (from the root "to see"). It can denote an enigmatic dream that conceals its true meaning and requires interpretation; or a dream that is literal, with no deciphering required; or an oracular, predictive dream in which God or an angel or some other venerated figure appears and reveals esoteric knowledge to the dreamer. [The dreams of Muhammad (PBUH) fall into this last category, as would Nursi's 1919 dream featuring the "great assembly" of Islamic authorities.] The single word *ruya* encompasses all of these kinds of dreams. Most of the time, the dream manuals are interested in the more enigmatic dreams that require a deciphering of the symbolism. This interpretive process is called in Arabic *ta'bir*. "It entails the 'transferring' of the dream from the symbol to its meaning, from the sign to the signified. We might even call this process an act of 'translating' the dream, a usage paralleled in Syriac."[30]

One of the authoritative Hadith collections, the *Sahih Al-Bukhari*, has a whole section entitled *Kitab Al-Ta'bir*, or *The Book of Dream Interpretation*. The Arabic-English Saudi edition translated by Dr. Muhammad Muhsin Khan includes this book in its ninth volume, with a total of sixty-six entries over forty pages.[31] Some teachings are very short, others quite lengthy. Some are sayings of the Prophet (PBUH), such as: "Narrated Abu Qatada: The Prophet (PBUH) said, 'A true dream is from Allah, and a bad dream is from Satan.'"[32] There are four citations, in the names of four different Companions, of the key statement referred to earlier: "The Prophet (PBUH) said, 'A (good) dream of a faithful believer is a part of the forty-six parts of *An-Nabuwwa* (Prophethood).'"[33] Other entries report a particular dream dreamt by Muhammad (PBUH), or one of his wives, or one of his Companions, together with its interpretation. If someone dreams of the Prophet, this is particularly auspicious, for one tradition reads, "The Prophet [PBUH] said, 'Whoever sees me [in a dream] then he indeed has seen the truth.'"[34] Objects that appear in dreams that are reported include a bowl of milk, shirts of different lengths, a green garden, a silken garment, the keys to the earth's treasures, a flowing spring, a well, a palace in Paradise, Jesus and the Dajjal in Mecca, a black woman with unkempt hair, and a sword waved by Muhammad (PBUH).

One of the striking aspects of this Hadith compilation is the ease with which the Prophet (PBUH) and those around him shared their dreams publicly. It was a regular practice, as we learn from this report: "Narrated Ibn 'Umar: Men from the Companions of Allah's Messenger (PBUH) used to see dreams during the lifetime of Allah's Messenger (PBUH) and they used to narrate those dreams to Allah's Messenger (PBUH). Allah's Messenger (PBUH) would interpret them as Allah wished him to interpret them." The report goes on to say that Ibn 'Umar himself had a dream featuring angels who showed him the gateway to Hell, but he was reassured that he would not end up there if he would pray more often. Ibn 'Umar told this dream to his sister Hafsa, who in turn told it to Muhammad (PBUH). "Allah's Messenger (PBUH) said, 'No doubt, 'Abdullah is a good man.' (Nafi' said, 'Since then, 'Abdullah bin 'Umar used to offer *Salat* [prayer] much.'"[35]

The last entry in Al-Bukhari's *Kitab Al-Ta'bir* starts with: "Narrated Samura bin Jundub: Allah's Messenger (PBUH) very often used to ask his Companions, 'Did anyone of you see a dream?' So dreams would be narrated to him by those whom Allah willed to relate." The rest of this Hadith conveys a lengthy dream that the Prophet (PBUH) himself had and related to his associates one morning. In it, two angels accompany him and show him all kinds of wondrous things. Then, after these very strange encounters, the angels interpret for Muhammad (PBUH), within the dream itself, what these experiences and phenomena symbolized—in each case with a homiletic message reinforcing Islamic moral values.[36]

From these various Hadith sources compiled by Al-Bukhari, and from the study on Muslim dream journals by John Lamoreaux, we can appreciate that Nursi's understanding of "true dreams" (including his own in 1919) has a long and honorable tradition behind it. So does his openness in sharing his own dreams publicly. Some questions worth asking are: Why have we moderns abandoned the practice of relating our dreams to others (except a psychotherapist), and inviting them to share theirs with us, for our mutual enrichment? Is it because we view dreams as nonsensical, or purely psychological without transcendent meaning and value? Or do we think that "true," powerful, life-transforming dreams are meant for our private edification alone? Have we given up the notion that at least some dreams convey prophetic messages and hence are relevant (as are sacred texts) to the wider society, and not only to ourselves as individuals? These questions are prompted by the Islamic teachings we have examined, beginning with the profound, discriminating, cautionary, and ultimately hopeful, even uplifting, insights of Nursi.

RESONANCES IN THE JEWISH TRADITION

The Islamic teachings on dreams and dream interpretation have their parallels in Jewish tradition. In the Hebrew Bible, prophetic personalities receive divine revelation through dreams, including the same Joseph who is the focus of *Sura Yusuf* in the Quran. (See Genesis chs. 28, 37, 40, and 41 for accounts of Jacob, Joseph, Pharaoh, and Joseph's fellow prisoners; Solomon's experiences in I Kings 3; and Nebuchadnezzar and the prophet Daniel in Daniel chs. 1, 2, 7, 8, and 10.) From these sacred stories, it is clear that the Hebrew Scriptures, at various stages of its composition, retained the belief in dreams as a prophetic medium—dreams dreamt by prophets and kings, as well as the dreams of people without exalted status. (For other references to dreams in the Hebrew Bible, see Joel 3:12, Zechariah 10:2, and Ecclesiastes 5:2 and 5:6).

In Numbers 12:6, the text reads: "If there be among you a prophet, I, the Eternal, will make myself known to him; in a vision, in a dream, will I speak to him." But the danger in heeding dream messages is also presented, in very clear and forceful terms, in Deuteronomy 13:2–4:

> If there arises among you a prophet (*navi*), or a dreamer of dreams (*cholem chalom*), and he gives you a sign or wonder, and the sign or wonder comes to pass, of which he spoke to you, saying, "Let us go after other gods, which you have not known, and let us serve them"; you shall not hearken to the words of that prophet, or that dreamer of dreams; for the Eternal your God is putting you to the test, to know whether you love the Eternal your God with all your heart and with all your soul. You shall walk after the Eternal your God, and be in awe of Him, and keep His commandments, and obey His voice, and you shall serve Him, and hold fast to Him. And that prophet, or dreamer of dreams, shall be put to death, because he has spoken to turn you away from the Eternal your God, who brought you out of the land of Egypt, and redeemed you out of the house of slavery . . . so shall you put the evil away from your midst.

In Rabbinic literature, the belief in the prophetic nature of some dream content is reaffirmed, but it is also seriously qualified by statements limiting or circumscribing the value of most dreams. One common view or principle is "the contents of dreams neither benefit nor harm" [literally, "neither raise nor lower"—*Divrei chalomot ein ma'alin ve-lo mordin*].[37] In the first tractate of the Babylonian Talmud, *Berakhot*, six pages or folio sides (55a to 57b) are devoted to the subject of dreams and their interpretation. Some sages give interpretations of particular dream imagery (as in the hadith sources examined earlier), while others offer more general statements about dreams as a phenomenon. Here are some examples of the latter:

> A dream that is not interpreted is like a letter that is not read. . . . Neither a good dream nor a bad dream is ever wholly fulfilled. . . . A bad dream is better than a good dream. (R. Hisda, *Berakhot* 55a).
>
> To a good person, bad dreams are shown, and to a bad person, good dreams are shown. (R. Huna, *Berakhot* 55b, conforming to a modernist understanding of how dreams are morally corrective messages, either countering ego-inflation by confronting the dreamer with charac-

ter flaws or giving a less-than-virtuous individual some moral instruction and inspiration)

Just as wheat can not be without straw, so there can not be a dream without some nonsense. (*devarim betaylim*, meaningless content: R. Yohanan in the name of R. Shimon bar Yochai, *Berakhot* 55a)

While part of a dream may be fulfilled, the whole of it is never fulfilled. (R. Berekhiah, *Berakhot* 55a)

When Shmuel had a bad dream, he used to say, "The dreams speak falsely" [quoting Zechariah 10:2]. When he had a good dream, he used to say, "Do the dreams speak falsely, seeing it is written [Numbers 12:6], 'I [God] will speak to him in a dream'? Raba pointed out a contradiction [since Zech. 10:2 and Num. 12:6 seem in opposition]. . . . There is no contradiction: in the one case it is through an angel, in the other through a demon. (*Berakhot* 55b)

R. Bana'ah said: There were twenty-four dream interpreters in Jerusalem. Once I dreamt a dream and I went round to all of them, and they all gave different interpretations, and all were fulfilled, thus confirming that which is said: All dreams follow the mouth. (*Berakhot* 55b, with scriptural justification for this claim, that dreams take on their meaning through verbal interpretation, offered from the story of Joseph and the two Egyptians imprisoned with him)

If one rises early and a Scriptural verse comes to his mouth, this is a kind of minor prophecy. . . . Three kinds of dreams are fulfilled: an early morning dream, a dream which a friend has about one, and a dream which is interpreted in the midst of a dream. (R. Yohanan, *Berakhot* 55b)

Dreams are one-sixtieth part prophecy. (R. Hananiah bar Yitzhak, *Berakhot* 57b and Genesis Rabbah 17:5—this is a close parallel, albeit with a different fraction stipulated, to the Islamic teaching of one-forty-sixth or one-forty-ninth or, in Nursi's case, one-fortieth part prophecy).

These excerpts serve to illustrate the range of views that the Talmudic sages expressed on dreams. Moshe Halevi Spero, in his essay, "Dream Psychology in Biblical and Rabbinic Thought," offers some synthesizing comments:

> In summary, there is a basis in the Bible for two attitudes on dreams: (1) dreams can carry messages of worth—especially when they are prophetic vehicles; and (2) dreams can be worthless—apparently when they are not clearly prophetic dreams . . . talmudic analysis further clarified this understanding of dreams . . .

Certain halakhic [legal] discussions reveal that the rabbis, despite individual statements which questioned the overall worthwhileness of dreams, accepted the psychological reality of the dream message for the dreamer. This acceptance is heightened when the dream message is felt to be a Divinely inspired presage. "If one saw a [bad] dream and if one is anxious over it [*ve-im nafsho agumah alav*], he should go and have it interpreted before three individuals." This law is omitted in the codes of Maimonides and Alfasi but noted in others. The Talmud details a precise liturgy for the process of hatabat or hatarat halom (lit., interpretation [or enhancement—YL] or nullification of a dream) comprising passages from Tanakh [i.e., Scripture—this liturgical formulation is still included in Orthodox prayer books, as a personal confession to be uttered during the priestly benediction that *cohanim*, male descendents of Aaron and his family, pronounce before the congregation on major holidays] . . .

In summary, this [essay shows] that biblical and rabbinic sources distinguish between fully prophetic dreams, dreams which retain some elements of prophetic import, and so-called normal dreams. The *devarim betaylim* [nonsense] contained in dreams have been interpreted as the manifest content of the dream, meaning that the latent content of the dream is not vitiated by the fact that all dreams have an esoteric symbolic structure. The "one-sixtieth prophecy" which characterizes dreams has halakhic ramifications . . . but also alludes to the fact that dreams are prophetic in that one tends to do what one dreams and to dream about what one wishes to do. Dreams are expressive of important personal issues whose significance may depend, not only on the understanding of the individual dreamer, but on the objective perspective others can add to it. [This last sentence reinforces the notion that sharing one's dreams, especially vivid and meaningful ones, can help clarify their messages and augment the chances of their prophetic promise being fulfilled.]

The central point is that the talmudic rabbis did not confine dreams to satisfying one wish—be it sexual wish-fulfillment, as in Freud's view, power motives, as in Adler's view, or cosmic and transcendental inspirations, as in C. G. Jung's view. Rather, they viewed dreams as expressive of the whole range of unworked day material and symbolism, irrational strivings as well as reason, morality, and unconscious wisdom; an important function of the mental processes, and a potential source of Divine inspiration. The Talmud, then, clearly indicates that dreams are the "royal road" to man's active subliminal workings.[38]

The Talmudic sages and Said Nursi share a certain faith orientation: they combine in one worldview mystical piety and rational norms of jurisprudence. They evince empirical this-worldly discernment, along with a solid belief in divine revelation as a reality that continues to bestow guidance and blessing on humankind. The Jewish mystics, in the corpus of writings known as Kabbalah, tended to lean toward the pole of supernaturalism and the esoteric, hidden in the workings of Creation or directed to this plane of reality from the unseen realms, often via angels. They would also speak more forthrightly about demons and dark forces emanating from "the other side' (*sitra achra* in Aramaic), intruding on the lives and consciousness of human beings (e.g., through bad or tempting dreams). In Kabbalah, there is a cosmology with four "worlds" or dimensions that parallels quite closely the four-level typology in Nursi's *Eighteenth Letter*:

the physical world of empirical events and actions (*Olam Ha'Asiyah*), the world of transcendent forms and forces that shape nature and history (*Olam HaYetzirah*), the world of creative, causal agency where angels and demons reside (*Olam HaBriyah*), and finally the world of pure spirit (*Olam Ha'Atzilut*) from which everything else originates and flows "downward" through the "lower" worlds until it reaches our plane of physical existence.[39] It is worth noting that there is also a four-dimensional or four-level typology of scriptural exegesis that "hears" the Torah speaking and teaching in four distinct voices, conveying complementary meanings: the *p'shat* (literal meaning), the *remez* (allusions or associations, sometimes cross-references to other Torah verses), the *drash* (the allegorical meaning, often interpreted through an exegetical parable called a *midrash*), and the *sod* (the mystical, esoteric, usually hidden meaning). Since the Jewish mystics see the Torah as God's blueprint for creation, the parallels between the four worlds and the four dimensions of meaning in any Torah text are not difficult to see and appreciate. And since the Torah for Jews, like the Quran for Muslims, is the most authoritative revelation of God's will, any other phenomenon that might have a revelatory function (such as dreams) would have to somehow "fit" within the Providential design linking sacred text and human experience. This is too broad a subject to adequately develop here.

The role of dreams in manifesting supernatural phenomena and conveying divine messages is discussed in Jewish mystical literature, just as it is in the Talmud. Spero, in the essay cited earlier, repeats a statement from the mystical Scripture commentary known as the *Zohar* (*Book of Illumination*), the core text in Kabbalah:[40] "'Now prophecy has ended and the *bat kol* [heavenly message] has ended, and man only uses the dream.' In other words, dreams may be the contemporary vehicle for Divine inspiration now that its traditional sources are unavailable. This is in accord with Maimoindes' view."[41] On Maimonides (Rabbi Moshe ben Maimon), Spero writes: "Maimoindes, who holds that prophecy is a perfection which may be acquired through dreaming—also considering dreams the 'unripe fruit [*nobelet*] of prophecy"—distinguishes between "revelatory dreams" and normal dreams."[42] His mention of Maimonides is significant, since this towering giant of the Middle Ages, who wrote in Arabic and was well versed in Islamic thought, was a rationalist by nature and wrote forceful legal opinions condemning occult practices like astrology.

The teaching from the *Zohar* brought by Spero parallels the hadith sources we examined, citing the announcement by Muhammad (PBUH), as he was dying, that dreams would henceforth complement the Quran as a medium of divine communication. This hadith teaching is probably the most sweeping statement, in either tradition, establishing a link between prophetic dreams and the authoritative revelations in the Quran or the Torah.

To conclude this section, I wish to mention a recent book by Vanessa Ochs, coauthored with her daughter Elizabeth and beautifully illustrated by Kristina Swarner. It is called *The Jewish Dream Book: The Key to Opening the Inner Meaning of Your Dreams*. It covers a wide range of subjects related to our general theme, aimed at inspiring contemporary Jews to take their dreams seriously and to share them with others. Here are the chapter headings: The Origin of Dreams; Classical Jewish Approaches to Dream Interpretation; Bedtime Rituals to Help Prepare for Dreaming; Dream Practices for Waking Up; Practices for Interpreting Dreams; Practices for Dream Incubation; Practices for Responding to Nightmares; Holding a *Rosh Chodesh* [the new moon festival, celebrated traditionally by Jewish women] Gathering Devoted to Dreaming; Seeking Healing through Dreams; Practices for Mourning; Blessings for Dreaming; Practices for Linking Your Dreams to Torah; and A Torah Practice That Honors Dreamers.[43]

Universal Implications and Intimations

Clearly, there is much food for thought, and for imagination (by day and by night), in the range of Islamic and Jewish teachings we have considered. What are their practical implications for us today? I offer here a brief reflection, hoping that others can further develop this subject.

We live in an era of genocide, weapons of mass destruction, and ecological threats caused mainly by human folly. In the imaginations of many people, apocalyptic fantasies are rampant, partly as a response to the insecurities of our present condition. The temptation of an instant upheaval, overturning this corrupt or "fallen" world, is very strong. And for groups or whole peoples suffering injustice, haunting memories and "victim scripts" generate ideologies of militant revenge.

Against this violent corruption of our imaginations, and the pathological symptoms we see reported in the mass media, are traditions of healing and hope in all our Abrahamic traditions. I would argue that the teachings on dreams and prophecy that we find in Islamic and Jewish (and Christian) sources are resources we can tap to redeem our precarious situation as vulnerable creatures on this planet.

But in order to become allies in this redemptive effort, we need to overcome the parochialism that has constrained us for centuries. We can no longer afford dreams or visions of triumph at another group's expense. Such fantasies are not "true dreams." They are expressions of our own insecure egos and our childish needs to "win" some kind of dualistic religious war. Such negative energies only feed the demonic forces within us, and make us susceptible to whatever destructive powers may be active in realms beyond this plane of existence—in classical terms, "Satan" or "demons."

The end-of-times dreams of global transformation through violence need to be countered by "true" messianic dreams of transformation through justice, compassion, and reconciliation. We need life-affirming and life-enhancing dreams, ones that we can together implement and fulfill.

All of us need to publicly share our dreams of redemption and see how they can nourish us and reinforce each other instead of competing in a zero-sum struggle for "victory" or vindication. The culmination of those dreams is called, in Jewish terms, the Messianic Redemption, and in Islamic terms, the arrival of the Mahdi followed by the Day of Judgment and Resurrection. (Some Jewish versions of the end-times also envision resurrection of the dead.) Meanwhile, we are killing an awful lot of people, too often in the name of some religious ideology, while some of us are focused either on resurrection or Paradise in some other realm of reality. The perverse paradoxes, or blatant contradictions, in these militant religious worldviews are too tragic for words. They guarantee that one group's dream of triumph will end up being a nightmare of colossal proportions for everyone else.

Our dreams can help heal us. But we need to humbly share them with our Abrahamic siblings. These neighbors can be interpretive mirrors and correctives for us. For each person, and for each faith community, subjectivity limits the field of vision. The field is broadened and enriched when we come together, as the Prophet Muhammad (PBUH) and his Companions did, to share dreams and possible interpretations of their symbolism. If each of us, at best, can aspire to one-fortieth, or one-forty-sixth, or one-sixtieth of prophecy, would not the odds of reaching a critical mass of true wisdom increase if we were to pool the visionary resources from our dreams? Muslims, Jews, and Christians can come together as allied dreamers and as partners in historical transformation—in fact they must, lest the extremists in our midst hijack our sacred texts, and our dreams, and ultimately our destinies, in the service of evil. As Nursi said, we must be "servants of the Sun," the Light of God, to which we are drawn as plants are drawn to the sun's rays. But our dreams, on occasion, can be informed, and our lives transformed, by that light—even at night, when the moon is shining in the sky, and while, as we sleep, we are more receptive to other sources of illumination.

I close with a passage by Rabbi Arthur Green, a long-time friend and teacher who initiated a postdenominational training program for rabbis at Hebrew College in Newton, Massachusetts. The theology developed by Green in his book *Seek My Face, Speak My Name* breaks through conventional categories of thought. It is informed by Kabbalah, by egalitarian impulses in our contemporary culture, and by the demythologizing that science and a critical reading of history have forced upon us. In the process, he offers us new interpretations of ancient dreams and visions:

> The figure of messiah remains our symbol of hopes and dreams still not abandoned, needed more than ever in a world that can see the face of its own destruction. But our vision of human perfectibility no longer culminates in a single human being, any more than our sense of origins really goes back to the primal pair in Eden. We see the evolution of our species continuing to move forward, however haltingly, toward the existence of humans who have ever greater depths of awareness or consciousness of divinity than we think possible. We see a human race, some thousands of years in the future, that looks upon us as one of the ancient empires, advanced for its day in technological matters, but rather primitive in its understanding of the universe, and quite awfully childish in its moral conduct. We see that later age dwarfed by still another, and yet another, beyond that. Somewhere in that ongoing growth of understanding and compassion, we glimpse [in dreams?—YL] messiah, the human self most fully open to the One, perhaps the human self that stands at the very edge of transcending what we understand as "human" altogether, reaching out to a presently unknown new world. Such fulfilled humanity will be that which is most fully aware of its role in joining together what the ancients would have called the "beyond" and "within," realizing and proclaiming the oneness of all being.[44]

NOTES

1. For Christian explorations of the spiritual significance of dreams, see Morton T. Kelsey, *God, Dreams and Revelation: A Christian Interpretation of Dreams* (Minneapolis, 1974); John A. Sanford, *Dreams: God's Forgotten Language* (New York, 1989); and Lois Lindsey Hendricks, *Discovering My Biblical Dream Heritage* (San Jose, 1989).
2. I wish to thank Mustafa Gurbuz and Gulsum Gurbuz for their assistance in researching this chapter.
3. Sukran Vahide, *Islam in Modern Turkey: An Intellectual Biography of Bediuzzaman Said Nursi*, edited with an introduction by Ibrahim M. Abu-Rabi' (Albany, 2005), 157. The source cited is *Sunuhat*, 41–47.
4. See Leighton McCutchen, "Psychology of the Dream: Dream without Myth," in *The Dialogue Between Theology and Psychology*, edited by Peter Homans (Chicago, 1968), 183–219. McCutchen writes (208, 212), "An understanding of the function of dreams has unquestionably given fresh insight into the nature of psychopathology and psychotherapy. Can we suggest a concomitant insight on the side of health? . . . The power tapped by dreams is that which is allied with the energy moving creativity, art, and higher forms of human expression. The dream is sometimes the direct source for literature and poetry (Blake, Coleridge), painting (Bosch), to say nothing of the visions of philosophy (Descartes), and religion (Jacob-Israel)."

   See also James Hillman's book *In Search: Psychology and Religion* (New York, 1967), for a discussion (60–61) of how to "befriend" our dreams, in order to deepen our understanding of "the myths which are operating in me, my real story, the story of my life from within, rather than my case history derived from without." What Hillman calls the "rediscovery of soul through the unconscious" entails a religious dimension: "the reawakened presence of inner myth and sense of destiny, the sense that one is somehow meant. To be meant implies a transcendent power that calls, chooses . . . a power which gives meaning" (66–67).
5. Bediuzzaman Said Nursi, *Letters 1928–1932*, from the *Risale-i Nur* Collection, vol. two, translated from the Turkish *Mektubat* by Sukran Vahide (Istanbul, 1997), 407. The emphasized couplet is based on a poem by Mevlana Jalaluddin Rumi (see *Kulliyyat-i Shams ya Diwan-i Kabir*, Tehran, 1338 sh, vol. three, ghazal 1621, 302–303) which was cited by one of Nursi's own spiritual authorities, Ahmad Sirhindi (*Maktubat-i Imam-i Rabbani*, Lucknow: Nawal Kishore, 1899, vol. one, number 130, 143). I am grateful to Professor Yohanan Friedmann of the Hebrew University and to Dr. Faris Kaya for their help in locating these references.
6. Ibid., 408.
7. Ibid.
8. Ibid., 408–409.
9. Ibid., 409–10.
10. Ibid., 410–11.
11. Ibid., 411–12.
12. Bediuzzaman Said Nursi, *The Words*, vol. two, t. Şükran Vahide, (Istanbul, 1992), 416.

13. Ibid., 407.
14. Ibid., 359.
15. Ibid., 355.
16. Ibid., 344.
17. See ibid., 344–50.
18. Ibid., 345, 350.
19. Nursi, *Letters*, 104.
20. Ibid., 104–105.
21. Ibid., 106.
22. I am indebted to Mustafa Gurbuz for calling this to my attention and for helping me with the translation.
23. Bediuzzaman Said Nursi, *Risale-I Nur Kulliyati*, vol. two (Istanbul, 1996), 2042.
24. The multiple Hadith sources are cited in his footnotes, cf. Nursi, *Letters,* 408, 409.
25. Nursi, *The Words*, op.cit., 344.
26. John C. Lamoreaux, *The Early Muslim Tradition of Dream Interpretation* (Albany, 2002), 28
27. Ibid., 83.
28. Ibid., 83–84.
29. Ibid., 84.
30. Ibid., 84–86.
31. *The Translation of the Meanings of Sahih al-Bukhari*, tr. Muhammad Muhsin Khan, vol. nine (Riyadh, 1997), 83–122.
32. Ibid., 86.
33. Ibid., 87, 93.
34. Ibid., 93.
35. Ibid., 110.
36. Ibid., 118–22.
37. Moshe Halevi Spero, "Dream Psychology in Biblical and Rabbinic Thought." In *Judaism and Psychology: Halakhic Perspectives* (New York, 1980), 100–105; Jacob Bazak, *Judaism and Psychological Phenomena* (New York, 1972), 30–31.
38. Spero, op. cit., 102, 104, 108.
39. For a discussion of the different worlds, see Rabbi Aryeh Kaplan, *Inner Space: Introduction to Kabbalah, Meditation, and Prophecy* (Jerusalem, 1990), chapter 3 ("The Universes"), 21–36.
40. See Daniel C. Matt, *Zohar: Annotated and Explained* (Woodstock, 2002), and Arthur Green, *A Guide to the Zohar* (Stanford, 2004).
41. Spero, op.cit., 101.
42. Ibid.
43. Vanessa L. Ochs with Elizabeth Ochs, *The Jewish Dream Book: The Key to Opening the Inner Meaning of Your Dreams* (Woodstock, 2003).
44. Arthur Green, *Seek My Face: A Contemporary Jewish Theology* (Northvale, 1994), 183.

NINE

"For you, illness is good health"

Said Nursi's Spirituality in His Approach to Physical Illness

Thomas Michel

In a recent survey conducted in Europe, respondents showed a decreasing interest in "religion" but, surprisingly, a corresponding increasing interest in "spirituality." Although this would appear to be an inconsistency, I believe that there is an explanation. In expressing a lack of interest, the respondents were probably thinking of *religion* as connoting unattractive elements of religiosity such as dry ritual, external conformity to social expectations, legalistic obedience, and repetition of dogmatic formulas. Conversely, in their show of interest for *spirituality*, the respondents were expressing a need for something transcendent in their lives, for internalized ethical norms, for a discipline that would give structure and order to their behavior, for a way to discover the divine in the midst of modern life, for an opening to encounter eternal values and wisdom.

Such felt needs underline the relevance of spirituality in modern life. A working definition might assert that spirituality is the way one internalizes the teaching and practice of religion so that it shapes, informs, and transforms that person's behavior. Without a spirituality, one's religious practice remains at the level of repetition of dry ritual, external to one's interior life and incapable of contributing to spiritual growth. It is spirituality that gives depth and roots to one's experience of God, without which that experience remains ephemeral and superficial. Spirituality implies a discipline, a conviction of the rightness of what one is doing that inspires a strong motivation. In this way, spirituality provides a solid foundation on which one can build habits of behavior and persevere at times of discouragement, boredom, and doubt.

Finally, it is spirituality that enables the believer to apply the lessons one has learned from faith to the trials and challenges that inevitably arise in daily life. It is one's spirituality that comes to the fore at moments of crisis, when the normal patterns of activity, work, and relaxation are disrupted, when relationships are strained, when thing are not "the way they should be." At such times, a person without faith must fall back on his or her own resources, but those resources are too often inadequate to face the challenge; the person gives up, admits defeat, and falls into despair. However, through spirituality, the believer is rooted in the divine message and nourished by faithful practice and as a result has access to additional resources of God's guidance and grace that can strengthen a believer to face the critical moment.

Illness and Spirituality

One moment of crisis that afflicts everyone at some point in their lives, and afflicts most people more than once, and some for lengthy periods, is physical illness. Even those fortunate few who manage to pass a whole lifetime in unbroken good health must still face the multiple crises that arise from illness as they accompany and care for spouses, parents, children, friends, and relatives who have been struck with poor health. A person's approach to this most common of human crises tells much about that person's spirituality. How one approaches the disruptive reality of illness displays the attitudes and perspectives that have been produced inside individuals through their internalization of the message of their faith.

My decision to try to learn what might be revealed about the spirituality of Said Nursi in his approach to the question of illness did not originate solely on academic grounds. A year ago I had what was probably a mild heart attack and my doctor sent me immediately to the hospital for emergency bypass surgery. While I was recovering, I was encouraged by the sympathy and kind words of various readers of the *Risale-i Nur*, who also shared with me some of the insights they had discovered in the writings of Bediuzzaman Said Nursi. This experience pushed me to read and study the *Risale-i Nur* more deeply in order to understand what Said Nursi's approach to sickness and human infirmity might disclose about his Quranic spirituality.

At one point in his treatise, "Message for the Sick," Nursi coins a startling paradox. "For you," he tells the readers of the *Risale-i Nur*, "illness is good health, while for some of your peers good health is a sickness."[1] In this chapter, I would like to explore Said Nursi's thought on the question of illness, to see what he wants to teach by this apparently unreasonable assertion. I hope to show that Said Nursi has a serious point to make, a point that is consistent with the way his Quranic spirituality leads him to regard the common human reality of illness.

SICKNESS OF THE HEART

First of all, it should be noted that Said Nursi is more concerned about what he calls "spiritual sickness" or "sickness of the spirit" than about physical illness, more interested in the causes of social ills than individual complaints.[2] He regards the identification of the weaknesses and incapacities of modern culture as one of the principal tasks of the community of his disciples, along with the presentation of Quranic teaching as a healing message for this world. As he stated in his defense in the Afyon court: "The collective personality of the *Risale-i Nur* has diagnosed the social, spiritual, and religious sicknesses of this age, and at a Divine command has offered to all humanity at this time the truths of the All-Wise Quran's in a way that will cure its chronic social ills."[3]

The sickness of the heart that Nursi sees as afflicting modern men and women is one caused by a lack of faith. It is the sense of ennui, a feeling of being without direction or hope, the incapacity to love, and a conviction of the absurdity of life that afflict those whose life is not informed by faith. Positivist materialism, belief in nothing beyond what one can see and touch, is thus a common spiritual sickness of our time.[4] This basic disorder arising from the lack of faith in God and a transcendent system of values precipitates multiple societal ills: Istanbul politics is a type of spiritual illness "like the Spanish flu";[5] racism is a disease;[6] even frigidity in marriage can be said to be a type of spiritual sickness.[7]

It is not only unbelievers who suffer from spiritual sickness; there are other sicknesses of the spirit, such as innovation,[8] scruples,[9] exclusivist and partisan mentalities,[10] or desire for acclaim,[11] which can afflict believers. Even saints and conscientious worshipers have lamented over the sickness of heart experienced in moments of tranquility.[12] One might ask whether in this last point Nursi is referring to the well-known state of soul described by the Sufi masters as *qabd*, the "dark night," when the believer is tested by God who, for a time, withholds from the *murid* all sensible delight in prayer and worship. Whether Nursi is referring to the Sufi state of *qabd*, there is no doubt that he regards Sufism as an effective remedy for treating the sickness of the heart.[13]

In this the Sufis have followed the example of the prophet Jesus who was granted the twin blessing of being able to act as God's agent to heal both physical and spiritual illnesses. However, Nursi saw this blessing not as a gift granted exclusively to Jesus; rather, it is one that the students of the *Risale-i Nur* can also obtain if they ask God and strive conscientiously for it. He states:

> Just as the Quran explicitly urges man to follow Jesus' (Pbuh) high morals, so it encourages him towards the elevated art and sovereign medicine of which Jesus was the master. "Remedies may be found for even the most chronic ills." . . . Don't despair! Whatever the ill, its cure is possible. Search for it and you will find it. . . . God is saying through the figurative tongue of this verse: "I gave two gifts to one of My servants who abandoned the world for Me. One was the remedy for spiritual ills, and the other the cure for physical sicknesses. Moribund hearts were raised to life through the light of guidance, and sick people who were as though dead found health through his breath and cure. You too may find the cure for every ill in the pharmacy of My wisdom. Work to find it! If you seek, you will certainly find."[14]

Praying for Health and Illness

There is much more that could be said about Said Nursi's approach to sicknesses of the spirit, but the above will have to suffice, for the main focus of this chapter is not on spiritual sickness, but rather on physical illness. It is to this aspect of Said Nursi's spirituality that I will now turn.

The first point to be noted is that Said Nursi does not idealize sickness in the manner of some nineteenth-century Romantic poets. He is quite realistic in holding that good health is a blessing from God for which the believer should hope and pray, whereas illness is never to be sought for its own sake, nor brought about by one's own effort. It is a pious act to ask that if it be God's will, one may enjoy good health. In one of his prayers included in the *Risale-i Nur*, Nursi makes such an appeal: "Forgive me my sins, O God, bear with me, and heal my ills. . . . Pardon all my sins, and grant me health from all sicknesses, and be pleased with me for all eternity!"[15]

On the other hand, good health is not an absolute good. The believer can also find himself asking God to grant ills and their remedies, if that be God's will. Nursi alludes to a prayer made in the Shafi'i rite during the *tasbihat* following the daily *namaz*, in which the faithful ask God to bestow on the family of the Prophet both ills as well as the remedies for those ills.

> "O God! Grant blessings to our master Muhammad and to the family of Muhammad, to the number of ills and their remedies; bless him and

> them, and grant them unending peace." . . . Just as illnesses are the most effective whip driving a person to the Divine Court, so also remedies, healing, and good health are the chief of the sweet bounties prompting him to give thanks earnestly and to truly offer praise. It is for this reason that this benediction is most meaningful and widely accepted. Sometimes when reciting the phrase "to the number of all ills and their remedies," I see the earth in the form of a hospital and sense the clearly obvious existence of the True Healer, Who supplies the remedies for all ills, physical and spiritual, and answers all needs, and His universal clemency and sacred all-embracing compassion.[16]

Nursi defends this unusual prayer by saying that just as illnesses are one of the surest means to drive someone to come before God in supplication and worship, so also release from illness is a privileged occasion for thanking and praising God. He goes on to note that the prayer inspires him to see the world as a huge hospital, full of sick people, who come before God as the compassionate healer who answers the needs of all. His spirituality leads him to understand that since both health and illness come from God, true faith consists of accepting willingly and patiently whatever God sends and placing one's trust in God who is the healer of bodies and souls.

Wisdom Arising from Experience

Said Nursi's understanding of physical illness is not the theoretical speculation of someone who has very seldom or never suffered from pain and infirmity. In the *Risale-i Nur* there are many references, too numerous for all of them to be cited, to the various illnesses that he suffered during his life. He experienced not only physical pain, but the lack of strength and stamina needed to accomplish the work he felt called to do. Because of his bad health and physical weakness, he had to refuse invitations to speak in the mosque,[17] and often felt too weak to teach and write.[18] At times he felt assailed by five or more illnesses at once.[19] Sometimes, the physical illness was compounded by the oppression and bad treatment he received during his periods of imprisonment, and he notes that several parts of the *Risale-i Nur* were written in such situations of psychological stress combined with physical pain and the discomfort of deprivations and mistreatment.[20] As he grew older, old age aggravated his illnesses[21] and made it more difficult to recover from them.

Beyond the purely physical effects of his illnesses, Nursi suffered the depression and anguish frequently experienced by those in poor health. He felt frustrated at being unable to continue his work. He tasted the powerlessness of ill persons who know that they can do nothing on their own to restore their health. He experienced the difficulty of concentrating and the mental exhaustion that often accompanies illness.[22] He was not a stranger to the common psychological effects of illness and a heightened awareness of the proximity of death, such as insomnia, nameless anguish, the feeling that one has wasted one's youth. He knew the loneliness, the feeling of being cut off from healthy friends and relatives that so often accompanies illness, a neediness that God alone can assuage. All this left him in a weakened, fragile condition that a tragedy such as the death of his nephew and spiritual son[23] could bring him almost to the point of despair.

In an intensely personal passage in the *Risale-i Nur*, Nursi shares his experiences of old age and sickness so that others might find in the teaching of the Quran the same hope that enabled him to endure and survive the spiritual crisis. He expresses beautifully the anguish and loneliness that are frequently the felt reality experienced by the aged in poor health. Nursi articulates his misery, and alludes to the universal human reality experienced therein, by quoting the seventeenth-century Mevlevi poet Niyazi Misri. Because of its eloquence, I include the passage in full:

> "Old age and illness attacked me in concert. Hitting me over the head, they chased away sleep. I had nothing binding me to the world like family, children, and possessions. Having wasted the fruits of my life's capital through the giddiness of youth, I saw those fruits to consist only of sins and mistakes. Crying out like Niyazi Misri, I said:
>
> *I had concluded no trade; the capital of life was all lost;*
> *I came to the road to find the caravan had moved on, unaware.*
> *Lamenting, I continued down the road, all alone, a stranger;*
> *My eyes weeping, my heart in anguish, my mind bewildered, unaware.*
>
> I was in exile at the time; I felt a despairing sorrow, a regretful penitence, a longing for assistance. Suddenly, the All-Wise Quran came to my aid. It opened a door of hope so powerful and afforded a light of consolation so true that it could have dispelled despair and darknesses a hundred times more intense than mine."[24]

It is to Said Nursi's credit that he does not hide or gloss over such weaknesses and spiritual crises, but includes them in the *Risale-i Nur* in the hope that such trials will serve as guidance and comfort for others similarly oppressed by age and poor health. Even at moments of what he acknowledges to be "extreme weakness, wretchedness, and powerlessness,"[25] he never doubted the truth of the divine favor and compassion he was receiving. It was this unshakeable conviction of God's power in his life that enabled Nursi to take consolation in God's presence, accept the illness, learn patience, and even "be content" with his situation of helplessness.

> Divine favor pointed out the above fact to me while, during a few days of material and spiritual affliction, illness and trial the like of which I had never before experienced in my life, I was being crushed in particular by the despair and distress of the heart and spirit which resulted from my being unable to serve the Quran and belief with the Risale-i Nur. I was then content with my distressing illness and imprisonment.[26]

LESSONS TO BE LEARNED IN TIMES OF SICKNESS

Nursi's view is that even though sickness is never to be sought, much less brought about self-destructively by one's own misuse of the body, when God in divine wisdom nevertheless allows illness to befall a person, there are some positive spiritual benefits that can be reaped and lessons to be learned. First, sickness is a salutary reminder of mortality without which people could go on for years in heedlessness and foolish complacency. "Since old-age, illness, disaster, and death open up frightful pain and are a reminder that even if the people who follow misguidance and vice enjoy a hundred thousand pleasures and delights, they most certainly experience a sort of hell in their hearts, although a profound stupor of heedlessness temporarily makes them insensible to it."[27] It is experiences like sickness, old age, and natural disasters that can be an occasion for egoistic, misguided people to wake up and realize the hellish existence they have made for themselves.

Second, sickness makes one appreciate the blessing of health. Those who enjoy unbroken health can easily take this great gift of God for granted and presume that it is the normal state for all humankind. It is only when one undergoes a period of bad health that one is able to understand the great favor that is contained in good health. Nursi quotes the proverb: "Light is indebted to darkness; pleasure is indebted to pain; there is no health without illness."[28]

In one passage of the *Risale-i Nur*, Nursi offers advice on why those who have been struck with sickness should not complain.[29] He offers three reasons. First, sickness, like hunger, is necessary so that God can display His Beautiful Names and qualities. God is the Compassionate One who consoles the sick, the healer who takes away illness, the provider who gives food to the hungry.

Second, illness is one of those events that show the value of life. Unbroken good health can become monotonous, flat, and empty; it resembles nonbeing more than the richness and fullness of life. Illness breaks the monotony and in doing so enriches, strengthens, and moves life forward. The third reason is that this world is a field of testing and service. Illness encourages the sick to become aware of their own powerlessness and their need for God, the compassionate sustainer. Their helpless situation leads them to take refuge in God, to meditate on God, and to offer petitions.

For the believer, states Nursi, sickness is like a veil[30] that shields humans from the harsh reality of death. Were people to live constantly in good health, death would loom as an ever more terrible prospect, a horrifying reality which no one would be prepared to face. The fears and complaints about death would take over one's consciousness and destroy the pleasure of life. However, sickness veils the horrors of death and serves to prepare people psychologically for its eventual reality.

Should the sick pray that they be healed? Nursi sees great value in this and takes the prophet Job as an example. Job prayed to be healed of his illness, not for selfish reasons of comfort and release from pain, but so that he would be able to worship and serve God better.[31] However, Nursi notes that the sick person should ask for healing with humility and trust, instead of accusing God and complaining about the unfairness of his situation. In contrast to complaining, which implies a criticism of God's nature as sustainer of life, trust in God is a form of worship by placing confidence in God's goodness and willingness to heal.

"Message for the Sick"

In addition to the many pieces of religious instruction found throughout the *Risale-i Nur* about the spirituality of illness, Nursi also devoted a lengthy treatise in the *Risale-i Nur* specifically aimed at offering guidance to those languishing in the throes of poor health and disease. This is his "Message for the Sick," found in the 25th Flash of the Flashes Collection. In this treatise, he brings together much of the teaching found dispersed in the *Risale-i Nur* and elaborates what he has said elsewhere at greater depth, and then adds new material and original observations.

In his introduction, Nursi confesses that he wrote this Flash more quickly than his other writings and did not find the time to correct the treatise. In fact, he comments that he chose not to revise the text so that it would retain the "natural" and provisional quality of a rough draft rather than the polished character of a finished manuscript. As a result, one should not expect a logical, carefully organized thesis on remedies for illness; instead, it is a collection of twenty-six remedies from which a sick person might draw profit.[32] The term "remedy" could be misleading. The reflections that Nursi offers are not remedies in the sense of medicinal or physical cures meant to remove the illness, but are rather remedies for the types of despair and distress to which those in poor health are often inclined. As such, they are spiritual remedies for the sickness of the soul that can sometimes follow upon that of the body.

Nursi recognizes that the two central problems for all those who suffer poor health are anxiety and impatience. Anxiety arises from a sense of helplessness, the inability to do anything to change the situation, the nagging fear that the illness will not be a transient state from which one will recover, but a permanent disability and ongoing affliction. Impatience comes from the sick person's feeling that time is passing too slowly and that she is wasting time that could be more profitably spent on other activities; consequently, the invalid harbors a desire to change the situation precipitately.

Most of the remedies that Nursi offers are aimed at helping the sick person to overcome anxiety by accepting his afflicted state tranquilly and find patience by placing his trust in God. By internalizing the implications of faith in God, the sick person can achieve peace of mind that, since it is conducive to physical well-being, can also help to bring about bodily recovery. The very personal nature of the remedies that he proposes indicates that these are reflections and insights that helped Nursi himself during his many periods of poor health. I will here briefly summarize each of the remedies.

1. Illness actually lengthens one's life. A life passed without trial or hardship is fleeting and insubstantial. The sick person should realize that God has given this opportunity to come to a deeper and richer appreciation of life.

2. The sick person who does not complain, but accepts illness patiently and takes refuge in God—that person is actually worshiping God. For worship is of two kinds: there is active worship, such as the daily *namaz* that one prays, or the Ramadan fast. Then there is what might be called passive worship, which consists of those periods of illness when the believer is simply aware of her own weakness and powerlessness and of God's power and compassion. By submitting to God's will and trusting in God's power to heal, the invalid is performing a very pleasing form of worship to God.

3. Illness is an occasion for the believer to give witness that we are not on this earth to enjoy ourselves. We are here to work hard and prepare an everlasting life. Moreover, sickness is a reminder of death. Heedless people, whose attention is fixated on a trivial pursuit of pleasure and success, do not want to think about death. Illness forces one to reflect on more serious questions of what life is all about.

4. Your body, along with its members and functions, does not belong to you. It belongs to God, who provides for it in God's own time and manner. Sickness is an occasion to learn that one's body is not a private possession to be disposed of according to one's whims, but is subject to the decrees of its true Owner and Provider.

5. Sickness can make people more mindful of their dissolute habits and of their duties to God. Illness is a time for waking up to what life is really about. For many sick people, Nursi states, the time of sickness is a privileged occasion of God's grace leading to conversion; for them, "*illness is good health, while for some of their peers good health is a sickness.*"

6. Sickness brings into sharp relief the previous times of good health and should lead one to thank God for such moments of happiness. Rather than giving in to bitterness and despair, the sick should reflect on the transient nature of their illness and place their hopes in God who will eventually restore the person to new times of good health and enjoyment.

6. (bis) Sickness reminds one that our bodies are not indestructible, we have no claim to immortality. By shattering the "myth of invincibility," illness is an antidote to natural human pride and an invitation to recognize humbly one's powerlessness before God.

7. Illness makes a person appreciate the great blessing involved in good health. Those who enjoy good health constantly are not able to value properly what they have. Good health is a wonderful blessing of God, but in order that people appreciate it fully, God allows illness to afflict people from time to time.

8. Sick people tend to bemoan their fate, but the really serious diseases are those of the soul, those that arise from unbelief and disobedience. By patiently accepting one's illness and placing one's trust in God, the sick person is actually distancing himself from these greater and more eternally threatening diseases.

9. Much of the anxiety felt by the sick is based on a fear of death. The believer, however, can overcome this fear by reflecting on the good things that await a person at death: rejoining friends and relations, returning to one's true homeland, accepting the invitation to the gardens of Paradise extended to those who remain faithful to God. By concentrating on what faith teaches about the reward awaiting steadfast believers, the invalid can come to accept death as a reality that need not be feared.

10. Many sick people make their situation worse by worrying about it constantly. The only way to stop excessive worry is to hand over one's life and cares to God. God is wise and compassionate and powerful. A believer can find no better solution to the self-destructive tendency to worry than that of placing one's trust in God, whereas obsessive anxiety is actually an accusation against God by implying that God is neither able nor willing to help.

11. This is an exhortation to remain patient and focused on the present moment. When the sick person thinks of the past, she should be grateful to God because she has been able to endure the illness up to this time. She should refrain from uselessly dwelling on future suffering, since that is something that does not exist and perhaps may never come to pass.

12. Sickness brings the benefit of knowing how much one is in need of God and how little one can count on one's own strength. The sick person discovers one's true significance and value in relation to the Creator. By pushing one to pray to God, sickness helps one to become aware that one's true glory is to be found, not in what one might have accomplished in life, but in one's very nature as creature of God.

13. Since no one knows one's appointed hour of death, sickness is beneficial in that it reminds a person to be heedful. Because of their suffering in this life, sick people are led to reflect on the life to come. Sickness thus increases their fear of God and leads them to be faithful and obedient, thus acting as a good preparation for eternity.

14. The loss of physical sight enables one to see spiritual realities more clearly. Physical sight can act as a veil that blinds one from a contemplation of Paradise. More broadly, whatever one lacks in the physical world can be used by God to teach and enlighten the sick person about deeper spiritual truths.

15. If illness were not good, God would not have granted it to God's most favored servants. Like the prophet Job, those holy people who suffer their illness as a kind of worship of God become, in a certain sense, martyrs. "They result in a degree of sainthood like martyrdom." Moreover, by lessening one's attachment to the world, sickness eases the pain of one's departure from the world.

16. Illness makes one more compassionate. Constant good health can make one feel self-sufficient. Sickness shows people their own weakness and need for others. They grow in respect and affection for those who help them and visit them. As a result of their own miseries, they experience greater fellow-feeling and are more ready to be compassionate toward other sick people and to disaster victims.

17. Some sick people complain that their illness deprives them from the opportunity of performing good deeds. However, in reality their illness makes them an occasion for others to do good works by assisting and visiting them and by praying for them. Especially in the case of close relatives, caring for the sick is an important act of worship. When the sick person prays for healing, that person's prayer is always heard and answered, but not always in the way the person seeks. However, the prayer, being sincere, is always acceptable to God.

18. Too often the sick person compares herself to those who are in good health and feels that her rights are being violated. However, the truth is that no one has the right to good health, which is a free gift from God. It is more

advantageous to compare oneself to those who are worse off, so that one will be led to thank God that one's health situation is not worse.

19. Life spent in permanent good health becomes monotonous and boring. It is change and variety in conditions of life that one can realize life's value and come to appreciate its true pleasures.

20. People make their health worse by confusing real and imaginary illnesses and treating them in the same way. In the case of real sicknesses, one must follow the advice of conscientious, believing doctors. On the other hand, hypochondria should be given no importance for, if one dwells on it, one's morale is destroyed and one is in danger of actually damaging one's health through excessive concentration on the imagined illness.

21. The invalid should try to identify and enjoy the pleasures that come with illness, such as the signs of affection and human kindness that come from friends and relatives and the opportunity to rest from taxing duties. If one focuses on such pleasures, the pain of sickness will seem less burdensome.

22. Illness reminds people of the fleeting nature of human life in this world. Through belief and submission to God, one can reap spiritual benefit from even the most serious illness.

23. One who feels lonely and abandoned in time of sickness should contemplate the compassionate presence of the Creator. The loneliness felt by a faithful believer in time of illness is not true loneliness. True loneliness, which no human medicine can cure, is separation from God, but the believer who has faith in God's healing presence is never really alone.

24. This remedy is directed toward caregivers. Those who tend sick children and the elderly should be aware that transient childhood illnesses are granted by God to build character in the child and are an integral part of the child's natural growth. Those who care for elderly parents will reap a special reward from God, both in this life and in the hereafter; care for aged parents is a form of worship especially pleasing to God.

25. Believers should take advantage of their illness to deepen their faith in God. Illness should be an occasion to cut down one's appetites, grow in heedfulness and reflection, and deepen one's prayer life.

Nursi concludes his treatise by praying for the sick: "May God restore you to health and make your illnesses atonement for sins. Amen."[33]

Said Nursi's Spirituality

Nursi's attitude toward physical illness should have become clear from this summary of the remedies proposed, and from them one can glean insights into his spirituality. For Nursi, sickness is a human reality that, like all human realities, should lead the believer to God. The frailty of the body is a forceful argument against all human tendencies toward self-sufficiency and complacent self-satisfaction. The sick person must confront a harsh but ultimately liberating reality: that one can do nothing to heal oneself, but must submit to what God ordains.

Nursi's appeals to the sick person to accept one's illness must not be construed as some kind of fatalism or defeatist passivity. He is very clear that when one is ill, that person must follow the prescriptions and advice of a well-trained doctor, must take proper care of oneself, and must pray for healing.[34] However, medical science cannot guarantee immediate cures and in many cases cannot bring about any improvement in fighting the disease. However, by working together with medical science, religious faith can often produce results that are impossible for the unbeliever. By accepting the fact that one is in the hands of a loving and compassionate God, the believer can overcome natural anxieties and attain peace of mind, which physicians agree to be the emotional and psychological state most conducive to bodily healing.

Moreover, Nursi is not guilty of romanticizing the sick person. In saying that "sickness makes one more compassionate," or "the sick person comes to a richer understanding of life," Nursi is not claiming that sickness gives people an inside track to virtue or that greater understanding and loving compassion are the automatic results of illness. What he is saying is that God can and does produce spiritual fruits such as compassion and understanding in the sick person who cooperates with God's grace, who submits to God's decrees, and who patiently accepts his or her condition without complaining or accusing the Creator. For such a person, God is able to use the time of illness to make that person more compassionate, for example, or to understand better what is really important in life.

Nursi sees that for someone without faith, the time of illness is often regarded as time wasted, an aberration from "normal" life when productive activity becomes impossible, an unhappy situation when pain, fear, and anxiety threaten to eliminate joy from life, a bitter condition where frustration, anger, and resentment can make a person irritable and disagreeable to others, a time of loneliness and alienation when one is tempted to despair and misery. However, faith in God provides the sick person with spiritual resources with which to transform the spiritual context of the illness. When the sick person is aware that he is worshiping God by his very act of submission and humility, this precludes his thinking of sickness as time wasted. By realizing that his life is in the hands of a just and compassionate God, he can overcome fear of death and obsessive worry about his state of health. Reflecting on the loving presence of God the Healer brings hope to the sick person and can prevent feelings of isolation and loneliness from leading to depression and despair. Rather than dwelling on pain and loss, the invalid should see the time of sickness as an opportunity, a chance to learn spiritual truths that would otherwise be hidden.

By allowing the basic teachings of the Quran to shape one's attitudes and reactions to this most common of human hardships, Nursi offers a spirituality that is practical and suited to the needs of ordinary believers. With the advice he offers, he shows his followers how the unhappy condition of illness can be transformed by God's guidance into an opportunity and occasion for spiritual growth and deeper submission to God's will.

Notes

1. *The Flashes*, 25th Flash "For the Sick," 269.
2. Nursi refers to "sicknesses of the spirit, mind, and heart" but often uses the terms interchangeably. In this chapter, I will make no attempt to distinguish between these terms. Cf. *The Flashes*, 11th Flash, 87.
3. Said Nursi, *The Rays*, The Fourteenth Ray, 441.
4. *The Words*, "A Flower of Emirdag," 474. Cf. Also, The Rays, Conclusion to 10th Topic, 272.
5. *The Letters*, "Seeds of Reality," 549.
6. *The Letters*, 29th Letter, 6th Section, 495.
7. *The Rays*, 15th Ray, 1st Station, 587.
8. *The Flashes*, 6th Flash, 44, 11th Flash, 80.
9. *The Words*, 21st Word, 2nd Station, 281–83.
10. *The Words*, "Gleams," 753; *The Letters*, 22nd Letter, 1st Topic, 317.
11. *The Flashes*, 21st Flash "On Sincerity," 220.
12. *The Letters*, 26th Letter, 4th Topic, 87.
13. *The Letters*, 5th Letter, 41.
14. *The Words*, 20th Word, 2nd Station, 263.
15. *The Words*, 32nd Word, 682.
16. *The Rays*, 2nd Ray, 1st Station, 16.
17. *The Flashes*, 24th Flash, 265.
18. *The Rays*, 15th Ray "The Shining Proof," 614.
19. *The Flashes*, 24th Flash, 260.
20. *The Letters*, 28th Letter, 7th Matter, 440. Cf. also *The Letters*, 28th Letter, 423, and *The Rays*, 7th Ray, 124.
21. *The Flashes*, 26th Flash "For the Elderly," 289.
22. *The Rays*, 15th Ray "The Shining Proof," 2nd Station, 622.
23. *The Flashes*, 26th Flash "For the Elderly," 310.
24. *The Flashes*, 26th Flash "For the Elderly," 289. Cf. a similar passage in *The Rays*: "Once, when a period of heedlessness coincided with my being shaken by various indispositions like old age, exile, illness, and defeat, I was overcome by a grievous anxiety that my very existence, to which I was intensely attached and by which I was

captivated, would cease to be. Again I had recourse to the verse: *For us God suffices*." *The Rays*, 4th Ray, 78.

25. *The Flashes*, 24th Flash, 260.
26. *The Rays*, 14th Ray, 475.
27. *The Words*, 13th Word, 2nd Station, 156. Cf. also *The Damascus Sermon*, 130.
28. *The Words*, "Gleams," 754.
29. *The Flashes*, 2nd Flash, Points 2–5, 23–26.
30. *The Words*, 22nd Word, 2nd Station, 301.
31. *The Flashes*, 2nd Flash, 5th Point, 26.
32. The remedies are numbered 1–25, but there are two separate remedies under #6.
33. *The Flashes*, 25th Flash, 285.
34. *The Flashes*, 25th Flash, 282.

TEN

Nursi on Hatred as the Root of Violence

Mustafa Ulusoy

We live in a world that is being constructed at the same time it is being destroyed. Symbols are made and symbols are destroyed. Houses are built and houses are pulled down. People are born, people are killed. Bonds are formed, bonds are severed. Peace is made, war destroys.

Humanity, having made so much progress in so many different ways, has failed to build a peaceful world. The period after the Age of Reason in the seventeenth century has been called that of "the articulate mind," that is, the Age of Enlightenment. The nineteenth century, on the other hand, is generally known as the Age of Revolutions. As for our century, the twentieth century, Bauman's answer to the question: "What have we been able to achieve in it?" is noteworthy: "In the present century we have learned this—modernity is not merely about increasing production, or traveling faster, or becoming more affluent, or living more freely; it is also about speedier and more effective killing and bloodshed being planned and carried out more scientifically."[1]

It is interesting to note that though oppression and bloodshed are not new and have existed throughout history, they have been on the increase in recent years. Modernity has not been able to eliminate hatred and aggression, which have roots thousands of years old. On the contrary, it has regenerated and nourished them. Taking into account the duration of wars, the forces employed, their size in relation to the populations of all sides taking part, and the numbers of casualties, the military historian Quincy Wright has demonstrated that wars have increased in Europe in modern times. The figures he gives are 18 in the twelfth century, 24 in the thirteenth, 60 in the fourteenth, 100 in the fifteenth, 180 in the sixteenth, 500 in the seventeenth, 370 in the eighteenth, 120 in the nineteenth, and 3080 in the twentieth century until 1945.[2]

Though World War Two with the terrifying destruction it brought about raised hopes that it would extinguish humanity's love for war, it was followed from 1945 to 1990 by 160 armed struggles in various parts of the world. Moreover, the countries taking part were not known as "despotic." Out of the total number of years from its foundation until 1965, there were only twenty in which the U.S. army or navy did not see active service anywhere in the world.[3]

Wars are a manifestation of destruction, but destructiveness is not particular to war, nor is it limited to it. Along with violence, destructiveness is a violation; in other words, it breaches the wholeness and integrity of beings. A raped woman, an unloved child, Palestinians dispossessed by the Israeli government, ghetto inhabitants subject to ugly police terror, workers alienated from their own manpower by capitalist production, forests polluted by acid rain; these should all be seen as having suffered violence and aggression, for the conditions of their existence have been violated. Some of them have suffered aggression only by the way. But all have suffered violence; the specific fate of each, springing from violence, has destined their actual suffering.

However, "The Absolutely Wise One, the Truly Just One, the All-Compelling and Glorious One, established justice, not only for men and jinn, but for all creatures." That is, "He bestowed on everything the right to exist and the right to life."[4] The notion of violence, therefore, requires correct and in-depth analysis and an ontological understanding: beings in this world have their own needs and integrity, that is, they have rights.[5] The violation of their rights constitutes violence.

Destruction is attractive because it is easy and because it excites the desire for power. This allows people with narcissistic egos in particular to experience the pleasure of possessing power and strength. "Destruction is easy, the weak person is destructive."[6] "They appear to have extraordinary power because destruction is easy."[7] For instance, a person who has both a match and the desire to destroy becomes gripped by his imaginary power. He burns with desire at the thought that what will be destroyed by the fire will never be the same again. This desire for strength and power first of all catches hold of his self. Destruction being easy and exciting a sense of power provides us with an important insight into understanding why those who deny God tend to be destructive and violent. I will discuss this in more detail later.

Among all living creatures it is only man who destroys for the sake of destruction.[8] He is capable of being cruel and ignorant.[9] It is interesting that a Polish survivor of the concentration camps expressed his amazement at the cruelty by saying: "They could kill people and treat it as quite normal." It was the comfortable way in which one person could kill another that amazed him. He added: "I couldn't understand it."[10]

These opposite poles of human behavior, that is, the capacity for both good and evil, poses a complex problem for modern psychology.[11] Nursi attributes this frightening truth to man's being created in the most perfect way, and to the multiplicity and comprehensiveness of his potentialities:

> Man has been created on 'the most excellent of patterns' and has been given comprehensive abilities. He has been cast into an arena of trial and examination in which he may rise or fall to stations, ranks, and degrees from the lowest of the low to the highest of the high, from the earth to the divine throne, and from minute particles to the sun. He has been sent to this world as a miracle of divine power, as the result of creation, and as a wonder of Divine art before whom have been opened two roads, leading either to infinite ascent or infinite descent.[12]

Man's potentialities and subtle faculties are not limited like those of the animals and this may lead narcissistic people with inflated, self-loving egos, who exist only for themselves and who act at the behest of their desires and caprices, to behave wildly and aggressively.[13] In other words, both constructive, disciplined behavior and such attributes as compassion and kindness, and unlimited destruction may result from man's comprehensive capabilities. The restricted nature and capabilities of animals limit both the good they do and the evil.

Down to the present, people have generally employed three methods for dealing with their enemies: war, flight, or finding a way to pacify them. None of these has succeeded in eliminating hostility from the world.[14] In my opinion, it would be naive to expect this. However, it is possible to establish areas of peace and to decrease the amount of conflict. I will now investigate the reasons for this.

WHY IS A WORLD WITHOUT TENSION LEFT TO THE AFTERLIFE?

This world is a place where opposites conflict. Good and evil, beauty and ugliness, benefit and harm, perfection and deficiency, light and darkness, guidance and misguidance, belief and unbelief, obedience and rebellion, light and fire, fear and love—tension has always existed between these opposites and it always will.[15]

Nursi states that basically what renders the earth amenable to conflicting opposites is the law of contest. Life is an "arena for the contest of life."[16] With the descent of man to earth, "since the time of Adam (Peace be upon him), two mighty conflicting currents have come down to us."[17] "One is that of the people of prophethood, righteousness, and belief, who, following the straight path, receive the bounty of happiness in this world and the next."[18] "The second current" is that group characterized by the verse in *Sūrat al-Fātiḥa*, "*maghdūbī 'alayhim wa la'ḍ-ḍāllīn* (those whose portion is wrath and those who go astray)"; that group that "deviates from the straight path, and, through excess and deficiency, transforms the intelligence into an instrument of torture amassing pains, casting humanity down to a degree lower than the animals."[19]

The tension between faith and unbelief is decreed by the Creator and is an imperative of the law of contest. Nursi says: "The All Powerful One of Glory, Who holds within the grasp of His power the breathing-in and breathing-out of the unbelievers, does not wipe them out with a single command, a single trumpet-blast. With His title of universal Lord and names of All-Wise and Controller, He inaugurates a field of examination and contest."[20] Nursi explains too: "[from] the contest between the inspirations and satanic whisperings around the heart to the contest between angels and devils on the bounds of the heavens, they require that law to be all-embracing."[21] He thus underlines that the struggle is necessitated by the Creator's attributes of glory and beauty, and is not limited to relations between humans but is played out in the micro-worlds and macro-worlds, from the angelic inspirations and satanic whisperings in the human heart to the struggle between the angels and Satans in the heavens.

In contrast to the profane understanding of history prevalent in the West, which views human history in terms of conflicting interests, the Quran interprets history as a process of struggle between the prophets, their communities, and those who founded their lives on principles of justice and obedience to Allah, and those who opposed them. The Quran characterizes these interest groups in terms of *mustakbir* or arrogance (31:7), *mutraf* or oppulence (43:23), and *ṭāghūt* or false idols (16:36).[22]

As long as opposites remain on the earth, contest and struggle will persist. There have been times in particular places when peace, security, and well-being prevailed, such as in the Age of Bliss, but there has never been a time when there have been no wars, tension, or conflict. At any rate, each person experiences constantly in his own heart the tension and struggle between satanic whisperings and angelic inspirations, and this continues until death, which marks the end of his trial and examination.

The fruits yielded by conflicting opposites will separate out in the eternal world into heaven and hell, and this sorting out will be completed on the Day of Judgment. "The branches and results, which are opposites, of those two elements will continue into eternity; they will become concentrated and separate from one another. Then they will be manifested in the form of paradise and hell."[23] This may well be one of the reasons heaven will be a place abounding in peace, tranquility, and well-being. For everything counter to peace and happiness will have been discharged into hell.

UNBELIEF AS A SOURCE OF AGGRESSION AND VIOLENCE

Nursi distinguishes between skeptical unbelief and absolute unbelief. He says that even absolute unbelievers may benefit from the Quran's mercy, for it allows them to transform their unbelief into a form of scepticism whereby they may have hope about an eternal life[24] and thereby obtain some pleasure from the present one.[25] Nursi also distinguishes between non-acceptance and denial as two forms of unbelief.[26] He considers nonacceptance to be indifference, whereas denial is a state of open unbelief, a judgment, and acceptance of nonexistence. The path of denial leads not just to the rejection of faith but to its opposite, whereas nonacceptance corresponds to doubting or skeptical unbelief.

What I am proposing in this chapter is that the tension between faith and unbelief is an understandable one, but that the translation of this tension into violence, aggression, oppression, and crime result from "absolute unbelief," which is not a question of only not accepting faith but leads to its opposite. Violence and oppression are the inherent characteristics of absolute unbelief, and are even necessitated by it.

The fact that Muslims have resorted to violence throughout human history does not mean that violence is particular to faith. Either faith or unbelief is rooted in a person's heart. It is then reflected in all the person's mental processes and behavior. However, not all the states and characteristics of unbelievers are marked by the traits of unbelief.[27] On the other hand, by stating: "Believers may be suffer from diseases of the heart. They too, like the people of misguidance, can give unnecessary importance to unimportant things. However, they realize their fault quickly, repent and do not insist,"[28] Nursi does not look on believers as being absolutely free of fault.

The underlying reason a Muslim resorts to violence is his failure to follow a faith-based path when trying to resolve his traumatic experiences, as desired by the Creator and indicated in the Quran. This is recorded in the person's personal history as unbelief, and as evil, injurious conduct, and will be taken into account in this world or the next. Being called to account is not restricted to the people of disbelief; it applies to everyone. The attempt to show that Muslims worldwide have become embroiled in violence and caused the deaths of innocent people because such involvement is an inherent part of faith and of Islam arises from ignorance of the true nature of faith and unbelief.

Violence and cruelty are the inherent characteristics of absolute unbelief, but unbelievers may still possess good qualities; and although faith yields absolute goodness and beauty, people with faith in their hearts may still display states that show their hearts are diseased. This may appear to be contradictory, but it does not alter the fact that violence is an inherent dimension of unbelief. I would like to emphasize the theory I am attempting to put forward, namely, that the source of aggression and violence is absolute unbelief—and not the people of unbelief—and I am implying that faith and unbelief are translated into practice in varying degrees and are not absolute. I would like this difference to be kept in mind as the remaining part of this study is read.

I will now show why violence and aggression are particular to unbelief and why they reflect a state of unbelief. Before moving onto the concept of hatred, I will discuss a less severe emotion, that of anger. When attempting to understand the psychodynamics of hatred I will be borrowing heavily from Otto Kernberg's studies on this topic.

Anger

Anger is the emotion that marks the activation of aggression. Irritation is a mildly aggressive emotion that signals that angry reactions are imminent, and its chronic form is irritability. Annoyance is a more intense emotion than irritation and is usually more differentiated in its cognitive content and in the nature of the object relationship that is activated.

Research carried out on infants has documented the early appearance of anger as an emotion. Its primordial function is to eliminate a source of pain or irritation. In this sense, anger seems to be used not so much for destruction as for the preservation of life. A later developmental function of anger is as a last resort to restore the feeling of autonomy. The violent assertion of will restores an internal state of narcissistic balance.

The Relationship between Aggression and Hatred

Hatred is a complex aggressive emotion. It is the most common motive for destroying things. It is what causes a person to be destructive. Contrary to anger and its reactions, which are spontaneous and have cognitive aspects that are changeable, hatred is cognitively fixed and deep-seated. It is a complex emotion that may overshadow other aggressive emotions such as envy and disgust, and be the main driving force of aggression.[29]

Hatred is not always pathological. As a response to the threat of physical or psychological harm or to dangers threatening the survival of a person and his loved ones, hatred follows on normally from anger and is designed to eliminate such dangers. However, if it becomes a chronic, ingrained tendency, it always reflects the psychopathology of aggression. I will focus on hatred as a fundamental trait and intrinsic part of a person's character, and as the root of aggression.

The primary aim of the person consumed by hatred is to destroy the object of his hatred, a specific object of unconscious fantasy, and the conscious derivatives of this object: at its depths the object is both needed and desired. Yet its destruction is also equally needed and desired. It is crucial to keep this paradox in mind if one is to understand hatred.

Hatred in its most extreme form demands: (1) the physical elimination of the object of hatred, as in murder. Also, (2) radically devaluing the object as an act of destruction or elimination may be another manifestation of hatred; and (3) sometimes destructive hatred may become generalized and take the form of the symbolic destruction of all objects of hatred. For instance, a good indication of destructive hatred is when the person concerned severs all relationships with people he deems worthwhile.

Sometimes hatred is expressed in suicide. The self is identified as the hated object and the only way to destroy it is to annihilate the self.

A less severe degree is expressed in sadistic tendencies and wishes. The person feels a desire to make the object of hatred suffer in some way and this is accompanied by a profound enjoyment, conscious or unconscious, at that suffering. Sadism may take the form of sexual perversion in which actual physical harm is inflicted on the object, or it may be part of the malignant narcissism syndrome, or a part of a sadomasochistic personality structure. In contrast to the earlier, more encompassing form of hatred, sadism is characterized by the wish not to eliminate the object of hatred but to maintain the relationship with it. This is the relationship of a sadistic agent and a paralyzed victim. The desire to inflict pain and the pleasure in doing so are central here.

A still milder form of hatred is manifested as the desire to dominate the hated object. The yearning to have power over it may include sadistic components, but attacks on it tend to end with the object's submission. In this way, the person's freedom and autonomy are reconfirmed. More frequent manifestations of this milder level include the assertion of hierarchical superiority and territoriality in social interactions and the aggressive aspects of regressive small-group and large-group processes.

Other forms of hatred include those of the aggressive assertion of idiosyncratic yet well-rationalized systems of morality, justified indignation, and primitive levels of commitment to vindictive ideologies. This degree of hatred forms a bridge with the exalting function of bold assertiveness in the service of and commitment to ideals and ethical systems.

Deep-seated, ingrained hatred and the desire to inflict pain on the hated object coexist with inveterate—and sometimes sexual—sadism and cruelty.

Primitive hatred may also be displayed as the attempt to ruin potentially satisfying human relationships and to eliminate the possibilities of learning something of value from them. Envy of the hated object underlies the desire to destroy the immediacy and communication of close relationships. This is particularly true if the hated object is not dominated by hatred.

The Relationship between Envy and Hatred

It was Melanie Klein who first identified envy as a dominant characteristic of patients with severe narcissistic psychopathology. She defined envy as an emotion akin to anger that arose due to the belief that a desired object was in the possession of someone else and that it afforded them pleasure and not us.[30] The envious person feels pain when he sees something he desires in the possession of another, and he tries to take it from him, or to spoil or mar it. Pleasurable and happy scenes give him pain. It is only other people's misery that gives him pleasure. This is why all attempts to satisfy an envious person are futile. For his envy arises from within himself and he will always find something to envy.

Klein states forcefully that considering envy as one of the seven deadly sins is fully justified psychologically.[31] Her quoting the following from Chaucer's *The Parson's Tale* is interesting: "Envy is undoubtedly the greatest sin; for all the others transgress against one virtue only, whereas envy contravenes all virtues and goodness."

Otto Kernberg writes that envy of a thing and hatred blend together in some way. He emphasizes that conscious or unconscious envy underlies the primitive hatred displayed as the attempt to destroy potentially gratifying human relationships and the possibility of learning something of value from them.[32]

Max Scheler emphasizes that if a person is only unhappy at someone else possessing something good, this feeling can encourage him to work for, buy, usurp, or steal it, whereas envy arises when he is unable to do this and so feels powerless.[33] If the desired values are unobtainable and incomparable, envy may lead to resentment, a concept especially favored by Scheler.

Underlying envy of something and the need to destroy and spoil anything good that might come from it, is identification with the originally hated—and needed—thing. Envy may be considered both the source of a primitive form of hatred and a complication of the hatred deriving from the fixation on trauma. On the surface, hatred of the envied object is often rationalized as fear of the object's destructive potential.

The Relationship between Hatred and Unbelief: The Envy of Unbelief toward Faith

In the Quran, the emotion of hatred is ascribed only to unbelievers.[34] For there are profound bonds and parallels between the psychodynamics of unbelief and the dynamics of hatred.

"Unbelief is an evil, a destruction."[35] Unbelief renders the universe meaningless. It negates all the attributes manifested in beings. Nursi considers this to be a violation, a stepping beyond the mark, an evil, and a crime. Unbelief severs the bonds that connect man both to himself and to all other beings. "Unbelief is so frigid it causes enmity even among brothers; it sows seeds of alienation in everything; it makes everything appear to be inimical to everything else."[36] Because faith establishes genuine brotherhood and relations between beings, "there is no hostility, spite, or brutality in the believer's spirit, he feels a sort of brotherhood with his greatest enemy even.[37] "In the unbeliever's spirit, however, are greed and hostility."[38] "Unbelief extinguishes the spirit and heart, and leaves them in darkness." This dark state is the source of hatred in the unbeliever's spirit. It is to not feel one's own existence and that of the universe due to their meaninglessness and to perceive being as nonbeing. This gives rise to a sense of inner emptiness.

Basing his view on numerous Quranic verses,[39] Nursi states that "the enmity of unbelievers towards Muslims and the people of the Quran is necessitated by their unbelief. For unbelief is the opposite of faith."[40] He thus shows that the enmity of unbelievers toward believers and the Quran is necessitated by their unbelief. For this reason he emphasizes that any love shown toward unbelievers, for whom it is not possible to have feelings of love or familiarity, will be to no avail, just as it is futile to expect love in return or to hope for help from them.[41]

Unbelief also destroys the relationship a person has with himself. "Should unbelief, which consists of the severance of the relation, enter man's being, then all those meaningful inscriptions of the divine names are plunged into darkness and become illegible."[42] The outlook of unbelief causes him to perceive himself as worthless, meaningless, and a nonentity. Unbelief awakens in man a profound feeling of emptiness, which is the primary cause of resentment, anger, aggression, destructiveness, greed, and envy. Arno Gruen considers this self-hatred to be the source of destructiveness in people. It is interesting to discover that what narcissistic people most hate is their own existence.[43] Unbelief first destroys the relation a person has with himself; his perceiving his existence to be meaningless, empty, and futile transforms it into a prison from which there is no escape. The unbelievers' confinement in it leads primarily to resentment and hatred of themselves. This state of hatred empties them and takes them to nothingness. The person who sees himself as nonexistent thus becomes hostile to existence and to goodness.

The psychodynamics of Satan assist in understanding the psychodynamics of the enmity of unbelief toward faith. The words of Satan, namely, that "I take of Thy servants a portion marked off and mislead them and create in them false desires"[44] are noteworthy. Why does Satan want to mislead people? Isn't it enough for him that he does not obey Allah's commands? In my opinion, as I have argued elsewhere,[45] this is entirely related to the psychology of unbelief.

Satan lost everything the moment he became proud and refused to obey his Lord's command to prostrate before Adam. He was deprived of everything, for beings acquire their richness by complying with their Lord's commands. Existence itself obtains through His command. Satan rebelled against this truth that was inherent in his existence and persisted in his rebellion. He came into existence through his Lord's command; he did not exist of himself. If beings do not come into existence by themselves, the One Who determines which of them is best and superior is their Creator. Satan rebelled against this situation, and refused to comply with His command—that man had been created superior and better—and he persisted in his rebellion. This is significant: his persistance meant he was deprived of his Lord's mercy.[46]

Satan's being deprived in this way was actually absolute deprivation and it gnawed away at him. His had nothing within him he felt to be positive. At this point he began to be filled with envy—envy at having lost everything. It consumed him, and he was henceforth the enemy of all existence. He became hostile to everything in which his Lord's mercy was manifested and he envied all beings. Out of envy he was consumed with the desire to destroy, annihilate, sully, and ruin every situation in which this mercy was manifested. He was ablaze within. From then on he wanted to annihilate goodness, mercy, beauty, and compassion, for he was deprived of all of them.

While Satan persisted in this, Adam and Eve were in paradise, the recipients of infinite varieties of mercy. Satan could not accept this; it was torture for him.

He could not abide a person he deemed inferior to himself living in the copious abundance of the Lord of Mercy in paradise, for he was created out of fire while Adam was created out of dust. He was overcome by envy. Moreover, Adam and Eve were to receive this endless mercy for all eternity, when for him there was to be endless deprivation in hell. This situation was a source of pain for Satan and engendered hatred in him. Envy and hatred were eating away at him. He wanted to take away the bounty from man and destroy it, that form of existence he did not possess and had not been given him.

Satan's first attempt was successful. He played with the lives of the two people he envied. The path had now been set for him. He turned his envy and hatred, directed at Adam and Eve (Peace be upon them), toward all of humanity. He then did not want any human being to receive mercy, compassion, benefit, beauty, or goodness. He wanted no one to have a good relationship with his Creator. The hatred and envy within him made him think: "If my relationship with my Creator is spoilt, everyone must have a bad relations with Him as well." He became jealous of everyone. He did not want people to be loved by their Creator or to receive bounties from Him. Deprived of eternity himself, he envies those called to it and makes every effort to prevent them obtaining it. He does not want people to love their Creator. He feels envy when people feel gratitude for and thank their Creator for what He has bestowed on them. He is the enemy of everything good. The hatred and envy within him long to destroy and ruin all goodness. All goodness occurs through the connection and relationship of man with his Creator. Satan, therefore, is bent on severing all the bonds people have with their Creator.

The emptiness felt at being expelled from the Lord's mercy, which is the source of envy, and the destructiveness of such emptiness gives rise to, are not particular to Satan. They characterize every sort of unbelief that goes so far as contesting the Creator, and are extensions of it. That is why everything good and beautiful in life is a source of envy for people who have become embroiled in unbelief. This inner deprivation underlies unbelief's hostility toward faith and everything related to it, and toward goodness and beauty.[47] The weakest envy is at the same time the worst type of envy. This is why the strongest source of resentment is the existential envy directed toward another's very nature. Envy constantly whispers: "I can forgive you for everything but I can never forgive you for what makes you—for what you have that I don't have—and for not being you."[48] Scheler states that close examination of this type of envy reveals it to be hostility to the other's very existence, for the envier feels that the other's existence oppresses him, rebukes him, and abases him intolerably. This is just like Satan's opposition to the existence of a being superior to himself, and unbelief generating existential envy of faith, something infinitely more valuable than itself, and its envy of everything related to belief.

Hatred as a Form of Attachment and the Trap of Hatred

The most important characteristic of intense hatred is an intense desire to maintain a bond with the object of hate. People who have undergone trauma and have not effectively resolved it become obsessed with the people who have violated them. They feel intense hatred for the one who subjected them to the traumatic experience, but at the same time become obsessed with them and try to prolong their attachment through hatred. Attachment to the enemy or oppressor gives birth to the universal belief that the only way not to be a victim is to become a tyrant. It is because of this attachment that people who have not effectively resolved their traumatic experiences may become the cruelest of people, if the opportunity arises. Paulo Freire underlined the danger of the oppressed internalizing their oppressors when he said: "The oppressed are at one and the same time themselves and the oppressor, whose consciousness they have internalized."[49]

This psychodynamic is also applicable in the case of the unbelievers' hatred toward the believers, even when they pose no concrete threat or danger. Hatred is the emotion felt for "something loved and needed from which love is expected but the frustration of such hope is evitable."[50] Such hatred corresponds exactly to Nursi's explanation of the unbelievers' resentment toward the Creator, and their enmity toward Him and rejection of Him, namely, "the deep wounds caused by eternal separation from an Absolute Beauty that he loves and whose value he appreciates."[51]

> An admirer condemned to irreversible separation will find his love turning to enmity once he conceives of separation. His admiration will yield to ridicule, his respect to contempt. For just as obstinate man is an enemy to what is unknown to him, so too he is opposed to all that lies beyond his reach, and love that is not infinite will respond to a beauty that deserves unending admiration with implicit enmity, hatred and rejection. From this we understand the profound reason for the unbeliever's enmity to God.

The anger felt toward the Creator by Satan and people who have become embroiled in unbelief, his playthings, arises from their need for the Creator and their need to be loved by Him on the one hand, and their narcissistic attitude on the other, which causes them to choose to live, not according to how He wants but according to their own desires and whims. They have been expelled from His mercy, yet they are in absolute need of it. But their desire to attain to this mercy in their own way—and not in that prescribed by the Creator—and their being deprived of it, leads to their feeling anger, resentment and extreme hatred toward the Creator, and those who believe in Him and want to live according to His wishes, and to any symbols that remind them of Him.

> Since the misguidance of those unfortunates arises from love of this world and obstinacy, they do not keep to themselves but transgress against others. Prompted by what they know, they harbor the hostile desire to dry up the sources of the religion to which their forefathers were dedicated, and to destroy its bases, and to block up the doors and paths leading to it.[52]

Nursi summarizes succinctly as follows what lies at the base of the anger felt by the people of misguidance: (1) Love of worldly life: Attachment to this world and disregard of the Creator gives rise to a feeling of offense. On the one hand, the person is so attached to the world he feels great passion for it, and, on the other, it is continuously parting from him and he will one day depart from it. The inability to solve this dilemma results in the person feeling disgust at existence being thus. On the other hand, (2) the person is obstinate and refractory, that is, he is narcissistic and persists in it despite his knowing that before his Maker he is absolutely powerless and insignificant. The unbelievers also assume this narcissistic attitude in the face of the believers. The latter's existence in this world unsettles the people of disbelief, and this makes them aggressive toward the believers.

If we pursue this second element, obstinacy, further, we see that the innate absolute powerlessness of the unbelievers prevents their acquiring the power they want and obtaining the things they desire. This wounds their narcissistic natures. "Since man and jinn are capable of infinite evil and exertion, they are infinitely obdurate and rebellious."[53] The Quran challenges this obstinacy and tyranny in the following manner: "O you assembly of jinn and men! If you can pass beyond the zones of the heavens and the earth, pass! Not without authority will you be able to pass."[54] Nobody can pass beyond the boundaries of the Almighty's dominions. Just as man cannot go beyond the universe spatially, so he cannot put himself outside the conditions determined by the Creator.

For example, no one can live without water or without breathing. Man's being condemned to abide within the conditions determined by the Creator awakens in him the feeling of powerlessness. This challenge causes severe narcissistic pain to Satan and the people of unbelief, since their egos are narcissistic. This situation overlaps with another side of hatred, which is that "more than anything, hatred is directed towards things that obstruct the hater."[55]

Nursi indicated clearly the unbelievers' state of mind when he said:

> Because their misguidance arises from science and philosophy, it has induced in them an extraordinary arrogance and made them as egotistical as the Pharaoh. It has inflated their souls to such an extent that they want to discover defects in the rays of the divine laws that govern the universe and in the principles of those truths in the human world, since they imagine they are opposed to their base desires and appetites.[56]

While this helpless state is felt by the believers and is accepted by them, it is rejected by Satan and the people of disbelief and rebelled against. This is why they are caught between experiencing absolute need for the Creator and the desire to be given importance by Him on the one hand, and rebelling against Him on the other. Their inability to escape His dominion is another source of anger and hatred for them.

Faith makes a person into the friend of both himself and the universe. "In the view of a believer, all beings are the friendly servants, amicable officials, and agreeable books of his Most Generous Lord and All-Compassionate Owner."[57] It is to be expected that the people of faith possess an inner richness. This makes them contented. Instead of envy, they are filled with gratitude. By definition, the people of belief are not expected to be aggressive. However, even if a believer is not himself aggressive, he may have to face up to suffering aggression at the hands of unbelievers, and be confronted with the problem of effectively resolving the trauma he experiences. The Quran encourages believers who are subject to "*laghw*," that is, flippancy, to respond with "*karam*" or generosity.[58] That is, it encourages them to rebuff those insulting them in the best manner possible.[59] If this doesn't work, they should part from them in the best way.[60] However, if the enemy persists in his aggression and threatens the believer's life, he should have recourse to *jihād* as it is commonly understood.[61]

If the people of belief do not respond suitably to the disbelievers' aggression and skip the step of "responding generously" or "parting from them in the best way possible," as indicated by Karabaşoğlu, they may well resort in the first instance to physical *jihād* rather than as a final solution, and deviate into perpetrating tyranny and injustice. If the people of faith do not reach an understanding that links the calamities they suffer at the hands of unbelievers to their Creator—in other words, if they do not resolve their traumatic experiences—

they risk becoming fixated on their traumas and fighting the weakness their trauma causes them, and responding to hatred with hatred. This may cause them to fall into the trap of hatred. For "the trap of hatred consists of becoming firmly attached to one's enemy."[62] The novelist Hermann Hesse was of the same opinion: "When we hate a person, we actually hate his image, which we have internalized. Something that is not within us cannot make us angry."[63] Hatred should not be the way the people of belief deal with the aggression and traumatic experiences they suffer at the hands of people of disbelief. For the hatred that arises due to the ineffective resolution of these traumas will at the same time bind the believers to the disbelievers. This is hatred's worst trap. In my opinion, some believers today resort to violence because they have been unable to come to terms with the oppression, injustice, and violence they have suffered, and have therefore internalized hatred—a characteristic of the disbelievers—and have responded to hatred with hatred and fallen into the trap of hatred. Nursi was someone who suffered similar oppression, so the solution he arrived at and the way he resolved his traumatic experiences and the meaning he gave them can provide us with a model.

PROTECTION AGAINST THE DESTRUCTIVE HATRED AND ENVY OF UNBELIEF TOWARD FAITH: THE SAID NURSI MODEL

There are two clear characteristics of Nursi's behavioral patterns:

1. Nursi rejected violence.
2. Nursi was an activist.

Nursi as a Person Who Confronted Violence with Helplessness

The traumas and calamities a person experiences in life are in a way ontological traumas. The person feels that his sense of existing as a living being with integrity and particular needs, that is, with rights, has been wounded.

Every ontological blow awakens in the person a feeling of helplessness. This helplessness is also an ontological posture. The question of to what his weakness and helplessness should be ascribed determines the trauma's effects. The trauma has to be resolved in relation to this helplessness.

There are two ways people generally respond to helplessness: (1) by rejecting it; (2) by accepting it. If the state and feeling of helplessness is perceived by the person as a weakness, or especially as a defect, he will attempt to reject it.

However, if the person looks on his helplessness as part of the human condition and as an ontological requirement of humanity, he will be able to face up to it. He will see his weakness and helplessness in the universe, and if he accepts that he is limited because of his helplessness, he will overcome the feelings of insignificance and unimportance, and rid himself of primal and destructive hatred. A reverse situation awakens feelings of hatred and destructiveness: as I tried to explain in the section entitled "Hatred as a form of attachment and the trap of hatred," by rejecting human ontological helplessness and powerlessness, absolute unbelief causes people to be overwhelmed by hatred. They especially feel hatred toward the Absolute Being, whom they try to reject yet feel an absolute need for.

In my opinion, Nursi's most prominent quality in this respect was his responding to his traumatic experiences (exile, imprisonment, surveillance, searches, and court cases) with his feelings of ontological helplessness. He used his traumatic experiences and the resultant feelings of helplessness, insignificance, and powerlessness as means of forming stronger bonds and relations with his Creator. If a person does not come to terms, through the Creator, with the helplessness he feels as a result of traumas, he will try to eliminate such feelings by trying to gain control and domination and by acquiring power. Every institution and person that takes this path inflicts violence on people and their progress. It is my view that Nursi's acceptance of his ontological helplessness lies at the base of his nonviolence.

In stating: "The concealed aggression of the irreligious has taken on a most ugly form," Nursi was emphasizing that the treatment he had suffered was "tyrannical aggression against the unfortunate people of belief and against religion."[64] The passage, from "Six Questions," begins with the verse: "No reason have we why we should not put our trust in Allah. Indeed He has guided us to the ways we follow. We shall certainly bear with patience all the hurt you may cause us. For those who put their trust should put their trust in Allah";[65] and finishes with the verse "Men said to them: 'A great army is gathering against you'; and frightened them; but it only increased their faith, they said: "For us God suffices, and He is the Best Disposer of Affairs.'"[66] He confided in his Creator the helplessness he felt due to the trauma, and took comfort in the existence of an Absolute Being. He escaped the trap of hatred because he did not attempt to eliminate his ontological helplessness and powerlessness by becoming powerful and dominant. When he said: "Another time when my life was being shaken by severe conditions," he focused not on the hardships and distress he suffered but on the aspect of his experiences that looked to the Ever-Living and Subsistent One. He said: "If one aspect of life looks to me, a hundred aspects look to the Ever-Living Bestower of Life. If one of its results concern me, a thousand pertain to my Creator."[67] He thus ascribed every stage of his life to Him and did not become obsessed with the calamities he faced.

He was asked: "How do you endure the difficulties and troubles with which you are faced?"[68] When a person spoke "insulting and contemptuous words" about him, he was not distressed since he directed the words at his person and soul, so they motivated him to train his soul and he forgave the man. He added, however: "If the man's insults were directed towards my belief and my attribute of being servant of the Quran, it does not concern me. I refer him to the Quran's Owner, Who employs me. He is Mighty, He is Wise." He concludes by divulging that he consulted the verse: "Soon will you remember what I say to you (now); my (own) affair I commit to Allah. For Allah (ever) watches over His servants."[69] In fact, by saying: "I thought of the incident as not having happened. But unfortunately it was later understood that the Quran had not forgiven him," he expressed his sadness at the person concerned suffering some misfortune. In this respect, Nursi is like the character in the parable in the Sura Ya. Sin., who according to some narrations is Habib Najjar of Antioch, who followed the messengers. Even at the moment he was being slain by his own people, he exclaimed: "If only my people had understood!"[70] He also resembled Abel, who said when set upon by his brother Cain: "If you stretch out your hand against me to slay me, it is not for me to stretch my hand against you to slay you, for I fear Allah the Cherisher of the Worlds."[71]

Joel Kovel claims that nonviolence is possible on acceptance of experiencing pain.[72] A person who adopts nonviolence concedes that he will suffer pain and he accepts the responsibility and tries to atone for it. Any act purified of violence is at the same time an act directed toward the sacred. Nursi said: "My life is a dominical missive,"[73] and with a sense of being a means to the manifestation of His names in all existential conditions, he made his helplessness the most effective vehicle of achieving this. For Nursi, everything that serves Him is acceptable and should be employed. The helplessness he was made to feel by his inability to do anything in the face of all the distress inflicted on him is meaningful here: it assisted in defining the limits imposed on man in the universe, and in understanding his existential position.

Nonviolence is not passivity or pacifism, nor does it lead to the elimination of life. Said Nursi was an activist who did not resort to violence; in other words, he was a nonviolent activist. He said: "If I join the opposition through the use of force or by provoking an incident, I might commit thousands of sins in order to reach a doubtful goal. Many people would be afflicted by disaster due to one person. [I]n conscience I could not sin and cause the innocent to sin due to a one or two chance in ten."[74] He avoided violence-based activism. His saying "I have bound everything to reliance on God"[75] indicates his reliance was not passivity in the face of the aggression he suffered, but a way of resolving his traumatic experiences. I will now focus on this aspect of his activism.

Said Nursi as Activist: Ontological Activism and the Risale-i Nur *as a Form of Activism*

Nursi's primary activism was a type of activism I call "ontological activism." Every aspect of existence is an act. As I attempted to explain earlier, when he was subject to aggression and when he felt helpless in other situations, he assumed the stance of being "a mirror to the power, strength, wealth, and mercy of the Creator of Life." This "ontological activism" of Nursi determined the form all his other activism took.

After "ontological activism," Nursi's most important act was the *Risale-i Nur*. He described it as "the result of my life, means of my happiness, and my natural duty,"[76] and related it to his own existence, making it a sort of act on which every part of his life was focused. He pointed out the link between his activism and service of the Quran with the words:

> Despite my faults, I have dedicated my life to this nation's happiness and to saving its religious belief. Saying, 'let my head too be sacrificed for a truth, that is, the truth of the Quran, for which millions of heroic heads have been sacrificed!' I worked with the *Risale-i Nur*. Through Divine assistance, I persisted in the face of all the cruel torments. I did not retreat.[77]

The service of religious belief that Nursi concentrated on without breaking its connection with his "ontological activism" freed him from mental preoccupation with the aggression of others and from internalizing it unconsciously, and from the addictive effects of internalizing the aggressors. Saying: "Since in their madness they do not condescend to show interest in our lofty affairs, why out of curiosity should we pursue their trivial matters and harm our sacred duty?," he avoided becoming mentally preoccupied with anything opposed to his ontological activism. Seeking refuge in the verse: "If you follow right guidance no hurt can come to you from those who stray,"[78] he declared: "We should spend all of our strength, curiosity, and time on this sacred service. We must realize that everything outside it is futile and not waste our time."[79] And saying: "I take no notice of the wrongs and tyranny perpetrated against my person and give them no importance. I say 'they are not worth worrying about' and I do not interfere in the world,"[80] he set out the guidelines for a plan of action that he followed in his life.

Nursi kept one of the most important features of the *Risale-i Nur*—compassion—in balance, and displayed clearly his attitude toward all that had been inflicted on him: "We may not be aggressive. If others are aggressive towards us, we respond with light. Our position is one of luminous defense."[81] He emphasized the fact that what had been done to him would not go unrecompensed by his Creator.

In this regard, Nursi's most significant acts were his not responding with hatred to those who ill treated him, and his not falling into the trap of hatred; his avoiding having a hate-obsessed mentality, which is particular to the people of disbelief and is unfitting for the believers; his not participating in the unbelievers' world; his avoiding such wrongs as oppression, injustice, violence, and repression, to which the misguided were addicted and into which they wished to draw him; and his turning to the afterlife and expending all his efforts for the truths of the Quran.

NOTES

1. Zygmunt Bauman, *Parçalanmış Hayat: Postmodern Ahlak Denemeleri* [Life in Fragments: Essays in Postmodern Morality] (Istanbul, 2001), 252.
2. Theodore Zeldin, *An Intimate History of Humanity* (New York, 1998), 213.
3. Zeldin, *An Intimate History of Humanity*, 213.
4. Bediuzzaman Said Nursi, *The Words* (Istanbul, 1998), 652.
5. Joel Kovel, *Tarih ve Tin. Özgürleşme Felsefesi Üzerine Bir İnceleme* [History and Spirit. An Inquiry into Philosophy of Liberation (Istanbul, 1994),165.
6. Nursi, *The Words*, 739.
7. Bediuzzaman Said Nursi, *The Rays Collection* (Istanbul, 1998), 106.
8. Arno Gruen, *Normalliğin Deliliği, Hastalık Olarak Gerçekçilik: İnsandaki Yıkıcılık Üzerine Bir Kuram* [Der Wahnsinn der Normalitat: Realismus als Krankheit: eine Theorie der menschlichen Destructivitat] (Istanbul, 2003), 8.
9. Quran, 33:72: "but man undertook it he was indeed unjust and foolish."
10. Gruen, *Normalliğin Deliliği*, 5.
11. Gruen, *Normalliğin Deliliği*, 8.
12. Nursi, *Rays*, 328.
13. Bediuzzaman Said Nursi, *Sünuhat* (Istanbul: Envar Neşriyat), 23.
14. Zeldin, *An Intimate History of Humanity*, 211.
15. Nursi, *The Words*, 552.
16. Bediuzzaman Said Nursi, *Münazarat*, 95.
17. Nursi, *Rays*, 529.
18. Nursi, *Rays*, 529.
19. Nursi, *Rays*, 529.

20. Nursi, *The Words*, 194.
21. Nursi, *The Words*, 195.
22. Mehmet Yolcu, *Kur'an'da İnkar Psikolojisi* [Psychology of Unbelief in Quran] (Istanbul, 1999), 225.
23. Nursi, *Rays*, 552.
24. Bediuzzaman Said Nursi, *Mesnevi-i Nuriye*, 81.
25. Nursi, *Flashes*, 114.
26. Bediuzzaman Said Nursi, *Letters 1928–1932* (Istanbul, 1997), 371.
27. Bediuzzaman Said Nursi, *İşaratü'l-İ'caz*, 164.
28. Bediuzzaman Said Nursi, *Barla Lahikası*, 273.
29. Otto Kernberg, Aggression in Personality Disorders and Perversions (Yale, 1992), 23.
30. Melanie Klein, *Haset ve Şükran* [Envy and Gratitude] (Istanbul, 1998), 23.
31. Melanie Klein, *Haset ve Şükran*, 33.
32. Otto Kernberg, *Aggression in Personality Disorders and Perversions*, 25.
33. Max Scheler, *Hınç* [Das Ressentiment im Aufbau der Moralen] (Istanbul, 1998), 13.
34. Quran, 17:41; 17:46; 25:60; 35:42; 67:21.
35. Nursi, *The Words*, 329.
36. Nursi, *Mesnevi-i Nuriye*, 90.
37. Ibid., 69.
38. Ibid., 69.
39. Quran, 3:118: "O you who have attained to faith! Do not take for your bosom-friends people who are not of your kind. They spare no effort to corrupt you; they would love to see you in distress. Vehement hatred has already come into the open from out of their mouths, but what their hearts conceal is yet worse. We have indeed made the signs [thereof] clear unto you, if you would but use your reason."

    Quran, 3:119: "Lo! It is you who [are prepared to] love them, but they will not love you, although you believe in all of the revelation. And when they meet you, they assert, 'We believe [as you believe];' but when they find themselves alone, they gnaw their fingers in rage against you. Say: 'Perish in your rage!' Behold, God has full knowledge of what is in the hearts [of men]!"

    Quran, 3:120: "If good fortune comes to you, it grieves them; and if evil befalls you, they rejoice in it. But if you are patient in adversity and conscious of God, their guile cannot harm you at all: for, verily, God encompasses [with His might] all that they do."
40. Nursi, *Mesnevi-i Nuriye*, 89.
41. Ibid., 89.
42. Nursi, *The Words*, 320.
43. Mustafa Ulusoy, *Aynalar Koridorunda Aşk* [Love in the Mirrors Hall] (Istanbul, 2004), 188.
44. Quran, 4:118–19.
45. Mustafa Ulusoy, *Ay Terapisi* [Moon Therapy] (Istanbul, 2005), 79.
46. Quran, 4:118: "Allah cursed him."
47. Quran, 2:109: "Out of their selfish envy, many among the followers of earlier revelation would like to bring you back to denying the truth after you have attained to faith—[even] after the truth has become clear unto them. None the less, forgive and

forbear, until God shall make manifest His will: behold, God has the power to will anything."

48. Max Scheler, *Hınç*, 13.
49. Paulo Freire, *Ezilenlerin Pedagojisi* [Pedagogia do oprimido] (Istanbul, 2003), 26.
50. Kernberg, *Aggression in Personality Disorders and Perversions*, 213.
51. Nursi, *Flashes*, 459.
52. Bediuzzaman Said Nursi, *Şualar*, 724.
53. Nursi, *The Words*, 195.
54. Quran, 55:33.
55. Kernberg, *Aggression in Personality Disorders and Perversions*, 213.
56. Nursi, *Şualar*, 724.
57. Nursi, *The Words*, 28.
58. Quran, 25:72.
59. Ibid., 41:34.
60. Ibid., 73:10.
61. Metin Karabaşoğlu, *Hadis Okumaları* (Istanbul, 2004), 37.
62. Milan Kundera, *Ölümsüzlük* (Istanbul, 2001), 33.
63. Hermann Hesse, *Demian* (Istanbul, 2002), 117.
64. Nursi, *Letters*, 502.
65. Quran, 14:12.
66. Ibid., 3:173.
67. Nursi, *Rays*, 80.
68. Nursi, *Letters*, 86.
69. Quran, 40:44.
70. Metin Karabaşoğlu, *Kur'an Okumaları: birinci kitap* (Istanbul, 2003), 86.
71. Quran, 5:28; Cevdet Said, *Adem'in Oğlu Habil Gibi Ol: Yeni Bir Kimliğin İnşası* (Istanbul, 2001), 94.
72. Joel Kovel, *Tarih ve Tin. Özgürleşme Felsefesi Üzerine Bir İnceleme* [History and Spirit. An Inquiry into Philosophy of Liberation] (Istanbul, 1994),180.
73. Nursi, *Rays*, 81.
74. Nursi, *Letters*, 84.
75. Ibid., *Letters*, 83.
76. Nursi, *Rays*, 73.
77. Ibid., 443.
78. Quran, 5:105.
79. Bediüzzaman Said Nursi, *Emirdağ Lahikası*, i, 44.
80. Nursi, *Letters*, 94.
81. Nursi, *Emirdağ Lahikası*, 44.

ELEVEN

TAKING FAITH TO HEART

Reconciliation and Peacebuilding in Islam

Asma Afsaruddin

Islam, like Judaism, is often characterized as a highly legalistic religion with an undue emphasis (in reference to Christianity in particular) on "orthopraxy," that is, on the correct performance of religiously incumbent acts of worship and punctilious observance of other duties prescribed by the religious law (Shari'ah). Such a perception arises largely from the fact that the outsider, for example, sees the devout Muslim mechanically bowing or prostrating in his daily prayers but cannot look into the worshiper's heart and read her silent communion with the Creator. Casual perceptions of this sort can be misleading as can be the casual inferences that they spawn: Muslims, some thereby assume, are not as much concerned with the cultivation of their inner spiritual lives and/or in practicing certain ethical and moral values, particularly forgiveness and love for one another, as they are with the physical performance of their religious obligations. Those who are of the spiritual bent, the casual observer might maintain, are the mystically inclined Sufis, who engage in supererogatory actions that are beyond the norm for the average Muslim.

A crosssection of Muslims might even agree with some of these assumptions, averring that a formal, literal adherence to prescribed religious duties is mainly what is required of the believer. Such Muslims may be regarded, with considerable justification, of reading their own scripture atomistically and doing a disservice to their religious tradition by downplaying the Quran's emphasis on the cultivation of one's inner life and establishing a personal relationship with the Almighty. The Quran asserts, as discussed below, that out of this close, loving relationship with God flows forgiveness and reconciliation among believers. A survey of some of the most important Quran commentaries from the premodern to modern periods establishes that these religious and ethical traits have always been recognized as important by Muslims. They have not, however, been adequately forefronted as ethical and social concepts to be deployed as a means to curb aggression and effect reconciliation among individuals and groups of people. Our discussion focuses on the most important Quranic verses to deal with this issue and analyzes some of their best-known exegeses through time. It will conclude with a brief assessment of the relevance of these verses to our conflict-ridden times as a foundation for the development of an Islamic peacebuilding model at the interpersonal and societal levels.

The Heart of Islam

One of the best known verses in the Quran with enormous implications for individual transformation and growth and ultimately social reform is from chapter 13, verse 11: "Indeed, God does not change people's circumstances unless they change what is in themselves." According to this verse, change is to be effected first internally in the individual before any meaningful external change can take root. From the Quranic perspective, the most important site for bringing about genuine individual change followed by social change is thus clearly the human heart—not to be understood of course merely as a physical organ but as the basic cognitive and emotive center of the human system.

An important consequence of the transformation of the human heart to make it receptive to God's will is the cultivation of fraternal bonds among fellow believers and genuine reconciliation between erstwhile enemies. The centrality of harmonious relationships and the importance of maintaining concord among believers is asserted in Quran 49:10: "Indeed the believers are brothers. Make peace among your brothers and fear God, so that you may be shown mercy." An incipient methodology of effecting reconciliation is contained in two significant Quranic verses 3:103 and 8:63, which refer to "the joining (or reconciliation) of hearts," a process known in Arabic as "*ta'līf al-qulūb*." Through the centuries, Muslim scholars and theologians have taken note of these crucial verses and focused on their conciliatory implications, both in their particular sociohistorical contexts and in their general applicability. This chapter will now proceed to selectively delineate exegeses of the two verses 3:103 and 8:63 by some of the most important Quran commentators from the medieval and modern periods in order to focus on the meanings of *ta'līf al-qulūb* and their implications for developing a methodology of faith-based reconciliation.

Exegeses of Quran 3:103

Hold fast, one and all, to the "rope of God" and let nothing divide you.
Remember the grace of God towards you, when you were enemies
He joined your hearts and you became through His grace brothers.

Al-Tabari's Exegesis

The famous medieval exegete Muhammad Jarir al-Tabari (d. 310/923) understands the "rope of God" to be the equivalent of "the religion of God which He has commanded you to follow," and as a consequence of which, believers are vouchsafed "cordiality [among them], unity based upon the word of Truth, and submission to God's commandment."[1] He understands the exhortation "Remember the grace of God" to mean "remember the blessing that He conferred on you of friendship and of being gathered together in Islam.[2] "Remember!" he explains, "O believers, the bounty of God towards you when you were enemies while polytheists. You killed one another out of tribal partisanship in disobedience to God and His messenger. Then God joined your hearts in Islam (submission [to God]) and made you the brothers of one another after you were enemies and you continue in the bonds of friendship in submission to God."[3]

Al-Tabari then cites two reports related by the Prophet's Companions in explication of this verse. The first one goes back to Qatada [b. Di'ama] who stated that the verse meant, "You used to slaughter one another in it (sc. in the pre-Islamic period, called in Arabic *Jāhiliyya*) and the strong used to prey on the weak until God brought forth Islam and made of you brothers and joined you together (or reconciled you). By God, and there is no god but He; indeed friendship is mercy and divisiveness is a punishment." The second variant report from Rabi' (b. Ka'b) states in explication, "You used to kill one another, with the strong among you preying upon the weak until God brought forth Islam and joined you together by it, assembled you together, and made of you brothers by means of it." These two reports, therefore, expound on the intrinsic benefit of the remembrance of God and making oneself receptive to submission to His will for believers in general.[4]

Al-Tabari provides further occasions of revelation that particularize the meaning of this verse to the specific situation of two key Medinan tribes before and after the advent of Islam. He comments that "the enmity" referred to in this verse refers to the enmity incurred during the wars waged between the two Medinan tribes of al-Aws and al-Khazraj before Islam. As the pre-Islamic *Ayyām al-'Arab* ("the Battle-Days of the Arabs") literature informs us, these wars had lasted for about 120 years. Al-Tabari refers to Ibn Ishaq (d. 767), the famous biographer of the Prophet, who recalled that these wars took place between al-Aws and al-Khazraj "even though they were full brothers." The intensity of their enmity was unprecedented, according to Ibn Ishaq, and "then God Almighty extinguished that (sc. their enmity) through Islam and brought them together through His messenger, Muhammad, peace and blessings be upon him." Through this verse, al-Tabari affirms, God was reminding the Ansars (the Medinan Muslims) of the misery and wretchedness that had afflicted them on account of their mutual hostility, their slaying and fear of one another. The verse is a further reminder of how submission to God and the guidance of the Prophet finally led to reconciliation and security and facilitated the development of the bonds of friendship and brotherhood between them.[5]

Al-Tabari concludes this section by commenting on the last part of the verse ("and thus you became brothers by His grace"). This means, he remarks,

> Because God, exalted is He, joined your hearts by means of Islam and the word of Truth. Through cooperation in aiding the people of faith and rallying against unbelievers who opposed you, so that there remained no malice and no enmity between you—you became sincere, truthful brothers.[6]

Al-Qurtubi's Exegesis

Like al-Tabari, the thirteenth-century Andalusian exegete al-Qurtubi (d.1273) understands the "rope of God" mentioned at the beginning of the verse to refer to the Quran on the basis of two hadiths narrated by Ibn Mas'ud, a well-known Companion of the Prophet. A third hadith, also narrated by Ibn Mas'ud, glosses the phrase as referring to "communal life" (Ar. *al-jamā'a*). Al-Qurtubi remarks that the meanings are intertwined and related, for God has enjoined sociability and forbidden separation from the community, for "separation is [equivalent to] destruction and communal affiliation is [equivalent to] salvation."[7]

The prohibition "do not become disunited" warns against the divisiveness that afflicted other religious communities in the practice of their religion and exhorts believers to remain brothers in "the religion of God" by not blindly following every whim and fancy. Al-Qurtubi goes on to clarify, however, that the verse does not rule out differences with regard to secondary matters of religion (Ar. *al-furū'*). If such differences do not lead to dissension and arise in the course of extrapolating legal rulings from and explicating the religious law, then they are not harmful in themselves. The Companions of the Prophet often differed with one another in the derivation of legal rulings in new circumstances, but despite that, remained amicable toward one another. Al-Qurtubi cites the well-known hadith: "The difference of my community is a mercy." The kind of difference God forbids is the kind that leads to corruption and sectarianism.[8]

The rest of the verse, al-Qurtubi continues, enjoins the believer to remember God's bounties, "the greatest of which is submission to God (Islam) and following Muhammad, upon whom be peace. It is thereby that enmity and dissension are dissolved and there is [instead] love and affection." The direct referents in this verse are the Aws and Khazraj, although the verse also has a general meaning. It is through God's blessings that the two former hostile tribes became brothers in religion.[9]

Ibn Kathir's Exegesis

In his commentary on 3:103, the popular fourteenth-century exegete Ibn Kathir (d. 1352) understands *habl Allah* as referring to God's covenant (*'ahd Allah*) and His protection (*dhimma*). According to a report from al-Harith al-A'war, this phrase refers to the Quran. The command "Do not become separated" is understood to specifically enjoin communal life and forbid withdrawal from society.[10]

The rest of the verse, according to Ibn Kathir, points to the Aws and Khazraj who were prone to much fighting in the Jahiliyya and, on account of their bitter enmity, harbored malignant hatred toward one another. All that was to change, however, "when God brought forth Islam, and those who entered it, entered it and became brothers, loving one another through the majesty of God, cooperating with one another in a spirit of piety and God-consciousness. Their disbelief in God, reflected in their constant feuding and fractiousness, had brought them to the edge of the Fire, from which they were delivered when God guided them to faith."[11] Ibn Kathir cross-references here Quran 8:63 (a discussion follows).

Ibn Kathir further points to the danger inherent in relaxing one's guard against potential fractiousness and thus allowing seditious elements to stir up enmity. He relates an anecdote in exegesis of Quran 3:103, according to which an individual of ill will, who was displeased to see the concord and amity reigning among the Aws and Khazraj tribes in Medina, dispatched one of his cohorts to sit among them and revive the memory of their prolonged wars during the Jahiliyya. The man did as he was told and, before long, he had succeeded in inflaming the passions of the Aws and Khazraj to the extent that they started chanting their battle slogans from the pre-Islamic period and reaching for their weapons. News of this reached the Prophet and he hurriedly approached them and began to calm them down. He asked, "Are you harking back to the pre-Islamic period while I am among you?" Then he recited to them Quran 3:103, at which they were filled with remorse. They began to make up with one another, and embraced one another after having cast away their weapons.[12]

This report powerfully demonstrates the recuperative power of the remembrance of God and His limitless grace toward humans, which effaces the memory of past wrongs and allows for reconciliation. But, it also warns, such memories can be resurrected by those malignantly inclined to sow dissension. The constant invocation of God in gratitude for His immeasurable benevolence toward humankind is, however, a potent shield against the incitements of troublemakers and helps preserve the unity of believers.

Muhammad 'Abduh's Exegesis

The nineteenth-century Muslim reformist and scholar Muhammad 'Abduh (d. 1905) also understands this verse to refer to the Aws and Khazraj tribes of Medina and their reconciliation in Islam after their bitter past of chronic hostility. He also sees this verse as containing a strong denunciation of the tribalism of the pre-Islamic period, termed in Arabic *al-'asabiyya*. He marshals two *hadith*s as proof-texts to further clarify his position. The first is recorded by al-Bukhari (d. 870) on the authority of Ibn 'Abbas, in which the Prophet states, "The most reprehensible of people before God are three: one who is a disbeliever in advanced age; one who wishes to resort to the customs of the Jahiliyya in Islam; and one who seeks to shed the blood of a Muslim without any rightful cause." In another hadith recorded by Abu Da'ud, the Prophet declares, "One who invokes tribalism is not one of us."[13]

'Abduh sees this pre-Islamic tribalism resurgent in his own time (the late nineteenth century) in the nationalisms of Europeans, which, he regretfully observes, is also in the process of being adopted by Westernized Muslims. The latter, he states, seeks to impose the idea of nationalism by attempting to delude others into thinking that this is the way to achieve national glory. 'Abduh regards this, however, as a relapse into pre-Islamic tribalism and asserts that true advancement of the nation lies rather in uniting all its citizens through submission to God, which ensures the well-being and welfare of all people, regardless of their religion or ethnicity. This is what "holding fast to the rope of God," as occurs in the verse, means and it is thereby that fraternity in God is achieved. It is through "holding fast to God's rope" that one may successfully resist divisiveness and sectarianism that leads to the shedding of blood, as happened in the pre-Islamic past. He reminds us that, according to the reports that have come down to us, the wars between the Aws and Khazraj lasted 120 years until Islam put an end to them, and "God reconciled their hearts through His messenger, [upon him be] blessings and peace."[14]

EXEGESES OF QURAN 8:63

> And He has joined (or reconciled) their hearts. If you had spent all that is in the earth, you could not have joined their hearts, but God has united them. Indeed He is Almighty, All-Wise.

Al-Tabari's Exegesis

Al-Tabari comments that the phrase in this verse "He joins their hearts" refers to the reconciliation of the hearts of the believers among the Aws and the Khazraj "based on [acceptance] of His true religion" after the severe dissensions and fractiousness that had plagued them. He thereby led them to become united and caused them to become "brothers after having been enemies."[15]

Al-Tabari remarks further that this verse indicates that the establishment of true amity and genuine reconciliation can only be effected through one's sincere belief in God and the divine guidance that one subsequently may hope for. Addressing the Prophet in this verse, God reminds him, "Were you to spend, O Muhammad, all that is on earth of gold, money, and worldly goods, you would not be able to reconcile their hearts with all your strength, for it is God Who joins them in guidance."[16]

The early exegete Mujahid b. Jabr (d. 720) was of the opinion that the statement "Were you to spend all that is on earth you would not be able to reconcile their hearts" meant that when two Muslims met and shook hands, their sins are forgiven. A variant exegesis attributed to Mujahid offers further elucidation of this somewhat elliptical comment. According to this variant, a man named 'Abda b. Abi Lubaba related that he met Mujahid and the latter took his hand in his own and said, "If you should see two individuals who harbor love for God (*mutahabbin fi'llah*) and one of them takes the hand of the other and smiles at him, their sins drop off them just as the leaves drop from the tree." 'Abda told Mujahid, "But indeed that is easy." Mujahid remarked, "Do not say that, for indeed God has stated, 'Were you to spend all that is on earth you would not be able to reconcile their hearts'." He thus impressed 'Abda with his perspicacity.[17]

The two reports taken together convey Mujahid's conviction that sincere faith in God results in genuine bonds of friendship and goodwill among believers, expressed outwardly in gestures of friendship toward one another, such as in shaking hands and exchanging smiles. But simply going through such motions does not automatically create a sense of bonhomie, unless they are firmly embedded in faith and love for God—this latter being a much harder task, as pointed out by Mujahid—and can only be effected by God Himself. Once firmly implanted in one's heart, love for God translates into love for one's fellow beings.

Another report suggests that effusive expressions of affection are a natural consequence of the believer's love for God and, as a consequence, for His created beings. Fudayl b. Ghazwan related that he encountered Abu Ishaq and greeted him, upon which the latter asked, "Do you know me?" Fudayl replied, "Yes. And if it were not for my bashfulness before you, I would have kissed you."[18]

Feelings of harmony and love toward one's fellow human beings are fragile, however, and must be constantly nurtured against the onset of divisiveness. For as one report on the authority of 'Umayr b. Ishaq warns, "the first [thing] to be removed from among people is concord and affection (*ulfa*)."[19]

Al-Qurtubi's Exegesis

In his exegetical work, al-Qurtubi focuses more briefly, in comparison with al-Tabari, on this verse and sees it essentially as parallel to 3:102. Thus, 8:63 is also understood to refer specifically to the reconciliation between the two tribes of Aws and Khazraj after the advent of Islam. Al-Qurtubi further points to the rabid enmity that existed between Arab tribes in the Jahiliyya and comments that its dissipation in the Islamic period must be considered "one of the miracles of the Prophet, peace and blessings be upon him," in view of the fact that "they were the most prone to violence among God's creation." But then "God reconciled their hearts through faith," so that they would fight only to safeguard religion from its enemies. Al-Qurtubi refers to the alternate explanation that reconciliation in this verse refers more specifically to the bonds of friendship between the Meccan Emigrants and the Medinan Helpers and remarks that the meaning of this explanation is similar to the former.[20]

Ibn Kathir's Exegesis

Ibn Kathir, like al-Tabari and other exegetes, also emphasizes the role of faith in God in extinguishing the rabid enmity between Aws and Khazraj in the pre-Islamic period and replacing it with "your obedience, and your mutual help and support of one another." It was God Himself, "Almighty and Wise," who brought about this reconciliation for "He does not dash the hopes of those who rely on Him." Those whose hearts are reconciled are "those who love one another for the sake of God," as related by the Companion ʿAbd Allah Ibn Masʿud. Further, Ibn ʿAbbas is quoted as saying that "the bonds of blood-relationship may be severed and [God's] bounty may be rejected, but when God brings hearts together, nothing can sway them." Ibn ʿAbbas then proceeded to recite, "Were you to spend all that is on earth, you would not be able to reconcile their hearts."[21]

The rest of Ibn Kathir's exegesis of this verse largely resembles that of al-Tabari's.

Muhammad ʿAbduh's Exegesis

Muhammad ʿAbduh, in tandem with the medieval exegetes, also understands the Medinan tribes of Aws and Khazraj to be the referents in this verse. But he also believes that 8:63 may be understood to refer more broadly to the Muhajirun (the Meccan Emigrants) and the Ansar (the Medinan Muslims) since "by God's grace, they became brothers[22] without mutual envy or hostility, as is otherwise often common in such situations."[23] He elaborates further on these two interpretive possibilities as follows.

"Were you to spend all that is on earth, you could not reconcile their hearts," means, Abduh explains, that it was only due to God's grace that the believers had become united in faith and in a brotherhood that was much stronger in regard to affection and depth of emotion than a brotherhood based on common descent and shared nationality. Given the duration of their internecine warfare and their deep-seated hostility, no amount of worldly goods or benefits could have eradicated such a grievous state of affairs. Only sincere faith—which engenders happiness in this world and the next—could have effaced such rancorous hostility.

ʿAbduh, as we mentioned before, understands this verse to also apply to the Meccan Muslims, who became brothers of the Medinan Muslims in faith, despite differences in social status and worldly rank. He underscores this dramatic transformation in the following way: "As for the Muhajirun, reconciliation (*ta'līf*) occurred among their rich and the poor, their masters and their clients, their nobility and their common people, in spite of the arrogance of the Jahiliyya that had previously existed among them." It was this concord among them that allowed them to endure the enmity of their fellow tribesmen and relatives for the sake of God. None of this could have been achieved by means of all the wealth and enticements of the world.[24]

'Abduh then goes on to point to the centrality of love in human relationships as asserted by wise people through the ages. They agree that "Love is the greatest of all bonds among humans and the most potent inducement to happiness is human social life and its refinement." They further concur that in the absence of love, nothing else can take its place in repelling evil, while the proper functioning of society is contingent on "the virtue of justice" (*faḍīlat al-'adl*). While love has been considered to be instinctual and not a matter of choice and justice regared as an act of deliberation (lit: "one of the acquired actions"; Ar. *min al-a'māl al-kasbiyya*), Islam made love a virtue and adherence to justice an obligatory duty. Justice in particular was the due of all who reside in the Islamic state, with no distinction between the Muslim and non-Muslim, pious and impious, rich and poor, and so on.[25]

In this important exegesis, 'Abduh goes further than his medieval predecessors and extends the concept of reconciliation based on love and justice to all human beings, regardless of their religious affiliation (or lack thereof). He argues that out of love for the Creator and adherence to justice the individual and the state must treat everyone even-handedly.

The Praxis of Reconciliation

The Quranic concept of *ta'līf al-qulūb* engendered the important sociolegal category of "those whose hearts are to be reconciled" (Ar. *mu'allafat al-qulūb*), referring to people whose friendship and alliance were to be nurtured and cultivated in a number of ways in the early period. This category of people included new converts to Islam and non-Muslims: Jews, Christians, and even "polytheists" (as they are termed in the literature), whose goodwill and friendship were deemed as contributing to the well-being of the community. As essential members of the polity, they were entitled to the charity (Ar. *zakāt;* also *ṣadaqa*) of Muslims and the revenues of the state.[26] The Prophet's administrative policy was thus deliberately inclusive of particularly "the People of the Book" of goodwill who wished to reside in Muslim lands, in reflection of the Quran's recognition of righteous Jews and Christians as constituting "a balanced community" (Ar. *umma muqtasida*) and "an upright community" (Ar. *umma qā'ima*).[27] His generosity also extended to the former staunch enemies of Islam, especially the nobility of the Quraysh, who were granted a general amnesty after the fall of Mecca in 630 C.E. and whose hearts were now to be reconciled to Islam. Such a policy of inclusiveness allowed Muslims to best represent the charitableness of their faith toward all who were needy and destitute, regardless of their religious orientation. "It is not righteousness," says the Quran (2:177), "that you turn your faces towards the East or West, but it is righteousness to believe in God and the Last Day, and the Angels, and the Book and the Messengers; to spend of your substance out of love for Him, for your kin, for orphans, for the needy, the wayfarer, for those who ask, and for the ransom of slaves." Charity toward all wedded to faith in and love for God constitutes true righteousness, according to this Quranic verse. No doubt, it also served for some as "the best of means" (Quran 29:46) for Muslims to invite others to learn about Islam and eventually enter its fold (as was the pious hope). But the moral imperative to practice charity toward all was not explicitly formulated in the Quran as a conversion strategy, although later extra-Quranic, particularly juridical, literature sometimes did.[28]

The Prophet's practice was continued by his early successors. According to early authorities, such as Abu Yusuf Ya'qub b. Ibrahim (d. 798), who have left us detailed accounts of early Islamic fiscal systems, the second caliph 'Umar b. al-Khattab (d. 644) recognized two categories of poor people who qualified for state support: the *fuqarā'* who were Muslims, and the *masākīn* who were the scriptuaries (Ar. *ahl al-kitāb*, literally People of the Book; besides Jews and Christians, this term also came to include Zoroastrians, Sabians, etc.) residing in Islamic realms. Both received provisions from the public treasury for their maintenance.[29] This was in accordance with the Quranic verse that states: "Verily the obligatory alms (*ṣadaqāt*)[30] are for the poor (*al-fuqarā'*), the destitute (*al-masākīn*), those who collect the alms/taxes, those whose hearts are to be reconciled, to ransom (slaves and prisoners of war), for those in debt, those who are engaged in the path of God, and for the wayfarer—a duty imposed by God; God is All-Knowing, All-Wise." According to this understanding of the verse, the non-Muslim poor would appear to be doubly advantaged in being both needy and belonging to the category of "those whose hearts are to be reconciled."

Adult, able-bodied male scriptuaries were normally required to pay a kind of poll tax called the *jizya* in return for state protection, military or otherwise, of their rights. Women, minors, the infirm, the old, the destitute, and religious personages, like monks, were normally exempt from its remittance. The infirm, the old, and the destitute among the scriptuaries instead received pensions from the state treasury as they were the equivalent of wards of the state, and their maintenance was consequently a basic, humane responsibility of the state.[31] Abu Yusuf relates how 'Umar, the second caliph, encountered an old, blind Jewish man begging for alms and brought him to his home out of pity. He offered the destitute man a modest sum of money (from his own funds) as alms and upon inquiry discovered that the latter had been paying taxes to the state. A shocked 'Umar proclaimed this to be an injustice and ordered the state treasury to immediately desist and instead treat him as one of the *masākīn* ("impoverished scriptuaries") entitled to state maintenance.[32] In this premodern system of state welfare, poor residents of Islamic lands, irrespective of religion, were thus entitled to a portion of the government's *zakat*-revenues. In the eleventh century, the Shafi'i jurist al-Mawardi (d. 1058) in his influential work, *The Governmental Ordinances*, continued to recognize the entitlement of "those whose hearts are to be reconciled," regardless of whether they were Muslim or "polytheist" (*mushrik*), to a portion of the taxes paid by Muslims to their state.[33]

This early inclusivist attitude toward non-Muslims and the special status of "those whose hearts are to be reconciled" were not always given due recognition in the later medieval period. This is reflected in the fact that most (but not all) of the later jurists would argue, in clear contradistinction to the *sunna* (practice) of the Prophet Muhammad, that Muslims should not give their obligatory alms (*zakat*) to needy non-Muslims (although voluntary alms could continue to be given). This position continues to be maintained by many jurists and jurisconsults until today.[34]

Bediuzzaman Said Nursi's (d. 1960) Thought

In his well-known work *Risale-i Nur*, Bediuzzaman Said Nursi in his *Twenty-Second Letter* deals with the issue of disunity and discord among believers and the virtue of inculcating among them feelings of fraternity and love. He states,

> Dispute and discord among the believers, and partisanship, obstinacy and envy, leading to rancor and enmity among them, are repugnant and vile, are harmful and sinful, by the combined testimony of wisdom and the supreme humanity that is Islam, for personal, social, and spiritual life. They are in short, poison for the life of man.[35]

Said Nursi underscores the centrality of reconciliation in the Quranic paradigm of harmonious coexistence on the basis of particularly Quran 49:10, 41:34, and 3:134, all of which stress the importance of maintaining concord and fraternal ties among believers. Verse 41:34, which states "Repel evil with what is better than it; then the one between whom and yourself enmity prevails will become like your friend," and 3:134, which states "Those who suppress their anger and forgive people—verily God loves those who do good" in particular counsel believers not to give in to the natural impulse to seek revenge for the infliction of some harm upon them, The suppression of one's possibly justifiable anger and subsequent forgiveness is a far superior course of action because it is selfless and strengthens the community of believers in unity rather than promoting divisiveness. In this commentary, Nursi echoes the opinions of the medieval exegete Ibn Kathir who remarked that according to verse 41:34, it is precisely the act of charitableness and kindness (*al-ihsan*) evident in repelling evil with good (i.e., by forsaking retaliation for some injury) that causes your adversary to seek reconciliation with you, to develop affection and sympathy for you, so much so that he or she now becomes transformed into "your intimate friend or your relative on account of [his or her] compassion for and charity towards you."[36]

In his detailed discussion of why rancor and enmity among believers are dangerous toxins, Bediuzzaman also emphasizes the heart as the locus for effecting sustained change in human relationships. He warns that the enmity within one's heart is far more detrimental to the spiritual and physical well-being of the believer than the enmity of an external enemy. He advises,

> If you wish to nourish enmity, then direct it against the enmity in your heart; attempt to rid yourself of it. Be an enemy to your evil-commanding soul and its caprice and attempt to reform it, for it inflicts more harm on you than all else. Do not engage in enmity against other believers on account of that injurious soul.[37]

The best way to defeat your enemy is in fact to "respond to his evil with good" as the Quran counsels. A quintessential trait of the sincere believer is nobility, both of intent and action. Treating your enemy with kindness and goodness is the nobler course of action, Nursi explains, and allows him or her the opportunity to repent and become a friend. Returning the hostility of one's enemy's causes him or her to persist in a state of enmity, for even if the enemy is outwardly defeated, hatred will continue to burn in his or her heart, and a true resolution of the hostility cannot be attained.[38]

Said Nursi also stresses, like the medieval exegetes before him, that when genuine love toward one's fellow human beings resides in one's heart, then "(t)he believer loves and should love his brother, and is pained by any evil he sees in him. He attempts to reform him not with harshness but with gentleness." How can that not be after all? The believers are united by a commonality of belief and purpose. "The unity of belief," Bediuzzaman declares, "necessitates also the unity of hearts, and the oneness of our creed demands the oneness of our society." Aggression toward a fellow believer is thus tantamount to transgressing against the entire community of the faithful that is built on a collectivity of fraternal bonds at the personal level.[39]

Like al-Qurtubi before him, Bediuzzaman endorses positive differences of opinion that seek not to destroy and dominate but to reform and improve the other. The first promotes partisanship that is extremely destructive of cordial social relationships while the latter promotes a healthy pluralism of ideas that are mutually reinforcing, wedded as they are to the pursuit of a common objective.[40] This common objective is to act for the sake of God and ward off the discord and anarchy associated with anti-God forces such as the Dajjal ("the anti-Christ") at the end of time. Nursi warns, "If one does not make the exalted rules, 'Love for the sake of God, dislike for the sake of God, judgment for the sake of God' the guiding principles of one's conduct, dissension and discord will result."[41]

Conclusion

The two principal Quranic verses under consideration and their exegeses by some of the most prominent Muslim commentators through time have much to tell us today about faith-based resolution of conflictual situations and harmonious coexistence with others. The verses locate the locus of both human love and animosity within the human heart—which of the two gets the upper hand within it is contingent on certain choices of the individual. The individual, on the one hand, may choose to believe in and submit to God, thereby cleansing his or her heart of resistance to His will and allowing one's heart to be flooded with love for Him and, consequently, for His creation. On the other, one can reject faith in God and harden one's heart against one's fellow human being and thus allow oneself to be swept away by worldly needs and desire for dominance. The two diametrically opposed states are exemplified by the Medinan tribes of Aws and Khazraj who were intractable enemies before the advent of Islam. But once faith entered their hearts through their submission to God, it was God Himself, as the exegetes, remind us, who transformed their inward state from one of animosity to fraternal love and reconciliation. The exegetes are thus alluding to the transformative power of selfless love unvitiated by ulterior motives other than the common pursuit and defense of a higher truth and reality.

In terms of generating social harmony, several reports relate that internal feelings of fraternal love need to be expressed in external gestures of bonhomie and affection toward one another, such as smiling, shaking hands, embracing, and kissing one another. For hearts to truly reconcile and strengthen social bonds, it is not enough, however, to simply go through these gestures of conciliation and rapprochement. If such gestures do not spring from a deep-seated conviction that one's fellow being must be loved for the sake of God, then they remain at the level of external social politesse and cannot effect social reform at the deepest, grassroots level. As the late seventh-century exegete Mujahid had counseled, transformation of one's heart as a prelude to genuine reconciliation is a much more difficult and challenging enterprise and requires that one be, above all, constantly receptive to God's guidance and His will. Reconciliation, once effected, requires constant vigilance and nurturing since, as 'Umayr b. Ishaq had warned, friendship and intimacy among people are susceptible to dissipation in adverse circumstances. This is further demonstrated in the example that the thirteenth-century exegete Ibn Kathir provides of the incitement of the Aws and Khazraj to the brink of violence because they allowed one skilled in the art of sedition to inflame their passions. It was the Prophet himself who intervened and reminded them of God's favor in creating bonds of fraternal love between them. This drew them back from the edge of violence and caused them to fling away their weapons and turn repentantly toward one another.

While medieval exegetes, understandably, focused on intra-Muslim reconciliation that would ensue from the implementation of the injunctions contained in these crucial verses, modern exegetes like Muhammad 'Abduh extend the exegetical purview of these verses to include believers of any faith and non-Muslims in general as the recipients of Muslim affection and fraternal sentiments. In a modernist vein, 'Abduh further comments that these verses with their emphasis on love for God, which creates in turn love for one's fellow beings, irrespective of their creedal affiliation, should be understood to guarantee non-Muslims full rights and privileges of citizenship in the modern Islamic polity.

'Abduh's views may be seen as a logical extension of the praxis of reconciliation that grew out of the Quranic commandment to extend charity and kindness to "those whose hearts are to be reconciled." As we have seen, the concept of "reconciliation of hearts" allowed non-Muslims to be included as members of the Islamic polity, whose well-being was a matter of concern to their Muslim administrators. Implementation of the principle of "reconciliation of hearts" as a social-legal-economic mandate created a premodern system of social welfare that at its best embraced all in their need, irrespective of religious affiliation, in the interest of generating intercommunal harmony and goodwill.

The Quranic concept of "the joining" or "reconciliation of hearts" (*ta'līf al-qulūb*), as expounded upon by exegetes from Mujahid to Said Nursi, is a particularly important one in the general context of quotidian human relationships and is potentially of special relevance today in the field of religious peacebuilding in our fractious world. It offers a preliminary methodology of effecting reconciliation among adversaries, rooted in love for God that translates (or should translate) into affection and respect for all God's created beings. Contemporary Muslims may use this concept as a useful springboard for developing more detailed procedures for constructive peacebuilding within their own faith communities as well as with other religious communities, both interpersonally and intersocietally, thereby taking to heart their faith and more effectively implementing its moral imperatives in contemporary settings.

Notes

1. Al-Tabari, *Jāmi' al-bayān fi tafsīr al-Qur'ān* ("The Compendium of Eloquence in Exegesis of the Qur'an") (Beirut, 1997), 3:378.
2. Ibid., 3:380.
3. Ibid.
4. Ibid., 380–81.
5. Ibid., 7:78.
6. Ibid., 7:84.
7. Al-Qurtubi, *Al-Jāmi' li-aḥkām al-Qur'ān* (("The Compendium of the Ordinances of the Qur'an") (Cairo, n.d.), 2:1401.
8. Ibid., 2:1402 ff.
9. Ibid.
10. Ibn Kathir, *Tafsīr al-Qur'ān al-'aẓīm* ("Exegesis of the Magnificent Quran") (Giza, 2002), 3:134.
11. Ibid., 3:136.
12. Ibid.
13. Muhammad 'Abduh, *Tafsīr al-manār* ("Exegesis of the Beacon") (Cairo, 1931), 4:21.
14. Ibid.
15. Al-Tabari, *Jāmi' al-bayān*, 6:280.
16. Ibid.
17. Ibid., 6:280–81.
18. Ibid., 6:281.
19. Ibid.
20. See his *al-Jāmi' li-aḥkām al-Qur'ān* (Cairo: Dar al-Sha'b, n.d.), 4:2881.
21. See his *Tafsīr al-Qur'ān al-'Aẓīm*, ed. Mustafa Sayyid Muhammad et al. (Giza, n.d.), 7:114–15.
22. This refers to the *mu'ākhāt* (the process of brothering) whereby the Prophet paired in most cases a Meccan Emigrant with a Medinan Helper to foster brotherly relations between them.
23. See his *Tafsīr al-Manār* (Cairo, 1349/1931), 10:70–71.
24. Ibid., 71.
25. Ibid.
26. See Ibn Hisham, *al-Sīra al-Nabawiyya* ("The Biography of the Prophet"), ed. Suhayl Zakkar (Beirut, 1992), 2:929–35; al-Tabari, *Ta'rikh al-umam wa-'l-muluk* ("History of the Nationas and Kings") (Beirut, 1997), 2:175.
27. This is in tandem with righteous Muslims who represent a "middle" or "moderate nation" (Ar. *umma wasat*).

28. See, for example, al-Mawardi, *al-Aḥkām al-Sulṭaniyya wa-' l-wilayat al-dīniyya* ("Governmental Ordinances and Religious Stewardship"); eds. 'Isam Faris al-Harastani and Muhammad Ibrahim al-Zaghli (Beirut, 1996), 194.
29. Abu Yusuf, *Kitāb al-Kharāj* ("The Book of Land Taxation") (Cairo, 1962), 122.
30. In the early period, this was the catch-all term for all obligatory alms or taxes paid by the Muslims, and used usually synonymously with *zakat*.
31. Cf. the *hadith* in which the Prophet states, "I am the guardian of a person who has no guardian"; recorded by al-Tirmidhi, *al-Jami'a al-Sahih* ("the Sound Compendium"), ed. Kamal Yusuf al-Hut (Beirut: Dar al-Kutub al-'Ilmiyya, n.d.), 4:367.
32. Abu Yusuf, *Kitāb al-Kharāj*, 126.
33. Al-Mawardi, *al-Aḥkām al-Sulṭāniyya*, 193–94.
34. See, for example, Sayyid Sabiq, *Fiqh al-sunna* (Beirut, 1992), 1: 328–32.
35. Bediuzzaman Said Nursi, *Letters*, tr. Sukran Vahide (Istanbul, 1997), 2:311.
36. Ibn Kathir, *Tafsīr* (Beirut, 1990), 4:103.
37. Nursi, *Letters*, 2:314.
38. Ibid., 2:314–15.
39. Ibid., 2:313.
40. Ibid., 2:317–18.
41. Ibid., 2:319.

TWELVE

SAID NURSI'S VISION FOR A NEW UNIVERSAL CULTURE OF DIALOGUE

Abdelaziz Berghout

This chapter highlights Said Nursi's conceptualization of dialogue between the West and the Muslim world. Certainly, these two civilizational blocks are on the verge of a grand historical transition that requires wisdom and dialogue. I believe that Nursi can shed some light on this important relationship. Indeed, in his spiritual journey, Nursi contemplated that the classical perception of power would shift from the condition of violence and hegemony to that of persuasion, dialogue, and love. Nursi argued that, "What I am certain of from my experience of social life and have learnt from my lifetime of study is the following: the thing most worthy of love is love, and the most deserving of enmity is enmity. That is, love and loving, which renders man's social life secure and lead to happiness are most worthy of love and being loved."[1] It is this new vision and spirit of love that has been advocated through the writings of Nursi, as Ian Markham aptly put it, "so we find in Said Nursi's writings, a strong commitment to love, coupled with an equally strong commitment to respecting the liberty of other."[2] Nursi maintains that the first step toward dialogue is to win the battle of souls and hearts first. Losing this battle would mean the loss of this world and the hereafter, as well.

Obviously, the issue of dialogue is of primary significance. Given the recent developments in the world and the intensity of problems that exist between the West and the Muslim world, dialogue gains a new momentum on the agenda of people of faith in order to rid humanity of destruction. I believe that Nursi has so much to offer in helping humanity eliminate conflict and achieve universal peace.

NURSI'S THOUGHT AND ESSENTIALITY OF UNIVERSAL DIALOGUE

Global Crisis and Nursi's Appeal for Universal Dialogue

Fathoming deeply the global changes that had been occurring in his time throughout the globe, Nursi foresaw the impact of those events and changes on the future of human civilization in general and the future of relations between religions and faiths in particular. Fully aware of the nature of those changes and their possible negative and destructive impact on civilizations, religions, and cultures, Nursi pondered deeply upon the main reasons, causes, and effects of those problems. According to him, given the nature of problems that humanity underwent during his time as well as the complexity of those problems and their global impact, the world will in the future face situations wherein all of humanity will be put on the verge of a global crisis. As a matter of fact, after more than half a century from his predications, the world today faces a global crisis. Indeed, it is a multidimensional global crisis that cripples the world relations and aspirations in various instances and situations. It is a crisis that spreads all over the body of human activities and enlarges the degree of human suffering at several levels, whether spiritual, moral, intellectual, social, economic, cultural, political, or civilizational. In the following passage, Nursi draws a clear picture of the situation:

> I shall allude briefly to a most extensive and lengthy truth which occurred to my heart on the Night of Power. Because of the extreme tyranny and despotism of this last World War and its merciless destruction, and hundreds of innocents being scattered and ruined on account of a single enemy, and the awesome despair of the defeated, and the fearsome alarm of the victors and their ghastly pangs of conscience arising from the supremacy they are unable to maintain and the destruction they are unable to repair, and the utter transitoriness and ephemerality of the life of this world and the deceptive, opiate nature of the fantasies of civilization becoming apparent to all, and the exalted abilities lodged in human nature and the human essence being wounded in a universal and awesome manner, and heedlessness and misguidance and deaf, lifeless nature being smashed by the diamond sword of the Qur'an, and the exceedingly ugly, exceedingly cruel true face of world politics becoming apparent, which is the widest and most suffocating and deceptive cover for heedlessness and misguidance, most certainly and without any shadow of a doubt, since the life of this world—which is the metaphorical beloved of mankind—is thus ugly and transient,

> man's true nature will search with all its strength for eternal life, which it truly loves and yearns for, just as there are signs of this occurring in the North, the West, and in America.[3]

In this passage, it seems that Nursi carried on his shoulder the burden of human despotism and dilemma. He felt the suffering and internalized the pain that millions of sufferers bore throughout the world. He knew that the crisis is not superficial and not just a mere setback that can be overcome quickly; rather he considered it as a deep crisis that infected the human soul,[4] mind, heart, and innate personality. Therefore, as I explain later on, he suggested the starting-point in redressing the failure and crisis to be from a clear and correct understanding of the problem per se.

In his appraisal of the human dilemma that undertakes its course in our life, Nursi believes that the crisis is not only a reflection of our material and physical failure, but basically reaches to the very core of our moral and ethical edifice. Accordingly, by his account, everyone should understand that the human problem is deeper than many people thought. In fact, Nursi saw with his own eye and sensed with his own noble heart and soul the tragedy of humanity in its traumatic composition. His inner perception of the dilemma of humanity assisted him to see the real nature of the problem that goes deep beyond mere actions of war and killing of innocents. It goes deeply to the souls and intrinsic natures of people who were behind it. In his own words, Nursi puts it clearly that "the exalted abilities lodged in human nature and the human essence being wounded in a universal and awesome manner."[5] Accordingly, one should think through the real human crisis that intermingles with our perception of human nature, personality, culture, worldview, civilization, and human relation.

Ideally, wise people of our present world will not miss the message that has been conveyed through the previous passage. Extremely aware of the fact that human civilization was at the threshold of a very huge shift and transformation, Nursi knew that despite the global tyranny and mischief that had been inflicted upon innocent people during his time, humanity will give birth to a new deep human call for reconciliation, peace, tolerance, mercy, cooperation, justice, equality, understanding, and dialogue. An author has aptly noted: "as has been pointed out previously, although Bediuzzaman always upheld and struggled for the independence of the Islamic world against the West and the maintenance of its cultural integrity, he foresaw the co-operation of Islam and sincere Christians in the face of aggressive atheism."[6] In line with this, one should underline the fact that Nursi's stand regarding dialogue and understanding between the West and the Muslim world is not a mere emotional reaction to the tyrannical oppression resulting from the evil side of the forces of modern Western civilization[7] represented in the forces of irreligion and atheism; instead it is a very wise and strategic stand. He views dialogue as an essential element in the process of propagating faith and not imposing it on people. Hence, to him, for Muslims, in particular, to undertake their responsibility of servicing faith and providing the evidence to others, dialogue is an important means of the process of knowing one another and experiencing peaceful coexistence.

In this regard, Nursi calls on sincere believers in general and the followers of the three Abrahamic faiths in particular to join their efforts to participate in solving the global crisis of human souls, hearts, minds, and senses as a preliminary step toward curing the diseases of human association and civilization. At this juncture, one important point needs to be addressed before any further analysis. I would like to draw the attention of the reader to the fact that Nursi's call for understanding and dialogue among religions and civilizations is not merely meant for political, economic, and material gains and consumption. Rather, it is a call that has been born out of his deep understanding of man's existence and mission in the world as well as his profound grasp of the movement of human civilization and the role of religion in keeping the equilibrium and balance of human civilization. Therefore, Nursi's view of understanding and dialogue stems from his realization of human existence, human psychology, and the function of religious and ethical texts in disseminating the seeds of universal peace culture.

Nursi Predication of Man's Search for Universal Peace

The above submission takes us to another important point regarding Nursi's view of dialogue and understanding between the Muslim world and the West. Referring back to the previous passage, Nursi says, "Man's true nature will search with all its strength for eternal life, which it truly loves and yearns for, just as there are signs of this occurring in the North, the West, and in America."[8] No doubt, there are many signs that testify to this view today. Despite the huge sufferings of humanity and the spread of conflicts and wars in many places, Nursi still believes that the truth and the conditions for the salvation of humanity will be born from within the womb of this seething turmoil that befalls humanity. He considers that committed believers and followers of religions will bear witness to a new birth of balanced and ethical oriented human civilization that strives for the success of the entire humanity in ethical and material terms. In further explanation, Nursi declares that "the Qur'an, which is a mercy for mankind, only accepts a civilization that comprises the happiness of all, or at least of the majority."[9] Additionally, he foresees a very crucial role attributed to

Islam in making this dream realizable. He says: "God willing, through the strength of Islam in the future, the virtues of civilization will prevail, the face of the earth cleansed of filth, and universal peace be secured."[10]

It is clear that Nursi predicts a glittering future and assumes that religions in general and Islam in particular will contribute to the progress of humanity. As mentioned aptly by one of Nursi's writers, "Bediuzzaman's eyes were on the future. It was a time of defeat for the Islamic world, a period of regression and darkness. But he knew the spring would come, and a golden age would dawn bringing true happiness, progress, and civilization for mankind. This return to life had begun. Flashes of light, signs of life could be seen."[11]

On the basis of this analysis, the issue of dialogue and understanding between the West and the Muslim world in particular and between Islam and the rest of religions in general is a strategic project and not a mere situational appeal. Based on his integral vision and understanding, Nursi believes that, as far as the Quran is concerned, dialogue with others is a part and parcel of its teachings. Indeed, the true teachings of the Holy Quran stand for dialogue and cooperation in order to uphold and advance the human values, such as dignity, justice, tolerance, freedom, love, forgiveness, mercy, dignity, equality, and so on. Hence, dialogue and understanding, at least from a Quranic perspective, among religions are crucial and inseparable from the basic teachings of Islam. Therefore, every sincere believer hopes that dialogue should become a part of his or her culture and life.

For that reason, Nursi argues that if this is the main call of Islam, then it is not outlandish to call other religions in general and the people of the Book in particular to become involved in a mutual understanding, cooperation, and common struggle to solve human problems. Differently put, his call for dialogue and understanding between Muslim and Christians stems not only from the critical situation of the world's alarming problems but initially and basically from the inner call of his innate appeals as well as from the deep wisdom that has been enshrined in the Quranic text. Osman Cilaci has aptly quoted Nursi, stating: "our being friendly to them springs from our admiration for their civilization and progress, and our borrowing these. Such friendship is certainly not included in the Qur'anic prohibition."[12]

NURSI'S ENVISIONING OF A UNIVERSAL CULTURE OF DIALOGUE

As already indicated, there are several necessities that urge our struggle together in certain areas and for certain ends that will benefit us as well as all of humanity. Indeed, "the way of the Risale-i Nur was peaceful jihad or (jihad of the word) in the struggle against aggressive atheism and irreligion. By working solely for the spread and strengthening of belief, it was to work also for the preservation of internal order and peace and stability in society in the face of the moral and spiritual destruction of communism and the force of irreligion."[13] In fact, working together and joint sincere cooperation would result in important benefits to humanity. However, it should be clear from the very beginning that for any dialogue to give birth to constructive activities and results it should be viewed as a culture other than a mere process or a given event or forum.

In other words, the partners in dialogue should aspire toward creating a culture that can enhance interaction and create the necessary conditions for its success. Subsequently, there is a need to correct certain perceptions and change certain mind-sets. Dialogue as a culture necessitates perceptual revision so as to make the processes of dialogue meaningful and with clear purposes that can be measured and achieved. Pondering over Nursi's view on a new culture of dialogue between the West and the Muslim world, one can underline several principles and elements that constitute the starting-point toward this new culture. The following is a brief account of some important principles that are needed for building a universal culture of dialogue.

Objective Judgment and Sincere Intention: Knowing Each Other

To go one step further in inquiring into the issue of dialogue, I will proceed to scrutinize the main principles that Nursi considers for building a universal culture of dialogue. To begin with, Nursi is of the view that any fruitful dialogue between the West and the Muslim world should be based on a clear and objective judgment of our cultures, worldviews, heritages, and faiths. Indeed, any misconception or misunderstanding of the Muslim world and its civilization as well as the Western world and its civilization will lead to fatal judgmental mistakes. Thus, it is important to make a clear distinction between the forces of good and evil in our judgment of the other partner of dialogue. Additionally, one should avoid any terms of generalization that destroy the entire credibility of a religion or a culture because of the wrongdoings of few people. Put more emphatically, Nursi urges the Muslims who attempt to study the Western modern civilization to distinguish between what is positive and what is negative in its perceptions, experiences, and achievements. He posits a clear distinction between the forces of evil, torture, and aggression and the forces of good, mercy, and progress in the modern Western civilization.[14] In his own words, Nursi declares that "it should not be misunderstood; Europe is two. One follows the sciences, which serve justice and right and the industries beneficial for the life of society through the inspiration it has received from true Christianity; this first Europe I am not addressing. I am rather addressing the second corrupt Europe which, through the darkness of the philosophy of Naturalism, supposing the evils of civilization to be its virtues, has driven mankind to vice and misguidance."[15] Thus, one may note that this distinction is particularly needed for an objective appraisal of the relations between the West and the Muslim world. Any misconception regarding this distinction will lead to misjudgment from both sides. In a broadly similar way, Nursi further clarifies his stand, saying, "You should understand that what I mean are the good things that are civilization's virtues and its benefits for mankind. Not its iniquities and evils that idiots have imagined to be its virtues, and imitating them, devastated our possessions. Giving religion as the bribe, they have not even gained the world. Through civilization's iniquities prevailing over its benefits and its evils being preferred to its virtues, mankind has suffered two calamitous blows in the form of two world wars, and overturning that sinful civilization men have been so utterly disgusted that they have smeared the face of the earth with blood."[16]

As a matter of fact, several Western scholars, particularly those who advocate the real teachings of Christianity, confirm Nursi's stand on this issue. As an example, Professor Tomas Michel, S. J., puts it clearly that:

> our present age has produced its own challenge to sincere believers in God who seek to do God's will in all things. These can be summed up in what is usually called "modern civilization." It is a civilization, which is not all evil, and has bought many benefits to humanity. Not all of its spiritual values are opposed to God's will, but it affirms and supports many good human qualities. However, modern civilization can include a way of thinking in which people no longer feel a need for God. Not only can people claim to feel no need to worship, thank, and seek help from God, but often they do not look to God's Word for guidance and instruction concerning the way to lead their lives. They may choose to follow their own self-conceived philosophies and ideologies. For those who desire to lead their lives in every respect according to God' will, a critique of modern civilization is an inescapable task.[17]

Further on, Nursi also urges the West to judge objectively the Muslim world and the religion of Islam. He attempts through his writings to show the real teachings of Islam that pioneer the human calls for justice, tolerance, freedom, equality, cooperation, dialogue, unity, upholding human dignity, and forgiveness. He forcefully declares: "I shall prove and demonstrate to the world that the Qur'an is an undying, inextinguishable Sun!" From that time, he strove to employ his superior knowledge of both the traditional religious and the modern sciences in the service of the Quran: to prove its miraculousness, defend it against the attacks that were largely in the name of science and progress, and relate its truths in the light of modern advances in knowledge. He sought to prove that, contrary to the claims of its enemies, the Quran was the source of true progress and civilization and, in addition, since this was the case, Islam would dominate the future, despite its relative decline and regression at that time.[18] In this key explanation of Nursi, one can sense his desire to see other people's judgment of Islam more objectively.

He further explains how the teachings of Islam advocate the material and spiritual progress of humanity. He says: "this strength, which teaches men exalted aims in the form of competition for exalted things, and causes them to strive on that way, which shatters despotism, excites exalted emotions, and destroys jealousy, envy, malice and rivalry, and is furnished with true awakening, the eagerness of competition, the tendency towards renewal and predisposition for civilization, consists of the freedom which is accordance with the Shari'a. That is to say, it has been fitted out with the desire for the highest accomplishments worthy of humanity."[19]

In another instance, Nursi further establishes clearly the fact that Islam is not against the material and technological advancement of humanity, rather he considers it as a major advocator of material and spiritual progress. Nursi states that "Almighty God's great bounties of the airplane, railway, and radio should be responded to with great thanks. . . . While thanks for the vast bounty of radio would be shown by making it a universal million-tongue reciter of the Qur'an, which would allow people all over the earth to listen to the Qur'an...Although I urged Muslims to work towards these wonders, I am accused of opposing modern advances like railway, airplane and radio."[20] However, Nursi urges Muslims to understand that the strength of Islam and its spiritual force depend, in its realization, on material and technological advancement. As Nursi puts it, "this is the dignity of Islam, which proclaims and upholds the Word of God. In this age, proclaiming the Word of God is contingent on material progress; it may be proclaimed only through achieving true civilization. It cannot be doubted that in the future the world of Islam's collective personality will carry out to the letter that categorical command issued by the dignity of Islam through belief."[21]

This last analysis raises the issue of the need to know one another in a proper manner so as to appreciate each other as well as to find the common ground for our shared activities. In his interpretation of the following verse of the Holy Quran: "O mankind! We created you from a single pair of a male and a female, and made you into nations and tribes, that you may know each other"

(49:13), Nursi says: "that is I created you as peoples, nations, and tribe, so that you should know one another and the relations between you in social life, and assist one another; not so that you should regard each other as strangers, refusing to acknowledge one another, and nurturing hostility and enmity."[22] Obviously, Nursi looks for a better understating that is built on a correct knowledge about one another. He aims for a dialogue that will lead to the dissemination of cooperation and peace instead of enmity and hostility. At this juncture, I trust a quotation from Thomas Michel is in order. "In my opinion, it is the lifetime achievement of Said Nursi that in the Risal-i Nur he was able to provide modern Muslims with the interpretive tools they need to analyze modern civilization, so that they can discern what is of genuine and lasting value in modern life and so that they can also clearly see the harmful and self-destructive tendencies that lie beneath its glittering surface."[23]Additionally, I trust that the appeal of Nursi goes beyond addressing the Muslims per se, but also other people of faith in the hope that everyone can exercise the utmost wisdom in judging one another's worldview and religion.

Past Experiences and Future Wonders of Civilization will Necessitate Dialogue

Another important principle of fruitful dialogue is to revisit our past experiences as well as to derive lessons from the huge achievements that have been made by our present civilization. Going back to the past will enable us to encounter the important moments when our religions and cultures had made tremendous efforts toward achieving a good deal of dialogue and understating. According to Nursi, the Islamic civilization has presented a good example of tolerance and goodwill in standing with the forces of dialogue with other civilizations and religions. He has further mentioned how modern civilization,[24] in its positive aspects, allowed its people to overcome many obstacles that hindered them from participating in fruitful dialogue with others. According to him, the past experience of the Muslim world and the new signs of the Western civilization[25] pave the way to a more dynamic and fruitful dialogue. Therefore, it is important to benefit from these opportunities to enhance our present dialogue. Perhaps the following quotation serves as an important focus on the issue: "In the middle Ages, Islam was compelled to be bigoted and hostile in the face of the Europeans' savagery, but it nevertheless maintained its justice and moderation. It never instituted inquisitions and such like. In this time of modern civilization, the Europeans are civilized and powerful, and harmful hostility and bigotry have therefore disappeared. For in respect of religion, the civilized are to be conquered through persuasion, not through force, and through showing by conforming to its commands in actions and conduct that Islam is elevated and lovable. Force and enmity are only to combat the barbarity of savages."[26]

It is obvious that Nursi calls for a better understanding of the roots and basics of our civilizations so that we may be able to learn from each other and complement one another in things that are common between us. In another breath, Nursi predicts that the cooperation and dialogue between the Muslim world and the sincere Western people will intensify because the causes for their poor dialogue and weak communication are receding little by little. It is obvious that all these factors will open new opportunities for dialogue and mutual understanding, particularly in combating irreligion and healing the wounds of the sufferers in our present world.

Acknowledging Unique Peculiarities of Our Worldviews and Cultures

The other leading principle that helps in building a new culture of dialogue is the need to recognize that our religions, cultures, and civilizations differ in many points. In fact, there are unique features that characterize each one of our civilizations to the extent that any attempts to amalgamate or infuse them in one single body will surely fail. Therefore, we should be able to cooperate and join forces to fight against the forces of irreligion and atheism without attempting to impose our styles of life on each other. Hence, Nursi assumes that to formulate a positive and fruitful dialogue and understanding between the West and the Muslim world does not necessarily imply the dissolution and infusion of both our worldviews and cultures in one single body or the attempt to ask one another to abandon our own religions for no reason. In the first place, Nursi in his call for Christianity to come in interaction and contact with Islam is not asking them to abandon their religion, rather he is requesting them to benefit from the Quran in completing their perceptions of the true religion. He says: "O people of the Book! There is no difficulty for you in accepting Islam; do not let it appear hard to you. For Qur'an does not order you to abandon your religion completely. It proposes only that you complete your faith and build it on the fundamentals of religion that you already possess. The Qur'an is a modifier and perfecter of basic principles. As for its nature as establisher, this only concerns such details as are subject to change and alteration because of differences of time and place; and this is in no ay unreasonable or illogical."[27] It is clear in the body of the previous passage that Nursi singles out one of the basic principles of mutual dialogue and understanding. Thus, as Professor Michel puts it, "the kind of purification that Said Nursi expects to occur in Christianity seems to be not that of abandoning their religion in order to enter Islam, but rather a completion of what they already have that is good."[28]

In another pivotal instance, Nursi hammers out another important principle of mutual dialogue and understanding, stating that it is crucial to know the unique features of our own worldviews and religions so that we may engage in the process of knowing each other. By his account, acknowledging our essential differences and the unique features that distinguish us from one another is a basic step toward a mature and dynamic dialogue. Ursula Spuler has argued that "despite being against the materialist and capitalist West, Said Nursi clearly differentiates between capitalist Europe and America and Christian European and American People of the Book who take Christianity seriously, and while criticizing the West, held these Christians as exception."[29] In the same breath, Nursi clearly states that: "How could it be that with its different source, origin, and place of appearance, the light of the Qur'an and guidance of the Shari'a should be reconciled with the genius of Rome, the spirit of modern civilization, and should join and combine with it?"[30] Moreover, Nursi goes on further to state some of the unique characteristics that distinguish both the modern Western civilization and the Islamic worldview. He says:

> like the proofs in the Twelfth Word, it is to summarize a number of principles. By reason of its philosophy, present-day civilization[31] accepts 'force' as the point of support in the life of society. It takes as its aim 'benefits,' and considers the principle of its life to be 'conflict.' It considers the bond between communities to be 'racialism and negative nationalism.' While its aim is to provide 'amusements' for gratifying the appetites of the soul and increasing man's needs. However, the mark of force is aggression. And since the benefits are insufficient to meet all needs, their mark is that everyone tussles and jostles over them. The mark of conflict is contention, and the mark of racialism, aggression, since it thrives on devouring others. Thus, it is because of these principles of civilization that despite all its virtues, it has provided a sort of superficial happiness for only twenty per cent of mankind and cast eighty per cent into distress and poverty.[32]

He then goes on to mention several unique characteristics of the Muslim world's worldview, saying: "it considers 'the principle of mutual assistance' to be fundamental in life, rather than conflict. In the ties between communities it accepts 'the bonds of religion, class, and country,' in place of racialism and nationalism. Its aims are to place a barrier before the illicit assaults of the soul's base appetites and to urge the spirit to sublime matters, to satisfy man's elevated emotions and encourage him towards the human perfections. And as for the truth, its mark is concord; the mark of virtue is mutual support, and the mark of mutual assistance, hastening to help one another. The mark of religion is brotherhood and attraction. And the result of reining in and tethering the evil-commanding soul and leaving the spirit free and urging it towards perfection is happiness in this world and the next. Thus, despite the virtues present-day civilization has acquired from the guidance of the Qur'an in particular, and from the preceding revealed religions, in point of fact it has thus suffered defeat before the Qur'an."[33] Indeed, the point should be clear from the ongoing analysis is that we should observe and consider our own unique characteristics while we are attempting to discover and enhance the common and mutual elements and features that can bring us together. In line with this, commenting on Nursi's view of dialogue, Ian Markkam has stated that "Nursi's achievement is he stands inside a deeply traditional form of Islam and yet affirms the importance of toleration and conversion. . . . Said Nursi arrives at a place where truth is reconciled with toleration."[34]

Need for Common Struggle against Irreligion

It should be clear that while we are trying to learn the differences and unique features that distinguish our worldviews and cultures, in the same breath we should attempt to discover our commonalities and the things that bring us closer and enable us to struggle for the sake of God. The Holy Quran clearly indicates the importance of joining together our efforts and forces and work for the sake of God. God says in the Holy Quran: "O People of the Book! Come to common terms as between us and you; that we worship none but God; that we associate no partner with Him; that we erect not, from among ourselves, lords and partners other than God" (3:64). Indeed, several commonalities make it incumbent on sincere believers to come collectively and work jointly for the sake of God. An author has clearly indicated that "on our looking from the point of view of the Risale-i-Nur, one of the basic conditions of Muslim-Christian dialogue emerges before every thing else: the shared points of the two religions. These shared points make it possible for Islam and Christianity to act together against atheism, materialism, communism, etc."[35]

By stating the distinguishing features of both the Muslim world and modern Western civilization as well as urging us to look for the commonalities, Nursi then declares the urgency of dialogue among the spiritual and moral forces of our world so as to fight jointly against the forces of irreligion and atheism. In this regard, he foresees a vital role to be assumed by Muslims and sincere Christians in their pursuit of the truth and only the truth.

Toward that end he first specifies the focus of our efforts—that is, to fight irreligion, atheism, tyranny, and the evil forces of modern civilization, not its virtues and good values that benefit all humanity, of all kinds. Nursi declares that "this malignant civilization vomited all at once the combined savagery and crimes, all the cruelty and treachery, of former centuries, and its stomach is still queasy."[36] Second, he underlines the joint task that should be undertaken by Muslims and Christians saying: "moreover, in the world of humanity, the secret society of the Dajjal will overturn civilization and subvert all mankind's sacred matters, with the intention of denying the Godhead. A zealous and self-sacrificing community known as a Christian[37] community but worthy of being called "Muslim Christians," will be the reality of Islam,[38] and will kill and rout that society of the Dajjal, thus saving humanity from atheism."[39] Expressing the nature and complexity of the mission of both sincere Christians and Muslims in a more detailed way, Nursi highlights the kind of wounds and dissipations caused by the evil side of the modern civilization saying:

> In short: since modern Western civilization has not truly heeded the revealed religions, it has both impoverished man and increased his needs. It has destroyed the principle of frugality and contentment, and increased wastefulness, greed, and covetousness. It has opened the way to tyranny and what is unlawful. And through encouraging people to take advantage of the means of dissipation, it has cast those needy unfortunates into total laziness. It has destroyed the desire for effort and work. It has encouraged depravity.[40]

Further on, Nursi advances his view stating, "It is essential that missionaries and pious Christians, as well as Nurcus are extremely careful. For certainly, with the idea of defending itself against the attacks of the religion of Islam and Christianity, the current from the North will try to destroy the accord of Islam and the missionaries."[41] Accordingly, dialogue and cooperation between Muslims and sincere Christians are an important means for fighting jointly the forces of irreligion and evil in the world. In his own words: "at that point when the current appears to be very strong, the religion of true Christianity, which comprises the collective personality of Jesus (Upon whom be peace), will emerge. That is, it will be purified in the face of reality; it will cast off superstition and distortion, and unite with the truths of Islam. Christianity will in effect be transformed into a sort of Islam. Following the Qur'an the collective personality of Christianity will be in the rank of follower, and Islam, in that of leader. True religion becomes a mighty force as a result of joining it."[42]

He further foresees a crucial role to be played by pious and sincere followers of Jesus in their fight to eradicate irreligion and its Dajjalic forms. He says: "it will be the truly pious followers of Jesus who will kill the gigantic collective personality of materialism and irreligion which the Dajjal will form and destroy his ideas and disbelief, which are atheistic. Those truly pious Christians will blend the essence of true Christianity with the essence of Islam and rout the Dajjal with their combined strength, in effect killing him."[43]

As a result of the coming development in the relations between Muslims and sincere Christians, Nursi predicts a more dynamic involvement of both in solving the problems of humanity. He says:

> for the recent times, as though it was a time between prophets, an attitude of indifferences has arisen towards religion and the religion of Muhammad (Peace be upon him). And, at the end of time, the true religion of Jesus (Upon whom be peace) will prevail and will stand shoulder to shoulder with Islam. Therefore, it may be said with all certainty that the calamity, which the oppressed among Christians suffer, those connected to Jesus who at present remains in an interregnum-like obscurity, is a sort of martyrdom for them. But, for sure, together with atoning for the sins arising from the dissipation of civilization, ingratitude, and misguidance of philosophy and unbelief, it is a hundredfold profit for them. I was informed thus by truth and reality.[44]

The Power of Persuasion, Love, and Knowledge

Another important element toward building a positive and effective culture of dialogue is the tendency of persuasion, love, and knowledge. Adopting persuasion as a strategy in our dialogue means a big shift in our perception of interaction, communication, and cooperation. This shift indicates that intrinsic weapons of war that have been used through out the course of history to defeat the enemies are changing dramatically. The people will shift from the weapons of mass destruction to the weapons[45] of persuasion, tolerance, patience, compassion, forgiveness, and love. Put more emphatically, Nursi says: "for in respect of religion, the civilized are to be conquered through persuasion, not through force, and through showing by conforming to its commands in actions and conduct that Islam is elevated and lovable. Force and enmity are only to combat the barbarity of savages"[46] As Nursi clearly puts it, "we shall therefore wage jihad with the weapons of science and industry on ignorance, poverty, and conflicting ideas, the worst enemies of upholding the Word of God. As foe us external jihad, we shall refer it to the decisive proofs of the illustrious Shari'a. For conquering the civilized is through persuasion, not through force as though they were savage who understand nothing. We are devotees of love; we do not have time for enmity."[47]

In another instance, Nursi stresses the importance of the new power of moral and spiritual forces in dialogue and mutual interaction among religions and civilizations. He skilfully declares that "the enemy is bigotry and obstinacy. Whereas in the future, in place of weapons, the immaterial, moral swords of true civilization, material progress, and truth and justice will defeat and scatter the enemies."[48] He further clarifies: "the ruler of the old times was strength; the one with the sharp sword and a stony heart would rise. But the motor, the soul, the strength, the ruler, and the boss of the times of freedom are righteousness, mind, knowledge, law, and public opinion. Only those with a sharp mind and a bright heart will rise to the top. . . . Those who stand on reason, utilize love instead of force, and keep their mind over their emotions, will not fall; they may even rise further. . . . You can beat them with the same weapons that they beat you: the mind."[49] It is so far clear that Nursi advocates a new way and approach in building the culture of dialogue and interaction. In line with this, as Professor Cengel argues, "Bediuzzman warns those who fail to see the necessities of the time and the direction of the world, and insist on using brutal force rather than the mind, love and conscience."[50] Put in more precise words, Nursi says: "As for one who strikes with the sword, the sword turns back and hits his own innocent. Now victory is not with the sword. There is a place for the sword, but it is the hand of the mind."[51]

Moreover, Nursi emphasizes the importance and need to use knowledge in the future of dialogue among religions in general and between Islam and the people of the Book in particular. As Bediuzzaman Said Nursi demonstrates, since Islam relies on reason and reasoned proof, it is the religion of the present and the future, for this is the age of science, technology, and reason. Many who realize that they cannot live without a true and complete religion understand this fact now. The causes for the decline of the Islamic world and its material backwardness in comparison to the West should be sought in the failure of Muslims to adhere to the teachings and truths of the Holy Quran and Islam. Just as Islam provides for the material progress of man, and indeed urges him toward it, so does it provide for man's true progress and development in moral and spiritual matters. This combination forms the basis of true civilization.[52] Further on, Nursi establishes clear guidelines for the dialogue between Muslims and Westerns to flourish and give birth to a new culture of dialogue. To him, mind, love, and human conscience are still the most powerful means of the new culture of relations. He says: "the biggest barrier between us and the Westerns is the baseless fears of clashing and refutation stemming from deceptive imagination related the extremities of Islam and scientific matters. Bravo to the enlightening support of schools and the factual support of sciences for equipping the truth with the tendency to investigate, the love of humanity, and the human conscience and for shattering those barriers then and now. Yes, the biggest causes that deprived us from the comfort of this world and the Westerns from the happiness in the hereafter and curtailed the sun of Islam are the misunderstandings and the baseless fears of clashing and opposition."[53]

On the other hand, Nursi explains how it is crucial to adopt the strategy of love, mercy, and patience in dealing with our opponents[54] and those who attempt to destroy our religious and civilizational strength. Nursi states that: "What I am certain of from my experience of social life and have learnt from my life-time of study is the following: the thing most worthy of love is love, and the most deserving of enmity is enmity. That is, love and loving, which renders man's social life secure and lead to happiness are most worthy of love and being loved."[55]

In another instance, Nursi delves deep in scrutinizing the need for love and wisdom in dealing with human problems. Nursi declares:

> in the present stormy century, the egotism and racialism proceeding from cruel civilization, and the military dictatorships resulting from the Great War, and the pitilessness arising from misguidance have led to such extreme tyranny and excessive despotisms that if the people of truth defend their rights through physical force, or through severe tyranny, numerous unfortunates will be burnt on the pretext of partisanship, and in that situation, they too will be excessively tyrannical and will be defeated. For those who act and attack out of the above feelings, on some petty pretext, strike at twenty to thirty people because of the mistakes of one or two, and destroy them. If on the way of truth and justice, the people of truth strike only at the one who struck, they win only one in the face of thirty losses, and are then in a position of defeat. If, in accordance with the unjust rule of responding in kind, the people of truth also crush twenty to thirty people due to the errors of one or two, they will then perpetrate a ghastly injustice in the name of right."[56]

By adopting this attitude and stand, Nursi opens a new chapter in the world of dialogue and understanding among Muslims themselves and between them and the West as well as the rest of the world. He urges us to reinvent a new culture of relation and interaction. Nursi states that "the basis of all human society, and especially the Islamic nation, are earnest love between relatives, concerned relations between tribes and groups, brotherhood and moral assistance for fellow believers arising from Islamic nationhood, self-sacrificing concern for one's fellow countrymen and the members of one's nation, and unshakable attachment and devotion to and support for the truths of the Qur'an."[57] By his account, Nursi sees love and mutual brotherhood as one of the basic requirements of faith and devotion. He argues that having this sense of love and affection toward one another reflects our understanding of the names and attribute of God as well as our closeness to Him.

> In accordance with the principles that 'the consequence of an illicit love is suffering a merciless torment' you are suffering a fully justified punishment, for you are unlawfully employing your innate capacity for love, knowledge, thanks and worship that relate properly to the essence, attributes and names of God Almighty, on your own soul and the life of this world. You have lavished the love that belongs to God Almighty on yourself. Your own soul has become your beloved and will cause you endless suffering: you are not giving true peace to that beloved.[58]

Winning the Battle of Souls and Hearts First

Another vital element in the process of formulating a new culture of dialogue between the West and the Muslim world is to win the battle of souls and hearts first. It is a call not for physical, material, and geographical expansion and envision but primarily a call for the conquering of hearts and souls. According to Nursi, losing this battle means losing everything in this world and in the hereafter as well. Indeed, it should be clear that "humanity is transposing from the age of savagery and ignorance to the age of civilization and knowledge. A world that has completed phase of civilization, any wars can only be with words rather than arms. Those who conquer the minds with reason and elegance will conquer the world."[59]

Taking into consideration the above submission, one can realize that the present tension, clash, and confrontation among different civilizational blocks are initially the result of that soul and moral shift in our innate personality and culture. Indeed, the crisis resets there in our souls, hearts, minds, and perceptions of the world of seen and unseen. Therefore, before addressing the question of solving the civilizational problems of humanity, one should redress the deep wounds and injuries of human souls, hearts, minds, and senses. Differently put, Nursi suggests that a pathological diagnosis of our souls, hearts, minds, and senses should be carried out so that one may have a clear analysis and mapping out of the disease. In other words, humanity should go to the pharmacy of the revealed knowledge. It should go to the doctors who can cure the diseases of souls, hearts, minds, and senses. Hence, given this nature of the problem and crisis, religion becomes the cementing power that can elevate and get rid of the fatal viruses of materialism, atheism, absolutism, positivism, naturalism, deconstructivism, barbarism, tribalism.

The necessity of dialogue and understanding between the West and the Muslim world should not only be seen as a measure to absorb tension and diffuse the blockade in relations but mainly as a huge step toward building a new culture of dialogue as well as revitalizing the role of our religions in solving the human problems. In other words, dialogue should be visualized as a dynamic process that aspires toward creating the necessary conditions for religions and ethical systems to play their vital role in solving world problems. Accordingly, Nursi maintains the view that dialogue and understanding between the West and the Muslim world should not be subjected to external dictations and pressures caused by certain quarters that are not aware of the dynamics of religion and the dynamics of dialogue within a religious framework. Therefore, there must be a clear vision about dialogue and understanding so as to be able to set down the integral vision and principles of meaningful and dynamic dialogue. It is his contention that our dialogue and understanding should go far beyond the boundaries of just having agreements here and there to stop aggression against each other or to defuse tension in another part of the world, but basically should address the issue of religion being the cementing power that stands behind a dynamic, balanced, moral, and successful society. To sum up Nursi's view on this point, the following passage is exemplary:

> with the deception of motivation and intimidation one can only have a superficial effect and keep the mind in line. Impinging into the depth of the heart, moving even the most delicate senses, flourishing the inner talents like a blossoming rose, shaking and mobilizing the hidden and dormant talents and tendencies, causing the essence of humanity to gush out, and exhibiting the value of articulation are from the glimpses of the rays of truth. Yes polishing of the hearts from revolting practices

> such as burying of the girls while alive, which is a monument of stone heartedness, and gilding the hearts with virtues like mercy to animals, even compassion to ants, which is a flash of delicacy and tenderness, are such great revolutions.[60]

Indeed, what this passage conveys is very deep and critically needed in our present situation. Hence, "the way to such solution passes from being civilized not only in the body but also in the soul; that is from virtues."[61]

Dialogue and the Responsibility of Vicegerents of God

Nursi adds one more brick to the already mentioned vision of dialogue between the West and Islam. According to him, our dialogue should not be distanced from our responsibility and duty as vicegerents of God. Hence, we should initiate dialogue not only to solve some recurring tensions and problems from time to time but also primarily to share our knowledge, wisdom, and deep experiences from being vicegerents of God. "According to Nursi, human being's role on this planet is that of a guarding or vicegerent."[62] Once we fathom this basic requirement of dialogue and understanding, we can situate and position our relations, duties, responsibilities, and aspirations in the right place. Thus, dialogue will become the necessity of necessities and the norm in the relation between people, cultures, religions, and faiths. When our vision of dialogue takes this course and inclines toward the essence of our existence—to be splendid and genuine vicegerents and servants of God—then the real dialogue and understanding will begin and it will assist us in recuperating the retardation and delay in our real and fruitful dialogue.

Indeed, this kind of understanding will give birth to a new moral and ethical culture of dialogue that will open the era of learning and exchanging of wisdom between our people. This ethical and moral culture is the only guarantee that assures the sincerity and success of our dialogue. It is all about practicing dialogue and understanding for the sake of God. Nursi affirms

> since the reality is thus, what compassion requires for them is to place in their hearts in the form of belief in God and belief in the hereafter, an extremely powerful support and inexhaustible place of recourse in the face of their infinite want and impotence. Kindness and compassion to them is in this way. Otherwise, through the drunkenness of nationalist patriotism, it has the meaning of slaughtering those wretched innocents,

> like a crazy mother slaughtering her child with a knife. It is a savage cruelty and wrong, like pulling out their brains and hearts and making them eat them to nourish their bodies.[63]

This indicates clearly that faith, belief, and working for the sake of God as His servants and vicegerents is an important condition for the success of our dialogue or any other activity that we do or intend to do. Professor Jane I. Smith has aptly grasped the essence of Nursi's message in this respect. She argues that "if belief involves protection, misguidance hurts everyone and, as Nursi goes on to say . . . (the universe becomes angry at the people of rebellion and misguidance, as do all beings and creatures). Faith for Nursi is not a solitary activity, but has inevitable consequence not only for those whom one knows, but for the universe itself."[64]

Additionally, Nursi declares:

> for our programme is this: the world is a guest-house, and as for man, he remains there only a short time. He is a guest with many duties and in a brief lifetime is charged with preparing all the necessities for eternal life. The most important and essential matters will be offered to you. But most of you see this fleeting world through a veil of heedlessness, as an eternal abode, coloured and shaped by worldly feelings. So your share of worship, the basis of which is love of the truth and thinking of the hereafter, is very small. However, if there are among you respected craftsmen and artists and inspired inventors, who, purely for the benefit of God's servants, serve the general interest and public well-being and betterment of social life, which is a valuable worship, these signs and indications of the Qur'an are surely sufficient for those sensitive people, who of course form a minority, in order to encourage their efforts and appreciate their art.[65]

Toward a Rereading of Nursi's Views on Dialogue

The Dynamic of the New Global Realities

On the basis of various insights provided by Nursi, one can conclude that the urgency of dialogue becomes an obligation on our part, particularly when we work for the sake of God and the sake of elevating the sufferings of people in this world and in the hereafter. Dialogue should not be only taken as an imposed reality on us, but considered as an inner call that originates from our deep souls and hearts as vicegerents of God. Dialogue should blossom and emanate from the essence of our religious teachings and responsibilities.

It should be clear that the development of human civilization and its achievements in terms of sciences, technology, and means of progress and communication underscore the the urgency of dialogue. Accordingly, the new global realities of our world as well as the new global interactions and relations among nations and religions show how the world is in need of understanding and dialogue.

Indeed, any misassessment of the world's complexity and problems may lead to unprecedented kinds of conflicts and clashes between the West and the Muslim world. Consequently, there is a genuine reason that makes it incumbent on all partners who are today leading the affairs of human civilization to think and act beyond their own boundaries and self-interests so as to work for the sake of saving the entire human civilization from total chaos. Be it the Christian world or the Muslim world or the Buddhist world or other worlds, the fact remains that humanity and human civilization are presently in need of everybody's soul and action to contribute to their salvation and safety in a very complicated and globalized world.

If one is to reread, in our new terms and conditions, Nursi's insights with regard to his vision of dialogue between the West and the Muslim world, one should emphasize the importance of four elements. First, our vision of dialogue should take into account the core principles of our religions far from any kind of compulsion or imposition of views. Second, our dialogue should go beyond our own interests and self-oriented agendas to embrace the issues that concern humanity and human civilization at large. Third, our dialogue should fall within the framework of our mission as vicegerents of God who are entrusted with the responsibility of worshiping God, upholding justice, and spreading mercy, tolerance, and freedom among people. Four, understanding the huge and tremendous complexities of our reality and civilization in the global age and finding ways of how to revitalize the role of religion and ethics in addressing human problems. As an explanation to this fourth element, one should understand how the dynamics of new global realities influenced the processes of dialogue and understanding between the West and the Muslim world.

As a matter of fact, challenges and conditions set by globalization, industrialization, modernization, information technology, digitized mass media, virtual realities, genetic engineering discoveries, science invocations, knowledge society and economic realities, clash of civilizations, end of history, end of state, end of civilizations, weapons of mass destruction, sophisticated warfare techniques, ethnic tensions, religious conflicts, poverty, environment problems, health problems, and so on should all be taken into consideration in pursuing the cause of dialogue and understanding.

In one word, our world, civilization, life, and relations are dramatically undergoing change, be it negative or positive. Whether one accepts this change or denies its legitimacy, the fact remains that no one can hide from its course of events. Therefore, the main issue is not to look for ways and means to stop this global change or categorically reject it, but rather to disentangle the ways and means of how to absorb and lessen the astonishing shock and heavy burden of these changes on our minds, cultures, souls, and relations. Unfortunately, the impact of various events and changes that have been taking place in our present situation has detonated and alarmed the very core of our moral and ethical edifice to the extent that a large segment of humanity is in the verge of losing control of its moral destiny in favor of physical and material expansion. In fact, the heavy burden of the sordid events that exploded in our life and endangered our relations as civilizations and worldviews should be rethought so as to avoid all sorts of unnecessary and manipulated tensions, conflicts, and clashes.

Islam, the Winning Victimized Religion

Generally speaking, a huge number of events that are taking place in our political, economic, social, cultural, religious, and civilizational spheres testify to the alarming tension that shadowed our relations and interests in the recent years. Today, the Muslim world and the Western world face a critical situation wherein the forces of clash and conflict seem to gain mileage over the forces of reconciliation, understanding, and dialogue. It is obvious that there is a trend in world relations that aspires toward recalling back the classical conflicts and confrontations that ran through the vein of a long history and resulted in the bloody relation between the Muslim world and the West. Despite the differences and contexts that had been the cementing power behind those conflicts and clashes, there are still those who attempt eagerly and systematically to use those events to fuel the present situation of tension.

In today's situation, the Muslim world and the West should fathom the urgency of their dialogue and understanding. The alarming global status quo demands new stands and attitudes toward each other's cultures, civilizations, and worldviews. Indeed, humanity and human civilization are in dire need of the wisdom of the Muslim world as well as the wisdom of the sincere people in the West.

In this respect, Nursi makes it clear that Islam is, indeed, a real cure to the disease of contemporary man. He urges people to fathom the real truths of Islam and learn the medicine of the Quran instead of accusing it. Nursi says:

> furthermore, as described above, illicit pleasure on the path of misguidance causes man to fall to the lowest of the low. Then no civilization, no philosophy can provide a remedy for him, and no human progress and scientific advances can deliver him from that deep, dark pit. Whereas, the All-Wise Qur'an elevates man, through belief and good deeds, from the lowest of the low to the highest of the high, and demonstrates that it does this with clear proofs. And it fills in that deep pit with rungs of inner development and spiritual progress.[66]

Certainly, the dwindling and quivering relations between the Muslim world and the West go deep into their histories, cultures, and worldviews. Hence, any attempt to treat the present dilemma of relations and civilizational interactions between the two civilizational blocks requires a deep understanding of each other's worldviews, cultures, histories, and civilizational dynamics. As a matter of fact, any superficial endeavors that overlook and undermine the civilizational dynamics of the Muslim world and the West will only add more fuel to the already burning relations. Our attempts at dialogue and understanding should revolve within the orbits of our distinctive cultural surroundings and dynamics so as to allow mature and genuine relations to grow and flourish. Otherwise, our efforts and attempts will only hold back and waste our potentials and throw us in the world of nothingness and wastage.

ISLAM AND THE NEW VISION FOR UNIVERSAL DIALOGUE

With this comprehensive vision in mind, one can deeply fathom Nursi's philosophy and perception of dialogue between the Muslim world and the West. To him, dialogue and understanding are basically a Quranic universal stand that is in accordance with the norms of human nature, the laws of God in the universe, and the patterns of history, culture, and society. Whatever the stand of the partner of dialogue, Nursi argues, the people of the Quran are ready to share their wisdom and experience. One can underscore how the *Risale-i Nur* is advocating dialogue and attempting to show the truths of the Quran that covers issues related to worlds of seen and unseen alike. Nursi says: "thus, all Bediuzzaman's endeavour was to prove and demonstrate the falseness of these accusations, and that far from being incompatible with science and progress, the Qur'an was the source of true progress and civilization, and in addition, since this was the case, Islam would dominate the future, despite its relative decline and regression at that time."[67]

However, while Nursi calls for dialogue and urges the people of the Quran to practice it, he is observant on those kinds of dialogues that are meant for worldly gain or oriented self-interest. In fact, he does not hide his dismay with such dialogues because he sees in them a mere demagogy and indoctrination that do not serve the human cause. According to him, the door of dialogue should remain open as long as our intention is to serve humanity and save it from eternal suffering. He is of the view that the main concern in dialogue and understanding between the West and the Muslim world is not the occurrence of dialogue here and there and in different places and times, but what matters most is the quality, content, nature, objective, aspiration, horizon, and the extent of reach of the dialogue and understanding.

Risale-i Nur: A Dynamic Approach to Dialogue

As already stated, the question of dialogue between the West and the Muslim world had never been a controversial issue in the writings of Nursi. On the contrary, the spirit and bottom line of the *Risale-i Nur* have not only been as an advocator of dialogue but also as a provider of deep insights on ways and methods of carrying it out in the best manner. In fact, the sense of propagating dialogue is one of the main features of the *Risale-i Nur* as well as one of its basic teachings. Having said this, however, one should eliminate any ambiguity that can transpire from our explanation of Nursi's perception of dialogue.

There are certain passages in the *Risale-i Nur* that commendably and systematically criticize and decisively judge certain groups and religions, such as various groups of the people of the Book, several aspects of modern civilization, many philosophers and naturalists, and irreligious people. This is true and undeniable, yet one should firmly distinguish between criticizing a group or an idea or a religious practice of this group or another one and the virtue of dialogue that Nursi advocates and advances with all kind of peoples whatever their religious stance and attitude. As a matter of fact, the *Risale-i Nur* never ceases from practicing dialogue and understanding with all sorts of ideas and people. Hence, it is important to acknowledge this feature in the work of Nursi and distinguish it from his responses to some specific questions or interpretations of some verses of the Quran and traditions of the Prophet.

One should underline the fact that runs through the vein of Nursi's works and testifies to his deep admiration of dialogue with all groups for the sake of God. It is his clear intention and will to involve in dialogue and understanding process with others so that he can explain to them clearly the diamonds that the Quran contains as well as show them the role of religion in improving and expanding their relations and understanding of each other. Pondering deeply over the *Risale-i Nur* engenders a new perception of dialogue and understanding among religions and believers in the world today. To me, dialogue between faiths and civilizations is a sign of religious maturity and civilizational wisdom. It seems that practicing sincere dialogue and understanding among faiths and religions constitutes the departing point in wisdom dissemination and knowledge generations for the benefit of all humanity. Indeed, sincere dialogue and understanding constitute one sort of pondering on the parables and patterns of God in life. In line with this, dialogue and exchange of ideas about our faiths, heritages, and cultures are one way of seeing the names and attributes of God perceived and manifested in our life. It is through dialogue that people of different faiths discover the beauty of God's names and attributes. Therefore, dialogue and understanding of each other is to Nursi a way of learning about the names, attributes, signs, and patterns and wisdom of God. Indeed, one should see in dialogue and understanding platforms and grounds for increasing our faith in God and increasing our efficiency in relieving the sufferings of the sufferers. Therefore, it is important to advance a new perception of dialogue that is spiritually and ethically oriented.

CONCLUSION

As humanity advances and progresses toward deep stages of globality and universality, people will acquire more knowledge about themselves, their nature, their lives, their universe, their destination, their total well-being and the rest of the creatures that live with them and surround their lives. In this stage, when knowledge becomes a real power and a powerful means of knowing and accessing the wisdom of creations, religion will, consequently, become the core of human life and its reservoir of strength and enlightenment. In this stage of human development, Nursi envisions a very imperative role of the Quran and its methods and truths about God, life, universe, man, seen and unseen worlds and so on. According to him, new global realities and new advancements in sciences, technology, and human communication will mark the era when the Quranic facts and teachings will stand and play their vital role in providing clear evidences about the truth of matters that humanity is disputing and squabbling over.

In fact, we should be aware of the unprecedented pattern in which these events and changes are occurring and shaping our present and future realities. Indeed, they pose a big question mark to the very core structure of our ethical edifice and moral destiny. The shocking impact of this transformation in our perception of things and events in life and reality gives raise to several moral and ethical questions about the destiny and role of our civilization. Indeed, the present situation of humanity bears witness to essential events and changes that have been evolving ever since the advent of modern civilization. Hence, it is the right time to indulge in fruitful dialogue so as to be able to share our wisdom about how to overcome the human dilemmas and create the proper environment for cooperation and understanding to flourish and blossom.

Last but not least, I would like to propose that an International Council or Center for International Dialogue and Cooperation be set up to involve the activities of interfaith and intercivilization dialogue. The center should consist of renowned scholars, religious figures, and ordinary people. The center also should aim, among other goals, to produce new books and material that integrate the views and perceptions of different religions and partners of dialogue about the different problems and issues that encounter humanity today.

Notes

1. Said Nursi, *The Damascus Sermon* (Istanbul, 1996), 49.
2. Ian Markham, "Truth and Toleration: The Said Nursi Achievement," *Bringing Faith, Meaning, and Peace to Life in a Multicultural World: The Risale-i Nur's Approach*, Seventh International Symposium on Bediuzzaman Said Nursi, October 3–5, 2004, Istanbul, 13.
3. Said Nursi, *The Words* (Istanbul, 2002), 167.
4. See Said Nursi, *The Rays Collection* (Istanbul, 2002), 105, 287; Said Nursi, *The Letters* (Istanbul, 2001), 493.
5. Said Nursi, *The Words*, 167.
6. Bediuzzaman Said Nursi, *The Biography of Bediuzzaman Said Nursi*, translated from the Turkish by Sükran Vahide.
7. "For believers, it is not simply that modern civilization tends to exile God to the margin of daily consciousness and activity. Modern civilization also offers a value system that is at odds with that of religion. It defines happiness differently from religious thought. Success and failure are counted in different terms. Self-fulfillment is regarded as a basic human motivation, and possession of consumer goods is considered a mark of personal achievement." See Thomas Michel, S. J., "Grappling with Modern Civilization: Said Nursi's Interpretive Key," *Bringing Faith, Meaning, and Peace to Life in a Multicultural World: The Risale-i Nur's Approach*, Seventh International Symposium on Bediuzzaman Said Nursi, October 3–5, 2004, Istanbul, 79.
8. Said Nursi, *The Words*, 167.
9. Said Nursi, *The Letters*, 548.
10. Said Nursi, *The Damascus Sermon*, 38
11. *The Biography of Badiuzzaman Said Nursi.*
12. See Osman Cilaci, "Comments on the Holy Bible in the Raisale-i Nur," *Contemporary Approach to Understanding the Qur'an: The Example of the Risale-i Nur* (Istanbul, 2000), 585.

13. Sukran Vahide, *The Author of the Risale-i Nur, Bediuzzaman Nursi*, part three (Istanbul, 1992).
14. Nursi says: "in my journey of the spirit at that time I said to Europe's collective personality, which apart from beneficial science and the virtues of civilization, holds in its hand meaningless, harmful philosophy and noxious, dissolute civilization." Nursi, *The Flashes*, 160; See also Nursi, *The Words*, 45.
15. Nursi, *The Flashes Collection* (Istanbul, 2000), 160.
16. Nursi, *The Damascus Sermon*, 38.
17. Tomas Michel, "Muslim-Christians Dialogue and Cooperation in the Thought of Bediuzzaman Said Nursi," International Symposium on A Contemporary Approach to Understanding the Qur'an: The Example of the Risale-I-Nur, Turkey, September 20–22, 1998, 554.
18. Said Nursi, *Letters*, 578.
19. Said Nursi, *The Damascus Sermon*, 37.
20. Said Nursi, *The Rays*, 300.
21. Said Nursi, *The Damascus Sermon*, 37.
22. Said Nursi, *Letters*, 397.
23. Thomas Michel, S. J., "Grappling with Modern Civilization," 80.
24. See Nursi, *Letters*, 95.
25. See Nursi, *The Rays*, 105, 287.
26. Said Nursi, *The Damascus Sermon*, 85.
27. Said Nursi, *Īşārātū'l-ī'caz*, (Istanbul, 1995), 50.
28. Thomas Michel, S.J. "Muslim-Christians Dialogue," 561.
29. Ursula Spuler, *Christian-Muslim Dialogue*, Marburg University, Germany.
30. Said Nursi, *The Words*, 747.
31. Nursi says: "Since modern civilization acts contrary to the fundamental laws of the revealed religion, its evils have come outweigh its good aspects, its errors and harmful aspects its benefits. General tranquility and a happy worldly life, the true aims of civilization, have been destroyed." Nursi, *Emirdag Lahikasi*, ii, 97–99.
32. Said Nursi, *The Words*, 420.
33. Said Nursi, *The Words*, 421.
34. Ian Markham, "Truth and Toleration," 17.
35. Ursula Spuler, *Christian-Muslim Dialogue*.
36. Said Nursi, *The Words*, 746.
37. See also Said Nursi, *Mūnāzarat* (Istanbul, 1977), 26–27.
38. See Said Nursi, *The Damascus Sermon*, 14.
39. Said Nursi, *Letters*, 515.
40. Said Nursi, *The Biography of Bediuzzaman Said Nursi*.
41. Said Nursi, *Emirdag Lahikast* (Istanbul, 1993), I, 147.
42. Said Nursi, *Letters* (Istanbul, 2nd ed., 1997), 137.
43. Said Nursi, *The Rays Collection* (Istanbul, 1998), 108.
44. Said Nursi, *Kastamonu Lahikast* (Istanbul, 1960), 75.
45. Nursi clearly states that: "A definite proof for the damage in this time and age being moral and this damage can possibly be counteracted only by curative moral atomic bombs is the Risale-i Nur's standing as barricade against the attacks of misguidance, materialistic philosophy, and atheism. . . . Risale-i Nur has become a restorer and moral atomic bomb against this morality damage." Nursi, *Emirdag Lahikast*, 186.

46. Said Nursi, *The Damascus Sermon*, 85.
47. Ibid., 78.
48. Ibid., 38.
49. Said Nursi, *Mūnāzarat* (Istanbul, n.d.), 33, 68.
50. Yunus A. Cengel, "Fighting Terror and Eliminating Weapons of Mass Destruction," *Bringing Faith, Meaning, and Peace to Life in a Multicultural World: The Risale-i Nur's Approach*, Seventh International Symposium on Bediuzzaman Said Nursi, October 3–5, 2004, Istanbul, 203.
51. Said Nursi, *Munazrat*, 68.
52. Said Nursi, *The Damascus Sermon*, 14.
53. Said Nursi, *Muhakemat*, 10. As quoted in Yunus A. Cengel, "Fighting Terror and Eliminating Weapons of Mass Destruction," op. cit., 205.
54. Nursi says: "there is no hostility, spite or brutality in the soul of a believer. There is a type of brotherhood even with one's greatest enemy." Said Nursi, *Mesevi-i Nuriye* (Istanbul), 69; see also, 89–90.
55. Said Nursi, *The Damascus Sermon*, 49.
56. Said Nursi, *The Rays*, 316.
57. Ibid., 415.
58. Sid Nursi, *The Words*, 663–64.
59. Yunus A. Cengel, "Fighting Terror," op cit., 207.
60. Said Nursi, *Muhakemt*, 151 as quoted in Yunus A. Cengel, "Fighting Terror," op. cit., 202.
61. Yunus A. Cengel, "Fighting Terror," 202.
62. Mohammad Aslam Parvaiz, "Environmental Ethics—The Human Roles Advocated by the Qur'an and Elucidated by Ustad Nursi," *Bringing Faith, Meaning, and Peace to Life in a Multicultural World: The Risale-i Nur's Approach*, Seventh International Symposium on Bediuzzaman Said Nursi, October 3–5, 2004, Istanbul, 237.
63. Said Nursi, *Letters*, 494.
64. Jane I. Smith, "At the Heart of the Matter: Faith and Belief in the Poetic Imagery of Said Nursi," *Bringing Faith, Meaning, and Peace to Life in a Multicultural World: The Risale-i Nur's Approach*, Seventh International Symposium on Bediuzzaman Said Nursi, October 3–5, 2004, Istanbul, 109.
65. Said Nursi, *The Words*, 274.
66. Nursi, *The Words*, 666.
67. Nursi, *The Flashes*, 377.

THIRTEEN

THE THREAT TO SPIRITUALITY

Fred A. Reed

This chapter is a nonacademic response to an invitation from the Istanbul Foundation for Science and Culture. In it, I strive to address the sense of deprivation written upon our lives as individuals and upon the lives of our societies: the need not only for a spiritual dimension, but also for a spiritual compass to our existence.

Today, the need for such a compass has grown more acute than ever. The collapse of communism, itself a by-product of the materialist dispensation that proclaims itself to "be the world" and acts accordingly, has set loose in the land dark and terrifying forces. Citizens of the prosperous democracies of Europe, and of the English-speaking world in particular, are now peremptorily informed that "terrorism"—and specifically "Islamic terrorism"—is a dire threat to their way of life. Citizens of the Muslim world, in all its vast social and doctrinal diversity, have come under fire as never before from powers who seek to direct the lives of their societies, to control and expropriate their wealth, and to challenge—and perhaps overturn—the most deeply held tenets of their belief.

An international torture gulag has been established, with the complicity of states that had undertaken, through solemn international instruments, to abolish all such practices. Lip service is paid to international law, but that law is described as "quaint" by the theoreticians of unrestrained American executive power.

Islam, the last of the three Abrahamic religions, is today accused of harboring, in its very fabric and at the heart of its universal message, a shadowy movement that contradicts one of its holiest tenets: the sacred nature of human life. The first of the three, Judaism must likewise face charges of sheltering within it a secularist ideology that has denied the humanity of a people it has expropriated, colonized, and humiliated. The third, Christianity, is fulsomely invoked to justify American and British atrocities in the Middle East, not to mention complex and elaborate schemes to visit the benefits of U.S.-style "democracy" on their societies.

These dire circumstances, I argue, constitute the greatest threat to spirituality in our day. Thus, to speak and write of the imperative of spirituality becomes a daring exercise. Some might well claim that it is an impossible task. Precisely because it appears impossible, it must be undertaken. But it must be undertaken without illusion.

Those who stand for the values of spirituality must confront an intimidating question: against the imperatives of blood and power—against what Bediuzzaman Said Nursi called "the club of politics," what can we hope to achieve? On the face of it, thinkers and writers can do very little: they hold no life-or-death power; they cannot mobilize armies or purchase the sympathies of decision-makers. And yet, paradoxically, there is much they can do.

For over a decade, the Istanbul Foundation for Science and Culture has awakened the participants in its biennial symposia to their obligation to give a new, actualized reading to the principles of interfaith dialogue; to lend fuller meaning to what Iran's previous president, Seyyed Mohammad Khatami, termed the "dialogue of civilizations." Participants learned to respect and admire, if not always agree with, the sincere views of scholars of the three monotheistic dispensations, and have explored the ways in which they speak to the spiritual crisis of our times. They have done so not with the vocabulary that excludes and stigmatizes, but with that which includes and embraces.

They have, in the words of the eminent European Muslim Reform scholar Tariq Ramadan, learned in face-to-face contact and respectful argument that, for spirituality to flourish, we must build bridges, not walls.

Symposium attendees have sought to understand, and have criticized, the phenomenon called globalization, and held up against it an alternative vision. Where the secular high priests of globalism drone on about inevitability, they have attempted to respond with the argument of patient resistance that must be waged in the name of spirituality.

Said Nursi puts it this way, as if addressing every individual man or woman, and our society as well: "Do you think, O heedless one, that the essential purpose for man's life is restricted to material progress, scientific and technological development, earning a livelihood and the like concerning the worldly life?"[1]

Yet, in the name of spirituality, we cannot reject the worldly life. If this life is, as Muslims believe, the way station along the path to a greater life in the hereafter, it is also the place where we are called upon to exercise the responsibility of our limited, God-given free will, and for this exercise we will ultimately be held to account.

Said Nursi, and later, the multifaceted movement that follows him and invokes his spirit, draw a distinction between the Sufi path, based on purification of the carnal self, spiritual illumination, and removal from the world, and the path he had chosen in the bitter years of secularist repression that marked the beginnings of Republican Turkey. When I first encountered the Nur movement, in Istanbul, in 1998, I asked a simple question that betrayed my legitimate confusion: was Said a Sufi? "Bediuzzaman was not a follower of any sect, scholar or Sufi order," my hosts replied. "He said our age is a time for reality, *ḥaqīqat*, not *ṭarīqat*. What he did was to provide us with a shorter path to enlightenment, a direct line to the Qur'an."[2]

Readers will have intuited that I am working toward a way of situating spirituality in the world; of making its practice accountable to the imperative of resistance to injustice. I submit that Said Nursi's definition is good enough for us; that the spirituality we are seeking to elucidate and to foster, in our lives and in the life of society, must be anchored in *ḥaqīqat*, in the reality of the world as it is. Not as an end in itself, of course—but as a shorter path to the enlightenment that alone can avert the present crisis.

Not for us the touchy-feely pseudospiritualism on offer in the global cultural supermarket. The values we pursue are at the farthest remove from this kind of prepackaged, genetically engineered spiritualist fast food. What draws us is not this year's most successful spiritual crash diet. In fact, everything the patient work of the Nur movement stands for militates against the free-floating, one-size-fits-all nostrums hawked by charismatic preachers.

Nor can we accept, or tolerate, those individuals whose pretention to spiritual presence conceals the hidden agenda of states and political parties, or those whose pronouncements conceal an obsession with self-promotion.

The path of reality is a demanding one. On it we encounter the victims of an unjust global order. On it we must avert our eyes and our faces from the unconscionable profiteers of this same order, and, worse, from those who justify it or deny their responsibility for it. On it our faith and our belief systems are challenged, our values ridiculed, derided as antiquated, narrow-minded, picturesque. Perhaps declared dangerous, singled out, stigmatized, attacked, forbidden, persecuted.

Though we may not entirely appreciate it, the obstacles we face are similar to those faced by Bediuzzanam Said Nursi in his life. Professor Ibrahim abu-Rabi' perceptively notes: "one can read the *Risale-i Nur* as a product of suffering, exile, imprisonment, and alienation, a process reflective of the deep historical and social changes engulfing the Muslim world since the nineteenth century."[3]

As the *Risale-i Nur* reflects the changes that engulfed the Muslim world, and particularly the Ottoman state in its author's lifetime, our contemporary reading of it should, in parallel fashion, be applied to the globalizing society we live in. For, as those who have plans for restructuring Islam will be happy to tell us, a standardized model is, even as we speak, being prepared. This time it will be applied not only in one country, but also throughout the Muslim world—and perhaps beyond, as a component of the doctrine of globalization as it is currently being applied, by economic constraint, by military force, or by cultural domination.

The parallels between Said's time of troubles and hardships and our era are striking. Then, the Ottoman Empire was considered the "sick man of Europe." The remedy for its illness would be dismemberment, and then distribution of its component parts among the "doctors," a consortium of European powers. The aim was full integration into the existing world system. Today, the "sick man" is the entire Islamic world, and the remedy envisaged promises to be more draconian still. The prescription—always the same—is for "constructive instability" leading to a complete restructuring of the Muslim heartland, and, ideally, of the minds and hearts of Muslims. Of one thing we may be certain: this process will be neither for the profit nor the betterment of its inhabitants.

It can be cogently argued that discussion of politics, in the broader sense, is inimical to the spiritual life. But, true to our recognition of the world as it is, we must acknowledge that political developments exercise a powerful, even a determinant influence on the life of the spirit. We may mistakenly choose not to see the political. However, the political sees us and structures the society of which we are a part.

Here lies the nub of the problem. Those who are drawn toward a spiritual vision intuit that life in this globalizing society has become, except for a tiny minority of the rich and powerful, one of suffering and humiliation, injustice, exile, and alienation. These are the very factors that create the conditions that drive men to desperate measures, conditions in which conflict, bloodshed, destruction, and self-destruction—what is today called "terrorism"—appear as the only solution.

Bediuzzaman Said Nursi describes this prospect in powerful language:

> Wherever we look, we see the same scene where the shouts of oppressors and the cries and lamentations of the oppressed are heard. Since a man feels pain because of the pain of others, a man's conscience cannot bear so much injustice and lamentation. So, the one who believes witnesses them, because of hopelessness and inability to do anything to stop them, abandons all his human feelings, and, with a heart no longer

> concerned about the destruction of all other men so long as he himself is safe, surrenders to the utmost degree of savagery.[4]

We should not be misled by the apparent bleakness of the picture of reality Said paints. True, he was concerned to depict the world into which he was born, and which, in the shape of Turkish republican extremism, did everything it could, having failed to kill him, to silence and marginalize him. But he was more concerned still with a spiritual response to this world. A close examination of Said's work, rather than allowing us to posit a distinct, remote spiritual realm, indicates that the two cannot be separated, and that any attempt to separate them would be a dereliction of the duty to which he implicitly summons us.

Some argue, against the background of the events of September 11, 2001, that the world of Islam alone is in crisis. These events, shocking yet unsurprising, should not be seen as causes, but as outcomes; as symptoms of extreme dysfunction, as evidence of incipient systemic breakdown, perhaps even precipitous collapse. Not in what can be broadly defined as Islamic society, but in the apparently impregnable, all-powerful West, which asserts, to employ the military jargon of the Pentagon, "full spectrum dominance."

Iran's former president, Mohammad Khatami, writing before the attack on the Twin Towers, put it thus: "when the dominant worldview cannot satisfy the psychological, material and social needs of its constituents, people begin to experience a troubling void and sterility. . . . The historically conditioned predilections that are rendered anachronistic will not be easily abandoned. This state of limbo can merely offer the veneer of a civilization. An existential void sets in that brings on a full-blown identity crisis."[5]

Mr. Khatami has accurately diagnosed the crisis that affects the West in every sphere of its existence. This crisis, for reasons I believe can be identified, has become the dominant aspect of relations between two cultures that should be linked through mutually enriching dialogue, but instead glare at one another in hostility and incomprehension.

For those whose watchword is the necessity of dialogue, the danger of becoming infected, as it were, is great indeed. The danger of accepting as a basis for dialogue or debate the premises of the Western culture described by Mohammad Khatami is greater still. As I understand it, the appropriate response to any crisis is, first, to understand its origins; second, to grasp its potential effects; third, to seek paths of resolution and, at the same time, of resistance.

With a central focus on the links between spirituality and Said's *Risale-i Nur*—which many regard as the outstanding Quranic commentary of the twentieth century—we should strive to sketch out a program for recentering the debate this crisis has forced upon us.

While the West may possess, as Mr. Khatami says, "the material and symbolic sources of power simultaneously,"[6] it cannot easily impose these sources of power on us, providing we recognize them for what they are. It certainly cannot make them appear pleasing to our eyes, provided our eyes are wide open.

In no way can these power sources respond to our spiritual concerns, which Tariq Ramadan defines in these terms: "There can be no question of denying anything about our being, nor about our body, nor about our spirit; nothing about this life, nor about the life to come. The great test of spirituality is the test of balance; the "straight path" is the most difficult path of all."[7]

The "straight path," the *ṣirāt ul-mustaqīm* that all Muslims strive to follow, was and is the path of Said Nursi. Those who have come to know him, love him, and seek his guidance, recognize a fierce and dedicated fighter for the life of the spirit. They also recognize the man who singled out enmity as that object most worthy of our enmity.

Among his many outstanding qualities was an uncanny ability of being able to confront us with the kind of questions we'd never thought of asking ourselves before; questions that penetrate suddenly, unexpectedly, to the heart of the matter. Questions that ask: are we the owners of ourselves?

Let us pay close attention to Said:

> Supposing himself to absolutely own his self, a person imagines a realm of dominion for himself and then, comparing other people and material causes to himself, he shares the rest of God's property or dominion against them. . . . O selfhood! Give up this false claim! . . . You are not the owner of yourself so that you can be the maker or creator of the body in which you dwell. Nor have material causes made it so that they claim to own it."[8]

To ask the question, and to follow it to its logical conclusion, is to arrive rapidly at the edge of the chasm that separates the spiritual world whose richness we seek from the world of absolute materiality as established by the Western dispensation that now defines itself as the "world culture." For if any single factor can be said to define this culture, it is the contention that we are, individually and collectively, the owners of ourselves.

Absolute materiality, as it is represented in a global system, today stands as the overarching threat that confronts spirituality today. Before turning our attention to the forms this threat takes—for they are multiple—we must attempt to locate the sources of what we can call the 'Western dispensation', and its claim to occupy the entire field of consciousness and discourse.

In his wide-ranging investigation into the sources of the Western narrative tradition, the late Thierry Hentsch argued that Westerners have been convinced that their culture and civilization exhaust the possibilities of life on earth: "The idea of truth, and the need to believe in it have been less affected by the decline of the Church and the Christian faith than is generally supposed. Both idea and need have shifted, along with the need for religion itself. The shift has taken place principally toward the sciences. Today, for all our scepticism and relativism, it is from them that we stand in expectation of salvation."[9]

That shift is the rise of humanism and instrumental rationality, the complex of ideas that has placed man at the center of creation—made him that which Said Nursi warns against: the person who claims to be the owner of himself.

Hentsch continues: "For better or for worse, by placing man and his earthly achievements at the center of its concerns, humanism has put man in control, and paved the way for the development of the technoscientific development that is ours today. [But] . . . in its ignorance of itself, the modern vision of history has created a vicious circle, one from which even today it is struggling to escape."

In fact, the modern vision of history cannot escape itself. Hentsch demonstrates, in a close, critical reading of the formative texts of the Western literary canon, how this vision has been transposed from belief in the sacrifice of Christ as a condition for Christian salvation, to the conviction that belief could be imposed upon those outside our cultural sphere by force; and ultimately, and by implication—as in the case of the Crusades, the colonial enterprise and now, the American blueprint for a Middle East initiative—by invasion, torture, and massacre.

The imperative of salvation remains. It has become secularized, "humanized." Its original form applied to the Christian believer alone: "*Truth or death*. On condition that the believer accepts Truth, death will be overcome. Failing that, death will irremediably strike whoever has not believed."[10]

Today, under a humanistic culture that has cast its lot, irrevocably, with a purportedly neutral technoscience, and whose credo is modernity, the injunction is directed toward those who decline the invitation to accept this particular Truth. The notion of 'salvation' has migrated from the spiritual to the temporal and material sphere. Those who would reject it must henceforth face the alternative, which is death.

Few, I believe, would be surprised to learn that those who are currently being offered this ultimatum in its most direct form are primarily, though not exclusively, Muslims. The 'salvation' on offer is nothing so crude as religious conversion, though that idea is popular among some Christian fundamentalists in the United States. No, the 'salvation' held out to believers in Islam is of a more symbolic and, at the same time, more immediate nature.

The demands of globalization, which could be described as the West's last Crusade, are such that the essential nature of Islam must be changed, adjusted to correspond to the dominant paradigm. Muslims can choose between several variants of this paradigm, but choose they must. Failure to do so, failure to accept Truth as defined by the humanist/technoscientific nexus can mean only one thing. On the geopolitical level, the Anglo-American invasion of Iraq—and the prospect of an American nuclear attack on Iran—can be taken as an example of this policy in practice.

In their introduction to a recent collection of essays on globalization, ethics and Islam from the perspective of the *Risale-i Nur*, editors Ian Markham and Ibrahim Özdemir—hardly radicals—depart from strictly academic concerns to sound a note of warning. Accurately, they single out Daniel Pipes for special consideration. (For those who might have forgotten, Pipes is the son of Richard Pipes, the architect of the strategic alliance between Turkey and Israel.)

"For Pipes," write Markham and Özdemir, "the only good Muslim is a secular Muslim. His hero is Mustafa Kemal Atatürk in Turkey; indeed, secular Turkey is the model as far as Pipes is concerned. Pipes is deeply suspicious of any Muslim who is committed to his or her tradition. If we allow ourselves to be infected by the Pipes worldview, then perhaps we are in for a long, desperate battle between Islam and the West."[11]

The measured alarm of Markham and Özdemir, as compilers of a learned anthology, may well be an understatement of the stakes. Daniel Pipes adopts the postures, the linguistic tics of academic discourse. But he should be seen first and foremost as a hired gun, the kind of character whom the Western ideological establishment can rely upon to apply to the letter the injunction of Truth or Death. It would be no exaggeration to say that the worldview presented by Pipes actually looks forward gleefully to a long, desperate battle between Islam and the West. Do those whose intellectual and ideological agenda helped shaped the invasion of Iraq and today continue to justify the denial of Palestinian rights have in mind a 'regime change' program for Muslims, for Islam itself?

Let us examine for a moment the campaign to destroy the career of Tariq Ramadan. Ramadan is the son of the eminent Islamic legal scholar Said Ramadan, and maternal grandson of the founder of the *Ikhwan al-Muslimin*, Hassan al-Banna. His family background gives him "the requisite stature and influence to . . . encourage Muslims to understand that action must be informed by context."[12]

Tariq Ramadan was scheduled to take up a teaching position at Notre Dame University in Indiana in the fall of 2004. His visa was rescinded several days before he was to begin his professorial duties. None other than Daniel Pipes, founder of "Campus Watch," a website that tracks and attacks academics critical of Israel and the Zionist agenda, claimed credit for convincing American authorities that Ramadan represented a 'security risk' while producing not a shred of evidence. More recently, he has been instrumental in an international campaign of denigration designed to make Ramadan, a European-born Muslim, persona non grata in France and elsewhere in his native Europe.

Of course, Tariq Ramadan is no more a security risk to the United States than was Bediuzzaman Said Nursi to Kemalist Turkey. Like Said Nursi, he "does not attack Islam as Luther attacked Catholicism, nor does he advocate a wholesale break with classical Islamic tradition."[13] What he does do is speak from inside the faith. At last, a modern European Muslim intellectual can and does talk of Islam with greater authority than the non-Muslim academic 'experts,' those modern-day neo-Orientalists who have monopolized the representation of Islam until now.

Tariq Ramadan's other outstanding characteristic is his ability to address Muslim discontent, and to "rechannel frustration away from extremism and towards moderation."[14] He can do this because Muslims recognize him as one of their own, as a man who shares the beliefs and practices of the common Muslim.

Markham and Özdemir make the same point, trenchantly, with regard to Said Nursi: "[He] is a mainstream, conservative Muslim. The temptation for non-Muslims is to find a liberal secular Muslim as a conversation partner. But the fact is that the majority of Muslims are not secular and liberal."[15]

Why did Kemalist fundamentalism attempt to muzzle Said Nursi? Why do the Western ideologues of civilizational conflict seek to silence Tariq Ramadan? To imagine that these forces are searching for moderate voices within Islam to facilitate dialogue and increase understanding is to nourish illusions. In fact, their intent is quite the opposite. Writes Firas Ahmed: "Pipes is not advocating against Tariq Ramadan because he is an extremist, but precisely because he is a moderate. What Ramadan offers is dangerous because it empowers Muslims from within their own tradition."[16]

The parallels with the case of Bediuzzaman Said Nursi under the Kemalist dictatorship are clear. While Said was writing the letters, exegetical texts, inspirational passages, and essays that would become the *Risale-i Nur*, he had no other text, no other source than the Quran on which to rely: that is, directly and exclusively from the revealed Book precious to all Muslims.

Like the Kemalists by whom they swear, for Daniel Pipes and those who espouse his strategic outlook, "there is no such thing as a moderate Islamist, for all Islamists share the same long-term goal; they differ only over means. For example, the Justice and Development Party in Turkey is very different from the Taliban in its means, but not so different in its ends. If the party gained full control over Turkey, it could be as dangerous as the Taliban were in Afghanistan."[17]

Outrageous on its face, Pipes's argument is indicative of the gravity and depth of the crisis of Western discourse on Islam. Worse yet, where we can smell the smoke of incendiary rhetoric, we will soon feel the fire of initiatives designed to transmute Pipes's musings into policy. And the intent of policy, as we know, is application.

In 2003, the RAND Corporation, a conservative American think-tank, published an eighty-seven-page pamphlet by Cheryl Benard entitled *Civil Democratic Islam: Partners, Resources and Strategies.* The title has an intimate ring to it. How could anyone not sympathize with the idea of a "civil, democratic" Islam? But this title can be read two ways: as an assertion that Islam is indeed civil and democratic, or that it is not, and should become so.

The plot thickens when we learn that author Benard is the wife of Zalmay Khalizad, the former American viceroy in post-Taliban Afghanistan and now satrap of Iraq, whom she thanks, along with others, for his comments, suggestions, and assistance. Far from being an obscure academic researcher, Cheryl Benard moves at the highest levels of the global order's policy directorate. In fact, it might be more accurate to characterize Benard's document as the ideological and moral equivalent of the public relations campaign leading to the American invasions of Afghanistan and Iraq. Instead of attempts at regime change, which in those countries involved the recruitment of pliable and willing allies, we are now dealing with a programmatic document for the remake of an entire religion along lines congenial to the strategic, economic, and ideological imperatives of the Super Power.

"There is no question," she writes, "that contemporary Islam is in a volatile state, engaged in internal and external struggle over its values, its identity and its place in the world. Rival versions are contending for spiritual and political dominance. This conflict has serious costs and economic, social, political and security implications for the rest of the world."[18]

We can quickly deconstruct the preceding paragraph by asking a few questions: (1) If contemporary Islam is in a volatile state, why is this so? (2) Do the rival forces contending for spiritual and political dominance have any connection with power centers in the West? (3) Why should a process internal to one world religion, and not to others (the impact of Zionism on Judaism, or of Evangelical fundamentalism on Christianity, for example), alone have economic, social, and security implications for the "rest of the world"?

Indeed, the United States, and the rest of the 'international community' that consists primarily of its vassals, "would prefer an Islamic world that is compatible with the rest of the system . . . [that] follows the rules and norms of international conduct."

Coming from within a superpower that has adopted torture as official policy, that has discarded the Geneva Convention as "quaint," that threatens other states with "regime change" and employs nuclear blackmail, the author's assertion is indeed breathtaking.

Couched in the polite, neutral language of high-level Washington bureaucrats, Benard's pamphlet is in fact a manifesto for the revamping of Islam along lines acceptable to the West, as incarnated in the supreme defender of its "values," the United States.

Her strategy is to divide Muslims into arbitrary categories, then to describe those categories, and finally, to offer tactics for playing off one group against another. First, and worst, are the fundamentalists, who are said to want "an authoritarian, puritanical state that will implement their extreme view of Islamic law and morality." Second are the traditionalists, who are "suspicious of modernity, innovation and change." Then there are the modernists, who "want the Islamic world to become a part of global modernity." Finally, there are the secularists, who want "religion relegated to the private sphere."[19]

The fundamentalists, she says, are hostile to the West; the traditionalists hold more moderate views, but are close to the fundamentalists with regard to the values of modernity. The modernists and secularists are closer to the West, but generally in a weaker position, lacking a public platform from which to propagate their views in the Muslim world.

To deal effectively with what we might call "the Islamic problem," Benard proposes a series of measures designed to help various potential allies advance their respective agendas.

- Support the modernists first, she argues. Publish and distribute their works; give them a mass audience, primarily among young people; give them a public platform; position secularism and modernism as a "counterculture" option for disaffected Islamic youth.
- Then support the traditionalists against the fundamentalists. Publicize traditionalist criticism of fundamentalist violence and extremism; discourage alliances between traditionalists and fundamentalists; increase the presence and profile of modernists in traditionalist institutions.
- Then confront and oppose the fundamentalists by challenging their interpretation of Islam, revealing their linkages to illegal groups and activities, and demonstrating their inability to rule; these messages should be addressed to young people, to pious traditionalists, to Muslim minorities in the West, and to women.

- Finally, selectively support secularists. This would be done by discouraging secularist alliance with anti-U.S. forces on such grounds as nationalism or social justice; give full support to the idea that religion and state can be separate in Islam.[20]

An analytical diagram that charts the manifold ramifications and identity markers of the various categories of Islamic belief and practice follow this exposition. These markers range from such issues as 'innovation' to polygamy and the covering of women.

While some of Benard's categories and even programmatic conclusions might at first glance seem sensible, it is more appropriate to view them with alarm, for they all flow through a single prism, that of the interests of the United States as standard-bearer for a West that is a figment of its own imagination. In fact, if we accept the broad diagnosis that I have attempted to make—that the Islamic world is being given the implicit choice between Truth and Death—they quickly become ominous. For, as we know, U.S. policy these days is formulated in words, but ultimately applied by state terror.

"The West thinks of nothing but its own interests," writes Mohammad Khatami, "and if a people turn away from its values and refuse to serve its interests, it focuses its vast capabilities to force them to surrender or risk annihilation."[21] Here, the speaker is clearly neither a fundamentalist nor even a traditionalist, but a reformer and advocate of religious democracy of impeccable credentials.

"It is no easy matter to transform a major world religion," writes Benard.[22] Here we have the merit of candor: so confident are these theoreticians of nation- and religion-building (or destruction) that they do not disdain to conceal either their aims or the methods they intend to employ. While even the most cursory reading of Benard's pamphlet reveals the immense variety and vitality of Islam—reveals in fact the multiplicity of Islams—her conclusions point to only one, caricatural Islam.

It will be an Islam not as defined, lived, and believed in by Muslims, for their opinions will not be sought, only made use of. It will be an 'Islam' redefined and restructured by the new global order. Among its loudest voices will be those of 'reformers' like the best-selling Canadian author Irshad Manji, self-styled 'progressive Muslims' whose challenges to mainstream practice curiously resemble Cheryl Benard's strategic design, and those 'militants' overcome by what Bediuzzaman Said Nursi terms "the hypocritical desire to be seen by people and hold a position in public view, which is the ambition for fame and acclaim and self-advertisement."[23]

In his analysis of efforts to silence Tariq Ramadan in the West, the essayist Firas Ahmed concludes that Pipes and people like him, in their efforts to remake Islam, may turn out to have launched an explosive experiment. I believe we can see around us just how explosive the experiment may turn out to be. "A more congenial alternative is to look to those within the Muslim world that seek to transcend the events of radicalism and fundamentalism."[24]

Our analyst may have fallen prey to a serious illusion: whether or not there are those within the Muslim world who seek to transcend the events of radicalism and fundamentalism—the vast majority of Muslims, in fact—is of little importance to the religion-builders. For Daniel Pipes, Tayyip Erdogan's Justice and Development Party is little more than a handful of Talibans simply waiting for the opportunity to transform Turkey into Afghanistan on the Bosphorus.

Who, we should ask, is more likely to have the ear of the decision-makers in Washington? Daniel Pipes and his Islamophobic initiatives, or that handful of earnest Muslims who actually believe they will be taken seriously? As I suggested earlier, there is one approved model for Islam today, and that model is the Kemalist one. The recipe is tried and true, the technique well known: if the turban offends, cut off the head.

It is precisely because of Said Nursi's intimate experience of Kemalism—his years of exile, imprisonment, repeated unjust accusations, privations, and persecutions—that he is, for us today, an exemplar of the pathway of resistance; a voice that we would ignore at our peril.

Ibrahim Abu-Rabi‘ has persuasively argued for a reading of the *Risale-i Nur* placed firmly within its historical context. Without contradicting him, I would expand and slightly modify that argument. Not only is Said Nursi's testament to Muslims—and thereby to humanity—a product of its time and place; it is also a major document of resistance to what Tariq Ramadan—but not only Tariq Ramadan—has called 'the unjust order of the world.'

And as Ramadan insists that the appropriate Muslim resistance to this unjust order is *jihad*, so did Bediuzzaman Said Nursi eighty years earlier. The *jihad* being proposed is not the wild-eyed call to arms so beloved of Western 'experts' in Islamic fundamentalism, but the appeal to moral and spiritual betterment, to striving against our overbearing ego, to seeking the light.

I have outlined what I consider to be the greatest threat to spirituality facing us today, and identified that threat as originating in the Western dispensation. For Said, writing from his lonely exile in Barla in 1934, the choice of means was clear: "a powerless person cannot employ both . . . the club and the light. For this reason I am compelled to embrace the light with all my strength, and cannot consider the club of politics, whatever form it is in. . . . In accordance with a person's way, a club is necessary to form a barrier against the assaults of the unbelievers and the apostates. But we have only two hands. Even if we had a hundred hands, they would be sufficient only for the light."

In words that ring powerfully today, he continues: "We want relief, happiness and victory—but not with the sword of the unbelievers. Let the unbelievers' swords be the end of them!"[25]

Far from the field of physical combat, isolated, Bediuzzaman Said Nursi found in the light of the Quran the concept that was to accompany him in each of the ordeals he would face: that of moral *jihad* in the defense of spirituality.

As is often his wont, Said adopts a military metaphor. When attacked by the enemy, he writes, Muslims must regard it as their primary duty to abandon internal dissension. "Practice the brotherhood, love and cooperation insistently enjoined by hundreds of Qur'anic verses and traditions of the Prophet! Establish with all of your powers a union with your fellows and brothers in religion that is stronger than the union of the worldly!"

After warning against falling into dispute, he exhorts his followers, and through them, the worshippers in the great mosque of the world:

> Do not say to yourself, "Instead of spending my valuable time on such petty matters, let me spend it on more valuable things such as the invocation of God and meditation"; thus withdrawing and weakening unity. For precisely what you imagine to be a matter of slight importance in this moral *jihad* may in fact be very great. In just the same way that under special and unusual conditions the watch kept by one soldier may be equal to a whole year's worship, in this age when the people of truth have been defeated, the precious day that you spend on some apparently minor matter concerning the moral struggle may be worth a thousand days, just like the hour of that soldier."[26]

If we agree that Islam—and in a broader sense, the idea of spirituality itself—is today under attack, and if we agree that our bonds of unity with our brothers and sisters in religion must be protected and strengthened, and if we believe that sincere dialogue among religions is not a luxury but an obligation, then each of us should consider herself or himself to be like that one soldier on watch.

Notes

1. Bediuzzaman Said Nursi. "A Flower from the Garden of the Qur'an," in *Epitomes of Light* (Mathnawi al-Nuriya), (Izmir, 1999), 267.

2. Fred A. Reed, *Anatolia Junction: A Journey into Hidden Turkey* (Vancouver, 1999), 39.
3. Ibrahim M. Abu-Rabi', ed., *Islam at the Crossroads: On the Life and Thought of Bediuzzaman Said Nursi* (Albany, 2003), x.
4. Bediuzzaman Said Nursi, "A Flower from the Garden of the Qur'an," 256–57.
5. Seyyed Mohammad Khatami, *Hope and Challenge: The Iranian President Speaks* (Binghamton, 1997), 4.
6. Ibid., 13.
7. Tariq Ramadan, *Entre l'homme et son cœur: la voie de l'Unique* (Lyon, 2001), 83 [my translation].
8. Bediuzzaman Said Nursi, "Four Significant Truths" in *Epitomes*, 99–100.
9. Thierry Hentsch, *Truth or Death: The Quest for Immortality in the Western Narrative Tradition*, translated by Fred A. Reed (Vancouver, 2004), 230.
10. Ibid., 220
11. Ian Markham and Ibrahim Özdemir, ed., *Globalization, Ethics and Islam: The Case of Bediuzzaman Said Nursi* (Aldershot, 2005), xvii.
12. Firas Ahmed, "Why Tariq Ramadan? " *Islamica*, No. 12, Spring 2005, 37.
13. Ibid., 37.
14. Ibid., 38.
15. Markham and Özdemir, xvii.
16. Firas Ahmed, *Islamica,* 39.
17. Daniel Pipes, cited in ibid., 38.
18. Cheryl Benard, *Civil Democratic Islam: Partners, Resources and Strategies* (Santa Monica, 2003), 9.
19. Ibid., 10.
20. Ibid., 16–18.
21. Seyyed Mohammad Khatami, *Hope and Challenge*, 38.
22. Ibid., 19.
23. Bediuzzaman Said Nursi, "29th Letter, 6th Section," *Letters 1928–1932*, translated by Sukran Vahide (Istanbul, 1997), 483.
24. Firas Ahmed, *Islamica*, 41.
25. Bediuzzaman Said Nursi, "The Sixteenth Flash," *The Flashes Collection*, translated by Sukran Vahide (Istanbul, 1995), 143–44.
26. Bediuzzaman Said Nursi, "The 20th Flash—on Sincerity," 208–209.

FOURTEEN

SHAYKH AHMAD SIRHINDĪ AND BEDIÜZZAMAN NURSI

Some Comparative Considerations

Yohanan Friedmann

Influences of of the Naqshbandiyya in general and of Shaykh Ahmad Sirhindī (1564–1624) in particular on Muslim thinkers in the Ottoman Empire have been discussed by several scholars. One may say that most scholars spoke about the institutional connections to the Naqshbandiyya, but did not identify the specific ideas associated with Sirhindī, which influenced a number of Ottoman religious figures. Albert Hourani surveys the arrival of the Naqshbandī order into the Ottoman Empire. He mentions Shaykh Murād (d. 1720), who received the Naqshbandi teachings from Sirhindī's son, Shaykh Muhammad Maʿṣūm.[1] The most famous link between the Naqshbandiyya and the Ottoman Empire is Mawlānā Khālid al-Naqshbandī who went to India in 1809, studied with Shāh ʿAbd al-ʿAzīz, and was intitiated into the Suhrawardiyya, the Kubrawiyya, the Chistiyya, and the *mujaddidī* branch of the Naqshbandiyya. The Ottoman Naqshbandiyya came to be known al-Khālidiyya after him.[2] A much more detailed treatment of Shaykh Khālid can be found in the work of Butrus Abu-Manneh.[3] According to him, Khālid was seen as the "renewer" (*mujaddid*) of the thirteenth century A.H. and also as the reviver of the Sunnah in Damascus.[4] In his letters, he stresses the importance of following the Sunnah of the Prophet and Shariʿah of Islam.[5] He also entertained rather intolerant views toward non-Muslims, urging his disciples to strive for the annihilation of the Jews, the Christians, the Zoroastrians, and even the Shīʿīs.[6] None of these scholars mentions

Nursi, but their work is essential to understand the background for the connection between Sirhindī and Nursi discerned by other scholars.

The most comprehensive work showing this connection is by Şerif Mardin who speaks about the existence of the Naqshbandī order in the Ottoman Empire since the fifteenth century, describes some of the teachings of Ahmad Sirhindī,[7] and quotes a reference to Sirhindī in Nursi's *al-Mathnawī al-'Arabī al-nūrī.*[8] He also mentions that Nursi saw in the *Maktūbāt* of Sirhindī and in the *Futūḥ al-Ghayb* of 'Abd al-Qādir al-Jīlānī works that helped him to resolve "his own confusion."[9] He compares the views of Nursi and Sirhindī on the question of the *quṭb*, an authoritative religious leader.[10] Finally, he sees a parallel between the sixteenth-century struggle against Hinduism in India and the nineteenth-century struggle against the growing influence of Western civilization in the Ottoman Empire.[11]

The material assembled by Şerif Mardin makes it clear that Nursi was aware of Shaykh Ahmad Sirhindī and viewed his *Maktūbāt* with favor. But Sirhindī was a multifaceted thinker. One can find in the three volumes of his letters material about the spiritual progress of the Sūfī, the relationship between Shari'ah and *Ṭarīqa*, or the transformation of the Sunnah into a Sūfī concept, together with stringent opinions on the treatment of the Hindūs and the Sikhs in the Mughul Empire. Therefore, when we discuss the influence of Sirhindī on Nursi, we need to answer the question: which aspect of Sirhindī's thought had some impact on him?

In Nursi's works, there are several passages in which Nursi makes references to Sirhindī. The most significant one relates an incident in which Nursi treated Sirhindī's *Maktūbāt* as if they were a sacred scripture, worthy of bibliomancy. He took the *Maktūbāt* volume in his hands and opened it at random in order to receive an omen. The book opened on a page including two letters to a certain Mīrzā Badī' al-Zamān.[12] In the *Maktūbāt*, only these two letters are addressed to this contemporary of Sirhindī, and Bediuzaman Nursi felt that the opening of the book on pages including letters to his namesake meant that Sirhindī is addressing him in particular. Furthermore, he felt that these letters are a cure for his ills.[13] More specifically, the passage in which Sirhindī says that one should focus his attention on a single *qibla*, otherwise his own personality may dissipate (*ammā ēk sharṭ mar'ī dārand wa an waḥdat-i qibla-yi tawajjuh ast qibla-yi tawajjuh-rā muta'addid sākhtan khwud-rā dar tafriqa andākhtan ast*),[14] made a great impression on him. Sirhindī's text is rather cryptic and there is no indication what he meant by this *qibla-yi tawajjuh*. After some consideration, Nursi made up his mind that this *qibla* should not be a spiritual master, but rather the Quran itself.[15] This passage is an excellent indication of the high esteem in which Nursi held Sirhindī's work.

In another passage quoted by Nursi, Sirhindī makes a comparison between passages from the prophetic *Hadīth* (*al-kalimāt al-marwiyya 'an al-rasūl 'aẓīm ṣal'am*) on the one hand, and Sūfī prayers and ecstatic expressions (*al-awrād al-'aẓīma wa al-ḥālāt al-bāhira*) on the other; he concludes that the glitter of the Sunnah on the former is absent on the latter and therefore the prophetic Sunnah is preferable to any other form of religious expression.[16] In the same vein, he quotes a passage in which Sirhindī maintains that Sūfīs who adopted the Sunnah as the basis for their Sūfī way are the most perfect and the most exalted. Therefore, the simple Sūfīs (*al-awliyā' al-'awāmm*) in this group are more radiant than the elect (*al-awliyā' al-khawāṣṣ*) in the other.[17] In view of this material, there is reason to believe that it was Sirhindī's view of the Sunnah that had an impact on Nursi and we may proceed by discussing Sirhindī's view of the prophetic Sunnah. It has to be remembered, however, that in Sirhindī's thinking Sunnah is closely related to Sharī'ah and, consequently, both will have to be considered together.

Before we proceed, a word of caution is called for. Since the earliest days of Islam, the revival of prophetic Sunnah is one of the most meritorious actions that can be performed by a Muslim. Leaders of modern movements in Islam support the revival of the prophetic Sunnah as a matter of principle; whatever the differences between the content of their particular messages may be, they tend to describe their views as a revival of the prophetic Sunnah. For instance, there is little similarity between the Sudanese *mahdī* Muhammad Ahmad (d. 1885) and Ghulām Ahmad (d. 1907), the founder of the Ahmadī movement. Muhammad Ahmad was a militant figure who saw himself as a *mahdī*, fought the British and the Ottomans, considered this war a *jihād*, and established a state that survived for more than a decade after his death. Ghulām Ahmad, on the other hand, who also claimed to be a *mahdī*, supported the British rule in India, and maintained that in the circumstances of India in his time, *jihād* should be waged with pen and tongue rather than with the sword. Yet both leaders saw their respective communities as having abandoned the Sunnah of the Prophet and saw its revival as the remedy for the ills of the Muslims. When both go into details, the prophetic Sunnah as defined by the Sudanese *mahdī* is quite different from the Sunnah as seen by the Ahmadīs. Many additional examples of this kind can easily be adduced. Therefore, it may be argued, the fact that Nursi spoke in favor of the Sunnah requires little explanation: one can barely find a Muslim thinker who does not follow this path to some extent. Nevertheless, Nursi mentions Sirhindī several times in this connection and it is therefore legitimate to explore Sirhindī's conception of the Sunnah and see whether scholars of Bediuzzaman can benefit from the results of such a procedure.

Numerous scholars have stressed that, in Sirhindī's view, the Sunnah and the Sharī'ah are the most important components of Islamic culture. In a sense, this is true and there are numerous statements to this effect in Sirhindī's works. While there is no doubt that Sirhindī was a Sūfī and most of his writings attest to this in an unquestionable manner, he is willing to say that "on the Day of Resurrection, people will be asked about their adherence to the Sharī'ah, not about *tasawwuf*."[18] He urged his disciples to read books of *fiqh* and affirmed that Sūfī experience is inferior to the Sharī'ah, because Sharī'ah is based on incontrovertible proof, while Sūfī experience is a result of fallible speculation only. One of his disciples recalls that when he was overwhelmed by mystical ecstasy, Sirhindī used to tell him: "Go study your lesson, because an ignorant Sūfī is the fool of Satan (*sabaq bi-khwān kih Ṣūfī -yi jāhil maskhara-yi shayṭān ast*).[19] This is reminiscent of a statement attributed to Nursi who is reported to have said that he is not a Sūfī *shaykh*, because the times are not times of Sūfī *Turuq*, but of saving the belief (*innī lastu shaykha ṭarīqa, fa-'l-waqt laysa waqta ṭuruqin Ṣūfiyya bal huwa waqt inqādh al-īmān*).[20] Sirhindī's *Maktūbāt* are full of exhortations to follow the Sunnah and comply with the Sharī'ah. Naturally enough, Sirhindī also speaks out against the *bid'ah*, though he gives only very few examples of "innovations" current among Indian Muslims of his times. In most cases, he discusses the problem on a theoretical level, adducing random examples only to prove a general point. In several places in the *Maktūbāt* he launches vigorous attacks on the distinction between good innovation (*bid'ah hasana*) and bad innovation (*bid'ah sayyi'ah*), asserting that either is certain to do away with a Sunnah and should therefore be avoided. All innovations are bad and should be shunned. As said in Quran 5:3, Islam has been made perfect by God and does not require any modifications or additions. This is his attitude in principle. However, when he was asked a specific question about Sūfī practices, he admitted that they were not part of the Sunnah, but rather the invention of the Sūfīs. Nevertheless, he refrained from condemning them.[20] In this respect he is similar to Nursi, who also speaks against "innovations" and even quotes the same Quranic verse in support, but is careful to add that certain Sūfī practices such as *awrād* and *adhkār* are acceptable and may be considered a "good innovation."[22] It is clear that on this point there is a substantial similarity in outlook between the two thinkers.

If we return to Sirhindī again, we find that his view of the Sharī'ah is deeply influenced by his Sūfī outlook. Sirhindī is not interested in the legal injunctions of the Sharī'ah, but rather strives to incorporate it, as a major Islamic concept, in his comprehensive worldview. Therefore he speaks of the Sharī'ah in a characteristically Sūfī way. Sharī'ah consists, in his view, of two parts: form (*Sūra*) and essence (*Haqīqa*). In other words, it has an outward (*zāhir*) aspect and an inner (*bātin*) aspect. The outward form of the Sharīʻah involves compliance with the Quranic commandments despite the opposition still mounted at this stage by the evil-bidding soul (*al-nafs al-ammāra*). Spiritually, this is a rather low stage, and it is only God's mercy that enables persons who do not transcend it to enter Paradise. Paradise and its pleasures, however, also have form and essence; those who in this world attain the stage of formal belief (*Ṣūrat-i īmān*) only, will not enjoy Paradise in the same way as the people of the essence (*arbāb-i haqīqat*). The essence of Sharīʻah (*haqīqat-i sharīʻat*) can be arrived at by properly understanding the ambiguous verses of the Quran (*mutashābihāt*). This understanding can bring about the perfections of prophecy (*kamālāt-i nubuwwat*), while the form of Sharīʻah is capable of producing the perfections of sainthood (*kamālāt-i wilāyat*) only.[23]

I have tried to highlight those aspects of Sirhindī's thought that may have relevance to scholars of Nursi. I have concentrated on the question of Sunnah, because Nursi mentioned Sirhindī explicitly in this connection. But there is one other issue in which Sirhindī is apparently not mentioned by Nursi, but, nevertheless, there seems to be a similarity between the two thinkers. Yvonne Haddad has highlighted a passage from *Lamaʻāt* in which Bediuzzaman Nursi delivered a scathing attack on the non-Muslims and on Westernizing trends in Turkey.[23] Since these trends were associated first and foremost with the government, the situation is in some ways comparable to the situation in India in Sirhindī's times and the whole issue bears relevance to the question whether Muslim religious leaders should attempt to influence the government under which they live. Classical Muslim tradition contains numerous utterances that frown upon connections between religious scholars and the rulers.[25] One can conveniently study this material in al-Ghazālī's *Ihyā' 'ulūm al-dīn,*[26] under the title "On the permissible and forbidden intercourse with the oppressive Sultans" (*fīmā yuḥallu min mukhālaṭat al-salāṭīn al-Ẓalama wa mā yuḥram*). India has not been an exception in this respect. Professor Khalīq Ahmad Nizāmī maintained that "the Naqshbandī *silsilah* alone considered it not only permissible but imperative to establish contacts with the rulers, and to attempt to influence their thought and policies."[27] It has been a near-consensus of modern Muslim historiography that Sirhindī's revivalist activities, directed at the Mughul nobility and carried out in accordance with the general outlook of the Naqshbandī order, effected a significant change in the direction of Islamic developments in India. Sirhindī is said to have paved the way for the gradual shift of the religious policy of the Mughul empire from the rank heresy of Akbar (1556–1605) to the strict orthodoxy of Awrangzēb (1658–1707). It must be said, however, that the relationship with the state is not a central theme in Sirhindī's thought, and his statements on the matter do not point always in the same direction. On certain occasions he objected to people who wanted to join the service of the ruler; he considered such occupation as worldly and therefore demeaning. He himself, however, conducted correspondence with the ruling circles and demanded that they seek advice from the *'ulamā'*, though he was not enthusiastic about joining the court. Several times he warned his disciples against any association with the rulers, arguing that this world and the next are two irreconcilable opposites: one can be enjoyed only at the expense of the other. In the same vein, he quotes the following classical warning concerning the rulers:

> Flee from their company more than you would flee from a lion; the lion causes [only] worldly death which might [even] be beneficial in the hereafter, while association with the kings necessarily brings about eternal perdition. Beware of their company, beware of their food, beware of their love, beware of their sight. (*firra min ṣuḥatihim akthar mimmā tafirru min al-asad fa-innahu yūjib al-mawt al-dunyawī wa huwa qad yufīd fī al-ākhira wa 'khtilāṭ al-mulūk yūjib al-halāk al-abadī wa al-khasāra* (sic) *al-sarmadī fa-iyyāka wa ṣuḥbatahum wa iyyāka wa luqmatahum wa iyyāka wa maḥabbatahum wa iyyāka wa ruḥyatahum*).[28]

On the other hand, Sirhindī sent to a few Mughul nobles several letters that included personal recommendations for some of his disciples. He asks a noble to take two persons into his service, recommends a certain learned man for a government position, expresses his hope that a certain man with a large family will receive a stipend and that another will be included in the *dīwān*. It is not known to what extent these recommendations were heeded.

Professor Mardin has quoted a letter by Bediuzzaman Nursi in which he addressed (in 1923) the Grand National Assembly, warning it against imitating the West and demanding that the members act according to the injunctions of Islam.[29] In light of this, scholars of Nursi may be interested in the ways in which Sirhindī attempted to influence the Islamic policies of the Mughal Empire during the reign of Akbar (1556–1605) and Jahāngīr (1605–1627). The most important documents for the evaluation of Sirhindī's role in this field are the letters sent to Mughul officials in which he expressed his views on the situation of Islam in India during the reigns of Akbar and Jahāngīr. He bemoans the ascendancy of infidelity during the reign of Akbar and and demands that Jahāngīr be prevailed upon by his ministers to abolish the heretical customs established at the imperial court. He lays much of the blame at the door of the wicked and worldly *ulamā* and demands that the "*ulamā* of the hereafter" assist the emperor in strengthening Islam.[30]

It is evident from the existence of these letters that Sirhindī tried to impress his views of Islam on some senior officials of the Mughul Empire. Unfortunately, as far as I know, we do not have at our disposal the answers sent to Sirhindī by these officials. We therefore cannot know to what extent his efforts were successful. His sweeping recommendations concerning the necessity to humiliate the Hindū inhabitants of the Mughul empires were clearly not carried out by Jahāngīr. In a letter written during the reign of Jahāngīr, Sirhindī is still highly critical of the situation of Islam.[31] As the source material stands now, we cannot go beyond saying that Sirhindī tried, with unknown results, to propagate his ideas among the top echelons of Mughul officialdom. As for the alleged attempts of Sirhindī's sons to exercise political influence on Awrangzēb, these cannot be substantiated either: during the meetings between Sirhindī's sons and Awrangzēb, the subject of discussion was the Naqshbandī spiritual discipline rather than the policies of the Mughul Empire toward its Hindu population.[32]

One other issue in Sirhindī's life that may be of interest to scholars of Nursi is Sirhindī's imprisonment by the Mughul emperor. In 1619, some time after he wrote a letter very critical of the situation of Islam under Jahāngīr, he was summoned to the emperor's presence. Following this meeting, Sirhindī was imprisoned. Jahāngīr refers to Sirhindī's imprisonment several times in his memoirs. The first reference is a scathing denunciation of Sirhindī as an arrogant impostor (*shayyād*) who is sending his disciples to every town and city to deceive the people. His book, the *Maktūbāt*, contains many idle theories, which lead people to heresy. Among other things, Sirhindī wrote that he transcended the spiritual stage of the "Righteous Caliphs" (*khulafā' rāshidūn*). According to Jahāngīr, Sirhindī was not able to give a satisfactory explanation to his theories, and the emperor therefore decided to imprison him so that his disturbed disposition and confused mind calm down a little and the agitation of the masses subside. After one year, Sirhindī was released, and the emperor gave him a robe of honor and a present of 1000 rupees. Sirhindī is said to have recognized that the punishment imposed on him was appropriate. In a subsequent passage, Jahāngīr mentions that he had given Sirhindī another gift of 2000 rupees, but nowhere does he acknowledge that Sirhindī had any influence on him or on his policies.[33]

Sirhindī also refers to his imprisonment several times, and it is clear that some of letters in the third volume of the *Maktūbāt* were written while he was imprisoned. He tends to see this episode in characteristically Sūfī terms. The imprisonment is in his eyes a manifestation of God's awe (*jalāl*), as distinguished from His beauty (*jamāl*). Sirhindī believes that he made great strides in his spiritual progress by experiencing both aspects of the Divine. In one place he says that "the cruelty of the Beloved gives more pleasure than His fidelity' (*jafā-yi maḥbūb az wafā-yi ū bīshtar ladhdhat-bakhsh ast*). Sirhindī does not see his imprisonment as as part of his struggle against the emperor or his policies: he sees entirely in terms of Ñūfī experience.

Imprisonment of Muslim religious leaders is not a rare event in Muslim history. Numerous Muslim religious thinkers were imprisoned by Muslim rulers who saw in the views of these thinkers a threat to their authority. Nursi himself, who endured imprisonment both as a prisoner of war in Russia and as prisoner in Turkey, mentions the imprisonment of Abū Hanīfa and Ahmad b. Hanbal.[34] The cases of al-Hallāj and Ibn Taymiyya are other famous instances. Modern times have also seen several cases of this kind. Like Sirhindī, Nursi also sees imprisonment as an opportunity for religious uplifting, if the prisoner uses his time for worship, or, in the case of Nursi's fellow prisoners, for the study of *Risāle-i Nūr*.[35] His reference to the prison as the *Medrese-yi Yūsufiyya*, alluding to the Quranic description of Joseph's imprisonment in Egypt,[33] is also a clear attempt to describe prison as an experience of religious leaders since time immemorial.

In conclusion, let me return again to the thought of Sirhindī and present my main conclusion concerning his historical role. As I have said earlier, it has been a consensus of modern historians that Sirhindī paved the way for the gradual shift of the religious policy of the Mughul Empire from the religiously lenient policy of Akbar (1556–1605) to the strict orthodoxy of Awrangzēb (1658–1707). We have seen that Sirhindī tried, with unknown results, to influence the religious policies of the Mughul Empire. I would also like to say that Sirhindī's image went through substantial changes since his own lifetime and until the modern period. It may be said that, during his lifetime, Sirhindī's ecstatic Sūfī views aroused the greatest interest and also the most severe criticism. In the seventeenth century, Sirhindī was accused of arrogance that involved gross infringement of the Prophet's honor. His demands to implement Sharī'ah in the Mughul Empire went unmentioned in that period. The hagiographic literature concentrates on Sirhindī's miracles, his ability to prevent disasters, to rescue people who lost their way in the desert, and his violent treatment of those who slighted him. Of particular interest is a miracle story connected with the destruction of a Hindū temple. A group of Sirhindī's disciples was engaged in the destruction of a temple according to their master's teachings. When they were surprised by a large number of infidels, Sirhindī miraculously brought a Muslim force to their rescue. This story is a faint indication that Sirhindī's views of the Hindūs began to filter down to the popular level. We should, however, keep in mind that this is the only story of its kind in the hagiographies that I examined. Sirhindī's image in the eyes of his disciples was by no means that of a fanatic iconoclast, but rather as a saint with diverse miraculous powers.

It is also important to point out that the idea that the emperor Awrangzēb (1658–1707) was inspired by Sirhindī in his orthodox reforms is untenable. In 1679, Awrangzēb issued a decree in which he stated that Sirhindī's *Maktūbāt* are apparently opposed to the views of the *ahl al-Sunnah wa'l jamā'ah* and prohibited their teaching on the pain of *sharī'* punishment. It may thus be said that the prevalent image of Sirhindī in the seventeenth century was that of an extravagant Sūfī, highly disrespectful of the Prophet. This was the reason for numerous controversies concerning Sirhindī that erupted during the seventeenth century.[37] In the eighteenth and nineteenth centuries, the interest in Sirhindī seems to have subsided. The twentieth century, on the other hand, saw a great revival of this interest and Sirhindī was transformed into a major figure in the history of Indian Islam. The person to be credited with this change is Abū 'l-Kalām Āzād (1888–1958), one of the important Muslim associates of Gandhi in the noncooperation and *khilāfat* movement in India in the 1920s. Āzād's *Tadhkira* seems to be the first work in which Sirhindī is described as the sole person who properly reacted to the religious corruption that spread in India during the reign of Akbar. According to Āzād, Sirhindī was the only person who had the courage and stamina to embark upon a campaign of reform and renewal and stand up to the emperor himself. Āzād views him not only as a radical reformer in the field of religion, but also an uncompromising and defiant rebel against the government in power. This new image of Sirhindī reflects the rebellious mood of the Indian Muslims in the wake of World War One and the political attitudes of Āzād who was at that time one of their most prominent leaders. The image of Sirhindī is no longer that of a man of religion solely interested in the exploration of divine mysteries; he is a religiously minded rebel against the government in power.

NOTES

1. Albert Hourani, *The Emergence of the Modern Middle East* (London, 1981), 80–81.
2. Hourani, op. cit., 82–83.
3. "The Naqshbandiyya-Mujaddidiyya in the Ottoman Lands in the Early 19th Century." *Die Welt des Islams* 22 (1982), 1–36.
4. Ibid., 10–11.
5. Ibid., 13–14.
6. Ibid., 15.

7. Mardin, *Religion and Social Change in Modern Turkey. The Case of Bediuzzaman Said Nursi* (Albany, 1989), 54–56.
8. Ibid., 92.
9. Ibid., 94.
10. Ibid., 188.
11. Ibid., 326–27.
12. Sirhindī, *Maktūbāt* (Lucknow, 1889), vol. 1, 94–96 (letters 74 and 75 of the first volume).
13. Nursi, *Letters, 1928–1932. Risale-i Nur Collection 2* (Istanbul 2001), 419. Cf. also ibid., 40–41. I am indebted to Şükran Vahide for drawing my attention to this passage.
14. Sirhindī, *Maktūbāt*, vol. 1, 96, ll. 3–4.
15. Nursi expresses the feeling of being addressed by Sirhindī personally and gives the same explanation of "the unification of the *qibla*" in his *Al-Mathnawī al-'Arabī al-nūrī*, al-Mawṣil (Mossul, 1988), 43.
16. Nūrsī, *Mirqāt al-sunna*, 25.
17. Nursi, *Mirqāt al-sunna*, 8–9; same text in idem, Majmū'at, *al-lamaāt min Kulliyyāt rasāil al-nūr*, 17.
18. Y. Friedmann, *Shaykh Ahmad Sirhindī: An Outline of His Thought and a Study of His Image in the Eyes of Posterity* (Montreal, 1971) (reprint New Delhi, 2003), 41.
19. Friedmann, *Sirhindī*, 41.
20. Bahjat Ahmad, *Rā'id al-haraka al-islāmiyya fī Turkiya. Al-mujāhid al-mujtahid al-shaykh Sa'īd al-Nursī, 1873–1960* (Cairo, 1992), 14.
21. Friedmann, *Sirhindī*, 44.
22. Nursi, *Mirqāt al-sunna wa tiryāq maraḍ al-bid'a*, 25.
23. Friedmann, *Sirhindī*, 45.
24. Haddad, Yvonne Y., "*Ghurba* as Paradigm for Muslim Life: a *Risale-i Nur* World-view." *The Muslim World* 99 (1999), 302.
25. See S. D. Goitein, "Attitudes towards Government in Islam and Judaism," in *Studies in Islamic History and Institutions* (Leiden, 1966), 197–213.
26. Ed. (Cairo, 1939), vol. 2, 140–54. See also al-Samarqandī, Abū al-Layth, *Tanbīh al-ghāfiīn fī al-maw'iza bi-aḥādīth sayyid al-anbiyā wa al-mursalīn* (Ammān, 2000), 251–53.
27. Nizami, "Naqshbandī Influence on Mughal Rulers and Politics," in *Islamic Culture* 39 (1965), 41.
28. Friedmann, *Sirhindī*, 78, quoted from Sirhindī, *Maktūbāt* (Lucknow, 1889), vol. 1, 148.
29. Şerif Mardin, *Religion and Social Change in Modern Turkey*, 95.
30. Friedmann, *Sirhindī*, 80.
31. Ibid., 82.
32. Y. Friedmann, "The Naqshbandīs and Awrangzēb: A Reconsideration." M. Gaborieau, A. Popovic, Th. Zarcone, *Naqshbandis. Historical Developments and Present Situation of a Muslim Mystical Order* (Istanbul and Paris, 1990), 209–20.
33. Friedmann, *Sirhindī*, 83–84; *Tūzuk-i Jahāngīrī*, ed. Sayyid Ahmad Khān (Aligarh, 1864), 272–73, 308, 161, 276; Alexander Rogers, translator, *The Tūzuk-i Jahāngīrī, or Memoirs of Jahāngīr* (London, 1914), vol. 2, 91–92.

34. Bediuzzaman Said Nursi, *The Flashes Collection*, translated by Şükran Vahide. CD ROM edition, 335–36.
35. Bediuzzaman Nursi, *The Words*, translated by Şükran Vahide. CD ROM edition, 162–63.
36. See Quran 12:35.
37. Friedmann, *Sirhindī*, 94–102.

FIFTEEN

"Visions of Plurality in Unity"

Said Nursi, Muhyiddin Ibn 'Arabi, and the Question of the Unity of Being

Stephen Hirtenstein

> Say: O my servants who have been immoderate against yourselves, do not despair of God's Mercy; surely God forgives sins altogether; surely He is the All-forgiving, the All-merciful.
>
> —Quran 39.53

There is a great and pressing need in the modern era to find an all-inclusive perspective that allows for difference without the desire to destroy it. While writing this chapter and thinking about what Islamic spirituality can bring to the modern world, I was reminded of the words of an old Arab proverb: "Even the narrowest of places is large enough for a thousand friends" (*makān al-dīq yasa'u alif al-sadīq*). As our earth is daily becoming a narrower place, where an estimated 6.5 billion people are all jostling for space,[1] it is increasingly important to learn how to view neighbors as friends. Much of human history is seen and taught to the young as a litany of wars and conquests, rather than the exchange of trade and cooperation that really characterizes people's lives. To be a friend involves loving, knowing, and understanding the other with all respect and dignity, without wishing them to conform to our own viewpoint or subtly putting them in a secondary position below our own. Friendship is the way to establish our similarity and common purpose and humanity, as fellow-students in the wonder of life. As outward globalization gathers pace and brings peoples of different nations, languages, beliefs, and cultures into ever-closer contact, inevitably there are tensions and fears of loss, amid which some in desperation resort to violence.

Many, however, realize that these outward tensions are also to be found within us, and seek to discover a new way of living that is in harmony with our deepest selves, and thus with others. They hope for a deeper understanding of the inner globality that can appreciate all the outer differentiation in a wise and compassionate way. By "inner globality" I mean that there is a reality behind the appearance that is already unified and integrated, already global and universal, and which governs the material world and all the processes we now call globalization. What we see today in the outer world is a reflection or expression of this deeper, spiritual reality. With today's world presenting more and more aspects of the global network, whether financial, scientific, technological, or cultural, we have unparalleled opportunities for knowledge of the Reality underlying all forms, a unified vision. "Life," as Nursi put it, "is a sort of manifestation of Unity within multiplicity, and therefore leads to unity. Life makes one the owner of everything."[2]

At the same time we face direct threats from those forces that view the 'other' not just as different but as an enemy to be destroyed. As one survivor of the recent bomb attacks in London put it, "the best way [to defeat the terrorists] . . . is to have no fear of other cultures or creeds. We should only be wary of the hate-filled, the nihilistic, the furiously angry who won't listen or engage." Variety is the supreme feature of Reality in manifestation: God, it is said, never manifests in the same way twice. That which is antireality prefers monolithic simplicity. One modern novelist puts it thus: "Reality outstrips simplicity through a constant flowering of unexpected lives. Evil thoughts and deeds cannot prevail against it."

In the light of these preliminary remarks, I should like to turn to two apparently very different figures who strove for a vision of the world that embraces pluralism through the principle of Unity: Said Nursi (d.1960) and Muhyiddin Ibn 'Arabi (d.1240). The comparison of two figures from eras many centuries apart is always difficult, requiring a thorough investigation of their lives, circumstances, thought, and milieu. Naturally this is far beyond the scope of what I am capable of or can offer in this brief chapter, and I will limit myself to certain observations on four subjects: their respective backgrounds, Nursi's attitude to Ibn 'Arabi as shown in his writings, the question of the Unity of Being (*waḥdat al-wujūd*), and their understanding of the Quran.

Background

It is important to have some understanding of historical context, even if someone towers above their times and reaches a level unbounded by time or place, since many aspects of a person's work cannot be properly understood except within those particular conditions. This is especially so in the case of Nursi because he lived through one of the most turbulent times of world history, spanning the last years of the Ottoman Empire, the overthrow of old power structures and the rise of communist ideologies, two world wars, and the emergence of a completely different political and social landscape. Initially, Nursi, whose roots in a Kurdish hamlet in eastern Anatolia gave him a deep connection with the natural world, saw himself fundamentally as an Ottoman, not a Kurd or a Turk—that is, someone who adhered not to a tribe or nation but to the ideal of a common humanity bound by faith in God and obedience to the Law. As the Old Said put it, "with us Muslims religion and nationality are united, although there is a theoretical, apparent and incidental difference between them. . . . Religious zeal and Islamic nationhood have completely fused in Turk and Arab and may not now be separated."[3] Of course this particular view did not stand the test of time well, under the impact of nationalist struggles in the twentieth century, the march of secularism, and the rise of fundamentalism, although it might be argued that out of the crucible of the collapse of the old order is being forged a new understanding of *umma, millet*, and *din*. In launching a project for the revival of traditional values in opposition to European cultural 'invasion', Nursi voiced the concerns of many of his time, coupling the idea of 'positive action' with a remarkable personal abstinence in a manner reminiscent of his Indian contemporary, Mahatma Gandhi. This project, in the form of the *Risale-i Nur*, was primarily to answer the needs of ordinary people seeking a full spiritual and religious identity within a world dominated by the materialism of modern science and technology. As Ibrahim Abu-Rabi' has put it, "[the *Risale*] is an inquiry into why the modern Muslim world has fallen into a religious abyss, and why the 'other', that is to say, Europe, superseded the Muslim world in matters of science and civilisation. It offers a creative, although subtle, method to reconstruct Islamic thought and practice in an era that was no longer dominated by Islamic doctrinal or political teachings."[4] Nursi's view of spirituality or spiritual teaching was not to oppose science and religion but to bring them together in a new unity; it is primarily founded on what is best for the whole community, and represents a strengthening and deepening of piety, rather than an entry into esoteric truths.

By contrast, Ibn 'Arabi was born some 700 years earlier in 560/1165 into a sophisticated, well-to-do urban Andalusian family that associated with people of power, at a time when Spain was under Arab rule. His father was one of the Almohad Sultan's elite guards, and he himself would have joined the army had not destiny intervened. Ibn 'Arabi lived during the final flowering of Andalusian culture under the Almohads, a time when Muslim culture and civilization was in the ascendancy over Europe and when Arabs had good cause to look down on the unwashed and often ill-educated inhabitants of the north. Despite the Christian Reconquista that began in earnest in Ibn 'Arabi's homeland less than twenty years after he departed, and the instability of the Levant and Anatolia under the impact of the Crusades and Mongol invasions, he lived in an era of immense Arab and Turko-Iranian self-confidence and expansion, as can be seen in Andalusi, Ayyubid, and Seljuk culture at the turn of the twelfth/thirteenth centuries. In the second half of his life, which was spent in the Mashriq, he was patronized and befriended by people in positions of power, from Ayyubid kings to Seljuk aristocrats.[5] Unlike Nursi, he moved from an intense abstinence in his youth to a fully engaged family life in Malatya and Damascus. His many works have come to be seen as the bedrock of Islamic spirituality, touching on every area of Muslim life and thought, from questions of jurisprudence (*fiqh*) to love-poems to the most elevated understanding of the nature of man and his relation to God and the world. Two in particular hold a special place: *al-Futūḥāt al-Makkiyya* (The Meccan Illuminations or Revelations), an enormous work in 560 chapters and thirty-seven volumes, which has been endlessly referred to and quoted from by later writers, and *Fuṣūṣ al-Ḥikam* (The Settings of the Wisdoms), the quintessence of his teaching written toward the end of his life under the inspiration of the Prophet Muhammad, which gave rise to many masterly commentaries by men such as the first Ottoman shaykh al-islam, Da'ud al-Qaysari, 'Abd al-Razzaq al-Kashani, and 'Abd Allah Bosnevi. These were definitely not works for the masses, especially since in the preprinting era copies were very hard to come by.

The contrast, then, between the outer lives of Ibn 'Arabi and Nursi could hardly be more stark: the one living in a time of relative security prior to the emergence of the tariqas, the other living through the greatest upheavals when the tariqas themselves had fallen in some decline. Both, however, shared several personal characteristics: a formidable intellect and ability to absorb the intellectual currents of the time; a deep spiritual connection to the Prophet[6] and adherence to his example; an inspiration that flowed into writing. They also both spoke eloquently and movingly of the absolute centrality of the Quran in their work, emphasising less its legalistic aspects and more its inner teachings.

Nursi and Sufism

Anyone reading Nursi's works for the first time, who has a background in the writings of earlier Sufi masters, cannot help being struck by the number of images, frames of reference, and technical terminologies that he draws from that tradition. This is despite the apparent passage of time, discontinuities of circumstance, and the fact that Nursi did not really consider himself as part of the Sufi tradition. Although he studied with Khalidi Naqshbandi shaykhs in his early years, he never seems to have entered into any kind of initiatic link with them. He seems to have retained a great affection for Sufi teaching, but it is important to understand that, unlike Ibn 'Arabi who had many spiritual teachers, Nursi never underwent proper training (*riyāda*) under a master—his retreats, for example, seem to have been entirely self-directed.

The basic terms he employs in his writings, being grounded in the Islamic sciences, Quran and Hadith, are unsurprisingly similar and even identical to those used in Sufi teaching: for example, the unseen and visible worlds (*'ālam al-ghayb* and *'ālam al-shahāda*), the principle of continuous creation (*khalq jadid*), the greatest name of God (*al-ism al-a'zam*), the creation of the world as mirror to divine beauty and perfection, man as mirror to the divine names, and so on. Given a long tradition of teaching in almost all Sufi orders that has drawn its frame of reference from the works of Ibn 'Arabi and his followers within the Ottoman world, this is hardly surprising and emphasises a remarkable continuity of teaching and learning across 700 years. However, Nursi was keen to distance himself from the development of the Sufi tariqas in his own time, as he seems, like some spiritual masters before him,[7] to have seen them as over-elaborate. His own teaching of the path based on the Quran is described as shorter, safer, and more general than others. It delineates four stages: inability (*'ajz/acz*) before the divine power, poverty (*faqr/fakr*) before His all-embracing mercy, tender compassion (*shafaqa/sefkat*) before His compassion, and contemplation or reflection (*tafakkur/tefekkur*) before His all-comprehensive wisdom. These are expressed as honest self-appraisal, remembrance of God, attributing all good to God and all ill to oneself, and becoming a complete mirror to the divine revelation.[8] Like Ibn 'Arabi and others before him, Nursi stressed the fundamental importance of reaching true annihilation, beyond the imaginings of self-existence, in order to find true existence, and that this annihilation in Truth is preferable to all unveiling and spiritual powers, which are mere favors bestowed in addition to this spiritual degree.

Scholars have understandably tended to focus on Nursi's relationship to three particular Sufi figures, those whom he himself calls his masters, 'Abd al-Qadir al-Jilani (d.1166), Mevlana Jalaluddin Rumi (d.1273),[9] or Shaykh Ahmad Sirhindi (or Imam-i Rabbani as he calls him, d.1624), who are often praised in his works and seem to have exercised a great influence on his thinking. For example, it is clear that Nursi saw himself as having a particularly close spiritual relationship with al-Jilani:

> However many *Fatihas* and supplications I have uttered in general in my life, after the person of the Prophet (PBUH), they have been offered

> for Ùeyh-i Geylani. While I am a Nakshi in three or four respects, the Kadiri way and love of it prevail in me involuntarily. But preoccupation [with study of the religious sciences] prevented my becoming involved with the *tarikat*.[10]

This devotion to al-Jilani in particular is more comprehensible when we bear in mind the extraordinary popularity of the latter's teaching and public preaching, a model that Nursi was keen to emulate. Nursi's self-description as a Naqshbandi derives from his upbringing in eastern Anatolia where he was trained by several Khalidi shaykhs. The Khalidiyya-Naqshbandiyya, a nineteenth-century offshoot that follows the teaching of Shaykh Khalid (d.1827),[11] derives much of its teaching from the specific form of Naqshbandiyya instituted by Shaykh Ahmad Sirhindi, the renovator (*mujaddid*) of the second millennium in Islam, who founded his own branch in India known as the Mujaddidiyya and emphasized the orthodox nature of the *tariqa*. The Naqshbandiyya defines itself as *tarīqat al-sahāba*, the path of the Prophet's Companions, and stresses servanthood before God (*'ubudiyya*). This servanthood has two aspects: an external one involving strict adherence to the sunna, observance of the shari'a and avoidance of innovation (*bid'a*) and dispensation (*rukhsa*); and an internal one, leaving all the space to God and not attributing anything to the self, neither action nor quality nor existence. In Nursi's case, as the above quotation shows, he did not consider himself to be following the Sufi path (*tarikat*) as such because of what he termed his "preoccupation." When answering the many charges from the Eskisehir Court in 1935, he stated: "This is not the time of Sufism; it is the time to save belief." What he had taught to a small number of students was "not training in Sufism (*tarikat*) but instruction in the direct way to reality (*hakikat*)."[12]

However he framed it for the courtroom, his application of Naqshi principles is all too evident, and we find again and again the motifs of adhering to the shari'a, following the example of the Companions and stressing servanthood as opposed to mystical ecstasy. Some scholars have compared Sirhindi's struggle to renew Islam in the face of pantheistic religious thinking with Nursi's project to revive the centrality of the Quran in the face of the challenge of materialistic philosophy and scientific humanism, projecting Nursi himself as a *mujaddid* of the contemporary age.[13]

Nursi's View of Ibn 'Arabi

Students of spiritual teachings in Anatolia from the time of the Seljuks onward could not avoid the influence, direct or indirect, of al-Jilani's near-contemporary,

Muhyiddin Ibn 'Arabi. Ibn 'Arabi not only spent several years living and teaching in Malatya,[14] but the line of remarkable masters who followed his teachings, beginning with Sadruddin al-Qunawi (d.1273) in Konya, set the parameters for almost all discussion of spiritual understanding through the introduction of a comprehensive, technical vocabulary that embraced the whole arena of Islam, from Quranic exegesis to jurisprudence (*fiqh*), from Sufi teachings to philosophical thinking. Unlike their contemporaries, Ibn 'Arabi and his followers did not establish set patterns of behavior or found a *tariqa*. Their aim was quite different, emphasizing the written text and oral commentary, and in part this can be explained by their focus on the fundamentals of Islam and the centrality of the Book of Quran. Here we may note that it is only in the last twenty years or so that this aspect of Ibn 'Arabi's teachings has been given prominence, through the writings of scholars such as Michel Chodkiewicz and William Chittick. As a consequence of new research, many traditional views of Ibn 'Arabi espoused by Western orientalists and Muslim readers, some of which Nursi undoubtedly shared, have been shown to be somewhat distorted: this is not only due to a reassessment of Ibn 'Arabi's Quranic roots and teachings but equally to a reevaluation of what he actually wrote, since many works copied in his name have been shown to be misattributions.[15]

The few places where Nursi does mention Muhyiddin Ibn 'Arabi show how much respect he had for his famed predecessor. He calls him a "wondrous individual" and grants him a special place within the history of Islam: "[the Prophet Muhammad] opened up a window onto knowledge of God as broad and brilliant and luminous as the World of Islam. Millions of purified and veracious scholars like Imam Ghazzali, Imam-i Rabbani, Muhyiddin [ibn] al-Arabi, and 'Abd al-Qadir Geylani, look through that window, and show it also to others."[16] We may also note that when Nursi went to Damascus in early 1911 and delivered his famous sermon at the Umayyad Mosque, he stayed in the Salihiyya district of the city, at the center of which is the mosque complex built by Sultan Selim, where Ibn 'Arabi and his two sons are buried. It is hard to imagine that he did not pay a visit to the tomb of his predecessor, as is common practice to this day. In addition, at the beginning of his famous sermon, he quoted the following verse from the Quran that in many ways also summarizes the great message of hope espoused by Ibn 'Arabi: "Do not despair of God's Mercy"[17] (Quran 39.53).

Nursi alludes to Ibn 'Arabi's greatness in his writings, for example when he is responding to a question on the reality of the spirit: "With this question you are compelling a powerless wretch like me to contest an awesome, brilliant scholar of reality and genius of the occult sciences like Muhyiddin al-Arabi. However, relying on the teachings of the Qur'an I can attempt the discussion; even if I am only a fly, I can fly higher than such an eagle."[18] There is therefore no doubting the admiration that Nursi had for Ibn 'Arabi, and his readiness to defend him when criticised by his contemporaries: "it is not right to denigrate someone like Muhyiddin who was a miracle of the Islamic sciences."[19]

As to the extent that Nursi himself read Ibn 'Arabi's works directly, this is extremely hard to estimate, just as it is difficult to say what his attitude to Sufism really was.[20] Certainly he never quotes Ibn 'Arabi except in the form of a question posed by someone else,[21] and it is likely that he had little contact with his works except as mediated by others such as Ahmad Sirhindi. However, one or two passages indicate a familiarity with Qunawi's teaching, either directly or indirectly: he speaks of "one group of saints like Muhyiddin al-'Arabi, who most seriously and for a serious purpose, met with spirits when they wanted." This may well have drawn on the following seventeenth-century description attributed to Qunawi himself: "He [Ibn 'Arabi] had the power of meeting with the spirit of any of the prophets or saints of the past whom he chose. He was able to do this in three ways: sometimes he made their spirit descend into this world, where he perceived them in a subtle corporeal form similar to the one they possessed when alive; sometimes he induced them to present themselves to him in his sleep; and at other times he cast off his own corporeal form in order to meet them."[22] Elsewhere Nursi writes: "although he [Ibn 'Arabi] was such an elevated and wondrous spiritual pole, a unique one of ages, it is as though his particular way was very short, and restricted to Sadruddin al-Qunawi, and that his works are only rarely benefited from by those on the straight path."[23] At first sight this cautionary assessment would appear to be his own or that of others he had read, but in fact it may well represent an understanding of the following remarks made by Qunawi himself in his Will: "I enjoin my companions not to take up after me the problematic questions in the intricacies of the intuitive sciences. Rather they should limit themselves to pondering that which is unambiguous and clearly determined without trying to interpret what is not plain and unambiguous, whether in my words or in the words of the Shaykh [Ibn 'Arabi]. For *after me these are closed passages*"[24] [my italics]. There is no doubt that many passages in both authors' works can be extremely difficult to understand, and Qunawi is here showing the best attitude for others to adopt in reading them: if they appear ambiguous, leave them alone until such time as they are clear; in other words, refrain from speculation. Such advice is a perfect example of proper tact (*adab*) toward Truth. It can equally be applied in the manner that Nursi advises his students, which is: do not try to read them, as they will only benefit those rare individuals with the right receptivity—an attitude that has been common among many Sufis when talking to the general public, though behind closed doors and with specific students a more open approach was often implemented.

Oneness of Being (*Waḥdat al-Wujūd*)—the Problem of Meaning

"Muhyiddin said: 'Those who are not one of us and do not know our station should not read our books, for it may be damaging for them.' Yes, at this time it is harmful to read Muhyiddin's books, especially the matters about the Unity of Existence."[25]

Leaving aside the interesting question of time, since there is no doubt that the time in which we live now is quite different from the one in which Nursi found himself,[26] the name of Ibn 'Arabi appears often in Nursi's work in connection with the doctrine of *waḥdat al-wujūd*, a doctrine to be avoided in his view. While this phrase tends to be linked with Ibn 'Arabi's name by both his supporters and detractors, it has to be approached with great caution.

There are three fundamental problems with regard to the term *wujūd*: first, it has several related meanings that will be more or less prominent depending on the context. The root *wajada* means "to find, experience, feel, love" or "to be found, to exist, to be." Ibn 'Arabi's own definition of it as a technical Sufi term displays his love of the Arabic language and his fidelity to the meanings implied in words, and follows the earlier Sufi tradition: "*wujūd*" he writes, "is feeling/experiencing the Real in ecstasy" (*wijdān al-haqq fi'l-wajd*).[27] In this sense *wahdat al-wujūd* would mean something like 'unity of experience in ecstasy', something that noone who has been in love would ever really find contentious as an intellectual proposal!

The second major problem is what the phrase might really mean if we take it as referring to existence or being. As William Chittick has explained, there are at least as many as seven possible ways of understanding it, depending on whether the person who uses it is pro or anti-Ibn 'Arabi.[28] He writes:

> It is obvious that Ibn 'Arabi did accept that *wujūd* is one. However, the *wujūd* he is talking about is *al-wujūd al-haqq*, the Real Being, or the Being that is God. Moreover, if it is true that Being is one (*al-wujūd wāhid*), we can turn this sentence into a nominal phrase, giving us the expression "the oneness of being" (*wahdat al-wujūd*). . . . The real issue is this: are we saying anything of significance? . . . There is nothing remarkable about the idea that the Real Being is one. We are simply saying "God is one" in the philosophical and theological language that was current among Muslim intellectuals. We are uttering the first principle of Islamic thought, *tawhīd*, the declaration of God's unity."[29]

By the time of Ghazali, who preceded Ibn 'Arabi by a century, for example, the term *wujūd* is often used to explain the meaning of *tawhīd* as understood by those who reach true knowledge and vision: "The Real Existent (*al-mawjūd al-haqq*) is God . . . the gnostics climb from the lowlands of metaphor to the highlands of reality, and they perfect their ascent. Then they see—witnessing with their own eyes—that there is none in existence (*wujūd*) save God and that 'Everything is perishing except His face' [Quran 28.88]."[30]

The third problem is that while such statements as Ghazali's were widely accepted and echoed among the mainstream Muslim elite, the actual term *wahdat al-wujūd* is generally now considered to be a subsequent elaboration.[31] Although there is one reference in Ibn 'Arabi's writings[32] and a couple in Qunawi's, there is no evidence to suggest that *waḥdat al-wujūd* ever appeared in their teachings or, if it did, that it was anything other than a way of expressing *tawhīd*. The term only came into prominence through the later writing of Ibn Taymiyya (d.1328), who used it to characterize the teaching of Ibn 'Arabi and others as suspect, atheistic, and heretical. The problem is that Ibn Taymiyya's critique was based on a misunderstanding of Ibn 'Arabi's teaching, and that has been perpetuated by later writers who do not necessarily read his actual writings in any detailed way. Ironically, by the time of 'Abd al-Rahman Jami, *waḥdat al-wujūd* itself had become so pervasive that the term was adopted by him and other adherents of Ibn 'Arabi's teaching as a shorthand self-descriptor. In the section of Qunawi in his *Nafaḥāt al-uns*, Jami writes: "He is the assayer (*naqqād*, i.e., examiner) of the words of the Shaykh [Ibn 'Arabi]. What the Shaykh meant in the question of *waḥdat al-wujūd* will not come to hand in a manner that accords with both reason (*'aql*) and the Shariah unless one studies Qunawi's verifications and understands them properly."[33] Having said this, I should add that there is no evidence at all that Nursi ever studied any of Qunawi's works directly.

Nursi's Views of Unity of Being

When we look at Nursi's actual critique of *waḥdat al-wujūd*, we should therefore be careful to distinguish between Ibn 'Arabi's own teaching and writing, on the one hand, and what came to be known as the 'school' of the Unity of Being, on the other. Nursi's is primarily a critique not of Ibn 'Arabi's doctrine but of the way that it has been identified:

> [Everyone should not read this Flash, for they will not see the subtle errors of the Unity of Existence, and are not in need of it.] . . . The way of the Unity of Existence considers the existence of things to be imagination.[34]

> Many of those who have investigated creation, like Muhyiddin al-'Arabi, have reduced the other levels of existence to the level of delusion and imagination; they said: "There is no existence save Him." That is, it must not be said of other things that they have existence in relation to the Necessary Existence.[35]

He summarizes the problems of the way of the Unity of Being into three categories:

> 1. The way of the Unity of Existence is quite simply denying the universe on account of Almighty God.
> 2. The way of the Unity of Existence rejects the dominicality (lordship) of anything other than God so vehemently that it denies all other than God and removes duality.
> 3. While the All-Glorious One is free and exempt from, pure of and exalted above all change, alteration, division, and being comprehended in time or place, it [the way of the Unity of Existence] gives rise to conceptions which are not fitting for His necessary existence, holiness, and being free of all defect, and leads to false teachings.[36]

In fact, these three objections raised by Nursi are more or less a repetition of earlier views. Ibn Taymiyya wrote: "As for faith in God, they (that is, the followers of *wahdat al-wujūd*) think that His *wujūd* is identical with the *wujūd* of the cosmos, and that the cosmos has no other maker than the cosmos itself."[37]

This critique leads Nursi to emphasize the path of Four Steps (impotence, poverty, compassion, and reflection) that he is propounding as "much broader and more universal. For in order to attain to a constant awareness of God's presence, a person is not compelled to imagine the universe to be condemned to non-existence and to declare: 'There is no existent but He', like those who believe in 'the unity of existence', nor to suppose the universe to be condemned to imprisonment in absolute oblivion and say 'There is nothing witnessed but He', like those who believe in 'the unity of witnessing'."[38]

The Teachings of Ibn 'Arabi

A close study of Ibn 'Arabi's works reveals that some of the accusations leveled at him, that he was a pantheist who believed that the world and God are identical, or that he denied the existence of the universe and reduced it to mere imagination, are simply reductionist distortions, stemming from an inability to face the paradoxes of his work. These perceptions, however, have shaped many generations since the time of Ibn Taymiyya, and almost always among people who never read Ibn 'Arabi's work directly.[39] So what did Ibn 'Arabi teach?

Being and Becoming

First of all, on the charge of the identity of God and world, Ibn 'Arabi himself makes the clearest possible distinction between two apparently contradictory points of view: according to the first, "there is nothing in *wujūd* except God,"[40] a formula used by others such as Ghazali, stating that God alone has Being; according to the second, complementary point of view, "it should not be said 'there is nothing in *wujūd* except God' because the possible things and the creatures are manifest,"[41] so that all things have been given existence and attributes and are His self-revelation. When discussing the famous lines from the Surat al-Ikhlas, for example, Ibn 'Arabi clearly distinguishes God's unity and the world's multiplicity: "It is we who beget and are begotten, and it is we who depend upon Him, and it is we who are alike, one to another. But this One (*wāhid*) is independent of these characteristics."[42] In addition, this total distinction between His oneness and the world's multiplicity is founded upon the divine Himself, for He is one in His essence and many through His names, leading to Ibn 'Arabi's formulation of God as "The One/Many" (*al-wāhid al-kathīr*).[43]

Ibn 'Arabi deconstructs all systems and reference points except for being itself, the essence of the real, that which is, the only one who can truly say "I am." This is the only Absolute, base for all phenomena, from which they have come and to which they return. Things can therefore only be in a state of becoming, of coming-to-be, whereas only God has being as such. According to Ibn 'Arabi, we may intellectually conceive of a second absolute, pure nonexistence (*'adam*): even if this cannot, by definition, actually exist, it is this conception that allows being itself to appear in relativity and allows us to distinguish different aspects. Sheer being or light cannot be perceived, embraced or understood by any other than Itself, so "none knows God but God." In fact, this "Absolute One" is a total negation of all things without exception, and we can say nothing about It except that It is. We refer to it by negation as absolutely nonmanifest, undetermined, unarticulated: even Allah, God, being a name, can only be considered as Its outward face with regard to things.

Being is refracted as "things," which lie in the relative ambiguity of being both existent/light and nonexistent/dark. Thus, the world of creation that is everything other than God, from the highest spirits to the densest matter, can be viewed as either dark or light, relative nonexistence or existence, or, perhaps better, both sides at once. In one respect, the thing is He; in another respect, it is not He. This is what Nursi expressed as the true cleansing of a person: "in his existence he is non-existent, and in his non-existence he is existent."[44] Duality and hence opposition of aspects are absolutely necessary in the world of relativity. This corresponds precisely to Nursi's teaching that a thing has two aspects: one in respect of itself as compound (*mana-yi ismi*), and one in respect of its true nature in regard to the Creator (*mana-yi harfi*).[45] The plurality of 'things' is one of aspects, not an ontological multiplicity. All aspects are manifestations of divine names, which refer to God, the one who is named by all the names, the One/Many.

Rather than the somewhat monolithic concept of "oneness" (*waḥda*), Ibn 'Arabi himself uses the word "unification" (*ittihad*, from the same Arabic root), a more dynamic term that suggests "uniting" or "becoming unified." He is keen to point out that this is not a unification of separate essences, but a realization of the already existing fact of unity: "light is not burned away by light. Rather, it is included within it, that is, it coheres with it because it is of the same genus. This is conjunction and unification."46 Unification can only mean the servant assuming the characteristics of the Real (*haqq*), so that the Real becomes manifest in the form of the servant and the servant becomes manifest in the form of the Real.

Imagination

Nursi's statement that people of *waḥdat al-wujūd* take the world to be imagination and delusion would appear then to be drawn originally from Ibn Taymiyya's simplistic interpretation, probably mediated through his readings of Sirhindi's *Mektubat*. It also owes much to the more general attack on the ecstatic profession that "all is He," which gained currency among Iranian mystics.[47] For Ibn 'Arabi, the situation is far more nuanced: "The whole cosmos is He/not He. The Real manifest through form is He/not He. He is the limited who is not limited, the seen who is not seen."[48] The reality of "He/not He" that all things partake in is most clearly expressed as an imaginal, not imaginary reality.[49] Imaginal realities lie between the realm of pure disengaged meaning and the realm of sensory forms. When we dream, for example, we see a combination of form and meaning, meaning and form: a table that is not physical; knowledge in the form of milk and so on. Likewise, the form we see when we look into the mirror is both ourselves and not ourselves. It is this inexorable ambiguity that constitutes imagination for Ibn 'Arabi. Continual creation at each instant (*khalq jadīd*) and its constant transformation is for him the nature of all existence.

> The reality of imagination (*khayāl*) is continual change in every state and manifestation in every form. There is no true existence that does not accept change except God, and there is nothing in verified Being except God. As for everything other than He, that dwells in imaginal existence (*al-wujūd al-khayālī*). But when the Real becomes manifest within this imaginal existence, He only becomes manifest in keeping with its reality, not in His Essence, which is True Being (*al-wujūd al-haqīqī*).[50]

Thus, the reality of the world lies in the paradox of He/not He, without ever impinging on true being. This paradox means that for both Ibn ʻArabi and Nursi and countless others, intellectual knowledge cannot fathom reality, since it can only work in terms of oppositions. God's presence can only be *felt* by those who have faith (without vision) and those whose faith results in vision.

"The creation (*khalq*) is intelligible," Ibn ʻArabi writes, "and God (*haqq*) is perceptible and visible, according to the people of faith (*imān*) and the people of unveiled insight and experience (*ahl al-kashf wa'l-wujūd*). As for those who are in neither of these two categories, God is intelligible and the creation is visible. These latter are like bitter salty water while the former are like sweet, pleasant water, fit to drink."[51] Intelligibility is not the same as an invention of our imagination or fantasy; it is a question of differing viewpoints.

The Affirmation of Names

Instead of being viewed as imaginary, the universe is seen as the place where the real manifests Himself in His names. Without the universe, the divine names would have no meaning, as it is the "place" in which they show their effects. These names must have their logical correlatives. If there is a Creator (*khāliq*), there must be a created (*makhlūq*); if there is a Lord (*rabb*), there must be a servant, one over which He is Lord (*marbūb*); and so on. These two mutually dependent sides must constantly be borne in mind, if the relationship between God and universe, Reality and appearance, is to be truly understood: on the side of nonexistence there are all the possibilities of being or immutable entities (*al-a'yān al-thābita*), which he says "have never smelt the breath of existence"; on the side of existence there are the divine names, attributes, qualities, and actions. This exactly parallels Nursi's statement: "the true natures or realities of things are established/permanent" (*haqā'iqu'l-ashyā'i thābitatun*) and "God the Almighty manifests Himself truly through all His Names."[52]

It is due to the side of nonexistence that God is described as transcendent (*tanzīh*), and due to existence that He is known as immanent (*tashbīh*). The first description is accomplished through the use of reason, while the second corresponds to the exercise of imagination. By employing both faculties, reason and imagination, together properly, the mystic becomes "the one with two eyes," that is, someone with perfectly balanced vision. These two points of view, transcendence and immanence, are summarized for Ibn 'Arabi by the Quranic verse "There is no thing like Him, and He is the Hearer, the Seer." In addition, he points out that this verse contains an extraordinary conjunction of aspects, which are reversible: the first part of the verse alludes to His immanence, since it can be understood from the Arabic as "There is no thing like His likeness," which indicates man as the image of God ("God created Adam in His image"), while the second part of the verse includes absolutely every place of hearing and seeing, and therefore alludes to His transcendence.

Ibn 'Arabi's creed of rigorous unity is at the same time one of supreme tolerance of diversity and openness to fresh understandings. As he is often fond of citing (and Nursi follows him in this), "in everything there is a sign pointing to the fact that He is One."[53] Each created thing is at once a "receiver" of divine being and a "place" where God is manifest (*mazhar*). Whether it is gnat or an angel, it has a particular dignity and closeness to God that demands respect. Insofar as it has no being of its own, its quality is what is implied by nonexistence, that is, total dependence and humility; insofar as it manifests the Divine Being, it is dressed in divine qualities such as knowing and living. Therefore, insofar as man, that is the complete human being, the only creature to have been created by the two hands of God, manifests the divine qualities through his positive qualities, man can be said to be the divine likeness; but insofar as being is concerned, the difference is absolute, since *wujūd* only belongs to God.

One can see through this metaphysical overview that there are many points in common between Nursi and Ibn 'Arabi, though never rendered explicit. It would be possible to find other contact points: for example, the critique of the role of reason and its limitations; the subjection of the light (*nūr*) of intellect to the illumination (*diyā'*) of the heart, and thereby following what Nursi called "an isthmus between reason and heart";[54] sobriety through faith and intoxication through perplexity; the emphasis on realisation (*tahqīq/tahkiki iman*) rather than on blind imitation belief (*taqlīd/taklidi iman*);[55] the Reality of Muhammad and so on.

One of the major differences between the two men seems to me to lie in the way they discuss imagination and reason: while Nursi is keen to emphasize the dangers of imagination and prefers, like his predecessor Ghazali, to give his explanations in accordance with sober logic and reason and faith, Ibn 'Arabi also possesses a poetic disposition and gives imagination a real use, as the counterpart to the true nature of existence, as that which goes beyond the oppositions that limit the intellect, since through it we can "cross over" from the form to the intended meaning. It is a highly ambiguous realm born of both sides, an isthmus (*barzakh*), like the line that separates shadow from sunlight, or perhaps more appropriately, like the Bosphorus that simultaneously unites and separates the city of Istanbul and the two continents of Europe and Asia. However, Ibn 'Arabi does make a sharp distinction between someone dominated by their own imagination, who creates God in the image of his own belief, and someone under the sway of wonderment and perplexity, who can face the truly unfathomable depth of God as both Manifest and Hidden, both First and Last.[56]

Quranic Understanding

Nursi and Ibn 'Arabi both affirm the supreme, pivotal status of the Quran as revelation. Without such an all-encompassing source of revelation, human beings would be left to aspire to truth through intellect alone, which cannot penetrate into the world of reality.

For Ibn 'Arabi, "Everything of which we speak in our meetings and in our writings comes from the Quran and its treasures."[57] "Our shaykh Abu Madyan said: the aspirant (*murīd*) is really an aspirant only when he finds in the Quran all that to which he aspires."[58] "The Quran is perpetually new for any of those who recite it."[59] But there is a world of difference between one who recites with the mind and one who recites with the heart, for only the latter experiences "an immeasurable sweetness that surpasses all joy." He says that all depends on the state of reception: "he whose understanding is identical in two successive recitations is losing. He whose understanding is new in each recitation is winning. As for him who recites without understanding anything, may God have mercy upon him."[60]

For Nursi also, the Quran is a living sacred text: it should be "read and listened to as though it were freshly revealed . . . as though listening to God, the Pre-eternal Speaker."[61] It also embodies all the knowledge that a person needs:

> the All-Wise Quran, which makes known to us our Sustainer, is as follows: it is the pre-eternal translator of the great Book of the Universe; the discloser of the treasures of the Divine Names concealed in the pages of the earth and the heavens; the key to the truths hidden beneath these lines of events; the treasury of the favours of the Most Merciful

> and of the pre-eternal addresses, which come forth from the World of the Unseen beyond the veil of this Manifest World; the sun, foundation, and plan of the spiritual world of Islam, and the map of the worlds of the hereafter; the distinct expounder, lucid exposition, articulate proof, and clear translator of the Divine Essence, attributes and deeds; the instructor, true wisdom, guide, and leader of the world of humanity.[62]

One aspect of their pluralism can be seen in the way both men understand the verses of the Quran to be susceptible of multiple meanings. There is no one right way of reading, and all readings that can be totally grounded in the text are fruitful. In order to look more specifically at the way which Nursi and Ibn 'Arabi expound their teaching, let us consider their treatment of the Quranic verse, "And the mountains for supports/pegs (*awtād*)" (Quran 78.7). Nursi's major focus[63] is on the extraordinary comprehensiveness of the Quran, and he prefaces his exposition with an explanation that the words of each verse are complete expositions, referring to the famous hadith "Each verse has an outer meaning, an inner meaning, a limiting and a rising." He says that the words of the Quran should be understood according to many aspects and that "it gives to all those it addresses their share from a different door." He then proceeds to describe the meaning of the pegs/supports according to different kinds of people: an ordinary person of literal understanding, a bedouin, a geographer, a sociologist, and a natural scientist. For example: "An ordinary person . . . sees the mountains which appear like stakes driven into the ground, thinks of the benefits and bounties in them, and offers thanks to his Creator." Each one is described as contemplating the Quranic verse according to their own knowledge and background, and coming to wonder at the Glorious Creator of the mountains. What is interesting in this explanation is how Nursi restricts his gaze to ordinary people who have faith in God, showing that no matter what outer job one does, it may come to be viewed as a profession of faith.

By contrast, Ibn 'Arabi's understanding is metaphorical and based on a vision that came to him during the recitation of this passage while with his first spiritual master, al-'Uryani, in Andalusia:

> One day I was praying with [my shaykh] at the house of my friend . . . when the imam was reciting the chapter of the Qur'an entitled 'The Tiding'. When he came to the place where God says, "Have We not made the earth a resting-place and the mountains for supports . . ." I became abstracted from the imam and his recitation and saw inwardly our Shaykh, Abū Ja'far [al-'Uryanī], saying to me, "The resting-place is the world and the supports are the believers; the resting-place is the

community of believers and the supports are the gnostics; the gnostics are the resting-place and the prophets are the supports; the prophets are the resting-place and the messengers/envoys are the supports; the messengers are the resting-place and then what?" . . . After the prayer I asked him about what I had seen and found that his thoughts concerning the verse had been the same as I had heard him express in my vision.[64]

This passage describes well the spiritual hierarchy that Ibn 'Arabi would later elaborate: the four degrees of believers, saints, prophets, and messengers, and their interrelationship. Elsewhere, he describes the particular degree of the four supports or pillars (*awtād*), one of the highest ranks of saints "whose abodes are according to the four corners of the world, East, West, North and South, and the station (*maqām*) of each of them is the station of that direction."[65] Ibn 'Arabī identifies these supports as the prophetic quartet who have not tasted death, who have remained "alive in their bodies within the abode of this lower world"[66]: Khidr, Ilyās (Elijah), 'Īsa (Jesus), and Idrīs (Enoch). However, most people, Ibn 'Arabī points out, are not aware of these four being the real supports and conflate them with their more visible deputies. "Through one of [these four] God preserves faith; through the second He preserves sainthood; through the third He preserves prophethood; and through the fourth He preserves envoyship. Through them all together God preserves the primordial religion."[67]

Interestingly, Nursi himself was not unaware of this teaching on these four ever-living supports and the different levels of existence. He alludes to them in response to a question regarding whether Khidr is still alive:

He is alive but there are five degrees of life. . . . The first level is that of our life, which is very restricted. The second level is that of the lives of Khidr and Ilyas, which is free to an extent. That is to say, they can be present in numerous places at the same time. . . . The third level is that of Idris and Jesus, which . . . rises to an angelic level of life and acquires a luminous fineness.[68]

Conclusion

In conclusion, we may summarize the points we have made earlier. While himself not a Sufi, Nursi clearly sees Ibn 'Arabi as one of the great figures of Islamic spirituality. There is little or no evidence that Nursi himself read Ibn 'Arabi's works or those of his main disciple, Qunawi, although he does make reference to them.

The question of how far Nursi was actually influenced by Ibn 'Arabi is extremely difficult to determine. Like most learned people of his time, he had read many works by Sufi masters and been more or less influenced by them—and many of these in their turn were often transmitting teachings that had been set in written form by Ibn 'Arabi. We may cite in this regard three people whom Nursi had certainly read and quotes with delight, all of whom were great defenders of Ibn 'Arabi: the fourteenth-century Egyptian Shadhili shaykh, author of the K. al-Hikam, Ibn 'Ata'illah; the fifteenth-century Persian poet, 'Abd al-Rahman Jami; and the eighteenth-century Ottoman author exiled to Lesbos, Niyazi Misri.[69]

On the subject of *waḥdat al-wujūd* there is little doubt that Nursi's interpretation of the doctrine follows in the tradition, common among certain Naqshbandi paths, that the unity of existence is misleading for most people because it denies the existence of the world. This has little to do with Ibn 'Arabi's actual writings, and much more with the perceived effect that his teaching is reckoned to have had on later generations. Nursi appears to have inherited this tradition of reserve toward Ibn 'Arabi from Ahmad Sirhindi, without questioning its basis. This point needs emphasizing, as most later commentators have taken Nursi's doctrine at face value, as if it accurately reflects the teaching of Ibn 'Arabi himself, rather than the milieu in which he found himself in twentieth-century Turkey.

A closer analysis of Nursi's teachings (as well as Sirhindi's) does, however, reflect some degree of influence from Ibn 'Arabi, almost certainly through the medium of mainstream Islamic thought, which had taken on board many of his teachings without rendering their source explicit. A great deal of detailed research would need to be done to discuss the extent to which this actually took place. But Nursi's main project was different: to establish the fundamentals of a spiritual vision of the world and humanity that ordinary people could relate to, to preserve the basics of real faith in the heart while using one's reason to the full, and to emphasize divine harmony and beauty in a world that was, and is, being bombarded by secular thinking. In this respect, Ibn 'Arabi surely would only have encouraged him wholeheartedly and unreservedly.

NOTES

1. In the mid-thirteenth century, world population is estimated to have been a mere 400 million. Compare these figures to the 9 billion estimated for 2050.
2. Bediuzzaman Said Nursi, *Letters* (Istanbul, 2001), Seeds of Reality 18, 543.
3. Şükran Vahide, *Bediuzzaman Said Nursi* (Istanbul, 2000), 108, quoting from *Hutbe-i amiye*, 56–65.

4. *Islam at the Crossroads*, ed. Ibrahim M. Abu-Rabi' (Albany, 2003), x.
5. For example, he had close relations to the kings of Aleppo, Damascus, and Konya, and especially to the vizier of the Seljuk sultan, Majduddin Ishaq al-Rumi, the father of Sadruddin al-Qunawi. See Stephen Hirtenstein, *The Unlimited Mercifier*, chapter 13 (Oxford, 1999).
6. For example, they both had dream-visions of Muhammad when they were in their teens: Nursi dreamed of the Prophet telling him "Knowledge of the Quran will be given you on condition you ask no questions of any of my community" (Vahide, 8) while Ibn 'Arabi had a vision of the Prophet telling him "Cling to me and you will be safe" (*Unlimited Mercifier*, 55).
7. We may cite in this regard the great spiritual teacher of Bursa, Muhyiddin Mehmed Uftade (d.1580), who was also critical of the ten stages of the Halvetiyye. See Paul Ballanfat's introduction to *The Nightingale in the Garden of Love* (Oxford, 2005).
8. See *Words*, 26th Word addendum, 491–94. See also Bilal Kuspinar, "Nursi's Evaluation of Sufism," in *Third International Symposium on Bediuzzaman Said Nursi*, vol 2 (Istanbul, 1995), 78–80.
9. See, for example, Bilal Kuspinar's article, "The Concept of Man: Mevlana Jalal al-Din and Said Nursi," in *Islam at the Crossroads*, 151–66.
10. Quoted in Vahide's biography, *Bediuzzaman Said Nursi*, 5.
11. For a full treatment of this *tariqa* and its connection to Ibn 'Arabi's teachings, see Itzchak Weismann, *Taste of Modernity: Sufism, Salafism and Arabism in Late Ottoman Damascus* (Leiden, 2000).
12. Quoted by Vahide, 240. This can be compared to the notion of *tahqīq* espoused by Ibn 'Arabi, verifying the truth of knowledge through unveiling and direct vision: "We followed the authority [of the Messenger and the Quran] in knowledge until the Real was our hearing and our sight, so that we came to know things through God and gained knowledge of how things are classified through God" (*Fut.* II. 298, Beirut, n.d.).
13. See Imtiyaz Yusuf's article, "Relationship between God and Human Being: The Spiritual Interface between Two *mujaddids*," in *Fifth International Symposium on Bediuzzaman Said Nursi* (Istanbul, 2000), 197–207.
14. He first came to Malatya in 602H/1205 at the invitation of the Seljuk court and raised his family there, leaving for Damascus in approximately 619H/1222. See *Unlimited Mercifier*, chapter 13.
15. It was common for scribes to attribute works to Ibn 'Arabi on the basis of finding them among a collection of his works, even if the original scribe had not mentioned the author. These are often attributed in other manuscripts to different authors. In many cases, we can utilize technical vocabulary and phrasing of ideas to ascertain attribution: for example, the famous hadith: "He who knows himself knows his Lord" is always written by Ibn 'Arabi as "*man 'arafa nafsahu 'arafa rabbahu*," whereas later commentators or others write it as "*man 'arafa nafsahu* ***faqad*** *'arafa rabbahu.*" See Chodkiewicz's introduction to Awhad al-Din Balyani's *Risalat al-wujudiyya* (*Épitre sur l'Unicité absolue*, trans. M. Chodkiewicz, Paris, 1982).
16. Bediuzzaman Said Nursi, *Words* (Istanbul, 2002), 32nd Window, 721. In all his references he calls him Muhyiddin al-'Arabi, rather than the more usual Ibn 'Arabi or technically more correct Ibn al-'Arabi.

17. Quran 39.53. Ibn 'Arabi had a vision in Murcia, Spain, in which God tells him: "What is it then with My servants that they should despair of My Compassion, when My Compassion embraces everything?" (see *Unlimited Mercifier*, 125).
18. Bediuzzaman Said Nursi, *Flashes* (Istanbul, 2001), 9th Flash. It is somewhat unfortunate that the translation into English of some technical terms that Nursi uses are often inappropriate, for example, "occult" sciences (= *asrār*?) when Ibn 'Arabi would have abhorred what we understand today by the term "occult."
19. *Flashes*, 28th Flash, criticizing the attitude of the conservative shaykh al-islam Mustafa Sabri.
20. See Kuspinar, "Nursi's Evaluation of Sufism," *Third International Symposium on Bediuzzaman Said Nursi* (Istanbul, 1997), 72–83.
21. See, for example, *Letters*, 104, where he refers to both Ibn 'Arabi and the great Yemeni follower of his school, 'Abd al-Karim al-Jili (d.1428), author of the celebrated *al-Insān al-Kāmil.*
22. Ibn al-'Imād (d.1678), *Shadharāt al-dhahab* V, 196—quoted in *Unlimited Mercifier*, 211. This may be an actual quotation from Qunawi's works, but I have been unable to trace it.
23. *Flashes*, 9th Flash.
24. William Chittick, "The Last Will and Testament of Ibn 'Arabi's Foremost Disciple and Some Notes on its Author," *Sophia Perennis* Vol IV, number 1, 53.
25. *Flashes*, 28th Flash. Some authors, such as Afifi, have used the term "Unity of Existence" in their translations, but we prefer to use being to clarify the distinction between that which is, the essence itself (being), and that which becomes, the world of things that literally ex-ist, that is, come from It (existence). This to some extent parallels the Arabic terms *wujūd* and *mawjūd.* I have not been able to trace the quotation from Ibn 'Arabi given here.
26. Here I am referring not only to the outer conditions, important though these may be, but also to the substantial changes that have taken place in the field of Ibn 'Arabi studies. One hundred years ago, Ibn 'Arabi's name was unknown in the West, apart from a handful of scholars, and, though known in the East, little direct study was done of his work. Even twenty-eight years ago, when the Muhyidddin Ibn 'Arabi Society was founded, there was little accurate information available, let alone comprehension of his teachings. This has changed dramatically as more translations and studies are done, and a more balanced assessment of Ibn 'Arabi's contribution can be made, although much remains to be done in the area of critical editions.
27. *K. Istilāhāt al-sūfiyya, Rasā'il Ibn 'Arabi* (Hyderabad, 1948) 532. Earlier writers such as al-Qushayri based their definitions on the literal sense of the verb *wajada* found in Quran 24:39: "He finds God."
28. William Chittick, "Rumi and *wahdat al-wujūd*," *Poetry and Mysticism in Islam: The Heritage of Rumi* (Cambridge, 1994), 70–111.
29. William Chittick, "The Central Point," *Journal of the Muhyiddin Ibn 'Arabi Society* XXXV, 2004, 27–29.
30. Al-Ghazali, *The Niche of Lights*, trans. David Buchman (Utah, 1998), 16.
31. See William Chittick's excellent article, "Rumi and *wahdat al-wujūd.*"
32. It is only in Ibn 'Arabi's book of prayers that we find the phrase *wahdat wujūdika*, "the Oneness of Your Being," referring simply to the affirmation that God, the real

being, is one. This implies that our being or that of any thing that exists, in contrast, is multiple through being uniquely itself and the sum of its parts and different from every other thing.

33. *Nafahat al-uns* (Tehran, 1991), 555, quoted in Chittick, "Central Point," 31 and Claude Addas, *Quest for the Red Sulphur* (Cambridge, 1993), 231.
34. *Flashes*, 9th Flash.
35. *Letters*, 20th Letter, 2nd Station, 296.
36. *Flashes*, 28th Flash, 371.
37. Ibn Taymiyya, *Majmu'a* IV, 73, quoted in Chittick, "Rumi and *wahdat al-wujūd*," 85.
38. *Words*, 26th Word addendum, 494. The distinction of these terms, *wahdat al-wujud* and *wahdat al-shuhud*, is essentially the work of Ahmad Sirhindi, who belonged to quite a different milieu and had a different agenda.
39. It is therefore surprising to find modern scholars such as Leaman ("Islam, The Environment and Said Nursi," in *Islam at the Crossroads*) trying to discuss Ibn 'Arabi's "*wahdat al-wujūd* idea."
40. *Fut.* II.148.
41. *Fut.* III.299.
42. *Fusus al-Hikam*, ed. Afifi (Beirut, 1946), 105.
43. For example, "There is nothing in *wujūd* but the One/Many," *Fut.* III.420.
44. *Words*, 26th Word addendum, 493.
45. This follows closely Ghazali's lines: "Each thing has two faces: a face towards itself, and a face toward its Lord. Viewed in terms of the face of itself, it is nonexistent (*'adam*); but viewed in terms of the face of God, it is existent (*mawjūd*)" (Niche of Lights, 17). The distinction between "name" or "noun" (*ism*) and "letter" (*harf*) is fundamental in Ibn 'Arabi's teaching, corresponding to the world of manifestation and the world of the unseen respectively. The letter which makes up a word in sound or speech represents a thing's origin, its fundamental nature.
46. *Fut.* II.184.
47. As Chittick points out, there is a major difference between the Persian poetical exclamation "all is He" (*hama ūst*) and the nuanced approach of "He/not He" THAT combines both God's similarity and His incomparability.
48. *Fut.* II.379, translated in Chittick's *Sufi Path of Knowledge* (Albany, 1989), 116.
49. It was Henri Corbin who first coined this word "imaginal" to convey the proper condition of imagination as opposed to "imaginary," which is suppositional.
50. *Fut.* II.313, translated in Chittick, *Sufi Path of Knowledge*, 118.
51. *Fusūs*, ed. Afifi, 108. This alludes to the Quranic verse: "He it is who let forth the two seas, this one sweet and pleasant to taste, that one salty and bitter to the tongue" (Quran 25.53).
52. *Mektūbat*, 85, quoted in Kuspinar, "Nursi's Evaluation of Sufism."
53. Originally a verse by the Arab poet, Abu Atahiya.
54. From the Preface to *al-Mathnawī al-'Arabī al-Nūrī*, trans. Redha Ameur, in *Islam at the Crossroads*, 335.
55. For example, "Blind conformity (*taqlīd*) is not permissible in matters of religion, in our opinion, regardless of whether the individual is dead or still living" (*Futuhat*, vhapter 88, trans *Meccan Revelations*, Volume II, ed. M. Chodkiewicz (New York, 2004).

56. See *Fusūs*, chapter on Noah, ed. Afifi, 73, where Ibn 'Arabi quotes the prayer of the Prophet: "Increase me in you in perplexity/wonderment (*hayra*)," this wonderment being for Ibn 'Arabi the greatest stage of spiritual life, moving one beyond all conceptions of opposition: "The person of the long way inclines away from the aim, seeking what he is already in, creating in imagination that which is his goal—he has a 'from' and a 'to' and what lies between them. But the master of the circular movement has no starting-point that 'from' would force upon him, and no goal that 'to' could rule over him. He has the most complete being/experience (*wujūd*), and he is the one to whom is given the totality of words and wisdoms."
57. It was again Ibn Taymiyya who accused Ibn 'Arabi of twisting the meaning of the Quran, a charge that is hard to sustain when one looks closely at his writings that are faithful to many layers of meaning of the revealed text.
58. *Fut.* III.94.
59. *Fut.* III.93.
60. *Fut.* III.129. He also writes: "Plunge into the ocean of the Qur'an if your breath is sufficiently powerful. And if not, limit yourself to the study of the commentaries on its apparent sense; but in this case do not plunge, for you will perish. The ocean of the Quran is deep, and if he who plunges into it did not limit himself to those places which are closest to the shore, he would never come back to the creatures." (*Fut.* I.328).
61. Quoted (without reference) in Ali Mermer, "Divine Speech in the Risale-i Nur," *Fifth International Symposium*.
62. *Letters*, First Addendum, 244.
63. Nursi, *The Words* (25th Word, 1st Light, 2nd Ray), 402.
64. *Sufis of Andalusia* (Sherborne, 1988), 66–67. It is instructive to relate these four levels to the levels mentioned in the hadith, outer, inner, limit, and rising.
65. *Istilāhāt*, definition, 20. These four directions equally apply to the four corners of the Ka'ba.
66. *Fut.* II.5. He considers Idrīs, whose abode is the fourth heaven, to be part of this world, since the heavens belong to this world.
67. Ibid.
68. *Letters*, First Letter, 21–22. This view goes back to Ibn 'Arabi's teachings on the supports.
69. Quoted, respectively, in *Letters*, 44; *Words*, 230; *Letters*, 351.

SIXTEEN

Exploring the Spiritual Dimensions of Nature

Ahmed-i Jiziri and Said Nursi

M. Sait Özervarlı

The seventeenth chapter of Nursi's major work *The Words*, which is about relations between soul and body, and the spiritual desire for eternity among creatures, includes some of his poetic essays in various languages.[1] They are mainly spiritual reflections that came to his mind through natural observation or Sufi inspirations. One of the poems was inspired by the lines of the seventeenth-century Kurdish Sufi and poet Ahmed-i Jiziri, following "a magnificent, delightful, and glamorous display of dancing" by a gentle breeze under majestic pine, cedar, and juniper trees in Barla.[2]

The verses of Jiziri quoted by Nursi on this occasion and its English translation are the following:

Her kes bi-temaşagihē husna te ji-her ca
Teşbihē nigaran bi-cemala te dinazin![3]
(Everyone by gazing at Your Beauty from everywhere,
they are like dancers acting coyly before Your Beauty.)

Remembering these lines of Jiziri, Nursi's heart "weeps" and he writes a long poem in Persian, describing the spiritual meanings of the movements and voices of the trees. This poem, which will be discussed with other examples, is a summary of Nursi's spiritual interpretation of nature.[4]

As those who read Nursi's writings would realize, his thought mainly relied on his modern explanations of the Quran and spiritual observations of the universe. He often employs one for constructing and formulating the other. In doing so, he does not strictly follow a specific scholar or a tradition of thought in Islamic intellectual history, although he seemed to be influenced by various personalities and Sufi movements, such as Abu Hamid al-Ghazzali, Mawlana Jalal al-Din al-Rumi, 'Abd al-Qadir Jilani, or Naqshibandi, Khalidi, and Qadiri orders. These great scholars and major orders are quite well known in Islamic learning, especially in the Ottoman and Anatolian cultural environment. Therefore, Nursi's awareness of them will not be a surprise for the scholars of modern Ottoman thought. However, Nursi has also a connection with local Kurdish scholars of eastern Anatolia, who are known in the region. This connection is touched upon by few experts so far,[5] but is not yet analytically and fully elaborated within theoretical studies on Nursi. Ahmed-i Jiziri is a good example of this connection. As Martin van Bruinessen puts it, Jiziri "was not an isolated phenomenon but simply the best remembered, and perhaps the best, of a much larger circle of metaphysical poets writing in Kurdish that flourished over a considerable period."[6] According to Ferhad Shakeli, the quality of his poetry and the profoundness of his Sufi thought earned him a dominant position in Kurdish literature.[7]

Jiziri, certainly, is not the only Kurdish Sufi scholar who was known to Nursi. The author of the literary epic *Mem u Zin*, the theological treatise *Aqida Iman*, and the Arabic-Kurdish dictionary *Nubihar*, Ahmed-i Khani (d. 1707) is another well-known Sufi poet in the region, who was born in Hakkari and died in Dogu Beyazid. Khani, too, seems to have some effects on Nursi's early spiritual upbringing.[8] Dogu Beyazid is the town where Nursi obtained his madrasa certificate (*ijaza/icazet*) from Shaykh Mehmed Jalali and became "Mulla Said," following three months of his final training in the Beyazid Madrasa. However, during this period of extensive study, Nursi did not spend all his time in the madrasa doing academic work, but was also interested in spiritual inspiration and purification. Vahide in her English biography of Nursi writes:

> While in Beyazid, Said passed much of his time, and even the nights, in the mausoleum of the Kurdish saint and poet Shaikh Ahmad Hani, so that the people said he was specially privileged with Ahmad Hani's spiritual radiance. One night Said's friends from the *medrese* missed him and started searching for him. Finally they looked in the mausoleum and found him there studying by the light of a candle. But he rebuked them for disturbing them.[9]

This interest in self-isolation (*inziva'* or *uzlah*) demonstrates Nursi's engagement in spiritual piety (*zuhd*) and the denial of the outside world (*tark al-dunya*) since his early years.[10] Later he had similar spiritual experiences of isolation in the Yusha Hill of Istanbul and the Erek Mountain of Van.[11] It became a sort of alienation or exile (*ghurba*), which represents, according to recent studies, one of the most important dimensions of Nursi's thought. Based on prophetic traditions and Sufi interpretations, the concept of exile is a major theme of Islamic spirituality, and like other spiritualist personalities Nursi found the knowledge of God in seclusion and alienation.[12] In fact, in his later life he was forced to spend long years in exile or in prison, which turned out to be an opportunity for him to produce his writing and spread a spiritual movement.

More examples can be cited among this kind of local Sufis, such as Shaykh Abdurrahman-i Taghi, Muhammed-i Kufrawi, Fehim Arwasi, who guided him in his early life on *tasawwuf* and spirituality.[13] Mulla Khalil-i Siirdi[14] is another local scholar, whose lines from *Nahj al-anam* are quoted by Nursi.[15] This chapter, however, will examine the spirituality of Nursi and its similarities with the writings of Ahmed-i Jiziri. Jiziri is the author of a large *Diwan* book, which is very popular among Kurds, up to today. In eastern Anatolia during the Seljukid and Ottoman period, along with three major languages (*alsina al-thalatha*, i.e., Arabic Persian, and Turkish), Kurdish was also one of the languages of Islamic literature. The existing poetical examples of the sixteenth- and seventeenth-century writings by Jiziri, Khani, and the transmission of popular *aqida* and *mawlid* treatises demonstrate the place of Kurdish in local culture and learning.[16] The well-known Ottoman traveler Evliya Celebi, who visited the region in the mid-seventeenth century, gives lively accounts in the latest completed edition of his *Seyahatname* of the cultural and religious atmosphere in several towns of the area, including Cizre, quoting some pieces of Kurdish poetry.[17]

The founding of several Kurdish principalities or emirates, such as Diyarbekir, Bitlis, Imadiye, and Cizre, which were established by traditional tribes and dynasties in the region at least since the sixteenth century,[18] was one of the main reasons for the emergence and development of classical Kurdish literature. In the courts, mosques, and madrasas of these dynasties, Kurdish culture, especially poetry, found patronage and flourished in the region.[19] Jiziri lived under the patronage of one of these dynasties, the Emirate of the South-Anatolian town of Cizre (known as Jazirat Ibn Omar in history).[20] There are various claims about Jiziri's lifetime, but some details in the existing sources provide certain information. First, in his book he addresses to the head of Cizre Emirate, Sharaf III (d. 1618),[21] and second, he enters into a poetic contest with his contemporary Faqi-ye Tayran in 1622.[22] Therefore, he lived, quite certainly, in the late sixteenth and the early seventeenth century. Jiziri was based in Cizre, and named after the town as "Mela-yi Jiziri."[23] He is believed to die by 1640 and is buried in the basement of the historical Red Madrasa (Medresa Sor) in Cizre, where he presumably taught his students. One may know that eastern Anatolian towns such as Diyarbakir, Hısna Kayfa (Hasankeyf), Meyafarqin (Silvan), and Mardin own some majestic old madrasas, some of which were built as early as the twelfth century. Built by Ayyubid, Artuqid, or even Iranian dynasties, these madrasas attracted students of various ethnic origins including Kurdish *ulama*. The number of madrasas grew under the local emirates; Bitlis, Cizre, Tillo, and Amediyye became major centers of learning.[24] The Red Madrasa of Cizre is one of them, built by the emir of the town in Anatolian Seljukid architectural style, which is known with its connection to Ahmed-i Jiziri.[25]

Said Nursi himself is a remarkable production of these eastern Anatolian madrasas in the late nineteenth century.[26] In fact, there is an interesting account about Cizre and its *ulama* in Nursi's life. When Nursi's fame grew in eastern madrasas as "Famous Mulla Said" during his visits to Shirvan and Tillo as early as his sixteenth year, he saw Abd al-Qadir al-Jilani in his dream ordering Nursi to go to Mustafa Pasha of the Miran tribe in Cizre, in order to invite the Pasha to justice and the performance of religious duties. Nursi immediately made his way to Cizre, and in the first meeting with the governor Mustafa Pasha he explained the purpose of the visit and threatened to kill him if he did not change his behaviors. Pasha was shocked by Nursi's unexpected courage and wanted to humiliate him publicly before deciding on a serious punishment. Therefore, he suggested a scholarly contest between Nursi and the *ulama* of Cizre, and promised to consider the request in case of a victory over them. However, Nursi successfully answered all forty questions of the invited scholars in a ceremonial gathering, even correcting a wrong answer, which was not realized by the admiring questioners. The result was outstanding, and after the contest some of the participant scholars decided to study under the teenager Said.[27] Although the biographies do not give details, it is highly probable that, during his stay in Cizre, Nursi visited the tomb of Jiziri in the town, and spent some time there to strengthen his spiritual awakening, as he did in Dogu Beyazid within the mausoleum of Khani. Jiziri is even more influential and respected Sufi than Khani in the region, and therefore Nursi would not miss the opportunity to get a similar spiritual radiance that he sought earlier.

The content and terminology of Jiziri's *Diwan*[28] show that, apart from his native Kurdish language, he knows Arabic, Persian, and Turkish. Besides, he seems well equipped with Islamic culture and the madrasa learning as he refers to various Muslim communities, particular historical events, and some fiqh books. His *Diwan* includes 114 poems (resembling the numbers of surahs in the Quran) mostly *ghazals*, some *qasidas*, and few *tarji-i bands*. The manuscripts also contain a poem by adding three lines rhyming with the first couplet (*takhmis*) by an unknown follower called Laghar, and an Arabic poem by Ahmed Pasha (d. 1492) of Bursa.

In his poetry, there is an obvious influence of Hafiz-i Shirazi (d. 1390), as the book starts with a *Terbi* adding two lines to each two lines of Shirazi's famous poem, which starts with "*Ela ya eyyuha's-saqi*."[29] However Jiziri claims that his poetry was superior to Shirazi's and there was no need any more for the latter's poems.[30] He also refers to Sa'di-yi Shirazi (d. 1292) and Mulla Abdurrahman-i Jami (d. 1492), and presents himself as "arif-i zaman" like Ma'ruf al-Karkhi (d. 816) of the early period. The commentators of Jiziri's *Diwan* compare the author to Ibn al-Fārid, Fuzuli, and Rumi in Arabic, Turkish, and Persian Sufi literatures.[31] Jiziri's mystical thought, especially his defense of *waḥdat al-wujūd* (or even *waḥdat al-muṭlaq* as he puts in one of his lines), is similar to Muhyiddin Ibn al-Arabi, although he never mentions the latter. It is unlikely that he was unaware of Ibn al-Arabi, who was well known in the region at that time; therefore, despite the similarities of thought, the absence of Ibn Arabi's name in *Diwan* remains a question. There is no evidence about his connection to any Sufi order, though Ferhad Shakeli suggests that he was a Nakshibendi without a confirmation or any source of information.[32] The major themes of Jiziri's poems are divine love, the ontological questions of his mystical philosophy, and the spiritual manifestations of God. In fact, in some pieces, he uses the penname "Nishani" to describe himself as the target of the arrows of love. The descriptions and interpretations of human and physical beauty are used in the book to remind us of their divine aspects, and the spiritual meanings behind the material appearances of beings.[33]

SPIRITUALITY THROUGH NATURE

As seen in the content of his long poem on Jiziri's previously quoted lines, one of the characteristics of Nursi's thought is to see and describe the natural beings from a spiritual and simply a believer's point of view. Ordinary philosophers or scientists while examining the universe, Nursi suggests, will attribute the qualities of the existent beings to themselves; however, believers will remember their Creator and praise the perfectness of His creation in all parts of the universe. In the second view, each object and each event is directly connected to its Creator. Thus, "a philosophy without religion is an untruthful sophistry and an insult to the universe."[34]

Therefore, Nursi does not see the physical world and its contents as existents per se, but as creatures of God, each of which performs its own duty, according to the commands of God, in order to serve God within the wise program of divine creation. Hence,

> Everything is like a soldier under His command. Everything turns through His strength. Everything acts through His command. Everything is set in order through His wisdom. Everything helps the others through His munificence. Everything hastens to the assistance of the others through His compassion, that is, they are made to hasten to it.[35]

God "has created everything beautifully and with perfect order. He has fitted them out beautifully, turned their faces towards beautiful aims, employed them in beautiful duties, caused them to utter beautiful glorifications and to worship beautifully." Therefore, according to Nursi, every natural action by the created beings is a performance of worship to their All-knowledgeable Creator and Wise Designer. Everything they do is in the name and permission of God with complete obedience:

> The glorification and worship they perform by carrying out the duties related to their lives in this wonderful fashion through the power of God Almighty are gifts and salutations, which they present to the Court of the All-Glorious Creator, the Bestower of Life.[36]

The creatures are not valuable because of their simple existence and actions, in Nursi's view, but because of their obedience to fulfill their mission in a worshiping manner. Thus, Nursi observes the physical world beyond its appearance, through the meaning and aim of its existence, which are, in his view, serving and contributing to a continuous, universal divine program of creation under God's will. The created beings are beautiful individually in their appearances, but they are meaningfully beautiful by being a part of a harmonious design within the universe. Therefore, the fact that how beautifully they are made and how wonderfully they are placed is more important than how beautiful they are. In this form, love toward the creatures "will give a pain-free pleasure, and in one respect, an unending union. Moreover, it will increase love of God."[37]

The spiritual description of natural events, by looking beyond their appearances, is also one of the points of Jiziri's poetry. Astonished by the perfect cosmological system of the universe, he praises God for designing the continuity of the motions of the stars and planets without a moment of disorder or interruption. Days and nights, according to Jiziri, by turning continuously, in fact, come to see their love (God) and they do not make any mistake or delay in their trip.

The writings of the universe are in fact an address title (refers to God), that does not permit the slightest incorrect writing.[38]

Apart from being conscious of the light and fire of Love of God, Jiziri emphasizes that one also needs to see the beauty of His creation. Without examining the artistic work in nature by divine power, no one would be able to reach God through a spiritual unification.[39] In the morning when the winds breeze from right and left, he says, the various types of flowers delightedly start performing whirling dances from right and left. Moreover, the birds, leaves, papers, and other things begin moving by trembling and ecstasy of the situation.[40]

The spiritual interpretation of nature and natural events comes from one of the major Quranic aspects, which is described as cosmic signs (*al-ayat al-kawniyya*). Several verses of the Quran call for observing the world in order to realize the wise creation and planning behind it. A careful examination of the universe, according to the Quran, will help the person to understand who has made the earth a resting-place for humans, and the sky a canopy. It is God who sent water from skies, provided fruits for our sustenance, and caused gardens of shining beauty to grow. Again He made waters to flow in the midst of earth, set mountain firm upon it, and placed a barrier between the two seas.[41] Therefore, the Quran aims to teach humans how to examine the universe, how to discover the power behind the natural beings and event and reach the Creator. Following the Quranic path and Islamic intellectual tradition, Muslim thinkers highlighted the spiritual dimensions of physical and human nature. Abu Hamid al-Ghazzali's monumental work *Iḥya' 'ulūm al-dīn*, for instance, contains examples of these kind of descriptions.[42] In Ibn Arabi's thought, as well, everything in the cosmos qualifies as a sign of God.[43] Thus, Jiziri and Nursi focused on this Quranic spiritual path and brought it to the center of their thought.

Manifestations and Stamps of Divine Names in Nature

In Nursi's thought, the spiritual origin of the physical existence comes from the manifestations (*tajalli/tecelli*) of the divine names in the various aspects of the created beings. The term *tajalli*, which is translated as "the Self-disclosure of God" by Chittick in his major book on Ibn al-Arabi, is employed in two verses of the Quran, one referring to God and the other to the daytime (7:143 and 92:3). Based mainly on the interpretations of the first verse, the term later became one of the central topics in Sufi thought. Following the Quranic and Sufi traditions, Nursi describes the physical life as "an index of wonders pertaining to the Divine Names; a scale for measuring the divine attributes, a balance of the worlds within the universe." It is written by the pen of divine power, and it acts as a mirror of divine manifestation, being the focus of all names comprehensively.[44]

It means that there is no single existence, which escapes a reflection or manifestation from one or more than one divine names, according to Nursi. In his words, "in every level of beings, many or few, great or small, particular or general, He has an appearance through a particular manifestation, a particular dominicality, a particular Name." However, despite this manifestation, there are also veils in the physical existence obscuring the direct appearance of divine manifestations. Therefore, only on condition that you leave the whole universe behind you and focus on its divine origin of creativity, "you may reach the limits of the Name of Creator and draw close to the sphere of attributes."[45]

Nursi emphasizes that the manifestations of the names differ "in respect of universality, particularity, shadow, or originality." For example, an adorned flower, a living droplet, and a translucent atom, which looks to the Sun, all have consciousness and some perfection, and allude to the spiritual voyaging of the soul, the mind, and the heart. The flower, droplet, and atom cannot see a sun, which looks to the whole world; the sun of that individual or species or genus appears to it within narrow confines and under limiting restrictions. In addition, it cannot ascribe to that restricted sun the works of the unrestricted, unconfined, absolute sun. For within those narrow restrictions and limited confines it cannot attribute to the sun with the certain witnessing of the heart its majestic works like furnishing the whole face of the earth with light and heat, stirring all plants and animals into life, and making the planets revolve around it. In a further thinking, it will be realized that a flower is a minuscule mirror of the sun, and the sun, too, is merely a drop-like flash manifesting in the seas of the skies the name of light of the pre-eternal sun.[46]

Jiziri, too, often employs the concept of *tajalli* in his interpretations, giving examples of divine manifestation both in the universe and the beloved one. The universe is "the mirror of the Divine names," according to Jiziri, which are reflected by the light of their manifestations.[47] "If one rose comes out from Your garden," he says referring to God, "all the famous gardens of the world, even the Iram paradise[48] will disappear from the scenes. The description of Your Beauty is not possible by words and numbers. The place that Your Beauty is manifested should be recognized immediately and prostrated by members of all sects and religions, as it will be so obvious and undeniable."[49] Referring to the divine manifestation to Moses in the Sina Mountain, Jiziri states that similar flashes come to the hearts of people, but they are not able to comprehend them.[50]

The explanation of God's manifestations is mostly beyond the capacity of human language, according to Jiziri, as they appear in physical beings from their divine sources. They are "meanings that could not be adapted into words due to the narrowness of linguistic expressions."[51] The comprehension of the secrets of the divine attributes on the physical beings is not possible without a spiritual love, as we need manifestations for understanding them.[52] However, God opens hundreds of windows of divine lights, which help understanding His wisdom. Jiziri becomes confused, he says, by people, who at least once in their life could not hear the voices that come from the deeper meanings of divine creation. If only they pass the veil of surmising, he suggests, they will even hear so many songs with musical tunes.[53]

The aim of these divine manifestations is to show reasoning people that there were the origins of the beings behind the material veils, and they could see the signs of their origins if they examine them carefully. Therefore, in Nursi's view, through the manifestations of the divine names, God places His stamps on the beings and seals them. And through placing a particular stamp, special seal, and an inimitable signet on every adorned work of art that is seen, "He wants to show that everything is particular to Him, and is the work of His own hand, and that He is single and unique and independent."[54] Like a seal of a hidden one, they through their tongues of disposition say: "We are the art of One, Who can make this entire world of ours as easily and simply as He created us."[55] It can be seen on all creatures that there are seals special to the maker, and on the levels of being written during night and day, or summer and winter, are inimitable, illustrious signatures of God.[56]

THE MANIFESTATION OF GOD'S ONENESS IN THE DIVERSITY OF CREATURES

The manifestation of divine names within the individual beings becomes very clear by God's oneness (*Ahadiyya/Ehadiyyet*) through its access to each being in the universe, according to Nursi, as it is different from His unity (*Wahidiyya/Vahidiyyet*):

> As for Unity, it is to say that all those creatures belong to One and they look to One and they are the creation of One. Whereas by Oneness is meant that most of the Names of the Creator of all things are manifested in all beings. For example, the light of the sun may be seen as analogous to Unity by reason of its comprehending the face of the earth While the fact that its light and heat, the seven colours in its light and some sort of shadow of it are found in all transparent objects and drops of water makes them analogous to Oneness. And the fact that most of

> the Maker's Names are manifested in each single thing, especially in each animate creature, and above all in man, points to Oneness.[57]

That is, with regard to unity, the sun encompasses all the things, which confront it, while with regard to oneness; the sun is present together with many of its attributes in everything through a sort of manifestation of its essence.[58] On the heads of all creatures, whether large or small, numerous or few, a seal of divine oneness is to be observed. All flowers, all fruits, all leaves, all plants, all animals are such seals of divine oneness and stamps of eternal besoughtedness. In order to show their scribe, stamps have been put on the groups of creatures to the number of individuals.[59] Since the living being is like a miniature sample of the universe and a fruit of the tree of creation, it shows a seal of divine eternal besoughtedness, which conveys altogether with ease to the tiny sphere of its life, which are as many as the universe.[60]

There is quite a close similarity between Nursi and Jiziri on the distinction of divine unity and oneness. In fact, Nursi quotes the first line of Jiziri's poem on this subject, which is:

> *Sirrē wehdet ji ezel girtiye hetta bi-ebed*
> (The secret of divine unity covers the existence both
> pre-eternally and eternally.)[61]

According to Jiziri, although they are the same in essence, the oneness of God is different from His unity in the position of His absolute self-reliance (*Samadiyya/Samediyyet*), which means He is dependent on nothing and all things and persons are dependent on Him.[62] In His oneness, therefore, every being is in need of Him for his manifestation to each single existence. The sun of oneness, Jiziri says, covers all existence; however, we do not see it sometimes, not because of a cloud in between, but because of our shortsightedness.[63]

One should know that the difference between the *Ahadiyyet* and *Wahidiyyet* is also a subject of Ibn al-Arabi's thought. All the names' attributes are unified and the same in the absolute existence of the oneness of God (*Zat-i ehadiyyet*), according to Ibn al-Arabi, however, they represent their own individuality and therefore distinctiveness in the degree of divine unity (*mertebe-i vahidiyyet*).[64] God is *Ahad* through His self as He is in need of nothing, but He is *Vahid* through His names as He possesses various names and attributes, which means in this respect He is not independent of them.[65] Therefore, the crucial word to understand God's oneness and its difference from His unity is the concept of *Samediyyet*, which is emphasized in *Surat al-Ikhlas* (112: 1–2): "Say: He is Allah, the *Ahad* (the One and Only). Allah is *Samad* (free of all needs, but everything else is in need of Him)." Thus, in *Ahadiyya* there is no plurality whatsoever, while in *Wahidiyya* there is a relative plurality through divine names and their manifestations.[66] When Ibn Arabi differentiates between the two words, the basic difference is that *Ahad* designates God's unity in respect of *tanzih*, while *Wahid* designates it in terms of *tashbih*.[67] Moreover, the *Ahadiyyet* consists of the oneness of God's essence, of His names and attributes, and His actions. The plurality of the shadows of these names and actions through manifestations does not affect the divine oneness.[68]

THE DESCRIPTION OF THE UNIVERSE AS A SPIRITUAL BOOK

Since the created beings are the stamps of God in Nursi's spirituality, the whole universe is a great book including His variety of signs, just as the revealed book. The parts, pieces, particles, elements, and components of the universe resemble chapters, sections, sentences, words, and letters of a book. Even the smallest elements of the existence, he says, such as "the letters of the mighty book of the universe point to themselves to the extent of their own size and physical beings, but describe the Names of the Pre-Eternal Inscriber like odes, and testify to the One they signify and point to His Names with fingers to the number of their attributes."[69] Each of the beings is a meaningful letter, as bearing the meaning of another, on account of their Maker, saying, "How beautifully they have been made! How exquisitely they point to their Maker's beauty!," and showing the universe's true beauty.[70]

The universe is an "inner-outer" notebook according to Nursi, in which the Eternal Writer repeatedly writes and rewrites. A single human being includes fragments of all elements within the physical world of nature, so it is actually a smaller example (*misal-i musağğar*) of the universe, as well as a core of inner qualities. Therefore, the individual man, like other creatures, becomes a living proof for the existence of God. Thus, Nursi prefers an experimental inductive method from the cause (*athar*) to the effect (*muaththir*) in order to understand the spirituality of the universe, rather than using philosophical deductions.[71] This approach is based on a similar classification in the Quran (41: 53), which divides "signs" (*ayat*) for the existence of God as found both in the characteristics of the physical universe (*afaq*) and within the substance, both physical and spiritual, of all human beings (*anfus*).[72]

In Nursi's thought, the Quran, which is the revealed book of God, is in fact a translation of the great book of the universe and its speaking language. It reads the book of the universe in its mosque, and it is the light (*nur*) of the life of the universe and the intellect of its conscience. On the other hand, the universe is the proof of the Quran and its expounder. The passage of time is the best interpreter throughout the ages, and many other meanings of the Quran are being discovered by only new scientific inventions in successive centuries. The universe is dependent on the Quran for its meaning to be understood, while interpretation of the Quran is mainly a reflection on the universe, which is symbolized by the metaphor of the book. Therefore, there is an interdependent relationship between the revealed book and the book of universe in Nursi's spiritual thought.[73]

Jiziri also uses the book metaphor for the universe. In his view, although the book of this universe formally has grammar, letters, and words of various things, "its real meaning" is human being. The human body itself is a scribe, according to Jiziri; it may sometimes look miserable, but with close examination, you will see it as a divine signature.[74] The writings of the book of the universe are an address title to discover and reach God, which does not permit the occurrence of any incorrect writing in it, which might lead to possible different directions.[75] Ibn Arabi when using the book metaphor for the universe refers especially to the opening verses of the Quran in Surat al-Tur. In Ibn Arabi's words, "The cosmos, all of it, is a *book inscribed*, since it is an orderly arrangement, parts of which have joined to other parts."[76] The whole cosmos "is *a book inscribed on a parchment unrolled* [52: 2–3] and it is *wujud*. It is manifest and spread out, not rolled up, so that it may be known through this outspreading that it was created for mercy. God made it a book [*kitab*] because some of its letters are joined to others—this is the order of the cosmos . . . and its meanings are joined to the letters."[77]

The Glorification of God by Natural Beings

As beautifully designed words and letters of a mighty book, the various parts and particles of the universe not only represent the signs of God, but also proclaim His sovereignty, and praises His glory. Nursi quite frequently refers to the Quranic verses related to the glorification of God by the beings in the heavens and earth (e.g., 17:44; 59:24; 62:1), and gives examples of them. He says:

> See how those dead or sleeping creatures of the world spring to life at the sound of *declares the praises and glory* in the minds of those listening, how they awake, spring up, and mention God's Names! And at the sound of, *The seven heavens and the earth and all within them extol and glorify Him* (17:44), the stars in those black skies, all lifeless pieces of fire, and the wretched creatures on the face of the earth, present the following view to those listening: the sky appears as a mouth and the stars each as wisdom-displaying words and truth-uttering lights. The

> earth appears as a head, the land and sea as tongues, and all animals and plants as words of glorification. Otherwise you will not appreciate the fine points and pleasure at looking from this time to that.[78]

As the suns, moons, and stars, so the animals, plants, and trees praise and glorify Him. The earth, which possesses thousands of heads containing thousands of tongues, certainly has an angel appointed to it who performs with each, and who represents and proclaims them in the World of Spirits.[79]

Even in one of his poetic texts Nursi points out that

> All things became familiar;
> See, all sounds are the mentioning of God.
>
> All the atoms in existence
> See, each recites God's praises and extols Him.[80]

Yet, in his Persian poem on Jiziri, regarding the dancing trees by a breeze, Nursi writes:

> Since the trees have all become bodies, their leaves have become tongues. At the touching of the breeze each recites over and over again: "It is He! It is He!" With the benedictions of their lives, they proclaim their Maker to be Ever-Living and Self-Subsistent.
>
> With the tongue of disposition they continuously declare "O God!," and seek the necessities of their lives from Him, from the treasury of mercy. And through the tongue of their manifesting life from top to bottom, they recite His Name of "O Living One!"[81]

Nursi is so sure about the actual glorification of God by the creatures, as he specifies the divine names or praises they recite:

> If you want to observe these elevated truths from close to, go and ask a stormy sea or the quaking earth: "What are you saying?" You will hear that they are saying: "O Glorious One! O Glorious One! O One of Might, All-Compelling!" Then ask the small animals and their young being raised with kindness and compassion in the sea and on the land: "What are you saying?" They will surely reply: "O Beauteous One! O Beauteous One! O Most Compassionate and Merciful One!"

In a footnote here Nursi goes further by reporting an anecdote of his experience:

> Even, one day I looked at the cats; all they were doing was eating, playing, and sleeping. I wondered: how is it these little monsters, which perform no duties, are known as blessed. Later, I lay down to sleep for the night. I looked; one of the cats had come. It lay against my pillow and put its mouth against my ear, and murmuring: "O Most Compassionate One! O Most Compassionate One!" in the most clear manner, as though refuted in the name of its species the objection and insult which had occurred to me, throwing it in my face. Then this occurred to me: I wonder if this recitation is particular to this cat, or is it general among cats? And is it only an unfair objector like me who hears it, or if anyone listens carefully, can they hear it?
>
> The next morning I listened to the other cats; it was not so clearly, but to varying degrees, they were repeating the same invocation. At first, "O Most Compassionate!" was discernible following their purring. Then gradually their purring and meowing became the same "O Most Merciful!" It became an unarticulated, eloquent, and sorrowful recitation. They would close their mouths and utter a fine "O Most Compassionate!" I related the story to the brothers who visited me, and they listened carefully as well, and said that they heard it to an extent. Later I wondered what this Name's special feature was, and why they recite it in the way of men and not in animal tongue. Then it imparted to my heart that since these animals are very delicate and petted like children and are a friend of man, they are in much need of kindness and compassion. When they are stroked and paid attention to in the way they like, as praise and thanks for the bounty, and unlike dogs, they proclaim the mercy of their All-Compassionate Creator in their own worlds. They warn men in the sleep of heedlessness, and through their cry of "O Most Compassionate!," they remind those who worship causes, Who it is that help comes from and from Whom mercy may be awaited.[82]

Nursi adds that a true human also recites all the most beautiful names, which are written on his forehead. If one looks carefully, one may read them, since "the universe is a huge orchestra celebrating the Divine Names, mixing the faintest song with the most powerful refrains."[83]

As another example, Nursi draws attention to the nightingale and its songs for the roses. According to Nursi, the nightingales, just like the angels, do not understand the meaning of their songs, but we can understand. He compares nightingales' songs to the rings of alarm clocks, which inform you of the time, without their own awareness of time. It serves perfectly its duty, and it is your responsibility to understand what it means. The nightingale's sorrowful song is not a complaint arising from animal grief; it is thanks in return for the gifts of the Most Merciful, which is the delight of gazing on the smiling, beautiful roses. The bee, the spider, the ant, creeping insects, which have numerous aims, can be compared with the nightingale. Apart from the animals and sects, Nursi claims that every sort of being, and even the stars, has a chief-reciting and light-scattering nightingale. He concludes:

> But, the most excellent, the most noble, the most luminous, the most dazzling, the greatest and the most honorable nightingale, whose voice was the most ringing, whose attributes the most brilliant, whose recitation the most complete, whose thanks the most universal, whose essence was the most perfect, and whose form the most beautiful, who brought all the beings of the heavens and the earth in the garden of the universe to ecstasy and rapture through his subtle poetry, his sweet song, his exalted glorification, was the glorious nightingale of human kind, the nightingale of the Qur'an: Muhammad the Arabian![84]

The nightingale, its relation with the rose, and its songs is also one of the examples of Jiziri for the spiritual love and glorification of God by the creatures. Although the substance of the nightingale's essence is the rose, he says, the brightness of the rose comes from the nightingale's sincere love and loyalty. It is not, only, the nightingale that demonstrates its feelings. The love, praise, and enthusiasm of other beings, in general, are like another nightingale joining the nightingale in singing.[85] But Jiziri admits that they make him amazed by representing the deepest love to the rose, which symbolizes the beauty of God.[86] However, some other creatures are not aware of the value of the rose; they lack the capacity and consciousness for that.[87]

CONCLUSION

To sum up, this chapter shows that Nursi's spiritual thought could not be connected to one source, or related only to the major thinkers of Islamic intellectual history, such as Rumi, Jilani, or Sirhindi. That though also has to be compared to the less known and little studied local personalities like Ahmed-i Jiziri through the similarities of their understanding, conception, and description of spirituality. The content of Nursi's writings show that he read and comprehended the text of Jiziri, which represents many similarities with Ibn Arabian thought. However, despite these parallels between Jiziri and Nursi's spiritual thought, there are also differences in their views. For instance, while Nursi has reservations about the doctrine of the unity of existence (*waḥdat al-wujūd*), Jiziri is a strict defender of the doctrine. Nursi does not focus on spiritual interpretations of human beloved characters as Jiziri does within the context of Sufi poetry. Moreover, Nursi is a modern thinker and therefore uses a new language and method, employing Sufi spirituality in revitalizing Islamic thought; however, Jiziri represents the classical Sufi culture in an impressive way of its expression, which attracted Nursi within the context of his cultural environment.

Notes

1. I thank my father Abdülkerim Özervarlı for reminding me of some of the important passages of Jiziri's book during this study and helping me to clarify the meanings of the various parts of his text. I also thank my friend and colleague Abdurrahim Alkış for his assistance in comparing Jiziri's and Nursi's views with Ibn Arabi's texts.
2. Said Nursi, "Sözler," *Risale-i Nur Kulliyatı* (Istanbul, 1996), 1: 86. See also its English translation *The Words* (Istanbul, 1998), 234.
3. Ahmed-i Jiziri, *Diwan* (Cairo, n. d.), 94.
4. The translation by Sukran Vahide of the Nursi's semipoetic verses written at Tepelice, in the mountains of Barla is the following:

"Living creatures have appeared from everywhere on the face of the earth, Your art, to gaze on You.
From above and below they emerge like heralds, and call out.
The herald-like trees take pleasure at the beauty of Your embroideries, and they dance.
They are filled with joy at the perfection of Your art, and utter most beautiful sounds.
It is as if the sweetness of their own voices fills them with joy too, and makes them perform a delicate melody.
In response, the trees have started dancing and are seeking ecstasy.
It is through these works of Divine mercy that all the living creatures receive instruction in the glorification and prayer particular to each.
After receiving instruction, on high rocks the trees raise their heads to the Divine Throne.
Each, like Shahbaz Qalandar, stretches out a hundred hands to the Court of God, and assumes an imposing position of worship.
They make their small tassel-like twigs and branches dance, so both they and those that watch them express their fine pleasure and elevated delight.
They give voice as though touching the most sensitive strings and veins of the veils of love: "Ah! It is He!"
From it a meaning such as this comes to mind: they recall both the weeping caused by the pain of the fading of metaphorical loves, and a profoundly sorrowful moaning.

They make heard the melancholy songs of all lovers parted from their beloveds, like Sultan Mahmud.

They seem to have a duty of making the dead hear the pre-eternal songs and sorrowful voices, who no longer hear worldly voices and words.

The spirit understands from this that beings respond with glorification to the manifestation of the Glorious Maker's Names; they perform a graceful chant.

The heart reads the mystery of Divine unity from these trees, each like an embodied sign, from the elevated word order of this miraculousness. That is, there is so wonderful an order, art, and wisdom in the manner of their creation, that if all the causes in existence had the power to act and choose, and they gathered together, they could not imitate them.

The soul, on seeing them, sees the whole earth as revolving in a clamorous tumult of separation, and seeks enduring pleasure. It receives the meaning: "You will find it in abandoning worship of this world."

The mind discovers from the chanting animals and trees and the vociferous plants and air, a most meaningful order of creation, embroidery of wisdom, and treasury of secrets.

The desirous soul receives such pleasure from the murmuring air and whispering leaves that it forgets all metaphorical pleasures, and through abandoning these, which endow it with life, wants to die in the pleasure of reality.

The imagination sees that appointed angels have entered these trees like bodies, from whose branches hang many flutes. It is as though an Eternal Monarch has clothed the angels in the trees for a splendid parade accompanied with the sounds of a thousand flutes. Thus, the trees show themselves to be not lifeless, unconscious bodies, but highly conscious and meaningful.

The flutes are pure and powerful as though issuing from a heavenly, exalted orchestra. The mind does not hear from them the sorrowful plaints of separation, that foremost Mawlana Jalaluddin Rumi and all lovers hear, but dominical praise and laudation and grateful thanks offered to the Most Merciful One, the Ever-Living, the Self-Subsistent.

Since the trees have all become bodies, their leaves have become tongues. At the touching of the breeze each recites over and over again: "It is He! It is He!" With the benedictions of their lives, they proclaim their Maker to be Ever-Living and Self-Subsistent.

With the tongue of disposition they continuously declare "O God!," and seek the necessities of their lives from Him, from the treasury of mercy. And through the tongue of their manifesting life from top to bottom, they recite His Name of "O Living One!" (*The Words*, 234–36)

5. Martin van Bruinessen, *Agha, Shaikh and State: The Social and Political Structures of Kurdistan* (London, 1992), 257–59; ibid., *Mullas, Sufis and Heretics: The Role of Religion in Kurdish Society* (Istanbul, 2000), 29–30; Hamid Algar, "Sufism and Tariqat in the Life and Work of Bediuzzaman Said Nursi," *Journal of the History of Sufism*, 3 (2002), 199–207.
6. Martin van Bruinessen, "Kurdistan in the 16th and 17th Centuries, as Reflected in Evliya Celebi's *Seyahatname*," *The Journal of Kurdish Studies*, 3 (2000), 1–11.

7. Cf. Ferhad Shakeli, "The Kurdish Qasida," *Qasida Poetry in Islamic Asia and Africa: Classical Traditions and Modern Meanings*, eds. Stefan Sperl and Christopher Shackle (Leiden, 1996), 1: 328.
8. On Khani see Izzeddin Mustafa Rasul, *Ahmad Khani sha'iran, mutasawwifan wa mutafakkiran* (Baghdad 1979); Th. Bois, "Coup d'oeil sur la litterature kurde," *al-Mashriq*, 49: 2 (1955), 204–205; M. Sait Özervarlı, "Hani, Seyh Ahmed," *Türkiye Diyanet Vakfı İslam Ansiklopedisi* (Istanbul, 1997), 16: 31–32; ibid., "Hani'nin Tasvirlerine Göre XVII. Yüzyılda Cizre," in *Hz. Nuh'tan Günümüze Cizre Sempozyumu*, ed. M. Sait Özervarlı (Istanbul, 1999), 161–64.
9. Sukran Vahide, *Islam in Modern Turkey: An Intellectual Biography of Bediuzzaman Said Nursi* (Albany, 2005), 11; cf. also Necmeddin Şahiner, *Bilinmeyen Taraflarıyle Bediüzzaman Said Nursi* (Istanbul, 1974), 53–55.
10. Serif Mardin, *Religion and Social Change in Modern Turkey: The Case of Bediuzzaman Said Nursi* (New York, 1989), 70.
11. "Emirdağ Lahikası," *Risale-i Nur Külliyati*, 2: 1906–1907.
12. Ibrahim M. Abu-Rabi', "How to Read Said Nursi's Risale-i Nur," in *Islam at the Crossroads*, ed. Ibrahim Abu-Rabi' (New York, 2003), 67–70; Yvonne Y. Haddad, "Ghurba as Paradigm for Muslim Life: A Risale-i Nur Worldview," *The Muslim World*, 89: 3–4 (July–October 1999), 297–313.
13. Algar, "Sufism and Tariqat in the Life and Work of Bediuzzaman Said Nursi," 199–207.
14. On the life and works of Si'irdi, see Bursalı Mehmet Tahir, "Teracim-i ahvāl: Molla Halil es-Siirdi," *Sirat-ı Müstakim*, 5:127 (1326 A.H.), 377; ibid., *Osmanlı Müellifleri* (Istanbul, 1333), 2: 37; Ismail Pasha al-Baghdadi, *Hadiyyat al-arifin: Asma al-muallifin wa athar al-musannifin* (Ankara, 1955), 1: 357; Omar Rida Kahhala, *Mu'jam al-muallifin*, 1: 683; Khayr al-Din al-Ziriklī, *al-A'lām: Qamus al-tarajim*, ed. Zuhayr Fethullah (Beirut, 1984), 2: 317; Omer Pakis, "Molla Halil-i Siirdi," *Türkiye Diyanet Vakfı İslam Ansiklopedisi* (Ankara, 2005), 30: 250–51.
15. The quotation is about the civil war among the Companions of the Prophet (*Sahaba*) in the first century of Islam, and literally means "Don't gossip about the war between the Companions, for both killer and killed were destined for Paradise."

    "*Ji-harba Sahaban mekin qal u qīl*
    Biheştīne hem qatil u hem qetīl."

    Said Nursi, *Letters*, trans. Şükran Vahide (Istanbul, 1997), 74; *Risale-i Nur Külliyati*, vol. 1, 370; cf. Mulla Khalil-i Si'irdi, *Nahj al-anam* (Damascus, 1957), 6.
16. van Bruinessen, *Mullas, Sufis, and Heretics*, 47–48.
17. See *Evliya Celebi Seyahatnamesi: Topkapı Sarayı Bağdat 305 Yazmasının Transkripsiyonu ve Dizini* (Istanbul, 2001), 4: 316–17 and 325–26; cf. van Bruinessen, "Kurdistan in the 16th and 17th Centuries, as Reflected in Evliya Celebi's *Seyahatname*," 1–11.
18. The primary source for the history of Kurdish emirates and dynasties is *Şerefname* written by a scholar-prince of Bidlis/Bitlis, Sharaf Khan-i Bidlisi: *Şerefname*, trans. into Turkish M. Emin Bozarslan (Istanbul, 1990). On the relation of these dynasties with the Ottoman state and other regional powers, see van Bruinessen, *Agha, Shaykh and State*, 133–204, and Hakan Ozoglu, "State-Tribe Relations: Kurdish Tribalism in

the 16th- and 17th- Century Ottoman Empire," *British Journal of Middle Eastern Studies*, 23:1 (1996), 5–27.

19. Shakeli, "The Kurdish Qasida," *Qasida Poetry in Islamic Asia and Africa*, 1: 328–29.
20. On the history of Cizre/Jazira see Yusuf Ghandur, *Tarikhu Jazirat Ibn 'Omar munzu ta'sisiha hatta'l-fath al-Othmani* (Beyrut Dar al-fikr al-Lubnani, 1990); M. Sait Özervarlı (ed.), *Hz. Nuh'tan Günümuze Cizre Sempozyumu* (Istanbul, 1999); Abdullah Yaşın, *Bütün Yönleriyle Cizre* (Istanbul, 1983).
21. He calls him "Ey Shahinshah-i Muazzam," and "Khan-i Khanan"—see Jiziri, *Diwan*, 143, 145. Emir Sheref b. Abdal was the best ruler of Cizre and was alive in 1597 according to Sharaf Khan-i Bidlisi (*Şerefname*, 166). For an important study on the activities of Emir Sheref and the place of Cizre in Ottoman administrative and regional divisions, see Aydogan Demir, "Osmanlı Döneminden Bir Kesit: XVI. Yuzyil Sonlarında Cizre" in *Hz. Nuh'tan Günümüze Cizre Sempozyumu*, 73–86.
22. M. Xalid Sadīnī, *Feqiyē Teyran* (Istanbul, 2003), 45–46, 220.
23. Mela is the Kurdish spelling of Mulla.
24. van Bruinessen, *Mullas, Sufis, and Heretics*, 46–47.
25. On the history and description of the Red Madrasa and the tomb of Jiziri in its basement see Orhan C. Tuncer, "Mardin-Cizre Kırmızı Medrese," *Vakıflar Dergisi*, 10 (1973), 425–34; Abdullah Yaşın, *Bütün Yönleriyle Cizre*, 46–51.
26. Mardin, *Religion and Social Change in Modern Turkey*, 65–69; van Bruinessen, *Mullas, Sufis, and Heretics*, 48–49.
27. Şükran Vahide, *Islam in Modern Turkey*, 18–20; Necmeddin Sahiner, *Bilinmeyen Taraflarıyla Bediüzzaman Said Nursi*, 40–44. Cf. Mardin, *Religion and Social Change in Modern Turkey*, 73–74.
28. *Diwan* has various manuscripts in libraries and private collections (see Bodleian Library, Ms. Asiat. Misc. d. 2.; Marburg Staatsbibliothek, Ms. Or. Quart. 1131; İstanbul Üniversitesi Merkez Kütüphanesi, FY, 40). The first photolithographic print of a manuscript was done by Martin Hartmann in *Der Kurdische Divan des Schech Ahmed* (Berlin, 1904); later Muhammed Şefīq Arwasī prepared a new print (Istanbul, 1318 [1919]). Apart from other various prints (Erbil 1964; Cairo, n. d.), Sadiq Muhammed Amedi edited and annotated it (Baghdad, n. p., 1977). The book is translated by K. R. Ayyubi into Russian (St. Petersburg, 1994), commentated by Ahmed b. Muhammed al-Zivingi in Arabic entitled *al-Iqd al-Jawhari fi sharh Diwan al-Shaykh al-Jazari* (Kamishlu, 1378/1959), and by Abdurrahman Sherefkandi (with his pen-name Hejar) in Kurdish entitled *Diwanē arifē Rabbanī Shaykh Ahmedē Jizīrī* (Tahran, 1361 A.H. [1982]).
29. Jiziri, *Diwan*, 1–2.
30. Jiziri, *Diwan*, 27.
31. Zivingī, "c"; Hejar, 11–12.
32. Shakeli, "The Kurdish Qasida," *Qasida Poetry in Islamic Asia and Africa*, 1: 329.
33. For more details on the significance of Jiziri and his *Diwan*, see Alexander Jaba, *Recueil de notices et récits kurdes* (St. Petersburg, 1860), 8–11; Thomas Bois, "Coup d'oeil sur la litérature kurde," *el-Meşrık*, 49:2 (1955), 203; D. N. MacKenzie, "Malā-ē Jizrī and Faqī Tayran," *Yadname-yi Irani-yi Minorsky*, eds. Mojtaba Minovī ve Iraj Afshar (Tehran, 1969), 125–30; M. Sait Özervarlı, "Molla Cezeri," *Türkiye Diyanet Vakfı Islam Ansiklopedisi* (Ankara, 2005), 30: 241–43.

34. *The Words*, 145; cf. M. Sait Özervarlı, "Said Nursi's Project of Revitalizing Contemporary Islamic Thought." In *Islam at the Crossroads: On the Life and Thought of Bediuzzaman Said Nursi*, ed. Ibrahim M. Abu-Rabi' (Albany, 2003), 324.
35. *The Words*, 292.
36. *The Words*, 365–67.
37. *The Words*, 670.
38. The related lines of Jiziri are the following:

    Allah Allah cerx ū dolabē dinē
    Nuqte qet nakit di dewranē xelet
    Roz ū şeb her seyrē dīdare tēn
    Nakirin ew dewr ū seyranē xelet
    . . .
    Nusxe'ē 'alem hemī 'unwanek e
    Nuqteyek nabit di 'unwanē xelet. (*Diwan*, 71–72)

39. *Bē nūr u narē muhbetē*
    Bē naqşu sun'ē qudretē
    Naçim maqamē wuslatē
    Nurun lana wa'l-laylu daj. (*Diwān*, 38)
40. *Lew seher cewlan didit bayē sabayē rast ū çep*
    Sosin ū sinbil bi mestī bēn semayē rast ū çep
    . . .
    Tayrik ū iqd ū şerab ū netrik ū berg ū wereq
    Hey bi lerz ū cezbeyēn yaqutē tayē rast ū çep (*Diwan*, 20).
41. *Quran*, 2: 22; 27: 60–61.
42. Abu Hamid al-Ghazzali, *Ihya 'ulum al-din* (Cairo, 1922), 4: 361–81.
43. See William C. Chittick, *The Self-Disclosure of God: Principles of Ibn Arabi's Cosmology* (Albany, 1998), 4–5.
44. *The Words*, 141.
45. *The Words*, 342.
46. *The Words*, 345–47.
47. *Diwan*, 195.
48. On the people of Iram mentioned in the Quran (89:7) and their gardens, see W. Montgomery Watt, "Iram," *The Encyclopaedia of Islam*, (2nd ed.), 3: 1303; Ömer Faruk Harman, *Türkiye Diyanet Vakfı İslam Ansiklopedisi*, 22: 223.
49. *Ji gulistana cemala te gulek bēte zuhurē*
    Ji dinē dē biçitin navē bihişta İremē
    Serha halē xema isqa te ji kū tēte nivīsīn
    Medhē ewsafē cemala te kuca tē reqemē
    Wē mecālē ku cemala xwe tecellā dikirī
    Lazime secde bibīn ber te wē gav u demī. (*Diwan*, 151–52)
50. *Diwan*, 41.
51. *Diwan*, 155.
52. *Kesfa esrarē sifatan bē mehebbet nabitin*
    Suretē esma divētin da bikin jē fehim raz. (*Diwan*, 56)

53. *Diwan*, 34–35. According to Chittick, the term *tajalli* plays such a central role in Ibn al-Arabi's teaching that, before he was known as the great spokesman for *wahdat al-wujud*, he had been called one of the companions of Self-Disclosure (*ashab al-tajalli*). He employs the term to mean that God shows Himself to the universe inasmuch as His names and attributes display traces (*athar*) and properties (*ahkam*) in the cosmos (Chittick, *The Self-Disclosure of God*, 52). On the meanings and classifications of *tajalli* in its historical context also see E. Geoffroy, "Tadjalli," *Encyclopaedia of Islam* (2nd ed.), 10: 60–61.
54. *The Words*, 134.
55. *The Words*, 289.
56. *The Words*, 301.
57. *Letters*, 278–79.
58. *The Words*, 209–10.
59. Said Nursi, *The Rays*, trans. Şükran Vahide (Istanbul, 1998), 41–42.
60. *The Words*, 305–306.
61. *Diwan*, 46; Said Nursi, *İctimai Reçeteler-I* (Istanbul, 1990), 76.
62. *Ferq e Wahid ji-Ehad lē di-meqamē Samedī*
Bi-heqiqet ko yek in herdu ci Wahid u ci-Ehad. (*Diwan*, 46)
63. *Afitabē ehadiyyet di xwe da girtiye kewn*
Ne ko 'ewrek heye lē girtiye cehvēn me remed. (*Diwan*, 46)
64. Ahmed Avni Konuk, *Fusūs'l-hikem Tercüme ve Şerhi*, eds. Mustafa Tahralı and Selçuk Eraydın (Istanbul, 1989), 2: 251–52.
65. Konuk, *Fusūs'l-hikem Tercüme ve Şerhi*, 2: 254–56.
66. Abd al-Rahman Jami, *Naqd al-nusus fi sharh naqsh al-Fusus*, ed. William C. Chittick (Tehran, 1977), 34–36.
67. Chittick, *The Self-Disclosure of God*, 168. The divine name *al-Wahid* means One, but *al-Ahad* designates the One inasmuch as He is uniquely, exclusively, and incomparably One (ibid., 53).
68. Konuk, *Fusūs'l-hikem Tercüme ve Şerhi*, 266–67 and 242–44. Cf also Jami, *Naqd al-nusus*, 183–84; Abu'l-A'la al-Afifi, *Taliqat ala Fusus al-hikam* (Beyrut, 1980), 110–20, and George M. Abd al-Masih, *Mu'jam al-mustalahat al-Sufiyya* (Beirut, 1993), 39.
69. *The Words*, 307.
70. *The Words*, 145.
71. "İşārātu'l-icāz," *Risale-i Nur Külliyatı*, 1216; cf. *The Words*, 281–98. Nursi sees a harmonious relation between the universe and human beings, comparing them to a huge tree and its fruits. According to Nursi, man is a most comprehensive, most wonderful part, and is the heart and center of the whole universe (*The Words*, 193).
72. See Özervarlı, "Said Nursi's Project of Revitilazing Contemporary Islamic Thought." In *Islam at the Crossroads*, 323.
73. Ibid., 327. On further details regarding the metaphor of the book of universe in Nursi's works see Şükran Vahide, "The Book of the Universe: Its Place and Development in Bediuzzaman's Thought," in *A Contemporary Approach to Understanding the Qur'an: The Example of Risale-i Nur*, ed. Şükran Vahide (Istanbul, 2000), 466–83.
74. *Zahir tu perisaniya hale me nebin*
Mecmu' di zatē xwe ū tuxrayim ez

Alem ci bi-i'rab u huruf u kelimatin
Ew nuqte di-nefsa xwe u ma'nayim ez. (*Diwan*, 55)

75. *Nusxe'ē 'alem hemī 'unwanek e*
Nuqteyek nabit di 'unwanē xelet. (*Diwan*, 71–72)
76. Chittick, *The Self-Disclosure of God*, 6.
77. Chittick, *The Self-Disclosure of God*, 294.
78. *The Words*, 152.
79. *The Words*, 179. According to Ibn Arabi, all things glorify God through their own created nature or through the knowledge given to them by their own specific faces (Chittick, *The Self-Disclosure of God*, 155).
80. *The Words*, 232.
81. *The Words*, 236.
82. *The Words*, 342–43.
83. *The Words*, 343.
84. *The Words*, 364–65.
85. *Gerci bilbil cewherē zatī gul e*
Lē gulē rewneq ji 'isqa bilbil e

. . .

Guh de zikrē hal ū cosa badeyē
Wē bi bilbil ra dixwīnit bilbil e. (*Diwan*, 127)
86. *Diwan*, 128.
87. *Diwan*, 64.

SEVENTEEN

Sincerity in the Thought of Muhammad Iqbal and Bediuzzman Said Nursi

Ahmet Albayrak

In the most general and plain terms, morality or ethics may be defined as "consciously assessing 'good' and 'evil'."[1] The judgments determined in the field of ethics by either divine or human authorities are all value judgments.[2] In such judgments, the proportion of 'knowledge' related to the 'mental' dimension is less than the 'belief' aspect, which is related to 'the heart'.[3] For values have both a transcendental side,[4] and a human one.[5] In determining values in respect of affecting man's psychological makeup, the role of the transcendent 'absolute' being is more far-reaching. It is because of this that "in psychology the importance of values is not whether or not they are based on objective criteria, but is related to the role they play in guiding human actions. From this point of view, the psychologist treats values as beliefs, and this suffices him."[6] That is, "in so far as values are belief, they are a combination of our perceptions, feelings, and knowledge about a particular part of our world. But in respect of values being specific forms of beliefs, they are a higher mental organization than beliefs."[7]

Being dependent on value judgments, ethical rules are functional and acceptable to everyone insofar as they have the common denominator of "humanity." Such formations are possible only if "religion," which proceeds from God Almighty, the Creator of all humanity, is combined with ethics, or if ethics rise from foundations of religion. When moral laws are not related to Almighty God, they cannot be universal since they lack the divine authority and this authority's power of sanctions.[8] "The human being attains at once to the highest sense of religion, the highest moral sense, and the highest joy at life. In fact, the religious sense, the moral sense, and joy at life are a part of his nature. The religious person is not opportunist, he is optimistic. Whereas the person with no religion . . . is pessimistic."[9]

"If religion is contained, ethics are the container. If religion is a lofty tree, ethics are its branches and fruits."[10] "All religions have moral precepts which aim to make individual and social behavior conform to their teachings. Belief and morals are practiced together in the thoughts and actions of a person who believes in religion and adheres to it. Religious belief is a psychological factor in morality."[11]

The Concept of Sincerity and Its Relevance to Moral Psychology

Harmony and integrity may be established in values and between these values and a person's actions only through sincerity. "Generally this harmony is the harmony in the values system between 'ends' and 'means'."[12]

In Islamic literature, sincerity is described as purifying the heart of hypocrisy, associating partners with God (*shirk*), false beliefs, bad feelings, self-interest, and the desire for ostentation in the general sense, and to undertake every sort of good work with a good intention, and in every situation to seek God's pleasure alone.[13] In short, sincerity is to strip something of other things that have become mixed in with it and reduce its value.[14] That is, to remove all extraneous things and make it pure and unalloyed.[15]

This verse about sincerity "Verily it is We who have revealed the Book to you in truth; so serve God offering Him sincere devotion. Is it not to God that sincere devotion is due? But those who take for protectors others than God [say]: 'We only serve them in order that they may bring us nearer to God.' Truly God will judge between them in that wherein they differ. But 'God guides not such as are false and ungrateful'"[16] suggests that the opposite of sincerity is hypocrisy.[17]

There are several words in the Quran derived from the word *khulūs*, with both its dictionary and technical meanings. In the phrase "offering Him sincere devotion," which appears in ten places, the concept of sincerity means "turning to God alone and serving Him. Trusting in Him and beseeching Him. Believing only in God's religion and dedicating oneself to God. Pure belief, and avoiding marring belief in divine unity with false beliefs." It is the opposite of both associating partners with God, and hypocrisy.[18]

Sincerity is a state of mind that dominates man to the degree he has absorbed and is resigned to all the truths of belief, and chiefly belief in God and the hereafter, both intellectually, and spiritually, and emotionally, and in his conscience. Someone who achieves this, lives solely seeking God's pleasure, and serves Him on this basis.

Sincerity is a hidden mystery in man's spirit. According to a sound hadith, Almighty God said this: "Sincerity is a mystery proceeding from My mystery. I lodge it in the hearts of those of My servants whom I love."[19]

Junayd al-Baghdadi said that sincerity was so hidden a secret that because the recording angel does not have knowledge of it, he does not write it; and because the Devil does not know it, he cannot corrupt it; and because a person's whims and desires do not know it, they cannot cause him to stray.[20] Thus, let alone others, the person himself does not know whether or not he is sincere. For this reason, he has to question his soul and himself constantly, and to control them.

In İslam'ın Dirilişi (*The Resurrection of Islam*), Sezai Karakoç states that sincerity is a basic factor, and he praises the *Risale-i Nur* movement for dwelling on this concept. "Sincerity, which the Nur movement lays most emphasis on, means beliefs becoming firmly rooted in the depths of the heart and the growth of heartfelt belief. Belief in God, the Prophet, the next world, divine determining and being called to account for one's actions, having heartfelt belief in the angels, the soldiers of divine power in unseen worlds; this is what sincerity is. There can be no true Muslims without sincere belief, nor will it be possible to raise Islam to life among humanity once again without it."[21]

Today, all humanity including, unfortunately, Muslims, is faced with a crisis of morality. Theoretically, Muslims should have "fine morals" but this is not seen to be the case.[22] Everyone knows that the chief reason for this is lack of sincerity. "The person who thinks only of his own interests will try to further them whatever the cost and think of nothing else. All his actions, activities, conversation, claims, and efforts are directed at achieving this aim. For people of this type, 'all roads' unite in 'a single way,' and that is the way of serving his interests."[23]

If the desired consciousness develops in tandem with morality, and is supported by sincerity and becomes deeper through it, the resulting attitude will be entirely moral. It is sincerity that bonds together the triad morality–consciousness–attitude. A person's value becomes apparent through the effectiveness of sincerity in his or her character. For a person is assessed in this life through what he or she does. "This assessment is a completely different dimension of existence."[24] "It shouldn't be forgotten that mostly in life, we are faced with people, not with events, incidents, or activities. It is important to understand this."[25]

In a hadith, the Prophet Muhammad (UWBP) emphasizes that knowledge, actions, and sincerity must come together: "People will perish and only those who know will be saved. And those who know will perish, and only those who act on their knowledge will be saved. And those who act according to their knowledge will perish, except the sincere. And the sincere are in constant danger [of losing their sincerity]."[26] "Those who have a sense of both 'high values' and 'instrumental values,' and subjugate instrumental values to high values, are always objective in their actions and activities."[27] This objectivity is necessary so that the person may assess himself and his actions and ideas, and is therefore important for his relations with his environment.

Honesty, which develops together with sincerity, matures the conscience. A powerful conscience develops through a person gaining insight about his own self, and his getting to know himself better through introspection. It is for this reason that those whose chief ideal is to acquire fine morality continuously examine their consciences and call themselves to account.[28] In Sufism, this is called self-examination (*nefis muhasebesi*). It means a person checking and examining himself at every opportunity,[29] and weighing up whether what he does and thinks is conformable with moral norms.

Inspired by Hasan Aycın,[30] we can say that sincerity is a person establishing sound relations between his mind and his heart.[31] This relation can be strengthened with the spiritual stores, acquired through sincerity. The person otherwise will not be freed from the influence of the instinctive soul, which resembles a snake that nibbles at forbidden fruits.[32]

An Overview of Said Nursi and Iqbal

Said Nursi lived between 1876 and 1960, while Iqbal lived between 1877 and 1938. They were born with only a year between them, but Nursi lived twenty-three years longer.

In a paper entitled 'Nursi's Place in the Ihya' Tradition,' presented at the 1998 International Symposium on Nursi, Oliver Leaman compared Bediuzzaman with Ghazali and Muhammad Iqbal. These persons all carried out similar functions: "Both Nursi and Iqbal lived in times when cultural domination by Europe threatened seriously the role of Islam in the lives of Muslims."[33]

At the end of the nineteenth century and the beginning of the twentieth, "Islamic thinkers for the most part defended Islam within the framework of the religious sciences and only used specialist language in the field of the orientalists in order to eliminate their influence. In order to defend the crumbling structure, Muhammad Iqbal, equipped with classic Islamic knowledge mostly resisted with ideas, particularly the West, in learned, scholarly fashion, using a controversialist style."[34] In his intellectual resistance, Iqbal profited from philosophy and Sufism and the power of Eastern poetry, while Nursi for the most part used the Quran's unequalled eloquence and the resources of the science of *kalām*.[35] However it should be noted here that they also applied new, original approaches, rather than existent forms.

According to 'Imaduddin Khalil, "The language Bediuzzaman used gives importance to the meaning rather the words. In its style it quite simply hums the rhythm of music in the heart of the universe. It uses a poetical style without adhering to poetical forms. It resembles versified prose."[36] Khalil considers Bediuzzaman's work *Lemeāt* (Gleams), which is included at the end of *The Words* and has the subtitle *Flowers from the Seeds of Reality*, to be a literary masterpiece. As three leading Nur students wrote in the 'Note' at the beginning of the piece, it is a sort of Mathnawi.[37] Bediuzzaman himself described it as "semi-verse."[38]

Iqbal with inspired versified works, and Nursi with his eloquent descriptions and "prose resembling verse,"[39] spoke of the divine beauties and unsurpassed riches in the depths of our human existence. Thus, "what is important is the material we call culture, the collective conscience, or collective consciousness, being able to remain alive when an original ground like this is secured."[40]

> When a new culture becomes established or when one culture is transformed into another one, a new, almost spellbinding language and style are necessary. All new movements in Islam have begun with a literary movement, a manifestation of rain, with the flow of a writer and his works. Culture is often held to be the same as literature. . . . The Risale-i Nur has a most powerful voice and style. From one point of view, it is on its own an Islamic culture. One has to admit that it re-educated large numbers of people in Anatolia, from the illiterate to intellectuals, in Islamic culture and beliefs, and instigated a new cultural movement and embarked on a cultural battle. In other Muslim countries too, Islamic leaders have very often been well-known writers and literary figures. Iqbal was a great thinker as much as he was a poet.[41]

We may say that, despite their different methods, both thinkers' defense of Islamic thought was on an academic level. Generally speaking, Iqbal's stand was to define the perspective of Islamic thought in the face of orientalist influence, while Nursi's stance was more one of defense, debate, and refutation. Possible reasons for these differences are as follows: Iqbal's struggle was in the Indian subcontinent where the British attached importance to cultural development,[42] while Said Nursi was in Turkey, where he attempted to defend Islam in the midst of ideological debates, and under the harshest conditions.

The Concept of Sincerity in the Works of Nursi and Iqbal, and Its Influence on Moral Formation

The importance Said Nursi attached to sincerity may be understood from these words:

> in this world sincerity is the most important principle in works pertaining to the hereafter in particular; it is the greatest strength, and the most acceptable intercessor, and the firmest point of support, and the shortest way to reality,[43] and the most acceptable prayer, and the most wondrous means of achieving one's goal, and the highest quality, and the purest worship."[44]

The ideal, model person for both Nursi and Iqbal was the moral, and therefore the sincere, person. They both considered sincerity to be the essence and summit of morality.[45] Sincerity may lead to a person's being saved: "the only means of salvation and deliverance is sincerity. It is of the greatest importance to gain sincerity.[46] The tiniest act performed with sincerity is preferable to tons performed without sincerity.[47] A person should think that what gains sincerity in his actions is doing them purely because they are a Divine command and that their result is Divine pleasure,[48] and he should not interfere in God's business."[49] Man's ultimate aim in this life is to perform his moral duties.[50]

According to Iqbal, religion consists of powerful belief, resolution, and sincerity: "Be strengthened by the perfections of the great religion of Islam. From beginning to end, religion is resolution, sincerity, and powerful belief."[51] The person who feels the attraction of religion is so transformed through sincerity and belief that he begins to represent his Maker in the station of the vicegerency: "The believer's pomp and splendour are ever new / He bears witness to Allah in his speech and actions."[52] Iqbal also explains man's functions as vicegerent while expounding the verse, "And there is none like unto Him,"[53] from Sura al-Ikhlas, in his book Rumūz-i Bīhudī.[54] This station is the highest point the believer can reach through religion. In his work, *Sikke-i Tasdik-i Gayb*, Bediuzzaman also indicates that through sincerity the believers may become competent to represent God and His Prophet.[55]

Iqbal says that sincerity is "to feel in your spirit and heart what your lips continuously utter."[56] He recounts that while he was writing the summary of the discussions in Mawlana's Mathnawi about expounding Sura al-Ikhlas, he dreamt of Abu Bakr (May God be pleased with him). He described in the following verses his conversation with him:

> I said to him: "O highests of the elite in questions of love! Your love is the glorious opening line of your poetry. / Our business has come to fruition at your hand. What is the cure for our distress? Tell us!" / He told me: "O you captive of desire, receive the effulgence of Sura al-Ikhlas! It has caused one single breath to be expelled from a hundred breasts a mystery of divine unity. / Be imbued with its hues and you'll come to resemble it; you'll come to reflect its beauty in the world!"[57]

With these lines, Iqbal is saying that sincerity is the remedy for all our problems. Sincerity leads a person to affirm divine unity. The relationship of sincerity and divine unity in respect of the believer is one of the questions Iqbal most dwelt on. In his view, a person has to move on from the cup to the pitcher.[58]

The moral training given by the Quran is such that a person seeks neither worldly happiness nor the happiness of the hereafter in return for the worship he performs and his good works. His sole aim is to carry out Almighty God's commands and to win His pleasure. He can only think of God's pleasure, the peak of morality, through sincerity.[59]

Humans perform his their worship before the Supreme Being, whose transcendence and absoluteness they accept. It is a question, psychologically, of accepting absolute authority. This relationship appears as the created being perceiving the existence of the Creator, and submitting to Him in impotence and wishing to be one with Him.[60] Iqbal described this union beautifully: "Through supplication and worship, the tiny islands of our personalities suddenly discover that they exist within a total life, which is bigger than ourselves."[61] Nursi says that this spirit, which should be a part of worship, may be gained through sincerity.[62]

Nursi states that love can persist only if it is adorned with sincerity. Love of God should be together with sincerity. "There is sincerity in everthing. A jot of love even with sincerity is superior to tons of official love for which return is wanted . . . for love which requires love in return is weak and short-lived."[63]

The sincere person's actions and speech are effective. Their sincerity reflects in other's hearts. In fact, this sincerity is not only felt by other people, it may also be felt by other levels of existence in the universe. That is, the words and acts of the sincere person unite with the universe.[64] Moreover, such a person is in a suitable state to draw back the veil of the universe and perceive the essence of reality as a whole. According to Iqbal, "the person whose self has reached relative perfection, truly holds creative divine power in his heart and thus has a rank far higher than the things around him."[65]

In the Twentieth Flash, Said Nursi explains seven reasons related to sincerity why, although the worldly and people of misguidance unite, the people of truth and the rightly guided oppose each other in rivalry. They may be summarized as follows.

Rivalry due to money and fame; considering oneself to be right because of one's profound love for one's own way; jealousy and discontentment due to a greedy desire for reward; not loving and supporting for God's sake; relying on one's own strength and not seeking help; looking for faults in others; envy and jealousy due to rivalry.[66] We can say easily that jealousy is the common factor in these seven faults.[67] It is a psychological malady arising from not preferring others to oneself, self-seeking, and egotism. Bediuzzaman explains as follows the reason for jealousy, the basic factor preventing sincerity:

> The reason for envy and jealousy is that when several hands reach out after a single object, when several eyes are fixed on a single position, when several stomachs hunger for a single loaf of bread, first envy arises as a result of conflict, dispute and rivalry, and then jealousy. Since many people desire the same thing in the world, and because the world, narrow and transitory as it is, cannot satisfy the limitless desires of man, people become rivals of each other.[68]

Jealousy can be intense enough to make one person inimical to another, so causing sincerity and justice to be lost.[69]

The main causes of hypocrisy, which destroy sincerity,[70] can be brought together in four concepts: rivalry,[71] fame,[72] fear,[73] and greed.[74] In the section of the *Twenty-ninth Letter* called "The Six Attacks," Bediuzzaman discusses six stratagems used by evil men and satans.[75] He lists them as follows:[76] The desire for fame and acclaim, and high position;[77] fear;[78] greed; racialist nationalism; egotism;[79] and laziness.

Muhammad Iqbal studies the concepts included in these six matters from both the moral and the psychological angle. To put it another way, these concepts both destroy sincerity and, related to this, they prevent a person's knowing himself and his being the Creator's vicegerent. One can find verses about all of them in Iqbal's poetry. So as not expand the discussion unduly, I mention several of them in summary form.

It is impossible for someone who knows clearly his position in the cosmos to be frightened. In contrast to ontological awareness, which is related to his existence, man's position in the cosmos is his status as regards other creatures. This manner of perception, which we can call cosmological awareness, is directed toward nature and the universe. That is, while ontological awareness reflects man's looking inwardly, the result of introspection, cosmological awareness reflects his looking outwardly, the result of extrospection.[80] As the levels of ontological and cosmological awareness develop and man attains to reality, his inward and outward observations have to be supported by 'expansiveness' (*inshirah*).

In Iqbal's view, fear is the chief negative factor weakening a person's ego and preventing sincerity. If he is unaware of the potentialities in his being and supposes himself to be inadequate, he cannot be bold and brave.[81] It is only the person who is aware of his ego who can courageously stand on his own two feet.[82] Advancing through life so full of dangers, if his aim is God's pleasure, he wwill find courage. He will also develop a sound understanding of reliance on God.[83]

Bediuzzaman mentions something else that reduces sincerity and drives people to hypocrisy: the concept of nationalism. It is the equivalent of Iqbal's exaltation of one's lineage (*nasabparasti*), or tribalism. According to Iqbal, the concept of the unity of man's origin has its ideal equivalent in the principle of divine unity,[84] and he attempts to explain it with verses related to a verse from Sura al-Ikhlas.[85]

Man's aim, in Iqbal's view, should not be only the place he lives, but the whole world. In this way, he will go beyond the concept of space. He may conceive of things without boundaries and observe the horizons.[86] As a love voyager, Muhammad Iqbal wanted to see the Muslims he was addressing following the same ideal; the ideal of being "one" on the road of love, and passing beyond narrow stereotypes.[87]

The equivalent of Bediuzzaman's concept of greed, covetousness, and desiring too much out of fear of poverty is Iqbal's concept of 'beggary,' which he uses frequently. He posits that to want too many of the benefits of this world weakens the ego. For in wanting them, a person becomes indebted to others, and then he cannot be expected to preserve his self-confidence and freedom. In Iqbal's work, *Asrar*, is a section headed by this: "By wanting something from someone else, the ego is weakened since it becomes needy for the other."[88]

Asking for things may become a habit. According to what a person asks for, it may in time cause a change in the person's character.[89] Moreover, it is not only a factor weakening the ego, it is also an obstacle on the way of his becoming a 'perfect man' (*insan-i kamil*). For the person is not sufficing with what has been given him.[90] Iqbal says that one reason for this frequently encountered act of asking for things is "worry about making ends meet." He advises "poverty" to someone in this situation. For, in his view, only in this way may the vitality of the person's heart be maintained.[91]

Iqbal has a poem called "The Beggar," in which he quotes from Sha'ir Anwari. In the poem he treats begging very broadly: "Whether almsgiving, or tax / Those asking are beggars, all beggars! / Whether you believe it or not, / The dictators and leaders are beggars, all beggars!"[92]

Although there are numerous points on which Nursi and Iqbal are in agreement on the question of sincerity, there are also points on which they differ. Rather than the Sufis' terms "annihilation in the shaikh," "annihilation in the Messenger," in respect of sincerity, Nursi preferred the concept of "annihilation in the brothers," that is, the annihilation of the brothers' selves in one another. However, when we study Iqbal, we see that the former two concepts have a place. For he believed that "annihilation in the shaikh" and "annihilation in the Messenger" should be realized, so that uniting in these common concepts, humanity might proceed correctly toward brotherhood. First, the person had to become conscious of his own self, that is, he had to become aware of his createdness (*Asrar-i Khudi*), then he had to dedicate this being to the society in which he lived (*Rumuz-i Bikhudi*). Nevertheless, this second stage may be seen as the equivalent of Nursi's "annihilation in the brothers."

Conclusion

In the contemporary world, Muslims are in need of a map of meaning. "This map has to be a guide that both depicts their line with the past, and orders their present."[93]

Both thinkers we have discussed deal with both the past and the present in terms of ideas. But in regard to emphasis, Nursi's is more on the past, and Iqbal's more on the present. That is, Nursi has wider knowledge of the basic Islamic sciences than does Iqbal. Iqbal's philosophical and Sufistic sides are preponderant. Nevertheless, both are attempting to discover and determine the future with the power of the past. Stepping on the firm supports of the past, yet disregarding the rotten spots, they call out to tomorrow.

Both Nursi and Iqbal dwell on Islam's rich religious and cultural stores. The basis of their proposed solutions is the spiritual and moral structure of the Muslim and believer. That is, the solution arises from "inside." It is primarily man's being perfected that should be sought, rather than society. If humanity's revival is a natural transformation, it will be more lasting.

With regard to sincerity, which we attempted to study and compare, Said Nursi lays more emphasis on "meaning," while Iqbal emphasizes "giving meaning to" or "explanation." Nursi gives importance to subjects that will assist Muslims to understand their religion.[94] He made fresh interpretations of key concepts that have existed for centuries in the Quran, but had started to collect dust, such as intention, viewpoint, and the significative meaning of things. As Ali Ulvi Kurucu said: "The successes that Imam Ghazzali achieved nine hundred years ago in the fields of morality and virtue, Bediuzzaman achieved this century in the areas of belief and sincerity."[95]

To understand is a psychological need. "This motif has been depicted in various ways, such curiosity, discovery, the need to control symbolically other people's worlds, the investigation of what is meaningful, the tendency towards determined organization and mental constructs."[96] To give meaning to, however, is a value judgment. "It is an assessment in various stages, or a value judgement, or giving value, or forming a value. A value judgement is understanding values that others have previously brought into being."[97]

"Said Nursi discussed moral terms and studied them. He used them in a way that would ensure the exalting of moral virtues like truthfulness, hope, patience, courage, and self-sacrifice, and the opening of such flowers. Said Nursi pointed out short ways to take man to God's pleasure, like the ways of thanks, humility, reliance on God, love, and sincerity."[98] In the Addendum of the *Twenty-sixth Word*, Bediuzzaman says that the ways leading to Almighty God are truly numerous, but of these ways he had benefited from those of "impotence, poverty, compassion, and reflection."[99]

Both these thinkers whom we have tried to study and compare preferred "poverty" in the question of sincerity in their lifestyles, and are examples for us. For them, this world is a bridge to eternity. In this world, we should strive not to amass riches, but attain to perfection. On studying their legacies, we see just how sensitive they were in this connection. When Nursi died, the relevant official recorded that he left a turban, gown, and twenty liras.[100] His true legacy, however, was the 6,000-page *Risale-i Nur* and his elevated cause, which could never fit in the offical's records. The room in which Iqbal passed his last years is still preserved in Lahore. All it contains is a bed, a small glass-fronted bookcase, a small round table, a wooden chair, and a hubble-bubble.

With its system of beliefs and morality, a civilization constitutes a whole:

> The question of the revival of Islamic civilization today is the question of Muslims becoming more conscious of the Islamic civilization's system of belief and eethics, and their correcting themselves accordingly. This exceptional civilization, the first and only true civilization, this system of belief and ethics revealed by God, is for all mankind. Islam is not the religion of any one people; it is the religion God has chosen for all men. It will be preserved until the end of the world as a source of mercy and wisdom of which everyone is in need who wants

> to reform himself and attain to happiness in this world and the next. Its protector is God. In which case, there is no reform in Islam. What has to be done is the renewal Muslims will carry out in their own spirits and lives in accordance with the system of belief and ethics which is the basis of Islamic civilization.[101]

For sincerity to be determinative and lasting in believing, moral persons, such people have to seek God's pleasure with love of Him, and they must be ready to sacrifice themselves for Him:

> The distinguishing mark of absolute value is sacrificing oneself. It is voluntarily sacrificing ones self, which is the highest degree of value. Thus, for one of the values to dominate completely, all the others have to be sacrificed. If this degree is expressed in psychological terms, we call it absolute love or passion. In love there is a sacrifice and a choice. In all loves, the beloved is seen as superior to all others, and all values are abandoned for it. Loving God means sacrificing all other values for Him.[102]

"Just as with his profound, deeply rooted metaphysical belief the Muslim is an individual person, so with his historical consciousness and heartfelt attachment to the web of society he is the most social human prototype. The Muslim's anonymity is not an unconscious anonymity, it is one born of Muslims all being turned to the same direction and their all gathering together in it. Furthermore, in the Muslim's ideas is an anonymity of virtue. The anonymity of dedicating himself to the idea of truth in society, and his melting away within that anonymity. Muslims' belief in metaphysical reality does arise from their symbolizing nature or their becoming isolated from it; it is born of their acceptance of the suprahuman, supranatural Absolute and their calling out to Him."[103]

"The web of 'every day' which creates the material of people's lives, and creates every day, are the hundreds of particles of place, behavior, conduct, aesthetics, and morality."[104]

At a time when moral sensitivity has to a large extent been abraded and value judgments are all confused, we are in even more need of the essence of morality, as we may call sincerity. I want to conclude my chapter with the prayer at the end of Bediuzzaman Said Nursi's *Twenty-first Flash*, which consists of his ideas about sincerity: "O God! For the sake of *Sūra al-Ikhlāṣ*, place us among those of Your sincere servants who are saved. Amen. Amen."[105]

NOTES

1. For definitions of ethics or morality (in Turkish: *ahlak*), see Ahmet Cevici, *Felsefe Sözlüğü* [The Dictionary of Philosophy] (Istanbul, 2000), 17; Selçuk Budak, *Psikoloji Sözlüğü* [The Dictionary of Psychology] (Ankara, 2000), 23; Meral Çileli, *Ahlak Psikolojisi ve Eğitimi* [The Psychology of Ethics and Ethical Education] (Ankara,1986), 10; Mustafa Çağrıcı, art. "Ahlak" [Ethics], *Türkiye Diyanet Vakfı İslam Ansiklopedisi* [The Encyclopedia of Islam], ii, 1–9. For a study of the concepts of good and evil in regard to the human being, see Ioanna Kuçuradi, *İnsan ve Değerleri* [The Man and His Values] (Ankara, 1998), 75–94.
2. Erol Güngör, *Değerler Psikolojisi* [The Psychology of Values] (Amsterdam, 1993), 21. "Moral behavior is most distinguished by its being dealt with within the framework of certain people's judgments about good and evil." Güngör, *Değerler Psikolojisi* [The Psychology of Values], 17–18.
3. Hilmi Ziya Ülken, *Değerler Kültür ve Sanat* [Values, Culture and Art] (Istanbul, 1965), 8.
4. Ülken, op. cit., 11–12.
5. Ülken, op. cit., 12.
6. Güngör, *Değerler Psikolojisi* [The Psychology of Values], 18. Ioanna Kuçuradi starts with a brief quote from Epictetos. The sentence determining a person's attitude toward the value concept is this: "What makes people nervous is not what has happened, but what they believe in connection with it." Ioanna Kuçuradi, *İnsan ve Değerleri* [The Man and His Values], opening page.
7. Güngör, *Değerler Psikolojisi* [The Psychology of Values], 19. "Values or value judgements complete a person's view of life. A person's philosophy of life is a values system that he lives. Such a system includes his aims, ideals, style of thought, and the principles that govern his actions." See Cavit Ünal, *Genel Tutumların veya Değerlerin Psikolojisi Üzerine bir Araştırma* [A Research on General Attitudes or The Psychology of Values] (Ankara, 1981), 17.
8. See Recep Kılıç, *Ahlakın Dini Temeli* [The Religious Foundation of Ethics] (Ankara, 1992), 140, 145. Erol Güngör defines religion as a moral system whose source is from God. For a comparison of religion and morality, see Erol Güngör, *Ahlak Psikolojisi ve Sosyal Ahlak* [The Psychology of Ethics and Social Ethics] (Istanbul, 1995), 115–17; Şahin Filiz, *Ahlakın İnsani ve Dini Temelleri* [The Humane and Religious Foundations of Ethics] (Konya, 1998), 69–75. "It is religion that conveys man to the loftiest feelings and life; it is belief and worship. While worshipping man experiences the most sincere emotions. He reaches the highest and most profound, the purest stage of emotion and thought. He rises above instinct. He goes beyond himself. In worship he realizes his own nothingness before the Infinite Power. The moment humility suffuses his heart he reaches the highest morality. He is overflowing with mercy and kindness. He is scathed with the most unalloyed of excitement. The solid universe has burned in the flame of love and become ashes. Man, a race, has melted in the divine music." Sezai Karakoç, *Ruhun Dirilişi* [The Resurrection of the Spirit] (Istanbul, 1985), 81.
9. Karakoç, *Ruhun Dirilişi* [The Resurrection of the Spirit], 82.

10. Osman Pazarlı, *Din Psikolojisi* [The Psychology of Religion] (Istanbul, 1982), 44. For an original study of the religion/morality relationship, see also Yasin Ceylan, "Etik Değerlerin İnsan Yaşamındaki Yeri" [The Place of the Ethical Values in the Life of Person], *İslamiyat Journal*, vol. 4, no. 3 (July–September, 2001), 156–57.
11. Hayati Hökelekli, *Din Psikolojisi* [The Psychology of Religion] (Ankara, 1998), 103.
12. Ülken, *Değerler Kültür ve Sanat* [Values, Culture and Art], 16. "One of the motifs that may be the basis of values is the need of a person or the mind for coherence. The Gestalt psychologists who discussed the principles of organization, mentioned the mind's tendency towards coherence." See Ünal, *Genel Tutumların veya Değerlerin Psikolojisi Üzerine bir Araştırma* [A Research on General Attitudes or The Psychology of Values], 7. Also, for the moral values theory, see Cevizci, *Felsefe Sözlüğü* [The Dictionary of Philosophy], 21.
13. Ibn Manzur (Abu Fadl Muhammad ibn Mukarram ibn Abdullah), art. "hls," *Lisan al-Arab* (Beirut 1995), iv, 173–75; Abu Hamid al-Ghazali, *Ihya' Ulum al-Din* (Beirut, 1982), iv, 379–80; Süleyman Uludağ, *Tasavvuf Terimleri Sözlüğü* [The Dictionary of the Terms of Tasawwuf] (Istanbul, 1991), 240.
14. Raghib al-Isfahani, art. "hls," *al-Mufradat fi Gharib al-Qur'an* [tahqiq M. Sayyid Gilani] (Beirut, n.d.), 154–55.
15. Ali Ünal, art. "ihlas," *Kur'an'da Temel Kavramlar* [The Basic Terms in Quran] (Istanbul, 1998), 476–77. See also Quran, 4:146, 38:2–3.
16. Quran, 39:2–3.
17. Ebu Süleyman Darani said: "If God's servant is sincere, most of his hypocrisy and the satanic whisperings within him would disappear." See Abd al-Karim ibn Hawazin al-Qushayri, *al-Risalat al-Qushayriyya* [Turk. trans. Süleyman Uludağ] (Istanbul, 1991), 356.
18. Süleyman Ateş, art. "İhlas," *Türkiye Diyanet Vakfı İslam Ansiklopedisi* [The Encyclopedia of Islam], xxi, 536; Quran, 7:29, 98:5.
19. Abd al-Karim ibn Hawazin al-Qushayri, *al-Risalat al-Qushayriyya*, 353. "Sincerity is a divine light; it is a consciousness that suffuses the heart and spirit; it is a dominical mystery; it is the finest gift Almighty God bestows on the servants He loves. Sincerity attracts every sort of good. Sincerity purifies the heart of such sicknesses as associating partners with God, hypocrisy, pride, and self-love. Sincerity is the only citadel Satan cannot enter." See Nurullah Toprak, "Marifetullah ve İhlas" [Gnosis of Allah and Sincerity], *Semerkand Journal*, no. 2 (February 1999), 24.
20. Abd al-Karim ibn Hawazin al-Qushayri, *al-Risalat al-Qushayriyya*, 355; Safer Baba, *Tasavvuf Terimleri* [The Terms of Tasawwuf] (Istanbul, 1998), 125–26.
21. Sezai Karakoç, *İslam'ın Dirilişi* [The Resurrection of Islam] (Istanbul, 1986), 35.
22. See Selim Sönmez, "Ahlak" [Ethics], *Köprü Journal* (Special Issue on Ethics), no. 75 (Summer 2001), 2.
23. Takiyettin Mengüşoğlu, *Değişmez Değerler ve Değişen Davranışlar* [Unchangeable Values and Changeable Behaviors] (Istanbul, 1965), 31.
24. Kuçuradi, *İnsan ve Değerleri* [The Man and His Values], 42.
25. Kuçuradi, op. cit., 66.
26. Abu al-Fida Ismail ibn Muhammad al-Ajluni, *Kashfa al-Khafa* (Beirut, n.d.), ii, 312. Yusuf ibn Husayn al-Razi, who was well known for his ideas about sincerity, said the most precious thing in the world was sincerity, but that although he had worked with all his might to uproot hypocrisy from his heart, it flourished there in another form,

thus indicating the difficulties in always remaining sincere. See, Abd al-Karim ibn Hawazin al-Qushayri, al-Risalat al-Qushayriyya (Cairo, 1966), 440.

27. Mengüşoğlu, *Değişmez Değerler ve Değişen Davranışlar* [Unchangeable Values and Changeable Behaviors], 31.
28. Güngör, *Ahlak Psikolojisi ve Sosyal Ahlak* [The Psychology of Ethics and Social Ethics], 64.
29. When embarking on spiritual journeying in Sufism, solitariness is preferred in order to prepare for self-examination and to plumb the depths of the self. In this way one progresses toward sincerity: "Loving solitariness and worshipping in places where one is unseen serves to induce sincerity." Abu Nasr al-Sarraj, *al-Luma'* (Cairo, 1960), 290.
30. Hasan Aycın, *Gece Yürüyüşü* [The March of the Night] (Istanbul, 1994), 34.
31. Quran, 22:46, says: "so that their hearts may thus learn wisdom."
32. "Man's soul or ego has two faces. One is faithful to the covenant with God, inclined to do praiseworthy acts and is naturally understanding. The other is inclined to do evil, is by nature animal, and is unconcerned with the covenant with God. The first is the rational soul, and the latter the worldly or animal soul. When the rational soul subjugates the animal soul and holds it under control, it means both are being held in their right places. In this way, a person is holding both souls in their rights places in his inner world. It is that person's correct conduct towards himself." Sayyed Muhammad Nakib al-Attas, "Opening Speech." In *Fourth International Symposium on Bediuzzaman Said Nursi*, Istanbul 1998 (Istanbul, 2000), 21.
33. Oliver Leaman, "Nursi's Place in the Ihya' Tradition." In *Fourth International Symposium on Bediuzzaman Said Nursi*, Istanbul 1998 (Istanbul, 2000), 707. Another scholar who has made a comparison of Bediuzzaman and Iqbal is Jalalizade. See Jalal Jalalizade, "A Comparison of the Thought of Bediuzzaman and Muhammad Iqbal," in *Third International Symposium on Bediuzzaman Said Nursi*, Istanbul 1995 (Istanbul, 1997), 160–73.
34. Karakoç, *İslam'ın Dirilişi* [The Resurrection of Islam], 31.
35. For a detailed discussion of Bediuzzaman's eloquence, see 'Imaduddin Khalil, "The Literary Beauty of Bediuzzaman's Works," *International Symposium on the Reconstruction of Islamic Thought in the Twentieth Century and Bediuzzaman Said Nursi*, Istanbul 1992 (Istanbul, 1993), 48–68.
36. 'Imaduddin Khalil, op. cit., 49.
37. Bediuzzaman Said Nursi, *The Words* [Eng. trans.] (Istanbul, 2002), 725.
38. Nursi, op. cit., 726.
39. Nursi, op. cit., 726. This harmonious musical quality is found in all Bediuzzaman's works. This must be the reason why on repeated reading it yields different pleasures every time.
40. Şerif Mardin, "The Collective Memory and Consciousness," *International Symposium on the Reconstruction of Islamic Thought in the Twentieth Century and Bediuzzaman Said Nursi*, Istanbul 1992 (Istanbul, 1993), 14.
41. Karakoç, *İslam'ın Dirilişi* [The Resurrection of Islam], 38.
42. Erol Güngör attributes the fact that compared to other Islamic countries at that time, India perpetuated its tradition of Islamic knowledge and thought and produced many worthy Muslim thinkers, to the freedom of thought that the British government permitted. Güngör states that the colonial administration was extremely tolerant toward

local cultures. See Erol Güngör, *İslam'ın Bugünkü Meseleleri* [The Present Questions of Islam] (Istanbul, 1990), 203.

43. "The most important basis of the ways of sainthood and the branches of the Sufi path is sincerity, for salvation from the hidden association of partners with God is through sincerity. One who does not obtain sincerity cannot travel those ways." Bediuzzaman Said Nursi, *Letters* 1928–1932 (Istanbul, 2001), 526.
44. Bediuzzaman Said Nursi, *The Flashes Collection* [Eng. trans.] (Istanbul, 2000), 212.
45. Despite all efforts, I was unable to obtain this article: Ghulam Sadiq, "Iqbal on the Concept of Morality," *Iqbal Review*, vol. 10, no. 3 (October, 1969), 45–54.
46. According to Bediuzzaman, "One of the most effective ways of attaining and preserving sincerity is 'contemplation of death'." The other is "attaining a sense of the divine presence." Contemplation of death is "to think of death and realize that this world is transient and so be saved from the tricks of the soul." Nursi, *Flashes*, 216–17. "You should take as your guide the following rules, in order to gain sincerity and preserve it: . . . (1) You should seek divine pleasure in your actions . . . (2) This is not to criticize your brothers who are employed in this service of the Qur'an . . . (3) All your strength lies in sincerity and truth . . . (4) To imagine your brothers' virtues and merits in your own selves, and to thankfully take pride at their glory." Nursi, *Flashes*, 213–16. "Each member of a true and sincere union may see also with the eyes of the other brothers and hear with their ears." Nursi, *Flashes*, 214–15.
47. See also "An atom expended in sincerity and for the sake of God's pleasure becomes like a star. What is important is not the nature of the means employed, but the result that it yields. As long as the result is God's pleasure and the substance employed is sincerity, any means to which recourse is had will be great, not small." Nursi, *Flashes*, 209.
48. 'Ubayd ibn 'Umayr (May God be pleased with him): "The sign of sincerity is to not expect anything from people nor hope for their commendation." Safer Baba, *Tasavvuf Terimleri* [The Terms of Tasawwuf], 125. "They ask for no recompense from people in return for their actions. They expect no thanks or praise or love. They are not afraid of being censured. They suffice with His knowing what they are; His love is enough for them." Toprak, "Marifetullah ve İhlas" [Gnosis of Allah and Sincerity], 24.
49. Nursi, *Flashes*, 181. "For genuine sincerity, even for the sake of evil, cannot fail to yield results, and whatever man seeks with sincerity, God will grant him it." Nursi, *Flashes*, 202.
50. "So look to your own duty and concern, and do not meddle with God's concerns." Nursi, *Flashes*, 204.
51. Muhammad Iqbal, *Pas Chai Bayad Kard Ey Aqwam-i Sharq* [Turk. trans. Ali Nihad Tarlan] (Istanbul, 1976), 102.
52. Iqbal, *Zarb-i Kalim* [Turk. trans. N. Ahmed Asrar] (Istanbul, 1981), 160.
53. Quran, 112:4.
54. Iqbal, *Rumuz-i Bekhudi* [Turk. trans. Ali Nihad Tarlan] (Istanbul, 1964), 135–36. "Adam in this world is the Truth's deputy. His word is in force in the elements of this world." Op. cit., 120. See also Iqbal, *Zabur-i Ajam* [Turk. trans. Ali Nihad Tarlan] (Istanbul, 1971), 223.
55. "These dominical officials confirm their positions through their actions and deeds. They carry out their duty of reflecting the firmness of their belief and their sincerity.

They display in their actions their degree of faith. They show that they follow to the letter the practices of Muhammad (PBUH) and that truly they have been invested with the Prophetic robe. In short: for the community of Muhammad (PBUH) they form perfect models in respect of deeds and morality and following and adhering to the Prophet's Sunna; they are examples worthy of being followed." Nursi, *The Rays Collection* [Eng. trans.] (Istanbul, 2002), 635. See also Nursi, *Tarihçe-i Hayat* (Istanbul, 1990), 531.

56. Iqbal, *Asrar-i Khudī* [Turk. trans. Ali Nihad Tarlan] (Istanbul, 1964), 130.
57. Ibid., 129–30.
58. Ibid., 130.
59. Mustafa Said İşeri, "Güzel Ahlakı Ararken" [While Seeking the Well-Ethics], *Köprü Journal*, No. 75 (Summer 2001), 114. "In Islam, the spirit of the tenets of belief is divine unity, the spirit of worship is sincerity, the spirit of worldly matters is justice." Uludağ, *Tasavvuf Terimleri Sözlüğü* [The Dictionary of the Terms of Tasawwuf], 240.
60. "In so far as the person performing the worship looks on it as a debt and duty towards God, worship effectively develops a sense of responsibility. When one thinks that it is only actions that are performed with a sense of responsibility that deserve to be called 'moral,' the importance of worship in the development of a person's moral self becomes apparent." Hökelekli, *Din Psikolojisi* [The Psychology of Religion], 243.
61. Muhammad Iqbal, *The Reconstruction of Religious Thought in Islam* (Lahore, 1996), 72.
62. "Sincerity in worship is this, that it is performed only because it is commanded, although it comprises numerous instances of wisdom [and benefits]. Each of these may be a reason ('illa) for performing worship, but sincerity makes it imperative that the [true] reason be the command to perform it. If the wisdom or benefit is made the reason, the worship is null and void, but if it merely encourages the person to perform the worship, it is permissible." Nursi, *Signs of Miraculousness*, 163. "Sincerity is the bondsman performing all his worship correctly and purely for God's pleasure." Toprak, "Marifetullah ve İhlas" [Gnosis of Allah and Sincerity], 24. "According to the Sufis, sincerity is the spirit of worship. Actions without sincerity and sincerity without action are both without benefit. Nevertheless, actions without sincerity are worse than sincerity without action, for it is sincerity that affords value to everything. A person may be saved through sincerity in his worship, not through abundant worship. He has to be sincere, but he should not claim that he is thus. This was one of the Sufi's principles. Abu Bakr al-Dakkak said that the belief that one was sincere sprang from deficiency in sincerity. When God Almighty wants to make a person's sincerity acceptable, He prevents him knowing this. Then the bondsman is not 'mukhlis (sincere)' but in the words of the Qur'an (19:51), he is 'mukhlas (saved).' A person gains sincerity through his own voluntary efforts, but the one who is saved has his sincerity bestowed on him by God Almighty." See Ateş, art. "İhlas," *Türkiye Diyanet Vakfı İslam Ansiklopedisi* [The Encyclopedia of Islam], xxi, 536. See also *al-Qushayrī, al-Risālat al-Qushayriyya*, 445; cf. [Turk. trans. Süleyman Uludağ], 352–56.
63. Nursi, *Flashes*, 181.
64. "If those words are brought to life in the air by sincerity and truthful intent, they will enter the ears of the spirit beings like some tasty fruit in the mouth. But if God's

pleasure and sincerity do not bring those words to life, they will not be heard, and reward will be had only for the single utterance made by the mouth." Nursi, *Flashes*, 205.

65. Iqbal, *Reconstruction of Religious Thought in Islam*, 58.
66. Nursi, *Flashes*, 200–11.
67. "My brothers! The most dangerous aspect of egotism for our work is jealousy. If it is not purely for God's sake, jealousy interferes and spoils it." Nursi, *Letters*, 498.
68. Nursi, *Flashes*, 209. "The sole remedy for this disease is to accuse your own soul before others raise these charges, and always to take the side of your fellow, not your own soul. The rule of truth and equity established by the scholars of the art of debate is this: 'Whoever desires, in debate on any subject, that his own word should turn out to be true, whoever is happy that he turns out to be right and his enemy to be wrong and mistaken such a person has acted unjustly.' Not only that, such a person loses, for when he emerges the victor in such a debate, he has not learned anything previously unknown to him, and his probable pride will cause him loss. But if his adversary turns out to be right, he will have learned something previously unknown to him and thereby gained something without any loss, as well as being saved from pride. In other words, one fair in his dealings and enamoured of the truth will subject the desire of his own soul to the demands of the truth. If he sees his adversary to be right, he will accept it willingly and support it happily." Nursi, *Flashes*, 211.
69. "Spiritual life and correctness of worship will suffer as a result of enmity and rancour, since the purity of intention that is the means of salvation will be damaged." Nursi, *Letters*, 320.
70. Nursi, *Flashes*, 212–21.
71. "Be aware that the attention of men cannot be demanded, but only given. If it is given, one should not delight in it. If one delights in it, sincerity is lost and hypocrisy takes its place. The attention of men, if accompanied by the desire for honour and fame, is not a reward and a prize, but a reproach and chastisement for lack of sincerity. Such attention of men, such honour and fame, harm sincerity, the source of vitality for all good deeds, and even though they yield a slight pleasure as far as the gate of the tomb, on the other side of that gate they take on the form of torment. One should not therefore desire the attention of men, but flee and shy away from it." Nursi, *Flashes*, 201 fn. 3. See also Nursi, *Letters*, 483–86.
72. For the concept of "fame-seeking" as a stratagem of diabolical humans and jinns, see Nursi, *Letters*, 483–86.
73. For the sense of fear, and its exploitation by tyrants, see Nursi, *Letters*, 486–89.
74. For anxiety at making ends meet as a satanic stratagem, see Nursi, *Letters*, 489–91.
75. Nursi, *Letters*, 483–99.
76. For Hulusi Bey's letter to Bediuzzaman summarizing the section 'The Six Attacks' in Letters and his suggestions for countering them, see Bediuzzaman Said Nursi, *Barla Lahikası* (Istanbul, 1994), 119.
77. "God's pleasure is won by sincerity alone," and not by a large following or great success. For these latter are a function of God's will; they cannot be demanded, although they are sometimes given. Sometimes a single word will result in someone's salvation and hence the pleasure of God. Quantity should not receive too much attention, for sometimes to guide one man to the truth may be as pleasing to God as guiding a thousand." Nursi, *Flashes*, 204.

78. In Bediuzzaman's own words: "Those who receive most wounds are those who abandon their trenches and run away. While those who receive fewest wounds are those who persevere in their trenches." Nursi, *Letters*, 489.
79. See also, Nursi, *Letters*, 497–98. Also, "because they have failed to rid themselves of egoism, and on account of deficiency and excess, they lose their union, that lofty source of power, and permit their sincerity to be shattered. Their duty in regard to the hereafter is also harmed. God's pleasure is not had easily. The cure and remedy for this serious disease is to be proud of the company of all those traveling the path of truth, in accordance with the principle of love for God's sake; to follow them and defer leadership to them; and to consider whoever is walking on God's path to be probably better than oneself, thereby breaking the ego and regaining sincerity. Salvation is also to be had from that disease by knowing that an ounce of deeds performed in sincerity is preferable to a ton performed without sincerity, and by preferring the status of a follower to that of a leader, with all the danger and responsibility that it involves. Thus sincerity is to be had, and one's duties of preparation for the hereafter may be correctly performed." Nursi, *Flashes*, 205–206.
80. "Bravely toss your lasso at the sun, the moon / Drape it round their necks! / Grab the star from the firmament, pin it on him as finery." Iqbal, *Zabur-i Ajam*, 215. See also Iqbal, *Javid-Namah* [Turk. trans. Annemarie Schimmel] (Ankara, 1989], 151; Iqbal, *Armughan-i Hijaz* [Turk. trans. N. Ahmed Asrar] (Istanbul, 1981), 221.
81. "If the stone thinks it is glass, it'll make a habit of breaking." Iqbal, *Asrar-i Khudi*, 53. Iqbal says that fear is a psychological state that prevents people FROM acting. For it generally induces them to either run away, or to bow in submission. See Pierre Mannoni, *Korku* [Fear] [Turk. trans. Işın Gürbüz] (Istanbul, n.d.], 10. According to Delpierre, the thoughts and actions of a person who experiences extreme fear undergo a profound change. Insufficiently relegating things to the subconscious leads to extreme changeability of the psychic process, to the preponderance of automatism, and to the release of the reflex chain operations. For these reasons, the ability to act is impaired. Not relegating things to the subconscious makes some people inactive, passive, slow of reactions, and devoid of effort and initiative. See Mannoni, *Korku* [Fear], 12, quoted from, La Pieuvre, *Essaie Sur la Logique de l'Imaginaire* (ed. de la Table Ronde) (Paris, 1973), 67.
82. "Be strong and without ties like mountain tops swathed in cloud. / Beware! don't stoop to beggary! The wind's fierce, the flame, scorching." Iqbal, *Payam-i Mashriq* [Turk. trans. Ali Nihad Tarlan] (Ankara, 1956), 62. Also, op. cit., 103; Iqbal, *Bal-i Jibrail* [Turk. trans. Yusuf Salih Karaca] (Istanbul, 1983), 79; Iqbal, *Zarb-i Kalim*, 178, 185.
83. Iqbal, *Zabur-i Ajam*, 256; Iqbal, *Bal-i Jibrail*, 56; Iqbal, *Pas Chai Bayad Kard Ey Aqwam-i Sharq*, 65.
84. "We aren't restricted by fatherland; we're the light of two eyes, yet we're one / We're from Hijaz, China, Iran, yet we're dew-droplets of the same joyous morn. / We're intoxicated by the eyes of the Meccan watercarrier." Iqbal, *Asrar-i Khudi*, 30. See also Iqbal, *Rumuz-i Bekhudi*, 137; Iqbal, *Javid-Namah*, 316.
85. Iqbal, *Rumuz-i Bekhudi*, 133–35.
86. Iqbal, *Bal-i Jibrail*, 66.
87. Iqbal, *Payam-i Mashriq*, 111; Iqbal, *Bang-i Dara*, 83.
88. Iqbal, *Asrar-i Khudi*, 32. See also 32–33.

89. Iqbal, *Asrar-i Khudi*, 41–42. See also Iqbal, *Payam-i Mashriq*, 116; Iqbal, *Pas Chai Bayad Kard Ey Aqwam-i Sharq*, 94.
90. Iqbal, *Rumuz-i Bekhudi*, 130–32. See also Iqbal, *Payam-i Mashriq*, 67; Iqbal, *Bal-i Jibrail*, 54, 72, 100, 133; Iqbal, *Pas Chai Bayad Kard Ey Aqwam-i Sharq*, 86.
91. Iqbal, *Zarb-i Kalim*, 178, 212; Iqbal, *Javid-Namah*, 224; Iqbal, *Pas Chai Bayad Kard Ey Aqwam-i Sharq*, 112.
92. Iqbal, *Bal-i Jibrail*, 118.
93. Mardin, "The Collective Memory and Consciousness," 15.
94. See also Şerif Mardin, "Bediuzzaman's Understanding of Striving (Jihad) Is Not Armed Struggle," *Panel I* (Istanbul, 1993), 25–26.
95. Ali Ulvi Kurucu, "Önsöz" [Foreword], *Bediuzzaman Said Nursi, Tarihçe-i Hayatı*, 13.
96. Ünal, *Genel Tutumların veya Değerlerin Psikolojisi Üzerine bir Araştırma* [A Research on General Attitudes or The Psychology of Values], 6.
97. Ülken, *Değerler Kültür ve Sanat* [Values, Culture and Art], 14.
98. Muhammad Rushdi 'Ubayd, "Methods of Teaching in the Risale-i Nur," *International Symposium on The Reconstruction of Islamic Thought in the Twentieth Century and Bediuzzaman Said Nursi*, 251.
99. Nursi, *The Words*, 491.
100. Burhan Bozgeyik, *Meşhurların Son Anları* [The Last Moments of the Famous Persons], (Istanbul, 2002), 222.
101. Yılmaz Özakpınar, "Qur'anic Civilization," *Fourth International Symposium on Bediuzzaman*, (Istanbul, 1998), 465.
102. Ülken, *Değerler Kültür ve Sanat* [Values, Culture and Art], 21.
103. Sezai Karakoç, *Diriliş Neslinin Amentüsü* [The Credo of the Generation of the Resurrection] (Istanbul, 1986), 33.
104. Mardin, "The Collective Memory and Consciousness," 15.
105. Nursi, *Flashes*, 221.

EIGHTEEN

Spirit and Spirituality

Linking the Lives of Two Twentieth-Century Pioneers

Miriam Therese Winter

In an increasingly violent and xenophobic world, it is vital that we share the stories of those who do not fit the distorted generalizations that we hear about one another.

In this chapter, I present for our consideration the complementary spirit and spirituality of two contemporary persons of faith who never knew each other—Said Nursi, a Muslim scholar, and Anna Dengel, a Roman Catholic physician.

This chapter will show how elements of the spirituality of two very different individuals deeply rooted in two very different religions are often in harmony; that spirit has the capacity to transcend every boundary, be it race, religion, culture, gender, historicity; that the spirit of Said and the spirit of Anna are manifestations of God's One Eternal Spirit; and that the impetus, theological and spiritual, for promoting a unified spirit in the One God is deeply embedded in the *Risale-i Nur*.

This narrative exploration will take the following shape: a consideration of religion and spirituality and the distinction between the two; a synopsis of the lives of Said Nursi and Anna Dengel by way of introduction for those unfamiliar with either one; a look at their spirit and spirituality in relationship to the *Risale-i Nur*; and conclusions drawn from the above.

Religion and Spirituality

The words religion and spirituality are often interchanged and most people do not realize there is a distinction between the two. We tend to identify faith in God and its outward expression with religion, not spirituality. A believer or a person of faith is generally understood to have a religious affiliation, that is, membership in one of the world's recognized religions, or an ancient earth-based religion, or an independent sect or cult, or any one of the myriad ways humans formally organize themselves as manifestly religious. Religion implies a collective participation that is founded on an understanding of the divine relative to a code of beliefs that may or may not emanate from a sacred text or creed, with one or more designated rites, specific mandated practices, some rules and regulations, and more often than not, unwritten expectations that are binding on everyone. Religion provides a framework for praising our Creator and for living as God intended, for knowing there is more to life than what one actually sees, for reaching out to those in need, for creating community.

To many Christians, a believer is one who regularly "goes to church." No matter how pious an individual might be, if he or she no longer goes to church to participate in its rites, that person is said to be "outside the faith," even lost, or left behind. In ancient times, when tribal religions were essentially a fusion of cult and culture, such a disassociation from one's religious heritage was inconceivable. Today it is ubiquitous, as children within a religious tradition walk away from it in droves.

Characteristic of religion is an understanding of being set apart. Our religion separates us from all other religions on the planet because that is what religion does. It places a wall between an individual and those of other faith traditions, no matter how much one might choose to resist any such demarcation. Religion tells us who we are and how we ought to be behaving, how and why we are different from those who honor God in any other way. I grew up believing I was different, essentially and eternally different, from others who were not Christian, different from all those Protestant Christians who simply were not Catholic, that the God who created me was different from the God of other religions, the one true God of all people who alone could make that claim. Separated by theology and doctrine from all other people of faith and segregated in ways of worship, an insular view of the wider world beyond was inevitable. Fortunately, I no longer feel that way. The advent of our modern age spearheaded a shift in consciousness that will eventually change us all.

That change is already occurring within my own tradition and in many religious traditions. Except in extreme cases, religious fidelity around the world is becoming less divisive, and ordinary people in everyday settings are beginning to step across those lines that once kept us apart. This attitudinal shift is essential to the emergence of a more harmonious world. If we will have global peace, religion must lead the way for people of all faiths to come together to effect systemic change, even though, by its very nature, religion, an agent of separation, is not a unifying force. Spirituality, on the other hand, is.

Both religion and spirituality are concerned about leading people to God, but they do it in different ways. Religion is systemic and definitively organized. Its elements apply to everyone affiliated within. Spirituality is personal and selective. Religion and spirituality are not incompatible and are often intertwined. For those with a religious affiliation, spirituality is the individual's way of applying religion's expectations to one's own daily life. Some choose to do this by embracing an ancient tradition of mystical or applied spirituality within an established religion. For example, in Christianity, many have pursued the path of Benedictine spirituality, which is rooted in the monastic practice known as the Divine Office, in which set prayers are said daily at certain hours to render the whole day sacred. Others embrace Franciscan spirituality with its love of nature—Brother Sun, Sister Moon—and compassionate affinity with the poor; or follow the Spiritual Exercises of Ignation spirituality, which leads the practitioner, step by step, to union with God. Liberation theology, which promotes a preferential option for the poor and in practice is spirituality, has influenced a generation of Christians to choose a liberating compassion as foundational to their spiritual path. Feminist spirituality, a global phenomenon, welcomes women of all faiths and every spiritual persuasion into community, where the Holy One is celebrated with a variety of Images and Names. Indigenous peoples and ethnic groups within Christianity have held onto the cultural characteristics of ancient spiritualities, adding a dynamic variation to traditionally uniform ways.

Spirituality is especially attractive to those who have become disillusioned with religion, or say they have outgrown the religious traditions of their past. Many are drawn by an expectation of establishing a meaningful and transformative relationship with the divine. Others say they are responding to a perceived call from God to forge a new path within an already established tradition as they seek to set out on their own. In the end, each of us is responsible for our own spiritual life. Whether in or beyond religion, spirituality offers a parallel path, more accurately, offers multiple paths where people of faith might travel together as we move into the future.

> Imagine a circle, and in the midst a center,
> and from this center rays extend; each one,
> each radius radiates from the center of the circle.

> The farther these radii extend from the center, the more they diverge,
> the more remote they become from one another.
> On the other hand, as they approach the center,
> they converge and come together.
> Now imagine that this circle is the world
> and the center of the circle is God,
> and the radii from center to circumference,
> from the innermost point to the outer edge,
> and from the outer edge to the very center,
> are the paths of life of people.
> When people withdraw from the center, from God,
> they withdraw from one another,
> and when they approach the center, when they seek after God,
> they come closer to one another.
> Such is the circle of love.
> If we do not love, we are distant from God,
> we are distant from one another.
> When we love God, when we are one with God,
> we are one in our love of each other.
> The converse is also true.
> The closer we are to each other, the closer we are to God.
> Such is the circle of love.[1]

There are as many paths as there are believers who seek affinity with the divine. The common denominator is to live faithfully and authentically, entrusting the means and the outcome to the One who made us all. Spirituality is about finding our path and, in the process, creating circles, conversation circles, all-inclusive circles, spirituality circles of peace and reconciliation. Circles of love.

The spirit of spirituality is rooted in God's Spirit and open to every spirit, and in this sense has no boundaries that others cannot cross, no rules to segregate and exclude, no preconceived conditions. It has an innate capacity for hospitality, will welcome anyone and everyone under its canopy, hold in harmony a multitude of diverse faith traditions, weave into community individuals from every culture, whatever their social status, if their spirits and their hearts are open to inclusivity.

To hold an interfaith conference on the theme of spirituality is both pioneering and prophetic. There is a lot of interest in world religions within traditional religion, but very little talk of spirituality on a global scale. Spirituality has the potential to take a cosmic leap away from that which leaves us stymied and into the hearts of those who are eager to bring about change. The *Risale-i Nur* may prove to be a resource for connectivity, for its underlying spirit is not necessarily limited to a single faith tradition. Passages here and there sometimes soar beyond their context, seeking and even achieving an innerconnectedness within the realm of the spirit, as has already happened with me.

PIONEERING SPIRITS

Said Nursi (1877–1960)[2] was born in Nurs in eastern Anatolia in what is now Turkey. The middle child of seven children, he left home to begin his studies when he was only nine years old. His path in life was revealed in a dream. He would explore and communicate the truths of the Quran. So extraordinary was his intelligence and his ability to memorize, that by the time he had turned fifteen, he had earned the right to wear the scholar's turban and gown. He met every test that was put to him by determined scholars and shaykhs and was given the name "Bediuzzaman," which means "Wonder of the Age."

As the young Said became aware of the major issues of his time, he became politically active, embarking on a journey that would take him in and out of prison for the remainder of his life. He also came to realize that his inspirational method of interpreting the Quran lacked a firm foundation in the exercise of reason and began to study the texts in depth to strengthen its analytical basis. He also studied and mastered various fields of modern science, the science of religion, and philosophy. From this time forward, his ideas on educational reform, as well as his teaching methodology, were influenced by science. He opened a school and began to teach students of his own, so that he might put his radically new ideas into practice. What he learned from science had shaped his understanding of the Quran and from now on would assist him in proving its words to be true.

His deep desire to withdraw and concentrate on his teaching and writing was overridden by the circumstances of the times. He took up arms, along with his students, and commanded a large military force against the Russian invasion in 1916. He was captured and imprisoned for two years. On his release, he returned to Istanbul and was hailed as a hero. As the New Said, from this time forward, he took the Quran as his sole guide, and through what he called the "jihad of the word," tried to influence the leaders of the newly independent nation to base its government on the Quran. Instead they chose to adopt a secular form of society modeled on the West and to eradicate all vestiges of their Islamic past. The government became more and more repressive, assuming dictatorial power, sending dissidents into exile, and eliminating even the remotest challenge to its hegemony. In such a climate, Said's popularity was a constant threat. At this time he began writing what would become the *Risale-i Nur*. Although he had retired from public life, he and his students would be imprisoned four more times before his death. Each time he was brought to trial, he was subsequently acquitted as a result of his written depositions prepared in his own defense.

Nursi's desire to found an Islamic university in the Eastern Provinces was yet another aspect of his pioneering spirit. He believed that students should specialize in subjects they had a special aptitude for, an idea that was in itself quite radical. Despite the many efforts to suppress his work, study centers spread throughout the country and beyond. He had many followers at the time of his death and their numbers are steadily increasing. What he will be remembered for is his service to the Quran.

The Words, The Letters, The Flashes, and *The Rays* are four separate collections that make up the *Risale-i Nur*, a Quranic commentary in which Bediuzzaman Said Nursi, using his own inspired method, incorporates the wisdom of science, religion, and the modern age to prove the truths of belief.

Anna Dengel (1892–1980) was born in the village of Steeg in the Austrian Tyrol. Her mother died when she was nine, leaving a hole in her heart that would never fully heal. Her father sent her away to boarding school to ensure her education, for she was the eldest of five children before he remarried and had four more, and he did not want her burdened with the care of her younger siblings. As she was growing up, Anna heard about Catholic missionaries and their many works of mercy, and she felt a bond with suffering people living in faraway lands. During a two-year sojourn in France, she learned that a female Scottish physician was looking for a woman to study medicine. She would sponsor that woman through medical school if, after graduation, she went to India to work in a hospital for women and children, for which no doctor could be found. Anna took up the challenge. After graduating with a medical degree from the University of Cork in Ireland in 1919, she went to Rawalpindi, which was in India at that time, and was the doctor in charge of St. Catherine's Hospital for nearly four years.

Anna's work among women in the Punjab region of India, the majority of whom were Muslim and could not be treated by a male physician because of their custom of *purdah*, was exhausting yet deeply satisfying and absolutely essential. She wanted to do this for the rest of her life, yet she knew she could not continue to do it on her own, for the needs were simply enormous. Many more people were required, doctors and nurses professionally trained and others who would train the local people to do the work themselves. There also had to be some kind of structure to assure continuity. Struggling with this dilemma, Anna left India and eventually arrived in the United States, where, by the grace of God, she was led to begin a new initiative within the Roman Catholic tradition in the field of medical missions.

In 1925, Anna Dengel founded a community called Medical Mission Sisters, whose primary purpose initially was to bring professional medical care to women of the Orient, especially Muslim women. The community was not recognized by Rome because canon law forbid the practice of obstetrics and the full range of surgical procedures to those with religious vows. Nevertheless, three women joined Anna, and, in 1926, one of them went to Rawalpindi as physician-in-charge of St. Catherine's Hospital with a mandate to build a larger hospital in a more viable location. The following year the two hospitals were merged into a single institution with special wards and a female staff to serve Muslim women. Three years later, Holy Family Hospital, a hospital for the whole family, had admitted more than 1000 patients and treated over 20,000 people in its outpatient dispensary, plus home visits and village work.

The community of sisters grew and expanded. Finally, in 1936, Rome approved the study and practice of medicine for mission sisters with public vows and Medical Mission Sisters were officially recognized as a religious community. Responding to numerous invitations, Anna's community of dedicated women built hospitals and opened training schools for nurses, midwives, and lab technicians throughout India and Africa, in Pakistan and Bangladesh, Indonesia and the Philippines, Burma and Vietnam, in Jordan and in South America, engaging the local people in their healing mission, opening clinics in isolated villages, facilitating emergency relief in crisis situations, working with oppressed peoples to change their social situation and wipe out the root causes of disease, empowering women to do what was needed to reach their full potential.

Anna relinquished her medical career to implement her vision of bringing professional medical care to women and their families in developing nations. Her urgent concern for systemic change meant helping to raise the level of health and the delivery of health services, as well as training indigenous people, not only in curative skills, but in nutrition and sanitation and other means of disease prevention. She founded the first Catholic medical mission journal in 1926 and was its editor for many years; was tireless in raising funds for the missions; gave talks to educate people about the needs of others; visited sites around the world before establishing new foundations. Today the majority of her community's members are women of India. Anna received many honors and awards, including four honorary doctorates, but she never spoke of such things. The alleviation of suffering was her all-consuming concern.

Spirit and Spirituality

When Bediuzzaman Said Nursi was still a boy, it was revealed to him in a dream that knowledge of the Quran would be given to him provided he asked questions of no one, and so he never did. This revelation was the foundation stone on which he would build the rest of his life, the centerpiece of his spirituality. God had extended an invitation directly to him. It was a call to be completely absorbed in the mystery of God's revelation. It came with a condition, as such calls often do. Spirituality is how we respond to God's call. It reflects the degree of faith and trust that accompanies not only our efforts to honor preconditions but the quality of our fidelity as we journey into the unknown. The core of Nursi's spirituality coalesced around two lifelong goals: to found an Islamic university and to prove the truths of the Quran. His unique interpretation of the Quran was the centering focus of his life.

> I knew and felt that the *Risale-i Nur*, which was the result of my life, means of my happiness, and my natural duty, was saved from being lost and without benefit and from annihilation and losing its meaning, and that it was fruitful and enduring. I realized that I am ever-ready to sacrifice my life and immortality for the immortality, continuance, statement, and acceptance of each of those treatises, which prove the truths of belief, and that my happiness lies in their serving the Qur'an.[3]

In his pioneering methodology, Bediuzzaman Said Nursi compared the Quranic way to reality. He took examples from the world around him, from nature and everyday life. This manner of reflective thought on the universe "opens up a window onto the knowledge of God in everything."[4] In contrast to a scholarly process, which is primarily intellectual, or the Sufi approach of the heart, Nursi's integrated Quranic way unfolded through "an alliance of the intellect and heart"[5] on a path as yet not traveled. One encounters at times a cascade of metaphors conjuring up vibrant images that make the soul sing, echoing a wide open invitation to the outsider to step inside. Said Nursi, the scholar, was a poet and a mystic, which may be why so many of his lyrical passages resonate with me.

> Then listen to the stars, listen to their harmonious address!
> See what wisdom has emblazed on the decree of its light.
> Altogether they start to speak with the tongue of truth,
> They address the majesty of the All-Powerful, All-Glorious One's
> sovereignty:
> We are each of us light-scattering proofs of the existence of our Maker,

We are witnesses both to His Unity and His Power,
We are subtle miracles gilding the face of the skies for the angels to
gaze upon.
We are the innumerable attentive eyes of the heavens
which watch the earth, which study Paradise.
We are the innumerable exquisite fruits which the hand of wisdom of
the All-Glorious and Beauteous One has fastened
To the celestial portion of the tree of creation, to all the branches of the
Milky Way.
For the inhabitants of the heavens,
We are each of us a traveling mosque, a spinning house, a lofty home;
Each is an illumining lamp, a mighty ship, an aeroplane.
We are each of us a miracle of power, a wonder of creative art
Created by the Powerful One of Perfection, the All-Wise One of Glory;
A rarity of His wisdom, a marvel of His creation, a world of light.[6]

He ends this poem with words that might serve as a centering mantra:

We are each of us in ecstasy,
a member of the mighty circle of the Milky Way.

Our present understanding of the universe, in harmony with quantum physics, confirms we are made of stardust, for the same raw matter that shaped the stars and planets of our galaxies gives rise to our earthly embodiment. Mystics have always known what Said Nursi intuitively understood. The inherent unity of all that is weaves thematically like a golden thread through the pages of his *Risale-i Nur*. "It is only through the mystery of Divine unity that it is known that the universe as a whole is a meaningful book of the Eternally Besought One."[7]

The universe—all that is—is revelatory of the Divine unity, reflecting back to us from all sides that we are all one.

> Through the mystery of Divine unity, a thousand and one Divine Names are concentrated in the furthest points and most scattered particulars of the sphere of multiplicity in the tiny missives known as living beings. The All-Wise Maker multiplies the copies of them extensively and publishes them everywhere.[8]

Scientists speak of a web of being, of particles and waves moving in and out of relationships, of innerconnectedness, thereby laying the foundation for positing the potentially transformative conclusion: we are all one. We are part of a cosmic whole. We are particles of one reality. Mystics push this further and say we originate from a single Source.

> We are all the same and we have one maker.
> We are the property of a single person.
> Whoever made one of us, made all of us.[9]

This claim in the *Risale-i Nur* is made by the seeds, the fruit, and all parts of a tree. It functions, however, as a metaphor for the relationship of humanity to its Maker, as we look individually, and collectively, "to the One Who holds the whole universe in the grasp of His power, and testify to His unity."[10]

From what I have been able to discern, Said Nursi's spirituality, firmly embedded in an uncompromising faith in the God of his tradition, has deep mystical roots and very practical implications that emanate from the Quran. He has been given the gift of seeing, and he sees far more than meets the eye. Here is an example.

> Then the world of humanity appeared to me as though on a cinema screen. I looked through the telescope of the people of misguidance and saw that world to be so dark and terrifying that I cried out from the depths of my heart. "Alas!" I cried. For they had desires and hopes that stretched to eternity, thoughts and imaginings that embraced the universe, the earnest desire for everlasting happiness and Paradise, an innate capacity and power on which no limit had been placed and which were free, yet despite their innumerable needs and their weakness and impotence they were exposed to the attacks of innumerable enemies and the blows of innumerable calamities.[11]

Such a horrendous vision could lead the seer to the pinnacle of despair, but immediately, the scenario shifts to an ecstasy of hope.

> I saw the Divine Name of All-Just rising like the sun in the sign of All-Wise, the Name of All-Merciful rising in the sign of Munificent, the Name of All-Compassionate rising in the sign of, that is, in the meaning of, All-Forgiving, the Name of Resurrector rising in the sign of Inheritor, the Name of Granter of Life rising in the sign of Bountiful, and the Name of Sustainer rising in the sign of Owner. They lit up the entire world of humanity and all the worlds within it. They dispelled those hellish states, opened up windows onto the luminous worlds of the

> hereafter, and scattered light over the world of humanity. I declared: "Praise and thanks be to God to the number of particles in existence!" I understood with complete certainty that in belief is a sort of paradise in this world too and in misguidance a sort of hell.[12]

Key to Nursi's spirituality and core to the *Risale-i Nur* are the divine names. They are the sum and substance of all that can be apprehended of the attributes of God. They are the song of the universe, the heartbeat of all that lives and moves and has inherent being, the causation and the linkages within and among us all. It is in the divine diversification of names that we are all one.

> Names such as All-Wise, Compassionate, Giver of Forms, Disposer, Quickener, and Nurturer, the impresses and manifestations of which are to be seen at work in every corner of the world, attributes such as wisdom, mercy, and grace, and acts such as formation, disposition and nurturing, are all one. . . . It is as if those Names and deeds were uniting in such fashion that power becomes identical with wisdom and mercy, and wisdom becomes identical with grace and life.[13]

Time and again the *Risale-i Nur* reveals how closely intertwined are the virtues and their expression with the divine names.

> As for mercy and gentleness, through displaying compassion and bounty, they impel the manifestation of the Names of Compassionate and Bestower. And compassion and bestowal require the qualities of making known and loved and impel the Names of Loving and Known One to be manifested.[14]

Nursi's climactic summation of the ubiquity of the divine names resounds like an orchestral reprise, leaving an imprint of the divine to reverberate in the heart.

> Go and ask a stormy sea or the quaking earth: "What are you saying?" You will hear that they are saying: "O Glorious One! O Glorious One! O One of Might, All-Compelling!" Then ask the small animals and their young being raised with kindness and compassion in the sea and on the land: "What are you saying?" They will surely reply: "O Beauteous One! O Beauteous One! O Most Compassionate and Merciful One!" Then listen to the skies; they say: "O Glorious One of Beauty!" And give your ear to the earth; it says: "O Beauteous One of Glory!"

> Listen carefully to the animals; they are saying: "O Merciful One! O Provider!" And ask the spring; you will hear many Names like: "O Gentle One! O Most Merciful one! O Most Compassionate One! O Most Generous One! O Gracious One! O Benevolent One! O Giver of Forms! O Giver of Light! O Bestower! O Adorner!" Then ask a human being who is a true human, and see how he recites all the Most Beautiful Names and how they are written on his forehead. If you look carefully, you too may read them. It is as if the universe is a huge orchestra celebrating the Divine Names. Mixing the faintest song with the most powerful refrains, it produces a sublime and subtle harmony.[15]

Bediuzzaman Said Nursi wrestled with the word of God and translated it into meaning in new and evocative ways. Such was the nature of his call.

Anna Dengel, on the other hand, felt called to reach out to suffering humanity long before the call took shape and she could clearly define it. For that reason she was ready to respond when the opportunity arose. "I was especially attracted to the idea of doing something only women could do for suffering women."[16]

Her call was tactile and practical, a call to action, so to speak, to become immersed as a Christian in the corporal works of mercy by tending with care and compassion to those who were in need. A spiritual advisor confirmed what God had already revealed to her. "You must devote yourself to the development of medical missions through establishing a congregation with permission of the church and under the church. You must never doubt that this is the will of God for you."[17] The impetus for her initiative was compelling and concrete. Bring the full scope of professional medicine to those who were deprived of it, in particular, Muslim women. "My work as a doctor in Northern India was predominantly among Muslims.[18] In fact the very reason for my going there was to attend the Muslim women who, on account of religious laws and customs could not receive medical aid from men."[19]

From the very beginning, Anna was determined to establish "good hospitals that would provide care for all kinds of medical needs of the Indian women, as there is none to my knowledge for native women, where surgical and obstetric cases of every kind can be satisfactorily treated."[20] The only way this could be done with any hope of continuity would be to found a new community, that is, begin a new tradition within an ancient tradition that was very slow to accept new ideas and even slower to change. She would plant the seed. God would give the increase.

> There is the hope that the seed here or there may fall on good ground and that in due time one more young woman will give her life to God

> as a member of the little band of medical missionaries who have pledged themselves to shun no disease, no medical need in any corner of the mission world.[21]

She began the "Holy Experiment" without official recognition and never doubted for a moment that the seed God had sown in her would come to fruition. "We were chosen by Providence to be the first in the Church to do this," she said at the time of the society's silver jubilee.[22] She also said on that occasion: "We, the pioneers, should thank God with all our heart for having led us so fatherly, so motherly, so wonderfully through these twenty-five years. How many graces and gifts have we not received collectively and individually?"[23]

Anna was not only a physician to women in the Orient, she was also their sister and friend, and when she had the time, she enjoyed their company.

> The Punjabi women were, I found, of sturdy character and sociable, so once I could string together sentences in Urdu, I ventured to invite some of them to my room for a friendly chat. One particularly encouraging feature about them was their inquisitiveness. They scrutinized everything within the four walls, even opening drawers, not realizing, of course, that this was "not done" according to western standards. However, I just took it for granted and let them look and look until by degrees they automatically and gracefully placed themselves in a circle on the floor. The topic of conversation was somewhat limited (only two percent of the forty million Muslim women in India are literate) but many questions were asked—what did we think and what did we do—and on their part much information about their customs and beliefs was simply and spontaneously given.[24]

Anna referred to these gatherings as "round floor" conferences. They gave her an opportunity to better understand the cultural context of the women she had come to serve, so that she might be a more effective advocate on their behalf.

> I am still on the road, so to say, traveling from place to place—trying to enlist sympathy for the women of India. Without getting into the meaning too deeply, one significance of sympathy is a friend's feeling for his friend's suffering. As a doctor it was my privilege to come in close contact with a variety of Indian women. I can honestly say that . . . one cannot help but loving them and feeling happy that one's life work is amongst them and for them. If I try to lay bare their physical suffering, their social status, their superstitious practices, the result of *purdah*, of

> child marriage and the peculiar hardships of Indian widowhood, it is not from a spirit of criticism, but a sister's love.[25]

She felt strongly that the root cause of so much of the physical and emotional illness in her female patients could be traced to oppressive conditions in which women failed to thrive. Consequently, she was a proponent of women's liberation from the beginning, giving talks and publishing articles in support of systemic change.

> One of the outstanding needs of the day is to stretch out a helping and guiding hand to the rapidly emancipating women of the East at this opportune time when many laws and customs in the non-Christian world are in the breaking and in the making.[26]

In 1928, Anna wrote an article about *purdah* in the journal she founded. In a brief overview of its current status, she made the following notation: "Turkey broke the ice in abolishing *purdah.* Slowly, other countries are following her example."[27]

The following story describes her efforts to learn the predominant language of the region, which was Hindustani, so that she might communicate directly with her patients about their ills and concerns.

> A *munshi*—a teacher—was hired, an affable man eager to teach his beautiful language, although it proved difficult to make him concentrate on such ordinary things as verbs or syntax. What he loved to do was talk about the origin of the tongue, of its Sanskrit base, its Arabic script. He explained to Dr. Dengel Hindu customs and Brahmin traditions. She learned of mental attitudes in India; she imbibed much valuable information on the religious and social practices of her patients. Eventually she gave up trying to learn much Hindustani from the *munshi.* It did not really matter, for a young Muslim[28] girl had constituted herself Dr. Dengel's guardian angel and hovered about her exactly like one. From her, she learned most of the Hindustani she eventually had.[29]

Over the years, her pioneering efforts for justice included the just treatment of local people employed in the hospitals of the Medical Mission Sisters.

> Another thing we cannot stress too much is fair compensation for those who are employed. It is a sin that cries to heaven. In the missions, we can lead in that way.[30]

> In India, it is not customary to give servants holidays. We give them two weeks holiday. When they don't receive a holiday, it forces them to lie and there are all kinds of tales about relatives who have died. But when you give them their proper holiday, they don't have to lie. I am sure that their parents die, but now only once.[31]

Characteristic of her spirituality, and that of her community, is a deep and abiding gratitude for all the gifts and blessings received from God and from others. Core qualities also include a spirit of joy and simplicity, compassion and a passion for justice on behalf of the poor and oppressed, at the heart of which is love. Anna spoke often of love to the sisters who were preparing to serve. "To the degree and intensity of our love, we will be united to God, for by loving, we are one thing with what we love."[32] Deeply embedded in the community's tradition from the very beginning were also a spirit of hospitality and a sense of humor, essential to a life of continual cross-cultural adaptation, which was often characterized by doing without what would seem absolutely essential. For instance, an Indian member of the community once wrote:

> The working conditions at the hospital [in Bharananganam] were very primitive, with no running water or electricity. We explained to Mother [Anna] how abdominal surgery was done by one person standing on a stool and shining a flashlight into the abdomen. In spite of all the difficulties, Mother said to carry on, bearing all in good faith with love, and that slowly things would improve, since it was God's work.[33]

The Gospel parable of the Good Samaritan[34] has been the scriptural and spiritual model for Anna's community. The parable, she wrote, "means to care for complete strangers of a different religion and nationality, at one's own personal inconvenience and cost and even to undertake a certain amount of responsibility."[35] She elaborates on its theme with a contemporary application.

> In the Orient today there are millions of human beings who are strangers to us, who profess a different religion, many of whom are suffering and lying helpless and voiceless. . . . Fevers, such as malaria, are so common that the loss of labor and income is a great economic problem and not only causes much suffering to the victim but to his whole family. There are thousands who die of cholera, plague, sleeping sickness, kalazaar, tuberculosis, etc. every year. All these are so many wounded by the roadside, stripped of happiness and usually unable to call out for assistance. In order to act like the Good Samaritan, whom Our Lord gave as

> example, we must stoop down and see and examine, and pour in the oil and wine of mercy and generosity and make arrangements not only for momentary relief, but for "seeing the case through," even at the cost of personal fatigue and expense. . . . The parable of the Good Samaritan teaches charity and mercy without alluding to conversion.[36]

Anna Dengel is remembered, not so much for her spirituality, but for her humanity. She once said: "To be human, that counts for very much—to be considerate and to know the human needs of people, to humanize humanity and humanize Christianity."[37] In my understanding, that is precisely what spirituality is, a human effort to live life as God would have us live it. The presence of God was the unifying force at the heart of Anna's humanity. "To make our daily life one harmonious whole in the service of God, we must make everything a service of God."[38] She was always optimistic, no matter how difficult the circumstance.

> Let us look at the world in the right way. For some it may be gloomy, hopeless. For us it is a paradise of opportunity to glorify God, to work out our love here and there, wherever we work, wherever we move about, wherever our literature, our anything and everything go.[39]

Anna's concern for human suffering was passionate and all-consuming. On returning from a trip to India and Pakistan, she described vividly the hordes of malnourished children "with bloated stomachs and hollow eyes" and the suffering of women, how much of it there was and how little was being done to alleviate its causes. She paused and sat in silence, then banged her fist on the table and shouted, "It eats me up!"[40]

When asked what it was like to found the Society, she replied, "It was simple—as simple as putting one foot in front of another. I saw the need."[41] She also told the sisters who were following in her footsteps. "We have only one life, and we must make the most of it."[42]

Anna's healing ministry was rooted in her faith in God's healing presence and her allegiance to Christ the healer. She would have deeply appreciated some of the spiritually empowering reflections of Said Nursi, her contemporary, for she, too, was a lover of nature who saw the sacred manifested everywhere around her. Prescriptions and pharmacies and other medicinal metaphors were among the images Nursi employed in his interpretive schema, which would have made Anna feel right at home. For example:

> The pharmacy of the globe of the earth with its living potions and medicaments in the jars which are the four hundred thousand species of

> plants and animals shows and makes known to eyes that are blind even—by means of the measure or scale of the science of medicine that you study—the All-Wise One of Glory, Who is the Pharmacist of the mighty pharmacy of the earth.[43]

He developed this theme in the first volume of the *Risale-i Nur*.

> If being healed of a dreadful disease is considered from the point of view of the affirmation of Divine unity, on the face of the bestowal of healing on all the sick in the huge hospital called the earth, through the remedies and medicines from the vast pharmacy called the world, the beautiful compassion of the Absolutely Compassionate One and the acts of His mercy become apparent in universal and splendid fashion.[44]

Healing has its place in the pantheon of possibility, and as is the case of all reality, receives its fundamental being in a divine name. "The realities of all beings and of the universe are based on the Divine Names. . . . True natural science is based on the name of All-Wise, true medicine on the Name of Healer."[45]

I cannot help wondering what a conversation between the two would have been like. In the following passage, Anna Dengel expounds on a theme that would strike a chord with Said Nursi, which is not too surprising between two such kindred spirits.

> For what else is science but the searching out of the secrets of God. Medical science, to mention only one, is so highly developed now that it can save and prolong life—prevent, alleviate and cure many ills. It could change the face of the earth if it could be made available to all.[46]

Implicit in her statement is the healing presence of God underlying scientific efforts to help others in God's name. The last word here belongs to Bediuzzaman Said Nursi. Listen for Anna's amen.

> The heat-giving lamp of this hospice that is the world is one; its candle that is the basis for the reckoning of time is one; its merciful sponge is one; its fiery cook is one; its life-giving beverage is one; its well-guarded field is one, as well as a thousand and one other instances of oneness. It follows from all of these instances of oneness that the Maker and Master of this hospice is also one, that He is extremely generous and hospitable.[47]

Conclusion

The vision and witness of two very different faith-filled individuals have been presented here for our inspiration and as models for our times. The contrast between the two is striking. They had markedly different starting points, diverse demographic realities, and traveled different paths. They were solidly rooted in and consistently molded by two different faith traditions, which over the course of history have seemed more like enemies than friends. With such diversity as credentials, what better example might we offer our world than these two pioneering spirits and their defining creed: we are all one. Said Nursi put the vision into words in his *Risale-i Nur*. His innovative text identifies a unifying spirit that reaches beyond its intended receivers to invite the other in. Anna Dengel put the vision into action, translating into merciful deeds and an institutionalized continuity a call to comfort the brokenhearted, to have mercy on the stranger, to tend to another's wounds. Together their lives speak loudly to us of the embodiment of God's word, which is the basis for living as though all that exists emanates from the One God of us all. If we would give this vision flesh, if we would have a pioneering spirit and take the risk of leading the way into a reconciling unity, we must be willing to step outside the lines, to insist there are no permanent boundaries to prevent our spirits and our hearts from embracing the other side.

Notes

1. Based on a text by Abba Dorotheus, seventh-century Eastern Orthodox mystic.
2. Source for the following information: Şükran Vahide, "Bediuzzaman Said Nursi and the Risale-i Nur" in *Globalization, Ethics, and Islam: The Case of Bediuzzaman Said Nursi*, ed. by Ian Markham and Ibrahim Ozdemir (Ashgate, 2005), 3–35.
3. *The Rays*, 73.
4. Ibid., 15.
5. Ibid.
6. *The Letters*, 48–49.
7. *The Rays*, 20.
8. *The Rays*, 18.
9. *The Rays*, 31.
10. Ibid.
11. *The Rays*, 641–42.
12. Ibid.
13. *The Rays*, 186.
14. *The Words*, 658.
15. *The Words*, 342–43.
16. *Fire and Flame: The Legacy of Anna Dengel* (Medical Mission Sisters, 1998), 54.
17. "The Course of Events" in *Fire and Flame*, 18–19.

18. The original says "Mohammedans."
19. *The Medical Missionary*, February 1945, 27.
20. Letter to Dr. Lyons, February 25, 1925, in *Fire and Flame*, 57.
21. *The Medical Missionary,* August 1928, 3.
22. Talk given to Professed Sisters, September 27, 1950.
23. Circular Letter to the community, 1949.
24. *The Medical Missionary*, February 1945, 27.
25. From her personal notes. Undated. In *Fire and Flame,* 56.
26. October 1927, from the printed statement announcing the publication of *The Medical Missionary.*
27. "Lifting the Veil," *The Medical Missionary,* September 1928.
28. The original says "Mohammedan."
29. Katherine Burton, *According to the Pattern* (New York, 1946), 157–58.
30. Talk given to the community, May 1950.
31. Ibid.
32. *Talks and Writings*, 1.
33. Josephine Vechyanical, *Fire and Flame,* 90.
34. Luke 10: 25–37.
35. *The Medical Missionary,* August 1928.
36. *The Medical Missionary*, October 1940.
37. *Fire and Flame,* 127.
38. Circular Letter to the community, January 1, 1953.
39. Ibid.
40. Mary Louise Lynch, "Justice and Compassion," in *Fire and Flame,* 99.
41. Ibid., 97.
42. Talk given to the community, April 28, 1952.
43. *The Words*, 169.
44. *The Rays*, 15.
45. *The Words*, 655.
46. *The Medical Missionary*, April 1940, 63.
47. *The Rays*, 186.

NINETEEN

Selections from Nursi's Writings on Spirituality

Tr. Şükran Vahide

The Fifth Letter

In His Name, be He glorified!
And there is nothing but it glorifies Him with praise.

In his *Letters* (*Maktubat*), Imam-i Rabbani[1] (May God be pleased with him), a sun of the Naqshbandi Order and its hero, said: "For me, the disclosure of a single matter of the truths of faith is preferable to thousands of illuminations, ecstasies, and instances of wonder-working."

He also said: "The final point of all the Sufi ways is the clarification and unfolding of the truths of faith."

He also said: "Sainthood (*velāyet*) is of three sorts: one is the lesser sainthood, which is the well-known sainthood. The others are the middle sainthood and the greater sainthood. Greater sainthood is to open up by way of the legacy of prophethood (*verāset-i nübüvvet*) a direct way to reality without entering the intermediate realm of Sufism."

He said also: "The Naqshi way is traversed with two wings." That is, "By having firm belief in the truths of faith, and by carrying out the religious obligations. The way cannot be covered if either of these two wings are defective." In which case, the Naqshi way consists of three veils:

The First and most important is to serve the truths of faith directly; Imam-i Rabbani travelled this way in his later years.

The Second is to [advance the cause of] the religious obligations and serve the glorious practices (Sunnah) of the Prophet (PBUH) under the veil of the Sufi way.

The Third is to strive to eliminate the sicknesses of the heart by way of Sufism and to journey with the feet of the heart.

Of these, the first is the equivalent of obligatory, the second, close to obligatory, and the third, *Sunnah*.

Since the reality of the matter is thus, my conjecture is that if such persons as Shaykh 'Abd al-Qadir Gilani[2] (May God be pleased with him) and Shah Naqshband[3] (May God be pleased with him) and Imam-i Rabbani (May God be pleased with him) were alive today, they would expend all their efforts on strengthening the truths of faith and tenets of Islam. For it is through them that eternal happiness is won. Any deficiency in them results in eternal misery. A person without faith will not enter Paradise, but very many will go there without Sufism. Man cannot live without bread, but he can live without fruit. Sufism is the fruit, the truths of Islam, basic sustenance. In former times, through spiritual journeying from forty days to as much as forty years, a person could rise to some of the truths of faith. But now, if through Almighty God's mercy there is a way to rise to those truths in forty minutes, it surely is not sensible to remain indifferent to it.

Thus, people who have studied the thirty-three Words closely state that they have opened up just such a Qur'anic way. Since this is a fact, I am of the opinion that the Words so far written about the mysteries of the Qur'an are a most appropriate medicine and salve for the wounds of this time, and a most beneficial light for Islam as a whole, which has been subject to the assaults of darkness, and a most right guide for those wandering bewildered in the valleys of misguidance.

You know that if misguidance arises from ignorance, it is easy to dispel. But if it results from science and learning, it is difficult to eliminate. In former times, only one person in a thousand was in the latter category, and only one in a thousand such people would be reformed through guidance. For such people fancy themselves. They do not know, but they think they do know. I think that Almighty God has bestowed the Words at this time, which are flashes of the Qur'an's miraculousness, as an antidote to this atheistic misguidance.

The Eternal One, He is the Eternal One!

Said Nursi

(A part of) The Nine Allusions
[from the Twenty-Ninth Letter]

[This section is about the paths of sainthood (*turuk-u velāyet*), and consists of nine Allusions.]

In the Name of God, the Merciful, the Compassionate.
Behold! Verily on the friends of God there is no fear, nor shall they grieve.[4]

First Allusion

Underlying the terms Sufism, path, sainthood, and spiritual journeying is an agreeable, luminous, joyful, and spiritual sacred truth. This truth has been proclaimed, taught, and described in thousands of books written by authoritative scholars (*muhakkikīn*) among the people of illumination (*zevk*) and unveiling (*keşf*), who have told the Muslim community and us about it. May God reward them abundantly! Now, because of some compelling circumstances at this time, we shall point out a few droplets, like sprinklings, from that vast ocean.

Question? What is the Sufi path?

The Answer: The aim and goal of the Sufi path is—knowledge of God and the unfolding of the truths of faith—through a spiritual journeying with the feet of the heart under the shadow of the Ascension of Muhammad (PBUH), to manifest the truths of faith and the Qur'an through 'tasting' (*zevkī*) and certain enhanced states (*halī*), and to an extent through direct vision (*şuhūdī*); it is an elevated human mystery and perfection called the Sufi path or Sufism.

Yes, since man is a comprehensive index of the universe, his heart resembles a map of thousands of worlds. For innumerable human sciences and fields of knowledge show that man's brain in his head is a sort of centre of the universe, like a telephone and telegraph exchange for innumerable lines. Similarly, the millions of light-scattering books written by incalculable saints show man's heart in his essential being to be the place of manifestation of innumerable truths of the universe, and to be their pivot, and seed.

Since the human heart and brain are thus central, and comprise the members of a mighty tree in the form of a seed, and within them are encapsulated the parts and components of an eternal, majestic machine pertaining to the hereafter, certainly the heart's Creator willed that it should be worked and brought out from the potential to the actual, and developed, and put into action, for that is what He did. Since He willed it, the heart will certainly work like the mind. And the most effective means of working it is to be turned towards the truths of faith on the Sufi path through the remembrance of God in the degrees of sainthood.

Second Allusion

The keys and means of this journeying of the heart and spiritual progress are remembrance of God and reflective thought. Their virtues are too numerous to be described. Apart from uncountable benefits in the hereafter and human attainments and perfections, a minor benefit pertaining to this tumultuous worldly life is as follows: everyone wants a solace and seeks enjoyment in order to be saved a little from the upheavals of life and its heavy burdens, and to take a breather; everyone searches out something friendly to banish the loneliness. For one or two people out of ten, the social gatherings in civilized life offer a temporary, but heedless, drunken familiarity, intimacy, and solace. Eighty per cent, however, live solitary lives in mountains or valleys, or are driven to distant places in search of a livelihood, or due to such agencies as calamities or old age that recall the hereafter, they are deprived of the companionship of human groups and societies. Their circumstances allow them no familiarity, friendliness, or consolation.

For such a person, true solace, intimacy, and sweet pleasure are to be found in addressing his own heart in those distant places and desolate mountains and distressing valleys, in working it through remembrance of God and reflection. Calling on God Almighty, he may become intimate with Him in his heart, and by virtue of that intimacy think of the things around him, which were regarding him savagely, as smiling on him familiarly. He will say: "My Creator, Whom I am recollecting, has innumerable servants here in my place of solitude, just as He has everywhere. I am not alone; loneliness has no meaning." Thanks to his faith, he receives pleasure from that sense of familiarity. He grasps the meaning of life's happiness, and he offers thanks to God.

Third Allusion

Sainthood is a proof of divine Messengership (*risalet*); the Sufi path is a proof of the Sharī'ah. For the truths of belief that Messengership preaches, sainthood sees and confirms with a sort of direct vision with the heart and tasting with the spirit at the degree of the vision of certainty (*aynelyakīn*). Its confirmation is a certain proof of the veracity of Messengership. Through the experiential knowledge of the Sufi path and its unveilings, and through its benefits and effulgences, it is a clear proof of the truths and the matters that the Sharī'ah teaches; it demonstrates that they are the truth and that they come from the truth. Yes, just as sainthood and the Sufi path are evidence and proof of Messengership and the Sharī'ah, so they are a perfection of Islam and a means of attaining to its lights, and through Islam, a source of humanity's progress and moral enlightenment.

Although this vast mystery holds such importance, certain deviant sects have tended to deny it. They have been deprived of those lights, and they have caused others to be deprived. The most regrettable thing is that making a pretext of abuses and faults they have seen committed by the followers of the Sufi path, some literalist Sunni scholars and some neglectful politicians who are also Sunnis are trying to close up that supreme treasury, indeed, to destroy it, and to dry up that source of Kawthar which distributes a sort of water of life. However, there are few things and ways and paths that are without fault and are good in every respect. They are bound to contain some faults and abuses. For if the uninitiated embark on something, they are sure to misuse it. But as with the accounting of deeds in the hereafter, Almighty God demonstrates His dominical justice through the weighing up of good deeds and bad deeds. That is to say, if good deeds preponderate and weigh heavier, He accepts them and grants reward; whereas if evil deeds preponderate, he punishes for them and rejects them. The balancing of good and evil deeds looks to quality rather than quantity. It sometimes happens that a single good deed will weigh heavier than a thousand evils, and cause them to be forgiven. Divine justice judges thus and reality too considers it right. Thus, the evidence that the good deeds of the Sufi path—that is, paths within the bounds of the Prophet's (PBUH) practices—definitely preponderate over their evils is that those who follow them preserve their belief when attacked by the people of misguidance. A sincere ordinary follower of the Sufi path preserves himself better than a superficial, apparent Muslim with a modern, scientific background. Through the illumination of the Sufi path and the love of the saints, he saves his belief. If he commits grievous sins, he becomes a sinner, but not an unbeliever; he is not easily drawn into atheism. No power at all can refute the chain of shaykhs he accepts, with a strong love and firm belief, to be spiritual poles. And because no power can refute it, his confidence in them cannot be shaken. And so long as his confidence is not shaken, he will not accept atheism. In the face of the atheists' stratagems at the present time, it has become difficult for a person unconnected with the Sufi path, whose heart has not been brought to action, to preserve himself completely, even if he is a learned scholar.

There is another thing; the Sufi path should not be condemned because of the evils of some orders that have adopted practices outside the bounds of *taqwah*, and even of Islam, and have wrongfully called themselves Sufi paths. Quite apart from the elevated religious and spiritual fruits of the Sufi path and those that look to the hereafter, Sufi orders were the first, and most effective and ardent means of spreading and strengthening brotherhood, the sacred bond of the Islamic world. They were also one of the three unassailable strongholds of Islam, which held out against the awesome attacks of the world of unbelief and the politics of Christendom. What preserved Istanbul, the centre of the Caliphate for five hundred and fifty years against the whole Christian world, were the lights of belief that poured out of five hundred places in Istanbul and the powerful faith of those who recited "Allah! Allah!" in the *tekkes* behind the big mosques, which were a firm source of support for the people of belief in that centre of Islam, and their spiritual love arising from knowledge of God, and their fervent murmurings.

O you unreasoning pseudo-patriots and false nationalists! What evils are there in the Sufi paths that can negate all this good in the life of your society? You say! . . .

Fifth Allusion

An extremely important way within Sufism is the Unity of Witnessing, which is another name for the Unity of Existence. This restricts the gaze to the existence of the Necessarily Existent, and sees other beings to be so weak and shadow-like in relation to Him that it declares that they do not deserve the name of existence. It envelops them in veils of imagination, and in the station of abandoning all things other than God, counts them as nothing. It even imagines them to be non-existent, and goes so far as to belittle the manifestations of the divine names, saying they are mere imaginary mirrors.

A significant fact about this way is that due to the powerful faith it inculcates and the elevated sainthood of those on it advancing to the degree of absolute certainty (*hakkalyakīn*), the existence of contingent beings is so diminished that nothing remains in its view other than imagination and non-existence; it is as though it denies the universe on account of the Necessarily Existent One.

But this way holds dangers, the first of which is this: there are six pillars of faith, and such pillars as belief in the Last Day and belief in God require the existence of contingent beings. These firmly-founded pillars of belief cannot be constructed on imagination! For this reason, when a person following this way re-enters the world of sobriety from the worlds of ecstasy and intoxication, he should not bring it with him, nor should he act in accordance with it.

Furthermore, he should not convert this way, which pertains to the heart and to illuminations and certain states, into a form that pertains to the reason, knowledge, and words. For the laws and principles related to reason, knowledge, and speech, which proceed from the Qur'an and the practices of the Prophet (PBUH), cannot sustain that way and are inapplicable to it. For this reason, the four Rightly-Guided Caliphs, and the leading authorities and interpreters of the law, and the authorities of the first generations of Islam were not seen to practise it. This means that it is not the most elevated way. It may be elevated, but it is also deficient. It is very important, but it is also very perilous and difficult. Yet, it is still very pleasurable. Those who embark on it for the pleasure, do not want to leave it, and because of their self-centredness, they suppose it to be the highest degree. We have explained the basis and nature of this way to an extent in the treatise called *Nokta Risalesi*, and in some of the *Words* and *Letters*, and shall suffice with them. Here, we shall describe one of the serious hazards on that important way. It is as follows:

For the highest of the elite, who pass beyond the sphere of causes and renouncing everything other than God, sever their attachment to contingent beings and enter a state of complete absorption in God, this way is a righteous way. But, to present it in terms of intellectual knowledge to people who are submerged in causes, are enamoured of the world, and are plunged into materialist philosophy and nature, will drown them in nature and materiality and distance them from the reality of Islam. For those people who love this transitory world and are attached to the sphere of causes want to ascribe a sort of permanence to them. They do not want to lose their beloved. On the pretext of the Unity of Existence, they imagine it to have permanent existence. On account of the world, their beloved, and by ascribing permanence and eternity to it, they make it an object of worship; and, I seek refuge with God, this paves the way to the abyss of denying God.

This century, materialism is so widespread, materiality is thought to be the source of everything. If in such an age, the elite believers consider materiality to be so unimportant as to be non-existent, thus furthering the way of the Unity of Existence, the materialists will lay claim to it, saying: "We say the same thing." Whereas, among all the ways in the world, the one furthest from that of the materialists and nature-worshippers, is the way of the Unity of Existence. For the followers of the Unity of Existence attach such importance, due to their belief, to the divine existence that they deny the universe and beings. Whereas the materialists attach so much importance to beings that on account of the universe they deny God. How can the two come together or be compared? . . .

Seventh Allusion

This consists of four points.

First Point: The Sharī'ah is directly, without shadow or veil, the result of the divine address, through the mystery of divine oneness (*ehadiyet*) in respect of absolute dominicality (*rubūbiyet*). The highest degrees of the Sufi path (*tarikat*) and of reality (*hakikat*) are like parts of the Sharī'ah. Or they are always like its means, introduction, and servant. Their results are the incontrovertible matters of the Sharī'ah. That is to say, the ways of the Sufi orders and of reality are like means, servants, and steps for reaching the truths of the Sharī'ah, till at the highest level they are transformed into the meaning of reality and essence of the Sufi way, which are at the heart of the Sharī'ah. So then they become parts of the Greater Sharī'ah. It is not right to think of the Sharī'ah as an outer shell and reality as its inner part and result and aim, as some Sufis do. Yes, the Sharī'ah unfolds according to the levels of men. It is wrong to suppose that what the mass of people imagine is the external aspect of the Sharī'ah is its reality, and to give the names of reality and Sufi path to the degrees of the Sharī'ah that are disclosed to the elite. The Sharī'ah has degrees which look to all classes.

It is in consequence of this that the further the Sufis and those who seek reality advance, their longing for the truths of the Sharī'ah increases, as does their captivation by them and their following them. They consider the most minor aspect of the Prophet's (PBUH) practices to be their greatest aim, and strive to follow them and imitate them. For however higher divine revelation is than inspiration, the conduct of the Sharī'ah, which is the fruit of revelation, is higher to the same degree than the conduct of the Sufi path, the fruit of inspiration. Therefore, following the Prophet's (PBUH) practices is the basis and principal element of the Sufi path.

Second Point: The Sufi path and way of reality should not exceed being means. If they become the ultimate aim, the incontrovertible teachings and actions of the Sharī'ah and following the practices of the Prophet (PBUH) become merely matter of form, while the heart looks beyond them. That is to say, such a person thinks of his circle for the remembrance of God rather than the obligatory prayers; he is drawn more to his recitations and supplications than to his religious obligations; he is more concerned with avoiding offending against his order's rules of behaviour than with avoiding grievous sins. Whereas the recitations of the Sufi path cannot be the equivalent of the obligatory acts that constitute the incontestable matters of the Sharī'ah; they cannot take their place. The etiquette of the Sufi path and the invocations of Sufism should be a solace and a way of obtaining true pleasure from the obligatory acts; they should not themselves be the source. That is, the *tekke* should lead a person to perform the five daily prayers assiduously in the mosque. If he performs them there hurriedly as a formality, thinking that he will find true pleasure and perfection in the *tekke*, he is drawing away from reality.

Third Point: It is sometimes asked: "Can there be any Sufi path outside the practices of the Prophet (PBUH) and matters of the Sharī'ah?"

The Answer: There are some such paths, and there are not. There are, because some of the highest saints were executed by the sword of the Sharī'ah. And there are not, because the authoritative scholars among the saints (*muhakkikīn-i evliya*) have agreed on this rule of Sa'di Shirazi: "It is impossible, Sa'di, to be victorious on the way of felicity, except by following the Chosen One." That is, it is impossible for one outside the highway of God's Messenger (Upon whom be blessings and peace), who does not follow him, to attain the true lights of reality. The meaning of this is as follows:

God's Messenger (Peace and blessings be upon him) was the Seal of the Prophets and the addressee of God in the name of all mankind; mankind, therefore, cannot advance outside his highway; it is essential to be under his banner. But since ecstatics and those immersed in divine contemplation are not responsible for their opposition; and since man possesses certain subtle faculties that are not held accountable, and when such faculties dominate a person, he cannot be held responsible for opposing the obligations of the Sharī'ah; and since man possesses subtle faculties that just as they are not accountable, so they are not under the jurisdiction of the will, and cannot be controlled by the mind, for they do not heed the heart or the mind; certainly, when those faculties dominate in a person,—but only at that time—he does not fall from the rank of sainthood by opposing the Sharī'ah, he is held excused. On condition, however, that he does not deny or insult the truths of the Sharī'ah and rules of belief, or display contempt towards them. Even if he does not carry out the injunctions, he has to acknowledge that they are right. But if he is overcome by that state and assumes a position, I seek refuge with God, which infers denial and giving the lie to those incontestible truths, it is the sign that he has deviated from the path!

In Short: There are two groups that follow the Sufi path outside the bounds of the Sharī'ah.

One group: As described above, these people are either overwhelmed by their mental state, immersion, or ecstasy or intoxication, or they are dominated by some of their subtle faculties that do not heed the injunctions of religion nor listen to the will; they therefore transgress the bounds of the Sharī'ah. But this is not due to their disliking its rulings or not wanting to follow them; they are rather compelled to, involuntarily. Among this group are people of sainthood some of whom have even been temporary saints of high rank. But the authoritative scholars from among the saints (*muhakkikīn-i evliya*) have ruled that of these some have been not only outside the bounds of the Sharī'ah, but outside the bounds of Islam. But they are considered people of sainthood on condition that they have not denied any of the injunctions brought by Muhammad (Peace and blessings be upon him). It is that they do not think of them, or cannot keep them in view, or are not aware of them. They cannot not accept them if they are aware of them.

As for the second group, they are carried away by the brilliant pleasures of the Sufi path and way of reality, and since they cannot attain to the pleasures of the truths of the Sharī'ah, which are far more elevated, they suppose them to be dull formalities and are indifferent towards them. They gradually accept the idea that the Sharī'ah is an external shell, and that the reality they have found is the essential goal. They say: "I have found it; it is enough for me," and act in a way contrary to the injunctions of the Sharī'ah. Any in this group who are in their right minds are responsible; they stray from the path, indeed, become the playthings of Satan to an extent.

Fourth Point: Some persons who belong to the divisions of the people of misguidance and innovation are found acceptable by the Muslim community, while others, just like them and not apparently different, are rejected. I always used to wonder about this. For example, although someone like Zamakhshari was one of the most bigoted members of the Mu'tazilite sect, the authoritative Sunni scholars did not pronounce him an unbeliever or misguided, despite his severe objections; they rather searched for a way to exonerate him. But then they held that Mu'tazilite authorities like Abu 'Ali Jubba'i, who was far less bigoted than Zamakhshari, should be rejected and refuted. I was curious about this for a long time. Then through divine grace I understood that Zamakhshari's objections about the Sunnis arose from his love of his way, which he looked on as right. That is to say, for example, in his view God could be truly declared free of all fault and defect by saying that animals create their own actions. It was out of love for declaring God free of all fault that he did not accept the Sunnis' principles concerning the creation of actions. Whereas the other Mu'tazilite authorities were rejected because their inadequate intelligences could not aspire to the elevated principles of the Sunnis and they could not fit the Sunni's extensive laws within their own narrow ideas, and so denied them. In the same way that the Mu'tazilites opposed the Sunnis in theology, so the opposition of some followers of the Sufi path outside the Prophet's (PBUH) practices is of two kinds:

The first: Like Zamakhshari, out of love for their way or state, they remain somewhat indifferent towards the conduct of the Sharī'ah, because through it they cannot obtain the same degree of pleasure.

As for the other kind: God forbid! They think the conduct of the Sharī'ah is unimportant relatively to the principles of the Sufi path. For their narrow understanding cannot comprehend those broad pleasures, and their short stations cannot attain to that elevated conduct.

Eighth Allusion

This describes eight Abysses.

The First: Some people who embark on spiritual journeying do not conform completely to the practices of the Prophet (PBUH), and fall into the abyss of preferring sainthood to prophethood. It is proved in the Twenty-Fourth and Thirty-First Words how elevated is prophethood, and how dull sainthood is in relation to it.

The Second: Some of followers of the Sufi path fall into the abyss of preferring extremist saints to the Prophet's (PBUH) Companions and even of believing those saints to be prophets. It is proved decisively in the Twelfth and Twenty-Seventh Words and in the Addendum on the Companions, that the Companions acquired such qualities through conversation with the Prophet (PBUH) that cannot be attained through sainthood, and that the Companions cannot be surpassed, and that the saints can never reach the degree of the Companions.

The Third: Some of those who are excessively bigoted concerning the Sufi path oppose the practices of the Prophet (PBUH) and give them up because of their preference for the customs, conduct, and recitations of the Sufi way, which they never give up. In this way, they become slack in practising the conduct of the Sharī'ah, and fall into that abyss.

As is proved in many of the *Words*, and as veracious authorities (*muhakkikīn*) of the Sufi path like Imam Ghazali and Imam-i Rabbani said: "The degree of acceptance gained by following a single of the Prophet's (PBUH) practices cannot be won through a hundred personal practices and supererogatory acts of worship. And just as a single obligatory act is superior to a thousand acts taken from the Prophet's practices, so a single of those practices is superior to a thousand practices of Sufism."

The Fourth: Some extremist Sufis suppose inspiration to be like divine revelation and of similar kind to revelation, and fall into an abyss. It has been proved most definitely in the Twelfth Word and in the Twenty-Fifth Word on the Miraculousness of the Qur'an, how elevated, universal, and sacred is divine revelation, and how insignificant and dull inspirations are in comparison.

The Fifth: Some Sufis who do not understand the essence of the Sufi path, in order to strengthen the weak, encourage the slack, and to lighten the hardships and weariness arising from strenuous service, find the lights, illuminations, and wonders, which are not sought but given, to be pleasurable, and they become captivated by them and fall into the abyss of preferring them to worship, acts of service, and recitation of supplications. It is mentioned briefly in the Third Point of the Sixth Allusion in the present treatise and proved decisively in others of the Words that this world is the realm of service and not the realm of reward. People who seek their recompense here, both transform enduring, perpetual fruits into a transitory and temporary form, and find permanence in this world pleasing, so they do not yearn for the Intermediate Realm. Quite simply, they love the life of this world in one respect, since they find a sort of hereafter within it.

The Sixth: Some of those who embark on spiritual journeying fall into an abyss by confusing the shades and shadows and partial samples of the stations of sainthood with its fundamental, universal stations. As is proved clearly in the Second Branch of the Twenty-Fourth Word and in others of the Words, the sun becomes numerous by means of mirrors and thousands of similitudes of the sun possess light and heat like the sun itself, despite their paltriness in relation to the actual sun. In exactly the same way, the stations of the prophets and the great saints possess shades and shadows. Those who journey with the spirit enter these, and see themselves as greater than those great saints, or even to have advanced further than the prophets, and so fall into an abyss. However, the way to avoid this is to always take the principles of belief and fundamentals of the Sharī'ah as one's basis and guide, and to look on one's illuminations and visions as opposed to them.

The Seventh: Some of the people of illumination and ecstasy fall into an abyss in their spiritual journeyings by preferring pride, complaint, ecstatic utterances, public regard, and being referred to, to offering thanks and supplication, beseeching Almighty God, and self-sufficiency. Whereas the highest degree is Muhammadan worship, which is termed "belovedness." The basis and essence of worship is to manifest the perfection of that reality by supplicating and beseeching Almighty God, showing deep humility before Him, offering thanks, and through impotence and want, and by displaying self-sufficiency in the face of others. Some of the great saints have involuntarily and temporarily become proud and made complaints and ecstatic utterances, but they should not be followed voluntarily on such points; they are rightly-guided but not the guide; their way may not be taken!

The Eighth: Some of those who journey spiritually are self-centred and precipitate and want to consume in this world the fruits of sainthood, which will be given in the hereafter; they fall into an abyss by seeking them on their spiritual journeyings. But, as such verses as, "The life of this world is but goods and chattels"[5] proclaim, and as is proved decisively in many of the Words, a single fruit in the realm of eternity is superior to a thousand gardens in this fleeting world. For this reason, those blessed fruits should not be consumed here. If without being sought they are given to eat here, they should be thanked for, and deemed divine favours bestowed, not as reward, but for encouragement.

Ninth Allusion

Here we shall describe briefly nine out of the truly numerous fruits and benefits of the Sufi path.

The First is the unfolding and clarification, by means of the Sufi paths that are on the straight way, of the truths of faith, which are the keys, sources, and springs of the eternal treasuries of everlasting happiness; it is their manifestation at the degree of the vision of certainty.

The Second: Since the Sufi path is a means of working the heart, the mainspring of the human machine, and of causing the heart to stir the other subtle faculties into motion, it drives them to fulfil the purposes of their creation, and thus makes a person into a true human being.

The Third: On the journey to the Intermediate Realm and the hereafter, it is to join one of the lines of the Sufi orders, and become a member of its luminous caravan on the road to eternity. The person is thus saved from loneliness and finds the friendship of the other members in this world and in the Intermediate Realm; and relying on their consensus and accord in the face of the attacks of doubts and fears, and seeing each of their masters as a powerful support and proof, he repulses through them those doubts and instances of misguidance.

The Fourth is to understand by means of the pure Sufi way the knowledge of God to be found in belief in God, and the pleasure of love of God within the knowledge of God, and by so understanding, to be saved from the desolation of this world and man's exile in the universe. We have proved in many of the Words that the happiness of both worlds, and pain-free pleasure, and intimacy untainted by loneliness, and true delight, and untroubled happiness are all to be found in faith and the reality of Islam. As is explained in the Second Word, faith produces the seed of a Tuba-tree of Paradise. It is through the training and nurturing of the Sufi path that the seed grows and develops.

The Fifth is to perceive through an awakening of the heart elicited by the Sufi path and remembrance of God, the subtle truths contained in the obligations of the Sharīʻah, and to appreciate them. Then the person obeys and performs his worship, not under compulsion, but with longing.

The Sixth is to rise to the station of reliance on God and the rank of submission to Him and winning His pleasure, which are the means of obtaining true delight, real solace, painfree pleasure, and friendship untainted by loneliness.

The Seventh is, through sincerity, which is the essential precondition for travelling the Sufi way and its most valuable result, to be delivered from base qualities like implicitly associating partners with God, hypocrisy, and artificiality. It is also to be saved, through purifying the soul, which is like the surgical operation of the Sufi path, from the dangers of the evil-commanding soul and the perils of egotism.

The Eighth: Through the regard, sense of the divine presence, and powerful intentions of the Sufi path, gained by recalling God with the heart and reflecting on Him with the mind, this is to transform customary actions into worship and make mundane dealings into actions benefiting the hereafter. Utilizing the capital of life, it is to make all its minutes into seeds that will produce the shoots of eternal happiness.

The Ninth is to struggle to be a perfect human being through journeying with the heart and striving with the spirit and spiritual progress; that is to say, to be a true believer and total Muslim; that is, to gain not superficial belief, but the reality of belief and the reality of Islam; that is, to be directly the bondsman of the Glorious Creator of the Universe, in the universe and in one respect as the universe's representative, and to be His addressee, and friend, and beloved, and to be a mirror to Him; and through showing man to be on the best of patterns, it is to prove man's superiority to the angels. It is to fly through the lofty stations with the Sharī'ah's wings of faith and works, and to behold eternal happiness in this world, and even to enter upon it. . . .

Second Important Matter [of the Eighteenth Letter]

Question: The Unity of Existence is considered by many people to be the most elevated station, but there was no explicit sign of it among the Companions and foremost the four Rightly-Guided Caliphs, who were at the level of the greatest sainthood (*velāyet-i kübra*), or among the Imams of the Prophet's Family and foremost the five People of the Cloak, or the great interpreters of the law and the generation following the Companions and foremost the founders of the four schools of law. So did those who lived later advance further than them? Did they find a better highway on which to proceed?

The Answer: God forbid! Nobody at all has the ability to advance further than those purified ones who were the stars and heirs closest to the Sun of Prophethood; the highway is indeed theirs.

As for the Unity of Existence (*Vahdet-ül-Vücud*), it is a way and a state, but it is deficient. However, because it is illuminating and pleasurable, most of those who have reached that degree on their spiritual journeyings have not wanted to leave it; they have remained there and supposed it to be the ultimate degree.

If the spirit of the person who takes this way is divested of materiality and intermediaries and he has rent the veil of causes, and is immersed in a state of witnessing (*şuhūd*: direct vision), then an experiential—not pertaining to knowledge—unity of existence that arises not from the Unity of Existence but from the Unity of Witnessing (*vahdet-üş-şuhūd*), may obtain for him a certain attainment, a spiritual station. He may even reach the degree of denying the universe for God's sake. But if he is submerged in causes and preoccupied with materiality, for him, the Unity of Existence may mean going so far as denying God on account of the universe.

Yes, the great highway is the highway of the Companions, and those that followed them, and the Purified Ones. Their universal rule was, "the reality of things is constant." In accordance with the sense of "There is nothing that resembles Him,"[6] Almighty God has absolutely nothing that resembles Him. He is utterly beyond being comprehended in place or class and being divided into parts. His relation with beings is creativity. Beings are not imaginings or fancies as those who followed the way of the Unity of Existence said. Visible things too are Almighty God's works. Everything is not "Him," everything is "from Him." For events cannot be pre-eternal. We shall make this matter easier to understand with two comparisons:

The First: For example, there is a king. Through his name of Just Judge he has a Ministry of Justice that shows the manifestation of that name. Another of his names is *Khalifa*, and the Shaykh al-Islam's Office and learned institution are the manifestations of that name. He has also the name of Commander-in-Chief, through which all the offices of the army perform their actions; the army is the manifestation of that name. Now, if someone were to appear and say: "The king is only the Just Judge, he has no office or ministry other than that of justice," then the attributes and states of the religious scholars in the Shaykh al-Islam's Office would have to be applied—not actually but theoretically—to the officials of the Ministry of Justice; a secondary and shadowy Shaykh al-Islam's Office would have an imaginary existence within the actual Ministry of Justice. Again in hypothetical fashion, the dealings and states of the Army Office would be ascribed to the officials of the Judiciary, an unreal Army Office would be imagined there, and so on. In this situation, the king's true name is the name of Just Judge and his true sovereignty is his sovereignty in the Ministry of Justice. His names like *Khalifa*, Commander-in-Chief, and Sultan are not actual, but hypothetical. However, the nature of kingship and reality of sovereignty demand all the names in actuality. And actual names require and necessitate actual offices.

Thus, the sovereignty of divinity necessitates in actuality numerous sacred names like All-Merciful, Provider, Bestower, Creator, Doer, Munificent, and Compassionate. And those true and actual names require actual mirrors. Now, since the followers of the Unity of Existence say: "There is no existent but He," they downgrade the reality of beings to the level of imagination. Almighty God's names of Necessary Existent, Existent, One, and Single have true manifestations and spheres of application. For sure, if their mirrors and spheres of application were not real and were imaginary and non-existent, it would not harm them. And perhaps if there were no colour of existence in the mirror of true existence, they would be purer and more brilliant, but the manifestations of such names as Merciful, Provider, Subduer, Compeller, and Creator would not be real, they would be hypothetical. However, those names are realities like the name of Existent, they cannot be shadows; they are essential, not secondary.

Thus, the Companions and great interpreters of the law and Imams of the Family of the Prophet said: "The reality of things is constant;" Almighty God has a manifestation through all His names in actuality. Through His creativity, all things have an accidental existence. For sure, in relation to the Necessarily Existent's existence their existence is an extremely weak and unstable shadow, but it is not imagination, it is not fancy. Almighty God gives existence through His name of Creator and He continues that existence.

Second Comparison: For example, on the four walls of this house are four full-length mirrors. However much the house is depicted together with the other three mirrors in all the mirrors, each holds the things in itself in accordance with its own makeup and colour; it reflects a similitude of the house that is particular to itself. Now, two men enter the house. One of them looks at one of the mirrors and says: "Everything is within it." When he hears of the other mirrors and the images in them, he applies what he hears to a tiny corner of the one mirror whose contents are shadows twice over, whose reality has shrunk and has changed. He also says: "I see it thus, in which case reality is thus." The other man says to him, "Yes, you see it like that and what you see is true. But in actuality and reality the true form of reality is not like that. There are other mirrors besides the one you looked at; they are not the shadow of shadows and as tiny as you saw."

Thus, each of the divine names requires a different mirror. And since Merciful and Provider, for example, are real and fundamental, they require beings worthy of them who are needy for sustenance and compassion. Just as All-Merciful requires real beings with spirits needy for sustenance in a real world, so too, All-Compassionate requires a paradise which is thus real. To maintain that only the names of Existent, Necessarily Existent, and Single One of Unity are real and that the other names are mere shadows within them, is a sort of injustice towards those other names.

It is due to this mystery that the great highway is surely the highway of the Companions, the Purified Ones, the Imams of the Prophet's Family, and the great interpreters of the law and founders of the four schools of law, who possessed greater sainthood, and were directly the first class of the Qur'an's students. . . .

An Addendum to the Second Matter

Question: Muhyi'l-Din al-'Arabi considered the Unity of Existence to be of the highest level. Likewise, some of the great saints who took the path of love followed him. However, you say that this matter is not of the highest level, and is not real; that it is rather the way, to a degree, of those who become intoxicated and immersed in the divine, and of the people of love and ecstasy. So what, briefly, is the high level of the affirmation of divine unity pointed out by the clear verses of the Qur'an, through the mystery of the legacy of prophethood (*verāset-i nübüvvet*)? Can you explain it?

The Answer: It is a hundred times beyond the ability of an utterly powerless unfortunate like myself to judge those elevated stations with his limited thought. I shall just explain one or two extremely brief points proceeding from the effulgence of the All-Wise Qur'an. Perhaps they will be useful in understanding the matter.

First Point: There are numerous reasons for becoming embroiled in the way of the Unity of Existence. One or two of them may be explained as follows:

The First Reason: Because they could not squeeze into their brains the maximum degree of the creativity of dominicality, nor entirely establish in their hearts the idea that everything, through the mystery of divine oneness (*ehadiyet*), is held directly in the grasp of dominicality (*rubūbiyet*) and that all things have existence through divine power, choice, and will, those who took that way were obliged to say that everything is either Him, or does not have existence, or is imaginary, or is His manifestation or emanation.

The Second Reason: The mark of passionate love is to want never to be separated from the beloved and to flee desperately from such separation; to tremble at the thought of parting, to fear distance from the beloved as though fearing Hell, and to abominate transience; to love union with the love of one's own spirit and life, and to yearn for nearness to the beloved as though longing for Paradise. Thus, through adhering to a manifestation of divine immediacy in all things, those who took the way of the Unity of Existence disregarded separation and distance; supposing union and meeting to be permanent, they said: "There is no existent but He"; through the intoxication of love and as demanded by the ecstasy of permanence, meeting, and union, they imagined that in the Unity of Existence was a most pleasurable way of illumination whereby they could be saved from the dreadfulness of separation.

That is to say, the first reason sprang from the fact that their intellects were unable to reach up to some of the truths of belief, which were extremely broad and elevated; they could not comprehend them and had not developed completely in regard to faith. And the source of the second reason was the extraordinary unfolding of their hearts in respect of love, and their wondrous expansion and breadth.

However, the supreme level of divine unity that the Purified Ones (*asfiya*)—who were the people of sobriety and great saints of the legacy of prophethood—saw through the clear expositions of the Qur'an is both extremely elevated, and shows both the maximum level of dominicality and creativity, and that all the divine names are real. It preserves the Qur'an's principles and does not spoil the balance of the decrees of dominicality. For they say that together with the oneness of His essence and His being free of space, with His knowledge Almighty God encompasses and determines directly all things together with all their attributes, and through His will He chooses and specifies them, and through His power He creates them. He creates and directs the whole universe as though it were a single being.

He creates the huge spring with the same ease as creating a flower. Nothing obstructs anything else. There is no fragmentation in His regarding things. He is present everywhere at the same instant through the disposal of His knowledge and power. There is no division or distribution in His disposal. This mystery has been expounded and proved completely in the Sixteenth Word and in the Second Stopping-Place of the Thirty-Second Word. Since, according to the rule, "Comparisons are incontestible," no attention should be paid to defects in comparisons and allegories, I shall set forth a very faulty comparison so that the difference between the two ways may be understood to a degree.

For example, let us imagine a huge, matchless, and wondrously adorned peacock that can fly from east to west in an instant, and opens and closes its wings, which stretch from north to south, are adorned with hundreds of thousands of fine patterns, and in every single feather of which are included brilliant arts. Now, there are two men observing it; they want to fly up with the wings of the intellect and heart to the elevated qualities of this bird, to its wondrous decorations. One looks at the peacock's appearance and form and the marvellous inscriptions of power on all its feathers; he loves it with extreme passion and ardour; he in part abandons his attentive reflective thought, and clings on to love. But then he sees that every day those lovable decorations change and are transformed. Those objects of his love, which he worships, disappear and are lost.

While he should have said that through true divine unity, which he could not encompass with his mind, and absolute dominicality and the oneness of the divine essence, they were the artistic decorations of an Inscriber possessing universal creativity, he said instead—in order to console himself—that the spirit of the peacock was so sublime that its maker was within it, or that the peacock had become Him, and that since its spirit had become one with its being, and its being combined with its outward appearance, its spirit's perfection and being's exaltedness displayed those manifestations, displaying every moment a different inscription and beauty; it was not a true creation through its will, but a manifestation, an emanation.

As for the other man, he said that those harmonious, orderly decorations so full of art definitely required will, choice, intention, and purpose. It was impossible for there to be a manifestation without will, an emanation without choice.

Yes, the peacock had a beautiful and elevated nature, but it could not be the doer; it was passive. It could not become one with the active agent. Its spirit was fine and exalted, but it could not be the creator and disposer, only receptive and a means. For observedly in each of its feathers was an art performed with infinite wisdom and an inscription and decoration made through an infinite power. And these could not occur without will and choice. The arts indicating perfect wisdom within perfect power, and perfect dominicality and mercy within perfect wisdom were not the work of some sort of manifestation. The scribe who had written that gilded notebook could not be inside it and be united with it. The notebook rather only had contact with the nib of the scribe's pen. In which case, the wondrous decorations of the similitude of the peacock known as the universe were a gilded missive of the peacock's Creator.

Now, look at the peacock and read the missive. Say to its Scribe: "What wonders God has willed! Blessed be God! Glory be to God!" The person who supposes the missive to be the scribe, or the scribe to be inside the letter, or fancies the missive to be imagination, has surely hidden his reason in the veils of love, and is unable to see the true form of reality.

Among the varieties of passionate love, the one most conducive to the way of the Unity of Existence, is love of this world. When it turns into true love, love of this world, which is temporary (*mecazī*), it is transformed into the Unity of Existence. A person loves his personal beloved with worldly (*mecazī*) love.

Then, unable to accept in his heart his beloved's transience and ephemerality, he consoles himself by saying that his beloved is a mirror reflecting the beauty of the True Object of Love and Worship, and attaches himself to a reality, so acquiring permanence for him through true love.

In the same way, when, due to the constant blows of death and separation, the strange love of the person who takes the huge world and the universe in its totality as his beloved is transformed into true love, he seeks refuge in the way of the Unity of Existence, in order to save that great beloved of his from death and separation. If he has extremely powerful and elevated faith, it becomes a pleasurable, luminous, acceptable level, as with those resembling Muhyi'l-Din al-'Arabi. However, there is the possibility of falling into various abysses, embracing materiality, and becoming submerged in causes. As for the Unity of Witnessing, it is harmless; it is an exalted way of the people of sobriety.

O God, show us what is indeed the truth, and make us follow it!

Glory be unto You! We have no knowledge save that which You have taught us; indeed, You are All-Knowing, All-Wise.[7]

Flashes 58–61
My Dear Brother!

A Summary of Your Second Question: Muhyiddin al-'Arabi said: "The spirit's createdness consists of its unfolding." With this question you are urging a powerless wretch like me to contest an awesomely brilliant scholar of reality and genius of the occult sciences like Muhyiddin al-'Arabi. However, relying on the teachings of the Qur'an I can attempt the discussion; even if I am only a fly, I can rise higher than that eagle.

My brother! You should understand that Hadhrat Muhyiddin would not deceive, but he could be deceived. He was rightly-guided, but could not act as guide with all his works. What he saw was correct, but it was not reality. The reality of man's spirit, about which you ask, is explained in the Twenty-Ninth Word, the discussion about the spirit.

Yes, in respect of its nature, the spirit is a law proceeding from the divine command, but it is a living law clothed in external existence and possessing external existence. Hadhrat Muhyiddin thought of it only from the point of view of its essential nature. The way of the Unity of Existence considers the existence of things to be imaginary. He had wondrous visions and unveiled the realities, but since he had chosen an independent way, he was compelled to apply, artificially and with forced interpretations, certain Qur'anic verses to his way and visions, thus marring the clarity of the verses. In others of his treatises he expounds the straight highway of the Qur'an and of the Sunnis. He was a holy man who held a position all his own, and he was one of the well-accepted, but he exceeded the mark in his unbalanced disclosures, and in many matters opposed the majority of the learned authorities (*muhakkikīn*).

It is because of this that although he was such an elevated and wondrous spiritual pole, unequalled down the ages, it is as though his particular way was very short and restricted to Sadruddin al-Qunawi, and that his works were only rarely benefited from by those on the straight path. Many of the authoritative purified scholars (*muhakkikīn-i asfiya*) do not encourage study of those valuable works, and some of them even prevent it.

Lengthy study and a very lofty, broad view are needed to show the fundamental differences together with their sources between the Hadhrat Muhyiddin's way and that of the exacting (lit. verifying) scholars (*ehl-i tahkik*). Yes, the differences are so fine and profound and the sources, so elevated and extensive that Hadhrat Muhyiddin has not been censured and has continued to be accepted. For if in regard to thought, scholarship, and illumination the difference and sources had become apparent, it would have been very humiliating for him, and he would have been seen to be seriously in error. Since the difference is so profound, we shall try to show it and the sources briefly by means of a comparison, as well as Hadhrat Muhyiddin's errors in the matter.

For example, the sun appears in a mirror. The mirror both contains the sun, and is qualified by it. That is to say, in one respect the sun is present in the mirror, and in another it adorns the mirror, becoming a brilliant colour, attribute and quality of it. If the mirror had been a camera, it would have fixed the sun's image on photographic paper. In both these cases, the sun appearing in the mirror, and its semblance on the photographic paper, and its aspect that adorns the mirror and becomes like a quality of the mirror, are other than the actual sun. They are not the sun, but the sun's manifestation, which has assumed another existence. As for the existence of the sun that is visible in the mirror, even if it is not identical with the sun that is visible outside, since it is tied to it and points to it, it is supposed to have the same existence.

In consequence of this comparison, it may be said: "There is nothing apart from the actual sun in the mirror," meaning that the mirror contains it and intending the sun's external existence in the mirror. But if it is said that the sun's extended reflection, which has become like an attribute or quality of the mirror, and its image which has been transposed to the photographic paper is the sun, it is wrong; it is an error to say: "There is nothing in them other than the sun." For there is the reflection on the mirror's shining face and the image formed on its back, and these have their own separate existences. For sure, those existences are from the sun's manifestation, but they are not the sun. The human mind and imagination resemble this example of the mirror. It is as follows:

The information in the mirror of man's thought also has two faces: in one respect it is knowledge, in another, it is known. If we suppose the mind to contain what is known, then the known thing becomes something known by the mind; its existence is something different to the mind. If we suppose the mind to be qualified by the thing, it becomes an attribute or quality of the mind; then the thing becomes knowledge and has an external existence. Even if the existence of the thing known is essential (*jawhari*), it has an accidental external existence like the knowledge.

Thus, according to these two comparisons, the universe is a mirror. The true nature of beings is also a mirror; they are subject to divine creation through pre-eternal power. In one respect, each being is a sort of mirror to one of the names of the Pre-Eternal Sun, displaying one of its embroideries. The followers of Hadhrat Muhyiddin's way unveiled them only in respect of being mirrors and containers, revealing the similitude of their existence in the mirror, from the point of view of denial. Supposing the reflection to be identical with the thing reflected, they did not think of other levels. They said: "There is no existent but He," and were in error. They almost went so far as to deny the fundamental rule: "The reality of beings is constant."

As for the people of reality, they have seen through the mystery of the legacy of prophethood and the definite statements of the Qur'an that the embroideries and inscriptions that come into existence in the mirrors of beings through divine power and will are His works. They are "all from Him"; they are not "all Him.8 Things have an existence and their existence is constant to a degree. For sure it is weak compared to that of the Necessary Existence, like an illusion or imagining, but through the Pre-Eternal All-Powerful One's creation, will, and power, it exists.

In the comparison, the sun in the mirror has an existence through its similitude apart from its external existence. And its expanded reflection also, which gives colour to and adorns the mirror, has an accidental and separate external existence. And the sun's image that is depicted on the photographic paper on the back of the mirror also has a separate and accidental external existence.

Similarly, the inscriptions of beings, which appear through the manifestations of the sacred divine names—occurring through will, choice, and power—in the mirror of the universe and mirrors of the quintessential natures of things, have a created existence separate from the Necessary Existence. And this existence has been given a permanence through pre-eternal power. But if the connection were to be severed, all things would at once cease to be. Because for their continued existence, all things are every instant in need of their Creator's preserving them. "The reality of things is constant," but it is constant and permanent only through His making it so.

Thus, Hadhrat Muhyiddin's saying that "Spirit is not created; it is a reality proceeding from the world of the divine command and from the attribute of will," is contrary to many clear statements of the Qur'an and Hadiths, and according to the investigation above, he was confused, deceived, and had not seen the weak existences of things.

The places of manifestation of such divine names as Creator and Provider cannot be illusions or imaginary. Since the names have a reality, their places of manifestation also have an external reality.

ADDENDUM
[TO THE TWENTY-SIXTH WORD]

In the Name of God, the Merciful, the Compassionate.

[This short Addendum has great importance; it is beneficial for everyone.]

The ways leading to Almighty God are truly numerous. While all true ways are taken from the Qur'an, some are shorter, safer, and more general than others. Of these ways taken from the Qur'an is that of impotence, poverty, compassion, and reflection, from which, with my defective understanding, I have benefited.

Like ecstatic love, impotence is a path which, by way of worship, leads to winning God's love; but it is safer. Poverty too leads to the divine name of All-Merciful. And, like ecstatic love, compassion leads to the name of All-Compassionate, but it is a swifter and broader path. Also like ecstatic love, reflection leads to the name of All-Wise, but it is richer, broader, and more brilliant path. This path consists not of ten steps like the ten subtle faculties of some of the Sufi paths employing silent recollection, nor of seven stages like the seven souls of those practising public recitation, but of four steps. It is reality (*hakikat*), rather than a Sufi way (*tarikat*). It is Sharī'ah.

However, let it not be misunderstood. It means to see one's impotence, poverty and faults before Almighty God, not to fabricate them or display them to people. The method of this short path is to follow the practices of the Prophet (PBUH), perform the religious obligations and give up serious sins. Especially, it is to perform the prescribed prayers correctly and with attention, and following them to say the *tesbihat*.

The verse, "Therefore, do not justify yourselves," points to the first step.

The verse, "And be not like those who forget God, and He therefore makes them forget their own selves," points to the second step.

The verse, "Whatever good happens to you is from God, but whatever evil befalls you is from yourself," points to the third step.

The verse, "Everything will perish save His countenance," points to the fourth step.

A brief explanation of these four steps is as follows:

The First Step

As the verse, "Therefore, do not justify yourselves" suggests, it is to not purify the soul. For on account of his nature and innate disposition, man loves himself. Indeed, he loves himself before anything else, and only himself. He sacrifices everything other than himself to his own soul. He praises himself in a manner befitting some object worthy of worship. He absolves and exonerates himself from faults in the same way. As far as he possibly can, he does not see faults as being appropriate for him, and does not accept them. He defends himself passionately as though worshipping himself. Even, using on himself the members and faculties given him as part of his nature in order to praise and glorify the True Object of Worship, he displays the meaning of the verse, "Who takes as his god his own desires." He considers himself, he relies on himself, he fancies himself. Thus, his purification and cleansing at this stage, in this step, is to not purify himself; it is not to absolve himself.

The Second Step

As the verse, "And be not like those who forget God, and He therefore makes them forget their own selves" teaches, man is oblivious of himself and not aware of himself. If he thinks of death, it is in relation to others. If he sees transience and decline, he does not attribute them to himself. His evil-commanding soul demands that when it comes to inconvenience and service of others, he forgets himself, but when it comes to receiving his recompense, and to benefits and enjoyment, he thinks of himself and takes his own part fervently. His purification, cleansing, and training at this stage is the reverse of this state. That is to say, when oblivious of himself, it is not to be oblivious. That is, to forget himself when it comes to pleasure, and ambition and greed, and to think of himself when it comes to death and service of others.

The Third Step

As the verse, "Whatever good happens to you is from God, but whatever evil befalls you is from yourself" teaches, the nature of the evil-commanding soul demands that it always considers goodness to be from itself and it becomes vain and conceited. Thus, in this Step, a person sees only faults, defects, impotence, and poverty in himself, and understands that all his good qualities and perfections are bounties bestowed on him by the All-Glorious Creator. He gives thanks instead of being conceited, and offers praise instead of boasting. According to the meaning of the verse, "Truly he succeeds who purifies it," his purification at this stage is to know his perfection to lie in imperfection, his power in impotence, and his wealth in poverty.

The Fourth Step

As the verse, "Everything will perish save His countenance" teaches, the evil-commanding soul considers itself to be free and independent and to exist of itself. Because of this, man claims to possess a sort of dominicality. He harbours a hostile rebelliousness towards his True Object of Worship. Thus, through understanding the following fact, he is saved from this. The fact is this:

According to the apparent meaning of things, which looks to each thing itself, everything is transitory, wanting, accidental, non-existent. But according to the meaning that signifies something other than itself and in respect of each thing being a mirror to the All-Glorious Maker's names and charged with various duties, each is a witness, it is witnessed, and it is existent. The purification and cleansing of a person at this stage is as follows:

In his existence he is non-existent, and in his non-existence he has existence. That is to say, if he values himself and attributes existence to himself, he is in the darkness of non-existence as great as the universe. That is, if he relies on his individual existence and is unmindful of the True Giver of Existence, he has an individual light of existence like that of a fire-fly and is submerged in an endless darkness of non-existence and separation. But if he gives up egotism and sees that he is a mirror of the manifestations of the True Giver of Existence, he gains all beings and an infinite existence. For he who finds the Necessarily Existent One, the manifestation of Whose names all beings display, finds everything.

CONCLUSION

The four steps in this way of impotence, poverty, compassion, and reflection have been explained in the twenty-six Words so far written, which are concerned with knowledge of reality, the reality of the Shari'a, and the wisdom of the Qur'an. So here, we shall allude briefly to only one or two points, as follows:

This path is shorter, because it consists of four steps. When impotence causes a person to give up the soul, it turns him directly to the All-Powerful One of Glory. Whereas, when a person on the way of ecstatic love, the swiftest way, gives up the soul, his way directs him to a temporary (*mecazī*) beloved. Only when he discovers the beloved's impermanence does he turn to the True Beloved.

Also, this path is much safer, because the ravings and high-flown claims of the soul are not present on it. For apart from impotence, poverty, and defect, the soul possesses nothing so that it oversteps its mark.

Also, this path is much broader and more universal. For in order to attain to a constant awareness of God's presence, a person is not compelled to imagine the universe to be condemned to non-existence and to declare: "There is no existent but He," like those who believe in the Unity of Existence, nor to suppose the universe to be condemned to imprisonment in absolute oblivion and to say, "There is nothing witnessed but He," like those who believe in the Unity of Witnessing. Rather, since the Qur'an has most explicitly pardoned the universe and released it from execution and imprisonment, the person on this path disregards the above, and dismissing beings from working on their own account and employing them on account of the All-Glorious Creator, and in the duty of manifesting the Most Beautiful Names and being mirrors to them, he considers them from the point of view of signifying something other than themselves; and being saved from absolute heedlessness, he enters the divine presence permanently; he finds a way leading to the Almighty God in everything.

In Short: Dismissing beings from working on account of other beings, this way is to not look at them as signifying themselves.

Second Matter
[of the Fourth Topic of the Twenty-Sixth Letter]

Explanations of the three questions asked by the former teacher (*hoja*) are to be found in various parts of the *Risale-i Nur*. For now we shall just make brief allusion to them.

His First Question: Muhyi'l-Din al-'Arabi said in his letter to Fakhr al-Din Razi: "To know God is different to knowing He exists." What does this mean and what did he intend by saying it?

Firstly: In the introduction to the Twenty-Second Word, which you read to him, the comparison and example showing the difference between the true affirmation of divine unity and its superficial affirmation point to what was intended.

While the Second and Third Stopping-Places of the Thirty-Second Word and its Aims, elucidate it.

And secondly: Muhyi'l-Din al-'Arabi said that to Fakhr al-Din Razi, who was a leading authority on theology, because the explications of the tenets of belief and the existence of the Necessary Existent and divine unity offered by the authoritative scholars of the principles of religion (*usūl-üd-din*) and theology (*kalām*) were insufficient in his view.

Yes, the knowledge of God gained through theology does not afford a complete knowledge and a complete sense of the divine presence. However, when gained through the method of the Qur'an of Miraculous Exposition, it affords both complete knowledge and a total sense of the divine presence. God willing, all the parts of the *Risale-i Nur* perform the duty of an electric lamp on that light-filled highway of the Qur'an of Miraculous Exposition.

Furthermore, however deficient in Muhyi'l-Din al-'Arabi's view was the knowledge of God Fakhr al-Din Razi obtained by means of theology, the knowledge of God attained on the Sufi way is similarly deficient in relation to the knowledge obtained through the legacy of prophethood directly from the All-Wise Qur'an. For in order to attain a constant sense of the divine presence, the way of Muhyi'l-Din al-'Arabi said: "There is no existent save He," going so far as to deny the existence of the universe. As for the others, again to gain a constant sense of the divine presence, they said: "There is none witnessed save He," entering a strange state as though casting the universe into absolute oblivion.

However, the knowledge of God obtained from the All-Wise Qur'an, in addition to affording a constant sense of the Divine presence, neither condemns the universe to non-existence, nor imprisons it in absolute oblivion. It rather releases it from its purposelessness and employs it in Almighty God's name. Everything becomes a mirror yielding knowledge of God. As Sa'di Shirazi said: "To the conscious gaze each leaf is a book yielding knowledge of the divine."

In everything a window opens up onto knowledge of God.

In some of the *Words* we have illustrated with the following comparison the differences between the way of the scholars of theology and the true highway taken from the Qur'an: in order to have water, some is brought from a distant place by means of pipes, digging down under mountains. And some of it is obtained by digging wells everywhere. The first sort is fraught with difficulties; the pipes become blocked or broken. But those who know how to dig wells and extract water can find water everywhere with no trouble.

In exactly the same way, utilizing the impossibility of causation and causal sequences, the scholars of theology cut the chains of causes at the extremities of the world and then they proved the existence of the Necessarily Existent One. They travelled a long road. However, the true highway of the Wise Qur'an finds water everywhere and extracts it. Each of its verses causes water to flow forth wherever it strikes, like the Staff of Moses. Each verse makes everything recite the rule: "In everything is a sign indicating that He is One."

Furthermore, faith is not gained only through knowledge; many of the subtle faculties have their share of faith. When food enters the stomach, it is distributed in various ways to various members. Similarly, after entering the stomach of the mind, the matters of faith that come through knowledge are absorbed by the spirit, heart, inner heart, soul, and other subtle faculties; each receives its share according to its degree. If they do not receive their share, faith is deficient. Muhyi'l-Din al-'Arabi was reminding Fakhr al-Din Razi of this point.

FOURTH MATTER
[OF THE FOURTH TOPIC OF THE TWENTY-SIXTH LETTER]

You ask concerning the wisdom contained in [the Hadith]: "Renew your belief by means of 'There is no god but God.'" The wisdom in it has been mentioned in many of the Words and one aspect of it is as follows:

Since man himself and the world in which he lives are being continuously renewed, he needs constantly to renew his faith. For in reality each individual human being consists of many individuals. He may be considered as a different individual to the number of the years of his life, or to the number of the days or even the hours of his life. For since a single individual is subject to time, he is like a model and each passing day clothes him in the form of another individual.

Furthermore, just as there is within man this plurality and renewal, so also is the world in which he lives in motion. It goes and is replaced by another. It varies constantly. Every day opens the door of another world. As for faith, it is both the light of the life of each individual in that person, and it is the light of the world in which he lives. And as for "There is no god but God," it is a key with which to turn on the light.

Then the instinctual soul, desire, doubts, and Satan exercise great influence over man. In order to damage his faith, they are much of the time able to take advantage of his negligence, to trick him with their wiles, and thus to extinguish the light of belief with doubts and uncertainty. Also, man is prone to act and utter words which apparently oppose the Sharī'ah, and which in the view of some religious authorities are no less then unbelief. Therefore, there is a need to renew belief all the time, every hour, every day.

Question: The masters of scholastic theology wrapped up the world in the abbreviated concepts of contingency and createdness and having disposed of it, so to speak, proved divine unity. And one school of Sufis, in order to experience God's presence and affirm His unity fully, said: "Nothing is observed but Him." They thus forgot the universe and drew the veil of oblivion over it, and then fully experienced the divine presence. Another school of Sufis, in order to truly affirm divine unity and enter God's presence at the highest degree, said: "There is no existent but Him." They relegated the universe to the level of imagination and cast it into non-existence, and then fully entered the divine presence. But you point out that in the Qur'an is a mighty highway besides these three ways. And you say that its mark is the phrases: "There is nothing sought but Him," and, "There is nothing worshipped but Him." Can you show me a brief proof of the affirmation of divine unity provided by this highway and point out a short way leading to it?

The Answer: All the *Words* and *Letters* in the *Risale-i Nur* point out that highway. For now, as you wish, we shall indicate concisely an extensive, lengthy and mighty proof of it.

Each thing in the world ascribes every other thing to its own Creator. And each artistically fashioned object in this world demonstrates that all such objects are the works of its own fashioner. And each creative act in the universe proves that all creative acts are the acts of its own author. And each name that is manifested in beings indicates that all names are the names and titles of the one whom it itself signifies. That is to say, each thing is a direct proof of divine unity and a window yielding knowledge of God.

Each object, especially if it is animate, is a miniature specimen of the universe, a seed of the world, and a fruit of the globe of the earth. Since this is so, the one who created the miniature specimen, seed and fruit must also be the one who created the universe. For the fruit's creator cannot be other than the creator of the tree that bears it.

And so, in the same way that each object ascribes all other objects to its own fashioner, each act ascribes all other acts to its author. For we see that each creative act appears as the tip of a law of creativity that is so extensive as to encompass most other creatures, and so long as to reach from particles to galaxies. That is to say, whoever performs the creative act must be the author of all the creative acts which are tied to the universal law that encompasses those beings and stretches from particles to galaxies.

For sure, the one who gives life to a fly must be the one who creates all insects and animals and who gives life to the earth. And whoever spins particles as though they were Mevlevi dervishes must be the one who sets successive beings in motion as far as the sun travelling through the skies with its planets. For the law is a chain and the creative acts are tied to it.

That is to say, just as each object ascribes all other objects to its fashioner, and each creative act attributes all acts to its author, in exactly the same way, each divine name manifested in the universe ascribes all names to the One Whom it itself describes and proves that they are His titles. For the names manifested in the universe are like intersecting circles, blending with one another like the seven colours in light; they assist one another and perfect and adorn one another's works of art.

For example, the instant the name of Giver of Life is manifested on a thing and life is given, the name of All-Wise also becomes manifest; it orders the body which is that animate creature's dwelling-place with wisdom. At the same time, the name of Munificent is manifested; it adorns the creature's dwelling-place. So too, the manifestation of the name of All-Compassionate appears; it presents the body's needs with tenderness. At the same instant, the manifestation of the name of Provider appears; it supplies the material and spiritual sustenance necessary for the continued existence of the animate creature in unexpected ways. And so on. That means to whomever the name of Giver of Life belongs, the name of All-Wise, which is luminous and comprehensive in the universe, is also His. The name of All-Compassionate, which nurtures all creatures with tenderness, is also His. And the name of Provider, which sustains all animate creatures with munificence, is His name and title. And so on.

That is to say, each name, each act, each object is a proof of divine unity, and such a proof that each is a stamp of divine unity (*vahdaniyet*) and each is a seal of divine oneness (*ehadiyet*) which has been inscribed on the pages of the universe and on the lines of the centuries. Each indicates that all the words of the universe, which are called beings, are inscriptions traced by the pen of its own scribe. . . .

On Thanks
[From the Twenty-Eighth Letter]

In the Name of God, the Merciful, the Compassionate.
And there is nothing but it glorifies Him with praise.

Will they not then give thanks? * Will they not then give thanks? * And we shall surely reward those who give thanks. * If you give thanks, I shall increase [my favours] to you. * Worship God and be of those who give thanks.[8]

By repeating verses like these, the Qur'an of Miraculous Exposition shows that thanks is what the All-Merciful Creator wants most from His servants. The Qur'an, the All-Wise Distinguisher between Truth and Falsehood, calls on men to offer thanks, giving it the greatest importance. It shows ingratitude to be a denial of bounties, and in Surat al-Rahman, utters a fearsomely severe threat thirty-three times with the verse, "So which of the favours of your Sustainer do you deny?" It demonstrates that ingratitude is denial and negation.

Indeed, just as the All-Wise Qur'an shows thanks to be the result of creation; so the universe, which is a mighty Qur'an, shows the most important result of the world's creation to be thanks. For if the universe is observed carefully, it is seen from the way it is arranged that everything results in thanks; each looks to thanks to an extent and is turned towards it. It is as if thanks is the most important fruit of the tree of creation, and gratitude is the most elevated product of the factory of the universe. The reason for this is as follows:

We see in the creation of the world that its beings are arranged as though in a circle with life as its central point. All beings look to life, and serve life, and produce the necessities of life. That is to say, the One Who created the universe chose life from it, giving it preference.

Then we see that He created the animal kingdom in the form of a circle and placed man at its centre. Simply, He centred the aims intended from animate beings on man, gathering all living creatures around him, and subjugating them to him. He made them serve him and him dominant over them. That is to say, the Glorious Creator chose man from among living beings, and willed and decreed this position for him in the world.

Then we see that the world of man, and the animal world too, are disposed like circles, with sustenance placed at their centre. He has made mankind and the animals enamoured of sustenance, has subjugated them to it, and made them serve it. What rules them is sustenance. And He has made sustenance such a vast, rich treasury that it contains all His innumerable bounties. Even, with the faculty called taste, He has placed on the tongue sensitive scales to the number of foods, so that they can recognize the tastes of the many varieties of sustenance. That is to say, the strangest, richest, most wonderful, most agreeable, most comprehensive, and most marvellous truth in the universe lies in sustenance.

Now we see that just as everything has been gathered around sustenance and looks to it, so does sustenance in all its varieties subsist through thanks, both material and immaterial and that offered by word and by state; it exists through thanks, it produces thanks, its shows thanks. For appetite and desire for sustenance are a sort of innate or instinctive thanks. Enjoyment and pleasure also are a sort of unconscious thanks, offered by all animals. It is only man who changes the nature of that innate thanks through misguidance and unbelief; he deviates from thanks and associates partners with God.

Furthermore, the exquisitely adorned forms, the fragrant smells, the wonderfully delicious tastes in the bounties which are sustenance invite thanks; they awake an eagerness in animate beings, and through eagerness urge a sort of appreciation and respect, and prompt thanks of a sort. They attract the attention of conscious beings and engender admiration. They encourage them to respect the bounties; through this, they lead them to offer thanks verbally and by act, and to be grateful; they cause them to experience the highest and sweetest pleasure within thanks. That is, they show that, as well as a brief and temporary superficial pleasure, through thanks, these delicious foods and bounties gain the favours of the Most Merciful One, which provide a permanent, true, boundless pleasure. They cause conscious beings to ponder over the infinite, pleasurable favours of the All-Generous Owner of the treasuries of mercy, and in effect to taste the everlasting delights of Paradise while still in this world. Thus, although by means of thanks sustenance becomes such a valuable, rich, all-embracing treasury, through ingratitude it becomes utterly valueless.

As is explained in the Sixth Word, when the sense of taste in the tongue is turned towards sustenance for the sake of Almighty God, that is, when it performs its duty of thanks, it becomes a grateful inspector of the numberless kitchens of divine mercy and a highly-esteemed supervisor full of praise. If it is turned towards it for the sake of the soul, that is, without thinking of giving thanks to the One Who has bestowed the sustenance, the sense of taste is demoted from being a highly-esteemed supervisor to the rank of a watchman of the factory of the stomach and a doorkeeper of the stable of the belly. Just as through ingratitude these servants of sustenance descend to such a level, so does the nature of sustenance and its other servants fall; they fall from the highest rank to the lowest; they sink to a state opposed to the Creator of the universe's wisdom.

The measure of thanks is contentment, frugality, and being satisfied and grateful. While the measure of ingratitude is greed, wastefulness and extravagance; it is disrespect; it is eating whatever one comes across, whether lawful or unlawful.

Like ingratitude, greed causes both loss and degradation. For example, it seems that it is because of greed that the blessed ant with its social life is crushed underfoot. For, although a few grains of wheat would suffice it for a year, it is not contented with this and collects thousands if it can. While the blessed honey-bee flies overhead due to its contentment, and at a divine command bestows honey on human beings for them to eat.

The name of All-Merciful—the greatest name after the name of Allah, which signifies the divine essence and is the greatest name of the Most Pure and Holy One—looks to sustenance, and is attained to through the thanks provoked by sustenance. Also, the most obvious meaning of All-Merciful is Provider.

There are different varieties of thanks, the most comprehensive of which are the prescribed prayers. The prescribed prayers are a universal index of the sorts of thanks.

Furthermore, thanks comprises pure belief and is a sincere affirmation of God's unity. For a person who eats an apple and utters, "Praise be to God!" is proclaiming through his thanks: "This apple is a souvenir bestowed directly by the hand of power, a gift directly from the treasury of mercy." By saying this and believing it, he is ascribing everything, particular and universal, to the hand of power. He recognizes the manifestation of mercy in everything. He announces through his thanks, his true faith and sincere affirmation of divine unity.

The heedless man incurs serious loss through ingratitude for bounties. We shall describe only one of its many aspects. It is as follows:

If someone eats a delicious bounty and gives thanks, by virtue of his thanks the bounty becomes a light and a fruit of Paradise in the hereafter. If, because of the pleasure it produces, he thinks of it as the work of Almighty God's favour and mercy, it affords a true, lasting delight and enjoyment. He sends kernels and essences of its meanings, and immaterial substances like these, to the abodes above, while the material husk-like residue, that is, the matter that has completed its duty and now is unnecessary, becomes excreta and goes to be transformed into its original substances, that is, into the elements. If he fails to give thanks, the temporary pleasure leaves behind a pain and sorrow at its passing, and itself becomes waste. Bounty, which is as precious as diamonds, is transformed into coal. Through thanks, transient sustenance produces enduring pleasures, everlasting fruits. But if bounty is met with ingratitude, it is turned from the very best of forms into the most distasteful. For according to the heedless person, after producing a fleeting pleasure, sustenance ends up as waste-matter.

Sustenance is indeed in a form worthy of love, and this form is to be seen through thanks. However, the passion of the misguided and heedless for sustenance is animality. You can make further comparisons in this way and see what a loss the heedless and misguided suffer.

Among animate species, the most needy for all the varieties of sustenance is man. Almighty God created man as a comprehensive mirror to all His names; as a miracle of power with the capacity to weigh up and recognize the contents of all His treasuries of mercy; and as His vicegerent on earth possessing the faculties to draw to the scales and evaluate all the subtleties of His names' manifestations. He therefore made man utterly resourceless, making him needy for the endless varieties of sustenance, material and immaterial. Thanks is the means of raising man to "the best of forms," which is the highest position in accordance with this comprehensiveness. If he does not give thanks, he falls to "the lowest of the low," and perpetrates a great wrong.

In Short: The most essential of the four fundamental principles of the way of worship and winning God's love, the highest and most elevated way, is thanks. These four principles have been defined as follows:

"Four things are necessary on the way of the impotent, my friend:

"Absolute impotence, absolute poverty, absolute fervour, and absolute thanks, my friend." . . .

Fifth Mystery [from the Second Station of the Fourteenth Flash]

There is a Hadith that goes something like this: "God created man in the form of the Most Merciful." It has been interpreted by some Sufis in an extraordinary way, unfitting for the tenets of belief. Some of them who were ecstatics even considered man's spiritual nature to be in the form of the All-Merciful. Ecstatics are mostly immersed in contemplation and confused, so they are perhaps to be excused if they hold views contrary to reality. But on consideration, people in their right senses cannot accept ideas of theirs that are contrary to the fundamentals of belief. If they do, they are in error.

Indeed, the Most Pure and Holy Deity, Who administers with order the whole universe as though it were a palace or house, and spins the stars as though they were particles and causes them to travel through space with wisdom and ease, and employs minute particles as though they were orderly officials, has no partner, match, opposite, or equal. So too, according to the meaning of the verse: "There is nothing whatever like unto Him, and He hears and sees [all things]," He has no form, like, or peer, and there is nothing resembling Him or similar to Him. However, according to the meaning of the following verse and its parabolic comparison, "And His is the highest similitude in the heavens and the earth, and He is Exalted in Might, Full of Wisdom," His actions, attributes, and names may be considered. That is to say, allegory and comparison may be used in connection with His actions. One of the many things intended by the above-mentioned Hadith is: "Man is in a form that displays the divine name of All-Merciful in its entirety." Yes, as we explained before, the divine name of All-Merciful is manifested through the rays of a thousand and one names on the face of the universe, and is apparent through the innumerable manifestations of God's absolute dominicality on the face of the earth. Similarly, its complete manifestation is apparent in a small measure in man's comprehensive form, the same as on the face of the earth and the face of the universe.

The Hadith suggests also that the evidences of the Necessarily Existent One offered by such proofs, mirrors, and manifestations of the Most Merciful as animate creatures and man are so certain, clear, and obvious that just as it may be said of a shining mirror which reflects the image of the sun: "That mirror is the sun," indicating the clarity of its brilliance and evidence, so it has been said and may be said: "Man is in the form of the All-Merciful One," indicating the clarity of his evidence and completeness of his relation. It is in consequence of this mystery that the more moderate of those who believed in the Unity of Existence said: "There is no existent but He," as a way of expressing the clarity of this evidence and perfection of the relation. . . .

ON THE COMPANIONS OF THE PROPHET (PBUH)
ADDENDUM TO THE TWENTY-SEVENTH WORD

> In the Name of God, the Merciful, the Compassionate.
> Muhammad is the Messenger of God, and those who are with him are strong against the unbelievers, [but] compassionate amongst each other. . . .

You Ask: There are some narrations which say: "At a time innovations are rife, some of the righteous from among the believers and those who fear God will be on a level with the Companions, or of even greater virtue." Are these narrations sound? And if so, what is their true meaning?

The Answer: The consensus of the Sunnis, that after the prophets the most virtuous of mankind are the Companions, is certain proof that the sound ones out of those narrations refer to minor virtues. For in the case of minor virtues and particular qualities, a person may be deemed preferable to others who are superior and in fact preferable. But from the point of view of general virtue (*fazilet-i külliye*) the Companions cannot be reached, for they are praised by God at the end of Surat al-Fath and applauded in the Torah, Gospels, and Qur'an. For now, out of very many instances of wisdom we shall explain three related to this truth, which comprise three reasons.

First Instance of Wisdom: The conversation of the Prophet was such an elixir that someone who experienced it for even a minute received lights of reality equivalent to years of spiritual journeying. For things are reflected and imparted through conversation. It is well-known that a truly exalted level may be reached through such reflection and through following and imitating, and through the sublime light of prophethood—just as through allegiance to his sovereign and following him, a sultan's servant may rise to a position so high a king cannot rise to it. It is because of this mystery that the greatest saints cannot aspire to the level of the Companions. Even saints like Jalaluddin Suyuti cannot reach them although he conversed many times with God's Noble Messenger (PBUH) while in a waking state; they still cannot even if they do this and are honoured in this world with his company. For the Companions' conversation was with the light of

Muhammad's (PBUH) prophethood (*nübüvvet*), that is, it was with him as Prophet. While the saints saw him (PBUH) after his death and conversed with him (PBUH) through the light of his sainthood (*velāyet*). That is to say, God's Noble Messenger (PBUH) was personified and appeared in their sight by virtue of his sainthood, not in respect of his prophethood. Since this is so, however much higher prophethood is than sainthood, the two sainthoods differ to that degree.

Just how luminous an elixir was the Prophet's company may be understood from the fact that a primitive man so savagely hard-hearted he buried his daughter alive would come and be honoured for an hour with the Prophet's (PBUH) conversation, and become too kind and compassionate to step on an ant. And an ignorant savage would spend a day in the Prophet's company, then go to lands like China and India and instruct civilized peoples in the realities and guide them in perfections.

Second Reason: As is explained and proved in the discussion about interpretation of the law in the Twenty-Seventh Word, the personal perfections of the vast majority of the Companions were at the highest level. For at that time in the mighty revolution of Islam, good and truth appeared in all their beauty, and evil and falsehood, in all their ugliness, and they were felt physically. Such a difference was apparent between good and evil and such a distance opened up between truth and falsehood that they became as distant from one another as belief is from unbelief, and Hell is from Paradise even. The Companions, with their naturally elevated sensitivities, were captivated by the highest morality, and inclined towards dignity and virtue; they would not have embraced evil and falsehood voluntarily, and have fallen to the level of Musaylima the Liar and his ridiculous utterances. For Musaylima was the herald of falsehood, evil, and lies, and their embodiment. Their characters demanded that they looked to the very highest rank of perfections, those of God's Beloved (PBUH), who was the herald and embodiment of truthfulness, good, and right, and that they pursued that way with all their might and strength.

For example, it sometimes happens that in the market of human civilization and shop of social life, everyone flees in disgust from the fearsome results and ugly consequences of certain things, like from a deadly poison, let alone buying them. Then the beautiful results and valuable consequences of other things and of immaterial goods attract the general view and create demand for themselves, as though they were a universal panacea and sparkling brilliant; everyone tries their utmost to buy them. In just the same way, in the Era of Bliss in the market of human social life, since it had become clear that goods like lying, evil, and unbelief gave rise to such results as everlasting misery and base buffoons like

Musaylima the Liar, certainly the Companions, being captivated by lofty qualities and love of exalted things, would flee from them with loathing as from fatal poison. With their pure natures and praiseworthy qualities, the Companions would be desirous of and customers for truth, truthfulness and belief with all their strength, emotions, and faculties. For they yielded results like eternal happiness and luminous fruits like God's Noble Messenger (PBUH), and were apparently the most effective panacea and precious as diamonds. However, after that time, the distance between truthfulness and lying gradually diminished until they became shoulder to shoulder. They began to be sold together in the same shop, and social morality deteriorated accordingly. The propaganda of politics created a greater demand for lying. Now that the awesome ugliness of lying has begun to be concealed and the shining beauty of truthfulness obscured, who can attain to the strength, constancy, and *taqwah* of the Companions in matters of justice, truthfulness, exaltedness, and right, or surpass their level? I shall explain something that occurred to me which will illuminate this to a degree. It was like this:

One time, it occurred to me, why could wondrous individuals like Muhyiddin al-'Arabi not attain to the levels of the Companions? Then, while declaring, "Glory be to my Sustainer, the Most High" during the prayers, the phrase's meaning was unfolded to me. Not completely, but its truth in part became clear to me. I said in my heart: "If only I could perform one of the five daily prayers in the way this phrase requires, it would be better than a year's worship." After the prayers I understood that the thought and my feelings had been guidance inferring that the Companions' degree in worship could not be reached. For during that mighty social revolution brought about by the lights of the Qur'an, opposites were separated from one another, and evils together with all their darkness, details and all who followed them, and good and perfections together with all their lights and results came face to face—at such an exciting time, all glorifications of God and recitations of His names expressed all the levels of their meanings freshly and newly and in a young and unfaded fashion. So too, under the crashing of that mighty revolution all the human senses and subtle inner faculties were awakened, even fancy and imagination, in an awakened and aware state, received the numerous meanings of those recitations and glorifications in accordance with their own perceptions, and absorbed them.

Due to this wisdom, when the Companions, whose senses were awakened and subtle faculties, alert, uttered those blessed words comprising the lights of belief and glorification, they did so in all their meaning and they partook of them with all their senses. However, subsequently to that revolution and upheaval, people's subtle faculties have gradually sunk into sleep and their senses have fallen from that point of realities into heedlessness; like fruits dulled by familiarity, those blessed words have gradually lost their delicacy and freshness. Simply, as though drying up through the air of superficiality, only a little freshness remains, and this may be restored to its former state only through drastic surgery of a reflective and reasoning kind. It is because of this that others can reach the virtue and level the Companions attained to in forty minutes, only in forty years.

Third Reason: As is proved in the Twelfth, Twenty-Fourth, and Twenty-Fifth Words, in comparison with prophethood, which is the sun itself, sainthood resembles the sun's reflection as it appears in mirrors. Thus, however much higher the sphere of prophethood is than that of sainthood, the servants of the sphere of prophethood and the Companions, the stars of that Sun, must be superior to the righteous of the sphere of sainthood to the same degree. The legacy of prophethood (*verāset-i nübüvvet*) and veracity, which is the supreme sainthood (*velāyet-i kübra*), is the sainthood of the Companions. Even if a saint attains to this, he still cannot reach the level of the Companions, the first rank. We shall explain three of this third reason's many aspects:

First Aspect: The Companions cannot be reached in interpretation of the law, that is, in deducing its ordinances, that is, in understanding what pleases Almighty God from His Word. Because that mighty divine revolution revolved on comprehension of the dominical wishes and divine ordinances. All minds were directed towards deducing the divine ordinances. All hearts were eager to know "What does our Sustainer want from us?" All that happened at that time did so in such a way as to make this known and understood. The discussions of the time were all about this. Thus, since everything and all situations and discussions and conversations occurred in such a way as to give some sort of instruction in these meanings; and since this perfected the Companions' capacities and illuminated their minds; and since their ability to interpret the law and deduce its ordinances was ready to be lit up like a match; someone at this time with their intelligence and capacity could not reach in ten years or perhaps in a hundred, the level of deduction and interpretation they reached in a day or a month. For now, attention is focussed on worldly happiness rather than eternal happiness. Mankind's attention is directed towards different goals. People's spirits have become stupified by the struggle for livelihood and by failing to rely on God, and their intellects have become blinded by naturalist and materialist philosophies, and the social environment does not strengthen their minds and augment their capacities in the question of interpreting the divine law, it confuses and scatters them. We proved in the discussion on interpretation of the law in the Twenty-Seventh Word, in the comparison between Sufyan ibn Uyayna and someone of his intelligence today that today's person could not acquire in a hundred years what Sufyan acquired in ten.

Second Aspect: The feet of sainthood cannot rise to the Companions' level in nearness to God. For Almighty God is infinitely near to us, nearer to us than everything, but we are infinitely distant from Him. Divine proximity may be gained in two ways:

The First is through the unfolding of divine immediacy (*akrebiyet*), to which the divine proximity (*kurbiyet*) in prophethood looks, and which the Companions manifested through the legacy of prophethood and conversation of the Prophet (PBUH).

The Second Way is to traverse the degrees of our distance from God and be honoured with divine proximity to an extent. Most of the spiritual voyaging of sainthood is in accordance with this, and illumination through the self and through the outside world proceeds in this way.

Thus, the first way is only given, it is not acquired; it is attraction, the drawing of the Most Merciful One; it is being loved by Him. This path is short, but very severe, very elevated, very pure, and without shadow. The other is acquired, lengthy, and in shadow. Even if its strange wonders are many, it cannot reach the first in respect of quality and divine proximity. For example, there are two ways of reaching yesterday. The first is not to be subject to the course of time. Through a sacred power, it is to rise above time, and see yesterday as present like today. The second is to traverse the distance of a year, to travel and turn, and come to yesterday. But still yesterday cannot be held on to; it leaves the person and departs. In just the same way, there are two ways of passing from the apparent to reality. The first is to be carried away directly on the attraction of reality, and, without entering the intermediate realm of the Sufi way, to find reality within the apparent itself. The second is to traverse many levels through spiritual journeying. For sure, the saints are successful in annihilating the soul and they kill the evil-commanding soul, but they still cannot reach the Companions. For the Companions' souls had been purified and cleansed, and by virtue of the many faculties within the soul, they manifested to a greater degree the varieties of worship, and thanks, and praise. After the saints have annihilated the soul, their worship acquires a simplicity and plainness.

Third Aspect: The Companions cannot be reached in regard to virtuous actions and good deeds pertaining to the hereafter. For just as in certain conditions when posted in a frightening, crucial position, a soldier may gain with one hour's watch the virtue of a year's worship, and if hit by a bullet may rise in one minute to a station equivalent to sainthood, which normally can by gained only in forty years; so too, the Companions' service in establishing Islam and propagating the Qur'an's decrees and their declaring war on the whole world for Islam, was so elevated that others cannot reach one minute of it in a year. It may even be said that all the minutes of their sacred service were the equivalent of that single minute of the martyred soldier. All their hours were equal to the one hour's watch of the faithful soldier in that terrifying post when the acts are few, but the recompense great, and the value high.

Indeed, since the Companions formed the first rank in the establishment of Islam and spreading of the lights of the Qur'an, in accordance with the rule "the cause is like the doer," they receive a share of all the good works performed by all the Islamic community. The fact that the Islamic community declares: "O God! Grant blessings to our master Muhammad and to his Family and Companions" shows that the Companions receive a share of all its good works.

Furthermore, an insignificant characteristic in a tree's root may become a large growth in the tree's branches, and larger than the largest branch; and a small protuberance at the beginning gradually forms a mass; and an excessive amount the size of a needle point at the central point of a circle may be longer than a metre at the circumference. Just like these four examples, since the Companions were at the roots and foundations of the luminous tree of Islam, and at the beginning of the luminous lines of the structure of Islam, and were among the leaders of the Islamic community and were the first of their number, and since they were close to the centre of the Sun of Prophethood and Lamp of Reality, a few of their actions were many and their small acts of service, great. To reach their level necessitates being a true Companion. . . .

Question: It is said, the Companions saw God's Noble Messenger (Peace and blessings be upon him), then they believed. However we have believed without seeing him, in which case our belief is stronger. Also, there are narrations mentioning the strength of our belief, are there not?

The Answer: At a time all ideas were opposed and hostile to the truths of Islam, the Companions believed so strongly—sometimes on only seeing the person of God's Messenger (PBUH) and without miracles—that all the generally held ideas in the world did not shake them. Let alone doubts, they did not cause them the slightest anxiety or scruple. You are comparing your belief with that of the Companions, but how can there be any comparison? For you see with the mind's eye, not the Messenger's (PBUH) humanity and bodily form, which was the seed of the Tuba-tree of his prophethood, but through all the lights of Islam and truths of the Qur'an, his luminous, magnificent collective personality, encompassed by a thousand miracles, yet you waver and fall into doubt at the word of a European philosopher. However, thanks to their belief, the Companions did not waver in the face of the attacks of the entire world of unbelief and of the Christians, Jews, and philosophers. And how can you compare the intense fear of God of the Companions and their complete righteousness, which demonstrated the strength of their belief and proceeded from it, and your dull belief, which due to your extreme weakness does not impel you to perform even the obligatory practices properly, O you who make such a claim!? However, the Hadith the meaning of which is: "Those people at the end of time who do not see me yet believe, are more acceptable," refers to particular virtues. It concerns certain special individuals. Our discussion, however, is in regard to general virtue and the majority.

Second Question: They say that the saints and possessors of perfection abandoned the world. It even says in a Hadith: "Love of this world is the source of all error." Whereas the Companions were very involved in the world. Let alone abandoning it, some of them were more advanced than the civilized people of the time, even. How is it that you say that even the least of such Companions was of greater worth than the greatest saint?

The Answer: It has been proved decisively in the Second and Third Stopping-Places of the Thirty-Second Word that to love the face of the world which looks to the hereafter and the face that looks to the divine names is not the cause of loss, but the means to perfection and attainment, and however far one goes in those two faces, the further one goes in worship and knowledge of God. The Companions' world was in those two faces. They saw this world as the arable field of the hereafter, and sowed and reaped it. They saw beings as mirrors of the divine names, and gazed on them yearningly. As for the world's ephemerality, it is its transitory face and looks to man's base desires.

Third Question: The Sufi paths are the ways of reality. Some of the heroes and leaders of the Naqshbandi Order, which is claimed to be the most famous, the most elevated, and the highway among Sufi ways, defined its basis as follows. They said: "On the Naqshbandi way four 'abandonings' are necessary: abandoning the world, abandoning the hereafter, abandoning existence, and abandoning abandoning." That is to say, on the Naqshi way one has to give up four things: both give up this world; and, on account of the soul, not make even the hereafter one's true aim; forget one's existence; and in order not to become vain and proud, not think about these acts of renunciation. This means that true knowledge of God and human perfections are attained through giving up what is other than God?

The Answer: If man consisted of only a heart, it would be necessary to give up everything other than God, and to leave behind even the divine names and attributes and bind one's heart to the divine essence alone. But man possesses many senses and subtle faculties such as the mind, spirit, soul, and others, which all have their functions. The perfect man is he who, driving all those subtle senses towards reality on the different ways of worship particular to them, marches heroically like the Companions in a broad arena and rich fashion towards the goal, with the heart as commander and the subtle faculties as soldiers. For the heart to abandon its soldiers in order to save itself alone and to proceed on its own is the cause not of pride, but of distress.

Fourth Question: Where does it spring from, this claim of the Companions' superiority? Who advanced it? Why should this question be discussed at this time? Also, why do some people claim to be the equals of the great interpreters of the law?

The Answer: There are two groups who say these things. Some are the sincere religious scholars and men of religion who, seeing certain Hadiths, open up such discussions in order to hearten the pious and the upright at this time. We do not have anything to say to them. They are anyway few and are quickly made aware of matters. The other group, however, consists of awesomely arrogant people who want to spread their denial of the schools of law by claiming equality with the great interpreters of the law, and to further their irreligion by claiming equality with the Companions. Firstly, those misguided people are depraved and are addicted to depravity. They cannot carry out the obligations of the Sharī'ah since they hinder them in their depravity. So in order to find a pretext for themselves, they say: "These questions may be interpreted. The schools of law are opposed to each other in these matters. The interpreters of the law were human beings like us and may have made mistakes. In which case, like them we shall interpret the divine law and perform our worship as we wish. Why should we be compelled to follow them?" Thus, due to such satanic wiles, those wretches put themselves outside the fold of the schools of law. It is demonstrated clearly in the Twenty-Seventh Word just how baseless and rotten their claims are, so we refer you to that.

Secondly: the above group of the people of misguidance saw that the matter does not end with the interpreters of the law, for the field of their exertions was restricted to the theoretical matters of religion. But this group wants to give up and change the essential teachings of religion. When they say: "We are better than them," the matter does not end there. For interpreters of the law may intervene in theoretical matters and in secondary matters that are not categorical, but these people of misguidance who follow no school of law want to mix their ideas in the essentials of religion as well, and to change matters that may not be changed, and to oppose the incontrovertible pillars of Islam. So they are bound to attack the Companions, who are the bearers and supports of the essentials of religion. Alas! It has been proved decisively in the Twenty-Seventh Word that not animals in human form like them, but true human beings and the greatest of the saints even, who are the most perfect of true human beings, cannot win the case claiming equality with the least of the Companions.

NOTES

1. Shaykh Ahmad Sirhindi was also known by the titles of Imam-i Rabbani, Ahmad Faruqi, and Regenerator of the Second Millennium. He lived in India 971/1563–1034/1624, where he purified the religion of Islam of polytheistic accretions and efforts to degenerate it. He is also famous for his efforts to reform Sufism.
2. Sayyid 'Abd al-Qadir Gilani (Geylani), known as the Gawth al-A'zam, was a towering spiritual figure in the history of Islam. He lived 470/1077–561/1166.
3. Muhammad Baha'uddin Naqshband. He was the founder of the Naqshbandi Order, and died in 791(1389) in Bukhara.
4. Quran, 10:62.
5. Quran, 3:185, etc.
6. Quran, 42:11.
7. Quran, 2:32.
8. Quran, 39:66

Bibliography

'Abd al-Masih, G. M. *Mu'jam al-mustalahat al-Sufiyya* (Beirut: Maktabat Lubnan,1993).

'Abduh, M. *al-Jami' li-ahkam al-Qur'an* (Cairo: Dar al-Sha'b, n.d.).

———. *Tafsir al-manar [Exegesis of the Beacon]* (Cairo: Dar al-Manar, 1931).

'Abduh, M. *Tafsir al-Qur'an al-'Azim* (Giza, n.p and n.d.).

Abu-Rabi', I. "How to Read Said Nursi's Risale-i Nur." In *Islam at the Crossroads: On the Life and Thought of Bediuzzaman Said Nursi* (New York: State University of New York Press, 2003).

Abu-Rabi', I. ed., *Islam at the Crossroads: On the Life and Thought of Bediuzzaman Said Nursi* (New York: State University of New York Press, 2003).

Abu Yusuf. *Kitab al-Kharaj [The Book of Land Taxation]* (Cairo, n.p., 1962).

Addas, C. *Quest for the Red Sulphur* (Cambridge: Islamic Texts Society, 1993).

Afifi, A., ed., *Fusus al-Hikam* (Beirut: Dar al-Kutub al-'Arabi, 1946).

Ahmad, B. *Rāshid al-Īaraka al-islāmiyya fī Turkiya. Al-Mujāhid al-Mujtahid al-Shaykh Sa'īd al-Nursī* (Cairo: Dar al-Turath, 1992).

Ahmed, F. "Why Tariq Ramadan? " in *Islamica*, no. 12 (Spring 2005).

Algar, H. "Said Nursi and the Risale-i Nur." In *Islamic Perspectives Studies in Honour of Sayyid Abu'l-A'la Mawdudi* (Leicester: Islamic Foundation, 1979).

———. "Sufism and Tariqat in the Life and Work of Bediuzzaman Said Nursi." In *Journal of the History of Sufism*, 3 (2002).

Allchin, A. M. "Anglican Spirituality." In *The Study of Anglicanism* (London: SPCK, 1988).

Allen, D. *Myth and Religion in Mircea Eliade* (London: Routledge, 2002).

Attas, Sayyed Muhammad Nakib al-. "Opening Speech." In *Fourth International Symposium on Bediuzzaman Said Nursi*, Istanbul 1998 (Istanbul: Sözler Publications, 2000).

Baba, S. *Tasavvuf Terimleri [The Terms of Tasawwuf]* (Istanbul: Ayrıntı Yayınları, 1998).

Ballanfat, P. "Introduction." *The Nightingale in the Garden of Love* (Oxford: Anqa Publishing, 2005).

Balyani, A. *Risalat al-wujudiyya* (*Épitre sur l'Unicité absolue*, trans. M. Chodkiewicz (Paris: Les Deux Oceans, 1982).

Bauman, Z. *Parçalanmış Hayat: Postmodern Ahlak Denemeleri [Life in Fragments: Essays in Postmodern Morality]* (Istanbul: Ayrıntı Yayınları, 2001).

Bazak, J. *Judaism and Psychical Phenomena* (New York: Garrett Publications, 1972).

Benard, C. *Civil Democratic Islam: Partners, Resources and Strategies* (Santa Monica: Rand Corporation, 2003).

Bolay, S. H. *Türkiye'de Ruhçu ve Maddeci Görüşün Mücadelesi* (Ankara: Akçağ Yayınları, 1995).

Bozgeyik, B. *Meşhurların Son Anları [The Last Moments of the Famous Persons]* (Istanbul: Ayrıntı Yayınları, 2002).

Burckhardt, T. *Mirror of the Intellect: Essays on Traditional Science and Sacred Art* (Albany: State University of New York Press, 1987).

Burton, K. *According to the Pattern* (New York: Longmans, 1946).

Carr, D. "Three Concepts of Spirituality." In *Spirituality, Philosophy and Education* (London: Routledge, 2003).

Çengel, Y. A. "Fighting Terror and Eliminating Weapons of Mass Destruction." In *Bringing Faith, Meaning, and Peace to Life in a Multicultural World: The Risale-i Nur's Approach, Seventh International Symposium on Bediuzzaman Said Nursi* (Istanbul: October 3–5, 2004).

Ceylan, Y. "Etik Değerlerin İnsan Yaşamındaki Yeri" [The Place of the Ethical Values in the Life of Person] in *İslamiyat Journal*, vol. 4, no. 3 (July–September, 2001).

Chittick, W. "Rumi and *wahdat al-wujūd*," *Poetry and Mysticism in Islam: The Heritage of Rumi*, eds. A. Banani, R. Hovanisian and G. Sabagh (Cambridge, Cambridge University Press, 1994).

———. *The Self-Disclosure of God: Principles of Ibn Arabi's Cosmology* (Albany: State University of New York Press, 1998).

Cobb M., Robshaw, V. *The Spiritual Challenge of Health Care* (London: Churchill Livingstone, 1998).

Crain, W. C. *Theories of Development: Concepts and Applications* (Englewood Cliffs, NJ: Prentice-Hall, 1985).

Dammen, J. McAuliffe's *Encyclopedia of the Qur'an* (Leiden: E.d. Brill, 2002).

Eickelman, D. "Qur'anic Commentary, Public Space, and Religious Intellectuals in the Writings of Said Nursi" in *The Muslim World* 89:3–4 (July–October 1999).

Fahlberg, L. "Exploring Spirituality and Consciousness with an Expanded Science: Beyond the Ego with Empiricism, Phenomenology, and Contemplation" in *American Journal of Health Promotion*, vol. 5, no. 4 (March/April 1991).

Fowler, J. W. *Stages of Faith: The Psychology of Human Development and the Quest for Meaning* (San Francisco: Harper & Row, 1981).

Frager, R. *Heart, Self, and Soul: The Sufi Psychology of Growth, Balance, and Harmony* (Wheaton, IL: Quest, 1999).

Freire, P. *Ezilenlerin Pedagojisi [Pedagogia do oprimido]* (Ayrıntı Yayınları, 2003).

Friedmann, Y. *Shaykh Ahmad Sirhindī. An Outline of His Thought and a Study of His Image in the Eyes of Posterity* (Montreal: McGill-Queens University Press 1971) (reprint New Delhi: Oxford University Press, 2003).

Ghazali, A. *Ihya' Ulum al-Din* (Beirut: Dar al-Kutub,1982).

Ghazali, A. H. *The Niche of Lights*, trans. David Buchman (Provo:Brigham Young University Press, 1998).

Goitein, S. D. "Attitudes towards Government in Islam and Judaism." In *Studies in Islamic History and Institutions* (Leiden: E. J. Brill, 1966).

Green, A. *A Guide to the Zohar* (Stanford: Stanford University Press, 2004).

———. *Seek My Face, Speak My Name: A Contemporary Jewish Theology* (Northvale, NJ: Jason Aronson, 1994).

Gruen, A. *Normalliğin Deliliği, Hastalık Olarak Gerçekçilik: İnsandaki Yıkıcılık Üzerine Bir Kuram [Der Wahnsinn der Normalitat: Realismus als Krankheit: eine Theorie der menschlichen Destructivitat]* (Istanbul: Çitlembik Yayınları, 2003).

Gümüşhaneli, Shaikh Ahmed Ziya'üddin (ed.). *Majmu'at al-Ahzab*, three vols. (Istanbul: IFAV, 1311).

Güngör, E. *Değerler Psikolojisi [The Psychology of Values]* (Amsterdam: Çitlembik Yayınları, 1993).

———. *İslam'ın Bugünkü Meseleleri [The Present Questions of Islam]* (Istanbul: Çitlembik Yayınları, 1990).

Haddad, I. *The Lives of Man* (Louisville: Fons Vitae, 1991).

Haddad, Y. "Ghurba as Paradigm for Muslim Life: A Risale-i Nur Worldview" in *The Muslim World*, 89: 3–4 (July–October 1999).

Hentsch, T. *Truth or Death: The Quest for Immortality in the Western Narrative Tradition* (Vancouver: Talonbooks, 2004).

Hillman, J. *Insearch: Psychology and Religion* (New York: Scribner's, 1967).

Hirtenstein, S. *The Unlimited Mercifier* (Oxford: Anqa Publishing, 1999).

Hökelekli, H. *Din Psikolojisi [The Psychology of Religion]* (Ankara, Türkiye Diyanet Vakfı Publications, 1998).

Hourani, A. *The Emergence of the Modern Middle East* (London: Macmillan, 1981).

Ibn al-'Imād (d.1678). *Shadharāt al-dhahab* (Beirut: al-Maktab al-Tijari li'l-Tiba'a wa'l-Nashr wa'l-Tawzi', 1966).

Ibn Hisham. *al-Sira al-Nabawiyya [The Biography of the Prophet]* (Beirut: 1992).

Ibn Kathir. *Tafsir al-Qur'an al-'azim [Exegesis of the Magnificent Qur'an]* (Giza: 2002).

Ibn Manzur. *Lisan al-Arab* (Beirut: Dar Ihya' al-Turath al-'Arabi, 1995).

Iqbal, M. *Asrar-i Khudī* [Turk. trans. Ali Nihad Tarlan] (Istanbul: Düşünce Publications, 1964).

———. *Bal-i Jibrail* [Turk. trans. Yusuf Salih Karaca] (Istanbul: Furkan Publications, 1983).

———. *Pas Chai Bayad Kard Ey Aqwam-i Sharq* [Turk. trans. Ali Nihad Tarlan] (Istanbul: M. İkbal Derneği, 1976).

———. *Payam-i Mashriq* [Turk. trans. Ali Nihad Tarlan] (Ankara: Türkiye İş Bankası Publications, 1956).

———. *Rumuz-i Bekhudi* [Turk. trans. Ali Nihad Tarlan] (Istanbul: Türkiye Pakistan Kültür Cemiyeti İstanbul Şb. Publications, 1964).

———. *The Reconstruction of Religious Thought in Islam* (Lahore: Iqbal Academy, 1996).

———. *Zabur-i Ajam* [Turk. trans. Ali Nihad Tarlan] (Istanbul: Türkiye İş Bankası Publications, 1971).

———. *Zarb-i Kalim* [Turk. trans. N. Ahmed Asrar] (Istanbul: Düşünce Publications, 1981).

İşeri, M. S. "Güzel Ahlakı Ararken" [While Seeking the Well-Ethics] in *Köprü Journal*, no. 75 (Summer 2001).

Jakobson R., Waugh, L. R. *The Sound Shape of Language* (Bloomington: Indiana University Press, 1979).

Jalalizade, J. "A Comparison of the Thought of Bediuzzaman and Muhammad Iqbal." In *Third International Symposium on Bediuzzaman Said Nursi*, Istanbul 1995 (Istanbul: Sözler Publications, 1997).

Jami, 'Abd al-Rahman. *Naqd al-nusus fi sharh naqsh al-Fusus* (Tehran: Imperial Academy of Science, 1977).

Karakoç, S. *Diriliş Neslinin Amentüsü [The Credo of the Generation of the Resurrection]* (Istanbul: Diriliş Publications, 1986).

Karakoç, S. *İslam'ın Dirilişi [The Resurrection of Islam]* (Istanbul: Diriliş Publications, 1986).

Kernberg, O. *Aggression in Personality Disorders and Perversions* (New Haven: Yale University Press, 1992).

Khalil, I. "The Literary Beauty of Bediuzzaman's Works." In *International Symposium on the Reconstruction of Islamic Thought in the Twentieth Century and Bediuzzaman Said Nursi*, Istanbul 1992 (Istanbul: Sözler Publications, 1993).

Khan, M. *The Translation of the Meanings of Sahih Al-Bukhari*, Arabic-English ed. (Riyadh: Darussalam, 1997).

Khatami, S. M. *Hope and Challenge: The Iranian President Speaks* (Binghamton, NY: Binghamton University Press, 1997).

Kılıç, R. *Ahlakın Dini Temeli [The Religious Foundation of Ethics]* (Ankara: Türkiye Diyanet Vakfı Publications,1992).

Klein, M. *Haset ve Şükran [Envy and Gratitude]* (Istanbul: Metis Yayınları, 1998).

Kohlberg, L. *The Psychology of Moral Development: The Nature and Validity of Moral Stages* (San Francisco: Harper & Row, 1984).

Konuk, A. *Fusūs'l-hikem Tercüme ve Şerhi* (Istanbul: IFAV, 1989).

Kovel, J. *Tarih ve Tin. Özgürleşme Felsefesi Üzerine Bir İnceleme [History and Spirit. An Inquiry into Philosophy of Liberation]* (Istanbul: Ayrıntı Yayınları, 1994).

Kuşpınar, B. "Nursi's Evaluation of Sufism." In *Third International Symposium on Bediuzzaman Said Nursi*, vol. 2 (Istanbul: Sözler, 1995).

———. "The Concept of Man: Mevlana Jalal al-Din and Said Nursi." In Ibrahim M. Abu-Rabi', ed., *Islam at the Crossroads* (Albany: State University of New York Press, 2003).

Lamoreaux, J. C. *The Early Muslim Tradition of Dream Interpretation* (Albany: State Univeristy of New York Press, 2002).

Leaman, O. "Nursi's Place in the Ihya' Tradition." In *Fourth International Symposium on Bediuzzaman Said Nursi*, Istanbul 1998 (Istanbul: Sözler Publications, 2000).

Lewis, F. D. *Rumi: Past and Present, East and West* (Oxford: Oneworld, 2000).

Maddi, S. *Personality Theories: A Comparative Analysis* (Long Grove, IL: Waveland, 1996).

Mannoni, Pierre. *Korku [Fear]* [Turk. trans. Işın Gürbüz] (Istanbul: İletişim Publications, n.d.].

Mardin, Ş. "Bediuzzaman's Understanding of Striving (Jihad) Is Not Armed Struggle." In *Panel I* (Istanbul: Sözler Publications 1993).

———. "The Collective Memory and Consciousness." In *International Symposium on The Reconstruction of Islamic Thought in the Twentieth Century and Bediuzzaman Said Nursi*, Istanbul 1992 (Istanbul: Sözler Publications, 1993).

———. *Religion and Social Change in Modern Turkey: The Case of Bediuzzaman Said Nursi* (New York: State University of New York Press, 1989).

Markham, I. "Truth and Toleration: The Said Nursi Achievement." In *Bringing Faith, Meaning, and Peace to Life in a Multicultural World: The Risale-i Nur's Approach, Seventh International Symposium on Bediuzzaman Said Nursi* (Istanbul: October 3–5, 2004).

Markham I., Özdemir, I. *Globalization, Ethics and Islam: The Case of Bediuzzaman Said Nursi* (Aldershot, UK: Ashgate, 2005).

Mawardi, A. *al-Ahkam al-Sultaniyya wa' l-wilayat al-diniyya [Governmental Ordinances and Religious Stewardship]* (Beirut: Dar al-Kutub, 1996).

McCutchen, L. "Psychology of the Dream: Dream without Myth." In *The Dialogue Between Theology and Psychology* (Chicago: University of Chicago Press, 1968).

Mengüşoğlu, T. *Değişmez Değerler ve Değişen Davranışlar [Unchangeable Values and Changeable Behaviours]* (Istanbul: Istanbul Press, 1965).

Mermer, A. "Divine Speech in the Risale-i Nur." In *Fifth International Symposium* (Istanbul: Sözler Yayınevi, 2000).

Michel S. J, T. "Grappling with Modern Civilization: Said Nursi's Interpretive Key." In *Bringing Faith, Meaning, and Peace to Life in a Multicultural World: The Risale-i Nur's Approach, Seventh International Symposium on Bediuzzaman Said Nursi* (Istanbul: October 3–5, 2004).

Najm al-Din al-Razi. *The Path of God's Bondsmen from Origin to Return* (North Haledon, NJ: Islamic Publications International, 1982).

Nizami. "Naqshbandī Influence on Mughal Rulers and Politics." In *Islamic Culture,* vol. 39 (1965).

Nursi, S. *Mūnāzarat* (Istanbul: Sözler Yayınevi, 1977).

———. "A Flower from the Garden of the Qur'an." In *Mathnawi al-Nuriya [Epitomes of Light]* (Izmir: Karnak, 1999).

———. *Risale-i Nur Külliyatı*, two volumes (Istanbul: Envar Neşriyat, 2004).

———. *Barla Lahikası* (Istanbul: Envar Neşriyat, 1994).

———. *Man and the Universe* (Istanbul: Sözler Neşriyat, 1987).

———. *Risale-i Nur Kulliyatı,* vol. 2 (Istanbul: Nesil Publishing, 1996).

———. *Sikke-i Tasdik-i Gaybī* (Istanbul: Envar Neşriyat, 1994).

———. *Tarihçe-i Hayat* (Istanbul: Sözler Publications, 1990).

———. *The Damascus Sermon* (Istanbul: Sözler Publications, 1996).

———. *The Letters* (Istanbul: Sözler Publications, 2001).

———. *The Rays Collection* (Istanbul: Sözler Publications, 2002).

———. *The Staff of Moses* (Istanbul: Sözler Publications, 2002).

———. *The Words* (Istanbul: Sözler Publications, 2002).

———. *The Flashes Collection* (Istanbul: Sözler Publications, 2000).

Ochs V. L., Ochs, E. *The Jewish Dream Book: The Key to Opening the Inner Meaning of Your Dreams* (Woodstock, VT: Jewish Lights Publishing, 2003).

Özakpınar, Y. "Qur'anic Civilization." In *Fourth International Symposium on Bediuzzaman* (Istanbul: Sözler Publications, 1998).

Özervarlı, M. S. "Hani, Seyh Ahmed." In *Türkiye Diyanet Vakfı İslam Ansiklopedisi* (Istanbul: Türkiye Diyanet Vakfı, 1997).

———. "Hani'nin Tasvirlerine Göre XVII. Yüzyılda Cizre" in *Hz. Nuh'tan Günümüze Cizre Sempozyumu* (Istanbul: Cizre Kaymakamlığı, 1999).

———. "Said Nursi's Project of Revitalizing Contemporary Islamic Thought." In Ibrahim M. Abu-Rabi', ed., *Islam at the Crossroads: On the Life and Thought of Bediuzzaman Said Nursi* (Albany: State University of New York Press, 2003).

Padwick, C. E. *Muslim Devotions: A Study of Prayer-Manuals in Common Use* (Oxford: Oneworld, 1996).

Parvaiz, M. A. "Environmental Ethics—The Human Role as Advocated by the Qur'an and Elucidated by Ustad Nursi." In *Bringing Faith, Meaning, and Peace to Life in a Multicultural World: The Risale-i Nur's Approach, Seventh International Symposium on Bediuzzaman Said Nursi* (Istanbul: October 3–5, 2004).

Pazarlı, O. *Din Psikolojisi [The Psychology of Religion]* (Istanbul: Remzi Kitabevi Publications, 1982).

Poston, L. *Islamic Da'wa in the West* (New York: Oxford, 1992).

Qummi, I., ed. *Kulliyāt-i Mafātīh al-Jinān* (Gulī Publications, Tehran, n.d.).

Qushayri, 'Abd al-Karim ibn Hawazin al-. *al-Risalat al-Qushayriyya* (Istanbul: Turath, 1991).

Rabbi Kaplan, A. *Innerspace: Introduction ti Kabbalah, Meditation and Prophecy* (Jerusalem: Moznaim Publishing Corporation, 1990).

Ramadan, T. *Entre l'homme et son cœur: la voie de l'Unique* (Lyon : Éditions Tawhid, 2001).

Reed, F. A. *Anatolia Junction: A Journey into Hidden Turkey* (Vancouver: Talonbooks, 1999)

Reed, P. "Spirituality and Mental Health in Older Adults: Extant Knowledge for Nursing." In *Family Community Health,* vol. 14, no. 2 (1991).

Roof, W. C. *A Generation of Seekers: The Spiritual Journeys of the Baby Boom Generation* (San Francisco: HarperSanFrancisco, 1993).

Rosenthal, F. *Sweeter than Hope: Complaint and Hope in Medieval Islam* (Leiden: E. J. Brill, 1997).

Ross, L. "The Spiritual Dimension: Its Importance to Patients' Health, Well-being and Quality of Life and Its Implications for Nursing Practice." In *International Journal of Nursing Studies*, vol. 32, no. 5 (1986).

Sadīnī, M. X. *Feqiyē Teyran* (Istanbul: Nubihar, 2003).

Sadiq, G. "Iqbal on the Concept of Morality." In *Iqbal Review*, vol. 10, no. 3 (October 1969).

Şahiner, N. *Bilinmeyen Taraflarıyle Bediüzzaman Said Nursi* (Istanbul: Yeni Asya Yayınları, 1974).

Sarraj, Abu Nasr al-. *al-Luma'* (Cairo: Turath, 1960).

Schimmel, A. *Mystical Dimensions of Islam* (Chapel Hill: University of North Carolina Press, 1975).

Sells, M. *Approaching the Qur'ān: The Early Revelations* (Ashland, OR: White Press, 1999).

Shabistari, M. M. *Dīn wa Āzādī* (Tehran: Gulī Publications,1999).

Shakeli, F. "The Kurdish Qasida." In *Qasida Poetry in Islamic Asia and Africa: Classical Traditions and Modern Meanings* (Leiden: E. J. Brill, 1996).

Şimşek, Ü. "The Style of Reflective Thought in the Risale-i Nur." In *The Reconstruction of Islamic Thought in the Twentieth Century and Bediuzzaman Said Nursi* (Istanbul: Sözler Neşriyat, 1997).

Smith, J. I. "At the Heart of the Matter: Faith and Belief in the Poetic Imagery of Said Nursi." In *Bringing Faith, Meaning, and Peace to Life in a Multicultural World: The Risale-i Nur's Approach, Seventh International Symposium on Bediuzzaman Said Nursi* (Istanbul: October 3–5, 2004).

Sönmez, S. "Ahlak" [Ethics] in *Köprü Journal*, no. 75 (Summer 2001).

Spero, M. H. "Dream Psychology in Biblical and Rabbinic Thought." In *Judaism and Psychology: Halakhic Perspectives* (New York: KTAV Publishing House, 1980).

Tabari, I. *Jami' al-bayan fi tafsir al-Qur'an [The Compendium of Eloquence in Exegesis of the Qur'an]* (Beirut: Risalah, 1997).

———. *Ta'rikh al-umam wa-'l-muluk [History of the Nationas and Kings]* (Beirut: 1997)

Tisdell, E. J. *Exploring Spirituality and Culture in Adult and Higher Education* (San Francisco: Jossey-Bass, 2003).

Toprak, N. "Marifetullah ve İhlas" [Gnosis of Allah and Sincerity] in *Semerkand Journal*, no. 2 (February, 1999).

Ülken, H. Z. *Değerler, Kültür ve Sanat [Values, Culture and Art]* (Istanbul: Istanbul Teknik University Publications, 1965)

Uludağ, S. *Tasavvuf Terimleri Sözlüğü [The Dictionary of the Terms of Tasawwuf]* (Istanbul: Marifet Publications, 1991).

Ünal, A. "ihlas." In *Kur'an'da Temel Kavramlar [The Basic Terms in Qur'an]* (Istanbul:1998)

Vahide, Ş. "Bediuzzaman Said Nursi and the Risale-I Nur" in *Globalization, Ethics, and Islam: The Case of Bediuzzaman Said Nursi* (London: Ashgate, 2005).

———. "The Book of the Universe: Its Place and Development in Bediuzzaman's Thought." In *A Contemporary Approach to Understanding the Qur'an: The Example of Risale-i Nur* (Istanbul: Sözler, 2000).

———. *Islam in Modern Turkey: An Intellectual Biography of Bediuzzaman Said Nursi*, ed. Ibrahim M. Abu-Rabi' (Albany: State University of New York Press, 2005).

———. *Signs of Miraculousness. The Inimitability of the Qur'an's Conciseness* (Istanbul: Sözler Publications, 2004).

———. *The Author of the Risale-i Nur, Bediuzzaman Nursi, part three* (Istanbul: Sozler Publications, 1992).

van Bruinessen, M. "Kurdistan in the 16th and 17th Centuries, as Reflected in Evliya Celebi's Seyahatname." In *The Journal of Kurdish Studies*, 3 (2000).

———. *Mullas, Sufis and Heretics: The Role of Religion in Kurdish Society* (Istanbul: ISIS Press, 2000).

———. *Agha, Shaikh and State: The Social and Political Structures of Kurdistan* (London: Zed Books, 1992).

Weismann, I. *Taste of Modernity: Sufism, Salafism and Arabism in Late Ottoman Damascus* (Leiden: E. J. Brill, 2000).

Yavuz, M. H. "Print-Based Islamic Discourse and Modernity: The Nur Movement." In *Third International Symposium on Bediuzzaman Said Nursi* (Istanbul: Sözler Press, 1997).

Yusuf, I. "Bediuzzaman Said Nursi's Discourse on Belief in Allah: A Study of Texts from *Risale-i Nur* Collection" in *The Muslim World*, 89:3–4 (July–October, 1999).

———. "Relationship Between God and Human Being: The Spiritual Interface Between Two Mujaddids." In *Fifth International Symposium on Bediuzzaman Said Nursi Proceedings* (Istanbul: Sözler, 2000).

Zeldin, T. *An Intimate History of Humanity* (New York: Vintage, 1998).

CONTRIBUTORS

Ibrahim M. Abu-Rabi' is the holder of the Edmonton Council of Muslim Communities Chair in Islamic Studies at the University of Alberta in Canada. He has published over fifteen books in several languages and numerous academic articles.

Asma Afsaruddin is Associate Professor of Arabic and Islamic Studies at the University of Notre Dame. Her fields of specialization are Islamic political and religious thought, Quran and hadith, Islamic intellectual history, and gender. She is the author or editor of four books, the most recent being *The First Muslim: A Short History*, and has also written numerous articles and essays on various aspects of Islamic thought. Afsaruddin's research has been funded by the Harry Frank Guggenheim Foundation and the Carnegie Corporation of New York, among others.

Ahmet Albayrak is Assistant Professor of Islamic Studies at Rize University in Turkey.

Abdelaziz Berghout is a lecturer of theology, civilization, and interdisciplinary studies associated with the Kulliyyah of Islamic Revealed Knowledge and Human Sciences, International Islamic University Malaysia. He has been awarded the title of the best lecture (2003, 2005, and 2005).

Yohanan Friedmann is Max Schloessinger Professor Emeritus of Islamic Studies at the Hebrew University of Jerusalem and a member of the Israel Academy of Sciences and Humanities. At the Hebrew University he served as Chair of the

Institute of Asian and African Studies, Chair of the Graduate School, Dean of Humanities, and Chair of the Department of Arabic Language and Literature. He served several times as visiting Professor at the University of Pennsylvania and at New York University. In 2002, he was a member at the Institute for Advanced Study in Princeton. In 2003, he received the Landau Prize in the Humanities. Since 1993, he has been the editor of *Jerusalem Studies in Arabic and Islam.*

Marcia Hermansen is Professor of Islamic Studies at the Department of Theology at Loyola University in Chicago. She has written on Islamic mysticism and Islam in South Asia.

Stephen Hirtenstein is the editor of *The Muhyiddin Ibn 'Arabi Society Journal.* He has been studying Ibn 'Arabi for over thirty years, translating, researching, and lecturing on his works.

Bilal Kuşpınar is currently lecturing at the Institute of Islamic Studies at McGill University. He has a special interest in Islamic philosophy and mysticism.

Yehezkel Landau is Faculty Associate in Interfaith Relations at Hartford Seminary, a position underwritten by the Henry Luce Foundation. He lectures internationally on Jewish-Christian-Muslim relations and Middle East peace issues, has authored numerous journal articles, co-edited the book *Voices from Jerusalem: Jews and Christians Reflect on the Holy Land,* and authored a research report entitled "Healing the Holy Land: Interreligious Peacebuilding in Israel/Palestine" (United States Institute of Peace, accessible at www.usip.org/reports). At Hartford Seminary, Professor Landau coordinates an interfaith training program for Jews, Christians, and Muslims called "Building Abrahamic Partnerships."

Ian Markham is Professor of Christian Ethics and Dean of Hartford Seminary, Hartford, Connecticut. He is the author of several books on comparative religion and religious ethics.

Thomas Michel is director of the interreligious dialogue office at the Vatican. He holds a Ph.D. in Islamic Studies from the University of Chicago and has been active in interreligious activities in the Middle East and Southeast Asia.

Lucinda Mosher holds a Th.D. from the General Theological Seminary. A Christian ethicist, she works as a consultant in interreligious relations for the

Interchurch center in New York, and teaches at Fordham University and the University of Michigan-Dearborn.

M. Sait Özervarlı received his Ph.D. in Islamic theology at Marmara University, Istanbul, in 1994 He did his postdoctoral studies at Harvard University and was a member of the Institute for Advanced Study in Princeton. Currently, he is Associate Professor at the Center for Islamic Studies in Istanbul and teaches graduate courses at Marmara University. He published a book in Turkish on the revitalization of Muslim theological thought in modern times, and edited *Lubab al-kalam*, a classical Arabic book by Alaaddin al-Usmandi. He has also published several book chapters and articles in various journals such as the *Muslim World* and the *Turkish Journal of Islamic Studies*.

Fred A. Reed is a Canadian journalist specializing in Islamic issues. He has written several books about Greece, Turkey, and Iran.

Jane I. Smith is Professor of Islam Studies and Christian-Muslim Relations at Hartford Seminary and the senior editor of *The Muslim World*. In addition to writing on Islamic thought, she has written on Islam in America and Europe and women in Islam.

Colin Turner is Lecturer in Islamic Studies and Persian at Durham University, UK. Trained as a historian of the medieval Muslim world, Dr. Turner has research interests that include Islamic theology and philosophy, Sufism, Quranic exegesis, and Shi'ite history, with particular reference to Safavid Iran. His most recent publication is *Islam: The Basics*.

Mustafa Ulusoy is a psychiatrist-psychotherapist, writer, and a man of literature. Dr. Ulusoy, who continues his therapies at his private office, specializes in the field of personality and personality disorders, separation anxiety, mourning reactions, bonding, and love. He is the author of *Love in the Mirrors' Hall* (novel), Nietzsche and My Grandmother (essay), Moon Therapy (story), and Intimacy (essay), and currently working on his newest book, psychobiography of Said Nursi.

Şükran Vahide is a writer and translator who has published a biography of Said Nursi (*Islam in Modern Turkey: An Intellectual Biography of Bediuzzaman Said Nursi*), and has translated a large part of the *Risale-i Nur* into English (six volumes to date). She has written extensively on Said Nursi and the *Risale-i*

Nur, and contributed articles to *The Blackwell Companion to Contemporary Islamic Thought* and *Islam at the Crossroads: On the Life and Thought of Bediuzzaman Said Nursi*, both edited by Ibrahim Abu-Rabi‘.

Miriam Therese Winter is professor of liturgy, worship, and spirituality, and director of the Women's Leadership Institute at Hartford Seminary in Connecticut. A Medical Mission Sister, she has published fifteen books, numerous articles, and over a dozen CDs of original songs and hymns that are sung around the world.

Index